Exploring Social Psychology

McGraw-Hill Series in Social Psychology

This popular series of paperback titles is written by authors about their particular field of expertise and are meant to complement any social psychology course. The series includes:

Exploring Social Psychology

SECOND EDITION

❖

David G. Myers

Hope College
Holland, Michigan

Boston   Burr Ridge, IL   Dubuque, IA   Madison, WI
New York   San Francisco   St. Louis
Bangkok   Bogotá   Caracas   Lisbon   London   Madrid   Mexico City
Milan   New Delhi   Seoul   Singapore   Sydney   Taipei   Toronto

McGraw-Hill Higher Education

A Division of The **McGraw-Hill** *Companies*

EXPLORING SOCIAL PSYCHOLOGY, SECOND EDITION

This book is printed on acid-free paper.

2 3 4 5 6 7 8 9 0 DOC/DOC 0 9 8 7 6 5 4 3 2 1 0 9

ISBN 0–07–234487–3

Editorial director: *Jane E. Vaicunas*
Executive editor: *Mickey Cox*
Senior developmental editor: *Sharon Geary*
Senior marketing manager: *James Rozsa*
Senior project manager: *Gloria G. Schiesl*
Senior production supervisor: *Mary E. Haas*
Coordinator of freelance design: *Rick Noel*
Photo research coordinator: *John C. Leland*
Senior supplement coordinator: *Candy M. Kuster*
Compositor: *Carlisle Communications, Ltd.*
Typeface: *10/12 Palatino*
Printer: *R. R. Donnelley & Sons Company/Crawfordsville, IN*

Cover/interior designer: *Ellen Pettengell*
Cover image: *©SuperStock "Springtime in Central Park" by Jane Wooster Scott*
Photo research: *Connie Mueller*

The credits section for this book begins on page 411 and is considered an extension of the copyright page.

Library of Congress Cataloging-in-Publication Data

Myers, David G.
　　Exploring social psychology / David G. Myers. — 2nd ed.
　　　　p.　　cm.
　　Includes bibliographical references and index.
　　ISBN 0–07–234487–3
　　1. Social psychology.　I. Title.
　　HM1033.M94　2000
　　302—dc21　　　　　　　　　　　　　　　　99—15842
　　　　　　　　　　　　　　　　　　　　　　　　CIP

www.mhhe.com

About the Author

❖

David G. Myers is the John Dirk Werkman Professor of Psychology at Michigan's Hope College, where students have voted him "Outstanding Professor." Myers's love of teaching psychology is manifest in his writings for the lay public. His articles have appeared in two dozen magazines and he has authored or co-authored a dozen books, including *The Pursuit of Happiness* (Avon, 1993) and *The American Paradox* (Yale University Press, 2000).

Also an award-winning researcher, Myers received the Gordon Allport Prize from Division 9 of the American Psychological Association for his work on group polarization. His scientific articles have appeared in more than two dozen journals, including *Science, American Scientist, Psychological Science,* and the *American Psychologist.* He has served his discipline as consulting editor to the *Journal of Experimental Social Psychology* and the *Journal of Personality and Social Psychology.*

In his spare time he has chaired his city's Human Relations Commission, helped found a community action agency that assists impoverished families, and spoken to dozens of collegiate and religious groups. David and Carol Myers are parents of two sons and a daughter.

Contents

———— ❖ ————

Foreword

————— ❖ —————

W hen social psychology works best, it touches the soul of society and the heartbeat of its individuals. Of course, it is an academic discipline with its own history, heroes, theories, methodologies, and jargon. As such, in recent years it has gradually moved to a central position within the field of psychology. In earlier days, it was looked upon as a peripheral curiosity, more akin to cultural anthropology than hard-nosed brass instrument and animal psychology that dominated a psychology proudly branded "Made in the U.S.A.," at least until the 1960s. As cognitive psychology has restored the mind and tongue to behaving organisms, social psychology has put them into a meaningful and lively social context. And as other domains of psychology have come to recognize the importance of the social setting and interpersonal dynamics in understanding the whys of human thought, feeling, and action, they too have added a social dimension to their studies. So we now have social-cognition, social-learning, social-developmental, social-personality, and many other hyphenated alliances that enrich the study of the individual. That person, though usually taken alone as the unit of psychology's research focus, is more fascinating when seen as part of the complex social fabric from which human nature is woven.

But what is unique among social psychologists is that their concern for experimental rigor and creativity in the laboratory equals their concerns for real-world relevance and viable interventions that may improve the quality of our lives. Virtually all of the most significant areas of application and extensions of psychology out of academia into the everyday life of ordinary people have come from, and are continuing to be energized by, social psychologists. What are those realms of social-psychologically inspired contributions to the human condition? Let us count but a few: health psychology, psychology and law, organizational behavior, environmental psychology, political psychology, peace psychology, and sports psychology. When a former president of the American Psychological Association urged his colleagues to "give psychology away" to the public, it was primarily the social psychologists who took his message to heart and went to work in the field of everyday little hassles and big-time troubles. So while some of us are proud to uncover a significant statistical effect in a laboratory test of key hypotheses derived from a theory, others are deriving joy from showing politicians how to negotiate more effectively, companies how to structure energy conservation programs, or the elderly how to take more control and personal responsibility over their lives.

We all recall the admonition of our inspirational leader, Kurt Lewin, who told us that there is nothing so practical as a good theory. But we now add to that intellectual call to arms that there is nothing as valuable as theoretically inspired practical applications. Furthermore, there is no reason not to embrace all of it—the abstract theory that unifies our singular observations and points us in new directions, the ingenious experimental test, the convincing demonstration of a social phenomenon, or the perceptive application of what we know to solving social problems facing our society and the world.

Despite this range of interests among social psychologists, most would agree on the basic "lessons" of social psychology that emerge from a variety of sources. Five principles can be identified. First, the power of the situation influences individual and group behavior more than we recognize in our individualistic, dispositionally oriented, culture. The second principle concerns the subjective construction of social reality, by which we mean that the social situation is a shared construal of a reality that does not exist "out there," but is created in our minds and passed on in gossip, rumors, ritual, folklore, school lessons, and racist tracts, among other sources of social communication. The third lesson is about the irrationality of some human behavior and the concurrent fallibility of human intuition—even among the best and brightest of us. Because we have shown that the presence of others, whether in groups of friends or coworkers, or in unstructured settings of strangers, influences the decisions and actions of individuals, our fourth lesson centers on group dynamism. Finally, social psychologists add the principle that it is possible to study complex social situations and generate practical solutions to some emerging problems, as well as apply what we already know to improve personal and societal functioning.

But such lessons are not merely the stuff of textbooks, they are the stuffing, or stories of life itself. Let me share a personal tale with you about the first two lessons, which, now that I think of it, also slips over into the rest of them.

Growing up in a South Bronx ghetto as a poor, sickly kid, I somehow learned the tactics and strategies of survival, known collectively as "street smarts." At first they were put to use to avoid being beaten up by the big tough guys through righteous utilization of ingratiation tactics and sensitivity to nonphysical sources of power. Then they worked to make me popular with the girls at school, which in turn enhanced my status with the less verbal neighboring big shots. By the time I got to junior high school, I was being chosen as class president, captain of this or that, and was generally looked to for advice and leadership. However, a strange thing happened along the path through adolescence. In 1948 my family moved to North Hollywood, California, for my junior year of high school. The initial wonder at being in this western paradise soon became a living nightmare. I was unable to make a single friend during the entire year, not one date. Nobody would even sit near me in the cafeteria! I was totally confused, bewildered, and of course very lonely. So much so that I became asthmatic. I became so with such intensity that my family used this newfound sickness as the excuse it needed to leave the polluted palms and general disillusionment we all felt to return to the dirty but comprehensible reality of the Bronx. Still more remarkable, within six months I was elected as the most popular boy in the senior class, "Jimmy Monroe" or James Monroe High School!

I was talking about this double transformation to my friend in homeroom class 12-H-3, Stanley Milgram, and we acknowledged that it wasn't me that had changed but the situation in which I was being judged by my peers, either as an alien New York Italian stereotype or a charming, reliable friend. We wondered how far someone could be changed by such divergent situations, and what was the stable constant in personality. "Just how much of what we see in others is in the eye of the beholder and the mouth of the judges?" Stanley wrote the senior class squibs for the Year Book and helped me to reclaim my California-lost ego by penning, "Phil's our vice president, tall and thin, with his blue eyes all the girls he'll win." So my Bronx street smarts were still working, at least sometimes, in some situations, for some people. Naturally, thereafter we both were heard to repeat loud and clear whenever asked about our predictions of what someone was like or might do: "It all depends on the situation."

Stanley went on to study conformity with Solomon Asch, a major contributor to early social psychology. At Yale, where we were on the faculty together for a short while, Milgram then conducted a series of now-classic studies on obedience to authority that have become the most cited experiments in our field because of their definitive demonstration of the power of the situation to corrupt good people into evil deeds. My way was not too divergent, since I studied how anonymity can lower restraints against antisocial acts and how putting normal, healthy young men in a mock prison ended up with their behaving in abnormal, pathological ways.

The irrationality lesson? It was the prejudice toward me created by applying an ill-fitting stereotype of being Mafia-like because of my ethnic identity and urban origins—by otherwise nice, intelligent white kids. The influence of the group prevented individual students from breaking through the constraints imposed by prejudiced thinking and group norms, even when their personal experience diverged from the hostile base rate. As a student at Brooklyn College I studied prejudice between allegedly liberal Whites and Blacks in their self-segregated seating patterns in the school cafeteria and also Black versus Puerto Rican prejudices in my neighborhood. Then when I became president of my White-Christian fraternity, I arranged to have it opened to Jews, Blacks, Puerto Ricans, and whoever made the new grade as a "good brother"—a first step in putting personal principles into social action.

You can see now why I feel that social psychology is not merely about the social life of the individual; for me, it is at the core of our lives. People are always crucial to the plot development of our most important personal stories.

The *McGraw-Hill Series in Social Psychology* has become a celebration of that basic theme. We have gathered some of the best researchers, theorists, teachers, and social change agents to write their stories about some aspect of our exciting field which they know best. They are encouraged to do so not just for their colleagues, as they do often in professional journals and monographs, but rather for intelligent undergraduates. With that youthful audience in mind, we all have tried to tap into their natural curiosity about human nature, to trigger their critical thinking, to touch their concerns for understanding the complexity of social life all about them, and to inspire them toward socially responsible utilization of their knowledge.

No one achieves those lofty goals better than the author of this text, David Myers. David writes with a clarity, precision of style, and graceful eloquence unmatched in all of psychology. He is the author of the best-selling introductory psychology textbook and also the best-selling social psychology text, a rare feat of effective writing and mind-boggling focused energy. What sets him apart from his talented peers is David's clear vision of his audience, to whom he talks as if they were welcomed guests at his dining table. We see him sharing his wealth of knowledge of psychology and of literature, posing just the right questions to pique their interest, or calling up the apt metaphor that clarifies a complex thought, and always integrating it all within a compelling story.

The *McGraw-Hill Series in Social Psychology* provided David Myers with a new option for his talents, enabling him to go beyond traditional textbook writing with its compressed, encyclopedic presentation of information. Why not tell a series of stories, each built around a distinctive theme of social psychological interest? They would be points-of-view pieces, personal perspectives of this senior researcher, writer, teacher. Taken as a whole, these modules would represent the breadth of the field while also enabling David the freedom to plumb some of its depths more fully than is possible in traditional texts. This new orientation freed David to burst out of the constraints imposed on textbook authors and fashion a novel approach to introducing students to the joys and challenges of social psychology.

In a sense, David Myers moved from master writer to master chef by creating wonderfully enticing little dishes, with 30 separate flavors, as in an Indonesian rice table, a rijstafel. Skillfully blended are many expected ingredients—attribution, persuasion, aggression, prejudice, and group dynamics—along with unfamiliar ones—pride, corruption of nice people, dislike of diversity, peacemakers, and psychology of religion, to name but a handful of his dishes.

These 30 "magical modules," as I have come to think of them, form a fabulous feast suitably rich for new students at the table of social psychology, yet quite satisfying for the more jaded tastes of mature faculty colleagues. Whole sets of research are skillfully summarized, critical questions posed for pondering, perceptive conclusions subtly extracted, and meaningful implications for students and society are adroitly drawn.

The success of the first edition of *Exploring Social Psychology* (1994) has inspired David Myers to try his hand at improving the module mix, blending them better within and across categories, while updating some to reflect contemporary research and theorizing. What was excellent earlier now becomes simply superb.

As with any gourmet feast, one enjoys the indulgence, but remains curious about what went into making it so memorable. In this instance, David Myers focused his analytical, philosophical, literary, and spiritual skills and values into creating a unique constellation of tasteful tales about social psychology. He presides over his feast as a dedicated teacher does in class, concerned for whetting, then sat-isfying, the enormous appetites for each guest-student for learning and enjoying the acquisition of knowledge-made-meaningful.

Before you start your first course, let me note one personal flaw of my own—this was not the first book I read in my undergraduate social psychology course. Had it been, I would have known instantly that there could be no more exciting ad-venture than to spend one's life as one of Them—social psychologists who make a difference through their research and theories in enhancing the quality of the Hu-man Condition. As Allen Funt's *Candid Camera Classics* reveal that it is possible to learn while laughing, David Myers's *Exploring Social Psychology* reveals that it is possible to be entertained while becoming educated. So sit back, read, and enjoy this master of the trade weaving his wonderful tales for your pleasure, each tasty in its own way.

Philip G. Zimbardo
Series Consulting Editor

Preface

———— ❖ ————

This is a book I secretly wanted to write. I have long believed that what is wrong with all psychology textbooks (including those that I have written) is their overlong chapters. Few can read a 40-page chapter in a single sitting, without their eyes glazing over and their mind wandering. So why not organize the discipline into digestible chunks—say, forty 15-page chapters rather than fifteen 40-page chapters—that a student *could* read in a sitting, before laying the book down with a sense of completion?

Thus when McGraw-Hill psychology editor Chris Rogers first suggested over bowls of New England clam chowder that I abbreviate and restructure my 15-chapter 600-page *Social Psychology* into a series of crisply written 10-page modules I said Eureka! At last a publisher willing to break convention by packaging the material in a form ideally suited to students' attention spans. By presenting concepts and findings in smaller bites, we also hoped not to overload students' capacities to absorb new information. And by keeping *Exploring Social Psychology* slim and economical, we sought to enable instructors to supplement it with other reading.

As the playful module titles suggest, I have also broken with convention by introducing social psychology in an essay format. Each is written in the spirit of Thoreau's admonition: "Anything living is easily and naturally expressed in popular language." My aim in the parent *Social Psychology*, and even more so here, is to write in a voice that is both solidly scientific and warmly human, factually rigorous and intellectually provocative. I hope to reveal social psychology as an investigative reporter might, by providing a current summary of important social phenomena, by showing how social psychologists uncover and explain such phenomena, and by reflecting on their human significance.

In selecting material, I have represented social psychology's scope, highlighting its scientific study of how we *think about*, *influence*, and *relate to* one another. I also emphasize material that casts social psychology in the intellectual tradition of the liberal arts. By the teaching of great literature, philosophy, and science, liberal education seeks to expand our thinking and awareness and to liberate us from the confines of the present. Social psychology can contribute to these goals. Many undergraduate social psychology students are not psychology majors; virtually all will enter other professions. By focusing on humanly significant issues such as belief and illusion, independence and interdependence, love and hate, one can present social psychology in ways that inform and stimulate all students.

A comprehensive teaching package accompanies *Exploring Social Psychology*. Julia Zuwerink Jacks, of the University of North Carolina, has revised the Instructor's Manual and Test Bank to accompany the second edition. In collaboration with Allen Funt and Philip Zimbardo, McGraw-Hill has developed *Candid Camera Classics in Social Psychology*, a videodisc (also available on videotape) of fifteen 3- to 5-minute clips from the original "Candid Camera" shows. Martin Bolt, of Calvin College, has revised the Student Study Guide to accompany this edition as well.

ACKNOWLEDGMENTS

I remain indebted to the community of scholars who have guided and critiqued the evolution of this material through six editions of *Social Psychology*. These caring colleagues, acknowledged individually therein, have enabled a better book than I, alone, could have created.

Special credit for this new book goes, of course, to psychology editor Christopher Rogers, whose brainchild it is. My thanks to Chris for his creativity and confidence, and to series editor Philip Zimbardo for his encouragement. As my friendship with Phil has grown, I have come to admire his gifts as one of psychology's premier communicators.

Psychology editor Mickey Cox encouraged this new edition, and Stephanie Cappiello supported us by gathering first-edition reviews from eight very thoughtful colleagues: Paul Allen, Central Connecticut State University; Carrie Fried, Indiana University of South Bend; J. Jurek Karylowski, University of North Florida; A. Julie Kiotas, Pasadena Area Community College; Eric Mankowski, Portland State University; Richard L. Miller, University of Nebraska at Kearney; Mark Templeton, Gardner-Webb University; and Timothy P. Tomczak, Genesee Community College.

Here at Hope College two key people played essential roles with their usual excellence and joy. Gretchen Rumohr-Voskuil helped digest the sixth-edition *Social Psychology* material into these modules, and then proofed the resulting manuscript and created the reference section. For Phyllis Vandervelde, loyal friend, this marks the nineteenth book for which she has prepared multiple manuscript drafts with timely excellence.

As in all five of my published social psychology books with McGraw-Hill, I again pay tribute to three significant people. Were it not for the invitation of McGraw-Hill's Nelson Black, it surely never would have occurred to me to try my hand at text writing. James Belser has patiently guided the process of converting all my McGraw-Hill books from manuscript into finished book. Finally, poet Jack Ridl, my Hope College colleague and writing coach, helped shape the voice you will hear in these pages.

To all in this supporting cast, I am indebted. Working with all these people has made my work a stimulating, gratifying experience.

David G. Myers

—— ❖ ——

PART ONE

Introducing Social Psychology

"We cannot live for ourselves alone," remarked the novelist Herman Melville," [for] our lives are connected by a thousand invisible threads." Social psychologists study those connections by scientifically exploring how we *think about, influence,* and *relate to* one another.

In the first two modules I explain how we do that exploring, how we play the social psychology game. As it happens, the ways we social psychologists form and test ideas can be carried into life itself, enabling us to think smarter as we analyze everyday social thinking, social influences, and social relations.

If intuition and common sense were utterly trustworthy, we would be less in need of scientific inquiry and critical thinking. But the truth, as Module 2 relates, is that whether we are reflecting on research results or everyday events, we readily succumb to a powerful hindsight bias, also called the I-knew-it-all-along phenomenon.

MODULE

1

❖

Doing Social Psychology

T here once was a man whose second wife was a vain and selfish woman. This woman had two daughters who were similarly vain and selfish. The man's own daughter, however, was sweet and kind. This sweet, kind daughter, whom we all know as Cinderella, learned early on that she had best do as she was told, accept insults, and not upstage her vain stepsisters.

But then, thanks to her fairy godmother, Cinderella was able to escape her situation and go to a grand ball, where she attracted a handsome prince. When the lovestruck prince later encountered a homelier Cinderella back in her degrading home, he at first failed to recognize her.

Implausible? The folk tale demands that we accept the power of the situation. In one situation, playing one role in the presence of her oppressive stepmother, meek and unattractive Cinderella was a different person from the charming and beautiful Cinderella whom the prince met. At home, she cowered. At the ball, Cinderella felt more beautiful and walked and talked and smiled as if she were.

The French philosopher-novelist Jean-Paul Sartre (1946) would have had no problem accepting the Cinderella premise. We humans are "first of all beings in a situation," he believed. "We cannot be distinguished from our situations, for they form us and decide our possibilities" (p. 59–60, paraphrased). Social psychology is a science that studies the influences of our situations, with special attention to how we view and affect one another. It does so by asking questions that have intrigued us all:

- How and what do people *think* of one another? How reasonable are the ideas we form of ourselves? of our friends? of strangers? How tight are the links between what we think and what we do?

3

- How, and how much, do people *influence* one another? How strong are the invisible threads that pull us? Are we creatures of our gender roles? our groups? our cultures? How can we resist social pressure, even sway the majority?

- What shapes the way we *relate to* one another? What leads people sometimes to hurt and sometimes to help? What kindles social conflict? And how might we transform the closed fists of aggression into the open arms of compassion?

A common thread runs through these questions: They all deal with how people view and affect one another. And that is what social psychology is all about. Social psychologists study attitudes and beliefs, conformity and independence, love and hate. To put it formally, **social psychology** is *the scientific study of how people think about, influence, and relate to one another.*

Unlike other scientific disciplines, social psychology has nearly 6 billion amateur practitioners. People-watching is a universal hobby—in parks, at the beach, at school. As we observe people, we form ideas about how human beings think about, influence, and relate to one another. Professional social psychologists do the same, only more systematically (by forming theories) and painstakingly (often with experiments that create miniature social dramas that pin down cause and effect).

FORMING AND TESTING THEORIES

Many of us are social psychologists because we simply are fascinated by human existence. If, as Socrates counseled, "The unexamined life is not worth living," then simply "knowing thyself" seems a worthy enough goal.

As we wrestle with human nature to pin down its secrets, we organize our ideas and findings into theories. A **theory** is an integrated set of principles that explain and predict phenomena. Theories are a scientific shorthand.

In everyday conversation, "theory" often means "less than fact"—a middle rung on a confidence ladder from fact to theory to guess. But to any kind of scientist, facts and theories are different things, not different points on a continuum. Facts are agreed-upon statements about what we observe. Theories are *ideas* that summarize and explain facts. "Science is built up with facts, as a house is with stones," said Jules Henri Poincaré, "but a collection of facts is no more a science than a heap of stones is a house."

Theories not only summarize, they also imply testable predictions, which we call **hypotheses.** Hypotheses serve several purposes. First, they allow us to *test* the theories on which they are based. By making specific predictions, a theory puts its money where its mouth is. Second, predictions give *direction* to research. Any scientific field will mature more rapidly if its researchers have a sense of direction. Theoretical predictions suggest new areas for research; they send investigators looking for things they might never have thought of. Third, the predictive feature of good theories can also make them *practical*. What, for example, would be of greater practical value today than a theory of aggression that would predict when to expect it and how to control it? As Kurt Lewin, one of modern social psychology's founders, declared, "There is nothing so practical as a good theory."

Consider how this works. Say we observe that people sometimes become violent when in crowds. We might therefore theorize that the presence of other people makes individuals feel anonymous and lowers their inhibitions. Let's let our minds play with this idea for a moment. Perhaps we could test it by constructing a laboratory experiment that modestly mimics execution by electric chair. What if we asked individuals in groups to administer punishing "shocks" to a hapless victim without their knowing which one of the group was actually shocking the victim (and without their knowing that no real shocks are administered)? Would these individuals administer stronger "shocks" than individuals acting alone, as our theory predicts?

We might also manipulate anonymity: Would people hiding behind masks deliver stronger shocks because they could not be identified? If the results confirm our hypothesis, they might suggest some practical applications. Perhaps police brutality could be reduced if officers were required to wear large name tags, drive cars labeled with large identifying numbers, and videotape their arrests.

But how do we conclude that one theory is better than another? A good theory does all these jobs well: (1) It effectively summarizes a wide range of observations. And (2) it makes clear predictions that we can use to (a) confirm or modify the theory, (b) generate new exploration, and (c) suggest practical applications. When we discard theories, usually it's not because they have been proved false. Rather, like an old car, they get replaced by newer, better models.

Most of what you will learn about social-psychological research methods you will absorb as you read later modules. But let us go backstage now and take a brief look at how social psychology is done. This glimpse behind the scenes will be just enough, I trust, for you to appreciate findings discussed later and to think critically about everyday social events.

Social-psychological research varies by location. It can take place in the *laboratory* (a controlled situation) or in the **field** (everyday situations). And it varies by method—**correlational research** asks whether two or more factors are naturally associated, and **experimental research** manipulates some factor to see its effect on another. If you want to be a critical reader of psychological research reported in newspapers and magazines, you will benefit from understanding the difference between correlational and experimental research.

CORRELATIONAL RESEARCH: DETECTING NATURAL ASSOCIATIONS

Using some real examples, let's first consider the advantages of *correlational research* (often involving important variables in natural settings) and the disadvantage (ambiguous interpretation of cause and effect). As we will see in a later module, today psychologists are relating personal and social factors to human health. Among these researchers are Douglas Carroll at Glasgow Caledonian University and his colleagues George Davey Smith and Paul Bennett (1994). In search of possible links between socioeconomic status and health, Carroll and his colleagues ventured into Glasgow's old graveyards. As a measure of health, they noted from grave markers the life spans of 843 individuals. As an indication of status, they measured the height of pillars over the grave, reasoning that height reflected cost and therefore affluence. As Figure 1-1 shows, higher markers were related to longer lives, for both men and women.

Carroll and his colleagues explain how other researchers, using contemporary data, have confirmed the status–longevity correlation. Scottish postal-code regions having the least overcrowding and unemployment also have the greatest longevity. In the United States, income correlates with longevity

Commemorative markers in Glasgow Cathedral graveyard.

(poor and lower-status people are more at risk for premature death). In contemporary Britain, occupational status correlates with longevity. One study followed 17,350 British civil service workers for 10 years. Compared to top-grade administrators, those at the professional-executive grade were 1.6 times more likely to have died, clerical workers were 2.2 times more likely, and laborers 2.7 times more likely to have died (Adler & others, 1993, 1994). Across times and places, the status–health correlation seems reliable.

Correlation Versus Causation

The status–longevity question illustrates the most irresistible thinking error made by both amateur and professional social psychologists: When two factors like status and longevity go together, it is terribly tempting to conclude that one is causing the other. Status, we might presume, somehow protects a person from health risks. Or might it be the other way around? Maybe health promotes vigor and success. Perhaps people who live longer accumulate more wealth (enabling them to have more expensive grave markers). Correlational research allows us to *predict*, but it cannot tell us whether changing one variable (such as social status) will *cause* changes in another (such as health).

Confusing correlation with causation is behind much muddled thinking in popular psychology. Consider another very real correlation—

Age at Death

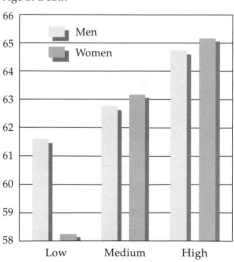

FIGURE 1-1
Status and Longevity. Tall grave pillars commemorated people who also tended to live longer. (Adapted from Carroll & others, 1994.)

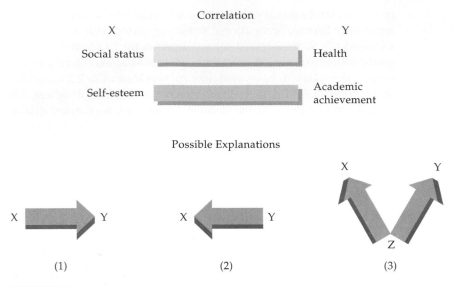

FIGURE 1-2
When two variables correlate, any combination of three explanations is possible.

between self-esteem and academic achievement. Children with high self-esteem tend also to have high academic achievement. (As with any correlation, we can also state this the other way around: High achievers tend to have high self-esteem.) Why do you suppose this is? (See Figure 1-2.)

Some people believe a "healthy self-concept" contributes to achievement, and that boosting a child's self-image can also boost their school achievement. Others argue that high achievement produces a favorable self-image. Do well, and you will feel good about yourself; goof off and fail, and you will feel like a schmuck. A study of 635 Norwegian school-children suggests that a string of gold stars by one's name on the spelling chart and constant praise from an admiring teacher can boost a child's self-esteem (Skaalvik & Hagtvet, 1990).

It's also possible that self-esteem and achievement correlate because both are linked to underlying intelligence and family social status. That possibility was raised in two studies—one a nationwide sample of 1,600 young American men, another of 715 Minnesota youngsters (Bachman & O'Malley, 1977; Maruyama & others, 1981). When the researchers statistically removed the effects of intelligence and family status, the correlation between self-esteem and achievement evaporated. Similarly, John McCarthy and Dean Hoge (1984) disputed the idea that the correlation between low self-esteem and delinquency means that low self-esteem causes delinquency; rather, their study of 1,658 teenagers suggested, delinquent acts lower self-esteem. Breaking rules leads to condemnation, which leads to lower self-esteem.

Advanced correlational techniques can *suggest* cause-effect relations. *Time-lagged* correlations reveal the *sequence* of events (for example, by indicating whether changed achievement more often precedes or follows changed self-esteem). Researchers can also use statistical techniques that extract the influence of "confounded" variables. Thus, the researchers just mentioned saw the correlation between self-esteem and achievement evaporate after extracting differences in intelligence and family status. (Among people of similar intelligence and family status, the relationship between self-esteem and achievement was minimal.) The Scottish research team wondered whether the status–longevity relationship would survive their removing the effect of cigarette smoking, which is now much less common among those higher in status. It did, which suggested that some other factors, such as increased stress and decreased feelings of control, must also account for the greater mortality of the poor.

So, the great strength of correlational research is that it tends to occur in real-world settings where we can examine factors like race, sex, and social status that we cannot manipulate in the laboratory. Its great disadvantage lies in the ambiguity of the results. The point is so important that, even if it fails to impress people the first 25 times they hear it, it is worth making a 26th time: Knowing that two variables change together enables us to predict one when we know the other; but correlation does not specify cause and effect.

*E*XPERIMENTAL RESEARCH: SEARCHING FOR CAUSE AND EFFECT

The near impossibility of discerning cause and effect among naturally correlated events prompts most social psychologists to create laboratory simulations of everyday processes whenever this is feasible and ethical. These simulations are roughly similar to how aeronautical engineers work. They don't begin by observing how flying objects perform in a wide variety of natural environments. The variations in both atmospheric conditions and flying objects are so complex that they would surely find it difficult to organize and use such data to design better aircraft. Instead, they construct a simulated reality that is under their control—a wind tunnel. Then they can manipulate wind conditions and ascertain the precise effect of particular wind conditions on particular wing structures.

Control: Manipulating Variables

Like aeronautical engineers, social psychologists experiment by constructing social situations that simulate important features of our daily lives. By varying just one or two factors at a time—called **independent variables**—the experimenter pinpoints how changes in these one or two things affect us. As the wind tunnel helps the aeronautical engineer discover principles of aerodynamics, so the experiment enables the social psychologist to discover principles of social thinking, social influence, and social relations. The ultimate aim of wind tunnel simulations is to understand and predict the flying characteristics of complex aircraft; social psychologists experiment to understand and predict human behavior.

Social psychologists have used the experimental method in about three-fourths of their research studies (Higbee & others, 1982), and in two out of three studies the setting has been a research laboratory (Adair & others, 1985). To illustrate the laboratory experiment, consider an issue we will explore in a later module: the effect of television violence on children's attitudes and behavior. Phrasing the issue like that suggests that there is a cause-effect explanation of the well-known correlation between television viewing and behavior. Figure 1-2 reminds us that there are two other cause-effect interpretations that do not implicate television as the cause of the children's aggression. (What are they?)

Social psychologists have therefore brought television viewing into the laboratory, where they control the amount of violence the children see. By exposing children to violent and nonviolent programs, researchers can observe how the amount of violence affects behavior. Robert Liebert and Robert Baron (1972) showed young Ohio boys and girls a violent excerpt from a gangster television show or an excerpt from an exciting track race. The children who viewed the violence were subsequently most likely to press vigorously a special red button that supposedly would heat a rod, causing a burning pain to another child. This measure of behavior we call the **dependent variable.** (Actually, there was no other child, so no one was harmed.) Such experiments indicate that television *can* be one cause of children's aggressive behavior.

So far we have seen that the logic of experimentation is simple: By creating and controlling a miniature reality, we can vary one factor and then another and discover how these factors, separately or in combination, affect people. Now let's go a little deeper and see how an experiment is done.

Every social-psychological experiment has two essential ingredients. One we have just considered—*control.* We manipulate one or two independent variables while trying to hold everything else constant. The other ingredient is *random assignment.*

Random Assignment: The Great Equalizer

Recall that we were reluctant, on the basis of a correlation, to assume viewing violence *caused* aggressiveness. A survey researcher might measure and statistically extract other possibly pertinent factors and see if the correlations survive. But one can never control for all the factors that might distinguish violence-viewers from nonviewers. Maybe violence-viewers differ in education, culture, intelligence—or in dozens of ways the researcher hasn't considered.

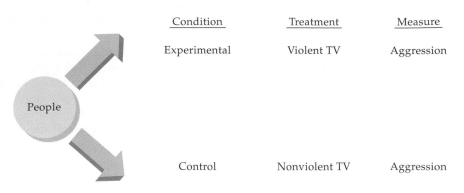

Condition	Treatment	Measure
Experimental	Violent TV	Aggression
Control	Nonviolent TV	Aggression

FIGURE 1-3
Randomly assigning people either to a condition that receives the experimental treatment or to a control condition that does not gives the researcher confidence that any later difference is somehow caused by the treatment.

In one fell swoop, **random assignment** eliminates all such extraneous factors. With random assignment, each person has an equal chance of viewing the violence or the nonviolence. Thus, the people in both groups would, in every conceivable way—family status, intelligence, education, initial aggressiveness—average about the same. Highly intelligent people, for example, are equally likely to appear in both groups. Because random assignment creates equivalent groups, any later aggression difference between the two groups must have something to do with the only way they differ—that is, whether they viewed violence (Figure 1-3).

The Ethics of Experimentation

Our television-viewing example illustrates why some experiments are ethically sensitive. Social psychologists would not, over long time periods, expose one group of children to brutal violence. Rather, they briefly alter people's social experience and note the effects. Sometimes the experimental treatment is a harmless, perhaps even enjoyable, experience to which people give their knowing consent. Sometimes, however, researchers find themselves operating in that gray area between the harmless and the risky.

Social psychologists often venture into that ethical gray area when they design experiments that really engage people's thoughts and emotions. Experiments need not have what Elliot Aronson, Marilynn Brewer, and Merrill Carlsmith (1985) call **mundane realism.** That is, laboratory behavior (such as delivering electric shocks as part of an experiment on aggression) need not be literally the same as everyday behavior. For many researchers, that sort of realism is indeed mundane—not important. But the experiment *should* have **experimental realism**—it should absorb and involve the participants. Experimenters do not want their participants consciously play-acting or ho-humming it; they want to engage real psychological processes. Forcing people to choose whether to give supposed intense or mild electric shock to someone else can, for example, be a realistic measure of aggression. It functionally simulates real aggression.

Achieving experimental realism often requires deceiving people with a plausible cover story. If the person in the next room is actually not receiving the shocks, the experimenter does not want the participants to know this. That would destroy the experimental realism. Thus, about one-third of social-psychological studies (though a decreasing number) have required deception (Korn & Nicks, 1993; Vitelli, 1988).

Experimenters also seek to hide their predictions lest the participants, in their eagerness to be "good subjects," merely do what's expected—or, in an ornery mood, do the opposite. In subtle ways, the experimenter's words, tone of voice, and gestures can call forth desired responses. To minimize such **demand characteristics**—cues that seem to "demand" certain behavior—experimenters typically standardize their instructions or even use a computer to present them.

Researchers often walk a tightrope in designing experiments that will be involving yet ethical. To believe that you are hurting someone, or to be subjected to strong social pressure to see if it will change your opinion or behavior, can be temporarily uncomfortable. Such experiments raise the age-old question of whether ends justify means. Do the insights gained justify deceiving and sometimes distressing people?

University ethics committees now review social-psychological research to ensure that it will treat participants humanely. Ethical principles developed by the American Psychological Association (1981, 1992) and the British Psychological Society (1991) urge investigators to do the following:

- Tell potential participants enough about the experiment to enable them to give **informed consent.**
- Be truthful. Use deception only if it is justified by a significant purpose and if there is no alternative.
- Protect participants from harm and significant discomfort.
- Treat information about the individual participants confidentially.
- Fully explain the experiment afterward, including any deception. The only exception to this rule is when the feedback would be distressing, say by making participants realize they have been stupid or cruel.

The experimenter should be sufficiently informative *and* considerate that people leave feeling at least as good about themselves as when they came in. Better yet, the participants should be repaid by having learned something about the nature of psychological inquiry. When treated respectfully, few participants mind being deceived (Christensen, 1988; Sharpe & others, 1992). Indeed, say social psychology's defenders, we provoke far greater anxiety and distress by giving and returning course exams than we now do in our experiments.

GENERALIZING FROM LABORATORY TO LIFE

As the research on children, television, and violence illustrates, social psychology mixes everyday experience and laboratory analysis. Throughout this book we will do the same by drawing our data mostly from the laboratory and our illustrations mostly from life. Social psychology displays a healthy interplay between laboratory research and everyday life. Hunches gained from everyday experience often inspire laboratory research, which deepens our understanding of our experience. This interplay appears in the children's television experiment. What people saw in everyday life suggested experimental research. Network and government policymakers, those with the power to make changes, are now aware of the results.

We need to be cautious, however, in generalizing from laboratory to life. Although the laboratory uncovers basic dynamics of human existence, it is still a simplified, controlled reality. It tells us what effect to expect of variable X, all other things being equal—which in real life they never are. Moreover, as you will see, the participants in many experiments are college students. This might help you identify with them, but college students are hardly a random sample of all humanity. Would we get similar results with people of different ages, educational levels, and cultures? This is always an open question.

Nevertheless, we can distinguish between the *content* of people's thinking and acting (their attitudes, for example) and the *process* by which they think and act (for example, how attitudes affect actions and vice versa). The content varies more from culture to culture than does the process. People of different cultures might hold different opinions yet form them in similar ways. Thus college students in Puerto Rico report greater loneliness than do collegians on the U.S. mainland, yet in both cultures the ingredients of loneliness are much the same—shyness, uncertain purpose in life, low self-esteem (Jones & others, 1985). Our behaviors can differ yet be influenced by the same social forces.

CONCEPTS TO REMEMBER

Social psychology   The scientific study of how people think about, influence, and relate to one another.

Theory   An integrated set of principles that explain and predict observed events.

Hypothesis   A testable proposition that describes a relationship that might exist between events.

Field research   Research done in natural, real-life settings outside the laboratory.

Correlational research   The study of the naturally occurring relationships among variables.

Experimental research   Studies that seek clues to cause-effect relationships by manipulating one or more factors (independent variables) while controlling others (holding them constant).

Independent variable   The experimental factor that a researcher manipulates.

Dependent variable   The variable being measured, so-called because it may *depend* on manipulations of the independent variable.

Random assignment   The process of assigning participants to the conditions of an experiment such that all persons have the same chance of being in a given condition. (Note the distinction between random *assignment* in experiments and random *sampling* in surveys. Random assignment helps us infer cause and effect. Random sampling helps us generalize to a population.)

Mundane realism   The degree to which an experiment is superficially similar to everyday situations.

Experimental realism   The degree to which an experiment absorbs and involves its participants.

Demand characteristics   Cues in an experiment that tell the participant what behavior is expected.

Informed consent   An ethical principle requiring that research participants be told enough to enable them to decide whether they wish to participate.

2

❖

Did You Know It All Along?

Anything seems commonplace, once explained.

Dr. Watson to Sherlock Holmes

D o social psychology's theories provide *new insight* into the human condition? Or do they only describe the obvious? Many of the conclusions presented in this book will probably have already occurred to you, for social psychology is all around you. We constantly observe people thinking about, influencing, and relating to one another. Much of our thinking aims to discern and explain relationships among social events. It pays to know what that facial expression predicts, how to get someone to do something, or whether to regard another person as friend or foe. For centuries, philosophers, novelists, and poets have observed and commented upon social behavior, often with keen insight. Social psychology is everybody's business! As English philosopher Alfred North Whitehead noted, "Everything important has been said before."

Might it therefore be said that social psychology is only common sense in different words? Social psychology faces two contradictory criticisms: One is that it is trivial because it documents the obvious; the second is that it is dangerous because its findings could be used to manipulate people. Is the first objection valid—does social psychology simply formalize what any amateur already knows intuitively?

Cullen Murphy (1990) thinks so: "Day after day social scientists go out into the world. Day after day they discover that people's behavior is pretty much what you'd expect." Nearly a half century earlier, historian Arthur

Schlesinger, Jr., (1949) reacted with similar scorn to social scientists' studies of American World War II soldiers, as reported in the two volumes of *The American Soldier.*

What were *The American Soldier's* findings? Another reviewer, Paul Lazarsfeld (1949), offered a sample with interpretive comments, a few of which I paraphrase:

1. Better-educated soldiers suffered more adjustment problems than less-educated soldiers. (Intellectuals were less prepared for battle stresses than were street-smart people.)

2. Southern soldiers coped better with the hot South Sea island climate than did Northern soldiers. (Southerners are more accustomed to hot weather.)

3. White privates were more eager to be promoted to noncommissioned officer than were Black privates. (Years of oppression take a toll on achievement motivation.)

4. Southern Blacks preferred Southern to Northern White officers (because Southern officers were more experienced and skilled in interacting with Blacks).

One problem with common sense, however, is that we invoke it *after* we know the facts. Events are far more "obvious" and predictable in hindsight than beforehand. Experiments reveal that when people learn the outcome of an experiment, that outcome suddenly seems unsurprising—certainly less surprising than it is to people who are simply told about the experimental procedure and the possible outcomes (Slovic & Fischhoff, 1977).

You perhaps experienced this phenomenon when reading Lazarsfeld's summary of *The American Soldier* findings. For actually, Lazarsfeld (1949) went on to say, *"every one of these statements is the direct opposite of what was actually found."* In reality, the book reported that poorly educated soldiers adapted more poorly. Southerners were *not* more likely than Northerners to adjust to a tropical climate. Blacks were *more* eager than Whites for promotion, and so forth. "If we had mentioned the actual results of the investigation first [as Schlesinger experienced], the reader would have labelled these 'obvious' also."

Likewise, in everyday life we often do not expect something to happen until it does. We *then* suddenly see clearly the forces that brought it about and feel unsurprised. After Ronald Reagan's presidential victory over Jimmy Carter in 1980, commentators—forgetting that the election had been "too close to call" until the campaign's final few days—found the Reagan landslide unsurprising. When Martin Bolt and John Brink (1991) invited Calvin College students to predict the U.S. Senate vote on controversial Supreme Court nominee Clarence

Thomas, 58 percent predicted his approval. A week after his confirmation, they asked other students to recall what they would have predicted. "I thought he would be approved," said 78 percent. As the Danish philosopher-theologian Sören Kierkegaard put it, "Life is lived forwards, but understood backwards."

If this **hindsight bias** (also called the I-knew-it-all-along phenomenon) is pervasive, you might now be feeling that you already knew about it. Indeed, almost any conceivable result of a psychological experiment can seem like common sense—*after* you know the result. Here's how you can demonstrate the phenomenon:

Tell one group one psychological finding and tell another group the opposite result. For example, tell one group:

> Social psychologists have found that, whether choosing friends or falling in love, we are most attracted to people whose traits are different from our own. There seems to be wisdom in the old saying, "Opposites attract."

Tell the other group:

> Social psychologists have found that, whether choosing friends or falling in love, we are most attracted to people whose traits are similar to our own. There seems to be wisdom in the old saying, "Birds of a feather flock together."

Ask each group first to explain the result. Then ask them to say whether it is "surprising" or "not surprising." Virtually all will find whichever result they were given "not surprising."

As this example shows, we can draw upon our stockpile of proverbs to make almost any result seem to make sense. Shall we say with John Donne, "No man is an island," or with Thomas Wolfe, "Every man is an island"? If a social psychologist reports that separation intensifies romantic attraction, Joe Public responds, "You get paid for this? Everybody knows that 'absence makes the heart grow fonder.' " Should it turn out that separation weakens attraction, Judy Public might say, "My grandmother could have told you, 'Out of sight, out of mind.' " No matter what happens, there will be someone who knew it would.

Karl Teigen (1986) must have had a few chuckles when asking University of Leicester (England) students to evaluate actual proverbs and their opposites. When given the actual proverb "Fear is stronger than love," most rated it as true. But so did students who were given its reversed form, "Love is stronger than fear." Likewise, the genuine proverb "He that is fallen cannot help him who is down" was rated highly; but so too was "He that is fallen can help him who is down." My favorites, however, were these two highly rated proverbs: "Wise men make proverbs and fools repeat them" (authentic) and its made-up counterpart, "Fools make proverbs and wise men repeat them."

The hindsight bias creates a problem for many psychology students. Sometimes results are genuinely surprising (for example, that Olympic bronze medalists take more joy in their achievement than do silver medalists). More often, when you read the results of experiments in your textbooks, the material often seems easy, even obvious. When you later take a multiple-choice test on which you must choose among several plausible conclusions, the task can become surprisingly difficult. "I don't know what happened," the befuddled student later moans. "I thought I knew the material." (A word to the wise: Beware of this phenomenon when studying for exams, lest you fool yourself into thinking that you know the material better than you do.)

The I-knew-it-all-along phenomenon not only can make social science findings seem like common sense. It also can have pernicious consequences, because it is conducive to arrogance—an overestimation of our own intellectual powers. Moreover, because outcomes seem as if they should have been foreseeable, we are more likely to blame decision makers for what are in retrospect "obvious" bad choices than to praise them for good choices, which also seem "obvious." *After* the 1991 Persian Gulf War, it seemed obvious that the overwhelming air superiority of the United States and its allies would rout the Iraqi military, though that was hardly clear to most politicians and pundits beforehand.

Likewise, we sometimes blame ourselves for "stupid mistakes," such as not having handled a situation or a person better. Looking back, we see how we should have handled it. But sometimes we are too hard on ourselves. We forget that what is obvious to us *now* was not nearly so obvious at the time. Physicians who are told both a patient's symptoms and the cause of death (as determined by autopsy) sometimes wonder how an incorrect diagnosis could have been made. Other physicians, given only the symptoms, don't find the diagnosis nearly so obvious (Dawson & others, 1988). (Would juries be slower to assume malpractice if they were forced to take a foresight rather than a hindsight perspective?)

So what do we conclude? That common sense is usually wrong? Sometimes it is. Until science dethroned the commonsense view, centuries of daily experience assured people that the sun revolved around the earth. Medical experience assured doctors that bleeding was an effective treatment for typhoid fever, until someone in the middle of the last century bothered to experiment—to divide patients into two groups, one bled, the other given mere bed rest.

Other times, conventional wisdom is right—or it falls on both sides of an issue: Does happiness come from knowing the truth, or preserving illusions? from being with others, or from living in peaceful solitude? from living a virtuous life, or from getting away with evil? Opinions are a dime a dozen; no matter what we find, there will be someone who foresaw it. But which of the many competing ideas best fit reality?

So the point is not that common sense is predictably wrong. Rather, common sense usually is right *after the fact.* We therefore easily deceive ourselves into thinking that we know and knew more than we do and did. And this is precisely why we need science—to help us sift reality from illusion, and genuine predictions from easy hindsight.

CONCEPT TO REMEMBER

Hindsight bias   The tendency to exaggerate, *after* learning an outcome, one's ability to have foreseen how something turned out. Also known as the *I-knew-it-all-along phenomenon.*

PART TWO

❖

Social Thinking

This book unfolds around its definition of social psychology: the scientific study of how we *think about* (Part II), *influence* (Part III), and *relate to* (Part IV) one another.

These modules on social thinking examine, first, the quite amazing and sometimes rather amusing ways in which we form beliefs about our social worlds. We have quite remarkable powers of intuition (or what social psychologists call automatic information processing), yet in at least a half-dozen ways our intuition often fails us. Knowing these ways not only beckons us to humility, it can help us sharpen our thinking, keeping it more closely in touch with reality.

Succeeding modules explore the interplay between our sense of self and our social worlds, by showing, for example, how self-interest colors our social judgments, and the correlates of a positive sense of self and personal control. We will also explore the links between attitudes and behaviors: Do our attitudes determine our behaviors? Do our behaviors determine our attitudes? Or does it work both ways?

3

❖

Intuition

The Power and Limits of Our Inner Knowing

W hat are our powers of intuition—of immediately knowing something without reasoning or analysis? Advocates of "intuitive management" believe we should tune in to our hunches. When judging others, they say, we should plug in to the nonlogical smarts of our "right brain." When hiring, firing, and investing, we should listen to our premonitions. In making judgments, we should follow the example of *Star Wars'* Luke Skywalker by switching off our computer guidance systems and trusting the force within.

Are the intuitionists correct that important information is immediately available apart from our conscious analysis? Or are the skeptics right in saying that intuition is "our knowing we are right, whether we are or not"?

*T*HE POWERS OF INTUITION

"The heart has its reasons which reason does not know," observed seventeenth-century philosopher-mathematician Blaise Pascal. Three centuries later, scientists have proved Pascal correct. We know more than we know we know. Studies of our unconscious information processing confirm our limited access to what's going on in our minds (Bargh, 1994; Greenwald & Banaji, 1995). Our thinking is partly *controlled* (deliberate and conscious) and, more than most of us once supposed, partly *automatic* (effortless and without our awareness). Automatic thinking occurs not "on screen" but off screen, out of sight, where reason does not know. Consider:

- *Schemas*—mental templates—automatically, intuitively, guide our perceptions and interpretations of our experience. Whether we hear

23

someone speaking of religious *sects* or *sex* depends not only on the word spoken but on how we automatically interpret the sound.

- *Emotional reactions* are often nearly instantaneous, before there is time for deliberate thinking. One neural shortcut takes information from the eye or ear to the brain's sensory switchboard (the thalamus) and out to its emotional control center (the amygdala) before the thinking cortex has had any chance to intervene (LeDoux, 1994, 1996).

  Simple likes, dislikes, and fears typically involve little analysis. Although our intuitive reactions sometimes defy logic, they can still be adaptive. Our ancestors who intuitively feared a sound in the bushes were usually fearing nothing, but compared to their more deliberative cousins they were more likely to survive to pass their genes down to us.

- Given sufficient *expertise*, people can intuitively know the answer to a problem. The situation cues information stored in their memory. Without knowing quite how we do it, we recognize a friend's voice after the first spoken word of a phone conversation. Master chess players intuitively recognize meaningful patterns that novices miss.

- Some things—facts, names, and past experiences—we remember explicitly (consciously). But other things—skills and conditioned dispositions—we remember *implicitly*, without consciously knowing and declaring that we know. It's true of us all, but most strikingly evident in brain-damaged persons who cannot form new explicit memories. Having learned how to solve a block-stacking puzzle or play golf, they will deny ever having experienced the task. Yet (surprisingly to themselves) they perform like practiced experts.

- Equally dramatic are the cases of *blindsight*. People who have lost a portion of the visual cortex to surgery or stroke can be functionally blind in part of their field of vision. Shown a series of sticks in the blind field, they report seeing nothing. After correctly guessing whether the sticks are vertical or horizontal, the patients are astounded when told, "You got them all right." Again, these people unconsciously know more than they know they know. There are, it seems, little minds—parallel processing units—operating unseen.

- *Prosopagnosia* patients suffer damage to a brain area involved in face recognition. They can see familiar people but are unable to recognize them as their spouses or children. Yet, shown these people, their heart knows them—their heart rate increases, as a bodily sign of unconscious recognition.

- For that matter, consider your own taken-for-granted capacity to intuitively recognize a face. As you look at a photo, your brain breaks down the visual information into subdimensions such as color, depth, movement, and form, and works on each aspect simultaneously before reassembling the components. Finally, some-how, your brain compares the perceived image with previously stored images. Voilà! Instantly and effortlessly, you recognize your grandmother. If intuition is immediately knowing something without reasoned analysis, perceiving is intuition par excellence.

- Although below our threshold for conscious awareness, *subliminal* stimuli can nevertheless have intriguing effects. Shown certain geometric figures for less than 0.01 second each, people will deny having seen anything more than a flash of light. Yet they will later express a preference for the forms they saw. Sometimes we intu-itively feel what we cannot explain. Likewise, invisible flashed words can *prime* or predispose our responses to later questions. If the word *bread* is flashed too briefly for us to recognize it, we might afterward detect a flashed, related word such as *butter* more easily than an unrelated word such as *bottle*.

To repeat, many routine cognitive functions occur automatically, un-intentionally, without awareness. Our minds function rather like big cor-porations: Our CEO—our controlled consciousness—attends to the most important or novel issues and assigns routine affairs to subordinates. This delegation of resources enables us to react to many situations quickly, effi-ciently, *intuitively,* without having to spend time reasoning or analyzing.

*T*HE LIMITS OF INTUITION

Although researchers affirm that unconscious information processing can produce flashes of intuition, they have their doubts about its brilliance. Elizabeth Loftus and Mark Klinger (1992) speak for today's cognitive sci-entists in reporting "a general consensus that the unconscious may not be as smart as previously believed." For example, although subliminal stim-uli can trigger a weak, fleeting response—enough to evoke a feeling, if not conscious awareness—there is no evidence that commercial subliminal tapes can "reprogram your unconscious mind" for success. (A mass of new evidence indicates that they can't—Greenwald & others, 1991.)

Moreover, our intuitive judgments err often enough that we can un-derstand why poet T. S. Eliot would speak of "The hollow man . . . Head-piece filled with straw." Social psychologists have explored our error-prone hindsight judgments (our intuitive sense, after the fact, that we knew it all along). Other domains of psychology have explored our capac-ity for illusion—perceptual misinterpretations, fantasies, and constructed beliefs. Michael Gazzaniga (1992) reports that patients whose brain hemi-spheres have been surgically separated will instantly fabricate, and be-lieve, explanations of puzzling behaviors. If the patient gets up and takes a few steps after the experimenter flashes the instruction "walk" to the patient's nonverbal right hemisphere, the verbal left hemisphere will instantly invent a plausible explanation ("I felt like getting a drink").

Illusory thinking also appears in the vast new literature on how we take in, store, and retrieve *social* information. As perception researchers study visual illusions for what they reveal about our normal perceptual mechanisms, social psychologists study illusory thinking for what it reveals about normal information processing. These researchers want to give us a map of everyday social thinking, with the hazards clearly marked. As we examine some of these efficient thinking patterns, remember this: Demonstrations of how people create counterfeit beliefs do not prove that all beliefs are counterfeit. Still, to recognize counterfeiting, it helps to know how it's done. So let's explore how efficient information processing can go awry, beginning with our self-knowledge.

WE OFTEN DO NOT KNOW WHY WE DO WHAT WE DO

"There is one thing, and only one in the whole universe which we know more about than we could learn from external observation," noted C. S. Lewis (1960, pp. 18–19). "That one thing is [ourselves]. We have, so to speak, inside information; we are in the know." Indeed. Yet sometimes we *think* we know, but our inside information is wrong. This is the unavoidable conclusion of some fascinating research.

Explaining Our Behavior

Why did you choose your college? Why did you lash out at your roommate? Why did you fall in love with that special person? Sometimes we know. Sometimes we don't know. Asked why we have felt or acted as we have, we produce plausible answers. Yet when causes and determinants are not obvious, our self-explanations are often wrong. Factors that have big effects we sometimes report as innocuous. Factors that have little effect we sometimes perceive as influential.

Richard Nisbett and Stanley Schachter (1966) demonstrated this by asking Columbia University students to take a series of electric shocks of steadily increasing intensity. Beforehand, some took a fake pill that, they were told, would produce heart palpitations, breathing irregularities, and butterflies in the stomach—the very symptoms that usually accompany being shocked. Nisbett and Schachter anticipated that people would attribute the shock symptoms to the pill and thus should tolerate more shock than people not given the pill. Indeed, the effect was enormous—people given the fake pill took four times as much shock.

When informed they had taken more shock than average, and asked why, their answers did not mention the pill. When pressed (even after the experimenter explained the hypotheses in detail), they denied the pill's influence. They would usually say the pill probably did affect some people, but not them. A typical reply was, "I didn't even think about the pill."

Sometimes people think they *have* been affected by something that has had no effect. Nisbett and Timothy Wilson (1977) had University of Michigan students rate a documentary film. While some of them watched, a power saw roared just outside the room. Most people felt that this distracting noise affected their ratings, but it didn't; their ratings were similar to those of control subjects who viewed the film without distraction.

Even more thought-provoking are studies in which people recorded their moods every day for two or three months (Stone & others, 1985; Weiss & Brown, 1976; Wilson & others, 1982). They also recorded factors that might affect their moods—the day of the week, the weather, the amount they slept, and so forth. At the end of each study, the people judged how much each factor had affected their moods. Remarkably (given that their attention was being drawn to their daily moods), there was little relationship between their perceptions of how important a factor was and how well the factor actually predicted their mood. These findings raise a disconcerting question: How much insight do we really have into what makes us happy or unhappy?

Predicting Our Behavior

People also err when predicting their behavior. Asked whether they would obey demands to deliver severe electric shocks or would hesitate to help a victim if several other people were present, people overwhelmingly deny their vulnerability to such influences. But as we will see, experiments have shown that many of us are vulnerable. Moreover, consider what Sidney Shrauger (1983) discovered when he had college students predict the likelihood of their experiencing dozens of different events (becoming romantically involved, being sick, and so forth) during the ensuing two months: Their self-predictions were hardly more accurate than predictions based on the average person's experience. The surest thing we can say about your individual future is that it is sometimes hard for even you to predict. When predicting yourself, the best advice is to consider your past behavior in similar situations (Osberg & Shrauger, 1986, 1990).

Predicting Our Feelings

Many of life's big decisions involve predicting our future feelings. Would marrying this person lead to lifelong contentment? Would entering this profession make for satisfying work? Would going on this vacation produce a happy experience? Or would the likelier results be divorce, job burnout, and holiday disappointment?

Sometimes we know how we will feel—if we fail that exam, win that big game, or soothe our tensions with a half-hour jog. But often we don't. George Loewenstein and David Schkade (1999) offer some examples:

- People overestimate how much their well-being would be affected by such things as gaining or losing weight, a changed climate, increased television channels, or more free time. Even extreme events, such as winning a state lottery or suffering a paralyzing accident, affect long-term happiness less than most people suppose.

- When people being tested for HIV predict how they will feel five weeks after getting the results, they expect to be feeling misery over bad news and elation over good news. Yet given devastating news, people cope better than they expected. And after adapting to good news, they feel not quite so elated as they anticipated.

- When male youths are shown sexually arousing photographs, then exposed to a hypothetical passionate date scenario in which their date asks them to "stop," they acknowledge the possibility that they might not stop. When they are not first shown sexually arousing pictures, male youths more routinely deny the possibility of their being sexually aggressive. When not aroused, one easily mispredicts how one will feel and act when aroused—a phenomenon that also leads to many unintended pregnancies.

CONSTRUCTING MEMORIES

Do you agree or disagree with this statement?

> Memory can be likened to a storage chest in the brain into which we deposit material and from which we can withdraw it later if needed. Occasionally, something is lost from the "chest," and then we say we have forgotten.

About 85 percent of college students agree (Lamal, 1979). As a 1988 ad in *Psychology Today* put it, "Science has proven the accumulated experience of a lifetime is preserved perfectly in your mind."

Actually, psychological research has proved the opposite. Many memories are not copies of experiences that remain on deposit in a memory bank. Rather, we construct memories at the time of withdrawal, for memory involves backward reasoning. It infers what must have been, given what we now believe or know. Like a paleontologist inferring the appearance of a dinosaur from bone fragments, we reconstruct our distant past by combining fragments of information using our current feelings and expectations (Hirt,

1990; Ross & Buehler, 1994). Thus we can easily (though unconsciously) revise our memories to suit our current knowledge. One of my sons complained, "The June issue of *Cricket* never came;" then he was then shown where it was, and he delightedly said, "Oh good, I knew I'd gotten it."

Reconstructing Past Attitudes

Five years ago, how did you feel about nuclear power? About Bill Clinton or Jean Chrétien? About your parents? If your attitudes have changed, do you know the extent of the change?

Experimenters have tried to answer such questions, and the results have been unnerving. People whose attitudes have changed often insist that they have always felt much as they now feel. Daryl Bem and Keith McConnell (1970) took a survey among Carnegie-Mellon University students. Buried in it was a question concerning student control over the university curriculum. A week later the students agreed to write an essay opposing student control. After doing so, their attitudes shifted toward greater opposition to student control. When asked to recall how they had answered the question before writing the essay, they "remembered" holding the opinion that they *now* held and denied that the experiment had affected them. After observing Clark University students similarly denying their former attitudes, researchers D. R. Wixon and James Laird (1976) commented: "The speed, magnitude, and certainty" with which the students revised their own histories "was striking."

University of Michigan researchers interviewed a national sample of high school seniors in 1973, and then reinterviewed them in 1982 (Markus, 1986). When recalling their 1973 attitudes on issues such as aid to minorities, the legalization of marijuana, and equality for women, people's reports were much closer to their 1982 attitudes than to those they actually expressed in 1973. As George Vaillant (1977, p. 197) noted after following some adults for a period of time: "It is all too common for caterpillars to become butterflies and then to maintain that in their youth they had been little butterflies. Maturation makes liars of us all."

The construction of positive memories does brighten our recollections. Terence Mitchell, Leigh Thompson, and their colleagues (1994, 1997) report that people often exhibit *rosy retrospection*—their *recall* of mildly pleasant events is more favorable than their experience of them was. College students on a three-week bike trip, older adults on a guided tour of Austria, and undergraduates on vacation all report enjoying their experiences as they have them. But they later recall such experiences even more fondly, minimizing the unpleasant or boring aspects and remembering the high points. Thus, the pleasant times during which I have sojourned in Scotland I now (back in my office facing deadlines and interruptions) romanticize as pure bliss. With any positive experience, some of the pleasure resides in the anticipation, some in the actual experience, and some in the rosy retrospection.

Cathy McFarland and Michael Ross (1985) found that we also revise our recollections of other people as our relationships with them change. They had university students rate their steady dating partners and then, two months later, rate them again. Students who were more in love than ever had a tendency to recall love at first sight. Those who had broken up were more likely to recall having recognized that the partner was somewhat selfish and bad-tempered.

Diane Holmberg and John Holmes (1994) discovered the same phenomenon among 373 newlywed couples, most of whom reported being very happy. When resurveyed two years later, those whose marriages had soured recalled that things had always been bad. The results are "frightening," say Holmberg and Holmes: "Such biases can lead to a dangerous downward spiral. The worse your current view of your partner is, the worse your memories are, which only further confirms your negative attitudes."

It's not that we are totally unaware of how we used to feel; it is just that when memories are hazy, current feelings guide our recall. Parents of every generation bemoan the values of the next generation, partly because they misrecall their youthful values as being closer to their current values.

Reconstructing Past Behavior

Memory construction enables us to revise our own histories. Michael Ross, Cathy McFarland, and Garth Fletcher (1981) exposed some University of Waterloo students to a message convincing them of the desirability of toothbrushing. Later, in a supposedly different experiment, these students recalled brushing their teeth more often during the preceding two weeks than did students who had not heard the message. Likewise, when representative samples of Americans are asked about their cigarette smoking and their reports are projected to the nation as a whole, at least a third of the 600 billion cigarettes sold annually are unaccounted for (Hall, 1985). Noting the similarity of such findings to happenings in George Orwell's *Nineteen Eighty-Four*—where it was "necessary to remember that events happened in the desired manner"—social psychologist Anthony Greenwald (1980) surmised that we all have "totalitarian egos" that revise the past to suit our present views.

Sometimes our present view is that we've improved, in which case we might misrecall our past as more *un*like the present than it actually was. This tendency resolves a puzzling pair of consistent findings: Those who participate in self-improvement programs (weight-control programs, antismoking programs, exercise programs, psychotherapy) show only modest improvement, on average. Yet they often claim considerable benefit (Myers, 1998). Michael Conway and Michael Ross (1985, 1986) explain why: Having expended so much time, effort, and money on self-improvement, people might think, "I may not be perfect now, but I was worse before; this did me a lot of good."

"Know thyself," urged the ancient Greek philosopher Thales. We try. But to a striking extent, we are often wrong about what has influenced us and what we will feel and do. Our intuitive self-knowledge errs.

This fact of life has two practical implications. The first is for psychological inquiry: Although the intuitions of clients or research subjects can provide useful clues to their psychological processes, *self-reports are often untrustworthy.* Errors in self-understanding limit the scientific usefulness of subjective personal reports.

The second implication is for our everyday lives: The sincerity with which people report and interpret their experiences is no guarantee of the validity of these reports. Personal testimonies are powerfully persuasive, but they can also unwittingly convey error. Keeping this potential for error in mind can help us feel less intimidated by others and can help us be less gullible.

MODULE

4

❖

Reasons for Unreason

What good fortune for those in power that people do not think.

Adolf Hitler

The mixed picture of our intuitive self-knowledge that we saw in Module 3 is paralleled by a mixed picture of our rationality. On the one hand, what species better deserves the name *Homo sapiens*—wise humans? Our cognitive powers outstrip the smartest computers in recognizing patterns, handling language, and processing abstract information. Our information processing is also wonderfully efficient. With such precious little time to process so much information, we specialize in mental shortcuts. Scientists marvel at the speed and ease with which we form impressions, judgments, and explanations. In many situations, our snap generalizations—"That's dangerous!"—are adaptive. They promote our survival.

But our adaptive efficiency has a trade-off; snap generalizations sometimes err. Our helpful strategies for simplifying complex information can lead us astray. To enhance our own powers of critical thinking, let's consider five reasons for unreason—five common ways in which people form or sustain false beliefs.

1. Our preconceptions control our interpretations.
2. We overestimate the accuracy of our judgments.
3. We often are swayed more by anecdotes than by statistical facts.
4. We misperceive correlation and control.
5. Our beliefs can generate their own conclusions.

OUR PRECONCEPTIONS CONTROL OUR INTERPRETATIONS

We earlier noted a significant fact about the human mind—that our pre-conceptions guide how we perceive and interpret information. People will grant that preconceptions influence social judgments, yet fail to realize how great the effect is. Preconceptions also affect the way people perceive and interpret information. This was tragically demonstrated in 1988 when the USS *Vincennes* crew mistook an Iranian passenger airliner for a hostile warplane and shot it down. As social psychologist Richard Nisbett (1988) noted in a congressional hearing on the incident, "The effects of expecta-tions on generating and sustaining mistaken hypotheses can be dramatic."

The same is true of social perception. An experiment by Robert Vallone, Lee Ross, and Mark Lepper (1985) reveals just how powerful preconcep-tions can be. They showed pro-Israeli and pro-Arab students six network news segments describing the 1982 killing of civilian refugees at two camps in Lebanon. As Figure 4-1 illustrates, each group perceived the networks as hostile to its side. The phenomenon is commonplace: Presidential candi-dates and their supporters nearly always view the news media as unsym-pathetic to their cause. A 1994 Gallup poll found African Americans twice

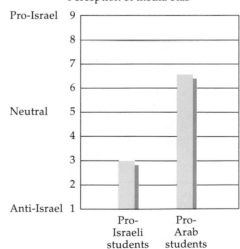

FIGURE 4-1
Pro-Israeli and pro-Arab students who viewed network news descriptions of the "Beirut massacre" believed the coverage was biased against their point of view. (Data from Vallone, Ross, & Lepper, 1985.)

as likely as other Americans to perceive media coverage of O. J. Simpson's arrest as too harsh. Sports fans perceive referees as partial to the other side. People in conflict (married couples, labor and management, opposing racial groups) see impartial mediators as biased against them.

Our shared assumptions about the world can even make contradictory evidence seem supportive. For example, Ross and Lepper assisted Charles Lord (1979) in asking students to evaluate the results of two supposedly new research studies. Half the students favored capital punishment and half opposed it. One study confirmed and the other disconfirmed the students' beliefs about the deterrence effect of the death penalty. The results: Both proponents and opponents of capital punishment readily accepted evidence that confirmed their belief but were sharply critical of disconfirming evidence. Showing the two sides an *identical* body of mixed evidence had therefore not lessened their disagreement but *increased* it. Each side ended up perceiving the evidence as supporting its belief and then believed even more strongly.

Is this why, in politics, religion, and science, ambiguous information often fuels conflict? Televised presidential debates in the United States have mostly reinforced predebate opinions. By nearly a 10-to-1 margin, those who already favored one candidate or the other in the 1960, 1976, and 1980 debates perceived their candidate as having won (Kinder & Sears, 1985).

FIGURE 4-2
"Kurt Walden," as shown by Myron Rothbart and Pamela Birrell. Judge for yourself: Is he cruel or kindly?

Experiments have manipulated preconceptions with astonishing effects upon how people interpret and recall what they observe. Myron Rothbart and Pamela Birrell (1977) had University of Oregon students assess the facial expression of the man shown in Figure 4-2. Those who were told that he was a Gestapo leader responsible for barbaric medical experiments on concentration camp inmates during World War II intuitively judged his expression as cruel. (Can you see that barely suppressed sneer?) Those told he was a leader in the anti-Nazi underground movement whose courage saved thousands of Jewish lives judged his facial expression as warm and kind. (On second thought, look at those caring eyes and that almost smiling mouth.) Bottom line: Our preconceptions control our interpretations.

W E OVERESTIMATE THE ACCURACY OF OUR JUDGMENTS

The "intellectual conceit" evident in judgments of past knowledge ("I knew it all along") extends to estimates of current knowledge. To explore this **overconfidence phenomenon,** Daniel Kahneman and Amos Tversky (1979) gave people factual questions and asked them to fill in the blanks, as in: "I feel 98 percent certain that the air distance between New Delhi and Beijing is more than _____ miles but less than _____ miles." Most subjects were overconfident: About 30 percent of the time, the correct answers lay outside the range they felt 98 percent confident about.

To find out whether overconfidence extends to social judgments, David Dunning and his associates (1990) created a little game show. They prepared Stanford University students to guess a stranger's answers to a series of questions, such as "Would you prepare for a difficult exam alone or with others?" and "Would you rate your lecture notes as neat or messy?" Knowing the types of questions that would be asked, but not the actual questions, the subjects first interviewed their target person about background, hobbies, academic interests, aspirations, astrological sign— anything they thought might be helpful. Then, while the targets privately answered 20 of the two-choice questions, the interviewers predicted their target's answers and rated their own confidence in the predictions.

The interviewers guessed right 63 percent of the time, beating chance by 13 percent. But, on average, they *felt* 75 percent sure of their predictions. When guessing their own roommates' responses, they were 68 percent correct and 78 percent confident. Moreover, the most confident people were most likely to be *over*confident. People also are markedly overconfident about their estimations of such things as the sexual history of their dating partner or the activity preferences of their roommates (Swann & Gill, 1997).

Are people better at predicting their own behavior? To find out, Robert Vallone and his colleagues (1990) had college students predict in September whether they would drop a course, declare a major, elect to live off campus next year, and so forth. Although the students felt, on average, 84 percent sure of these self-predictions, they were wrong nearly twice as often as they expected to be. Even when feeling 100 percent sure of their predictions, they erred 15 percent of the time.

In estimating their chances for success on a task, such as a major exam, people's confidence runs highest when removed in time from "the moment of truth." By exam day, the possibility of failure looms larger and confidence typically drops (Gilovich & others, 1993). Roger Buehler and his colleagues (1994) report that most students also confidently underestimate how long it will take them to complete papers and other major assignments. They are not alone:

- Planners routinely underestimate the time and expense of projects. In 1969, Montreal Mayor Jean Drapeau proudly announced that a $120 million stadium with a retractable roof would be built for the 1976 Olympics. The roof was completed in 1989, and the roof alone cost $120 million.

- Investment experts market their services with the confident presumption that they can beat the stock market average, forgetting that for every stockbroker or buyer saying "Sell!" at a given price there is another saying "Buy!" A stock's price is the balance point between these mutually confident judgments. Thus, incredible as it might seem, economist Burton Malkiel (1985, 1995) reports that mutual fund portfolios selected by investment analysts have not outperformed randomly selected stocks.

- Overconfident decision makers can wreak havoc. It was a confident Adolf Hitler who from 1939 to 1945 waged war against the rest of Europe. It was a confident Lyndon Johnson who in the 1960s invested U.S. weapons and soldiers in the effort to salvage democracy in South Vietnam. It was a confident Saddam Hussein who in 1990 marched his army into Kuwait.

What lessons can we draw from research on overconfidence? One lesson is to be careful about other people's dogmatic statements. Even when people seem sure they are right, they might be wrong. Confidence and competence need not coincide.

Two techniques have successfully reduced the overconfidence bias. One is prompt feedback (Lichtenstein & Fischhoff, 1980). In everyday life, weather forecasters and those who set the odds in horse racing receive clear, daily feedback. Experts in both groups, therefore, do quite well at estimating their probable accuracy (Fischhoff, 1982).

When people think about why an idea *might* be true, it begins to seem true to them (Koehler, 1991). Thus, another way to reduce overconfidence is to get people to think of one good reason *why their judgments might be wrong*: force them to consider disconfirming information (Koriat & others, 1980).

Managers might foster more realistic judgments by insisting that all pro-posals and recommendations include reasons why they might not work.

Still, we should be careful not to undermine people's self-confidence to a point where they spend too much time in self-analysis or where their self-doubts begin to cripple their decisiveness. In times when their wis-dom is needed, those lacking self-confidence might shrink from speaking up or making tough decisions. *Over*confidence can cost us, but realistic self-confidence is adaptive.

WE OFTEN ARE SWAYED MORE BY ANECDOTES THAN BY STATISTICAL FACTS

Anecdotal information is persuasive. A research team led by Richard Nis-bett (1976) explored the tendency to overuse such information. They showed University of Michigan students videotaped interviews of people who supposedly had participated in an experiment in which most subjects failed to assist a seizure victim. Learning how *most* subjects acted had little effect upon people's predictions of how the individual they observed acted. The apparent niceness of this individual was more vivid and compelling than the general truth about how most subjects really acted: "Ted seems so pleasant that I can't imagine him being unresponsive to another's plight."

This experiment illustrates the **base-rate fallacy:** *Focusing upon the specific individual can push into the background useful information about the population the person came from and distort our perception of what is generally true.*

There is, of course, a positive side to viewing people as individuals and not merely as statistical units. The problem arises when we formulate our beliefs about people in general from our observations of particular persons. Focusing on individuals distorts our perception of what is gener-ally true. Our impressions of a group, for example, tend to be overly in-fluenced by its extreme members. One man's attempt to assassinate Pres-ident Reagan caused people to say, "It's not safe to walk the streets anymore," and to conclude, "There's a sickness in the American soul." As psychologist Gordon Allport put it, "Given a thimbleful of facts we rush to make generalizations as large as a tub."

Nevertheless, research reveals a basic principle of social thinking: People are slow to deduce particular instances from a general truth but are remark-ably quick to infer general truth from a vivid instance. No wonder that, after hearing and reading about countless instances of rapes, robberies, and beat-ings, 9 out of 10 Canadians overestimate—usually by a considerable margin—the percentage of crimes that involve violence (Doob & Roberts, 1988).

Sometimes the vivid example is a personal experience. Before buying a new Honda, I consulted the *Consumer Reports* survey of car owners and found the repair record of the Dodge Colt, which for a time I considered, to be quite good. A short while later, I mentioned my interest in the Colt to a student. "Oh no," he moaned, "don't buy a Colt. I worked in a garage last summer and serviced two Dodge Colts that kept falling apart and being brought in for one thing after another." How did I use this information—and the glowing testimonies from two friends who were Honda owners? Did I simply add to the *Consumer Reports* surveys of Colt and Honda owners two more people each? Although I knew that, logically, that is what I should have done, it was nearly impossible to ignore my awareness of those vivid accounts. I bought the Honda.

The Availability Heuristic

Consider: Does the letter *k* appear in print more often as the first letter of a word or as the third letter? Do more people live in Cambodia or Tanzania?

You probably answered in terms of how readily instances of them come to mind. If examples are readily *available* in our memory—as words beginning with *k* and as Cambodians tend to be—then we presume that the event is commonplace. Usually it is, so we are often well served by this cognitive rule of thumb, called the **availability heuristic.**

The availability heuristic explains why powerful anecdotes are often more compelling than base-rate statistical information, and why perceived risk is therefore often badly out of joint with real risks. News footage of airplane crashes is a readily available memory for most of us, so we often suppose we are more at risk traveling in a commercial airplane than in a car. Actually, U.S. travelers during the 1980s were 26 times more likely to die in a car crash than on a commercial flight covering the same distance (National Safety Council, 1991). In the 27 months following March 22, 1992, major U.S. airlines had more than *16 million* flights without a single death. For most air travelers, the most dangerous part of the journey is the drive to the airport.

Or consider this: Three fatal crashes every day of jumbo jets full of passengers would not equal tobacco's death toll. If the deaths caused by tobacco occurred in horrible accidents, the resulting uproar would long ago have eliminated cigarettes. Because, instead, the deaths are disguised as "cancer" and "heart disease" and diffused on obituary pages, we hardly notice. Thus, rather than eliminating the hazard, the U.S. government continues to subsidize the tobacco industry's program for quietly killing its customers. The point: Dramatic events stick in our minds, and we use ease of recall—the availability heuristic—when predicting the likelihood that a certain event will happen.

WE MISPERCEIVE CORRELATION AND CONTROL

Another influence on everyday thinking is our search for order in random events, a tendency that can lead us down all sorts of wrong paths.

Illusory Correlation

It's easy to see a correlation where none exists. When we expect significant relationships, we easily associate random events, perceiving an **illusory correlation.** William Ward and Herbert Jenkins (1965) showed people the results of a hypothetical 50-day cloud-seeding experiment. They told their subjects which of the 50 days the clouds had been seeded and which days it rained. This information was nothing more than a random mix of results: Sometimes it rained after seeding; sometimes it didn't. People nevertheless became convinced—in conformity with their ideas about the effects of cloud seeding—that they really had observed a relationship between cloud seeding and rain.

Other experiments confirm that people easily misperceive random events as confirming their beliefs (Crocker, 1981; Jennings & others, 1982; Trolier & Hamilton, 1986). If we believe a correlation exists, we are more likely to notice and recall confirming instances. If we believe that premonitions correlate with events, we notice and remember the joint occurrence of the premonition and the event's later occurrence. We seldom notice or remember all the times unusual events do not coincide. If, after we think about a friend, the friend calls us, we notice and remember this coincidence. We don't notice all the times we think of a friend without any ensuing call, or receive a call from a friend about whom we've not been thinking.

Illusion of Control

Our tendency to perceive random events as related feeds an **illusion of control**—the idea that chance events are subject to our influence. This is what keeps gamblers going, and what makes the rest of us do all sorts of superstitious acts.

Gambling

Ellen Langer (1977) demonstrated the illusion of control with experiments on gambling. Compared to those given an assigned lottery number, people who chose their own number demanded four times as much money when asked to sell their ticket. When playing a game of chance against an awkward and nervous person, they bet significantly more than when playing against a dapper, confident opponent. In these and other ways, more than 50 experiments have consistently found people acting as if they can predict or control chance events (Presson & Benassi, 1996). Moreover, the more people *need* a random outcome (a food prize for the hungry rather than for the well-fed participants, in one experiment), the more illusory confidence they feel (Biner & others, 1995).

Observations of real-life gamblers confirm these experimental findings. Dice players might throw softly for low numbers and hard for high numbers (Henslin, 1967). The gambling industry thrives on gamblers' illusions. Gamblers attribute wins to their skill and foresight. Losses become "near misses" or "flukes"—perhaps (for the sports gambler) a bad call by the referee or a freakish bounce of the ball (Gilovich & Douglas, 1986).

Regression Toward the Average

Tversky and Kahneman (1974) noted another way by which an illusion of control can arise: We fail to recognize the statistical phenomenon of **regression toward the average.** Because exam scores fluctuate partly by chance, most students who get extremely high scores on an exam will get lower scores on the next exam. Because their first score is at the ceiling, their second score is more likely to fall back ("regress") toward their own average than to push the ceiling even higher. (This is why a student who does consistently good work, even if never the best, will sometimes end a course at the top of the class.) Conversely, the lowest-scoring students on the first exam are likely to improve. If those who scored lowest go for tutoring after the first exam, the tutors are likely to feel effective when the student improves, even if the tutoring had no effect.

Indeed, when things reach a low point, we will try anything, and whatever we try—going to a psychotherapist, starting a new diet-exercise plan, reading a self-help book—is more likely to be followed by improvement than by further deterioration. (When we're extremely high or low, we tend to fall back toward our normal average.)

OUR BELIEFS CAN GENERATE THEIR OWN CONFIRMATION

There's one additional reason why our intuitive beliefs resist reality: They sometimes lead us to act in ways that produce their apparent confirmation. Our beliefs about other people can therefore become **self-fulfilling prophecies.**

In his well-known studies of "experimenter bias," Robert Rosenthal (1985) found that research subjects sometimes live up to what is expected of them. In one study, experimenters asked subjects to judge the success of people in various photographs. The experimenters read the same instructions to all their subjects and showed them the same photos. Nevertheless, experimenters who had been led to expect high ratings obtained higher ratings than did those who expected their subjects to see the photographed people as failures. Even more startling, and controversial, are reports that teachers' beliefs about their students similarly serve as self-fulfilling prophecies.

Do Teacher Expectations Affect Student Performance?

Teachers do have higher expectations for some students than for others. Perhaps you have detected this after having a brother or sister precede you in school, after receiving a label such as "gifted" or "learning disabled," or after being tracked with "high-ability" or "average-ability" students. Perhaps conversation in the teachers' lounge sent your reputation ahead of you, or your new teacher scrutinized your school file or discovered your family's social status. Do such teacher expectations affect student performance? It's clear that teachers' evaluations *correlate* with student achievement: Teachers think well of students who do well. That's mostly because teachers accurately perceive their students' abilities and achievements (Jussim, 1989, 1991; Jussim & others, 1996). But do expectations also affect performance? Often they don't. But in 39 percent of the 448 published experiments they do (Rosenthal, 1991).

Why do expectations sometimes matter? Rosenthal and other investigators report that teachers look, smile, and nod more at "high-potential students." A random 10-second clip of either the teacher's voice or face was enough to tell viewers—both children and adults—whether this was a good or poor student and how much the teacher liked the student. (You read that right: 10 seconds.) Although teachers might think they can conceal their feelings, students are acutely sensitive to teachers' facial expressions and body movements. Teachers also might teach more to their "gifted" students, set higher goals for them, call on them more, and give them more time to answer (Cooper, 1983; Harris & Rosenthal, 1985, 1986; Jussim, 1986).

Reading the experiments on teacher expectations makes me wonder about the effect of *students'* expectations upon their teachers. You no doubt begin many of your courses having heard "Professor Smith is interesting" and "Professor Jones is a bore." To see whether such effects might also occur in actual classrooms, a research team led by David Jamieson (1987) experimented with four Ontario high school classes taught by a newly transferred teacher. During individual interviews they told students in two of the classes that both other students and the research team rated the teacher very highly. Compared to the control classes, whose expectations they did not raise, the students given positive expectations paid better attention during class. At the end of the teaching unit, they also got better grades and rated the teacher as clearer in her teaching. The attitudes that a class has toward its teacher are as important, it seems, as the teacher's attitude toward the students.

Do We Get What We Expect from Others?

So, the expectations of experimenters and teachers, though usually reasonably accurate assessments, occasionally act as self-fulfilling prophecies. How general is this effect? Do we get from others what we expect of them? There are times when negative expectations of someone lead us to be extra nice to that person, which induces them to be nice in return—thus *dis*confirming our expectations. But a more common finding in studies of social interaction is that, yes, we do to some extent get what we expect (Olson & others, 1996).

In laboratory games, hostility nearly always begets hostility: People who *perceive* their opponents as noncooperative will readily induce them to *be* noncooperative (Kelley & Stahelski, 1970). Self-confirming beliefs abound when there is conflict. Each party's perception of the other as aggressive, resentful, and vindictive induces the other to display these behaviors in self-defense, thus creating a vicious self-perpetuating circle. Whether I expect my wife to be in a bad mood or in a warm, loving mood might affect how I relate to her, thereby inducing her to confirm my belief.

So do intimate relationships prosper when partners idealize one another? Are positive illusions of the other's virtues self-fulfilling? Or are they more often self-defeating, by creating expectations that can't be met and that ultimately spell doom? Among University of Waterloo dating couples followed by Sandra Murray and her associates (1996), positive ideals of one's partner were good omens. Idealization helped buffer conflict, bolster satisfaction, and turn self-perceived frogs into princes or princesses. When someone loves and admires us, it helps us become more the person they imagine us to be.

Several experiments conducted by Mark Snyder (1984) at the University of Minnesota show how, once formed, erroneous beliefs about the social world can induce others to confirm those beliefs, a phenomenon called **behavioral confirmation.** In a now-classic study, Snyder, Elizabeth Tanke, and Ellen Berscheid (1977) had men students talk on the telephone with women they thought (from having been shown a picture) were either attractive or unattractive. Analysis of just the women's comments during the conversations revealed that the supposedly attractive women spoke more warmly than the supposedly unattractive women. The men's erroneous beliefs had become a self-fulfilling prophecy by leading them to act in a way that influenced the women to fulfill their stereotype that beautiful people are desirable people.

Expectations influence children's behavior, too. After observing the amount of litter in three classrooms, Richard Miller and his colleagues (1975) had the teacher and others repeatedly tell one class that they should be neat and tidy. This persuasion increased the amount of litter placed in wastebaskets from 15 to 45 percent, but only temporarily. Another class, which also had been placing only 15 percent of its litter in wastebaskets, was repeatedly congratulated for being so neat and tidy. After eight days of hearing this, and still two weeks later, these children were fulfilling the expectation by putting more than 80 percent of their litter in wastebaskets. Repeatedly tell children they are hardworking and kind (rather than lazy and mean), and they might live up to your words.

These experiments help us understand how social beliefs, such as stereotypes about people with disabilities or about people of a particular race or sex, can be self-confirming. We help construct our own social realities. How others treat us reflects how we and others have treated them.

CONCLUSIONS

We could extend our list of reasons for unreason, but surely this has been a sufficient glimpse at how people come to believe what might be untrue.

What we believe about someone can lead us to treat the person in ways that create a self-fulfilling prophecy.

We cannot easily dismiss these experiments: Most of their participants were intelligent people, mostly students at leading universities. Moreover, these predictable distortions and biases occurred even when payment for right answers motivated people to think optimally. As one researcher concluded, the illusions "have a persistent quality not unlike that of perceptual illusions" (Slovic, 1972).

Research in cognitive social psychology thus mirrors the mixed reviews given humanity in literature, philosophy, and religion. Many research psychologists have spent a lifetime exploring the awesome capacities of the human mind. We are smart enough to have cracked our own genetic code, to have invented talking computers, to have sent people to the moon. Three cheers for human reason.

Well, two cheers—because the mind's premium on efficient judgment makes our intuition more vulnerable to *mis*judgment than we suspect. With remarkable ease, we form and sustain false beliefs. Led by our preconceptions, overconfident, persuaded by vivid anecdotes, perceiving correlations and control even where none might exist, we construct our social beliefs and then influence others to confirm them. "The naked intellect," observed novelist Madeline L'Engle, "is an extraordinarily inaccurate instrument."

*C*ONCEPTS TO REMEMBER

Overconfidence phenomenon   The tendency to be more confident than correct— to overestimate the accuracy of one's beliefs.

Base-rate fallacy   The tendency to ignore or underuse base-rate information (information that describes most people) and instead to be influenced by distinctive features of the case being judged.

Availability heuristic   An efficient but fallible rule of thumb that judges the likelihood of things in terms of their availability in memory. If instances of something come readily to mind, we presume it to be commonplace.

Illusory correlation   Perception of a relationship where none exists, or perception of a stronger relationship than actually exists.

Illusion of control   Perception of uncontrollable events as subject to one's control or as more controllable than they are.

Regression toward the average   The statistical tendency for extreme scores or extreme behavior to return toward one's average.

Self-fulfilling prophecy   The tendency for one's expectations to evoke behavior that confirms the expectations.

Behavioral confirmation   A type of self-fulfilling prophecy whereby people's social expectations lead them to act in ways that cause others to confirm their expectations.

5

❖

Clinical Intuition
The Perils of Psychologizing

Clinical psychologists—psychologists who study, assess, and treat people with psychological difficulties—struggle to make accurate judgments, recommendations, and predictions in any number of real situations: Is Susan suicidal? Should John be committed to a mental hospital? If released, will Tom be a homicide risk?

Such clinical judgments are also *social* judgments. Like all social judgments clinical judgments are vulnerable to illusory correlations, overconfidence bred by hindsight, and self-confirming diagnoses.

*I*LLUSORY CORRELATIONS

Consider the following court transcript in which a seemingly confident psychologist (PSY) is being questioned by an attorney (ATT):

ATT: You asked the defendant to draw a human figure?

PSY: Yes.

ATT: And this is the figure he drew for you? What does it indicate to you about his personality?

PSY: You will note this is a rear view of a male. This is very rare, statistically. It indicates hiding guilt feelings, or turning away from reality.

ATT: And this drawing of a female figure, does it indicate anything to you; and, if so, what?

PSY: It indicates hostility toward women on the part of the subject. The pose, the hands on the hips, the hard-looking face, the stern expression.

ATT: Anything else?

PSY: The size of the ears indicates a paranoid outlook, or hallucinations. Also, the absence of feet indicates feelings of insecurity. (Jeffery, 1964)

The assumption here, as in so many clinical judgments, is that test results reveal something important. Do they? There is a simple way to find out. Have one clinician administer and interpret the test. Have another clinician assess the same person's symptoms. Repeat this process with many people. The proof is in the pudding: Are test outcomes in fact correlated with reported symptoms? Some tests are indeed predictive. Others, such as the Draw-a-Person test above, have correlations far weaker than their users suppose. Why, then, do clinicians continue to express confidence in uninformative or ambiguous tests?

Pioneering experiments by Loren Chapman and Jean Chapman (1969, 1971) help us see why. They invited both college students and professional clinicians to study some test performances and diagnoses. If the students or clinicians *expected* a particular association, they generally *perceived* it, regardless of whether the data supported that association. For example, clinicians who believed that suspicious people draw peculiar eyes on the Draw-a-Person test perceived such a relationship—even when shown cases in which suspicious people drew peculiar eyes *less* often than nonsuspicious people. Believing that a relationship existed between two things, they were more likely to notice confirming instances. To believe is to see.

HINDSIGHT AND OVERCONFIDENCE

If someone we know commits suicide, how do we react? One common reaction is to think that we, or those close to the person, should have been able to predict and therefore to prevent the suicide: "We should have known." In hindsight, we can see the suicidal signs and the pleas for help. One experiment gave people a description of a depressed person who later committed suicide. Compared to those not informed of the suicide, those told the person committed suicide were more likely to say they "would have expected" it (Goggin & Range, 1985). Moreover, if they were told of the suicide, their reactions to the victim's family were more negative. After a tragedy, an I-should-have-known-it-all-along phenomenon can leave family, friends, and therapists feeling guilty.

David Rosenhan (1973) and seven associates provided a striking example of potential error in after-the-fact explanations. To test mental health workers' clinical insights, they each made an appointment with a different mental hospital admissions office and complained of "hearing voices." Apart from giving false names and vocations, they reported their life histories and emotional states honestly and exhibited no further symptoms. Most got diagnosed as schizophrenic and remained hospitalized for two to three weeks. Hospital clinicians then searched for early incidents in the pseudo-patients' life histories and hospital behavior that "confirmed" and "explained" the diagnosis. Rosenhan tells of one pseudo-patient who truthfully explained to the interviewer that he

> had a close relationship with his mother but was rather remote from his father during his early childhood. During adolescence and beyond, however, his father became a close friend, while his relationship with his mother cooled. His present relationship with his wife was characteristically close and warm. Apart from occasional angry exchanges, friction was minimal. The children had rarely been spanked.

The interviewer, "knowing" the person suffered from schizophrenia, explained the problem this way:

> This white 39-year-old male . . . manifests a long history of considerable ambivalence in close relationships, which begins in early childhood. A warm relationship with his mother cools during his adolescence. A distant relationship to his father is described as becoming very intense. Affective stability is absent. His attempts to control emotionality with his wife and children are punctuated by angry outbursts and, in the case of the children, spankings. And while he says that he has several good friends, one senses considerable ambivalence embedded in those relationships also.

Rosenhan later told some staff members (who had heard about his controversial experiment but doubted such mistakes could occur in their hospital) that during the next three months one or more pseudo-patients would seek admission to their hospital. After the three months, he asked the staff to guess which of the 193 patients admitted during that time were really pseudo-patients. Of the 193 new patients, 41 were accused by at least one staff member of being pseudo-patients. Actually, there were none.

SELF-CONFIRMING DIAGNOSES

So far we've seen that mental health workers sometimes perceive illusory correlations and that hindsight explanations are often questionable. A third problem with clinical judgment is that people might also supply information that fulfills clinicians' expectations. In a clever series of experiments at the University of Minnesota, Mark Snyder (1984), in collaboration with William Swann and others, gave interviewers some hypotheses to test concerning individuals' traits. To get a feel for their experiments, imagine yourself on a blind date with someone who has been told that you are an uninhibited, outgoing person. To see whether this is true, your date slips questions into the conversation, such as "Have you ever done anything crazy in front of other people?" As you answer such questions, will your date meet a different "you" than if you were probed for instances when you were shy and retiring?

Snyder and Swann found that people often test for a trait by looking for information that confirms it. If they are trying to find out if someone is an extravert, they often solicit instances of extraversion ("What would you do if you wanted to liven things up at a party?"). Testing for introversion, they are more likely to ask, "What factors make it hard for you to really open up to people?" Such questions feel more empathic than would questions that don't match the person's presumed traits (Leyens & others, 1975). But they also lead those being tested for extraversion to behave more sociably and those being tested for introversion to appear more shy and reserved. *Our behavior sometimes creates the kind of people we expect to see.*

At Indiana University, Russell Fazio and his colleagues (1981) reproduced this finding and also discovered that those asked the "extraverted questions" later perceived themselves as actually being more outgoing than did those who had been asked the "introverted questions." Moreover, they really became noticeably more outgoing. An accomplice of the experimenter later met each participant in a waiting room and 70 percent of the time correctly guessed from the person's behavior which condition the person had come from. Likewise, the framing of questions asked of an alleged rape victim—"Did you dance with Peter?" versus "Did Peter dance with you?"—can subtly influence who gets perceived as responsible (Semin & De Poot, 1997).

In other experiments, Snyder and his colleagues (1982) tried to get people to search for behaviors that would *disconfirm* the trait they were testing. In one experiment, they told the interviewers "it is relevant and informative to find out ways in which the person . . . may not be like the stereotype." In another experiment Snyder (1981) offered "$25 to the person who develops the set of questions that tell the most about . . . the interviewee." Still, confirmation bias persisted: People resisted choosing "introverted" questions when testing for extraversion.

This illustrates **confirmation bias.** When testing our beliefs, we seek information that will verify them before we seek disconfirming information. P. C. Wason (1960) demonstrated this, as you can, by giving people a sequence of three numbers—*2, 4, 6*—which conformed to a rule he had in mind (the rule was simply *any three ascending numbers*). To enable the people to discover the rule, Wason invited each person to generate sets of three numbers. Each time Wason told the person whether the set did or did not conform to his rule. When they were sure they had discovered the rule, the people were to stop and announce it. The result? Seldom right but never in doubt: 23 of the 29 people convinced themselves of a wrong rule. They typically formed some erroneous belief about the rule (for example, counting by twos) and then searched for *confirming* evidence (for example, by testing 8, 10, 12) rather than attempting to *disconfirm* their hunches.

Based on Snyder's experiments, can you see why the behaviors of people undergoing psychotherapy come to fit the theories of their therapists (Whitman & others, 1963)? When Harold Renaud and Floyd Estess (1961) conducted life-history interviews of 100 healthy, successful adult men, they were startled to discover that their subjects' childhood experiences were loaded with "traumatic events," tense relations with certain people, and bad decisions by their parents—the very factors usually used to explain psychiatric problems. When Freudian therapists go fishing for traumas in early childhood experiences, they often find their hunches confirmed. Thus, surmises Snyder (1981):

> The psychiatrist who believes (erroneously) that adult gay males had bad childhood relationships with their mothers may meticulously probe for recalled (or fabricated) signs of tension between their gay clients and their mothers, but neglect to so carefully interrogate their heterosexual clients about their maternal relationships. No doubt, any individual could recall some friction with his or her mother, however minor or isolated the incidents.

Nineteenth-century poet Robert Browning anticipated Snyder's conclusion:

> As is your sort of mind,
> So is your sort of search:
> You'll find
> What you desire.

CLINICAL VERSUS STATISTICAL PREDICTION

Given these hindsight- and diagnosis-confirming tendencies, it will come as no surprise that most clinicians and interviewers express more confidence in their intuitive assessments than in statistical data. Yet when researchers pit statistical prediction (as when predicting graduate school success using a formula that includes grades and aptitude scores) against intuitive prediction, the statistics usually win. Statistical predictions are indeed unreliable, but human intuition—even expert intuition— is even more unreliable (Dawes & others, 1989; Faust & Ziskin, 1988; Meehl, 1954).

Three decades after demonstrating the superiority of statistical over intuitive prediction, Paul Meehl (1986) found the evidence stronger than ever:

> There is no controversy in social science which shows [so many] studies coming out so uniformly in the same direction as this one. . . . When you are pushing 90 investigations, predicting everything from the outcome of football games to the diagnosis of liver disease and when you can hardly come up with a half dozen studies showing even a weak tendency in favor of the clinician, it is time to draw a practical conclusion.

So, why do so many clinicians continue to interpret Rorschach inkblot tests and offer intuitive predictions about parolees, suicide risks, and likelihood of child abuse? Partly out of sheer ignorance, says Meehl, but also partly out of "mistaken conceptions of ethics":

> If I try to forecast something important about a college student, or a criminal, or a depressed patient by inefficient rather than efficient means, meanwhile charging this person or the taxpayer 10 times as much money as I would need to achieve greater predictive accuracy, that is not a sound ethical practice. That it feels better, warmer, and cuddlier to me as a predictor is a shabby excuse indeed.

Such words are shocking. Do Meehl and the other researchers underestimate our intuition? To see why their findings are apparently true, consider the assessment of human potential by graduate admissions interviewers. Dawes (1976) explained why statistical prediction is so often superior to an interviewer's intuition when predicting certain outcomes such as graduate school success:

> What makes us think that we can do a better job of selection by interviewing (students) for a half hour, than we can by adding together relevant (standardized) variables, such as undergraduate GPA, GRE score, and perhaps ratings of letters of recommendation. The most reasonable explanation to me lies in our overevaluation of our cognitive capacity. And it is really cognitive conceit. Consider, for example, what goes into a GPA. Because for most graduate applicants it is based on at least $3\frac{1}{2}$ years of undergraduate study, it is a composite measure arising from a minimum of 28 courses and possibly, with the popularity of the quarter system, as many as 50. . . . Yet you and I, looking at a folder or interviewing someone for a half hour, are supposed to be able to form a better impression than one based on $3\frac{1}{2}$ years of the cumulative evaluations of 20–40 different professors. . . . Finally, if we do wish to ignore GPA, it appears that the only reason for doing so is believing that the candidate is particularly brilliant even though his or her record may not show it. What better evidence for such brilliance can we have than a score on a carefully devised aptitude test? Do we really think we are better equipped to assess such aptitude than is the Educational Testing Service, whatever its faults?

*I*MPLICATIONS

Professional clinicians are "vulnerable to insidious errors and biases," concludes James Maddux (1993). They

- are frequently the victims of illusory correlation,
- are too readily convinced of their own after-the-fact analyses,
- often fail to appreciate that erroneous diagnoses can be self-confirming, and
- often overestimate the predictive powers of their clinical intuition.

The implications for mental health workers are more easily stated than practiced: Be mindful that clients' verbal agreement with what you say does not prove its validity. Beware of the tendency to see relationships that you expect to see or that are supported by striking examples readily available in your memory. Rely on your notes more than your memory. Recognize that hindsight is seductive: It can lead you to feel overconfident and sometimes to judge yourself too harshly for not having foreseen outcomes. Guard against the tendency to ask questions that assume your preconceptions are correct; consider opposing ideas and test them, too (Garb, 1994).

Research on illusory thinking has implications not only for mental health workers but for all psychologists. What Lewis Thomas (1978) said of biology may as justly be said of psychology:

> The solidest piece of scientific truth I know of, the one thing about which I feel totally confident, is that we are profoundly ignorant about nature. Indeed, I regard this as the major discovery of the past 100 years of biology. . . . It is this sudden confrontation with the depth and scope of ignorance that represents the most significant contribution of 20th century science to the human intellect. We are, at last, facing up to it. In earlier times, we either pretended to understand how things worked or ignored the problem, or simply made up stories to fill the gaps.

Psychology has crept only a little way across the edge of insight into our human condition. Ignorant of their ignorance, some psychologists invent theories to fill gaps in their understanding. Intuitive observation seems to support these theories, even if they are mutually contradictory. Research on illusory thinking therefore leads us to a new humility: It reminds research psychologists why they must test their preconceptions before presenting them as truth. To seek the hard facts, even if they threaten cherished illusions, is the goal of every science.

I am *not* arguing that the scientific method can answer all human questions. There are questions that it cannot address and ways of knowing that it cannot capture. But science *is* one means for examining claims about nature, human nature included. Propositions that imply observable results are best evaluated by systematic observation and experiment—which is the whole point of social psychology. We also need inventive genius, or we might test only trivialities. But whatever unique and enduring insights psychology can offer will be hammered out by research psychologists sorting through competing claims. Science always involves an interplay between intuition and rigorous test, between creative hunch and skepticism.

CONCEPT TO REMEMBER

Confirmation bias   A tendency to search for information that confirms one's preconceptions.

MODULE

6

❖

The Fundamental Attribution Error

As later modules will reveal, social psychology's most important lesson concerns how much we are affected by our social environment. At any moment, our internal state, and therefore what we say and do, depends on both the situation and what we bring to the situation. In experiments, a slight difference between two situations sometimes greatly affects how people respond. I have seen this when teaching classes at both 8:30 A.M. and 7:00 P.M. Silent stares would greet me at 8:30; at 7:00 I had to break up a party. In each situation some individuals were more talkative than others, but the difference between the two situations exceeded the individual differences.

Attribution researchers have found that we often fail to appreciate this important lesson. When explaining someone's behavior, we underestimate the impact of the situation and overestimate the extent to which it reflects the individual's traits and attitudes. Thus, even knowing the effect of the time of day on classroom conversation, I found it terribly tempting to assume that the people in the 7:00 P.M. class were more extraverted than the "silent types" who come at 8:30 A.M.

This discounting of the situation, dubbed by Lee Ross (1977) the **fundamental attribution error,** appears in many experiments. In the first such study, Edward Jones and Victor Harris (1967) had Duke University students read debaters' speeches supporting or attacking Cuba's leader, Fidel Castro. When the position taken was said to have been chosen by the debater, the students logically enough assumed it reflected the person's own attitude. But what happened when the students were told that the debate coach had assigned the position?

People write stronger statements than you'd expect from those feigning a position they don't hold (Allison & others, 1993; Miller & others,

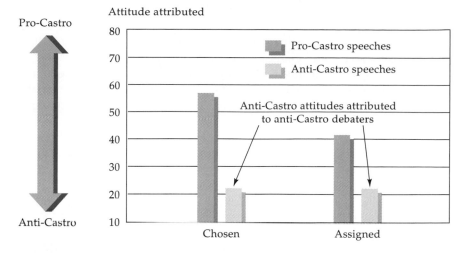

FIGURE 6-1
The fundamental attribution error. When people read a debate speech supporting or attacking Fidel Castro, they attributed corresponding attitudes to the speech writer, even when the debate coach assigned the writer's position. (Data from Jones & Harris, 1967.)

1990). Thus, even knowing that the debater had been told to take a pro-Castro position did not prevent students' inferring that the debater in fact had some pro-Castro leanings (Figure 6-1). People seemed to think, "Yeah, I know he was assigned that position, but to some extent I think he really believes it."

Peter Ditto and his colleagues (1997) replicated the phenomenon when they asked men to meet a woman who was actually working for the experimenters. The woman wrote her supposed impressions of each man, who was then to guess how much she liked him. When she wrote only negative statements, the men discounted her criticisms when told she was under orders to be negative. But when the woman wrote only positive impressions, the typical man inferred she *really* liked him—and it didn't matter whether he believed she wrote positive things freely or under orders. The fundamental attribution error looms large when it serves our self-interest.

The error is so irresistible that even when people know they are causing someone else's behavior, they still underestimate external influences. If subjects dictate an opinion that someone else must then express, they still tend to see the person as actually holding that opinion (Gilbert & Jones, 1986). If subjects are asked to be either self-enhancing or self-deprecating during an interview, they are very aware of why they are acting so. But they are *un*aware of their effect on another person. If Juan acts modest, his naive partner Bob is likely to exhibit modesty as well. Juan will easily understand his own behavior, but he will think that poor Bob suffers low self-esteem (Baumeister & others, 1988). In short, we tend to presume that others *are* the way they act. Observing Cinderella cowering in her oppressive home, people infer she is meek; dancing with her at the ball, the Prince sees a suave and glamorous person.

We commit the fundamental attribution error when explaining *other people's* behavior. We often explain our own behavior in terms of the situation while holding others responsible for their behavior. So John might attribute his behavior to the situation ("I was angry because everything was going wrong"), while Alice might think, "John was hostile because he is an angry person." When referring to ourselves, we typically use verbs that describe our actions and reactions ("I get annoyed when . . ."). Referring to someone else, we more often describe what that person *is* ("He is nasty") (Fiedler & others, 1991; McGuire & McGuire, 1986; White & Younger, 1988).

THE FUNDAMENTAL ATTRIBUTION ERROR OCCURS IN EVERYDAY LIFE

If we know the checkout cashier is programmed to say "Thank you and have a nice day," do we nevertheless automatically conclude that the cashier is a friendly, grateful person? We certainly know how to discount behavior that we attribute to ulterior motives (Fein & others, 1990). Yet consider what happened when Williams College students talked with a supposed clinical psychology graduate student who acted either warm and friendly or aloof and critical. Researchers David Napolitan and George Goethals (1979) told half the students beforehand that her behavior would be spontaneous. They told the other half that for purposes of the experiment she had been instructed to feign friendly (or unfriendly) behavior. The effect of the information? None. If she acted friendly, they assumed she was really a friendly person; if she acted unfriendly, they assumed she was an unfriendly person. As when viewing a dummy on the ventriloquist's lap or a movie actor playing a "good-guy" or "bad-guy" role, we find it difficult to escape the illusion that the programmed behavior reflects an inner disposition. Perhaps this is why Leonard Nimoy, who played Mr. Spock on the original *Star Trek*, entitled his book *I Am Not Spock*.

The discounting of social constraints was further revealed in a thought-provoking experiment by Lee Ross and his collaborators (Ross & others, 1977). The experiment re-created Ross's firsthand experience of moving from graduate student to professor. His doctoral oral exam had proved a humbling experience as his apparently brilliant professors quizzed him on topics they specialized in. Six months later, *Dr.* Ross was himself an examiner, now able to ask penetrating questions on *his* favorite topics. Ross's hapless student later confessed to feeling exactly as Ross had a half year before—dissatisfied with his ignorance and impressed with the apparent brilliance of the examiners.

In the experiment, with Teresa Amabile and Julia Steinmetz, Ross set up a simulated quiz game. He randomly assigned some Stanford University students to play the role of questioner, some to play the role of contestant, and others to observe. The researchers invited the questioners to make up difficult questions that would demonstrate their wealth of knowledge. It's fun to imagine the questions: "Where is Bainbridge Island?" "What is the seventh book in the Old Testament?" "Which has the longer coastline, Europe or Africa?" If even these few questions have you feeling a little uninformed, then you will appreciate the results of this experiment.[1]

Everyone had to know that the questioner would have the advantage. Yet both contestants and observers (but not questioners) came to the erroneous conclusion that the questioners *really were* more knowledgeable than the contestants (Figure 6-2). Follow-up research shows that these misimpressions are hardly a reflection of low social intelligence. If anything, intelligent and socially competent people are *more* likely to make the attribution error (Block & Funder, 1986).

In real life, those with social power usually initiate and control conversation, which often leads underlings to overestimate their knowledge and intelligence. Medical doctors, for example, are often presumed to be experts on all sorts of questions unrelated to medicine. Similarly, students often overestimate the brilliance of their teachers. (As in the experiment, teachers are questioners on subjects of their special expertise.) When some of these students later become teachers, they are usually amazed to discover that teachers are not so brilliant after all.

To illustrate the fundamental attribution error, most of us need look no further than our own experience. Determined to make some new friends, Bev plasters a smile on her face and anxiously plunges into a party. Everyone else seems quite relaxed and happy as they laugh and talk with one another. Bev wonders to herself, "Why is everyone always so at ease in groups like this while I'm feeling shy and tense?" Actually, everyone else is feeling nervous, too, and making the same attributional error in assuming that Bev and the others *are* as they *appear*—confidently convivial.

Attributions of responsibility are at the heart of many judicial decisions (Fincham & Jaspars, 1980). During the week following O. J. Simpson's 1994 arrest for the murders of his ex-wife and another man, a UCLA research team led by Sandra Graham (1997) questioned a sample of Los Angeles people who believed Simpson committed the crimes. Those who perceived his alleged act as an uncontrollable response to the situation advocated a relatively mild punishment. Those who believed he committed a self-initiated act, advocated more severe punishment. The case

---

[1]Bainbridge Island is across Puget Sound from Seattle. The seventh Old Testament book is Judges. Although the African continent is more than double the area of Europe, Europe's coastline is longer. (It is more convoluted, with lots of harbors and inlets, a geographical fact that contributed to its role in the history of maritime trade.)

Rating of general knowledge

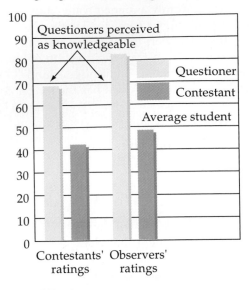

FIGURE 6-2
Both contestants and observers of a
simulated quiz game assumed that a
person who had been randomly assigned
the role of questioner was actually far more
knowledgeable than the contestant.
Actually the assigned roles of questioner
and contestant simply made the questioner
seem more knowledgeable. The failure to
appreciate this illustrates the fundamental
attribution error. (Data from Ross, Amabile,
& Steinmetz, 1977.)

exemplifies many judicial controversies: The prosecution argues, "You
are to blame, for you could have done otherwise"; the defendant replies,
"It wasn't my fault; I was a victim of the situation" or "Under the circumstances I did no wrong."

WHY DO WE MAKE THE ATTRIBUTION ERROR?

So far we have seen a bias in the way we explain other people's behavior:
We often ignore powerful situational determinants. Why do we tend to
underestimate the situational determinants of others' behavior but not of
our own?

Differing Perspectives

Attribution theorists point out that we have a different perspective when observing others than when acting (Jones & Nisbett, 1971; Jones, 1976). When we act, the environment commands our attention. When we watch another person act, that *person* occupies the center of our attention and the situation becomes relatively invisible. To use the perceptual analogy of figure and ground, the person is the figure that stands out from the surrounding environmental ground. So the person seems to cause whatever happens. If this theory is true, what might we expect if the perspectives were reversed? What if we could see ourselves as others see us and if we saw the world through their eyes? Shouldn't this eliminate or reverse the typical attribution error?

See if you can predict the result of a clever experiment conducted by Michael Storms (1973). Picture yourself as a subject in Storms's experiment. You are seated facing another student with whom you are to talk for a few minutes. Beside you is a TV camera that shares your view of the other student. Facing you from alongside the other student are an observer and another TV camera. Afterward, both you and the observer judge whether your behavior was caused more by your personal characteristics or by the situation.

Question: Which of you—subject or observer—will attribute the least importance to the situation? Storms found it was the observer (another demonstration of the fundamental attribution tendency). What if we reverse points of view by having you and the observer each watch the videotape recorded from the other's perspective? (You now view yourself, while the observer views what you saw.) This reverses the attributions: The observer now attributes your behavior mostly to the situation you faced, while you now attribute it to your person. *Remembering* an experience from an observer's perspective—by "seeing" oneself from the outside—has the same effect (Frank & Gilovich, 1989).

In another experiment, people viewed a videotape of a suspect confessing during a police interview. If they viewed the confession through a camera focused on the suspect, they perceived the confession as genuine. If they viewed it through a camera focused on the detective, they perceived it as more coerced (Lassiter & Irvine, 1986). In courtrooms, most confession videotapes focus on the confessor. As we might expect, note Daniel Lassiter and Kimberly Dudley (1991), such tapes yield a nearly 100 percent conviction rate when played by prosecutors. Perhaps a more impartial videotape would show both interrogator and suspect.

Time can change observers' perspectives. As the once-visible person recedes in their memory, observers often give more and more credit to the situation. Immediately after hearing someone argue an assigned position, people assume that's how the person really felt. A week later they are much more likely to credit the situational constraints (Burger, 1991). The day after the 1988 U.S. presidential election, Jerry Burger and Julie Pavelich (1994) asked Santa Clara, California, voters why the election turned out as it did. Most attributed the outcome to the candidates' personal traits and positions (Bush was likeable; challenger Dukakis ran a poor campaign). When they asked other voters the same question a year later, only a third attributed the verdict to the candidates. More people now credited circumstances, such as the country's good mood and the robust economy.

Editorial reflections on the six U.S. presidential elections from 1964 to 1988 show the same growth in situational explanations with time (Burger & Pavelich, 1994). Just after the 1978 election, editorial pundits focused on Ford's and Carter's campaigns and personalities. Two years later the situation loomed larger: "The shadows of Watergate . . . cleared the way for [Carter's] climb to the Presidency," noted one editorial in the *New York Times.*

Circumstances can also shift our perspective on ourselves. Seeing ourselves on television redirects our attention to ourselves. Seeing ourselves in a mirror, hearing our tape-recorded voices, having our pictures taken, filling out biographical questionnaires similarly focus our attention inward, making us *self*-conscious instead of *situation*-conscious. All these experiments point to a reason for the attribution error: *We find causes where we look for them.*

To see this in your own experience, consider: Would you say your social psychology instructor is a quiet or a talkative person?

My guess is you inferred that he or she is fairly outgoing. But consider further: Your attention focuses on your instructor while he or she behaves in a public context that demands speaking. The instructor also observes his or her own behavior in many different situations—in the classroom, in meetings, at home. "Me talkative?" your instructor might say. "Well, it all depends on the situation. When I'm in class or with good friends, I'm rather outgoing. But at conventions and in unfamiliar situations I feel and act rather shy."

If we are acutely aware of how our behavior varies with the situation, we should also see ourselves as more variable than other people. And that is precisely what studies in the United States, Canada, and Germany have found (Baxter & Goldberg, 1987; Kammer, 1982; Sande & others, 1988). Moreover, the less opportunity we have to observe people's behavior in context, the more we attribute to their personalities. Thomas Gilovich (1987) explored this by showing people a videotape of someone and then having them describe the person's actions to other people. The second-hand impressions were more extreme, partly because retellings focus attention on the person rather than the situation (Baron & others, 1997). Similarly, people's impressions of someone they have heard about from a friend are typically more extreme than their friend's firsthand impressions (Prager & Cutler, 1990).

Culture Differences

Cultures also influence the attribution error (Ickes, 1980; Watson, 1982). A Western worldview predisposes people to assume that people, not situations, cause events. Jerald Jellison and Jane Green (1981) reported that among University of Southern California students, internal explanations are more socially approved. "You can do it!" we are assured by the pop psychology of positive-thinking Western culture.

The assumption here is that, with the right disposition and attitude, anyone can surmount almost any problem: You get what you deserve and deserve what you get. Thus we often explain bad behavior by labeling the person as "sick," "lazy," or "sadistic." As children grow up in Western culture, they increasingly explain behavior in terms of the other's personal characteristics (Rholes & others, 1990; Ross, 1981). As a first-grader, one of my sons brought home an example. He unscrambled the words "gate the sleeve caught Tom on his" into "The gate caught Tom on his sleeve." His teacher, applying the Western cultural assumptions of the curriculum materials, marked this wrong. The "right" answer located the cause within Tom: "Tom caught his sleeve on the gate."

Some languages promote external attributions. Instead of "I was late," Spanish idiom allows one to say "The clock caused me to be late." In collectivist cultures, people less often perceive others in terms of personal dispositions (Lee & others, 1996; Zebrowitz-McArthur, 1988). They are less likely to spontaneously interpret a behavior as reflecting an inner trait (Newman, 1993). When told of someone's actions, Hindus in India are less likely than Americans to offer dispositional explanations ("She is kind") and more likely to offer situational explanations ("Her friends were with her") (Miller, 1984).

HOW FUNDAMENTAL IS THE FUNDAMENTAL ATTRIBUTION ERROR?

Like most provocative ideas, the presumption that we're all prone to a fundamental attribution error has its critics. Granted, say some, there is an attribution *bias*. But in any given instance, this might or might not produce an "error," just as parents who are biased to believe their child does not use drugs might or might not be correct (Harvey & others, 1981). We can be biased to believe what is true. Moreover, some everyday circumstances, such as being in church or on a job interview, are like the experiments we have been considering: As actors realize better than observers, the circumstances involve clear constraints. Hence the attribution error. But in other settings—in one's room, at a park—people exhibit their individuality. In such settings, people might see their own behavior as *less* constrained than do observers (Monson & Snyder, 1977; Quattrone, 1982; Robins & others,

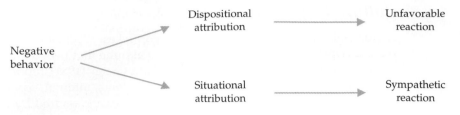

FIGURE 6-3
Attributions and reactions. How we explain someone's negative behavior determines how we feel about it.

1996). So it's an overstatement to say that at all times and in all settings observers underestimate situational influences. For this reason, many social psychologists follow Edward Jones in referring to the fundamental attribution error—seeing behavior as corresponding to an inner disposition—as the *correspondence bias.*

Nevertheless, experiments reveal that the bias occurs even when we are aware of the situational forces—when we know that an assigned debate position is not a good basis for inferring someone's real attitudes (Croxton & Morrow, 1984; Croxton & Miller, 1987; Reeder & others, 1989) or that the questioners' role in the quiz game gives them an advantage (Johnson & others, 1984). It is sobering to think that you and I can know about a social process that distorts our thinking and still be susceptible to it. Perhaps that's because it takes more mental effort to assess social effects on someone's behavior than merely to attribute it to a disposition (Gilbert & others, 1988, 1992; Webster, 1993). It's as if the busy person thinks, "This isn't a very good basis for making a judgment, but it's easy and all I've got time to look at."

The attribution error is, however, *fundamental* because it colors our explanations in basic and important ways. For example, researchers in Britain, India, Australia, and the United States have found that people's attributions predict their attitudes toward the poor and unemployed (Feather, 1983; Furnham, 1982; Pandey & others, 1982; Wagstaff, 1983; Zucker & Weiner, 1993). Those who attribute poverty and unemployment to personal dispositions ("They're just lazy and undeserving") tend to adopt political positions unsympathetic to such people (Figure 6-3). Their views differ from those who make external attributions ("If you or I were to live with the same overcrowding, poor education, and discrimination, would we be any better off?"). French investigators Jean-Leon Beauvois and Nicole Dubois (1988) report that "relatively privileged" middle-class people are more likely than less advantaged people to assume that people's behaviors have internal explanations. (Those who have made it tend to assume that you get what you deserve.)

Can we benefit from being aware of the attribution error? I once assisted with some interviews for a faculty position. One candidate was interviewed by six of us at once; each of us had the opportunity to ask two or three questions. I came away thinking, "What a stiff, awkward person he is." The second candidate I met privately over coffee, and we immediately discovered we had a close mutual friend. As we talked, I became increasingly impressed by what a "warm, engaging, stimulating person she is." Only later did I remember the fundamental attribution error and reassess my analysis. I had attributed his stiffness and her warmth to their dispositions; in fact, I later realized, such behavior resulted partly from the difference in their interview situations. Had I viewed these interactions through their eyes instead of my own, I might have come to different conclusions.

CONCEPT TO REMEMBER

Fundamental attribution error   The tendency for observers to underestimate situational influences and overestimate dispositional influences upon others' behavior. (Also called *correspondence bias,* because we so often see behavior as corresponding to a disposition.)

MODULE

7

---❖---

A New Look at Pride

I t is widely believed that most of us suffer low self-esteem. A generation ago, humanistic psychologist Carl Rogers (1958) concluded that
most people he knew "despise themselves, regard themselves as
worthless and unlovable." Many popularizers of humanistic psychology
concur. "All of us have inferiority complexes," contends John Powell
(1989). "Those who seem not to have such a complex are only pretending."
As Groucho Marx (1960) lampooned, "I don't want to belong to any club
that would accept me as a member."

SELF-SERVING BIAS: "HOW DO I LOVE ME? LET ME COUNT THE WAYS"

Actually, most of us have a good reputation with ourselves. In studies of
self-esteem, even low-scoring people respond in the midrange of possible
scores. (A low-self-esteem person responds to such statements as "I have
good ideas" with a qualifying adjective, such as "somewhat" or "sometimes.") Moreover, one of social psychology's most provocative yet firmly
established conclusions concerns the potency of **self-serving bias**—a tendency to perceive oneself favorably.

Attributions for Positive and Negative Events

Time and again, experimenters have found that people readily accept
credit when told they have succeeded (attributing the success to their
ability and effort), yet attribute failure to such external factors as bad

luck or the problem's inherent "impossibility" (Whitley & Frieze, 1985). Similarly, athletes commonly credit themselves for their victories but attribute losses to something else: bad breaks, bad referee calls, or the other team's super effort or dirty play (Grove & others, 1991; Lalonde, 1992; Mullen & Riordan, 1988). And how much responsibility do you suppose car drivers tend to accept for their accidents? On insurance forms, drivers have described their accidents in words such as these: "An invisible car came out of nowhere, struck my car and vanished"; "As I reached an intersection, a hedge sprang up, obscuring my vision and I did not see the other car"; "A pedestrian hit me and went under my car" (*Toronto News*, 1977).

Michael Ross and Fiore Sicoly (1979) observed a marital version of self-serving bias. They found that young married Canadians usually felt they took more responsibility for such activities as cleaning the house and caring for the children than their spouses credited them for. In a survey of Americans, 91 percent of wives but only 76 percent of husbands credited the wife with doing most of the food shopping (Burros, 1988). In another study, husbands estimated they did slightly more of the housework than their wives did; the wives, however, estimated their efforts were more than double their husbands' (Fiebert, 1990). Every night, my wife and I pitch our laundry at the foot of our bedroom clothes hamper. In the morning, one of us puts it in the hamper. When she suggested that I take more responsibility for this, I thought, "Huh? I already do it 75 percent of the time." So I asked her how often she thought she picked up the clothes. "Oh," she replied, "about 75 percent of the time." Small wonder that divorced people usually blame their partner for the breakup (Gray & Silver, 1990), or that managers usually blame poor performance on workers' lack of ability or effort (Imai, 1994; Rice, 1985). (Workers are more likely to blame something external—inadequate supplies, excessive workload, difficult co-workers, ambiguous assignments.) Small wonder, too, that people evaluate reward distributions such as pay raises as fairer when they receive more rather than less than most others (Diekmann & others, 1997).

Students also exhibit self-serving bias. After receiving an exam grade, those who do well tend to accept personal credit. They judge the exam to be a valid measure of their competence (Arkin & Maruyama, 1979; Davis & Stephan, 1980; Gilmor & Reid, 1979; Griffin & others, 1983). Those who do poorly are much more likely to criticize the exam.

Reading this research, I couldn't resist a satisfied "knew-it-all-along" feeling. But consider teachers' ways of explaining students' good and bad performances. When there is no need to feign modesty, those assigned the role of teacher tend to take credit for positive outcomes and blame failure on the student (Arkin & others, 1980; Davis, 1979). Teachers, it seems, are likely to think, "With my help, Maria graduated with honors. Despite all my help, Melinda flunked out."

Can We All Be Better Than Average?

Self-serving bias also appears when people compare themselves to others. If the sixth-century B.C. Chinese philosopher Lao-tzu was right that "at no time in the world will a man who is sane over-reach himself, over-spend himself, over-rate himself," then most of us are a little insane. For on nearly any dimension that is both *subjective* and *socially desirable,* most people see themselves as better than average. This is especially so when comparing oneself to people in general rather than to known individuals (Alicke & others, 1995). Consider:

- Most businesspeople see themselves as more ethical than the average businessperson (Baumhart, 1968; Brenner & Molander, 1977). One national survey asked, "How would you rate your own morals and values on a scale from one to 100 (100 being perfect)?" Fifty percent of people rated themselves 90 or above; only 11 percent said 74 or less (Lovett, 1997).

- Ninety percent of business managers rate their performance as superior to that of their average peer (French, 1968). In Australia, 86 percent of people rate their job performance as above average, 1 percent as below average (Headey & Wearing, 1987).

- In the Netherlands, most high school students rate themselves as more honest, persistent, original, friendly, and reliable than the average high school student (Hoorens, 1993, 1995).

- Most drivers—even most drivers who have been hospitalized for accidents—believe themselves to be safer and more skilled than the average driver (Guerin, 1994; McKenna & Myers, 1997; Svenson, 1981).

- Most people perceive themselves as more intelligent than their average peer (Wylie, 1979), as better looking (*Public Opinion,* 1984), and as less prejudiced than others in their communities (Fields & Schuman, 1976; Lenihan, 1965; Messick & others, 1985; O'Gorman & Garry, 1976).

- Most adults believe they support their aging parents more than their siblings do (Lerner & others, 1991).

- Los Angeles residents view themselves as healthier than most of their neighbors, and most college students believe they will outlive their actuarially predicted age of death by about 10 years (Larwood, 1978; C. R. Snyder, 1978).

Every community, it seems, is like Garrison Keillor's fictional Lake Wobegon, where "all the women are strong, all the men are good-looking, and all the children are above average." Perhaps one reason for this optimism is that although 12 percent of people feel old for their age, many more—66 percent—think they are young for their age (*Public Opinion,*

1984). All of which calls to mind Freud's joke about the man who told his wife, "If one of us should die, I think I would go live in Paris."

Subjective dimensions (such as "disciplined") trigger greater self-serving bias than objective behavioral dimensions (such as "punctual"). Students are more likely to rate themselves superior in "moral goodness" than in "intelligence" (Allison & others, 1989; Van Lange, 1991). And community residents overwhelmingly see themselves as *caring* more than most others about the environment, about hunger, and about other social issues, though they don't see themselves as *doing* more, such as contributing time or money to those issues (White & Plous, 1995). Education doesn't eliminate self-serving bias; even social psychologists exhibit it, by believing themselves to be more ethical than most social psychologists (Van Lange & others, 1997).

Subjective qualities give us leeway in constructing our own definitions of success (Dunning & others, 1989, 1991). Rating my "athletic ability," I ponder my basketball play, not the agonizing weeks I spent as a Little League baseball player hiding in right field. Assessing my "leadership ability," I conjure up an image of a great leader whose style is similar to mine. By defining ambiguous criteria in our own terms, each of us can see ourselves as relatively successful. In one College Entrance Examination Board survey of 829,000 high school seniors, 0 percent rated themselves below average in "ability to get along with others" (a subjective, desirable trait), 60 percent rated themselves in the top 10 percent, and 25 percent saw themselves among the top 1 percent!

We also support our self-image by assigning importance to the things we're good at. Over a semester, those who ace an introductory computer science course come to place a higher value on their identity as a computer-literate person in today's world. Those who do poorly are more likely to scorn computer geeks and to exclude computer skills as pertinent to their self-image (Hill & others, 1989).

Unrealistic Optimism

Many of us have what researcher Neil Weinstein (1980, 1982) terms "an unrealistic optimism about future life events." At Rutgers University, for example, students perceive themselves as far more likely than their classmates to get a good job, draw a good salary, and own a home, and as far less likely to experience negative events, such as developing a drinking problem, having a heart attack before age 40, or being fired. In Scotland, most late adolescents think they are much less likely than their peers to become infected by the AIDS virus (Abrams, 1991). After experiencing the 1989 earthquake, San Francisco Bay–area students did lose their optimism about being less vulnerable than their classmates to injury in a natural disaster, but within three months their illusory optimism had rebounded (Burger & Palmer, 1991).

Linda Perloff (1987) notes how illusory optimism increases our vulnerability. Believing ourselves immune to misfortune, we do not take sensible precautions. In one survey, 137 marriage license applicants accurately estimated that half of marriages end in divorce, yet most assessed their chance of divorce as zero percent (Baker & Emery, 1993). Sexually active undergraduate women who don't consistently use contraceptives perceive themselves, compared to other women at their university, as much *less* vulnerable to unwanted pregnancy (Burger & Burns, 1988). Those who cheerfully shun seat belts, deny the effects of smoking, and stumble into ill-fated relationships remind us that blind optimism, like pride, can, as the ancient proverb warns, go before a fall.

Optimism definitely beats pessimism in promoting self-efficacy, health, and well-being (Armor & Taylor, 1998). Yet a dash of realism can save us from the perils of unrealistic optimism. Self-doubt can energize students, most of whom, especially those destined for low grades, exhibit excess optimism about upcoming exams (Prohaska, 1994; Sparrell & Shrauger, 1984). (Such illusory optimism often disappears as the time approaches for receiving the exam back—Shepperd & others, 1996.) Students who are overconfident tend to underprepare. Their equally able but more anxious peers, fearing that they are going to bomb on the upcoming exam, study furiously and get higher grades (Goodhart, 1986; Norem & Cantor, 1986; Showers & Ruben, 1987). The moral: Success in school and beyond requires enough optimism to sustain hope and enough pessimism to motivate concern.

False Consensus and Uniqueness

We have a curious tendency to further enhance our self-image by overestimating or underestimating the extent to which others think and act as we do—a phenomenon called the **false consensus effect.** On matters of *opinion*, we find support for our positions by overestimating the extent to which others agree (Krueger & Clement, 1994; Marks & Miller, 1987; Mullen & Goethals, 1990). If we favor a Canadian referendum or support New Zealand's National Party, we wishfully overestimate the extent to which others agree (Babad & others, 1992; Koestner, 1993). When we behave badly or fail in a task, we reassure ourselves by thinking that such lapses are common. We guess that others think and act as we do: "I do it, but so does everyone else." If we cheat on our income taxes or smoke, we are likely to overestimate the number of other people who do likewise. If we harbor negative ideas about another racial group, we presume that many others also have negative stereotypes; thus our perceptions of others' stereotypes might reveal something of our own (Krueger, 1996).

False consensus can occur because we generalize from a limited sample, which prominently includes ourselves and our like-minded friends

(Dawes, 1990). But on matters of *ability* or when we behave well or successfully, a **false uniqueness effect** more often occurs (Goethals & others, 1991). We serve our self-image by seeing our talents and moral behaviors as relatively unusual. Thus those who drink heavily but use seat belts will *over*estimate (false consensus) the number of other heavy drinkers and *under*estimate (false uniqueness) the commonality of seat belt use (Suls & others, 1988). Simply put, people see their failings as normal, their virtues as rare.

Other Self-Serving Tendencies

These tendencies toward self-serving attributions, self-congratulatory comparisons, and illusory optimism are not the only signs of favorably biased self-perceptions. Earlier we noted that most of us overestimate how desirably we would act in a given situation. We also display a "cognitive conceit" by overestimating the accuracy of our beliefs and judgments, and by misremembering our own past in self-enhancing ways.

Additional streams of evidence converge to form a river:

- If an undesirable act cannot be misremembered or undone, then, as we will see, we might justify it.
- The more favorably we perceive ourselves on some dimension (intelligence, persistence, sense of humor), the more we use that dimension as a basis for judging others (Lewicki, 1983).
- The more favorably we view ourselves, the more we think others perceive us in flattering ways (Kenny & DePaulo, 1993).
- If a test or some other source of information—even a horoscope—flatters us, then we believe it, and we evaluate positively both the test and any evidence suggesting that the test is valid (Ditto, 1994; Glick & others, 1989; Pyszczynski & others, 1985).
- Most university students, however, think the Scholastic Assessment Test underestimates their ability (Shepperd, 1993). (In fact, however, the higher scores they *think* they deserved would *less* accurately predict their obtained grades.)
- When we judge on the basis of photos, we not only guess that attractive people have desirable personalities, we also guess that their personalities are more like our own than the personalities of unattractive people are (Marks & others, 1981).
- We like to associate ourselves with others' success. We bask in reflected glory if some famous person attended our school. If we find ourselves linked with (say, born on the same day as) some reprehensible person, we boost ourselves by softening our view of the rascal (Finch & Cialdini, 1989).

FALSE MODESTY

Perhaps you have by now recalled times when someone was not self-praising but self-disparaging. Such put-downs can be subtly self-serving, for often they elicit reassuring "strokes." "I felt like a fool" can trigger a friend to reassure that "you did fine!" Even a remark such as "I wish I weren't so ugly" might elicit at least a "Come now. I know a couple of people who are uglier than you."

There is another reason people disparage themselves and praise others. Think of the coach who, before the big game, extols the opponent's strength. Is the coach utterly sincere? When coaches publicly exalt their opponents, they convey an image of modesty and good sportsmanship, and set the stage for a favorable evaluation no matter what the outcome. A win becomes a praiseworthy achievement; a loss is attributable to the opponent's "great defense." Modesty, said seventeenth-century philosopher Francis Bacon, is but one of the "arts of ostentation." Thus, Robert Gould, Paul Brounstein, and Harold Sigall (1977) found that, in a laboratory contest, their University of Maryland students similarly aggrandized their anticipated opponent, but only when the assessment was made publicly. Anonymously, they credited their future opponent with much less ability.

Self-Handicapping

Sometimes people sabotage their chances for success by creating impediments that make success less likely. Far from being deliberately self-destructive, such behaviors typically have a self-protective aim (Arkin & others, 1986; Baumeister & Scher, 1988; Rhodewalt, 1987): "I'm really not a failure—I would have done well except for this problem."

Why would people handicap themselves with self-defeating behavior? Recall that we eagerly protect our self-images by attributing failures to external factors. Can you see why, *fearing failure*, people might handicap themselves by partying half the night before a job interview or playing video games instead of studying before a big exam? When self-image is tied up with performance, it can be more self-deflating to try hard and fail than to procrastinate and have a ready excuse. If we fail while working under a handicap, we can cling to a sense of competence; if we succeed under such conditions, it can only boost our self-image. Handicaps protect our self-esteem and public image by allowing us to attribute failures to something temporary or external ("I was feeling sick"; "I was out too late the night before") rather than to lack of talent or ability.

This analysis of **self-handicapping,** proposed by Steven Berglas and Edward Jones (1978), has been confirmed. One experiment was said to concern "drugs and intellectual performance." Imagine yourself in the position of their Duke University subjects. You guess answers to some difficult aptitude questions and then are told, "Yours was one of the best scores seen to date!" Feeling incredibly lucky, you are then offered a choice between two drugs before answering more of these items. One drug will aid intellectual performance and the other will inhibit it. Which drug do you want? Most students wanted the drug that would supposedly disrupt their thinking and thus provide a handy excuse for anticipated poorer performance.

Researchers have documented other ways in which people self-handicap. Fearing failure, people will:

- Reduce their preparation for important individual athletic events (Rhodewalt & others, 1984)
- Give their opponent an advantage (Shepperd & Arkin, 1991)
- Report feeling depressed (Baumgardner, 1991)
- Perform poorly at the beginning of a task in order not to create unreachable expectations (Baumgardner & Brownlee, 1987)
- Not try as hard as they could during a tough ego-involving task (Hormuth, 1986; Pyszczynski & Greenberg, 1983; Riggs, 1992; Turner & Pratkanis, 1993)

After losing to some younger rivals, tennis great Martina Navratilova confessed, "[I was] afraid to play my best. . . . I was scared to find out if they could beat me when I'm playing my best because if they can, then I am finished" (Frankel & Snyder, 1987).

WHY SELF-SERVING BIAS?

Self-serving bias has been explained in three ways: as an effort to *present* a positive image, as a by-product of how we *process information*, or as *motivated* by our desire to protect and enhance our self-esteem.

Self-Presentation

Self-presentation refers to our wanting to present a desired image both to an external audience (other people) and to an internal audience (ourselves). We work at managing the impressions we create. We excuse, justify, or apologize as necessary to shore up our self-esteem and verify our self-image (Schlenker & Weigold, 1992).

No wonder, say self-presentation researchers, that people will self-handicap when failure might make them look bad (Arkin & Baumgardner, 1985). No wonder that people take health risks—tanning their skin with wrinkle- and cancer-causing radiation, becoming anorexic, failing to obtain and use condoms, yielding to peer pressures to smoke, get drunk, and do drugs (Leary & others, 1994). No wonder people express more modesty when their self-flattery is vulnerable to being debunked, perhaps by experts who will be scrutinizing their self-evaluations (Arkin & others, 1980; Riess & others, 1981; Weary & others, 1982). Professor Smith will express less confidence in the significance of her work when presenting it to professional colleagues than when presenting to students.

Presenting oneself in ways that create a desired impression is a very delicate matter. People want to be seen as able, but also as modest and honest (Carlston & Shovar, 1983). Modesty creates a good impression, and unsolicited boasting creates a bad impression (Forsyth & others, 1981; Holtgraves & Srull, 1989; Schlenker & Leary, 1982). Thus, the false modesty phenomenon: We often display *less* self-esteem than we privately feel (Miller & Schlenker, 1985). But when we have obviously done extremely well, false disclaimers ("I did well, but it's no big deal") can come across as feigned humility. To make good impressions—as modest yet competent—requires social skill.

The tendency to present modesty and restrained optimism is especially great in cultures that value self-restraint, such as those of China and Japan (Heine & Lehman, 1995, 1997; Lee & Seligman, 1997; Markus & Kitayama, 1991; Wu & Tseng, 1985). There, people's identity and feelings of success are linked more with their group's performance. But self-serving bias is hardly restricted to North America. Self-serving bias has been noted among Dutch high school and university students, Belgian basketball players, Indian Hindus, Japanese drivers, Israeli and Singaporean schoolchildren, Australian students and workers, Chinese students, Hong Kong sports writers, and French people of all ages (Codol, 1976; de Vries & van Knippenberg, 1987; Falbo & others, 1997; Feather, 1983; Hagiwara, 1983; Hallahan & others, 1997; Jain, 1990; Lefebvre, 1979; Liebrand & others, 1986; Murphy-Berman & Sharma, 1986; and Ruzzene & Noller, 1986, respectively).

Information Processing

Why do people also *perceive* themselves in self-enhancing ways? One explanation sees self-serving bias as a by-product of how we process and remember information about ourselves.

Recall the study in which married people gave themselves credit for doing more housework than their spouses did. Might this not be due, as Michael Ross and Fiore Sicoly (1979) believe, to our greater recall for what we've actively done and our lesser recall for what we've not done or what we've merely observed others doing? I can easily picture myself picking up the laundry, but I have difficulty picturing myself absentmindedly overlooking it.

Self-Esteem Motivation

But are the biased perceptions simply a perceptual error, an unemotional bent in how we process information? Or are self-serving *motives* also involved? It's now clear from research that we have multiple motives. Questing for self-knowledge, we're eager to *assess* our competence (Dunning, 1995). Questing for self-confirmation, we're eager to *verify* our self-conceptions (Sanitioso & others, 1990; Swann, 1996, 1997). Questing for self-affirmation, we're *especially* motivated to *enhance* our self-image (Sedikides, 1993).

Experiments confirm that a motivational engine powers our cognitive machinery (Kunda, 1990). For example, Abraham Tesser (1988) at the University of Georgia reports that a "self-esteem maintenance" motive predicts a variety of interesting findings, even friction among brothers and sisters. Do you have a sibling of the same sex who is close to you in age? If so, people probably compared the two of you as you grew up. Tesser presumes that people's perceiving one of you as more capable than the other will motivate the less able one to act in ways that maintain his or her self-esteem. (Tesser thinks the threat to self-esteem is greatest for an older child with a highly capable younger sibling.) Men with a more or less able brother typically recall not getting along well with him; men with a similarly able brother are more likely to recall very little friction.

Self-esteem threats occur among friends and married partners, too. Although shared interests are healthy, *identical* career goals can produce tension or jealousy (Clark & Bennett, 1992). Similarly, people feel greater jealousy toward a romantic rival whose achievements are in the domain of their own aspirations (DeSteno & Salovey, 1996).

REFLECTIONS ON SELF-EFFICACY AND SELF-SERVING BIAS

No doubt many readers are finding all this either depressing or contrary to their own occasional feelings of inadequacy. To be sure, the most of us who exhibit self-serving bias might still feel inferior to specific individuals, especially those who are a step or two higher on the ladder of success, attractiveness, or skill. And not everyone operates with self-serving bias. Some people *do* suffer from low self-esteem.

Moreover, when feeling good about ourselves, we are less defensive (Epstein & Feist, 1988). We are also less thin-skinned and judgmental—less likely to inflate those who like us and berate those who don't (Baumgardner & others, 1989). In experiments, people whose self-esteem is temporarily bruised—say, by being told they did miserably on an intelligence test—are more likely to disparage others (Beauregard & Dunning, 1998). Those whose ego has recently been wounded also are more prone to self-serving explanations of success or failure than are those whose ego has recently received a boost (McCarrey & others, 1982). So, threats to self-esteem can provoke self-protective defensiveness. When feeling unaffirmed, people might offer self-affirming boasts, excuses, and put-downs of others. More generally, people who are down on themselves tend also to be down on others (Wills, 1981). Mockery says as much about the mocker as the one mocked.

Nevertheless, high self-esteem goes hand in hand with self-serving perceptions. Those who score highest on self-esteem tests (who say nice things about themselves) also say nice things about themselves when explaining their successes and failures (Ickes & Layden, 1978; Levine & Uleman, 1979; Rosenfeld, 1979; Schlenker & others, 1990), when evaluating their group (Brown & others, 1988), and when comparing themselves to others (Brown, 1986).

Self-Serving Bias as Adaptive

Self-serving bias and its accompanying excuses help protect people from depression (Snyder & Higgins, 1988). Nondepressed people excuse their failures on laboratory tasks, or perceive themselves as being more in control than they are. Depressed people's self-appraisals are more accurate: sadder but wiser.

And consider: Thanks to people's reluctance to criticize, it's easy to overestimate how others are really perceiving us (DePaulo & others, 1987; Kenny & Albright, 1987). Mildly depressed people are less prone to illusions; they generally see themselves *as* other people see them—which can, at times, be understandably depressing (Lewinsohn & others, 1980). This prompts the unsettling thought that Pascal may have been right: "I lay it down as a fact that, if all men knew what others say of them, there would not be four friends in the world."

As this new research on depression suggests, there can be some practical wisdom in self-serving perceptions. It can be strategic to believe we are smarter, stronger, and more socially successful than we are. Cheaters might give a more convincing display of honesty if they believe themselves to be honorable. Belief in our superiority can also motivate us to achieve—creating a self-fulfilling prophecy—and can sustain a sense of hope in difficult times.

Self-Serving Bias as Maladaptive

Although self-serving pride can help protect us from depression, it can at times be maladaptive. People who blame others for their social difficulties are often unhappier than people who can acknowledge their mistakes (C. A. Anderson & others, 1983; Newman & Langer, 1981; Peterson & others, 1981). Moreover, the most self-enhancing people often come across to others as egotistical, condescending, and deceitful (Colvin & others, 1995). In human history, expansive egos have marked genocidal dictators, White supremacists, and drunken spouse-abusers (Baumeister & others, 1996). When someone's inflated self-esteem is challenged by others' criticisms or taunts, the result is sometimes an abusive or murderous rage.

Such self-deception can lead individual group members to expect greater than average rewards when their organization does well and less

than average blame when it does not. If most individuals in a group believe they are underpaid and underappreciated relative to their contributions, disharmony and envy are likely. College presidents and academic
deans will readily recognize the phenomenon. Ninety percent or more of
college faculty members rate themselves as superior to their average colleague (Blackburn & others, 1980; Cross, 1977). It is therefore inevitable
that when merit salary raises are announced and half receive an average
raise or less, many will feel that they are victims of injustice.

Self-serving biases also inflate people's judgments of their groups.
When groups are comparable, most people consider their own group superior (Codol, 1976; Jourden & Heath, 1996; Taylor & Doria, 1981). Thus:

- Most university sorority members perceive their sorority sisters as
  far less likely to be conceited and snobby than members of other
  sororities (Biernat & others, 1996).

- 66 percent of Americans give their oldest child's public schools a
  grade of A or B. But nearly as many—64 percent—give the *nation's*
  public schools a grade of C or D (Whitman, 1996).

- 53 percent of Dutch adults rate their marriage or partnership as
  better than most; only 1 percent rate it as worse than most (Buunk
  & van der Eijnden, 1997).

- Most corporation presidents and production managers overpre-
  dict their own firms' productivity and growth (Kidd & Morgan,
  1969; Larwood & Whittaker, 1977).

Such overoptimism sometimes goes before a fall. If those who deal in
the stock market or in real estate perceive their business intuition to be superior to that of their competitors, they can be in for severe disappointment. Even seventeenth-century economist Adam Smith, a defender of
human economic rationality, foresaw that people would overestimate
their chances of gain. This "absurd presumption in their own good fortune," he said, arises from "the overweening conceit which the greater part
of men have of their own abilities" (Spiegel, 1971, p. 243).

That people see themselves with a favorable bias is hardly new. This
tragic flaw was portrayed in ancient Greek drama as *hubris,* or pride. Like
the subjects of our experiments, the Greek tragic figures were not self-
consciously evil; they merely thought too highly of themselves. In literature, the pitfalls of pride are portrayed again and again. In religion, pride
has long been first among the "seven deadly sins."

If pride is akin to self-serving bias, then what is humility? Is it self-
contempt? Can we be self-affirming and self-accepting without self-serving
bias? To paraphrase the English scholar-writer C. S. Lewis, humility is not
handsome people trying to believe they are ugly and clever people trying to
believe they are fools. False modesty can actually be a cover for pride in

one's better-than-average humility. (James Friedrich [1996] reports that most students congratulate themselves on being better than average at not thinking themselves better than average!) True humility is more like self-forgetfulness than false modesty. It leaves people free to rejoice in their special talents and, with the same honesty, to recognize special talents in others.

CONCEPTS TO REMEMBER

Self-serving bias   The tendency to perceive oneself favorably.

False consensus effect   The tendency to overestimate the commonality of one's opinions and one's undesirable or unsuccessful behaviors.

False uniqueness effect   The tendency to underestimate the commonality of one's abilities and one's desirable or successful behaviors.

Self-handicapping   Protecting one's self-image with behaviors that create a handy excuse for later failure.

Self-presentation   The act of expressing oneself and behaving in ways designed to create a favorable impression or an impression that corresponds to one's ideals.

8

❖

The Power of Positive Thinking

We have considered two potent biases uncovered by social psychologists: a tendency to ignore situational forces when explaining others' behavior (the fundamental attribution error) and a tendency to perceive ourselves favorably (self-serving bias). The first can dispose us to misunderstand others' problems (for example, by assuming that unemployed people are necessarily lazy or incompetent). The second can fuel conflict among people and nations when all see themselves as more moral and deserving than others.

Studies of the fundamental attribution error and self-serving bias expose deep truths about human nature. But single truths seldom tell the whole story, because the world is complex. Indeed, there is an important complement to these truths. High self-esteem—a sense of self-worth—is adaptive. Compared to those with low self-esteem, people with high self-esteem are happier, less neurotic, less troubled by ulcers and insomnia, and less prone to drug and alcohol addictions (Brockner & Hulton, 1978; Brown, 1991). Many clinical psychologists report that underneath much human despair is an impoverished self-acceptance.

Additional research on "locus of control," optimism, and "learned helplessness" confirms the benefits of seeing oneself as competent and effective. Albert Bandura (1986) merges much of this research into a concept called **self-efficacy,** a scholarly version of the wisdom behind the power of positive thinking. An optimistic belief in our own possibilities pays dividends. People with strong feelings of self-efficacy are more persistent, less anxious and depressed, and more academically successful (Gecas, 1989; Maddux, 1991; Scheier & Carver, 1992).

*L*OCUS OF CONTROL

"I have no social life," complained a 40-something single man to student therapist Jerry Phares. At Phares's urging, the patient went to a dance, where several women danced with him. "I was just lucky," he later reported, "it would never happen again." When Phares reported this to his mentor, Julian Rotter, it crystallized an idea he had been forming. In Rotter's experiments and in his clinical practice, some people persistently seemed to "feel that what happens to them is governed by external forces of one kind or another, while others feel that what happens to them is governed largely by their own efforts and skills" (quoted by Hunt, 1993, p. 334).

What do you think? Are people more often captains of their destinies or victims of their circumstances? the playwrights, directors, and actors of their own lives or prisoners of invisible situations? Rotter called this dimension **locus of control.** With Phares, he developed 29 paired statements to measure a person's locus of control. Imagine yourself taking their test. Which do you more strongly believe?

In the long run people get the respect they deserve in this world.	or	Unfortunately, people's worth often passes unrecognized, no matter how hard they try.
What happens to me is my own doing.	or	Sometimes I feel that I don't have enough control over the direction my life is taking.
The average person can have an influence in government decisions.	or	This world is run by the few people in power, and there is not much the little guy can do about it.

Do your answers to such questions (from Rotter, 1973) indicate that you believe you control your own destiny (*internal* locus of control)? or that chance or outside forces determine your fate (*external* locus of control)? Those who see themselves as internally controlled are more likely to do well in school, successfully stop smoking, wear seat belts, practice birth control, deal with marital problems directly, make lots of money, and delay instant gratification in order to achieve long-term goals (Findley & Cooper, 1983; Lefcourt, 1982; Miller & others, 1986).

*L*EARNED HELPLESSNESS VERSUS SELF-DETERMINATION

The benefits of feelings of control also appear in animal research. Dogs taught that they cannot escape shocks while confined will learn a sense of helplessness. Later these dogs cower passively in other situations when they *could* escape punishment. Dogs that learn personal control (by escaping their first shocks successfully) adapt easily to a new situation. Researcher Martin Seligman (1975, 1991) notes similarities to this **learned helplessness** in human situations. Depressed or oppressed people, for example, become passive because they believe their efforts have no effect. Helpless dogs and depressed people both suffer paralysis of the will, passive resignation, even motionless apathy.

Here is a clue to how institutions—whether malevolent, like concentration camps, or benevolent, like hospitals—can dehumanize people. In hospitals, "good patients" don't ring bells, don't ask questions, don't try to control what's happening (Taylor, 1979). Such passivity might be good for hospital efficiency, but it is bad for people. Feelings of efficacy, of an ability to control one's life, enhance health and survival. Losing control over what you do and what others do to you can make unpleasant events profoundly stressful (Pomerleau & Rodin, 1986). Several diseases are associated with feelings of helplessness and diminished choice. So is the rapidity of decline and death in concentration camps and nursing homes. Hospital patients who are trained to believe in their ability to control stress require fewer pain relievers and sedatives and nurses see them as exhibiting less anxiety (Langer & others, 1975).

Ellen Langer and Judith Rodin (1976) showed the importance of personal control by treating elderly patients in a high-rated Connecticut nursing home in one of two ways. With one group the benevolent caregivers stressed "our responsibility to make this a home you can be proud of and happy in." They gave the passive patients their normal well-intentioned, sympathetic care. Three weeks later, most were rated by themselves, by interviewers, and by nurses as further debilitated. Langer and Rodin's other treatment promoted personal control. It stressed opportunities for choice, the possibilities for influencing nursing-home policy, and the person's responsibility "to make of your life whatever you want." These patients were given small decisions to make and responsibilities to fulfill. Over the ensuing three weeks, 93 percent of this group showed improved alertness, activity, and happiness.

The experience of the first group must have been similar to that of James MacKay (1980), an 87-year-old psychologist:

> I became a nonperson last summer. My wife had an arthritic knee which put her in a walker, and I chose that moment to break my leg. We went to a nursing home. It was all nursing and no home. The doctor and the head nurse made all decisions; we were merely animate objects. Thank heavens it was only two weeks. . . . The top man of the nursing home was very well trained and very compassionate; I considered it the best home in town. But we were nonpersons from the time we entered until we left.

Studies confirm that systems of governing or managing people that promote self-efficacy will indeed promote health and happiness (Deci & Ryan, 1987).

- Prisoners given some control over their environments—by being able to move chairs, control TV sets, and switch the lights—experience less stress, exhibit fewer health problems, and commit less vandalism (Ruback & others, 1986; Wener & others, 1987).
- Workers given leeway in carrying out tasks and making decisions experience improved morale (Miller & Monge, 1986).
- Institutionalized residents allowed choice in such matters as what to eat for breakfast, when to go to a movie, whether to sleep late or get up early, might live longer and certainly are happier (Timko & Moos, 1989).
- Homeless shelter residents who perceive that they have little choice in when to eat and sleep, and little control over their privacy, are more likely to have a passive, helpless attitude regarding finding housing and work (Burn, 1992).

REFLECTIONS ON SELF-EFFICACY

Although this psychological research and comment on perceived self-control is new, the emphasis on taking charge of one's life and realizing one's potential is not. The you-can-do-it theme of Horatio Alger's rags-to-riches books is an enduring American idea. We find it in Norman Vincent Peale's 1950s best-seller, *The Power of Positive Thinking*. ("If you think in positive terms you will get positive results. That is the simple fact.") We find it in the many self-help books and videos that urge people to succeed through developing positive mental attitudes.

Research on self-control gives us greater confidence in traditional virtues such as perseverance and hope. Yet Bandura emphasizes that self-efficacy does not grow primarily by self-persuasion ("I think I can, I think I can") or by puffing people up like hot-air balloons ("You're terrific!"). Its chief source is the experience of success. If your initial efforts to lose weight, stop smoking, or improve your grades succeed, your self-efficacy increases.

After mastering the physical skills needed to repel a sexual assault, women feel less vulnerable, less anxious, and more in control (Ozer & Bandura, 1990). After experiencing academic success, students develop higher appraisals of their academic ability, which in turn often stimulate them to work harder and achieve more (Felson, 1984; Marsh & Young, 1997). To do one's best and achieve is to feel more confident and empowered.

So there is a power to positive thinking. But let us remember the point at which we began our consideration of self-efficacy: Any truth, separated from its complementary truth, is a half-truth. The truth embodied in the concept of self-efficacy can encourage us to not resign ourselves to bad situations, to persist despite initial failures, to exert effort without being overly distracted by self-doubts. But lest the pendulum swing too far toward *this* truth, we had best remember that it, too, is not the whole story. If positive thinking can accomplish *anything*, then if we are unhappily married, poor, or depressed, we have only ourselves to blame. For shame! If only we had tried harder, been more disciplined, less stupid. Failing to appreciate that difficulties sometimes reflect the oppressive power of social situations can tempt us to blame people for their problems and failures, or even to blame ourselves too harshly for our own. Ironically, life's greatest disappointments, as well as its highest achievements, are born of the highest expectations. The bigger we dream, the more we might attain—and the more we risk falling short.

Moreover, critics question popular psychology's assumption that positive self-esteem is the secret to successful, happy living. If children are underachieving, unruly, unpopular, or overbearing, pop psychology assumes that the child has a self-esteem deficit. From this perspective, the solution is to bolster the child's self-esteem, in part by positive affirmations that assure our children they are wonderful just as they are. Adults, too, can boost their self-esteem by chanting self-esteem mantras, such as "I'm terrific," or "Every day, in every way, I'm getting better and better."

Low self-esteem, as we have seen, does correlate with drug abuse, delinquency, and underachievement. Nevertheless, psychologists William Damon (1995), Robyn Dawes (1994), Mark Leary (1998), Roy Baumeister (1996), and Martin Seligman (1994) wonder about cause and effect. They doubt that positive-thinking self-esteem is really "the armor that protects kids" from such problems. Perhaps it's the other way around: Perhaps problems and failures cause low self-esteem. Perhaps self-esteem reflects the reality of how things are going for us. Perhaps the best boost of self-esteem comes from hard-won achievements.

Contrary to popular opinion, low self-esteem hardly plagues our culture as a whole. (Recall our discussion of self-serving bias.) Moreover, self-esteem also has its dark side. Teen males who engage in sexual activity at an "inappropriately young age" tend to have *higher* than average self-esteem. So do teen gang leaders, extreme ethnocentrists, and terrorists, notes Robyn Dawes (1998). A youth who develops a big ego, which then gets threatened or deflated by social rejection, is potentially dangerous (Bushman & Baumeister, 1998).

"The enthusiastic claims of the self-esteem movement mostly range from fantasy to hogwash," says Baumeister (1996), who suspects that he has "probably published more studies on self-esteem than anybody else." The effects of self-esteem are "small, limited, and not all good." High-self-esteem folks, he reports, are more likely to be obnoxious, to interrupt, and to talk *at* people rather than *with* them (in contrast to the more shy, modest, self-effacing folks with low self-esteem). "My conclusion is that self-control is worth 10 times as much as self-esteem."

The healthiest attitude, then, is neither an inflated self nor cynical self-denigration. Rather, it mixes ample positive thinking with enough realism to discriminate those things we can control from those we cannot. It was for such wisdom that theologian Reinhold Niebuhr offered his famous Serenity Prayer: "O God, give us grace to accept with serenity the things that cannot be changed, courage to change the things which should be changed, and the wisdom to distinguish the one from the other."

CONCEPTS TO REMEMBER

Self-efficacy   A sense that one is competent and effective. Distinguished from self-esteem, a sense of one's self-worth. A bombardier might feel high self-efficacy and low self-esteem.

Locus of control   The extent to which people perceive outcomes as internally controllable by their own efforts and actions, or as externally controlled by chance or outside forces.

Learned helplessness   The hopelessness and resignation learned by humans or animals who perceive themselves as having no control over repeated bad events.

MODULE

9

❖

Behavior and Belief

W hich comes first, belief or behavior? inner attitude or outer action? character or conduct? What is the relationship between
who we *are* (on the inside) and what we *do* (on the outside)?
Opinions on this chicken-and-egg question vary. "The ancestor of
every action is a thought," wrote American essayist Ralph Waldo Emerson
in 1841. To the contrary, said British Prime Minister Benjamin Disraeli,
"Thought is the child of Action." Most people side with Emerson. Underlying our teaching, preaching, and counseling is the assumption that private beliefs determine public behavior: If we want to alter people's actions,
we therefore need to change their hearts and minds.

*D*O ATTITUDES INFLUENCE BEHAVIOR?

Attitudes are beliefs and feelings that can influence our reactions. If we *believe* that someone is threatening, we might *feel* dislike and therefore *act* unfriendly. "Change the way people think," said South African civil rights
martyr Steve Biko (echoing Emerson), "and things will never be the same."
Believing this, social psychologists during the 1940s and 1950s studied
factors that influence attitudes. Thus they were shocked when dozens of
studies during the 1960s revealed that what people say they think and feel
often has little to do with how they act (Wicker, 1971). In these studies, students' attitudes toward cheating bore little relation to the likelihood of
their actually cheating. People's attitudes toward the church were but
modestly linked with church attendance on any given Sunday. Self-
described racial attitudes predicted little of the variation in behavior that

occurred when people faced an actual interracial situation. People, it seemed, were talking and playing different games.

This realization stimulated more studies during the 1970s and 1980s, which revealed that our attitudes *do* influence our actions in some circumstances:

- *When external influences on our words and actions are minimal.* Sometimes we adjust our attitude reports to please our listeners. This was vividly demonstrated when the U.S. House of Representatives once overwhelmingly passed a salary increase for itself in an off-the-record vote, and then moments later overwhelmingly defeated the same bill on a roll-call vote. Fear of criticism had distorted the true sentiment on the roll-call vote. Other times social pressure diverts our behavior from the dictates of our attitudes, leading people even to do cruelties toward people they do not dislike. When external pressures do not blur the link between our attitudes and actions, we can see that link more clearly.

- *When the attitude is specific to the behavior.* People readily profess honesty while cheating in reporting their taxes, cherish a clean environment while not recycling, or applaud good health while smoking and not exercising. But their more specific attitudes toward jogging better predict whether they jog (Olson & Zanna, 1981), their attitudes toward recycling do predict whether they recycle (Oskamp, 1991), and their attitudes toward contraception predict their contraceptive use (Morrison, 1989).

- *When we are conscious of our attitudes.* Attitudes can lie dormant as we act out of habit or as we flow with the crowd. For our attitudes to guide our action, we must pause to consider them. Thus, when we are self-conscious or reminded of how we feel, we act truer to our convictions (Fazio, 1990). Likewise, attitudes formed through a significant experience are more often remembered and acted upon.

So, an attitude will influence our behavior *if* other influences are minimal, *if* the attitude specifically relates to the behavior, and *if* the attitude is potent, perhaps because something brings it to mind. Under these conditions, we *will* stand up for what we believe.

DOES BEHAVIOR INFLUENCE ATTITUDES

Do we also come to believe in what we've stood up for? Indeed. One of social psychology's big lessons is that we are likely not only to think ourselves into a way of acting but also to act ourselves into a way of thinking. Many streams of evidence confirm that *attitudes follow behavior.*

Role Playing

The word **role** is borrowed from the theater and, as in the theater, refers to actions expected of those who occupy a particular social position. When stepping into a new social role, we must perform its actions, even if we feel phony. But our unease seldom lasts.

Think of a time when you stepped into some new role—perhaps your first days on a job, or at college, or in a sorority or fraternity. That first week on campus, for example, you might have been supersensitive to your new social situation and tried valiantly to act appropriately and root out your high school behavior. At such times we feel self-conscious. We observe our new speech and actions because they aren't natural to us. Then one day an amazing thing happens: We notice that our sorority enthusiasm or our pseudo-intellectual talk no longer feels forced. The role has begun to fit as comfortably as our old jeans and T-shirt.

In one study, college men volunteered to spend time in a simulated prison constructed in Stanford's psychology department by Philip Zimbardo (1971). Zimbardo, like so many others, wondered whether prison brutality is a product of evil prisoners and malicious guards, or whether the institutional roles of guard and prisoner would embitter and harden even compassionate people. Do the people make the place violent? Or does the place make the people violent?

By a flip of a coin, he designated some students as guards. He gave them uniforms, billy clubs, and whistles and instructed them to enforce the rules. The other half, the prisoners, were locked in cells and made to wear humiliating outfits. After a jovial first day of "playing" their roles, the guards and prisoners, and even the experimenters, got caught up in the situation. The guards began to disparage the prisoners, and some devised cruel and degrading routines. The prisoners broke down, rebelled, or became apathetic. There developed, reported Zimbardo (1972), a "growing confusion between reality and illusion, between role-playing and self-identity. . . . This prison which we had created . . . was absorbing us as creatures of its own reality." Observing the emerging social pathology, Zimbardo was forced to call off the planned two-week simulation after only six days. The deeper lesson of role-playing studies concerns how what is unreal (an artificial role) can evolve into what is real.

Saying Becomes Believing

In 1785, Thomas Jefferson hypothesized that shaded messages can affect the messenger: "He who permits himself to tell a lie once finds it much easier to do it a second and third time, till at length it becomes habitual; he tells lies without attending to it, and truths without the world's believing him. This falsehood of the tongue leads to that of the heart, and in time depraves all its good dispositions." Experiments have proved Jefferson right.

People induced to give spoken or written witness to something about which they have real doubts will often feel bad about their deceit. Nevertheless, they begin to believe what they are saying—*provided* they weren't bribed or coerced into saying it. When there is no compelling external explanation for one's words, saying becomes believing (Klaas, 1978).

Tory Higgins and his colleagues (Higgins & Rholes, 1978; Higgins & McCann, 1984) illustrated how saying becomes believing. They had university students read a personality description of someone and then summarize it for someone else who was believed either to like or dislike this person. The students wrote a more positive description when the recipient liked the person, and, having said positive things, then liked the person more themselves. Asked to recall what they had read, they remembered the description as being more positive than it was. In short, it seems that we are prone to adjust our messages to our listeners, and having done so, to believe the altered message.

The Foot-in-the-Door Phenomenon

Most of us can recall times when, after agreeing to help out with a project or an organization, we ended up more involved than we ever intended to be, vowing that in the future we would say no to such requests. How does this happen? Experiments suggest that if you want people to do a big favor for you, one technique is to get them to do a small favor first. In the best-known demonstration of this **foot-in-the-door principle,** researchers posing as safety-drive volunteers asked Californians to permit the installation of a huge, poorly lettered "Drive Carefully" sign in their front yards. Only 17 percent consented. Others were first approached with a small request: Would they display a 3-inch "Be a Safe Driver" window sign? Nearly all readily agreed. When approached two weeks later to allow the large, ugly sign in their front yards, 76 percent consented (Freedman & Fraser, 1966). One project helper who went from house to house later recalled that, not knowing who had been previously visited, "I was simply stunned at how easy it was to convince some people and how impossible to convince others" (Ornstein, 1991).

Other researchers have confirmed the foot-in-the-door phenomenon with altruistic behaviors.

- Patricia Pliner and her collaborators (1974) found 46 percent of Toronto suburbanites willing to give to the Cancer Society when approached directly. Others, asked a day ahead to wear a lapel pin publicizing the drive (which all agreed to do), were nearly twice as likely to donate.

- Joseph Schwarzwald and his colleagues (1983) asked some Israelis to donate to a collection for the mentally impaired. Fifty-three percent gave. Two weeks earlier, other Israelis had been approached to sign a petition supporting a recreation center for the impaired; among these, 92 percent now gave.

- Anthony Greenwald and his co-researchers (1987) approached a sample of registered voters the day before the 1984 U.S. presidential election and asked them a small question: "Do you expect that you will vote or not?" All said yes. Compared to other voters not asked their intentions, they were 41 percent more likely to vote.
- Angela Lipsitz and others (1989) reported that ending blood-drive reminder calls with "We'll count on seeing you then, OK? [pause for response]" increased the show-up rate from 62 to 81 percent.

Note that in these experiments the initial compliance—signing a petition, wearing a lapel pin, stating one's intention—was voluntary. We will see again and again that when people commit themselves to public behaviors *and* perceive these acts to be their own doing, they come to believe more strongly in what they have done.

Robert Cialdini [chal-DEE-nee] and his collaborators (1978) demonstrated a variation of the foot-in-the-door phenomenon by experimenting with the **low-ball technique,** a tactic reportedly used by some car dealers. After the customer agrees to buy a new car because of its great price and begins completing the sales forms, the salesperson removes the price advantage by charging for options the customer thought were included or by checking with a boss who disallows the deal because, "We'd be losing money." Folklore has it that more customers now stick with the higher-priced purchase than would have agreed to it at the outset.

Marketing researchers and salespeople have found that the principle works even when we are aware of a profit motive (Cialdini, 1988). A harmless initial commitment—returning a card for more information and a gift, agreeing to listen to an investment possibility—often moves us toward a larger commitment. While I was writing this module, a life insurance salesperson came to my office and offered a thorough analysis of my family's financial situation. He did not ask whether I wished to buy his life insurance, or even whether I wished to try his free service. His question was instead a small foot-in-the-door, one carefully calculated to elicit agreement: Did I think people should have such information about their financial situation? I could only answer yes, and before I realized what was happening, I had agreed to the analysis. But I'm learning. Just the other evening a paid fund-raiser came to my door, first soliciting a petition signature supporting environmental cleanup, then welcoming my contribution to what I had signed my support of. (I sign but, resisting manipulation, don't give.)

Salespeople might exploit the power of small commitments when trying to bind people to purchase agreements. Many states now have laws that allow customers of door-to-door salespeople a few days to think over their purchases and cancel. To combat the effect of these laws, many companies use what the sales-training program of one encyclopedia company calls "a very important psychological aid in preventing customers from backing out of their contracts" (Cialdini, 1988, p. 78). They simply have the customer, rather than the salesperson, fill out the agreement. Having written it themselves, people usually live up to their commitment.

The foot-in-the-door phenomenon is well worth learning about. Someone trying to seduce us—financially, politically, or sexually—usually will try to create a momentum of compliance. Before agreeing to a small request, think about what might follow.

Evil Acts and Attitudes

The attitudes-follow-behavior principle works with more immoral acts as well. Evil sometimes results from gradually escalating commitments. A trifling evil act can make a less trifling evil act easier. Evil acts gnaw at the moral sensitivity of the actor. To paraphrase La Rochefoucauld's *Maxims* (1665), it is not as difficult to find a person who has never succumbed to a given temptation as to find a person who has succumbed only once.

For example, cruel acts corrode the consciences of those who perform them. Harming an innocent victim—by uttering hurtful comments or delivering electric shocks—typically leads aggressors to disparage their victims, thus helping them justify their behavior (Berscheid & others, 1968; Davis & Jones, 1960; Glass, 1964). We tend not only to hurt those we dislike but to dislike those we hurt. In studies establishing this, people would justify an action especially when coaxed, not coerced, into it. When we voluntarily agree to do a deed, we take more responsibility for it.

The phenomenon almost always appears in wartime, as soldiers denigrate their victims: American World War II soldiers called their enemy "the Japs." In the 1960s American soldiers dehumanized the Vietnamese people as "gooks." This is another instance of spiraling action and attitude: The more one commits atrocities, the easier it becomes. Conscience mutates.

The same holds for prejudice. If one group holds another in slavery, it is likely to perceive the slaves as having traits that justify their oppression. Actions and attitudes feed one another, sometimes to the point of moral numbness.

If evil acts shape the self, so, thankfully, do moral acts. Character, it is said, is reflected in what we do when we think no one is looking. Researchers have tested character by giving children temptations when it seems no one is watching. Consider what happens when children resist the temptation. They internalize the conscientious act *if* the deterrent is strong enough to elicit the desired *behavior* yet mild enough to leave them with a sense of *choice*. In a dramatic experiment, Jonathan Freedman (1965) introduced elementary school children to an enticing battery-controlled robot, instructing them not to play with it while he was out of the room. Freedman used a severe threat with half the children and a mild threat with the others. Both were sufficient to deter the children.

Several weeks later a different researcher, with no apparent relation to the earlier events, left each child to play in the same room with the same toys. Of the 18 children who had been given the severe threat, 14 now freely played with the robot; but two-thirds of those who had been given the mild deterrent still resisted playing with it. Having earlier made a conscious choice *not* to play with the toy, the mildly deterred children apparently internalized their decision. This new attitude controlled their subsequent action. Thus, moral action, especially when chosen rather than coerced, affects moral thinking.

Interracial Behavior and Racial Attitudes

If moral action feeds moral attitudes, will positive interracial behavior reduce racial prejudice? This was part of social scientists' testimony before the U.S. Supreme Court's 1954 decision to desegregate schools. Their argument ran like this: If we wait for the heart to change—through preaching and teaching—we will wait a long time for racial justice. But if we legislate moral action, we can, under the right conditions, indirectly affect heartfelt attitudes.

This idea runs counter to the presumption that "you can't legislate morality." Yet attitude change has, in fact, followed desegregation. Consider some correlational findings from the mammoth social experiment of U.S. desegregation:

- Since the Supreme Court decision, the percentage of White Americans favoring integrated schools has more than doubled, and now includes nearly everyone.

- In the 10 years after the Civil Rights Act of 1964, the percentage of White Americans who described their neighborhoods, friends, co-workers, or other students as all-White declined by about 20 percent for each of these measures. Interracial behavior was increasing. During the same period, the percentage of White Americans who said that Blacks should be allowed to live in any neighborhood increased from 65 percent to 87 percent (*ISR Newsletter,* 1975). Attitudes were changing, too.

- More-uniform national standards against discrimination were followed by decreasing differences in racial attitudes among people of differing religions, classes, and geographic regions. As Americans came to act more alike, they came to think more alike (Greeley & Sheatsley, 1971; Taylor & others, 1978).

Experiments confirm that positive behavior toward someone fosters liking for that person. Doing a favor for an experimenter or another subject, or tutoring a student, usually increases liking of the person helped (Blanchard & Cook, 1976). In 1793, Benjamin Franklin tested the idea that doing a favor engenders liking. As clerk of the Pennsylvania General

Assembly, he was disturbed by opposition from another important legislator. So Franklin set out to win him over:

> I did not . . . aim at gaining his favour by paying any servile respect to him but, after some time, took this other method. Having heard that he had in his library a certain very scarce and curious book I wrote a note to him expressing my desire of perusing that book and requesting he would do me the favour of lending it to me for a few days. He sent it immediately and I return'd it in about a week, expressing strongly my sense of the favour. When we next met in the House he spoke to me (which he had never done before), and with great civility; and he ever after manifested a readiness to serve me on all occasions, so that we became great friends and our friendship continued to his death. (Rosenzweig, 1972, p. 769)

"BRAINWASHING"

Many people assume that the most social indoctrination comes through *brainwashing,* a term coined to describe what happened to American prisoners of war (POWs) during the 1950s Korean war. Actually, the Chinese "thought-control" program, developed to reeducate the Chinese populace into communism, was not nearly as irresistible as this term suggests. But the results still were disconcerting. Hundreds of prisoners cooperated with their captors. Twenty-one chose to remain after being granted permission to return to America. And many of those who did return came home believing that "although communism won't work in America, I think it's a good thing for Asia" (Segal, 1954).

Edgar Schein (1956) interviewed many of the POWs during their journey home and reported that the captors' methods included a gradual escalation of demands. The Chinese always started with trivial requests and gradually worked up to more significant ones. "Thus after a prisoner had once been 'trained' to speak or write out trivia, statements on more important issues were demanded." Moreover, they always expected active participation, be it just copying something or participating in group discussions, writing self-criticism, or uttering public confessions. Once a prisoner had spoken or written a statement, he felt an inner need to make his beliefs consistent with his acts. This often drove prisoners to persuade themselves of what they had done. The "start-small-and-build" tactic was an effective application of the foot-in-the-door technique, as it continues to be today in the socialization of terrorists and torturers.

In Nazi Germany, too, participation in mass meetings, wearing uniforms, demonstrating, and especially the "German greeting" ("Heil Hitler") established for many a profound inconsistency between behavior and belief. Historian Richard Grunberger (1971, p. 27) reports that for those who had their doubts about Hitler "the 'German greeting' was a powerful conditioning device. Having once decided to intone it as an outward token of conformity, many experienced schizophrenic discomfort at the contradiction between their words and their feelings. Prevented from saying what they believed, they tried to establish their psychic equilibrium by consciously making themselves believe what they said."

From these observations—of the effects of role playing, the foot-in-the-door experience, moral and immoral acts, interracial behavior, and brainwashing—there is a powerful practical lesson: If we want to change ourselves in some important way, it's best not to wait for insight or inspiration. Sometimes we need to act—to begin writing that paper, to make those phone calls, to see that person—even if we don't feel like acting. To strengthen our convictions, it helps to enact them. In this way, faith and love are alike: If we keep them to ourselves, they shrivel. If we enact and express them, they grow.

WHY DOES BEHAVIOR AFFECT ATTITUDES?

Social psychologists agree: Our actions influence our attitudes, sometimes turning foes into friends, captives into collaborators, and doubters into believers. Social psychologists debate: Why?

One idea is that, wanting to make a good impression, people might merely express attitudes that *appear* consistent with their attitudes. Let's be honest with ourselves. We do care about appearances—why else all the money we spend on clothes, cosmetics, and weight control? To manage the impression we're creating, we might adjust what we say to please rather than offend. To appear consistent we might at times feign attitudes that harmonize with our actions.

But this isn't the whole story. Experiments suggest that some genuine attitude change follows our behavior commitments. Cognitive dissonance theory and self-perception theory offer two explanations.

Cognitive dissonance theory, developed by the late Leon Festinger (1957), proposes that we feel tension ("dissonance") when two simultaneously accessible thoughts or beliefs ("cognitions") are psychologically inconsistent—as when we decide to say or do something we have mixed feelings about. Festinger argued that to reduce this unpleasant arousal, we often adjust our thinking.

Dissonance theory pertains mostly to discrepancies between behavior and attitudes. We are aware of both. Thus, if we sense some inconsistency, perhaps some hypocrisy, we feel pressure for change. That helps explain why, in a British survey, half of cigarette smokers disagreed with the near-consensus among nonsmokers that smoking is "really as dangerous as people say" (Eiser & others, 1979) and why the perception of risk among those who have quit declines after relapsing (Gibbons & others, 1997).

So if we can persuade others to adopt a *new* attitude, their behavior should change accordingly; that's common sense. Or if we can induce people to behave differently, their attitude should change (that's the self-persuasion effect we have been reviewing).

Cognitive dissonance theory assumes that our need to maintain a consistent and positive self-image motivates us to adopt attitudes that justify our actions. Assuming no such motive, **self-perception theory** says simply that when our attitudes are unclear to us, we observe our behaviors and then infer our attitudes from them. As Anne Frank wrote in her diary, "I can watch myself and my actions just like an outsider." Having done so—having noted how we acted toward that person knocking at our door—we infer how we felt.

In proposing self-perception theory, Daryl Bem (1972) assumed that when we're unsure of our attitudes, we infer them, much as we make inferences about others' attitudes. So it goes as we observe our own behavior. What we freely say and do can be self-revealing. To paraphrase an old saying, How do I know what I think till I hear what I say or see what I do?

The debate over how to explain the attitudes-follow-behavior effect has inspired hundreds of experiments that reveal the conditions under which dissonance and self-perception processes operate. Dissonance theory best explains what happens when our actions openly contradict our well-defined attitudes. When, say, we hurt someone we like, we feel tension, which we might reduce by viewing the other as a jerk. Self-perception theory best explains what happens when we are unsure of our attitudes: We infer them by observing ourselves. If we lend our new neighbors, whom we neither like nor dislike, a cup of sugar, our helpful behavior can lead us to infer that we like them.

As often happens in science, each theory provides a partial explanation of a complex reality. If only human nature were simple, one simple theory could describe it. Alas, but thankfully, we are not simple creatures, and that is why there are many miles to go before psychological researchers can sleep.

CONCEPTS TO REMEMBER

Attitude   A favorable or unfavorable evaluative reaction toward something or someone, exhibited in one's beliefs, feelings, or intended behavior.

Role   A set of norms that define how people in a given social position ought to behave.

Foot-in-the-door phenomenon   The tendency for people who have first agreed to a small request to comply later with a larger request.

Low-ball technique   A tactic for getting people to agree to something. People who agree to an initial request will often still comply when the requester ups the ante. People who receive only the costly request are less likely to comply with it.

Cognitive dissonance theory Cognitive dissonance is tension that arises when one is simultaneously aware of two inconsistent cognitions, as when we realize that we have, with little justification, acted contrary to our attitudes. Cognitive dissonance theory proposes that we act to reduce such tension, as when we adjust our attitudes to correspond with our actions.

Self-perception theory The theory that when unsure of our attitudes, we infer them much as would someone observing us—by looking at our behavior and the circumstances under which it occurs.

PART THREE

❖

Social Influence

Social psychologists study not only how we think about one another—our topic in the preceding modules—but also how we influence and relate to one another. In Modules 10 through 18 we therefore probe social psychology's central concern: the powers of social influence.

What are these unseen social forces that push and pull us? How powerful are they? Research on social influence helps illuminate the invisible strings by which our social worlds move us about. This unit reveals these subtle powers, especially the cultural sources of gender attitudes, the forces of social conformity, the routes to persuasion, and the consequences of being with others and participating in groups.

When we see how these influences operate in everyday situations, we can better understand why people feel and act as they do. And we can ourselves become less vulnerable to unwanted manipulation, and more adept at pulling our own strings.

MODULE

10

❖

Gender, Genes, and Culture

There are many obvious dimensions of human diversity—height, weight, hair color, to name just a few. But for people's self-concepts and social relationships, the two dimensions that matter most, and that people first attune to, are race and, especially, sex (Stangor & others, 1992).

Later, we will look closely at how race and sex affect the way others regard and treat us. For now, let's consider **gender**—the behaviors people associate with being male or female. What behaviors *are* universally characteristic and expected of males? of females?

"Of the 46 chromosomes in the human genome, 45 are unisex," notes Judith Rich Harris (1998). Females and males are therefore similar in many physical traits, such as age of sitting, teething, and walking. They also are alike in many psychological traits, such as overall vocabulary, creativity, intelligence, happiness, and self-esteem. So, shall we conclude that men and women are essentially the same, except for a few anatomical oddities that hardly matter apart from special occasions?

Actually, there are some differences, and it is these differences, not the many similarities, that capture attention and make news. In both science and everyday life, differences excite interest. Compared with the average man, the average woman has 70 percent more fat, possesses 40 percent less muscle, and is 5 inches shorter. Compared to the average woman, the average man enters puberty two years later, is 20 times more likely to have color-deficient vision, and dies five years sooner. Women are twice as vulnerable to anxiety disorders and depression. Women have a slightly better sense of smell. They more easily become re-aroused immediately after orgasm. Men are three times more likely to commit suicide, and five times more likely to become alcoholic. Men also are much more likely to suffer

hyperactivity or speech disorders as children, to display antisocial personalities as adults, and to be able to wiggle their ears.

During the 1970s, many scholars worried that studies of such gender
differences might reinforce stereotypes and that gender differences might
be construed as women's deficits. Although the findings confirm some
stereotypes of women—as less aggressive, more nurturant, more sensitive,
and so forth—those are traits that many feminists celebrate and most people prefer (Swim, 1994). Small wonder, then, that most people rate their
feeling regarding women as more *favorable* than their feelings regarding
men (Eagly, 1994; Haddock & Zanna, 1994).

GENDER DIFFERENCES

Let's compare men's and women's social connections, dominance, aggressiveness, and sexuality. Having described these differences, we can then
consider how evolutionary and cultural perspectives might explain them.
Do gender differences reflect tendencies predisposed by natural selection?
Or are they culturally constructed—a reflection of the roles that women
and men often play and the situations in which they act?

Independence Versus Connectedness

Individual men display outlooks and behaviors varying from fierce com-
petitiveness to caring nurturance. So do individual women. Without denying that, psychologists Nancy Chodorow (1978, 1989), Jean Baker Miller
(1986), and Carol Gilligan and her colleagues (1982, 1990) contend that
women more than men give priority to close, intimate relationships.

The difference surfaces in childhood. Boys strive for independence,
girls for *inter*dependence. Boys' play often involves group activity. Girls'
play occurs in smaller groups, with less aggression, more sharing, more
imitation of relationships, and more intimate discussion (Lever, 1978).
Adult relationships extend this gender difference. In conversation, men
more often focus on tasks and connections with large groups, women on
personal relationships (Tannen, 1990). In groups, men talk more to give information; women talk more to share lives, give help, or show support
(Dindia & Allen, 1992; Eagly, 1987). Among first-year college students, 5 in
10 males and 7 in 10 females say it is *very* important to "help others who
are in difficulty" (Sax & others, 1996).

In general, report Felicia Pratto and her colleagues (1997), women
gravitate to jobs that reduce inequalities (public defender, advertising
work for a charity); men disproportionately gravitate to jobs that enhance
inequalities (prosecuting attorney, corporate advertising). Indeed, in most
of the U.S. caregiving professions, such as social worker, teacher, and nurse,
women outnumber men. Women also seem more charitable: Among indi-

viduals leaving estates worth more than $5 million, 48 percent of women and 35 percent of men make a charitable bequest, and women's colleges have unusually supportive alumni (National Council for Research on Women, 1994).

Women's connections as mothers, daughters, sisters, and grandmothers bind families together (Rossi & Rossi, 1990). Women spend more time caring for both preschoolers and aging parents (Eagly & Crowley, 1986). They buy most birthday gifts and greeting cards (DeStefano & Colasanto, 1990; Hallmark, 1990). Asked to provide photos that portray who they are, women include more photos of themselves as parents and of themselves with others (Clancy & Dollinger, 1993).

When surveyed, women are far more likely to describe themselves as having **empathy,** as being able to feel what another feels—to rejoice with those who rejoice and weep with those who weep. Although to a lesser extent, the empathy difference extends to laboratory studies. Women are more likely to cry or report feeling distressed at another's distress (Eisenberg & Lennon, 1983). This helps explain why, compared to friendships with men, both men and women report friendships with women to be more intimate, enjoyable, and nurturing (Rubin, 1985; Sapadin, 1988). When they want empathy and understanding, someone to whom they can disclose their joys and hurts, both men and women usually turn to women.

One explanation for this male-female empathy difference is that women tend to outperform men at reading others' emotions. In her analysis of 125 studies of men's and women's sensitivity to nonverbal cues, Judith Hall (1984) discerned that women are generally superior at decoding others' emotional messages. For example, shown a two-second silent film clip of the face of an upset woman, women guess more accurately whether she is criticizing someone or discussing her divorce.

Women also are more skilled at *expressing* emotions nonverbally, reports Hall. This is especially so for positive emotion, report Erick Coats and Robert Feldman (1996). They had people talk about times they had been happy, sad, and angry. When shown five-second silent video clips of these reports, observers could much more accurately discern women's than men's emotions when recalling happiness. (Men, however, were slightly more successful in expressing anger.)

SOCIAL DOMINANCE

Imagine two people: One is "adventurous, autocratic, coarse, dominant, forceful, independent, and strong." The other is "affectionate, dependent, dreamy, emotional, submissive, and weak." If the first person sounds more to you like a man and the second like a woman, you are not alone, report John Williams and Deborah Best (1990a, p. 15). All around the world, people rate men as more dominant, driven, and aggressive.

In essentially every society, men *are* socially dominant. In no known societies do women dominate men (Pratto, 1996). Women are 12 percent of the world's legislators (Briscoe, 1997), 3 percent of the U.N. ambassadors, less than 1 percent of the national presidents and prime ministers, and 0 percent of the economics Nobel laureates since the prize began in 1901 (Sivard, 1995). Men are more concerned than women with social dominance, and are more likely to favor conservative political candidates and programs that preserve group inequality (Pratto & others, 1997). Men are half of all jurors but 90 percent of elected jury leaders and most of the leaders of ad hoc laboratory groups (Davis & Gilbert, 1989; Kerr & others, 1982). As is typical of those in higher-status positions, men do most of the inviting for dates.

Men's style of communicating undergirds their social power. As leaders in situations where roles aren't rigidly scripted, men tend to be directive, women to be democratic (Eagly & Johnson, 1990). Men tend to excel as directive, task-focused leaders, women as social leaders who build team spirit (Eagly & Karau, 1991; Eagly & others, 1995; Wood & Rhodes, 1991).

In everyday conversations, men are more likely to act as powerful people often do—talking assertively, interrupting, touching with the hand, staring more, smiling less (Carli, 1991; Ellyson & others, 1991; Major & others, 1990). Stating the results from a female perspective, women's influence style tends to be more indirect—less interruptive, more sensitive, more polite, less cocky.

So, is it right to declare (in the words of one 1990s best-seller) that *men are from Mars, women are from Venus?* Actually, note Kay Deaux and Marianne LeFrance (1998), women's and men's conversational styles vary with the social context. Much of the style we attribute to men is typical of people (men or women) in positions of status and power. Moreover, individuals vary; some men are characteristically hesitant and deferential, some women direct and assertive. Clearly, it oversimplifies to suggest that women and men are from different planets.

Aggression

By **aggression,** psychologists mean behavior intended to hurt. Throughout the world, hunting, fighting, and warring are primarily male activities. In survey, men admit to more aggression than do women. In laboratory experiments, men indeed exhibit more physical aggression, for example, by administering what they believe are hurtful electric shocks (Knight & others, 1996). In Canada, the male-to-female arrest rate is 11 to 1 for murder and 8 to 1 for assault (Colombo, 1994). In the United States, it is 9 to 1 for murder and 6 to 1 for assault (FBI, 1994). Across the world, murder rates vary. Yet in all regions, men are roughly 20 times more likely to murder men than women are to murder women (Daly & Wilson, 1989).

Sexuality

There is also a gender gap in sexual attitudes and assertiveness. It's true that in their physiological and subjective responses to sexual stimuli, women and men are "more similar than different" (Griffitt, 1987). Yet Susan Hendrick and her colleagues (1985) report that many studies, including their own, reveal that women are "moderately conservative" about casual sex and men are "moderately permissive." The American Council on Education's recent survey of a quarter million first-year college students is illustrative. "If two people really like each other, it's all right for them to have sex even if they've known each other for only a very short time," agreed 54 percent of men but only 32 percent of women (Sax & others, 1996). And in a survey of 3,400 randomly selected 18- to 59-year-old Americans, half as many men (25 percent) as women (48 percent) cited affection for the partner as a reason for first intercourse. How often do they think about sex? "Every day" or "several times a day," said 19 percent of women and 54 percent of men (Laumann & others, 1994).

The gender difference in sexual attitudes carries over to behavior. "With few exceptions anywhere in the world," report cross-cultural psychologist Marshall Segall and his colleagues (1990, p. 244), "males are more likely than females to initiate sexual activity." Among homosexual people, gay men likewise report more engagement in uncommitted sex than do lesbian women (Bailey & others, 1994). Casual hit-and-run sex is most common among males with traditional masculine attitudes (Pleck & others, 1993). Not only in sexual relations but also in courtship and touching, males tend to take more initiative (Hendrick, 1998; Kenrick 1987).

Sexual fantasies express the gender difference (Ellis & Symons, 1990). In male-oriented erotica, women are unattached and lust-driven. In romance novels, whose primary market is women, a tender male is emotionally consumed by his devoted passion for the heroine. Social scientists aren't the only ones to have noticed. "Women can be fascinated by a four-hour movie with subtitles wherein the entire plot consists of a man and a woman yearning to have, but never actually having a relationship," observes humorist Dave Barry (1995). "Men HATE that. Men can take maybe 45 seconds of yearning, and they want everybody to get naked. Followed by a car chase. A movie called 'Naked People in Car Chases' would do really well among men."

*E*VOLUTION AND GENDER: DOING WHAT COMES NATURALLY?

"What do you think is the main reason men and women have different personalities, interests, and abilities?" asked the Gallup Organization (1990) in a national survey. "Is it mainly because of the way men and women are raised, or are the differences part of their biological makeup?" Nearly equal numbers answered "upbringing" and "biology."

There are, of course, those salient biological sex differences. Men have penises; women have vaginas. Men produce sperm; women, eggs. Men have the muscle mass to hunt game; women can breast-feed. Are biological sex differences limited to these obvious distinctions in reproduction and physique? Or do women's and men's genes, hormones, and brains differ in ways that also contribute to behavior differences? Social scientists have recently been giving increased attention to biological differences on social behavior. Consider the bisocial view of gender differences.

Gender and Mating Preferences

Since Darwin, most biologists have assumed that for millions of years organisms have competed to survive and leave descendants. Genes that increased the odds of leaving descendants became more abundant. In the snowy Arctic environment, for example, polar bear genes that program a thick coat of camouflaging fur have won the genetic competition and now predominate.

Simplified, Darwin assumed that the way organisms evolve is adaptive: otherwise they wouldn't be here. Organisms well adapted to their environment are more likely to leave their genes for descendants. **Evolutionary psychology** studies how this process might predispose not just adaptive physical traits, such as polar bear coats, but also psychological traits and social behavior (Buss, 1991).

Evolutionary theory offers a ready explanation for why males exert more sexual initiative. The average male produces many trillions of sperm in his lifetime, making sperm cheap compared to eggs. Moreover, during the time when a female brings one fetus to term and then nurses it, a male can spread his genes wide and far by fertilizing many females. Thus females invest their reproductive opportunities carefully, by looking for signs of health and resources in males. Males compete with other males for chances to win the genetic sweepstakes by sending their genes into the future. Men, say the evolutionists, seek to reproduce widely, women wisely.

Moreover, evolutionary psychology suggests, physically dominant males gained more access to females, which over generations enhance male aggression and dominance. If our ancestral mothers benefited from being able to read their infants' and suitors' emotions, then natural selection may have similarly favored emotion-detecting ability in females. Underlying all these presumptions is the principle that nature selects traits that help send one's genes into the future.

Mind you, little of this is conscious. No one stops to calculate, "How can I maximize the number of genes I leave to posterity?" Rather, say evolutionary psychologists, our natural yearnings are our genes' way of making more genes. And that, these psychologists believe, helps explain not only male aggression but also the differing sexual attitudes and behaviors of females and males.

Evolutionary psychology also predicts that men will strive to offer what women will desire—external resources and physical protection—and that women will strive to offer men the youthful, healthy appearance (connoting fertility) that men will desire. And sure enough, note Buss (1994a) and Alan Feingold (1992), women's and men's mate preferences confirm these predictions.

Studies in 37 cultures, from Australia and Zambia, reveal that men everywhere feel attracted to women whose physical features, such as youthful face and form, suggest fertility. Women everywhere feel attracted to men whose wealth, power, and ambition promise resources for protecting and nurturing offspring.

Without disputing natural selection—nature's selecting physical and behavioral traits that enhance gene survival—critics see two problems with evolutionary explanations. First, these explanations sometimes start with an effect (such as the difference between females and males in sexual initiative) and then work backward to construct an explanation for it. This approach is reminiscent of functionalism, a dominant theory in psychology during the 1920s. "Why does that behavior occur? Because it serves such and such a function." The theorist can hardly lose at this game.

The way to prevent such hindsight bias is to imagine things turning out otherwise. Let's try it. If human males were never known to have extramarital affairs, might we not see the evolutionary wisdom behind their fidelity? After all, there is more to bringing offspring to maturity than merely depositing sperm in a fertile woman. Males who are loyal to their mates and offspring are more apt to ensure that their young will survive to perpetuate their genes. (This is, in fact, an evolutionary explanation for why humans, and certain other species whose young require a heavy parental investment, tend to pair off and be monogamous.)

Evolutionary psychologists reply that hindsight plays no less a role in cultural explanations: Why do women and men differ? Because their culture *socializes* their behavior! As we will see, when people's roles vary across time and place, "culture" *describes* those roles better than it explains them. And far from being mere hindsight conjecture, say evolutionary psychologists, their field is an empirical science that tests evolutionary predictions with data from animal behavior, cross-cultural observations, and hormonal and genetic studies. Also, the evolutionary psychologist reminds us, evolutionary wisdom is *past* wisdom. It tells us what behaviors worked in the past. Whether such tendencies are still adaptive is a different question.

Evolutionary psychology's critics acknowledge that evolution helps explain both our commonalties and our differences (a certain amount of diversity aids survival). But they contend that our common evolutionary heritage does not, by itself, predict the enormous cultural variation in human marriage patterns (from one spouse to a succession of spouses to

multiple wives to multiple husbands to spouse swapping). Nor does it explain cultural changes in behavior patterns over mere decades of time.
The most significant trait that nature has endowed us with, it seems, is the
capacity to adapt—to learn and to change. Therein lies what all agree is
culture's shaping power.

Gender and Hormones

The results of architectural blueprints appear in physical structures, so the
effects of our genetic blueprints appear in the sex hormones that differen-
tiate females and males. Do hormone differences predispose psychological gender differences?

The gender gap in aggression does seem influenced by testosterone. In
various animals, administering testosterone heightens aggressiveness. In
humans, violent male criminals have higher than normal testosterone levels; so do National Football League players and boisterous fraternity members (Dabbs & others, 1990, 1993). Moreover, for both humans and monkeys,
the gender difference in aggression appears early in life (before culture has
much effect) and wanes as testosterone levels decline during adulthood. No
one of these lines of evidence is conclusive. Taken together, they convince
most scholars that sex hormones matter. But so does culture, as we will see.

CULTURE AND GENDER

Culture is what's shared by a large group and transmitted across generations—ideas, attitudes, behaviors, and traditions. We can see the shaping
power of culture in ideas about how men and women should behave. In
countries everywhere, girls spend more time helping with housework and
child care, boys spend more time in unsupervised play (Edwards, 1991).
Even in contemporary, dual-career, North American marriages, men do
most of the household repairs and women arrange the child care (Biernat
& Wortman, 1991). In fact, women do most household work "everywhere," reports the United Nations (1991). And "everywhere, cooking and
dishwashing are the least shared household chores." Such behavior expectations for males and females define **gender roles.**

In an experiment with Princeton University undergraduate women,
Mark Zanna and Susan Pack (1975) showed the impact of gender-role expectations. The women answered a questionnaire on which they described
themselves to a tall, unattached, male senior they expected to meet. Those
who had been led to believe that his ideal woman was home-oriented and
deferential to her husband presented themselves as more traditionally
feminine than did women expecting to meet a man who liked strong, ambitious women. Moreover, given a problem-solving test, those expecting to

meet the nonsexist man behaved more intelligently: They solved 18 percent more problems than those expecting to meet the man with the traditional views. This adapting of themselves to fit the man's image was much less pronounced if the man was less desirable—a short, already attached freshman. In a companion experiment by Dean Morier and Cara Seroy (1994), men similarly adapted their self-presentations to meet desirable women's gender-role expectations.

But does culture construct gender roles? Or do gender roles merely reflect behavior that is naturally appropriate for men and women? The variety of gender roles across cultures and over time shows that culture indeed constructs our gender roles.

Gender Roles Vary with Culture

Should women do the housework? Should they be more concerned with promoting their husband's career than with their own? John Williams, Debra Best, and their collaborators (1990b) asked such questions of university students in 14 cultures. In nearly every one, women students had slightly more egalitarian views than their male peers. But the differences among the countries were far greater. Nigerian and Pakistani students, for example, had much more traditional ideas about distinct roles for women and men than did Dutch and German students.

Gender Roles Vary Over Time

In the last half-century—a thin slice of our long history—gender roles have changed dramatically. In 1938, 1 in 5 American approved "of a married woman earning money in business or industry if she has a husband capable of supporting her." By 1996, 4 in 5 approved (Niemi & others, 1989; NORC, 1996)—although nearly 2 in 3 still think that for children the "ideal family situation" is "father has a job and mother stays home and cares for the children" (Gallup, 1990). In 1967, 57 percent of first-year American college students agreed that "the activities of married women are best confined to the home and family." In 1997, 25 percent agreed (Astin & others, 1987; Sax & others, 1997).

Behavior changes have accompanied this attitude shift. Between 1960 and 1995, the proportion of 40-year-old married U.S. women in the workforce doubled—going from 38 to 76 percent (U.S. Bureau of the Census, 1996). A similar influx of women in the workforce has occurred in Canada, Australia, and Britain. Since 1970, increasing numbers of women have been training to become lawyers, doctors, and dentists. This striking variation of roles across cultures and over time signals that evolution and biology do not fix gender roles: Culture also bends the genders.

CONCLUSIONS: BIOLOGY AND CULTURE

We needn't think of evolution and culture as competitors. Cultural norms subtly but powerfully affect our attitudes and behavior, but they don't do so independently of biology. Everything social and psychological is ultimately biological. If others' expectations influence us, that is part of our biological programming. Moreover, what our biological heritage initiates, culture might accentuate. If genes and hormones predispose males to be more physically aggressive than females, culture might amplify this difference through norms that expect males to be tough and females to be the kinder, gentler sex.

Biology and culture can also **interact.** In humans, biological traits influence how the environment reacts. People respond differently to a Sylvester Stallone than to a Woody Allen. Men, being 8 percent taller than women and having almost twice the proportion of muscle mass as women, might likewise have different experiences than women. Or consider this: A very strong cultural norm dictates that males should be taller than their female mates. In one study, only 1 in 720 married couples violated this norm (Gillis & Avis, 1980). With hindsight, we can speculate a psychological explanation: Perhaps being taller (and older) helps men perpetuate their social power over women. But we can also speculate evolutionary wisdom that might underlie the cultural norm: If people preferred partners of the same height, tall men and short women would often be without partners. As it is, evolution dictates that men tend to be taller than women, and culture dictates the same for couples. So the height norm might well be a result of biology *and* culture.

In *Sex Differences in Social Behavior,* Alice Eagly (1987, 1997) theorizes how biology and culture interact (Figure 10-1). She believes that a variety

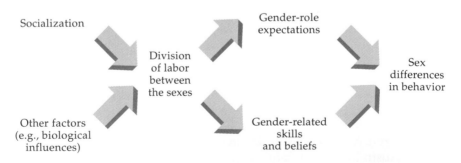

FIGURE 10-1
A social-role theory of gender differences in social behavior. Various influences, including childhood experiences and biologic factors, bend males and females toward differing roles. It is the expectations and the skills and beliefs associated with these differing roles that affect men's and women's behavior. (Adapted from Eagly, 1987, and Eagly & Wood, 1991.)

of factors, including biological influences and childhood socialization, predispose a sexual division of labor. In adult life, the immediate causes of gender differences in social behavior are the *roles* that reflect this sexual division of labor. Men tend to be found in roles that demand social and physical power, and women tend to be found in more nurturant roles. Each sex then tends to exhibit the behaviors expected of those who fill such roles and to have their skills and beliefs shaped accordingly. The effects of biology and socialization might be important insofar as they influence the social roles that people play, for the roles we play influence who we become.

CONCEPTS TO REMEMBER

Gender   In psychology, the characteristics, whether biologically or socially influenced, by which people define female and male. Because "sex" is a biological category, social psychologists sometimes refer to biologically based gender differences as "sex differences."

Empathy   The vicarious experience of another's feelings; putting oneself in another's shoes.

Aggression   Physical or verbal behavior intended to hurt. In laboratory experiments, this might mean delivering electric shocks or saying something likely to hurt another's feelings. By this social psychological definition, one can be socially assertive without being aggressive.

Evolutionary psychology   The study of how natural selection predisposes adaptive traits and behavior tendencies.

Culture   The enduring behaviors, ideas, attitudes, and traditions shared by a large group of people and transmitted from one generation to the next.

Gender role   A set of behavioral expectations (norms) for males or females.

Interaction   A relationship in which the effect of one factor (such as biology) depends on another factor (such as environment).

11

❖

How Nice People Get Corrupted

Researchers who study conformity construct miniature social worlds, laboratory microcultures that simplify and stimulate important features of everyday social influence. Two famous sets of experiments—Solomon Asch's studies of conformity and Stanley Milgram's studies of obedience—illustrate the process. They also offer startling evidence of the powers of social influence.

ASCH'S STUDIES OF CONFORMITY

From his boyhood, Asch recalls a traditional Jewish seder at Passover:

> I asked my uncle, who was sitting next to me, why the door was being opened. He replied, "The prophet Elijah visits this evening every Jewish home and takes a sip of wine from the cup reserved for him."
>
> I was amazed at this news and repeated, "Does he really come? Does he really take a sip?"
>
> My uncle said, "If you watch very closely, when the door is opened you will see—you watch the cup—you will see that the wine will go down a little."
>
> And that's what happened. My eyes were riveted upon the cup of wine. I was determined to see whether there would be a change. And to me it seemed—it was tantalizing, and of course, it was hard to be absolutely sure—that indeed something was happening at the rim of the cup, and the wine did go down a little. (Quoted by Aron & Aron, 1989, p. 27)

Years later, social psychologist Asch re-created his boyhood experience in his laboratory. Imagine yourself as one of Asch's volunteer subjects. You are seated sixth in a row of seven people. After explaining that

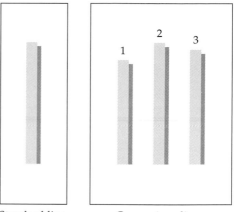

Standard line   Comparison lines

FIGURE 11-1
Sample comparison from Solomon Asch's conformity procedure. The participants judged which of three comparison lines matched the standard.

you will be taking part in a study of perceptual judgments, the experimenter asks you to say which of the three lines in Figure 11-1 matches the standard line. You can easily see that it's line 2. So it's no surprise when the five people responding before you all say "line 2."

The next comparison proves as easy, and you settle in for what seems a simple test. But the third trial startles you. Although the correct answer seems just as clear-cut, the first person gives a wrong answer. When the second person gives the same wrong answer, you sit up in your chair and stare at the cards. The third person agrees with the first two. Your jaw drops; you start to perspire. "What is this?" you ask yourself. "Are they blind? Or am I?" The fourth and fifth people agree with the others. Then the experimenter looks at you. Now you are experiencing an epistemological dilemma: "How am I to know what is true? Is it what my peers tell me or what my eyes tell me?"

Dozens of college students experienced this conflict during Asch's experiments. Those in a control condition who answered alone were correct more than 99 percent of the time. Asch wondered: If several others (confederates coached by the experimenter) gave identical wrong answers, would people declare what they would otherwise have denied? Although some people never conformed, three quarters did so at least once. All told, 37 percent of the responses were conforming (or should we say "*trusting* of others"?). Of course, that means 63 percent of the time people did not conform. Despite the independence shown by many of his subjects, Asch's (1955) feelings about the conformity were as clear as the correct answers to his

In one of Asch's conformity experiments, the subject, number 6, experienced uneasiness and conflict after hearing incorrect responses from the five persons who answered a question before him.

questions: "That reasonably intelligent and well-meaning young people are willing to call white black is a matter of concern. It raises questions about our ways of education and about the values that guide our conduct".

Asch's results are startling because in none of them is there any open, obvious pressure to conform; there are no rewards for "team play," no punishments for individuality. If people are this compliant in response to such minimal pressure, how much more compliant will they be if they are directly coerced? Could someone force the average American or British Commonwealth citizen to perform cruel acts? I would have guessed not: Their humane, democratic, individualistic values would make them resist such pressure. Besides, the easy verbal pronouncements of these experiments are a giant step away from actually harming someone; you and I would never yield to coercion to hurt another. Or would we? Social psychologist Stanley Milgram wondered.

MILGRAM'S OBEDIENCE EXPERIMENTS

Milgram's (1965, 1974) experiments on what happens when the demands of authority clash with the demands of conscience have become social psychology's most famous and controversial experiments. "Perhaps more than any other empirical contributions in the history of social science," notes Lee Ross (1988), "they have become part of our society's shared intellectual legacy—that small body of historical incidents, biblical parables, and classic literature that serious thinkers feel free to draw on when they debate about human nature or contemplate human history."

Here is the scene staged by Milgram, a creative artist who wrote stories and stage plays: Two men come to Yale University's psychology laboratory to participate in a study of learning and memory. A stern experimenter in a gray technician's coat explains that this is a pioneering study of the effect of punishment on learning. The experiment requires one of them to teach a list of word pairs to the other and to punish errors by delivering shocks of increasing intensity. To assign the roles, they draw slips out of a hat. One of the men, a mild-mannered, 47-year-old accountant who is the experimenter's confederate, pretends that his slip says "learner," and he is ushered into an adjacent room. The "teacher" (who has come in response to a newspaper ad) takes a mild sample shock and then looks on as the experimenter straps the learner into a chair and attaches an electrode to his wrist.

Teacher and experimenter then return to the main room where the teacher takes his place before a "shock generator" with switches labeled to indicate that they deliver shocks ranging from 15 to 450 volts in 15-volt increments. The switches are labeled "Slight Shock," "Very Strong Shock," "Danger: Severe Shock," and so forth. Under the 435- and 450-volt switches appears "XXX." The experimenter tells the teacher to "move one level higher on the shock generator" each time the learner gives a wrong answer. With each flick of a switch, lights flash, relay switches click, and an electric buzz sounds.

If the participant complies with the experimenter's requests, he hears the learner grunt at 75, 90, and 105 volts. At 120 volts the learner shouts that the shocks are painful. And at 150 volts he cries out, "Experimenter, get me out of here! I won't be in the experiment anymore! I refuse to go on!" By 270 volts his protests have become screams of agony, and he continues to insist to be let out. At 300 and 315 volts he screams his refusal to answer. After 330 volts he falls silent. In answer to the "teacher's" inquiries and pleas to end the experiment, the experimenter states that the nonresponses should be treated as wrong answers. To keep the participant going, he uses four verbal prods:

PROD 1: "Please continue" (or "Please go on").
PROD 2: "The experiment requires that you continue."
PROD 3: "It is absolutely essential that you continue."
PROD 4: "You have no other choice; you *must* go on."

How far would you go? Milgram described the experiment to 110 psychiatrists, college students, and middle-class adults. People in all three groups guessed that they would disobey by about 135 volts; none expected to go beyond 300 volts. Recognizing that self-estimates can reflect self-serving bias, Milgram asked them how far they thought *other* people would go. Virtually no one expected anyone to proceed to "XXX" on the shock panel. (The psychiatrists guessed about one in a thousand.)

But when Milgram conducted the experiment with 40 men—a vocational mix of 20- to 50-year-olds—25 of them (63 percent) went clear to 450 volts. In fact, all who reached 450 volts complied with a command to *continue* the procedure until, after two further trials, the experimenter called a halt.

Given this disturbing result, Milgram next made the learner's protests even more compelling. As the learner was strapped into the chair, the teacher heard him mention his "slight heart condition" and heard the experimenter's reassurance that "although the shocks may be painful, they cause no permanent tissue damage." The learner's anguished protests were to little avail; of 40 new men in this experiment, 26 (65 percent) fully complied with the experimenter's demands (Figure 11-2).

The obedience of his subjects disturbed Milgram, and the procedures he used disturbed many social psychologists (Miller, 1986). The "learner" in these experiments actually received no shock (he disengaged himself from the electric chair and turned on a tape recorder that delivered the protests). Nevertheless, some critics said that Milgram did to his participants what they thought they were doing to their victims: He stressed them against their will. Indeed, many of the "teachers" did experience agony. They sweated, trembled, stuttered, bit their lips, groaned, or even broke into uncontrollable nervous laughter. A *New York Times* reviewer complained that the cruelty inflicted by the experiments "upon their unwitting subjects is surpassed only by the cruelty that they elicit from them" (Marcus, 1974). Critics also argued that the experiment may have altered the participants self-concepts. One participant's wife told him, "You can call yourself Eichmann" (referring to Nazi death-camp administrator Adolf Eichmann). CBS television depicted the results and controversy in a two-hour dramatization starring William Shatner of *Star Trek* fame as Milgram. "A world of evil so terrifying no one dares penetrate its secret. Until Now!" declared a *TV Guide* ad for the program (Elms, 1995).

In his own defense, Milgram pointed to the lessons taught by his nearly two dozen experiments with a diverse sample of more than a thousand participants. He also reminded critics of the support he received from the participants after the deception was revealed and the experiment explained. When surveyed afterward, 84 percent said they were glad to have participated; only 1 percent regretted volunteering. A year later, a psychiatrist interviewed 40 of those who had suffered most and concluded that, despite the temporary stress, none was harmed.

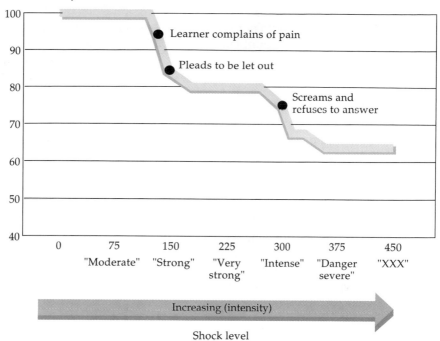

Percent of subjects still obedient

FIGURE 11-2
The Milgram obedience experiment. The percentage of subjects complying despite the learner's cries of protest and failure to respond. (From Milgram, 1965.)

The ethical controversy was "terribly overblown," Milgram felt. Actually, he wrote in a letter,

> there is less consequence to subjects in this experiment from the standpoint of effects on self-esteem, than to university students who take ordinary course examinations, and who do not get the grades they want. . . . It seems that [in giving exams] we are quite prepared to accept stress, tension, and consequences for self-esteem. But in regard to the process of generating new knowledge, how little tolerance we show. (quoted by Blass, 1996)

What Breeds Obedience?

Milgram did more than reveal the extent to which people will obey an authority; he also examined the conditions that breed obedience. In further experiments, he varied the social conditions and got compliance ranging from 0 to 93 percent fully obedient. The determining factors were these four: the victim's emotional distance, the authority's closeness and legitimacy, whether or not the authority is institutionalized, and the liberating effects of a disobedient fellow subject.

Emotional Distance of the Victim

Milgram's subjects acted with least compassion when the "learners" could not be seen (and could not see them). When the victim was remote and the "teachers" heard no complaints, nearly all obeyed calmly to the end. When the learner was in the same room, "only" 40 percent obeyed to 450 volts. Full compliance dropped to 30 percent when teachers were required to force the learner's hand into contact with a shock plate.

In everyday life, too, it is easiest to abuse someone who is distant or depersonalized. People will be unresponsive even to great tragedies. Executioners depersonalize those being executed by placing hoods over their heads. The ethics of war allow one to bomb a helpless village from 40,000 feet but not to shoot an equally helpless villager. In combat with an enemy they can see, many soldiers either do not fire or do not aim. Such disobedience is rare among those given orders to kill with the more distant artillery or aircraft weapons (Padgett, 1989).

On the positive side, people act most compassionately toward those who are personalized. This is why appeals for the unborn or the hungry are nearly always personalized with a compelling photograph or description. Perhaps even more compelling is an ultrasound picture of one's own developing fetus. When queried by John Lydon and Christine Dunkel-Schetter (1994), expectant women expressed more commitment to their pregnancy if they had earlier seen an ultrasound picture of their fetus that clearly displayed body parts.

Closeness and Legitimacy of the Authority

The physical presence of the experimenter also affected obedience. When Milgram gave the commands by telephone, full obedience dropped to 21 percent (although many lied and said they were obeying). Other studies confirm that when the one making the request is physically close, compliance increases. Given a light touch on the arm, people are more likely to lend a dime, sign a petition, or sample a new pizza (Kleinke, 1977; Smith & others, 1982; Willis & Hamm, 1980).

The authority, however, must be perceived as legitimate. In another twist on the basic experiment, the experimenter received a rigged telephone call that required him to leave the laboratory. He said that the equipment recorded data automatically, so the "teacher" should just go ahead. After the experimenter left, another person who had been assigned a clerical role (actually a second confederate) assumed command. The clerk "decided" that the shock should be increased one level for each wrong answer and instructed the teacher accordingly. Now 80 percent of the teachers refused to comply fully. The confederate, feigning disgust at this defiance, sat down in front of the shock generator and tried to take over the teacher's role. At this point most of the defiant participants protested. Some tried to unplug the generator. One large man lifted the zealous confederate from his chair and threw him across the room. This rebellion against an illegitimate authority contrasted sharply with the deferential politeness usually shown the experimenter.

It also contrasts with the behavior of hospital nurses who in one study were called by an unknown physician and ordered to administer an obvious overdose of a drug (Hofling & others, 1966). The researchers told one group of nurses and nursing students about the experiment and asked how they would react. Nearly all said they would not have given the medication as ordered. One explained that she would have replied, "I'm sorry, sir, but I am not authorized to give any medication without a written order, especially one so large over the usual dose and one that I'm unfamiliar with. If it were possible, I would be glad to do it, but this is against hospital policy and my own ethical standards." Nevertheless, when 22 other nurses were actually given the phoned-in overdose order, all but one obeyed without delay (until being intercepted on their way to the patient). Although not all nurses are so compliant (Krackow & Blass, 1995; Rank & Jacobson, 1977), these nurses were following a familiar script: Doctor (a legitimate authority) orders; nurse obeys.

Compliance with legitimate authority was also apparent in the strange case of the "rectal ear ache" (Cohen & Davis, 1981, cited by Cialdini, 1988). A doctor ordered that ear drops be given to a patient suffering infection in the right ear. On the prescription, the doctor abbreviated "place in right ear" as "place in *R ear*." Reading the order, the compliant nurse put the required drops in the compliant patient's rectum.

Institutional Authority

If the prestige of the authority is this important, then perhaps the institutional prestige of Yale University legitimized the Milgram experiment commands. In postexperimental interviews, many participants volunteered that had it not been for Yale's reputation, they would not have obeyed. To see whether this was true, Milgram moved the experiment to Bridgeport, Connecticut. He set himself up in a modest commercial building as the "Research Associates of Bridgeport." When the usual "heart disturbance" experiment was run with the same personnel, what percentage of the men do you suppose fully obeyed? Though reduced, the rate remained remarkably high—48 percent.

The Liberating Effects of Group Influence

These classic experiments give us a negative view of conformity. Can conformity be constructive? Perhaps you can recall a time you felt justifiably angry at an unfair teacher, or with someone's offensive behavior, but you hesitated to object. Then one or two others objected, and you followed their example. Milgram captured this liberating effect of conformity by placing the teacher with two confederates who were to help conduct the procedure. During the experiment, both defied the experimenter, who then ordered the real subject to continue alone. Did he? No. Ninety percent liberated themselves by conforming to the defiant confederates.

REFLECTIONS ON THE CLASSIC STUDIES

The common response to Milgram's results is to note their counterparts in recent history: the "I was only following orders" defense of Adolf Eichmann in Nazi Germany; of Lieutenant William Calley, who in 1968 directed the unprovoked slaughter of hundreds of Vietnamese in the village of My Lai; and of the "ethnic cleansing" occurring more recently in Iraq, Rwanda, and Bosnia. A Bosnian victim explains:

> I was raped and tortured too, because they knew that I am a wife of a leader of the Muslim party. My neighbor tortured me the most, the one my husband respected as his own brother. By the end of June, Chetniks brought another neighbor of ours and with a gun pointed at him they [demanded he] rape a 14-year-old girl. He stood trembling and stuttering with fear. Then he turned to a Chetnik he believed was a leader and said: "Don't make me do it. I have known her since she was born.". . . They beat him in front of us until he died. It was an example to the other Serbs that there is no pity, that one must do what leaders order them to do. (Drakulic, 1992)

The obedience experiments differ from the other conformity experiments in the strength of the social pressure: Compliance is explicitly commanded. Without the coercion, people did not act cruelly. Yet the Asch and Milgram experiments share certain commonalities. They show how compliance can take precedence over moral sense. They succeeded in pressuring people to go against their own conscience. They did more than teach us an academic lesson; they sensitized us to moral conflicts in our own lives. And they illustrate and affirm some familiar social psychological principles: the link between behavior and attitudes, the power of the situation, and the strength of the fundamental attribution error.

Behavior and Attitudes

In Module 9 on behavior and belief, we noted that attitudes fail to determine behavior when external influences override inner convictions. These experiments vividly illustrate this principle. When responding alone, Asch's subjects nearly always gave the correct answer. It was another matter when they stood alone against a group. In the obedience experiments, a powerful social pressure (the experimenter's commands) overcame a weaker one (the remote victim's pleas). Torn between the pleas of the victim and the orders of the experimenter, between the desire to avoid doing harm and the desire to be a good subject, a surprising number chose to obey.

Why were the participants unable to disengage themselves? How had they become trapped? Imagine yourself as the teacher in yet another version of Milgram's experiment, one he never conducted. Assume that when the learner gives the first wrong answer, the experimenter asks you to zap him with 330 volts. After flicking the switch, you hear the learner scream, complain of a heart disturbance, and plead for mercy. Do you continue?

I think not. Recall the step-by-step entrapment of the foot-in-the-door phenomenon (see Module 9) as we compare this hypothetical experiment to what Milgram's subjects experienced. Their first commitment was mild (15 volts) and it elicited no protest. You, too, would agree to do that much. By the time they delivered 75 volts and heard the learner's first groan, they already had complied five times. On the next trial the experimenter asked them to commit an act only slightly more extreme than what they had already repeatedly committed. By the time they delivered 330 volts, after 22 acts of compliance, the subjects had reduced some of their cognitive dissonance. They were therefore in a different psychological state from that of someone beginning the experiment at that point. External behavior and internal disposition can feed one another, sometimes in an escalating spiral. Thus, reported Milgram (1974, p. 10):

> Many subjects harshly devalue the victim *as a consequence* of acting against him. Such comments as "He was so stupid and stubborn he deserved to get shocked" were common. Once having acted against the victim, these subjects found it necessary to view him as an unworthy individual, whose punishment was made inevitable by his own deficiencies of intellect and character.

During the early 1970s, the military junta then in power in Greece used this "blame-the-victim" process to train torturers (Haritos-Fatouros, 1988; Staub, 1989). In Greece, as in the training of SS officers in Nazi Germany, the military selected candidates based on their respect for and submission to authority. But such tendencies alone do not a torturer make. Thus they would first assign the trainee to guard prisoners, then to participate in arrest squads, then to hit prisoners, then to observe torture, and only then to practice it. Step by step, an obedient but otherwise decent person evolved into an agent of cruelty. Compliance bred acceptance.

From his study of human genocide across the world, Ervin Staub (1989) shows where this process can lead. Too often, criticism produces contempt, which licenses cruelty, which, when justifications are produced, leads to brutality, then killing, then systematic killing. Evolving attitudes both follow and justify actions. Staub's disturbing conclusion: "Human beings have the capacity to come to experience killing other people as nothing extraordinary" (p. 13).

But then humans also have a capacity for heroism. During the Holocaust, 3,500 French Jews and 1,500 other refugees destined for deportation to Germany were sheltered by the villagers of Le Chambon. These villagers were mostly Protestants, descendants of a persecuted group, and people whose own authorities, their pastors, had taught them to "resist whenever our adversaries will demand of us obedience contrary to the orders of the Gospel" (Rochat, 1993; Rochat & Modigliani, 1995). Ordered to divulge the locations of the sheltered Jews, the head pastor modeled disobedience: "I don't know of Jews, I only know of human beings." Without knowing how terrible the war would be or how much they would suffer, the resisters made an initial commitment and then—supported by their beliefs, by their own authorities, and by one another—remained defiant to the war's end. Here and elsewhere, the ultimate response to Nazi occupation usually came early. The first acts of compliance or resistance bred attitudes that influenced behavior, which strengthened attitudes. Initial helping heightened commitment, leading to more helping.

The Power of the Situation

The most important lesson of the modules on individualism and gender (that culture is a powerful shaper of lives) and this module's most important lesson (that immediate situational forces are just as powerful) reveal the strength of the social context. To feel this for yourself, imagine violating some minor norms: standing up in the middle of a class; singing out loud in a restaurant; greeting some distinguished senior professors by their first names; wearing shorts to church; playing golf in a suit; munching caramel corn at a piano recital; shaving half your head. In trying to break with social constraints, we suddenly realize how strong they are.

Some of Milgram's own students learned this lesson when Milgram and John Sabini (1983) asked their help in studying the effects of violating a simple social norm: asking riders on the New York City subway system for their seats. To their surprise, 56 percent gave up their seats, even when no justification was given. The students' own reactions to making the request were as interesting: Most found it extremely difficult. Often, the words got stuck in their throat, and they had to withdraw. Once having made a request and gotten a seat, they sometimes justified their norm violation by pretending to be sick. Such is the power of the unspoken rules governing our public behavior.

The students in a recent Pennsylvania State University experiment found it similarly difficult to get challenging words out of their mouths. Some students imagined themselves discussing with three others who to select for survival on a desert island. They were asked to imagine one of the others, a man, injecting three sexist comments, such as "I think we need more women on the island to keep the men satisfied." How would they react to such sexist remarks? Only 5 percent predicted they would ignore each of the comments or wait to see how others reacted. But when Janet Swim and Lauri Hyers (1998) engaged other students in discussions where such comments were actually made by a male confederate, 56 percent (not 5 percent) said nothing. This once again demonstrates the power of normative pressures and how hard it is to predict behavior, even our own behavior.

Milgram's experiments also offer a lesson about evil. Evil sometimes results from a few bad apples. That's the image of evil symbolized by depraved killers in suspense novels and horror movies. In real life we think of Hitler's extermination of Jews, of Saddam Hussein's extermination of Kurds, of Pol Pot's extermination of Cambodians. But evil also results from social forces—from the heat, humidity, and disease that help make a whole barrel of apples go bad. As these experiments show, situations can induce ordinary people to agree to falsehoods or to act cruelly.

This is especially true when, as happens often in complex societies, the most terrible evil evolves from a sequence of small evils. German civil servants surprised Nazi leaders with their willingness to handle the paperwork of the Holocaust. They were not killing Jews, of course; they were merely pushing paper (Silver & Geller, 1978). When fragmented, evil becomes easier. Milgram studied this compartmentalization of evil by involving yet another 40 men more indirectly. Rather than trigger the shock, they had only to administer the learning test. Now, 37 of the 40 fully complied.

So it is in our everyday lives: The drift toward evil usually comes in small increments, without any conscious intent to do evil. Procrastination involves a similar unintended drift, toward self-harm (Sabini & Silver, 1982). A student knows the deadline for a term paper is weeks ahead. Each diversion from working on the paper—a video game here, a TV program there—seems harmless enough. Yet gradually the student veers toward not doing the paper at all, without ever consciously deciding not to do it.

The Fundamental Attribution Error

Why do the results of these classic experiments so often startle people? Is it not because we expect people to act in accord with their dispositions? It doesn't surprise us when a surly person is nasty, but we expect those with pleasant dispositions to be kind. Bad people do bad things; good people do good things.

When you read about Milgram's experiments, what impressions did you form of the subjects? Most people attribute negative qualities to them. When told about one or two of the obedient subjects, people judge them to be aggressive, cold, and unappealing—even after learning that their behavior was typical (Miller & others, 1973). Cruelty, we presume, is inflicted by the cruel at heart.

Günter Bierbrauer (1979) tried to eliminate this underestimation of social forces (the fundamental attribution error). He had university students observe a vivid reenactment of the experiment or play the role of obedient teacher themselves. They still predicted that, in a repeat of Milgram's experiment, their friends would be only minimally compliant. Bierbrauer concluded that although social scientists accumulate evidence that our behavior is a product of our social history and current environment, most people continue to believe that people's inner qualities reveal themselves—that only good people do good and that only evil people do evil.

It is tempting to assume that Eichmann and the Auschwitz death-camp commanders were uncivilized monsters. But after a hard day's work, the commanders would relax by listening to Beethoven and Schubert. Eichmann himself was outwardly indistinguishable from common people with ordinary jobs (Arendt, 1963). Or consider the German police battalion responsible for shooting nearly 40,000 Jews in Poland, many of them women, children, and elderly people who were shot in the back of the head, gruesomely spraying their brains about. Christopher Browning (1992) portrays the "normality" of these men. Like the many, many others who ravaged Europe's Jewish ghettos, operated the deportation trains, and administered the death camps (Goldhagen, 1996), they were not Nazis, SS members, or racial fanatics. They were laborers, salesmen, clerks, and artisans—family men who were too old for military service, but who, when directly ordered to kill, were unable to refuse.

Milgram's conclusion also makes it hard to attribute the Holocaust to unique character traits in the German people: "The most fundamental lesson of our study," he noted, is that "ordinary people, simply doing their jobs, and without any particular hostility on their part, can become agents in a terrible destructive process" (Milgram, 1974, p. 6). As Mister Rogers often reminds his preschool television audience, "Good people sometimes do bad things." Perhaps, then, we should be more wary of political leaders whose charming dispositions lull us into supposing they would never do evil. Under the sway of evil forces, even nice people are sometimes corrupted.

12

❖

Two Routes to Persuasion

O ur opinions have to come from somewhere. Persuasion, whether it be education or propaganda, is therefore inevitable. Indeed, persuasion is everywhere—at the heart of politics, marketing, courtship, parenting, negotiation, evangelism, and courtroom decision making. Social psychologists therefore seek to understand what makes a message effective: What factors influence us to change? And how, as persuaders, can we most effectively "educate" others?

Imagine that you are a marketing or advertising executive, one of those responsible for the nearly $300 billion spent annually worldwide on advertising (Brown & others, 1993). Or imagine that you are a preacher, trying to increase love and charity among your parishioners. Or imagine that you want to promote energy conservation, encourage breast-feeding, or campaign for a political candidate. What could you do to make yourself, and your message, persuasive? Or, if you are wary of being manipulated by such appeals, what tactics should you be alert to?

THE TWO ROUTES

In choosing tactics, you must first decide: Should you focus mostly on building strong *central arguments*? Or should you make your message appealing by associating it with favorable *peripheral cues*, such as sex appeal? Persuasion researchers Richard Petty and John Cacioppo (1986; Petty & Wegener, 1998) and Alice Eagly and Shelly Chaiken (1993) report that people who are able and motivated to think through an issue are best persuaded through a **central route** to persuasion—one that marshals systematic arguments to stimulate favorable thinking. Computer ads, for example, seldom feature Hollywood stars or great athletes; instead they offer customers information on competitive features and prices.

Some people are analytical, note Petty and Cacioppo. They like to think about issues and mentally elaborate them. Such people rely not just on the cogency of persuasive appeals but on their own cognitive responses to them as well. It's not so much the arguments that are persuasive as what they get people thinking. And when people think deeply rather than superficially, any changed attitude will more likely persist, resist attack, and influence behavior (Petty & others, 1995; Verplanken, 1991).

On issues that won't engage people's thinking, a **peripheral route**— one that provides cues that trigger acceptance without much thinking— works better. Instead of providing information, soft drink ads promote "the real thing" or "the Pepsi generation" with images of youth, vitality, and joy.

Even analytical people sometimes form tentative opinions using peripheral heuristics, such as "Trust the experts" or "Long messages are credible" (Chaiken & Maheswaran, 1994). Residents of my community recently voted on a complicated issue involving the legal ownership of our local hospital. I didn't have the time or interest to study this question myself (I had this book to write), but I noted that referendum supporters were all people I either liked or regarded as experts. So I used a simple heuristic— friends and experts can be trusted—and voted accordingly. We all make snap judgments using other rule-of-thumb heuristics: If a speaker is articulate and appealing, has apparently good motives, and has several arguments (or better, if the different arguments come from different sources), we take the easy peripheral route and accept the message without much thought (Figure 12-1).

*T*HE ELEMENTS OF PERSUASION

Among the central and peripheral ingredients of persuasion explored by social psychologists are these four: (1) the communicator, (2) the message, (3) how the message is communicated, and (4) the audience. In other words, who *says* what by what means to whom?

Who Says? The Communicator

Imagine the following scene: I. M. Wright, a middle-aged American, is watching the evening news. In the first segment, a small group of radicals is shown burning an American flag. As they do, one shouts through a bullhorn that whenever any government becomes oppressive, "it is the Right of the People to alter or to abolish it. . . . It is their right, it is their duty, to throw off such government!" Angered, Mr. Wright mutters to his wife, "It's sickening to hear them spouting that Communist line." In the next seg-

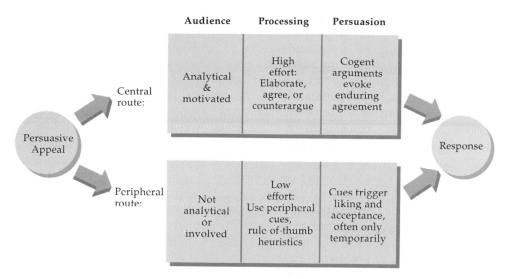

Audience	Processing	Persuasion
Central route:	Analytical & motivated	High effort: Elaborate, agree, or counterargue	Cogent arguments evoke enduring agreement
Peripheral route:	Not analytical or involved	Low effort: Use peripheral cues, rule-of-thumb heuristics	Cues trigger liking and acceptance, often only temporarily

FIGURE 12-1

The central and peripheral routes to persuasion. Computer ads typically take the central route, by assuming their audience wants to systematically compare features and prices. Soft-drink ads usually take the peripheral route, by merely associating their product with glamour, pleasure, and good moods.

ment, a presidential candidate speaking before an antitax rally declares, "Thrift should be the guiding principle in our government expenditure. It should be made clear to all government workers that corruption and waste are very great crimes." An obviously pleased Mr. Wright relaxes and smiles: "Now that's the kind of good sense we need. That's my kinda guy."

Now switch the scene. Imagine Mr. Wright hearing the same revolutionary line at a July 4 oration of the Declaration of Independence (from which the line comes) and hearing a Communist speaker read the thrift quote from *Quotations from Chairman Mao Zedong* (from which they come). Would he now react differently?

Social psychologists have found that who is saying something makes a big difference. In one experiment, when the Socialist and Liberal leaders in the Dutch parliament argued identical positions using the same words, each was most effective with members of his own party (Wiegman, 1985). It's not just the central message that matters, but a peripheral *cue*—who says it. But what makes one communicator more persuasive than another?

Credibility

Any of us would find a statement about the benefits of exercise more believable if it came from the National Academy of Sciences rather than a tabloid newspaper. Credible communicators seem both *expert* (confidently knowledgeable) and *trustworthy*. They speak unhesitatingly and without any selfish motive. Some television ads are obviously constructed to make the communicator appear both expert and trustworthy. Drug companies peddle pain relievers using a white-coated speaker who declares confidently that most doctors recommend their ingredient (the ingredient, of course, is aspirin). Given such peripheral cues, people who don't care enough to analyze the evidence might reflexively infer that the product has value.

The effects of source **credibility** often diminish after a month or so. If a credible person's message is persuasive, its impact can fade as its source is forgotten or dissociated from the message. The impact of a noncredible person can correspondingly *increase* over time, if people remember the message better than the reason for discounting it (Cook & Flay, 1978; Gruder & others, 1978; Pratkanis & others, 1988). This delayed persuasion, after people forget the source or its connection with the message, is called the **sleeper effect.**

Attractiveness
Most people deny that endorsements by star athletes and entertainers affect them. Everyone knows that stars are seldom knowledgeable about the products. Besides, we know the intent is to persuade us; we don't just accidentally eavesdrop on Jordan enjoying a Big Mac. Such ads are based on another characteristic of an effective communicator: attractiveness. We might think we are not influenced by attractiveness or likeability, but researchers have found otherwise. Our liking can open us up to their arguments (central route persuasion) or can trigger positive associations when we later see the product (peripheral route persuasion).

Attractiveness varies in several ways. *Physical appeal* is one. Arguments, especially emotional ones, are often more influential when they come from beautiful people (Chaiken, 1979; Dion & Stein, 1978; Pallak & others, 1983). *Similarity* is another. As a later module will emphasize, we tend to like people who are like us. We also are influenced by them. For example, Theodore Dembroski, Thomas Lasater, and Albert Ramirez (1978) gave African American junior high students a taped appeal for proper dental care. When a dentist assessed the cleanliness of their teeth the next day, those who heard the appeal from an African American dentist had cleaner teeth. As a general rule, people respond better to a message that comes from someone in their group (Van Knippenberg & Wilke, 1992; Wilder, 1990).

What Is Said? The Message Content

It matters not only who says a thing (a peripheral cue), but *what* that person says. If you were to help organize an appeal to get people to vote for school taxes, or to stop smoking, or to give money to world hunger relief, you might wonder how to concoct a recipe for central-route persuasion. Common sense can be made to argue on either side of these questions:

- How discrepant (different) should the message be from the audience's existing opinions? Will you get more opinion change by advocating a position only slightly discrepant from the listeners'
  existing opinions? or by advocating an extreme point of view?
  (That depends on the communicator's credibility. Highly credible
  people elicit the greatest opinion changes when they argue an extreme position; less credible people are more successful when they
  advocate positions closer to those of the audience.)

- Should the message express your side only, or should it acknowledge and attempt to refute opposing views? (This depends on the
  listeners. When the audience already agrees with the message, is
  unaware of opposing arguments, and is unlikely later to consider
  the opposition, then a one-sided appeal is most effective. With
  more sophisticated audiences or with those not already agreeing,
  two-sided messages are most successful.)

- If people present both sides, say in successive talks at a community
  meeting, is there an advantage to going first or last? (Information
  presented early is often the most potent, especially when it affects
  one's interpretation of later information. However, if a time gap
  separates the two sides, the effect of the early information diminishes; if a decision is also made right after hearing the second side,
  which is still fresh in mind, the advantage will likely go to the second presentation.)

Let's look closer at a fourth question: Which is more persuasive, a carefully reasoned message or one that arouses emotion?

Reason Versus Emotion

Suppose you were campaigning in support of world hunger relief. Would
it be best to itemize your arguments and cite an array of impressive statistics? Or would you be more effective presenting an emotional approach—
say, the compelling story of one starving child? Of course, an argument can
be both reasonable and emotional. You can marry passion and logic. Still,
which is more influential—reason or emotion? Was Shakespeare's
Lysander right: "The will of man is by his reason sway'd"? Or was Lord
Chesterfield's advice wiser: "Address yourself generally to the senses, to
the heart, and to the weaknesses of mankind, but rarely to their reason"?

The answer: It depends on the audience. Well-educated or analytical
people are more responsive to rational appeals than are less educated or
less analytical people (Cacioppo & others, 1983, 1996; Hovland & others,
1949). Thoughtful, involved audiences travel the central route; they are
most responsive to reasoned arguments. Disinterested audiences travel
the peripheral route; they are more affected by how much they like the
communicator (Chaiken, 1980; Petty & others, 1981).

To judge from interviews before major elections, many voters are un-involved. Americans' voting preferences have been more predictable from emotional reactions to the candidates (for example, whether Ronald Reagan ever made them feel happy) than from their beliefs about the candidates' traits and likely behaviors (Abelson & others, 1982).

The Effect of Good Feelings

Messages also become more persuasive through association with good feelings. Irving Janis and his colleagues (1965; Dabbs & Janis, 1965) found that Yale students were more convinced by persuasive messages if they were allowed to enjoy peanuts and Pepsi while reading them. Similarly, Mark Galizio and Clyde Hendrick (1972) found Kent State University students more persuaded by folk-song lyrics accompanied by pleasant guitar music than by unaccompanied lyrics. Those who like conducting business over sumptuous lunches with soft background music can celebrate these results.

Good feelings enhance persuasion, partly by enhancing positive thinking (when people are motivated to think) and partly by linking good feelings with the message (Petty & others, 1993). In a good mood, people view the world through rose-colored glasses. They also make faster, more impulsive decisions; they rely more on peripheral cues (Bodenhausen, 1993; Schwarz & others, 1991). Unhappy people ruminate more before reacting, so they are less easily swayed by weak arguments. Thus, if you can't make a strong case, it's a smart idea to put your audience in a good mood and hope they'll feel good about your message without thinking too much about it.

The Effect of Arousing Fear

Messages also can be effective by evoking negative emotions. In trying to convince people to cut down on smoking, brush their teeth more often, get a tetanus shot, or drive carefully, a fear-arousing message can be potent (Muller & Johnson, 1990). Showing cigarette smokers the horrible things that sometimes happen to people who smoke too much adds to persuasiveness. But how much fear should you arouse? Should you evoke just a little fear, lest people become so frightened that they tune out your painful message? Or should you try to scare the daylights out of them? Experiments by Howard Leventhal (1970) and his collaborators at the University of Wisconsin and by Ronald Rogers and his collaborators at the University of Alabama (Robberson & Rogers, 1988) show that, often, the more frightened people are, the more they respond.

The effectiveness of fear-arousing communications is being applied in ads discouraging smoking, drinking and driving, and risky sexual behaviors. Dawn Wilson and her colleagues (1987, 1988) had doctors send a letter to their patients who smoked. Of those who received a positively framed message (explaining that by quitting they would live longer), 8 percent tried to quit smoking. Of those who received a fear-framed message (explaining that by continuing to smoke they would likely die sooner), 30 percent tried to quit. Similarly, when Claude Levy-Leboyer (1988) found that attitudes toward alcohol and drinking habits among French youth were effectively changed by fear-arousing pictures, the French government incorporated this kind of information in its TV spots. But playing on fear will not always make a message more potent. People might respond with denial, because if they aren't told how to avoid the danger, the frightening messages can be overwhelming (Leventhal, 1970; Rogers & Mewborn, 1976). Fear-arousing messages are more effective if you lead people not only to fear the severity and likelihood of a threatened event but also to perceive an effective protective strategy (Maddux & Rogers, 1983). Many ads aimed at reducing sexual risks aim both to arouse fear—"AIDS kills"—and to offer a protective strategy: abstain or wear a condom or save sex for a committed relationship with an uninfected partner. During the 1980s, fear of AIDS did persuade many men to alter their behavior. One study of 5,000 gay men found that as the AIDS crisis mushroomed between 1984 and 1986, the number saying they were celibate or monogamous rose from 14 percent to 39 percent (Fineberg, 1988).

To Whom Is It Said? The Audience

It also matters who *receives* a message. Let's consider two other characteristics of those who receive a message: their age and their thoughtfulness.

How Old Are They?

People today tend to have different social and political attitudes depending on their age. There are two explanations for the difference. One is a *life-cycle explanation:* Attitudes change (for example, become more conservative) as people grow older. The other is a *generational explanation:* The attitudes older people adopted when they were young persist largely unchanged; because these attitudes are different from those now being adopted by young people today, a generation gap develops.

The evidence mostly supports the generational explanation. In surveying and resurveying groups of younger and older people over several years, the attitudes of older people usually change less than do those of young people. As David Sears (1979, 1986) puts it, researchers have "almost invariably found generational rather than life cycle effects."

The point is not that older adults are inflexible; most people in their fifties and sixties have more liberal sexual and racial attitudes than they had in their thirties and forties (Glenn, 1980, 1981). Few of us are utterly uninfluenced by changing cultural norms. The point is that the teens and early twenties are important formative years (Krosnick & Alwin, 1989), and the attitudes formed then tend to be stable thereafter. Young people might therefore be advised to choose their social influences—the groups they join, the media they imbibe, the roles they adopt—carefully.

Experiences during adolescence and early adulthood are formative partly because they make deep and lasting impressions. When Howard Schuman and Jacqueline Scott (1989) asked people to name the one or two most important national or world events over the last half century, most recalled events from their teens or early twenties. For those who experienced the Great Depression or World War II as 16- to 24-year-olds, those events overshadowed the civil rights movement and the Kennedy assassination of the early sixties, the Vietnam War and moon landing of the late sixties, and the women's movement of the seventies—each of which was imprinted on the minds of those who experienced it as 16- to 24-year-olds. We can therefore expect that for today's young adults the memorable turning points in world history might be the fall of the Berlin Wall or the explosive growth of e-mail and the World Wide Web.

What Are They Thinking?

In central-route persuasion, what's crucial is not the message itself but what responses it evokes in a person's mind. Our minds are not sponges that soak up whatever pours over them. If the message summons favorable thoughts, it persuades us. If it provokes us to think of contrary arguments, we remain unpersuaded.

Forewarned Is Forearmed—If You Care Enough to Counterargue   What circumstances breed counterarguing? One is a *warning* that someone is going to try to persuade you. If you had to tell your family that you wanted to drop out of school, you would likely anticipate their pleading with you to stay. So, you might develop a list of arguments to counter every conceivable argument they might make. Jonathan Freedman and David Sears (1965) demonstrated the difficulty of their trying to persuade you under such circumstances. They warned one group of California high schoolers that they were going to hear a talk entitled "Why Teenagers Should Not Be Allowed to Drive." Those forewarned did not budge. Others, not forewarned, did.

Sneak attacks on attitudes are especially useful with involved people. Given several minutes' forewarning, such people will prepare defenses (Chen & others, 1992; Petty & Cacioppo, 1977, 1979). But when people regard an issue as trivial, even blatant propaganda can be effective. Would you bother to construct counterarguments for two brands of toothpaste? Similarly, when someone slips a premise ("Why was Sue hostile to Mark?") into a casual conversation, people often accept the premise (that Sue was, in fact, hostile) (Swann, Giuliano, & Wegner, 1982).

Distraction Disarms Counterarguing   Verbal persuasion is also enhanced by distracting people with something that attracts their attention just enough to inhibit counterarguing (Festinger & Maccoby, 1964; Keating & Brock, 1974; Osterhouse & Brock, 1970). Political ads often use this technique. The words promote the candidate, and the visual images keep us occupied so we don't analyze the words. Distraction is especially effective when the message is simple (Harkins & Petty, 1981; Regan & Cheng, 1973). This research on how persuasion increases as counterarguing decreases makes me wonder: Does television shape important attitudes more through its subtle messages (for example, concerning gender roles) than through its explicit persuasive appeals? After all, if we don't notice a message, we cannot counterargue against it.

Uninvolved Audiences Use Peripheral Cues Recall again the two routes to persuasion—the central route of systematic thinking and the peripheral route of heuristic cues. Like the road through town, the central route has starts and stops as the mind analyzes arguments and formulates responses. Like the freeway around town, the peripheral route zips people to their destination. Analytical people, those with a high *need for cognition,* prefer central routes (Cacioppo & others, 1996). Image-conscious people, who care less about whether they're right or wrong than what sort of impression they are making, are quicker to respond to such peripheral cues as the communicator's attractiveness and the pleasantness of the surroundings (Snyder, 1989).

But the issue matters, too. All of us struggle actively with issues that involve us while making snap judgments about things that matter little (Johnson & Eagly, 1990). As we mentally elaborate upon an important issue, the strength of the arguments and of our own thoughts determine our attitudes.

This basically simple theory—that *what we think in response to a message is crucial, especially if we are* motivated and able to think about it—helps us understand several findings. For example, we more readily believe expert communicators, because when we trust the source we think favorable thoughts and are less likely to counterargue. When we mistrust the source, we are more likely to defend our preconceptions by refuting the disagreeable message.

The theory has also generated many predictions, most of which have been confirmed by Petty, Cacioppo, and others (Axsom & others, 1987; Harkins & Petty, 1987; Leippe & Elkin, 1987). Many experiments have explored ways to stimulate people's thinking—by using *rhetorical questions,* by presenting *multiple speakers* (for example, having three speakers each give one argument instead of one speaker giving three), by making people *feel responsible* for evaluating or passing along the message, by using *relaxed* rather than standing postures, by *repeating* the message, and by getting people's *undistracted attention.* The consistent finding with each of these techniques: *stimulating thinking makes strong messages more persuasive and* (because of counterarguing) *weak messages less persuasive.*

The theory also has practical implications. Effective communicators care not only about their images and their messages but also about how their audience is likely to react. How they will react depends not only on their interest in the issue but also on their dispositions—their analytical inclinations, their tolerance for uncertainty, their need to be true to themselves (Cacioppo & others, 1996; Kruglanski & others, 1993; Snyder & DeBono, 1987; Sorrentino & others, 1988).

So, are people likely to think and remember thoughts that favor the persuader's point of view? If the answer is yes, quality arguments will be persuasive. During the final days of a closely contested 1980 presidential campaign, Ronald Reagan effectively used rhetorical questions to stimulate desired thoughts in voters' minds. His summary statement in the presidential debate began with two potent rhetorical questions that he repeated often during the campaign's remaining week: "Are you better off than you were four years ago? Is it easier for you to go and buy things in the stores than it was four years ago?" Most people answered no, and Reagan, thanks partly to this bit of central-route persuasion, won by a bigger-than-expected margin.

*T*HE TWO ROUTES TO PERSUASION IN THERAPY

One constructive use of persuasion powers is in counseling and psychotherapy, which social-counseling psychologist Stanley Strong (1978) views "as a branch of applied social psychology" (p. 101). By the 1990s, more and more psychologists had accepted the idea that social influence, one person affecting another, is at the heart of therapy.

Early analyses of psychotherapeutic influence focused on how therapists establish credible expertise and trustworthiness and how their credibility enhances their influence (Strong, 1968). More recent analyses have focused less on the therapist than on how the interaction affects the client's thinking (Cacioppo & others, 1991; McNeill & Stoltenberg, 1998; Neimeyer & others, 1991). Peripheral cues, such as therapist credibility, can open the door for ideas that the therapist can now get the client to think about. But the thoughtful central route to persuasion provides the most enduring attitude and behavior change. Therapists should therefore aim not to elicit a client's superficial agreement with their expert judgment but to change the client's own thinking.

Fortunately, most clients entering therapy are motivated to take the central route, to think deeply about their problems under the therapist's guidance. The therapist's task is to offer arguments and raise questions calculated to elicit favorable thoughts. The therapist's insights matter less than the thoughts they evoke in the client. The therapist needs to put things in ways that a client can hear and understand, ways that will prompt agreement rather than counterargument, and that will allow time and space for the client to reflect. Questions such as "How do you respond to what I just said?" can stimulate the client's thinking.

Martin Heesacker (1989) illustrates with the case of Dave, a 35-year-old male graduate student. Having seen what Dave denied—an underlying substance-abuse problem—the counselor drew on his knowledge of Dave, an intellectual person who liked hard evidence, in persuading him to accept the diagnosis and join a treatment support group. The counselor said, "OK, if my diagnosis is wrong, I'll be glad to change it. But let's go through a list of the characteristics of a substance abuser to check out my accuracy." The counselor then went through each criterion slowly, giving Dave time to think about each point. As he finished, Dave sat back and exclaimed, "I don't believe it: I'm a damned alcoholic."

In an experiment, John Ernst and Heesacker (1993) showed the effectiveness of escorting participants in an assertion training workshop through the central route to persuasion. One group of participants experienced the typical assertiveness workshop by learning and rehearsing concepts of assertiveness. Another group learned the same concepts but also volunteered information about a time when they hurt themselves by being unassertive. Then they heard arguments that Ernst and Heesacker knew were likely to trigger favorable thoughts (for example, "By failing to assert yourself, you train others to mistreat you"). At the workshop's end, Ernst and Heesacker asked the people to stop and reflect on how they now felt about all they had learned. Compared to those in the first group, those who went through the thought-evoking workshop left the experience with more favorable attitudes and intentions regarding assertiveness. Moreover, their roommates noticed greater assertiveness during the ensuing two weeks.

In his 1620 *Pensées*, the philosopher Pascal foresaw this principle: "People are usually more convinced by reasons they discover themselves than by those found by others." It's a principle worth remembering in our own lives.

CONCEPTS TO REMEMBER

Central-route persuasion   Persuasion that occurs when interested people focus on the arguments and respond with favorable thoughts.

Peripheral-route persuasion   Persuasion that occurs when people are influenced by incidental cues, such as a speaker's attractiveness.

Credibility   Believability. A credible communicator is perceived as both expert and trustworthy.

Sleeper effect   A delay in the impact of a message; occurs when we remember the message but forget a reason for discounting it.

Attractiveness   Having qualities that appeal to an audience. An appealing communicator (often someone similar to the audience) is most persuasive on matters of subjective preference.

13

❖

Indoctrination and Inoculation

Persuasion principles have been and are being applied, consciously or not, in ways that reveal their power. Consider Joseph Goebbels, Nazi Germany's minister of "popular enlightenment" and propaganda. Given control of publications, radio programs, motion pictures, and the arts, he undertook to persuade Germans to accept Nazi ideology. Julius Streicher, another Nazi, published *Der Stürmer*, a weekly anti-Semitic (anti-Jewish) newspaper with a circulation of 500,000 and the only paper read cover to cover by his intimate friend Adolf Hitler. Streicher also published anti-Semitic children's books and, with Goebbels, spoke at the mass rallies that became a part of the Nazi propaganda machine.

How effective were Goebbels, Streicher, and other Nazi propagandists? Did they, as the Allies alleged at Streicher's Nuremberg trial, "inject poison into the minds of millions and millions" (Bytwerk, 1976)? Most Germans were not persuaded to feel raging hatred for the Jews. But many were. Others became sympathetic to anti-Semitic measures, and most of the rest became either sufficiently uncertain or sufficiently intimidated to staff the huge genocidal program, or at least to allow it to happen. Without the complicity of millions of people, there would have been no Holocaust (Goldhagen, 1996).

CULT INDOCTRINATION

On March 22, 1997, Marshall Herff Applewhite and 37 of his disciples decided the time had come to shed their bodies—mere "containers"—and be whisked up to a UFO trailing the Hale-Bopp comet, en route to heaven's gate. So they put themselves to sleep by taking phenobarbital mixed into pudding or applesauce, washing it down with vodka, and then fixing plastic bags over their heads so they would suffocate in their slumber. On that same day, a cottage in the French Canadian village of St. Casimir exploded in an inferno, consuming five people—the latest of 74 members of the Order of the Solar Temple to have committed suicide in Canada, Switzerland, and France. All were hoping to be transported to the star Sirius, nine light-years away. With a new millennium nearly upon us as this book is being written, predictions abound of more cult mythology and mass suicides to come. Fringe religion meets the *X-Files.*

The question on many minds: What persuades people to leave behind their former beliefs and join these mental chaingangs? Shall we attribute their strange behaviors to strange personalities? Or do their experiences illustrate the common dynamics of social influence and persuasion?

Bear two things in mind: First, this is hindsight analysis. It uses persuasion principles as categories for explaining, after the fact, a fascinating social phenomenon. Second, explaining *why* people believe something says nothing about the *truth* of their beliefs. Truth is a logically separate issue. A psychology of religion might tell us *why* a theist believes in God and an atheist disbelieves, but it cannot tell us who is right. Explaining either belief does not explain it away. So if someone tries to discount your beliefs by saying, "You just believe that because . . .," you might recall Archbishop William Temple's reply to a questioner who opened the discussion after the archbishop's address with this challenge: "Well, of course, Archbishop, the point is that you believe what you believe because of the way you were brought up." To which the Archbishop replied: "That is as it may be. But the fact remains that you believe I believe what I believe because of the way I was brought up, because of the way you were brought up."

In recent decades, several **cults**—which social scientists often call **New Religious movements**—have gained much publicity, including Sun Myung Moon's Unification Church, Jim Jones's People's Temple, David Koresh's Branch Davidians, and Marshall Applewhite's Heaven's Gate. The Reverend Moon's mixture of Christianity, anticommunism, and glorification of Moon himself as a new messiah attracted a worldwide following. In response to Moon's declaration "What I wish must be your wish," many committed themselves and their incomes to the Unification Church. How were they persuaded to do so?

In 1978 in Guyana, 914 followers of the Reverend Jones, who had followed him there from San Francisco, shocked the world when they died by following his order to swallow a fruit-flavored drink laced with tranquilizers, painkillers, and a lethal dose of cyanide.

In 1993, high school dropout David Koresh used his talent for memorizing scripture and mesmerizing people to seize control of a faction of a sect called the Branch Davidians. Over time, members were gradually relieved of their bank accounts and possessions. Koresh also persuaded the men to live celibately while he slept with their wives and daughters, and he convinced his 19 "wives" that they should bear his children. Under siege after a shootout that killed six members and four federal agents, Koresh told his followers they would soon die and go with him straight to heaven. When the federal agents rammed the compound with tanks, hoping to inject tear gas, cult members set it a fire, consuming 86 people in the flames.

Marshall Applewhite was not similarly tempted to command sexual favors. Having been fired from two music teaching jobs for homosexual affairs with students, he sought sexless devotion by castration, as had 7 of the other 17 Heaven's Gate men who died with him (Chua-Eoan, 1997; Gardner, 1997). While in a psychiatric hospital in 1971, Applewhite had linked up with nurse and astrology dabbler Bonnie Lu Nettles, who gave the intense and charismatic Applewhite a cosmological vision of a route to "the next level." Preaching with passion, he persuaded his followers to renounce families, sex, drugs, and personal money with promises of a spaceship voyage to salvation.

How could such things happen? Shall we make disposition explanations by blaming the victims? Shall we dismiss them as gullible kooks or dumb weirdos? Or can familiar principles of conformity, compliance, dissonance, persuasion, and group influence explain their behavior, putting them on common ground with the rest of us who in our own ways are shaped by such forces?

Attitudes Follow Behavior

Compliance Breeds Acceptance

As we saw in Module 9's discussion of behavior and belief, people usually internalize commitments they have made voluntarily, publicly, and repeatedly. Cult leaders seem to know this. New converts soon learn that membership is no trivial matter. They are quickly made active members of the team. Rituals within the cult community, and public canvassing and fund-raising, strengthen the initiates' identities as members. As those in social-psychological experiments come to believe in what they bear witness to (Aronson & Mills, 1959; Gerard & Mathewson, 1966), so cult initiates become committed advocates. The greater the personal commitment, the more the need to justify it.

The Foot-in-the-Door Phenomenon

How are we induced to make commitments? Seldom by an abrupt, conscious decision. One does not just decide, "I'm through with mainstream religion. I'm gonna find a cult." Nor do cult recruiters approach people on the street with, "Hi. I'm a Moonie. Care to join us?" Rather, the recruitment strategy exploits the foot-in-the-door principle. Unification Church recruiters would invite people to a dinner and then to a weekend of warm fellowship and discussions of philosophies of life. At the weekend retreat, they encouraged the attenders to join them in songs, activities, and discussion. Potential converts were then urged to sign up for longer training retreats. Eventually the activities became more arduous—soliciting contributions and attempting to convert others.

Jim Jones also used this foot-in-the-door technique with his People's Temple members. At first their monetary offerings were voluntary. Next Jones inaugurated a required contribution of 10 percent of income, which soon increased to 25 percent. Finally, he ordered members to turn over to him everything they owned. Workloads also became progressively more demanding. Grace Stoen recalls the gradual progress:

> Nothing was ever done drastically. That's how Jim Jones got away with so much. You slowly gave up things and slowly had to put up with more, but it was always done very gradually. It was amazing, because you would sit up sometimes and say, wow, I really have given up a lot. I really am putting up with a lot. But he did it so slowly that you figured, I've made it this far, what the hell is the difference? (Conway & Siegelman, 1979, p. 236)

Persuasive Elements

We can also analyze cult persuasion using the factors discussed in Module 12: *Who* (the communicator) said *what* (the message) to *whom* (the audience)?

The Communicator

Successful cults have a charismatic leader, someone who attracts and directs the members. As in experiments on persuasion, a credible communicator is someone the audience perceives as expert and trustworthy—for example, as "Father" Moon.

Jim Jones used "psychic readings" to establish his credibility. Newcomers were asked to identify themselves as they entered the church before services. Then one of his aides would call the person's home and say, "Hi. We're doing a survey, and we'd like to ask you some questions." During the service, one ex-member recalled, Jones would call out the person's name and say:

> Have you ever seen me before? Well, you live in such and such a place, your phone number is such and such, and in your living room you've got this, that, and the other, and on your sofa you've got such and such a pillow. . . . Now do you remember me ever being in your house? (Conway & Siegelman, 1979, p. 234)

Trust is another aspect of credibility. Cult researcher Margaret Singer (1979) noted that middle-class Caucasian youths are more vulnerable because they are more trusting. They lack the "street smarts" of lower-class youths (who know how to resist a hustle) and the wariness of upper-class youths (who have been warned of kidnappers since childhood). Many cult members have been recruited by friends or relatives, people they trust (Stark & Bainbridge, 1980).

The Message

To lonely or depressed people, the vivid, emotional messages and the warmth and acceptance with which the group showers them can be strikingly appealing: Trust the master, join the family; we have the answer, the "one way." The message echoes through channels as varied as lectures, small-group discussions, and direct social pressure.

The Audience

Many recruits are young—people under 25 who are still in that comparatively open period before attitudes and values stabilize. Some, such as the followers of Jim Jones, are less educated people who like the simplicity of the message and find it difficult to counterargue. But most are educated, middle-class people who, taken by the ideals, overlook the contradictions in those who profess selflessness and practice greed, who pretend concern and behave indifferently.

Potential converts often are at a turning point in their lives, facing a personal crisis, or vacationing or living away from home. They have needs; the cult offers to fulfill them (Singer, 1979; Lofland & Stark, 1965). Gail Maeder joined Heaven's Gate after her T-shirt shop had failed. David Moore joined when he was 19, just out of high school and searching for direction. Times of social and economic upheaval are especially conducive to an ayatollah or a "father" who can make apparent simple sense out of the confusion (O'Dea, 1968; Sales, 1972).

Group Effects

Cults illustrate a theme of several modules to come: the power of a group to shape members' views and behavior. The cult typically separates members from their previous social support systems and isolates them with other cultists. There can then occur what Rodney Stark and William Bainbridge (1980) call a "social implosion": External ties weaken until the group socially collapses inward, each person engaging only with other group members. Cut off from families and former friends, they lose access to counterarguments. The group now offers identity and defines reality. Because the cult frowns on or punishes disagreements, the apparent consensus helps eliminate any lingering doubts.

Marshall Applewhite and Bonnie Nettles (who died of cancer in 1985) at first formed their own group of two, reinforcing each other's aberrant thinking in a phenomenon that psychiatrists call *folie à deux* (French for "insanity of two"). As others joined them, the group's social isolation facilitated more peculiar thinking. As conspiracy theory Internet discussion groups illustrate (Heaven's Gate was skilled in Internet recruiting), virtual groups can likewise foster paranoia.

Contrary to the idea that cults turn hapless people into mindless robots, these techniques—increasing behavioral commitments, persuasion, and group isolation—do not have unlimited power. The Unification Church has successfully recruited fewer than 1 in 10 people who attend its workshops (Ennis & Verrilli, 1989). Most who had joined Heaven's Gate had left before that fateful day of "container shedding." David Koresh ruled with a mix of persuasion, intimidation, and violence. As Jim Jones made his demands more extreme, he, too, increasingly had to control people with intimidation. He used threats of harm to those who fled the community, beatings for noncompliance, and drugs to neutralize disagreeable members. By the end, he was as much an arm twister as a mind bender.

Moreover, cult influence techniques are in some ways similar to techniques used by groups more familiar to us. Fraternity and sorority members have reported that the initial "love bombing" of potential cult recruits is not unlike their own "rush" period. Members lavish attention on prospective pledges and make them feel special. During the pledge period, new members are somewhat isolated, cut off from old friends who did not pledge. They spend time studying the history and rules of their new group. They suffer and spend time on its behalf. They are expected to comply with all its demands. Not surprisingly, the result is usually a committed new member.

Much the same is true of some therapeutic communities for recovering drug and alcohol abusers. Zealous self-help groups form a cohesive "social cocoon," have intense beliefs, and exert a profound influence on members' behavior (Galanter, 1989, 1990).

I chose the examples of fraternities, sororities, and self-help groups not to disparage them but to illustrate two concluding observations. First, if we attribute the pull of New Religious movements to the leader's mystical force or to the followers' peculiar weaknesses, we might delude ourselves into thinking we are immune to social control techniques. In truth, our own groups—and countless salespeople, political leaders, and other persuaders—successfully use many of these tactics on us. Between education and indoctrination, enlightenment and propaganda, conversion and coercion, therapy and mind control, there is but a blurry line.

Second, that Jim Jones abused the power of persuasion does not mean persuasion is intrinsically bad. Nuclear power enables us to light up homes or wipe out cities. Sexual power enables us to express and celebrate committed love or exploit people for selfish gratification. Persuasive power enables us to enlighten or deceive. That these powers can be harnessed for evil purposes should alert us to guard against their immoral use. But the powers themselves are neither inherently evil nor inherently good; how we use them determines whether their effect is destructive or constructive.

RESISTING PERSUASION: ATTITUDE INOCULATION

This consideration of persuasive influences has perhaps made you wonder if it is possible to *resist* unwanted persuasion. Of course it is. If the repair person's uniform or the doctor's title has an aura of credibility that has intimidated us into unquestioning agreement, we can rethink our habitual responses to authority. We can seek more information before committing time or money or committing to a course of treatment. We can question what we don't understand.

Stimulate Commitment

There is another way to resist: Before encountering others' judgments, make a public commitment to your position. Having stood up for your convictions, you will become less susceptible (or should we say less "open"?) to what others have to say.

Challenge Beliefs

How might we stimulate people to commit themselves? From his experiments, Charles Kiesler (1971) offers one possible way: Mildly attack their position. Kiesler found that when committed people were attacked strongly enough to cause them to react, but not so strongly as to overwhelm them, they became even more committed. Kiesler explains:

> When you attack a committed person and your attack is of inadequate strength, you drive him to even more extreme behaviors in defense of his previous commitment. His commitment escalates, in a sense, because the number of acts consistent with his belief increases. (p. 88)

Perhaps you can recall a time when this happened in an argument, as those involved escalated their rhetoric, committing themselves to increasingly extreme positions.

Develop Counterarguments

There is a second reason a mild attack might build resistance. When someone attacks one of our cherished attitudes, we typically feel some irritation and contemplate counterarguments (Zuwerink & Devine, 1996). Like inoculations against disease, even weak arguments will prompt counterarguments, which are then available for a stronger attack. William McGuire (1964) documented this in a series of experiments. McGuire wondered: Could we inoculate people against persuasion much as we inoculate them against a virus? Is there such a thing as **attitude inoculation?** Could we take people raised in a "germ-free ideological environment"—people who hold some unquestioned belief—and stimulate their mental defenses? And would subjecting them to a small dose of belief-threatening material inoculate them against later persuasion?

That is what McGuire did. First, he found some cultural truisms, such as "It's a good idea to brush your teeth after every meal if at all possible." He then showed that people were vulnerable to a massive, credible assault upon these truisms (for example, prestigious authorities were said to have discovered that too much toothbrushing can damage one's gums). If, however, before having their belief attacked, they were "immunized" by first receiving a small challenge to their belief, *and* if they read or wrote an essay in refutation of this mild attack, then they were better able to resist the powerful attack.

Case Studies: Large-Scale Inoculation Programs

Inoculating Children Against Peer Pressure to Smoke

In a clear demonstration of how laboratory research findings can lead to practical application, a research team led by Alfred McAlister (1980) had high school students "inoculate" seventh-graders against peer pressures to smoke. The seventh-graders were taught to respond to advertisements implying that liberated women smoke by saying, "She's not really liberated if she is hooked on tobacco." They also acted in role-plays; after being called "chicken" for not taking a cigarette, they answered with statements like "I'd be a real chicken if I smoked just to impress you." After several such sessions during the seventh and eighth grades, the inoculated students were half as likely to begin smoking as uninoculated students at another junior high school that had an identical parental smoking rate (Figure 13-1).

Other research teams have confirmed that such inoculation procedures, sometimes supplemented by other life-skills training, reduce teen smoking (Botvin & others, 1995; Evans & others, 1984; Flay & others, 1985). Most newer efforts emphasize strategies for resisting social pressure. One study exposed sixth-, seventh-, and eighth-graders to antismoking films or to information about smoking, together with role-plays of student-generated ways of refusing a cigarette (Hirschman & Leventhal, 1989). A year and a half later, 31 percent of those who watched the antismoking films had taken up smoking. Among those who role-played refusing, only 19 percent had done so. Another study involved all seventh-graders in a diverse sample of 30 junior high schools. It warned students about pressures to smoke and use drugs and offered them strategies for resisting (Ellickson & Bell, 1990). Among nonusers of marijuana, the training curbed initiation by a third; among users, it reduced usage by half.

Antismoking and drug education programs apply other persuasion principles, too. They use attractive peers to communicate information. They trigger the students' own cognitive processing ("Here's something you might want to think about"). They get the students to make a public commitment (by making a rational decision about smoking and then announcing it, along with their reasoning, to their classmates). Some of these smoking-prevention programs require only two to six 1-hour class sessions, using

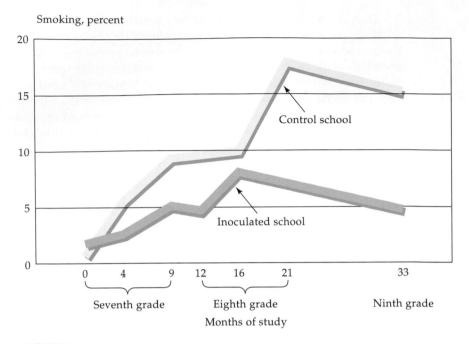

Smoking, percent

FIGURE 13-1
The percentage of cigarette smokers at an "inoculated" junior high school was much less than at a matched control school using a more typical smoking education program. (Data from McAlister & others, 1980; Telch & others, 1981.)

prepared printed materials or videotapes. Today any school district or teacher wishing to use the social-psychological approach to smoking prevention can do so easily, inexpensively, and with the hope of significant reductions in future smoking rates and associated health costs.

Inoculating Children Against the Influence of Advertising

Researchers have also studied how to immunize young children so they can more effectively analyze and evaluate television commercials. This research was prompted partly by studies showing that children, especially those under 8 years of age, (1) have trouble distinguishing commercials from programs and fail to grasp their persuasive intent, (2) trust television advertising rather indiscriminately, and (3) desire and badger their parents to buy advertised products (Adler & others, 1980; Feshbach, 1980; Palmer & Dorr, 1980). Children seem to be an advertiser's dream: gullible, vulnerable, an easy sell. Moreover, half of the 20,000 ads the typical child sees in a year are for low-nutrition, often sugary, foods.

Armed with such data, citizens' groups have given the advertisers of such products a chewing out (Moody, 1980): "When a sophisticated advertiser spends millions to sell unsophisticated, trusting children an unhealthy product, this can only be called exploitation. No wonder the consumption of dairy products has declined since the start of television, while soft-drink consumption has almost doubled." On the other side are the commercial interests, who claim that such ads allow parents to teach their children consumer skills and, more importantly, finance children's television programs. In the United States, the Federal Trade Commission has been in the middle, pushed by research findings and political pressures while trying to decide whether to place new constraints on TV ads aimed at young children.

Meanwhile, researchers have wondered whether children can be taught to resist deceptive ads. In one such effort, a team of investigators led by Norma Feshbach (1980; Cohen, 1980) gave small groups of Los Angeles–area elementary school children three half-hour lessons in analyzing commercials. The children were inoculated by viewing ads and discussing them. For example, after viewing a toy ad, they were immediately given the toy and challenged to make it do what they had just seen in the commercial. Such experiences helped breed a more realistic understanding of commercials.

Implications

Inoculation research also has some provocative implications. Contrary to what some U.S. senators thought after the Korean War, the best way to build resistance to brainwashing might not be to have more courses on patriotism. William McGuire advised teachers to use inoculation techniques: Challenge the concepts and principles of democracy and explain alternatives such as communism and constitutional monarchy, and so help students to develop defenses.

For the same reason, religious educators should be wary of creating a "germ-free ideological environment" in their churches and schools. An attack, if refuted, is more likely to solidify one's position than to undermine it, particularly if the threatening material can be examined with like-minded others. Cults apply this principle by forewarning members of how families and friends will attack the cult's beliefs. When the expected challenge comes, the member is armed with counterarguments.

Another implication is that, for the persuader, an ineffective appeal can be worse than none. Can you see why? Those who reject an appeal are inoculated against further appeals. Consider an experiment in which Susan Darley and Joel Cooper (1972) invited students to write essays advocating a strict dress code. Because this was against the students' own positions and the essays were to be published, all chose *not* to write the essay—even those offered money to do so. After turning down the money, they became even more extreme and confident in their anti-dress-code opinions. Having made an overt decision against the dress code, they became even more resistant to it. Those who have rejected initial appeals to quit smoking can likewise become immune to further appeals. Ineffective persuasion can be counterproductive because it stimulates the listener's defenses, "hardening the heart" against later appeals.

Inoculation research has a personal implication, too. Do you want to build your resistance to persuasion without becoming closed to valid messages? Be an active listener and a critical thinker. Force yourself to counterargue. After hearing a political speech, discuss it with others. In other words, don't just listen; react. If the message cannot withstand careful analysis, so much the worse for it. If it can, its effect on you will be the more enduring for your having done the analytical work.

CONCEPTS TO REMEMBER

Cult (also called New Religious movement) A group typically characterized by (1) a distinctive ritual of its devotion to a god or a person, (2) isolation from the surrounding "evil" culture, and (3) a charismatic leader. (A *sect*, in contrast, is a spinoff from a major religion.)

Attitude inoculation Exposing people to weak attacks upon their attitudes so that when stronger attacks come, they will have refutations available.

MODULE

14

❖

The Mere Presence of Others

Our world contains not only 5.9 billion individuals, but also 200 nation-states, 4 million local communities, 20 million economic organizations, and hundreds of millions of other formal and informal groups—couples on dates, families, churches, housemates in bull sessions, and so on. How do these groups influence individuals?

Let's begin with social psychology's most elementary question: Are we affected by the mere presence of another person? "Mere presence" means people are not competing, do not reward or punish, and in fact do nothing except be present as a passive audience or as **co-actors.** Would the mere presence of others affect a person's jogging, eating, typing, or exam performance? The search for the answer is a scientific mystery story.

*T*HE PRESENCE OF OTHERS

A century ago, Norman Triplett (1898), a psychologist interested in bicycle racing, noticed that cyclists' times were faster when the cyclists were racing together than when they were racing alone against the clock. Before he peddled his hunch that the presence of others boosts performance, Triplett conducted one of social psychology's early laboratory experiments he found that children told to wind string on a fishing reel as rapidly as possible wound faster when they worked with co-actors than when they worked alone.

Subsequent experiments in the early decades of this century found that the presence of others also improves the speed with which people do simple multiplication problems and cross out designated letters. And it improves the accuracy with which people perform simple motor tasks, such

141

as keeping a metal stick in contact with a dime-sized disk on a moving turntable (F. H. Allport, 1920; Dashiell, 1930; Travis, 1925). This **social-facilitation** effect, as it came to be called, also occurs with animals. In the presence of others of their species, ants excavate more sand and chickens eat more grain (Bayer, 1929; Chen, 1937). In the presence of other sexually active rat pairs, mating rats exhibit heightened sexual activity (Larsson, 1956).

Other studies revealed that on other tasks the presence of others hinders performance. In the presence of others, cockroaches, parakeets, and green finches learn mazes more slowly (Allee & Masure, 1936; Gates & Allee, 1933; Klopfer, 1958). This disruptive effect also occurs with people. The presence of others diminishes efficiency at learning nonsense syllables, completing a maze, and performing complex multiplication problems (Dashiell, 1930; Pessin, 1933; Pessin & Husband, 1933).

Saying that the presence of others sometimes facilitates performance and sometimes hinders it is about as satisfying as a weather forecast predicting that it might be sunny but then again it might rain. By 1940, research activity in this area had ground to a halt. It lay dormant for 25 years until awakened by the touch of a new idea.

Social psychologist Robert Zajonc (pronounced *Zy-ence,* rhymes with *science*) wondered whether these seemingly contradictory findings could be reconciled. As often happens at creative moments in science, Zajonc (1965) used one field of research to illuminate another. In this case the illumination came from a well-established principle in experimental psychology: Arousal enhances whatever response tendency is dominant. Increased arousal enhances performance on easy tasks for which the most likely ("dominant") response is the correct one. People solve easy anagrams, such as *akec,* fastest when they are anxious. On complex tasks, for which the correct answer is not dominant, increased arousal promotes *incorrect* responding. On harder anagrams people do worse when anxious.

Could this principle solve the mystery of social facilitation? It seemed reasonable to assume what evidence now confirms—that others' presence will arouse or energize people (Mullen & others, 1997). (Most of us can recall feeling more tense or excited before an audience.) If social arousal facilitates dominant responses, it should boost performance on easy tasks and hurt performance on difficult tasks. Now the confusing results made sense. Winding fishing reels, doing simple multiplication problems, and eating were all easy tasks for which the responses were well learned or naturally dominant. And sure enough, having others around boosted performance. Learning new material, doing a maze, and solving complex math problems were more difficult tasks for which the correct responses were initially less probable. And sure enough, the presence of others increased the number of *incorrect* responses on these tasks. The same general rule—that *arousal facilitates dominant responses*—worked in both cases. Suddenly, what had looked like contradictory results no longer seemed contradictory.

Zajonc's solution, so simple and elegant, left other social psychologists thinking what Thomas H. Huxley thought after first reading Darwin's *On the Origin of Species:* "How extremely stupid not to have thought of that!" It seemed obvious—once Zajonc had pointed it out. Perhaps, however, the pieces appeared to merge so neatly only because we viewed them through the spectacles of hindsight. Would the solution survive direct experimental tests?

After almost 300 studies conducted with the help of more than 25,000 volunteer subjects, it has survived (Bond & Titus, 1983; Guerin, 1993). Several experiments in which Zajonc and his associates manufactured an arbitrary dominant response confirmed that an audience enhanced this response. In one, Zajonc and Stephen Sales (1966) asked people to pronounce various nonsense words between 1 and 16 times. Then they told the people that the same words would appear on a screen, one at a time. Each time, they were to guess which had appeared. When the people were actually shown only random black lines for a hundredth of a second, they "saw" mostly the words they had pronounced most frequently. These words had become the dominant responses. People who took the same test in the presence of two others were even more likely to guess the dominant words (Figure 14-1).

Average number of responses

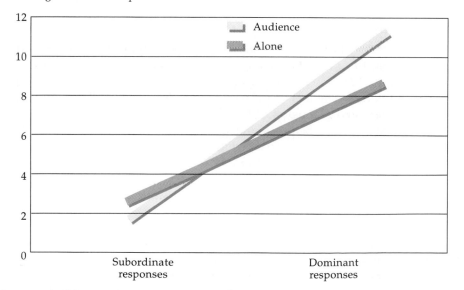

FIGURE 14-1
Social facilitation of dominant responses. People responded with dominant words (practiced 16 times) more frequently, and subordinate words (practiced but once) less frequently, when observers were present. (Data from Zajonc & Sales, 1966.)

In various ways, later experiments confirmed that social arousal facilitates dominant responses, whether right or wrong. Peter Hunt and Joseph Hillery (1973) found that in the presence of others, University of Akron students took less time to learn a simple maze and more time to learn a complex one (just as cockroaches do). And James Michaels and his collaborators (1982) found that good pool players in the Virginia Polytechnic Institute student union (who had made 71 percent of their shots while being unobtrusively observed) did even better (80 percent) when four observers came up to watch them play. Poor shooters (who had previously averaged 36 percent) did even worse (25 percent) when closely observed.

Athletes perform well-practiced skills, which helps explain why they often perform best when energized by the responses of a supportive crowd. Studies of more than 80,000 college and professional athletic events in Canada, the United States, and England reveal that home teams win about 6 in 10 games (somewhat fewer for baseball and football, somewhat more for basketball and soccer) (Zillmann & Paulus, 1993).

CROWDING: THE PRESENCE OF MANY OTHERS

So people do respond to the presence of others. But does the presence of observers really arouse people? In times of stress, a comrade can be comforting. Nevertheless, researchers have found that with others present, people perspire more, breathe faster, tense their muscles more, and have higher blood pressure and a faster heart rate (Geen & Gange, 1983; Moore & Baron, 1983).

The effect of other people increases with their number (Jackson & Latané, 1981; Knowles, 1983). Sometimes the arousal and self-conscious attention created by a large audience interferes even with well-learned, automatic behaviors, such as speaking. Given extreme pressure, we're vulnerable to choking. Stutterers tend to stutter more in front of larger audiences than when speaking to just one or two people (Mullen, 1986). College basketball players become slightly *less* accurate in their free-throw shooting when highly aroused by a packed rather than near-empty fieldhouse (Sokoll & Mynatt, 1984).

Being *in* a crowd also intensifies positive or negative reactions. When they sit close together, friendly people are liked even more, and *un*friendly people are *dis*liked even more (Schiffenbauer & Schiavo, 1976; Storms & Thomas, 1977). In experiments with Columbia University students and with Ontario Science Center visitors, Jonathan Freedman and his coworkers (1979, 1980) had an accomplice listen to a humorous tape or watch a movie with other subjects. When all sat close together, the accomplice could more readily induce them to laugh and clap. As theater directors and sports fans know, and as researchers have confirmed (Aiello & others, 1983; Worchel & Brown, 1984), a "good house" is a full house.

Perhaps you've noticed that a class of 35 students feels more warm and lively in a room that seats just 35 than when spread out in a room that seats 100. This occurs partly because when others are close by, we are more likely to notice and join in their laughter or clapping. But crowding also enhances arousal, as Gary Evans (1979) found. He tested 10-person groups of University of Massachusetts students, either in a room 20 by 30 feet or in one 8 by 12 feet. Compared to those in the large room, those densely packed had higher pulse rates and blood pressure (indicating arousal). Though their performance on simple tasks did not suffer, on difficult tasks they made more errors. In a study of university students in India, Dinesh Nagar and Janak Pandey (1987) similarly found that crowding hampered performance only on complex tasks, such as solving difficult anagrams.

WHY ARE WE AROUSED IN THE PRESENCE OF OTHERS?

To this point we have seen that what you do well, you will be energized to do best in front of others (unless you become hyperaroused and self-conscious). What you find difficult can seem impossible in the same circumstances. What is it about other people that causes arousal? Is it their mere presence? Evidence supports three possible factors: evaluation apprehension, distraction, and mere presence.

Evaluation Apprehension

Nickolas Cottrell surmised that observers make us apprehensive because we wonder how they are evaluating us. To test whether **evaluation apprehension** exists, Cottrell and his associates (1968) repeated Zajonc and Sales's nonsense-syllable study at Kent State University and added a third condition. In this "mere presence" condition they blindfolded observers, supposedly in preparation for a perception experiment. In contrast to the effect of the watching audience, the mere presence of these blindfolded people did *not* boost well-practiced responses.

Other experiments confirmed Cottrell's conclusion: The enhancement of dominant responses is strongest when people think they are being evaluated. In one experiment, joggers on a University of California at Santa Barbara jogging path sped up as they came upon a woman seated on the grass—*if* she was facing them rather than sitting with her back turned (Worringham & Messick, 1983).

Evaluation apprehension also helps explain these findings:

- People perform best when their co-actor is slightly superior (Seta, 1982).

- Arousal lessens when a high-status group is diluted by adding people whose opinions don't matter to us (Seta & Seta, 1992).
- People who worry most about others' evaluations are the ones most affected by their presence (Gastorf & others, 1980; Geen & Gange, 1983).
- Social-facilitation effects are greatest when the others are unfamiliar and hard to keep an eye on (Guerin & Innes, 1982).

The self-consciousness we feel when being evaluated can also interfere with our performance of behaviors that we perform best automatically (Mullen & Baumeister, 1987). If self-conscious basketball players analyze their body movements while shooting critical free throws, they are more likely to miss.

Driven by Distraction

Glenn Sanders, Robert Baron, and Danny Moore (1978; Baron, 1986) carried the investigation of evaluation apprehension a step further. They theorized that when people wonder how co-actors are doing or how an audience is reacting, they get distracted. This *conflict* between paying attention to others and paying attention to the task overloads the cognitive system, causing arousal. Evidence that people are indeed "driven by distraction" comes from experiments that produce social facilitation not just by the presence of another person but even by a nonhuman distraction, such as bursts of light (Sanders, 1981a, 1981b).

Mere Presence

Zajonc, however, believes that the mere presence of others produces some arousal even without evaluation apprehension or arousing distraction. For example, people's color preferences are stronger when they make judgments with others present (Goldman, 1967). On such a task, there is no "good" or "right" answer for others to evaluate and thus no reason to be concerned with their reactions.

Recall that facilitation effects also occur with nonhuman animals. This hints at an innate social-arousal mechanism common to much of the zoological world. (Animals probably are not consciously worrying about how other animals are evaluating them.) At the human level, most joggers feel energized when jogging with someone else, even someone who neither competes nor evaluates.

This is a good time to remind ourselves of the purpose of a theory. A good theory is a scientific shorthand: It simplifies and summarizes a variety of observations. Social-facilitation theory does this well. It is a simple summary of many research findings. A good theory also offers clear predictions that (1) help confirm or modify the theory, (2) guide new exploration, and (3) suggest practical applications. Social-facilitation theory has definitely generated predictions that have had the first two types of results: (1) The basics of the theory (that the presence of others is arousing, and that this social arousal enhances dominant responses) have been confirmed, and (2) the theory has brought new life to a long-dormant field of research. Does it also suggest (3) some practical applications?

Application is properly the last research phase. In their study of social facilitation, researchers have not yet worked much on this. But we can make some educated guesses about possible applications. Many new office buildings have replaced private offices with large, open areas divided by low partitions. Might the resulting awareness of others' presence help boost the performance of well-learned tasks, but disrupt creative thinking on complex tasks? Can you think of other possible applications?

CONCEPTS TO REMEMBER

Co-actors A group of people working simultaneously and individually on a non-competitive task.

Social facilitation (1) Original meaning: the tendency of people to perform simple or well-learned tasks better when others are present. (2) Current meaning: the strengthening of dominant (prevalent, likely) responses owing to the presence of others.

Evaluation apprehension Concern about how others are evaluating us.

15

❖

Many Hands Make Diminished Responsibility

In a team tug-of-war, will eight people on a side exert as much force as the sum of their best efforts in individual tugs of war? If not, why not? And what level of individual effort can we expect from members of work groups?

Social facilitation usually occurs when people work toward individual goals and when their efforts, whether winding fishing reels or solving math problems, can be individually evaluated. These situations parallel some everyday work situations, but not those where people cooperatively pool their efforts toward a *common* goal and where individuals are *not* accountable for their efforts. A team tug-of-war provides one such example. Organizational fund-raising, such as pooling candy-sale proceeds to pay for the class trip, provides another. So does a class project where all get the same grade. On such "additive tasks"—tasks where the group's achievement depends on the sum of the individual efforts—will team spirit boost productivity? Will bricklayers lay bricks faster when working as a team than when working alone? One way to attack such questions is with laboratory simulations.

MANY HANDS MAKE LIGHT WORK

Nearly a century ago, French engineer Max Ringelmann (reported by Kravitz & Martin, 1986) found that the collective effort of such teams was but half the sum of the individual efforts. This suggests, contrary to the common notion that "in unity there is strength," that group members might actually be *less* motivated when performing additive tasks. Maybe, though, poor performance stemmed from poor coordination—people

FIGURE 15-1
The rope-pulling apparatus. People in the first position pulled less hard when
they thought people behind them were also pulling. (Data from Ingham,
Levinger, Graves, & Peckham, 1974. Photo by Alan G. Ingham.)

pulling a tug-of-war rope in slightly different directions at slightly different times. A group of Massachusetts researchers led by Alan Ingham (1974)
cleverly eliminated this problem by making individuals think others were
pulling with them, when in fact they were pulling alone. Blindfolded participants assigned the first position in the apparatus shown in Figure 15-1
and told to "pull as hard as you can" pulled 18 percent harder when they
knew they were pulling alone than when they believed that behind them
two to five people were also pulling.

Researchers Bibb Latané, Kipling Williams, and Stephen Harkins
(1979; Harkins & others, 1980) kept their ears open for other ways to in-
vestigate this phenomenon, which they labeled **social loafing.** They observed that the noise produced by six people shouting or clapping "as loud
as you can" was less than three times that produced by one person alone.
However, like the tug-of-war task, noisemaking is vulnerable to group in-
efficiency. So Latané and his associates followed Ingham's example by
leading their Ohio State University participants to believe others were
shouting or clapping with them, when in fact they were doing so alone.

Their method was to blindfold six people, seat them in a semicircle,
and have them put on headphones, over which they were blasted with the
sound of people shouting or clapping. People could not hear their own
shouting or clapping, much less that of others. On various trials they were

instructed to shout or clap either alone or along with the group. People who were told about this experiment guessed the subjects would shout louder when with others, because they would be less inhibited (Harkins, 1981). The actual result? Social loafing: When the participants believed five others were also either shouting or clapping, they produced one third less noise than when they thought they were doing it alone. Social loafing occurred even when the subjects were high school cheerleaders who believed themselves to be cheering together or alone (Hardy & Latané, 1986).

John Sweeney (1973), a political scientist interested in the policy implications of social loafing, obtained similar results in an experiment at the University of Texas. Students pumped exercise bicycles more energetically (as measured by electrical output) when they knew they were being individually monitored than when they thought their output was being pooled with that of other riders. In the group condition, people were tempted to be **free riders.**

In this and some 160 other studies (Karau & Williams, 1993), we see a twist on one of the psychological forces that makes for social facilitation: evaluation apprehension. In the social loafing experiments, individuals believe they are evaluated only when they act alone. The group situation (rope pulling, shouting, and so forth) *decreases* evaluation apprehension. When people are not accountable and cannot evaluate their own efforts, responsibility is diffused across all group members (Harkins & Jackson, 1985; Kerr & Bruun, 1981). By contrast, the social-facilitation experiments *increased* exposure to evaluation. When made the center of attention, people self-consciously monitor their behavior (Mullen & Baumeister, 1987). So the principle is the same: When being observed *increases* evaluation concerns, social facilitation occurs; when being lost in a crowd *decreases* evaluation concerns, social loafing occurs.

To motivate group members, one strategy is to make individual performance identifiable. Some football coaches do this by individually filming and evaluating each player. The Ohio State researchers had group members wear individual microphones while engaged in group shouting (Williams & others, 1981). Whether in a group or not, people exert more effort when their outputs are individually identifiable: University swim team members swim faster in intrasquad relay races when someone monitors and announces their individual times (Williams & others, 1989). Even without pay consequences, actual assembly line workers in one small experiment produced 16 percent more product when their individual output was identified (Faulkner & Williams, 1996).

SOCIAL LOAFING IN EVERYDAY LIFE

How widespread is social loafing? In the laboratory, the phenomenon occurs not only among people who are pulling ropes, cycling, shouting, and clapping but also among those who are pumping water or air, evaluating poems or editorials, producing ideas, typing, and detecting signals. Do these results generalize to everyday worker productivity?

On their collective farms under communism, Russian peasants worked one field one day, another field the next, with little direct responsibility for any given plot. For their own use, they were given small private plots. In one analysis, the private plots occupied 1 percent of the agricultural land, yet produced 27 percent of the Soviet farm output (H. Smith, 1976). In Hungary, private plots accounted for only 13 percent of the farmland but produced one third of the output (Spivak, 1979). When China began allowing farmers to sell food grown in excess of that owed to the state, food production jumped 8 percent per year—2½ times the annual increase in the preceding 26 years (Church, 1986).

In North America, workers who do not pay dues or volunteer time to their union or professional association nevertheless are usually happy to accept its benefits. So, too, are viewers of public television who don't respond to their station's fund drives. This hints at another possible explanation of social loafing. When rewards are divided equally, regardless of how much one contributes to the group, any individual gets more reward per unit of effort by free-riding on the group. So people can be motivated to slack off when their efforts are not individually monitored and rewarded.

In a pickle factory, for example, the key job is picking the right-size dill pickle halves off the conveyor belt and stuffing them in jars. Unfortunately, workers are tempted to stuff any size pickle in, because their output is not identifiable (the jars go into a common hopper before reaching the quality-control section). Williams, Harkins, and Latané (1981) note that research on social loafing suggests "making individual production identifiable, and raises the question: 'How many pickles could a pickle packer pack if pickle packers were only paid for properly packed pickles?' "

But surely collective effort does not always lead to slacking off. Sometimes the goal is so compelling and maximum output from everyone is so essential that team spirit maintains or intensifies effort. In an Olympic crew race, will the individual rowers in an eight-person crew pull their oars with less effort than those in a one- or two-person crew?

The evidence assures us they will not. People in groups loaf less when the task is *challenging, appealing,* or *involving* (Karau & Williams, 1993). On challenging tasks, people might perceive their efforts as indispensable (Harkins & Petty, 1982; Kerr, 1983; Kerr & Bruun, 1983). When people see others in their group as unreliable or as unable to contribute much, they work harder (Vancouver & others, 1991; Williams & Karau, 1991). Adding incentives or challenging a group to strive for certain standards also promotes collective effort (Harkins & Szymanski, 1989; Shepperd & Wright, 1989).

Groups also loaf less when their members are *friends* rather than strangers (Davis & Greenlees, 1992). Latané notes that Israel's communal kibbutz farms have actually outproduced Israel's noncollective farms. Cohesiveness intensifies effort. So, will there be no social loafing in group-centered cultures? To find out, Latané and his co-researchers (Gabrenya & others, 1985) headed for Asia, where they repeated their sound-production experiments in Japan, Thailand, Taiwan, India, and Malaysia. Their findings? Social loafing was evident in all these countries, too.

Sixteen later studies in Asia reveal that people in collectivist cultures exhibit less social loafing than people in individualist cultures (Karau & Williams, 1993). As we noted earlier, loyalty to family and work groups runs strong in collectivist cultures. Likewise, women exhibit less social loafing than men (who tend to be more individualistic).

Some of these findings parallel those from studies of everyday work groups. When groups are given challenging objectives, when they are rewarded for group success, and when there is a spirit of commitment to the "team," group members work hard (Hackman, 1986). Keeping work groups small and forming them with equally competent people can also help members feel their contributions are indispensable (Comer, 1995). So, while social loafing is a common occurrence when group members work collectively and without individual accountability, many hands need not always make light work.

CONCEPTS TO REMEMBER

Social loafing   The tendency for people to exert less effort when they pool their efforts toward a common goal than when they are individually accountable.

Free riders   People who benefit from the group but give little in return.

16

❖

Doing Together What We Would Never Do Alone

I n 1991 an eyewitness videotaped four Los Angeles police officers hitting unarmed Rodney King more than 50 times—fracturing his skull in nine places with their nightsticks and leaving him brain damaged and missing teeth—while 23 other officers watched passively. Replays of the tape shocked the nation into a prolonged discussion of police brutality and group violence. People wondered: Where was the officers' humanity? What had happened to standards of professional conduct? What could provoke such behavior?

DEINDIVIDUATION

Social-facilitation experiments show that groups can arouse people. So-cial-loafing experiments show that groups can diffuse responsibility. When arousal and diffused responsibility combine and normal inhibitions diminish, the results can be startling. Acts can range from a mild lessening of restraint (throwing food in the dining hall, snarling at a referee, screaming during a rock concert) to impulsive self-gratification (group vandalism, orgies, thefts) to destructive social explosions (police brutality, riots, lynchings). In a 1967 incident, 200 University of Oklahoma students gathered to watch a disturbed fellow student threatening to jump from a tower. They began to chant "Jump! Jump! . . . " The student jumped to his death (UPI, 1967).

These unrestrained behaviors have something in common: They are somehow provoked by the power of a group. Groups can generate a sense of excitement, of being caught up in something bigger than oneself. It is

The beating of Rodney King by Los Angeles police officers made people wonder: How do group situations release people from normal restraints?

harder to imagine a single rock fan screaming deliriously at a private rock concert, a single Oklahoma student trying to coax someone to suicide, or even a single police officer beating a defenseless motorist. In certain kinds of group situations people are more likely to abandon normal restraints, to lose their sense of individual responsibility, to become what Leon Festinger, Albert Pepitone, and Theodore Newcomb (1952) labeled **deindividuated.** What circumstances elicit this psychological state?

Group Size

A group has the power not only to arouse its members but also to render them unidentifiable. The snarling crowd hides the snarling basketball fan. A lynch mob enables its members to believe they will not be prosecuted; they perceive the action as the *group's*. Rioters, made faceless by the mob, are freed to loot. In an analysis of 21 instances in which crowds were present as someone threatened to jump from a building or bridge, Leon Mann (1981) found that when the crowd was small and exposed by daylight, people usually did not try to bait the person. But when a large crowd or the cover of night gave people anonymity, the crowd usually baited and jeered. Brian Mullen (1986) reports a similar effect of lynch mobs: The bigger the mob, the more its members lose self-awareness and become willing to com-

FIGURE 16-1
Anonymous women delivered more shock to helpless victims than did
identifiable women.

mit atrocities, such as burning, lacerating, or dismembering the victim. In
each of these examples, from sports crowds to lynch mobs, evaluation apprehension plummets. And because "everyone is doing it," all can attribute
their behavior to the situation rather than to their own choices.

Philip Zimbardo (1970) speculated that the mere immensity of
crowded cities produces anonymity and thus norms that permit vandalism. He purchased two 10-year-old cars and left them with the hoods up
and license plates removed, one on a street near the old Bronx campus of
New York University and one near the Stanford University campus in Palo
Alto, a much smaller city. In New York the first auto strippers arrived
within 10 minutes; they took the battery and radiator. After three days and
23 incidents of theft and vandalism (by neatly dressed White people) the
car was reduced to a battered, useless hulk of metal. By contrast, the only
person observed to touch the Palo Alto car in over a week was a passer-by
who lowered the hood when it began to rain.

Physical Anonymity

How can we be sure that the crucial difference between the Bronx and Palo
Alto is greater anonymity in the Bronx? We can't. But we can experiment with
anonymity to see if it actually lessens inhibitions. In one creative experiment,
Zimbardo (1970) dressed New York University women in identical white
coats and hoods, rather like Ku Klux Klan members (Figure 16-1). Asked to

Percent transgressing

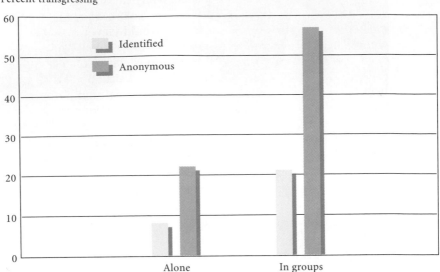

Percent transgressing

FIGURE 16-2
Children were more likely to transgress by taking extra Halloween candy when in a group, when anonymous, and, especially, when deindividuated by the combination of group immersion and anonymity. (Data from Diener & others, 1976.)

deliver electric shocks to a woman, they pressed the (fake) shock button twice as long as did women who were visible and wearing large name tags.

A research team led by Ed Diener (1976) cleverly demonstrated the effect both of being in a group *and* being physically anonymous. At Halloween, they observed 1,352 Seattle children trick-or-treating. As the children, either alone or in groups, approached 1 of 27 homes scattered throughout the city, an experimenter greeted them warmly, invited them to "take *one* of the candies," and then left the room. Hidden observers noted that, compared to solo children, those in groups were more than twice as likely to take extra candy. Also, compared to children who had been asked their names and where they lived, those left anonymous were also more than twice as likely to transgress. As Figure 16-2 shows, the transgression rate thus varied dramatically with the situation. When deindividuated by group immersion combined with anonymity, most children stole extra candy.

These experiments make me wonder about the effect of wearing uniforms. Preparing for battle, warriors in some tribal cultures (like rabid fans of some sports teams) depersonalize themselves with body and face paints or special masks. After the battle, some cultures kill, torture, or mutilate any remaining enemies; other cultures take prisoners alive. Robert Watson (1973) scrutinized anthropological files and discovered that the cultures with depersonalized warriors were also the cultures that brutalized the enemy. The uniformed Los Angeles police officers who beat Rodney King were angered and aroused by his defiant refusal to stop his car, enjoying one another's camaraderie, and unaware that outsiders would view their actions. Thus, forgetting their normal standards, they were swept away by the situation.

Does becoming physically anonymous *always* unleash our worst impulses? Fortunately, no. For one thing, the situations in which some of these experiments took place had clear antisocial cues. Robert Johnson and Leslie Downing (1979) point out that the Klan-like outfits worn by Zimbardo's subjects might have encouraged hostility. In an experiment at the University of Georgia, they had women put on nurses' uniforms before deciding how much shock someone should receive. When those wearing the nurses' uniforms were made anonymous, they became *less* aggressive in administering shocks than when their names and personal identities were stressed. Evidently, being anonymous makes one less self-conscious and more responsive to cues present in the situation, whether negative (Klan uniforms) or positive (nurses' uniforms). Given altruistic cues, deindividuated people even give more money (Spivey & Prentice-Dunn, 1990).

This helps explain why wearing black uniforms—which are traditionally associated with evil and death and worn by medieval executioners, Darth Vader, and Ninja warriors—have an effect opposite to that of wearing a nurse's uniform. Mark Frank and Thomas Gilovich (1988) report that, led by the Los Angeles Raiders and the Philadelphia Flyers, black-uniformed teams consistently ranked near the top of the National Football and Hockey Leagues in penalties assessed between 1970 and 1986. Follow-up laboratory research suggests that just putting on a black jersey can trigger wearers to behave more aggressively.

Arousing and Distracting Activities

Aggressive outbursts by large groups are often preceded by minor actions that arouse and divert people's attention. Group shouting, chanting, clapping, or dancing serve both to hype people up and to reduce self-consciousness. One Moonie observer recalls how the "choo-choo" chant helped deindividuate:

> All the brothers and sisters joined hands and chanted with increasing intensity, choo-choo-choo, Choo-choo-choo, CHOO-CHOO-CHOO! YEA! YEA! POWW!!! The act made us a group, as though in some strange way we had all experienced something important together. The power of the choo-choo frightened me, but it made me feel more comfortable and there was something very relaxing about building up the energy and releasing it. (Zimbardo & others, 1977, p. 186)

Ed Diener's experiments (1976, 1979) have shown that such activities as throwing rocks and group singing can set the stage for more disinhibited behavior. There is a self-reinforcing pleasure in doing an impulsive act while observing others doing it also. When we see others act as we are acting, we think they feel as we do, which reinforces our own feelings (Orive, 1984). Moreover, impulsive group action absorbs our attention. When we yell at the referee, we are not thinking about our values; we are reacting to the immediate situation. Later, when we stop to think about what we have done or said, we sometimes feel chagrined. Sometimes. At other times we seek deindividuating group experiences—dances, worship experiences, group encounters—where we can enjoy intense positive feelings and feel close to others.

DIMISHED SELF-AWARENESS

Group experiences that diminish self-consciousness tend to disconnect behavior from attitudes. Experiments by Ed Diener (1980) and Steven Prentice-Dunn and Ronald Rogers (1980, 1989) reveal that people who are not self-conscious, and are deindividuated are less restrained, less self-regulated, more likely to act without thinking about their own values, more responsive to the situation. These findings complement and reinforce the experiments on *self-awareness*. Self-awareness is the opposite of deindividuation. Those made self-aware, say by acting in front of a mirror or TV camera, exhibit *increased* self-control, and their actions more clearly reflect their attitudes. In front of a mirror, people taste-testing cream cheese varieties eat less of the high-fat alternative (Sentyrz & Bushman, 1997). People made self-aware are also less likely to cheat (Beaman & others, 1979; Diener & Wallbom, 1976). So are those who generally have a strong sense of themselves as distinct and independent (Nadler & others, 1982). People who are self-conscious, or who are temporarily made so, exhibit greater consistency between their words outside a situation and their deeds in it.

Circumstances that decrease self-awareness, as alcohol consumption does, therefore increase deindividuation (Hull & others, 1983). And deindividuation decreases in circumstances that increase self-awareness: mirrors and cameras, small towns, bright lights, large name tags, undistracted quiet, individual clothes and houses (Ickes & others, 1978). When a teenager leaves for a party, a parent's parting advice could well be: "Have fun, and remember who you are." In other words, enjoy being with the group, but be self-aware; don't become deindividuated.

CONCEPT TO REMEMBER

Deindividuation   Loss of self-awareness and evaluation apprehension; occurs in group situations that foster anonymity and draw attention away from the individual.

17

✦

How Groups Intensify Decisions

W hich effects—good or bad—does group interaction more often have? Police brutality and mob violence demonstrate its destructive potential. Yet support-group leaders, management consultants, and educational theorists proclaim its benefits. And social and religious movements urge their members to strengthen their identities by fellowship with like-minded others.

Research helps clarify our understanding of such effects. From studies of people in small groups, a principle emerges that helps explain both destructive and constructive outcomes: Group discussion often strengthens members' initial inclinations (good or bad). The unfolding of this research on "group polarization" illustrates the process of inquiry—how an interesting discovery often leads researchers to hasty and erroneous conclusions, which ultimately get replaced with more accurate conclusions. This is one scientific mystery I can discuss firsthand, having been one of the detectives.

*T*HE CASE OF THE "RISKY SHIFT"

A research literature of more than 300 studies began with a surprising finding by James Stoner (1961), then an MIT graduate student. For his master's thesis in industrial management, Stoner compared risk taking by individuals and groups. To test the commonly held belief that groups are more cautious than individuals, Stoner posed decision dilemmas faced by fictional characters. The participant's task was to advise the imagined character how much risk to take. Put yourself in the participant's shoes: What advice would you give the character in this situation?

> Helen is a writer who is said to have considerable creative talent but who so far has been earning a comfortable living by writing cheap westerns. Recently she has come up with an idea for a potentially significant novel. If it could be written and accepted, it might have considerable literary impact and be a big boost to her career. On the other hand, if she cannot work out her idea or if the novel is a flop, she will have expended considerable time and energy without remuneration.
>
> Imagine that you are advising Helen. Please check the *lowest* probability that you would consider acceptable for Helen to attempt to write the novel.
>
> Helen should attempt to write the novel if the chances that the novel will be a success are at least:

> _____ 1 in 10
>
> _____ 2 in 10
>
> _____ 3 in 10
>
> _____ 4 in 10
>
> _____ 5 in 10
>
> _____ 6 in 10
>
> _____ 7 in 10
>
> _____ 8 in 10
>
> _____ 9 in 10
>
> _____ 10 in 10 (Place a check here if you think Helen should attempt the novel only if it is certain that the novel will be a success.)

After making your decision, guess what this book's average reader would advise.

Having marked their advice on a dozen such items, five or so individuals would then discuss and reach agreement on each item. How do you think the group decisions compared to the average decision before the discussions? Would the groups be likely to take greater risks? be more cautious? stay the same?

To everyone's amazement, the group decisions were usually riskier. Dubbed the "risky-shift phenomenon," this finding set off a wave of investigation into group risk taking. The studies revealed that this effect occurs not only when a group decides by consensus; after a brief discussion, individuals, too, will alter their decisions. What is more, researchers successfully repeated Stoner's finding with people of varying ages and occupations in a dozen different nations.

During discussion, opinions converged. Curiously, however, the point toward which they converged was usually a lower (riskier) number than their initial average. Here was a delightful puzzle. The small risky-shift effect was reliable, unexpected, and without any immediately obvious explanation. What group influences produce such an effect? How widespread is it? Do discussions in juries, business committees, and military organizations also promote risk taking?

After several years of study and speculation about group risk taking, we became aware that the risky shift was not universal. We could write decision dilemmas on which people became more *cautious* after discussion. One of these featured "Roger," a young married man with two school-age children and a secure but low-paying job. Roger can afford life's necessities but few of its luxuries. He hears that the stock of a relatively unknown company might soon triple in value if its new product is favorably received or might decline considerably if it does not sell. Roger has no savings. To invest in the company, he is considering selling his life insurance policy.

Can you see a general principle that predicts both the tendency to give riskier advice after discussing Helen's situation and the tendency to give more cautious advice after discussing Roger's?

If you are like most people, you would advise Helen to take greater risk than Roger, even before talking with others. It turns out there is a strong tendency for discussion to accentuate these initial leanings.

We therefore began to realize that this group phenomenon was not, as originally assumed, a consistent shift to risk, but rather a tendency for group discussion to *enhance* the individuals' initial leanings. This idea led investigators to propose what Serge Moscovici and Marisa Zavalloni (1969) called a **group polarization** phenomenon: Discussion typically strengthens the average inclination of group members.

*D*O GROUPS INTENSIFY OPINIONS?

Group Polarization Experiments

This new view of the changes induced by group discussion prompted experimenters to have people discuss statements that most of them favored or most of them opposed. Would talking in groups enhance their initial inclinations as it did with the decision dilemmas? That's what the group polarization hypothesis predicts (Figure 17-1).

Dozens of studies confirm group polarization. Moscovici and Zavalloni (1969) observed that discussion enhanced French students' initially positive attitude toward their premier and negative attitude toward Americans. Mititoshi Isozaki (1984) found that Japanese university students gave more pronounced judgments of "guilty" after discussing a traffic case. And Glen Whyte (1993) reports that groups exacerbate the "too much invested to quit" phenomenon that has cost many businesses huge sums of money. Canadian business students imagined themselves having to decide whether to invest more money in the hope of preventing losses in various

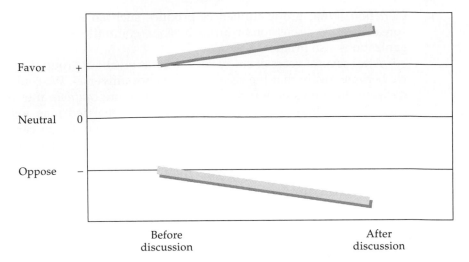

FIGURE 17-1
The group polarization hypothesis predicts that discussion will strengthen an attitude shared by group members. If people initially tend to favor something (say, risk on a life dilemma question), they tend to favor it even more after discussion. If they tend to oppose something, they tend to oppose it even more after discussion.

failing projects (for example, whether to make a high-risk loan to protect an earlier investment). They exhibited the typical effect: 72 percent reinvested money they would seldom have invested if they were considering it as a new investment on its own merits. When making the same decision in groups, 94 percent opted for reinvestment.

Another research strategy has been to pick issues on which opinions are divided and then cluster people who hold the same view. Does discussion with like-minded people strengthen shared views? Does it magnify the attitude gap that separates the two sides?

George Bishop and I wondered. So we set up groups of relatively prejudiced and unprejudiced high school students and asked them to respond, before and after discussion, to issues involving racial attitudes, such as property rights versus open housing (Myers & Bishop, 1970). We found that the discussions among like-minded students did indeed increase the initial gap between the two groups (Figure 17-2).

Naturally Occurring Group Polarization

In everyday life, people associate mostly with others whose attitudes are similar to their own. (Look at your own circle of friends.) So, does everyday group interaction with like-minded friends intensify shared attitudes?

Prejudice

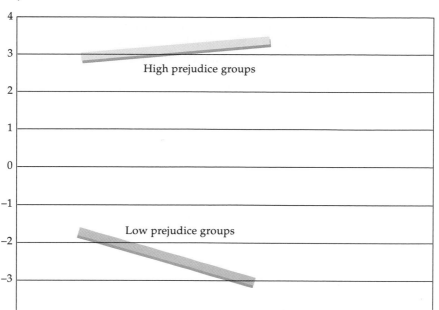

FIGURE 17-2
Discussion increased polarization between homogeneous groups of high- and low-prejudice high school students. Talking over racial issues increased prejudice in a high-prejudice group and decreased it in a low-prejudice group. (Data from Myers & Bishop, 1970.)

In natural situations it's hard to disentangle cause and effect. But the laboratory phenomenon does have real-life parallels.

One such parallel is what education researchers have called the "accentuation phenomenon": Over time, initial differences among college-student groups become accentuated. If the students at college X are initially more intellectual than the students at college Y, that gap is likely to grow during college. Likewise, compared to fraternity and sorority members, independents tend to have more liberal political attitudes, a difference that grows with time in college (Pascarella & Terenzini, 1991). Researchers believe this results partly from group members reinforcing shared inclinations (Chickering & McCormick, 1973; Feldman & Newcomb, 1969; Wilson & others, 1975).

Polarization also occurs in communities. During community conflicts, like-minded people increasingly associate with one another. This amplifies their shared tendencies. Gang delinquency emerges from a process of mutual reinforcement within neighborhood gangs, whose members have a common socioeconomic and ethnic background (Cartwright, 1975). From their analysis of terrorist organizations around the world, Clark Mc-Cauley and Mary Segal (1987) note that terrorism does not erupt suddenly. Rather, it arises among people whose shared grievances bring them together. As they interact in isolation from moderating influences, they become progressively more extreme. The social amplifier brings the signal in stronger. The result is violent acts that the individuals, apart from the group, would never have committed.

EXPLAINING GROUP POLARIZATION

Why do groups adopt stances that are more exaggerated than the average opinions of their individual members? Researchers hoped that solving the mystery of group polarization might provide some insights. Solving small puzzles sometimes provides clues for solving larger ones.

Among several proposed theories of group polarization, two survived scientific scrutiny. One deals with the arguments presented during a discussion, the other with how members of a group view themselves vis-à-vis the other members. The first idea is an example of what in Module 6 was called *informational influence* (influence that results from accepting evidence about reality). The second is an example of *normative influence* (influence based on a person's desire to be accepted or admired by others).

Informational Influence

According to the best-supported explanation, group discussion elicits a pooling of ideas, most of which favor the dominant viewpoint. Ideas that were common knowledge to group members will often be brought up in discussion or, even if unmentioned, will jointly influence their discussion (Gigone & Hastie, 1993; Larson & others, 1994; Stasser, 1991). Other ideas might include persuasive arguments that some group members had not previously considered. When discussing Helen the writer, someone might say, "Helen should go for it, because she has little to lose. If her novel flops, she can always go back to writing cheap westerns." Such statements often entangle information about the person's *arguments* with cues concerning the person's *position* on the issue. But when people hear relevant arguments without learning the specific stands other people assume, they still shift their positions (Burnstein & Vinokur, 1977; Hinsz & others, 1997). *Arguments,* in and of themselves, matter.

Normative Influence

A second explanation of polarization involves comparison with others. As Leon Festinger (1954) argued in his influential theory of **social comparison,** it is human nature to want to evaluate our opinions and abilities, something we can do by comparing our views with those of others. We are most persuaded by people in our "reference groups"—groups we identify with (Abrams & others, 1990; Hogg & others, 1990). Moreover, wanting people to like us, we might express stronger opinions after discovering that others share our views.

Perhaps you can recall a time when you and others were guarded and reserved in a group, until someone broke the ice and said, "Well, to be perfectly honest, I think. . . . " Soon you were all surprised to discover strong support for your shared views. When people are asked (as I asked you earlier) to predict how others would respond to items such as the Helen dilemma, they typically exhibit social ignorance: They don't realize how much others support the socially preferred tendency (in this case, writing the novel). A typical person will advise writing the novel even if its chance of success is only 4 in 10, but estimate that most other people would require 5 or 6 in 10. When the discussion begins, most people discover they are not outshining the others as they had supposed. In fact, some others are ahead of them, having taken an even stronger position for writing the novel. No longer restrained by a misperceived group norm, they are liberated to voice their preferences more strongly.

This social comparison theory prompted experiments that exposed people to others' positions but not to their arguments. This is roughly the experience we have when reading the results of an opinion poll. When people learn others' positions without discussion, will they adjust their responses to maintain a socially favorable position? When people have made no prior commitment to a particular response, seeing others' responses *does* stimulate a small polarization (Goethals & Zanna, 1979; Sanders & Baron, 1977). This polarization from mere social comparison is usually less than that produced by a lively discussion. Still, it's surprising that, instead of simply conforming to the group average, people often go it one better.

Group polarization research illustrates the complexity of social-psychological inquiry. As much as we like our explanations of a phenomenon to be simple, one explanation seldom accounts for all the data. Because people are complex, more than one factor frequently influences an outcome. In group discussions, persuasive arguments predominate on issues that have a factual element ("Is she guilty of the crime?"). Social comparison sways responses on value-laden judgments ("How long a sentence should she serve?") (Kaplan, 1989). On the many issues that have both factual and value-laden aspects, the two factors work together. Discovering that others share one's feelings (social comparison) unleashes arguments (informational influence) supporting what everyone secretly favors.

GROUPTHINK

Do the social-psychological phenomena we so far considered in Part Three occur in sophisticated groups like corporate boards or the president's cabinet? Is there likely to be self-justification? self-serving bias? a cohesive "we feeling" provoking conformity and rejection of dissent? public commitment producing resistance to change? group polarization? Social psychologist Irving Janis (1971, 1982a) wondered whether such phenomena might help explain good and bad group decisions made by some twentieth-century American presidents and their advisers. To find out, he analyzed the decision-making procedures that led to several major fiascos:

- *Pearl Harbor.* In the weeks preceding the December 1941 Pearl Harbor attack that put the United States into World War II, military commanders in Hawaii received a steady stream of information about Japan's preparations for an attack on the United States somewhere in the Pacific. Then military intelligence lost radio contact with Japanese aircraft carriers, which had begun moving straight for Hawaii. Air reconnaissance could have spotted the carriers or at least provided a few minutes' warning. But complacent commanders decided against such precautions. The result: No alert was sounded until the attack on a virtually defenseless base was under way. It claimed 18 ships, 170 planes, and 2,400 lives.

- *The Bay of Pigs Invasion.* In 1961, President John Kennedy and his advisers tried to overthrow Fidel Castro by invading Cuba with 1,400 CIA-trained Cuban exiles. Nearly all the invaders were soon killed or captured, the United States was humiliated, and Cuba allied itself even closer to the Soviet Union. After learning the outcome, Kennedy wondered aloud, "How could we have been so stupid?"

- *The Vietnam War.* From 1964 to 1967, President Lyndon Johnson and his "Tuesday lunch group" of policy advisers escalated the war in Vietnam on the assumption that U.S. aerial bombardment, defoliation, and search-and-destroy missions would bring North Vietnam to the peace table with the appreciative support of the South Vietnamese populace. They continued the escalation despite warnings from government intelligence experts and nearly all U.S. allies. The resulting disaster cost 47,000 American and more than 1 million Vietnamese lives, polarized Americans, drove the president from office, and created huge budget deficits that helped fuel inflation in the 1970s.

Janis believed these blunders were bred by the tendency of decision-making groups to suppress dissent in the interests of group harmony, a phenomenon he called **groupthink.** In work groups, camaraderie boosts productivity (Mullen & Copper, 1994). Moreover, team spirit is good for morale. But when making decisions, close-knit groups can pay a price. Janis believed that the soil from which groupthink sprouts includes an amiable, *cohesive* group; relative *isolation* of the group from dissenting viewpoints; and a *directive leader* who signals what decision he or she favors. When planning the ill-fated Bay of Pigs invasion, the newly elected President Kennedy and his advisers enjoyed a strong esprit de corps. Arguments critical of the plan were suppressed or excluded, and the president himself soon endorsed the invasion.

Symptoms of Groupthink

From historical records and the memoirs of participants and observers, Janis identified eight groupthink symptoms. These symptoms are a collective form of dissonance reduction that surfaces as group members try to maintain their positive group feeling when facing a threat (Turner & others, 1992, 1994). The first two groupthink symptoms lead group members to *overestimate their group's might and right:*

- *An illusion of invulnerability.* The groups Janis studied all developed an excessive optimism that blinded them to warnings of danger. Told that his forces had lost radio contact with the Japanese carriers, Admiral Kimmel, the chief naval officer at Pearl Harbor, joked that maybe the Japanese were about to round Honolulu's Diamond Head. They were, but Kimmel's laughing at the idea dismissed the very possibility of its being true.

- *Unquestioned belief in the group's morality.* Group members assume the inherent morality of their group and ignore ethical and moral issues. The Kennedy group knew that adviser Arthur Schlesinger, Jr., and Senator J. William Fulbright had moral reservations about invading a small, neighboring country. But the group never entertained or discussed these moral qualms.

Group members also become *closed-minded,* as shown in the next two groupthink symptoms:

- *Rationalization.* The groups discount challenges by collectively justifying their decisions. President Johnson's Tuesday lunch group spent far more time rationalizing (explaining and justifying) than reflecting upon and rethinking prior decisions to escalate. Each initiative became an action to defend and justify.

- *Stereotyped view of the opponent.* Participants in these groupthink tanks consider their enemies too evil to negotiate with or too weak and unintelligent to defend themselves against the planned initiative. The Kennedy group convinced itself that Castro's military was so weak and his popular support so shallow that a single brigade could easily overturn his regime.

Finally, the group suffers from *pressures toward uniformity,* as shown in these symptoms:

- *Conformity pressure.* Group members rebuffed those who raised doubts about the group's assumption and plans, at times not by argument but by personal sarcasm. Once, when President Johnson's assistant Bill Moyers arrived at a meeting, the president derided him with, "Well, here comes Mr. Stop-the-Bombing." Most people fall into line when faced with such ridicule.

● *Self-censorship.* Because disagreements were often uncomfortable and the groups seemed in consensus, members withheld or discounted their misgivings. In the months following the Bay of Pigs invasion, Arthur Schlesinger (1965, p. 255) reproached himself "for having kept so silent during those crucial discussions in the Cabinet Room, though my feelings of guilt were tempered by the knowledge that a course of objection would have accomplished little save to gain me a name as a nuisance."

● *Illusion of unanimity.* Self-censorship and pressure not to puncture the consensus create an illusion of unanimity. What is more, the apparent consensus confirms the group's decision. This appearance of consensus was evident in these three fiascos and in other fiascos before and since. Albert Speer (1971), an adviser to Adolf Hitler, described the atmosphere around Hitler as one where pressure to conform suppressed all deviation. The absence of dissent created an illusion of unanimity:

> In normal circumstances people who turn their backs on reality are soon set straight by the mockery and criticism of those around them, which makes them aware they have lost credibility. In the Third Reich there were no such correctives, especially for those who belonged to the upper stratum. On the contrary, every self-deception was multiplied as in a hall of distorting mirrors, becoming a repeatedly confirmed picture of a fantastical dream world which no longer bore any relationship to the grim outside world. In those mirrors I could see nothing but my own face reproduced many times over. No external factors disturbed the uniformity of hundreds of unchanging faces, all mine. (p. 379)

● *Mindguards.* Some members protect the group from information that would call into question the effectiveness or morality of its decisions. Before the Bay of Pigs invasion, Robert Kennedy took Schlesinger aside and told him, "Don't push it any further." Secretary of State Dean Rusk withheld diplomatic and intelligence experts' warnings against the invasion. They thus served as the president's "mindguards," protecting him from disagreeable facts rather than physical harm.

Groupthink in Action

Groupthink symptoms can produce a failure to seek and discuss contrary information and alternative possibilities (Figure 17-3). When a leader promotes an idea and when a group insulates itself from dissenting views, groupthink can produce defective decisions (McCauley, 1989).

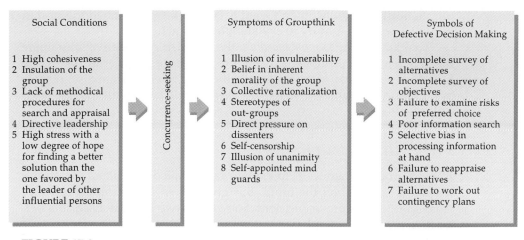

FIGURE 17-3
Theoretical analysis of groupthink. (Data from Janis & Mann, 1977, p. 132.)

Groupthink was tragically evident in the decision process by which NASA decided to launch the space shuttle *Challenger* in January 1986 (Esser & Lindoerfer, 1989). Engineers at Morton Thiokol, which makes the shuttle's rocket boosters, and at Rockwell International, which manufactures the orbiter, opposed the launch because of dangers posed to equipment by the subfreezing temperatures. The Thiokol engineers feared the cold would make the rubber seals between the rocket's four segments too brittle to contain the superhot gases. Several months before the doomed mission, the company's top expert had warned in a memo that it was a "jump ball" whether the seal would hold, and that if it failed, "the result would be a catastrophe of the highest order" (Magnuson, 1986).

In a telephone discussion the night before the launch, the engineers argued their case with their uncertain managers and with NASA officials, who were eager to proceed with the already delayed launch. One Thiokol official later testified: "We got ourselves into the thought process that we were trying to find some way to prove to them [the booster] wouldn't work. We couldn't prove absolutely that it wouldn't work." The result was an *illusion of invulnerability.*

Conformity pressures also operated. One NASA official complained, "My God, Thiokol, when do you want me to launch, next April?" The top Thiokol executive declared, "We have to make a management decision," and then asked his engineering vice-president to "take off his engineering hat and put on his management hat."

To create an *illusion of unanimity,* this executive then proceeded to poll only the management officials and ignore the engineers. The go-ahead decision now made, one of the engineers belatedly pleaded with a NASA official to reconsider: "If anything happened to this launch," he said prophetically, "I sure wouldn't want to be the person that had to stand in front of a board of inquiry to explain why I launched."

Thanks, finally, to *mindguarding*, the top NASA executive who made the final decision never learned about the engineers' concerns, nor did he hear the reservations of the Rockwell officials. Protected from disagreeable information, he confidently gave the go-ahead to launch the *Challenger* on its tragic flight.

Preventing Groupthink

Flawed group dynamics help explain many failed decisions; sometimes too many cooks spoil the broth. But given open leadership, a cohesive team spirit can improve decisions. Sometimes two or more heads are better than one.

In search of conditions that breed good decisions, Janis also analyzed two seemingly successful ventures: the Truman administration's formulation of the Marshall Plan for getting Europe back on its feet after World War II, and the Kennedy administration's handling of the Soviet Union's attempts to install missile bases in Cuba in 1962. Janis's (1982) recommendations for preventing groupthink incorporate many of the effective group procedures used in both cases:

- Be impartial—do not endorse any position.
- Encourage critical evaluation; assign a "devil's advocate."
- Occasionally subdivide the group, then reunite to air differences.
- Welcome critique from outside experts and associates.
- Before implementing, call a "second-chance" meeting to air any lingering doubts.

When such steps are taken, group decisions may take longer to make yet ultimately prove less defective and more effective.

CONCEPTS TO REMEMBER

Group polarization   Group-produced enhancement of members' preexisting tendencies; a strengthening of the members' *average* tendency, not a split within the group.

Social comparison   Evaluating one's opinions and abilities by comparing oneself to others.

Groupthink   "The mode of thinking that persons engage in when concurrence-seeking becomes so dominant in a cohesive in-group that it tends to override realistic appraisal of alternative courses of action" (Janis, 1971).

MODULE

18

❖

Power to the Person

"There are trivial truths and great truths," declared physicist Niels Bohr. "The opposite of a trivial truth is plainly false. The opposite of a great truth is also true." Each module in this unit on social influence teaches a great truth: the power of the social situation. This great truth about the power of external pressures would sufficiently explain our behavior if we were passive, like tumbleweed. But unlike tumbleweed, we are not just blown here and there by the environment. We act; we react. We respond, and we get responses. We can resist the social situation and sometimes even change it. Thus, each of these modules on social influence concludes by calling attention to the opposite of the great truth: the power of the person.

Perhaps stressing the power of culture leaves you somewhat uncomfortable. Most of us resent any suggestion that external forces determine our behavior; we see ourselves as free beings, as the originators of our actions (well, at least of our good actions). We sense that believing in social determinism can lead to what philosopher Jean-Paul Sartre called "bad faith"—evading responsibility by blaming something else or someone else for one's fate.

Actually, social control (the power of the situation) and personal control (the power of the person) no more compete with one another as explanations than do biological and cultural explanations. Social and personal explanations of our social behavior are both valid, for at any moment we are both the creatures and the creators of our social worlds. We might well be the products of our genes and environment. But it is also true that the future is coming, and it is our job to decide where it is going. Our choices today determine our environment tomorrow.

171

INTERACTING PERSONS AND SITUATIONS

Asking whether external situations or inner dispositions (or culture or evo-lution) determine behavior is like asking whether length or width deter-mines the area of a field. Social situations do profoundly influence individ-uals. But individuals also influence the social situation. The two *interact*.

The interaction occurs in at least three ways (Snyder & Ickes, 1985). First, a given social situation can *affect different people differently*. Because our minds do not see reality identically, we each respond to a situation as we construe it. And some people are more sensitive and responsive to social situations than others are (M. Snyder, 1983). The Japanese, for example, are more re-sponsive to social expectations than the British (Argyle & others, 1978).

Second, many interactions between persons and situations occurs be-cause the people have *chosen the situation* (Ickes & others, 1990). Given a choice, sociable people elect situations that evoke social interaction. When you chose your college, you were also choosing to expose yourself to a spe-cific set of social influences. Ardent political liberals are unlikely to settle in Orange County, California, and join the Chamber of Commerce. They are more likely to live in Toronto and join Greenpeace—in other words, to choose a social world that reinforces their inclinations.

Third, people often *create their situations*. Recall again that our precon-ceptions can be self-fulfilling: If we expect someone to be extraverted, hos-tile, feminine, or sexy, our actions toward the person can induce the very behavior we expect. What, after all, makes a social situation but the peo-ple in it? A liberal environment is created by liberals. What takes place in the sorority is created by the members. The social environment is not like the weather—something that just happens to us. It is more like our homes—something we make for ourselves.

The reciprocal causation between situations and persons allows us to see people as either *reacting to* or *acting upon* their environment. Each per-spective is correct, for we are both the products and the architects of our so-cial worlds. However, is one perspective wiser? In one sense, it is wise to see ourselves as the creatures of our environments (lest we become too proud of our achievements and blame ourselves too much for our problems) and to see others as free actors (lest we become paternalistic and manipulative).

However, we often do well to assume the reverse—to view ourselves as free agents and to view others as influenced by their environments. We would then assume self-efficacy as we view ourselves and seek under-standing and social reform as we relate to others. (If we view others as in-fluenced by their situations, we are more likely to understand and em-pathize than smugly to judge unpleasant behavior as freely chosen by "immoral," "sadistic," or "lazy" persons.) Most religions encourage us to take responsibility for ourselves but to refrain from judging others. Does religion teach this because our natural inclination is to excuse our own fail-ures while blaming others for theirs?

RESISTING SOCIAL PRESSURE

Social psychology offers other reminders of the power of the person. We are not just billiard balls. Knowing that someone is trying to coerce us can even prompt us to react in the *opposite* direction.

Reactance

Individuals value their sense of freedom and self-efficacy (Baer & others, 1980). When social pressure becomes so blatant that it threatens their sense of freedom, they often rebel. Think of Romeo and Juliet, whose love was intensified by their families' opposition. Or think of children asserting their freedom and independence by doing the opposite of what their parents ask. Savvy parents therefore offer their children choices instead of commands: "It's time to clean up: Do you want a bath or a shower?"

The theory of psychological **reactance**—that people do indeed act to protect their sense of freedom—is supported by experiments showing that attempts to restrict a person's freedom often produce a "boomerang effect" (Brehm & Brehm, 1981; Nail & Van Leeuwen, 1993). Suppose someone stops you on the street and asks you to sign a petition advocating something you mildly support. While considering the petition, you are told that someone else believes "people absolutely should not be allowed to distribute or sign such petitions." Reactance theory predicts that such blatant attempts to limit freedom will actually increase the likelihood of your signing. When Madeline Heilman (1976) staged this experiment on the streets of New York City, that is precisely what she found.

Reactance can also contribute to underage drinking. In the United States, where it is illegal to sell alcohol to persons under age 21, a survey of 3,375 students on a cross section of 56 campuses revealed a 25 percent rate of abstinence among students of legal drinking age but only a 19 percent abstinence rate among students under 21. The researchers, Ruth Engs and David Hanson (1989), also found that 15 percent of the legal-age students and 24 percent of the underage students were heavy drinkers. They suspect this reflects a reactance against the restriction. It probably also reflects peer influence. With alcohol use, as with drugs, peers influence attitudes, provide the substance, and offer a context for its use. This helps explain why college students, living in a peer culture that often supports alcohol use, drink more alcohol than their noncollege peers (Atwell, 1986).

Reactance can escalate into social rebellion. Like obedience, rebellion can be produced and observed in experiments. That's what William Gamson, Bruce Fireman, and Steven Rytina (1982) learned when they posed as members of a commercial research firm. They recruited people from towns near the University of Michigan to come to a hotel conference room for "a group discussion of community standards." Once there, the people learned that the discussions were to be videotaped on behalf of a

large oil company seeking to win a legal case against a local station manager who had spoken out against high gas prices.

In the first discussion, virtually everyone sided with the station manager. Hoping to convince the court that people in the local community
were on its side, the "company representative" then began to tell more and
more group members to defend the company. In the end, he told everyone
to attack the station manager and asked them to sign an affidavit giving
the company permission to edit the tapes and use them in court. By leaving the room from time to time, the experimenter gave the group members
repeated opportunities to interpret and react to the injustice.

Most rebelled, objecting to and resisting the demand that they mis-
represent their opinions to help the oil company. Some groups even mobi-
lized themselves to stop the whole effort. They made plans to go to a newspaper, the Better Business Bureau, a lawyer, or the court.

By brewing small social rebellions, the researchers saw how a revolt is
born. They found that successful resistance often begins very quickly; the
more a group complies with unjust demands, the harder it later is to break
free. And someone must be willing to seed the process by expressing the
reservations the others are feeling.

These demonstrations of reactance reassure us that people are not
puppets. Sociologist Peter Berger (1963) expressed the point vividly:

> We see the puppets dancing in their miniature stage, moving up and down as
> the strings pull them around, following the prescribed course of their various
> little parts. We learn to understand the logic of this theater and we find ourselves
> in its motions. We locate ourselves in society and thus recognize our own posi-
> tion as we hang from its subtle strings. For a moment we see ourselves as pup-
> pets indeed. But then we grasp a decisive difference between the puppet theater
> and our own drama. Unlike the puppets, we have the possibility of stopping in
> our movements, looking up and perceiving the machinery by which we have
> been moved. In this act lies the first step towards freedom. (p. 176)

Asserting Uniqueness

Imagine a world of complete conformity where there were no differences
among people. Would such a world be a happy place? If nonconformity
can create discomfort, can sameness create comfort?

People feel uncomfortable when they appear too different from others.
But, at least in Western cultures, they also feel uncomfortable when they appear exactly like everyone else. As experiments by C. R. Snyder and Howard
Fromkin (1980) have shown, people feel better when they see themselves as
unique. Moreover, they act in ways that will assert their individuality. In one
experiment, Snyder (1980) led Purdue University students to believe that
their "10 most important attitudes" were either distinct from or nearly identical to the attitudes of 10,000 other students. When they then participated
in a conformity experiment, those deprived of their feeling of uniqueness
were most likely to assert their individuality by nonconformity. In another

experiment, people who heard others express attitudes identical to their own altered their positions to maintain their sense of uniqueness.

Seeing oneself as unique also appears in people's "spontaneous self-concepts." William McGuire and his Yale University colleagues (McGuire & Padawer-Singer, 1978; McGuire & others, 1979) report that when children are invited to "tell us about yourself," they are most likely to mention their distinctive attributes. Foreign-born children are more likely than others to mention their birthplace. Redheads are more likely than black- and brown-haired children to volunteer their hair color. Lightweight and heavy children are the most likely to refer to their body weight. Minority children are the most likely to mention their race. Likewise we become more keenly aware of our gender when we are with people of the other sex (Cota & Dion, 1986).

The principle, says McGuire, is that "one is conscious of oneself insofar as, and in the ways that, one is different." Thus, "If I am a Black woman in a group of White women, I tend to think of myself as a Black; if I move to a group of Black men, my blackness loses salience and I become more conscious of being a woman" (McGuire & others, 1978). This insight helps us understand why any minority group tends to be conscious of its distinctiveness and how the surrounding culture relates to it. The majority group, being less conscious of race, might see the minority group as "hypersensitive." I occasionally live in Scotland, where my American accent marks me as a foreigner; there I am conscious of my national identity and sensitive to how others react to it.

When the people of two cultures are nearly identic' ' they still will notice their differences, however small. Even trivial distinct. ˑ can provoke scorn and conflict. Jonathan Swift satirized the phenomenoṇ   Gulliver's Travels—the Little-Endians war against the Big-Endians. Their dɯ ʳence: The Little-Endians preferred to break their eggs on the small end, the ʳ-Endians on the large end. On a world scale, the differences might not seem great between Scots and English, Hutus and Tutsis, Serbs and Croatians, or Catholic and Protestant Northern Irish. But small differences can mean big conflict (Rothbart & Taylor, 1992). Rivalry is often most intense when the other group most closely resembles you.

So it seems that although we do not like being greatly deviant, ironically, we are all alike in wanting to feel distinctive and in noticing how we are distinctive. But as research on self-serving bias makes clear, it is not just any kind of distinctiveness we seek but distinctiveness in the right direction. Our quest is not merely to be different from the average, but *better* than average.

MINORITY INFLUENCE

We have seen that although cultural situations mold us, we also help create and choose these situations; that although pressures to conform sometimes overwhelm our better judgment, blatant pressure can motivate us to assert our individuality and freedom; and that, although persuasive forces are indeed powerful, we can resist persuasion by making public commitments and by anticipating persuasive appeals. Consider, finally, how individuals can influence their groups.

At the beginning of most social movements, a small minority will sometimes sway, and then even become, the majority. "All history," wrote Ralph Waldo Emerson, "is a record of the power of minorities, and of minorities of one." Think of Copernicus and Galileo, of Martin Luther, Jr., of the suffragettes. The American civil rights movement was ignited by the refusal of one African American woman, Rosa Parks, to relinquish her seat on a Montgomery, Alabama, bus. Technological history is also made by innovative minorities. As Robert Fulton developed his steamboat—"Fulton's Folly"—he endured constant derision: "Never did a single encouraging remark, a bright hope, a warm wish, cross my path" (Cantril & Bumstead, 1960).

What makes a minority persuasive? Experiments initiated by Serge Moscovici in Paris have identified several determinants of minority influence: consistency, self-confidence, and defections from the majority.

Consistency

More influential than a minority that wavers is a minority that sticks to its position. Moscovici and his associates (1969, 1985) have found that if a minority consistently judges blue slides as green, members of the majority will occasionally agree. But if the minority wavers, saying "blue" to one-third of the blue slides and "green" to the rest, virtually no one in the majority will ever agree with "green."

The nature of this influence is still debated (Clark & Maass, 1990; Levine & Russo, 1987). Moscovici believes that a minority's following the majority usually reflects just public compliance, but a majority's following a minority usually reflects genuine acceptance—really recalling the blue slide as greenish. In public, people might wish not to align themselves with a deviant minority view (Wood & others, 1994, 1996). A majority can also give us a rule of thumb for deciding truth ("All those smart cookies can't be wrong"), while a minority influences us by making us think more deeply (Burnstein & Kitayama, 1989; Mackie, 1987). Minority influence is therefore more likely to take the thought-filled central route to persuasion.

Experiments show—and experience confirms—that nonconformity, especially persistent nonconformity, is often painful (Levine, 1989). If you set out to be Emerson's minority of one, prepare yourself for ridicule, especially when you argue an issue that's personally relevant to the majority and when the group wants to settle an issue by reaching consensus (Kameda & Sugimori, 1993; Kruglanski & Webster, 1991; Trost & others, 1992). People might attribute your dissent to psychological peculiarities (Papastamou & Mugny, 1990). When Charlan Nemeth (1979) planted a minority of two within a simulated jury and had them oppose the majority's opinions, the duo was inevitably disliked. Nevertheless, the majority acknowledged that the persistence of the two did more than anything else to make them rethink their positions. In so doing, a minority can stimulate creative thinking (Martin, 1996; Mucchi-Faina & others, 1991; Peterson & Nemeth, 1996). With dissent from within one's own group, people take in more information, think about it in new ways, and often make better decisions. Believing that one need not win friends to influence people, Nemeth quotes Oscar Wilde: "We dislike arguments of any kind; they are always vulgar, and often convincing."

A persistent minority is influential, even if not popular, partly because it soon becomes the focus of debate (Schachter, 1951). Being the center of conversation allows one to contribute a disproportionate number of arguments. And Nemeth reports that in experiments on minority influence, as in the studies dealing with group polarization, the position supported by the most arguments usually wins. Talkative group members are usually influential (Mullen & others, 1989).

Self-Confidence

Consistency and persistence convey self-confidence. Furthermore, Nemeth and Joel Wachtler (1974) reported that any behavior by a minority that conveys self-confidence, such as taking the head seat at the table, tends to raise self-doubts among the majority. By being firm and forceful, the minority's apparent self-assurance can prompt the majority to reconsider its position. This is especially so on matters of opinion rather than fact. In research at Italy's University of Padova, Anne Maass and her colleagues (1996) report that minorities are less persuasive regarding fact ("From which country does Italy import most of its raw oil?") than regarding attitude ("From which country should Italy import most of its raw oil?").

Defections from the Majority

A persistent minority punctures any illusion of unanimity. When a minority consistently doubts the majority wisdom, majority members become freer to express their own doubts and might even switch to the minority position. In research with University of Pittsburgh students, John Levine (1989) found that a minority person who had defected from the majority was more persuasive than a consistent minority voice. In her jury-simulation experiments, Nemeth found that once defections begin, others often soon follow, initiating a snowball effect.

Are these factors that strengthen minority influence unique to minorities? Sharon Wolf and Bibb Latané (1985; Wolf, 1987) and Russell Clark (1995) believe not. They argue that the same social forces work for both majorities and minorities. Informational and normative influence fuels both group polarization and minority influence. And if consistency, self-confidence, and defections from the other side strengthen the minority, such variables also strengthen a majority. The social impact of any position depends on the strength, immediacy, and number of those who support it. Minorities have less influence than majorities simply because they are smaller.

Anne Maass and Russell Clark (1984, 1986) agree with Moscovici that minorities are more likely to convert people to *accepting* their views. And from their analyses of how groups evolve over time, John Levine and Richard Moreland (1985) conclude that new recruits to a group exert a different type of minority influence than do longtime members. Newcomers exert influence through the attention they receive and the group awareness they trigger in the oldtimers. Established members feel freer to dissent and to exert leadership.

There is a delightful irony in this new emphasis on how individuals can influence the group. Until recently, the idea that the minority could sway the majority was itself a minority view in social psychology. Nevertheless, by arguing consistently and forcefully, Moscovici, Nemeth, and others have convinced the majority of group-influence researchers that minority influence is a phenomenon worthy of study.

*I*S LEADERSHIP MINORITY INFLUENCE?

One example of the power of individuals is **leadership,** the process by which certain individuals mobilize and guide groups. Leadership matters, note Robert Hogan and associates (1994). In 1910, the Norwegians and English engaged in an epic race to the South Pole. The Norwegians, effectively led by Roald Amundsen, made it. The English, ineptly led by Robert Falcon Scott, did not; Scott and three team members died. Abraham Lincoln's Civil War army was going nowhere until Lincoln appointed Ulysses S. Grant as its leader. Some coaches move from team to team, transforming losers into winners each time.

Some leaders are formally appointed or elected; others emerge informally as the group interacts. What makes for good leadership often depends on the situation—the best person to lead the engineering team might not make the best leader of the sales force. Some people excel at *task leadership*—at organizing work, setting standards, and focusing on goal attainment. Others excel at *social leadership*—at building teamwork, mediating conflicts, and being supportive.

Task leaders often have a directive style, which can work well if the leader is bright enough to give good orders (Fiedler, 1987). Being goal oriented, such leaders also keep the group's attention and effort focused on its mission. Experiments show that the combination of specific, challenging goals and periodic progress reports helps motivate high achievement (Locke & Latham, 1990).

Social leaders often have a democratic style—one that delegates authority, welcomes input from team members, and, as we have seen, helps prevent groupthink. Many experiments reveal that such leadership is good for morale. Group members usually feel more satisfied when they participate in making decisions (Spector, 1986; Vanderslice & others, 1987). Given control over their tasks, workers also become more motivated to achieve (Burger, 1987). People who value good group feeling and take pride in achievement therefore thrive under democratic leadership.

Democratic leadership can be seen in the move by many businesses toward participative management, a management style common in Sweden and Japan (Naylor, 1990; Sundstrom & others, 1990). Ironically, a major influence on this "Japanese-style" management was MIT social psychologist Kurt Lewin. In laboratory and factory experiments, Lewin and his students demonstrated the benefits of inviting workers to participate in decision making. Shortly before World War II, Lewin visited Japan and explained his findings to industrial and academic leaders (Nisbett & Ross, 1991). Japan's collectivist culture provided a receptive audience for Lewin's ideas about teamwork. Eventually, his influence circled back to North America.

The once-popular "great person" theory of leadership—that all great leaders share certain traits—has fallen into disrepute. Effective leadership styles, we now know, vary with the situations. People who know what they are doing might resent task leadership, those who don't know what they're doing might welcome it. Recently, however, social psychologists have again wondered if there might be qualities that mark a good leader in many situations (Hogan & others, 1994). British social psychologists Peter Smith and Monir Tayeb (1989) report that studies done in India, Taiwan, and Iran have found that the most effective supervisors in coal mines, banks, and government offices score high on tests of *both* task and social leadership. They are actively concerned with how work is progressing *and* sensitive to the needs of their subordinates.

Studies also reveal that many effective leaders of laboratory groups, work teams, and large corporations exhibit the behaviors that help make a minority view persuasive. Such leaders engender trust by *consistently* sticking to their goals. And they often exude a *self-confident* charisma that kindles the allegiance of their followers (Bennis, 1984; House & Singh, 1987). Charismatic leaders typically have a compelling *vision* of some desired state of affairs, an ability to *communicate* this to others in clear and simple language, and enough optimism and faith in their group to *inspire* others to follow.

To be sure, groups also influence their leaders. Sometimes those at the front of the herd have simply sensed where it is already heading. Political candidates know how to read the opinion polls. A leader who deviates too radically from the group's standards might be rejected. Smart leaders usually remain with the majority and spend their influence prudently. Nevertheless, effective individual leaders can sometimes exhibit a type of minority influence by mobilizing and guiding their group's energy.

In rare circumstances, the right traits matched with the right situation yield history-making greatness, notes Dean Keith Simonton (1994). To have a Winston Churchill or a Margaret Thatcher, a Thomas Jefferson or a Karl Marx, an Abraham Lincoln or a Martin Luther King, Jr., takes the right person in the right place at the right time. When an apt combination of intelligence, skill, determination, self-confidence, and social charisma meets a rare opportunity, the result is sometimes a championship, a Nobel Prize, or a social revolution. Just ask Rosa Parks.

CONCEPTS TO REMEMBER

Reactance   A motive to protect or restore one's sense of freedom. Reactance arises when someone threatens our freedom of action.

Leadership   The process by which certain group members motivate and guide the group.

PART FOUR

❖

Social Relations

Having explored how we do social psychology (Part One), and how we think about (Part Two) and influence (Part Three) one another, we come to social psychology's third facet—how we relate to one another. Our feelings and actions toward other people are sometimes negative, sometimes positive.

The upcoming modules on prejudice, aggression, and conflict examine the unpleasant aspects of human relations: Why do we dislike, even despise, one another? Why and when do we hurt one another?

Then in the modules on conflict resolution, liking, loving, and helping, we explore the more pleasant aspects: How can social conflicts be justly and amicably resolved? Why do we like or love particular people? When will we offer help to others?

MODULE

19

❖

The Dislike of Diversity

P rejudice comes in many forms—against "northeastern liberals" or "southern rednecks," against Arab "terrorists" or Christian "fundamentalists," against people who are short, or fat, or homely. Consider a few actual examples:

- In 1961, African American Charlayne Hunter, now PBS newscaster Charlayne Hunter-Gault, needed a federal judge to compel the University of Georgia to admit her. A week after she enrolled, state officials asked the court whether they also were compelled to allow her to eat on campus (Menand, 1991).

- Prejudice against girls and women is sometimes subtle, sometimes devastating. Nowhere in the modern world is it an accepted practice to leave female infants on a hillside to die of exposure, as was the occasional practice in ancient Greece. Yet in many developing countries, death rates for girls exceed those for boys.

- When men seek roles traditionally associated with women, discrimination can run in the other direction. Elizabeth Turner and Anthony Pratkanis (1994) sent identical job-inquiry letters, which pretended to be from a community-college student in a child-care program, to 56 child-care centers and preschools in seven cities. When the letter was signed "Mary E. Johnson," nearly half the centers returned a stamped postcard, checking "we would be interested in discussing a position." When the letter was signed "David E. Johnson," only 1 in 10 replied with similar encouragement.

- A group of homosexual students at the University of Illinois announced that the motto for one spring day would be: "If you are gay, wear blue jeans today." When the day dawned, many students who usually wore jeans woke up with an urge to dress up in a skirt or slacks. The gay group had made its point—that attitudes toward homosexuals are such that many students would rather give up their usual clothes than be suspected of being gay (*RCAgenda*, 1979).

WHAT IS PREJUDICE?

Prejudice, stereotyping, discrimination, racism, sexism: The meanings of the terms often overlap. Before seeking to understand prejudice, let's clarify the terms. Each of the situations just described involved a negative evaluation of some group. And that is the essence of **prejudice:** a negative prejudgment of a group and its individual members. Prejudice biases us against a person based solely on our identifying the person with a particular group.

Prejudice is an attitude. An attitude is a distinct combination of feelings, inclinations to act, and beliefs. This combination is the ABC of attitudes: *a*ffect (feelings), *b*ehavioral tendency (inclination to act), and *c*ognition (beliefs). Prejudiced people might *dislike* people who are different from themselves and *behave* in a discriminatory manner, *believing* them to be ignorant or dangerous or the like.

The negative evaluations that mark prejudice can stem from emotional associations, from the need to justify behavior, or from negative beliefs, called **stereotypes.** To stereotype is to generalize. To simplify the world, we generalize all the time: The British are reserved; Americans are outgoing. Professors are absentminded. Women who assume the title *Ms.* are more assertive and ambitious than those who call themselves "Miss" or "Mrs." (Dion, 1987; Dion & Cota, 1991; Dion & Schuller, 1991). Such generalizations can have a germ of truth. People do in fact differ.

A problem with stereotypes arises when they are *overgeneralized* or just plain wrong. To presume that most American welfare clients are African American is to overgeneralize, because it just isn't so. Another problem arises when people attribute negatively evaluated differences to racial biology, ignoring toxic social forces. People might see that race correlates with violent crime, but not see an underlying corroding factor: poverty. Take out the "confounding" poverty factor (for example, by comparing middle-class Blacks and Whites) and the race difference often disappears. Violence is rather like tuberculosis, which occurs more often among African Americans but has nothing to do with race per se (Eron & others, 1997). Rather, both violence and tuberculosis come with poverty and the associated poor housing and poor health care. Rich Black folks aren't at risk for TB. Poor White folks are.

Prejudice is a negative *attitude;* **discrimination** is negative *behavior.* Discriminatory behavior often, but not always, has its source in prejudicial attitudes (Dovidio & others, 1996). As an earlier module emphasized, attitudes and behavior are often loosely linked, partly because our behavior reflects more than our inner convictions. Prejudiced attitudes need not breed hostile acts, nor does all oppression spring from prejudice. **Racism** and **sexism** are institutional practices that discriminate, even when there is no prejudicial intent.

If word-of-mouth hiring practices in an all-White business have the effect of excluding potential non-White employees, the practice could be called racist—even if an employer intended no discrimination. This module explores the roots and fruits of prejudiced attitudes. Mindful that racist and sexist policies need not spring from prejudiced attitudes (though in time they often feed such), I leave it to sociologists and political scientists to explore racism and sexism in their institutional forms.

HOW PERVASIVE IS PREJUDICE?

Is prejudice inevitable? Let's look at the most heavily studied examples, racial and gender prejudice.

Racial Prejudice

In the context of the whole world, every race is a minority. Non-Hispanic Whites, for example, are but one-fifth of the world's people and will be but one-eighth within another half-century. Thanks to mobility and migration during the past two centuries, the world's races now intermingle, in relations that are sometimes hostile, sometimes amiable.

To a molecular biologist, skin color is a pretty trivial human characteristic, one controlled by a minuscule genetic difference between races. Moreover, nature doesn't cluster races in neatly defined categories. It is we and he, not nature, that labels Tiger Woods (whose ancestry is 25 percent African) as "African American" rather than "Asian American" (he is also 25 percent Thai and 25 percent Chinese)—or even as Native American or Dutch (he is one-eighth each). (He has labelled himself as "Cablinasian," representing his *C*aucasian, *Bl*ack, *In*dian, and *Asian* ancestry.)

Is Racial Prejudice Disappearing?
In 1942, most White Americans agreed: "There should be separate sections for Negroes on streetcars and buses" (Hyman & Sheatsley, 1956). Today, the question would seem bizarre, because such blatant prejudice has nearly disappeared. In 1942, fewer than a third of all Whites (only 1 in 50 in the South) supported school integration; by 1980, support for it

was 90 percent. Considering what a thin slice of history is covered by the years since 1942, or even since slavery was practiced, the changes are dramatic. In Canada, too, acceptance of ethnic diversity and various immigrant groups has increased in recent decades (Berry & Kalin, 1995).

African Americans' attitudes also have changed since the 1940s, when Kenneth Clark and Mamie Clark (1947) demonstrated that many held anti-Black prejudices. In making its historic 1954 decision declaring segregated schools unconstitutional, the Supreme Court found it noteworthy that when the Clarks gave African American children a choice between Black dolls and White dolls, most chose the White. In studies from the 1950s through the 1970s, Black children were increasingly likely to prefer Black dolls, and adult Blacks came to view Blacks and Whites as similar in traits such as intelligence, laziness, and dependability (Jackman & Senter, 1981; Smedley & Bayton, 1978).

So, shall we conclude that racial prejudice is extinct in countries such as the United States and Canada? No. Although no longer fashionable, racial prejudice still exists. It usually surfaces when a person thinks it is safe to express it.

In the United States, prejudice appears among the small proportion of Whites who, as Figure 19-1 shows, openly disdain Blacks. In other cultures, open ethnic hostilities are still common, as illustrated by Serbs and Muslims in the former Yugoslavia, and Tutsis and Hutus in Rwanda.

Questions concerning intimate interracial contacts still detect prejudice. "I would probably feel uncomfortable dancing with a Black person in a public place" detects more racial feeling than "I would probably feel uncomfortable riding a bus with a Black person." Thus many people who welcome diverse people as co-workers or classmates still socialize, date, and marry within their own race. This helps explain why, in a survey of students at 390 colleges and universities, 53 percent of African American students felt excluded from social activities (Hurtado & others, 1994). (Such feelings were reported by 24 percent of Asian Americans, 16 percent of Mexican Americans, and 6 percent of European Americans.) Such majority-minority relationships transcend race. On NBA basketball teams, minority players (in this case, Whites) feel similarly detached from their group's socializing (Schoenfeld, 1995).

This phenomenon of *greatest prejudice in the most intimate social realms* seems universal. In India, people who accept the caste system will typically allow someone from a lower caste into their home but would not consider marrying such a person (Sharma, 1981). In a national survey of Americans, 75 percent said they would "shop at a store owned by a homosexual" but only 39 percent would "see a homosexual doctor" (Henry, 1994).

Subtle Forms of Prejudice

Much prejudice remains hidden, until evoked by circumstance. When White students indicate racial attitudes while hooked up to a supposed lie detector, they admit to prejudice. Other researchers have invited people to

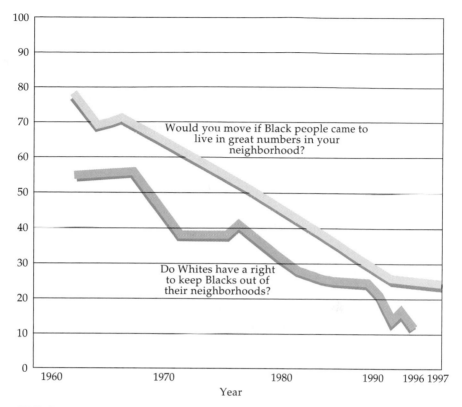

FIGURE 19-1
Expressed racial attitudes of White Americans from 1963 to 1997. (Data from
Gallup and National Opinion Research Center Surveys Schuman & others, 1998).

evaluate someone's behavior, that someone being either White or Black.
Birt Duncan (1976) had White students at the University of California,
Irvine, observe a videotape of one man lightly shoving another during a
brief argument. When a White shoved a Black man, only 13 percent of the
observers rated the act as "violent behavior." They interpreted the shove
as "playing around" or "dramatizing." Not so when a Black shoved a
White man: Then, 73 percent said the act was "violent."

Many experiments have assessed people's *behavior* toward Blacks
and Whites. Whites are equally helpful to any person in need—except
when the needy person is remote (say, a wrong-number caller with a
Black accent who needs a message relayed). Likewise, when asked to use
electric shocks to "teach" a task, White people give no more (if anything,
they give less) shock to a Black than to a White person—except when
they are angered or when the recipient can't retaliate or know who did it
(Crosby & others, 1980; Rogers & Prentice-Dunn, 1981) (Figure 19-2).

Intensity and duration of shock

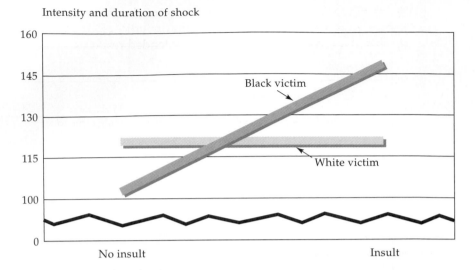

FIGURE 19-2
Does anger trigger latent prejudice? When White students administered electric
shock, supposedly as part of a "behavior-modification experiment," they
behaved less aggressively toward an agreeable Black victim than toward a White
victim. But when the victim insulted the subjects, they responded with more
aggression if the victim was Black. (Data from Rogers & Prentice-Dunn, 1981.)

Thus, discriminatory behavior surfaces when a prejudiced behavior can
hide behind the screen of some other motive.

As blatant prejudice subsides, automatic emotional reactions linger.
Patricia Devine and her colleagues (1989, 1995) report that persons low
and high in prejudice are aware of the same stereotypes and often have
similar automatic reactions. They differ because the low-prejudice person
consciously tries to suppress prejudicial thoughts and feelings. It's like
breaking a bad habit, says Devine. Try as we might to suppress unwanted
thoughts—thoughts about food, thoughts about romance with a friend's
partner, judgmental thoughts about another group—they sometimes refuse to go away (Macrae & others, 1994; Wegner & Erber, 1992). Unwanted
thoughts and feelings often persist.

A raft of new experiments by researchers at Yale University (Blair &
Banaji, 1996), Indiana University (Fazio & others, 1995), the University of
Colorado (Wittenbrink & others, 1997), and New York University (Bargh
& others, 1996) have confirmed the phenomenon of automatic stereotyping and prejudice. These studies briefly flash words or faces that "prime"
(automatically activate) stereotypes of some racial, gender, or age group.
Without the person's awareness, their activated stereotypes might then
bias their behavior. Having been primed with images associated with
African Americans, for example, they might react with more hostility to an

experimenter's annoying request. Many of the subjects, mind you, are people who usually express little or no prejudice. Rather, their prejudice operates largely as an unconscious, unintended response.

Gender Prejudice

How pervasive is prejudice against women? In Module 10, we examined gender-role norms—people's ideas about how women and men *ought* to behave. Here we consider gender *stereotypes*—people's beliefs about how women and men *do* behave.

Gender Stereotypes

From research on stereotypes, two conclusions are indisputable: Strong gender stereotypes exist, and, as often happens, members of the stereotyped group accept the stereotypes. Men and women agree that you *can* judge the book by its sexual cover. Analyzing responses from a University of Michigan survey, Mary Jackman and Mary Senter (1981) found that gender stereotypes were much stronger than racial stereotypes. For example, only 22 percent of men thought the two sexes are equally "emotional." Of the remaining 78 percent, those who believed females are more emotional outnumbered by 15 to 1 those who thought males are. And what did the women believe? To within 1 percentage point, their responses were identical.

Consider, too, a study by Natalie Porter, Florence Geis, and Joyce Jennings Walstedt (1983). They showed students pictures of "a group of graduate students working as a team on a research project" (Figure 19-3). Then they gave them a test of "first impressions," asking them to guess who contributed most to the group. When the group was either all male or all female, the students overwhelmingly chose the person at the head of the table. When the group was mixed sex, a man occupying that position was again overwhelmingly chosen but a woman occupying that position was usually ignored. Each of the men in Figure 19-3 received more of the leadership choices than all three of the women combined! This stereotype of men as leaders was true not only of women as well as men, but also of feminists as well as nonfeminists. How pervasive are gender stereotypes? Very.

Remember that stereotypes are generalizations about a group of people and can be true, false, or overgeneralized from a kernel of truth. As we previously noted, the average man and woman do differ somewhat in social connectedness, empathy, social power, aggressiveness, and sexual initiative (though not in intelligence). Do we then conclude that gender stereotypes are accurate? Often they are, observed Janet Swim (1994). She found that Pennsylvania State University students' stereotypes of men's and women's restlessness, nonverbal sensitivity, aggressiveness, and so forth were reasonable approximations of actual gender differences. Moreover, such stereotypes have persisted across time, leading some evolutionary psychologists to believe they reflect innate, stable reality (Lueptow & others, 1995).

FIGURE 19-3
Which one of these people would you guess is the group's strongest contributor?
Shown this picture, college students usually guessed one of the two men,
although those shown photos of same-sex groups most commonly guessed the
person at the head of the table.

But sometimes gender stereotypes exaggerate small differences, as
Carol Lynn Martin (1987) concluded after surveying visitors to the University of British Columbia. She asked them to check which of several traits described them and to estimate what percentage of North American males
and females had each trait. Males were indeed slightly more likely than females to describe themselves as assertive and dominant and were slightly
less likely to describe themselves as tender and compassionate. But stereotypes of these differences were exaggerated: The people perceived North
American males as almost twice as likely as females to be assertive and
dominant and roughly half as likely to be tender and compassionate.

Stereotypes (beliefs) are not prejudices (attitudes). Stereotypes can
support prejudice. But then again one might believe, without prejudice,
that men and women are "different yet equal." Let us therefore see how researchers probe for gender prejudice.

Gender Attitudes
Judging from what people tell survey researchers, attitudes toward
women have changed as rapidly as racial attitudes. In 1937, one-third of
Americans said they would vote for a qualified woman whom their party
nominated for president; by 1988, 9 in 10 said they would (Figure 19-4). In

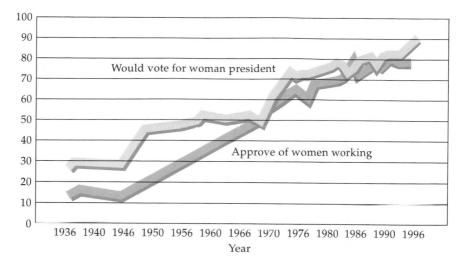

FIGURE 19-4
Prejudice against women: An idea whose time has passed? The percentage of
Americans who say that they approve of a married woman's working for money
if she has a capable husband and that they would vote for a qualified woman
candidate for president has steadily increased since the mid 1930s. (Data from
Niemi & others, 1989; Smith, 1997)

1967, 56 percent of first-year American college students agreed that "The
activities of married women are best confined to the home and family"; by
1996, only 24 percent agreed (Astin & others, 1987; Sax & others, 1997).

Alice Eagly and her associates (1991) and Geoffrey Haddock and Mark
Zanna (1994) also report that people don't respond to women with gut-
level negative emotions as they do to certain other groups. Most people like
"women" more than they like "men." They perceive women as more understanding, kind, and helpful. Thus, a *favorable* stereotype—which Eagly
(1994) dubs the *women-are-wonderful effect*—results in a favorable attitude.

So, is gender bias fast becoming extinct in Western countries? Has the
women's movement nearly completed its work? As with race prejudice,
blatant gender prejudice is dying, but subtle bias lives. The bogus-pipeline
method, for example, exposes bias. Men who believe an experimenter can
read their true attitudes with a sensitive lie detector express less sympathy
toward women's rights. Even on paper-and-pencil questionnaires, Janet
Swim and her co-researchers (1995, 1997) have found a subtle ("modern")
sexism that parallels subtle ("modern") racism. Both appear in denials of
discrimination and in antagonism toward efforts to promote equality.

We can also detect bias in behavior. That's what a research team led by
Ian Ayres (1991) did while visiting 90 Chicago-area car dealers and using
a uniform strategy to negotiate the lowest price on a new car that cost the
dealer about $11,000. White males were given a final price that averaged

$11,362; White females were given an average price of $11,504; Black males were given an average price of $11,783; and Black females were given an average price of $12,237.

Most women know that gender bias exists. They believe that sex discrimination affects most working women, as shown by the lower salaries for women and especially for jobs, such as child care, that are filled mostly by women. Garbage haulers (mostly men) make more than preschool teachers (mostly women). Curiously, however, Faye Crosby and her colleagues (1989) have repeatedly found that most women deny feeling personally discriminated against. Discrimination, they believe, is something *other* women face. Their employer is not villainous. They are doing better than the average woman. Hearing no complaints, managers—even in discriminatory organizations—can persuade themselves that justice prevails. Similar denials of *personal* disadvantage, while perceiving discrimination against one's *group,* occur among unemployed people, out-of-the-closet lesbians, African Americans, and Canadian minorities (Dion & Kawakami, 1996; Taylor & others, 1990).

In the world beyond democratic Western countries, gender discrimination is sometimes drastic, as in countries where expectant parents act on their preference for a boy. In South Korea, male births exceed female births by 14 percent, in China by 18 percent. Sex-selective abortions and infanticide in China and India have led to 76,000,000—let's say that slowly . . . seventy-six *million*—"missing women" (Klasen, 1994; Kristof, 1993).

To conclude, overt prejudice against people of color and against women is far less common today than it was four decades ago. The same is true of prejudice against homosexual people. Nevertheless, techniques that are sensitive to subtle prejudice still detect widespread bias. And in parts of the world, gender prejudice is literally deadly. We therefore need to look carefully and closely at the problem of prejudice and its causes.

CONCEPTS TO REMEMBER

Prejudice   A negative prejudgment of a group and its individual members.

Stereotype   A belief about the personal attributes of a group of people. Stereotypes can be overgeneralized, inaccurate, and resistant to new information.

Discrimination   Unjustifiable negative behavior toward a group or its members.

Racism   (1) An individual's prejudicial attitudes and discriminatory behavior toward people of a given race, or (2) institutional practices (even if not motivated by prejudice) that subordinate people of a given race.

Sexism   (1) An individual's prejudicial attitudes and discriminatory behavior toward people of a given sex, or (2) institutional practices (even if not motivated by prejudice) that subordinate people of a given sex.

20

❖

The Roots of Prejudice

Within recent memory, whole countries have been ripped apart by ethnic tensions. Israel's Palestinians and Jews, Bosnia's Serbs and Muslims, Rwanda's Tutsis and Hutus, have murdered, bombed, and pillaged one another. Around the world, gender prejudice and discrimination persist, too. Worldwide, two-thirds of children without basic schooling are girls; thus, 80 percent of the world's men, but only 64 percent of women are illiterate (*Women of our World*, 1998). What are the roots of such prejudice?

Prejudice springs from several sources. Prejudice might express our sense of who we are and gain us social acceptance. It might defend our sense of self against anxiety that arises from insecurity or inner conflict. And it might promote our self-interest by supporting what brings us pleasure and opposing what doesn't. Consider first how prejudice can function to defend self-esteem and social position.

SOCIAL SOURCES OF PREJUDICE

Unequal Status and Prejudice

A principle to remember: *Unequal status breeds prejudice.* Masters view slaves as lazy, irresponsible, lacking ambition—that is, as having traits that they believe justify slavery. Historians debate the forces that create unequal status. But once these inequalities exist, prejudice helps justify the economic and social superiority of those who have wealth and power. You tell me the economic relationship between two groups, and I'll predict the intergroup attitudes. Stereotypes rationalize unequal status (Yzerbyt & others, 1997).

In times of conflict, attitudes easily adjust to behavior. People often view enemies as subhuman and depersonalize them with a label. During World War II, the Japanese people became, to many Americans, "the Japs." After the war was over, they became "the intelligent, hardworking Japanese." Attitudes are amazingly adaptable.

Gender stereotypes, too, help rationalize gender roles. After studying these stereotypes worldwide, John Williams and Deborah Best (1990b) noted that if women provide most of the care to young children, it is reassuring to think women are naturally nurturant. And if males run the businesses, hunt, and fight wars, it is comforting to suppose that men are aggressive, independent, and adventurous. In experiments, people perceive members of unknown groups as having traits that suit their roles (Hoffman & Hurst, 1990).

Discrimination's Impact: The Self-Fulfilling Prophecy

Attitudes can coincide with the social hierarchy not only as a rationalization for it but also because discrimination affects its victims. "One's reputation," wrote Gordon Allport (1958), "cannot be hammered, hammered, hammered into one's head without doing something to one's character" (p. 139). If we could snap our fingers and end all discrimination, it would be naive then to say: "The tough times are all over, folks! You can now put on suits or dresses and be attaché-carrying executives and professionals." When the oppression ends, its effects linger, like a societal hangover.

In his classic book *The Nature of Prejudice*, Allport catalogued 15 possible effects of victimization. Allport believed these reactions were reducible to two basic types—those that involve blaming oneself (withdrawal, self-hate, aggression against one's own group) and those that involve blaming external causes (fighting back, suspiciousness, increased group pride). If the net results are negative—say, higher rates of crime—people can use them to justify the discrimination that helps maintain them: "If we let those people in our nice neighborhood, property values will plummet."

Does discrimination affect its victims in this way? We must be careful not to overstate the point. The soul and style of Black culture is for many a proud heritage, not just a response to victimization (Jones, 1983). Thus while White youth are learning to deemphasize ethnic differences and avoid stereotypes, African American youth "are increasingly taking pride in their ethnicity and positively valuing ethnic differences," report Charles Judd and his co-researchers (1995). Cultural differences need not imply social deficits.

Nevertheless, social beliefs *can* be self-confirming, as demonstrated in a clever pair of experiments by Carl Word, Mark Zanna, and Joel Cooper (1974). In the first experiment, Princeton University White men interviewed White and Black job applicants. When the applicant was Black, the interviewers sat farther away, ended the interview 25 percent sooner, and made 50 percent more speech errors than when the applicant was White. Imagine being interviewed by someone who sat at a distance, stammered, and ended the interview rather quickly. Would it affect your performance or your feelings about the interviewer?

To find out, the researchers conducted a second experiment in which trained interviewers treated students as the interviewers in the first experiment had treated either the White or Black applicants. When videotapes of the interviews were later rated, those who were treated like the Blacks in the first experiment seemed more nervous and less effective. Moreover, the interviewees could themselves sense a difference; those treated as were the Blacks judged their interviewers as less adequate and less friendly. The experimenters concluded that part of "the 'problem' of Black performance resides . . . within the interaction setting itself."

Recall, too, that social beliefs can be self-fulfilling. Prejudice affects its targets (Swim & Stangor, 1998). Placed in a situation where others expect you to perform poorly, your anxiety might cause you to confirm the belief. I am a short mid-fifties guy. When I join a pickup basketball game with bigger, younger players, my suspecting that they expect me to be a detriment to their team tends to undermine my confidence and performance. Claude Steele and his colleagues call this phenomenon **stereotype threat**—*a self-confirming apprehension that one's behavior will verify a negative stereotype.*

In several experiments, Steven Spencer and Steele (1997) gave a very difficult math test to men and women students who had similar math abilities and course experience. Told that men and women usually perform equally on the test, the women's performance consistently equaled the men's. Told that women usually underperform men on the test, the women dramatically confirmed the stereotype. Frustrated by the extremely difficult items, they apparently felt added apprehension, which undermined their performance.

SOCIAL IDENTITY

We humans are a group-bound species. Our ancestral history prepares us to feed and protect ourselves—to live—in groups. Humans cheer on their groups, kill for their groups, die for their groups. We define ourselves by our groups, note Australian social psychologists John Turner (1981, 1987, 1991) and Michael Hogg (1992, 1996). Our self-concept—our sense of who we are—contains not just our personal identity (our sense of our personal attributes and attitudes) but our social identity. Fiona identifies herself as a woman, an Aussie, a labourite, a Melbourne University student, a member of the MacDonald family. We carry such **social identities** like playing cards, playing them as appropriate.

Working with the late British social psychologist Henri Tajfel, Turner proposed *social identity theory.* Turner and Tajfel [pronounced TOSH-fel] assumed the following:

- *We categorize:* We find it useful to put people, ourselves included, into categories. To label someone as a Hindu, a Scot, or a bus driver is a shorthand way of saying some other things about the person.
- *We identify:* We associate ourselves with certain groups (our **in-groups**).
- *We compare:* We contrast our groups with other groups (**outgroups**), with a favorable bias toward our own group.

We evaluate ourselves partly by our group memberships. Having a sense of "we-ness" strengthens our self concept. It *feels* good. We seek not only *respect* for ourselves but *pride* in our groups (Smith & Tyler, 1997). Moreover, seeing our groups as superior helps us feel even better.

Lacking a positive personal identity, people often seek self-esteem by identifying with a group. Thus, many youths find pride, power, and identity in gang affiliations. Many superpatriots define themselves by their national identities (Staub, 1997). And some people feeling at loose ends find identity in their associations with new religious movements, self-help groups, or fraternal clubs.

Ingroup Bias

The group definition of who you are—your race, religion, sex, academic major—implies a definition of who you are not. The circle that includes "us" (the ingroup) excludes "them" (the outgroup). Thus, the mere experience of being formed into groups can promote **ingroup bias.** Ask children, "Which are better, the children in your school or the children at [another school nearby]?" Virtually all will say their own school has the better children.

In a series of experiments, Tajfel and Michael Billig (1974; Tajfel, 1970, 1981, 1982) discovered how little it takes to provoke favoritism toward *us* and unfairness toward *them.* In one study Tajfel and Billig had British teenagers evaluate modern abstract paintings and then told them that they and some others had favored the art of Paul Klee over that of Wassily Kandinsky. Finally, without ever meeting the other members of their group, the teens divided some money among members of both groups.

In these experiments and others since, defining groups even in this trivial way produced favoritism. David Wilder (1981) summarized the typical result: "When given the opportunity to divide 15 points [worth money], subjects generally award 9 or 10 points to their own group and 5 or 6 points to the other group." This bias occurs with both sexes and with people of all ages and nationalities, though especially with people from individualist cultures (Gudykunst, 1989). (People in communal cultures identify more with all their peers and so treat everyone more the same.)

We also are more prone to ingroup bias when our group is small and lower in status relative to the outgroup (Ellemers & others, 1997; Mullen & others, 1992). When we're part of a small group surrounded by a larger group, we are also more conscious of our group membership; when our ingroup is the majority, we think less about it. To be a foreign student, to be gay or lesbian, or to be of a minority race at some social gathering is to feel one's social identity more keenly and to react accordingly.

Even forming conspicuous groups on *no* logical basis—say, merely by composing groups X and Y with the flip of a coin—will produce some ingroup bias (Billig & Tajfel, 1973; Brewer & Silver, 1978; Locksley & others, 1980). In Kurt Vonnegut's novel *Slapstick*, computers gave everyone a new middle name; all "Daffodil-11's" then felt unity with one another and distance from "Raspberry-13's." Self-serving bias rides again, enabling people to achieve a more positive social identity: "We" are better than "they," even when "we" and "they" are alike.

Conformity

Once established, prejudice is maintained largely by inertia. If prejudice is socially accepted, many people will follow the path of least resistance and conform to the fashion. They will act not so much out of a need to hate as out of a need to be liked and accepted.

Thomas Pettigrew's (1958) studies of Whites in South Africa and the American South revealed that during the 1950s those who conformed most to other social norms were also most prejudiced; those who were less conforming mirrored less of the surrounding prejudice. The price of nonconformity was painfully clear to the ministers of Little Rock, Arkansas, where the U.S. Supreme Court's 1954 school desegregation decision was implemented. Most ministers favored integration but usually only privately; they feared that advocating it openly would lose them church members and contributions (Campbell & Pettigrew, 1959). Or consider the Indiana steelworkers and West Virginia coal miners of the same era. In the mills and the mines, the workers accepted integration, but in their neighborhoods, the norm was rigid segregation (Minard, 1952; Reitzes, 1953). Prejudice was clearly *not* a manifestation of "sick" personalities but simply of the social norms.

Conformity also maintains gender prejudice. "If we have come to think that the nursery and the kitchen are the natural sphere of a woman," wrote George Bernard Shaw in an 1891 essay, "we have done so exactly as English children come to think that a cage is the natural sphere of a parrot—because they have never seen one anywhere else." Children who *have* seen women elsewhere, such as children of employed women, have less stereotyped views of men and women (Hoffman, 1977).

Segregation is one way that social institutions (schools, government, the media) bolster widespread prejudice. Politics is another. Political leaders can both reflect and reinforce prevailing attitudes. When Arkansas Governor Orval Faubus barred the doors of Central High School in Little Rock, he was doing more than representing his constituents; he was legitimating their views. When advertisers, photographers, and artists picture men's faces and women's bodies, this "face-ism" makes men seem more intelligent and ambitious (Archer & others, 1983; Schwarz & Kurz, 1989).

In all of this, there is a message of hope. If prejudice is not deeply ingrained in personality, then as fashions change and new norms evolve, prejudice can diminish. And so it has.

EMOTIONAL SOURCES OF PREJUDICE

Although prejudice is bred by social situations, emotional factors often add fuel to the fire: Frustration can feed prejudice, as can personality factors like status needs and authoritarian tendencies. Let's see how.

Frustration and Aggression: The Scapegoat Theory

Pain and frustration (the blocking of a goal) often evoke hostility. When the cause of our frustration is intimidating or vague, we often redirect our hostility. This phenomenon of "displaced aggression" might have contributed to the lynchings of African Americans in the South after the Civil War. Between 1882 and 1930, there were more lynchings in years when cotton prices were low and economic frustration was therefore presumably high (Hepworth & West, 1988; Hovland & Sears, 1940).

Targets for this displaced aggression vary. Following their defeat in World War I and their country's subsequent economic chaos, many Germans saw Jews as villains. Long before Hitler came to power, one German leader explained: "The Jew is just convenient. . . . If there were no Jews, the anti-Semites would have to invent them" (quoted by G. W. Allport, 1958, p. 325). In earlier centuries people vented their fear and hostility on people they labeled as witches, whom they sometimes burned or drowned in public.

A famous experiment by Neal Miller and Richard Bugelski (1948) confirmed the scapegoat theory. They asked college-age men working at a summer camp to state their attitudes toward Japanese and Mexicans. Some did so before, and then after, being forced to stay in camp to take tests rather than attend a long-awaited free evening at a local theater. Compared to a control group that did not undergo this frustration, the deprived group afterward displayed increased prejudice. As new studies confirm, people put in unhappy moods often think and act more negatively toward outgroups (Esses & Zanna, 1995; Forgas & Fiedler, 1996). Passions provoke prejudice.

One source of frustration is competition. When two groups compete for jobs, housing, or social prestige, one group's goal fulfillment can become the other group's frustration. Thus, **realistic group conflict theory** suggests that prejudice arises when groups compete for scarce resources. A corresponding ecological principle, Gause's law, states that maximum competition will exist between species with identical needs. In western Europe, for example, some people agree to the statement that "over the last five years people like yourself have been economically worse off than most [name of country's minority group]." These frustrated people express relatively high levels of blatant prejudice (Pettigrew & Meertens, 1995). In Canada, opposition to immigration since 1975 has gone up and down with the unemployment rate (Palmer, 1996). In America, the strongest anti-Black prejudice occurs among Whites who are closest to Blacks on the socioeconomic ladder (Greeley & Sheatsley, 1971; Pettigrew, 1978; Tumin, 1958). When interests clash, prejudice pays, for some people.

Personality Dynamics

Any two people, with equal reason to feel frustrated or threatened, will often not be equally prejudiced. This suggests that prejudice serves other functions besides advancing competitive self-interest.

Need for Status and Belonging

Status is relative: To perceive ourselves as having status, we need people below us. Thus one psychological benefit of prejudice, or of any status system, is a feeling of superiority. Most of us can recall a time when we took secret satisfaction in another's failure—perhaps seeing a brother or sister punished, or a classmate fail a test. In Europe and North America, prejudice is often greater among those low or slipping on the socioeconomic ladder and among those whose positive self-image is being threatened (Lemyre & Smith, 1985; Pettigrew & others, 1997; Thompson & Crocker, 1985). In one study at Northwestern University, members of lower-status sororities were more disparaging of other sororities than were members of higher-status sororities (Crocker & others, 1987). Perhaps people whose status is secure have less need to feel superior.

But other factors associated with low status could also account for prejudice. Imagine yourself as one of the Arizona State University students who took part in an experiment by Robert Cialdini and Kenneth Richardson (1980). You are walking alone across campus. Someone approaches you and asks your help with a five-minute survey. You agree. After the researcher gives you a brief "creativity test," he deflates you with the news that "you have scored relatively low on the test." The researcher then completes the survey by asking you some evaluative questions about either your school or its traditional rival, the University of Arizona. Would your feelings of failure affect your ratings of either school? Compared with those in a control group whose self-esteem was not threatened, the students who experienced failure gave higher ratings to their own school and lower ratings to their rival.

Apparently, asserting one's social identity by boasting about one's own group and denigrating outgroups can boost one's ego.

James Meindl and Melvin Lerner (1984) found that a humiliating experience—accidentally knocking over a stack of someone's important computer cards—provoked English-speaking Canadian students to express increased hostility toward French-speaking Canadians. And Teresa Amabile and Ann Glazebrook (1982) found that Dartmouth College men who were made to feel insecure judged others' work more harshly. Thinking about your own mortality—by writing a short essay on dying and the emotions aroused by thinking about death—also can provoke enough insecurity to intensify your favoritism toward your ingroup and your prejudice against an outgroup (Greenberg & others, 1990, 1994; Harmon-Jones & others, 1996).

The Authoritarian Personality

The emotional needs that contribute to prejudice are said to predominate in the "authoritarian personality." In the 1940s, University of California, Berkeley, researchers—two of whom had fled Nazi Germany—set out on an urgent research mission: to uncover the psychological roots of an anti-Semitism so poisonous that it caused the slaughter of millions of Jews and turned many millions of Europeans into indifferent spectators. In studies of American adults, Theodor Adorno and his colleagues (1950) discovered that hostility toward Jews often coexisted with hostility toward other minorities. Prejudice appeared to be less an attitude specific to one group than a way of thinking about those who are different. Moreover, these judgmental, **ethno-centric** people shared authoritarian tendencies—an intolerance for weakness, a punitive attitude, and a submissive respect for their ingroup's authorities, as reflected in their agreement with such statements as "Obedience and respect for authority are the most important virtues children should learn."

As children, authoritarian people often were harshly disciplined. This supposedly led them to repress their hostilities and impulses and to "project" them onto outgroups. The insecurity of authoritarian children seemed to predispose them toward an excessive concern with power and status and an inflexible right/wrong way of thinking that made ambiguity difficult to tolerate. Such people therefore tended to be submissive to those with power over them and aggressive or punitive toward those beneath them.

Scholars criticized the research for focusing on right-wing authoritarianism and overlooking dogmatic authoritarianism of the left. Still, its main conclusion has survived: Authoritarian tendencies, sometimes reflected in ethnic tensions, surge during threatening times of economic recession and social upheaval (Doty & others, 1991; Sales, 1973). In contemporary Russia, individuals scoring high in authoritarianism have tended to support a return to Marxist-Leninist ideology and to oppose democratic reform (McFarland & others, 1992, 1996).

Moreover, contemporary studies of right-wing authoritarians by University of Manitoba psychologist Bob Altemeyer (1988, 1992) confirm that there *are* individuals whose fears and hostilities surface as prejudice. Feelings of moral superiority can go hand in hand with brutality toward perceived inferiors.

Different forms of prejudice—toward Blacks, gays and lesbians, women, old people, fat people, AIDS victims, the homeless—*do* tend to coexist in the same individuals (Bierly, 1985; Crandall, 1994; Peterson & others, 1993; Snyder & Ickes, 1985). As Altemeyer concludes, right-wing authoritarians tend to be "equal-opportunity bigots." The same is true of those with a "social dominance orientation" who view people in terms of hierarchies of merit or goodness. By contrast, those with a more communal or universal orientation—who attend to people's similarities and presume that "universal human rights" are enjoyed by "all God's children"—are more welcoming of affirmative action and accepting of those who are different (Phillips & Ziller, 1997; Pratto & others, 1994; Sidanius & others, 1996; Whitley & Lee, 1997).

COGNITIVE SOURCES OF PREJUDICE

Much of the explanation of prejudice so far could have been written in the 1960s, but not what follows. This new look at prejudice, fueled by 1,500 research articles on stereotyping in the last 10 years (Dovidio & others, 1996), applies the new research on social thinking. The basic point is this: Stereotyped beliefs and prejudiced attitudes exist not only because of social conditioning and because they enable people to displace hostilities, but also as by-products of normal thinking processes. Many stereotypes spring less from malice than from how we simplify our complex worlds. They are like perceptual illusions, a by-product of our knack for interpreting the world.

Categorization

One way we simplify our environment is to "categorize"—to organize the world by clustering objects into groups. As a biologist classifies plants and animals, we all tend to classify people. This helps us think about them more easily. If persons in a group are similar, knowing their group can provide useful information with minimal effort (Macrae & others, 1994). Customs inspectors and airplane antihijack personnel are therefore given "profiles" of kinds of individuals they should be suspicious of (Kraut & Poe, 1980).

We find it especially easy and efficient to rely on stereotypes when we are

- pressed for time (Kaplan & others, 1993),
- preoccupied (Gilbert & Hixon, 1991),
- tired (Bodenhausen, 1990),
- emotionally aroused (Esses & others, 1993b; Stroessner & Mackie, 1993), or
- too young to appreciate diversity (Biernat, 1991).

In our current world, ethnicity and sex are powerful ways of categoriz-ing people. Imagine Tom, a 45-year-old African American real estate agent in New Orleans. I suspect that your image of "Black male" predominates over the categories "middle-aged," "businessperson," and "southerner."

Experiments expose our spontaneous categorization of people by race. When subjects view different people making statements, they often forget who said what, yet remember the race of the person who made each state-ment (Hewstone & others, 1991; Stroessner & others, 1990; Taylor & oth-ers, 1978). By itself, such categorization is not prejudice, but it does provide a foundation for prejudice.

Perceived Similarities and Differences

Picture the following objects: apples, chairs, pencils.

There is a strong tendency to see objects within a group as being more uniform than they really are. Were your apples all red? your chairs all straight-backed? your pencils all yellow? It's the same with people. Once we assign people to groups—athletes, drama majors, math professors—we are likely to exaggerate the similarities within groups and the differ-ences between them (S. E. Taylor, 1981; Wilder, 1978). Mere division into groups can create an **outgroup homogeneity effect**—a sense that *they* are "all alike" and different from "us" and "our" group (Ostrom & Sedikides, 1992). Because we generally like people we think are similar to us and dis-like those we perceive as different, the natural result is ingroup bias (Byrne & Wong, 1962; Rokeach & Mezei, 1966; Stein & others, 1965).

When the group is our own, we are more likely to see diversity:

- Many non-Europeans see the Swiss as a fairly homogeneous peo-ple. But to the people of Switzerland, the Swiss are diverse, en-compassing French-, German-, and Italian-speaking groups.

- Many Anglo-Americans lump "Latinos" together. Mexican Amer-icans, Cuban Americans, and Puerto Ricans see important differ-ences, especially between their own subgroup and the others (Huddy & Virtanen, 1995). (Those in a minority nevertheless tend to feel more shared identity and similarity than do those in the majority—Haslam & Oakes, 1995; Ryan, 1996).

- Sorority sisters perceive the members of any other sorority as less diverse than the mix in their own (Park & Rothbart, 1982). And business majors and engineering majors overestimate the unifor-mity of the other group's traits and attitudes (Judd & others, 1991).

In general, the greater our familiarity with a social group, the more we see its diversity (Brown & Wootton-Millward, 1993; Linville & others, 1989). The less our familiarity, the more we stereotype.

Perhaps you have noticed: *They*—the members of any racial group other than your own—even *look* alike. Many of us can recall embarrassing ourselves by confusing two people of another racial group, prompting the person we've misnamed to say, "You think we all look alike." Experiments by John Brigham, June Chance, Alvin Goldstein, and Roy Malpass in the United States and by Hayden Ellis in Scotland reveal that people of other races do in fact *seem* to look more alike than do people of one's own race (Brigham & Williamson, 1979; Chance & Goldstein, 1981; Ellis, 1981). When White students are shown faces of a few White and a few Black individuals and then asked to pick these individuals out of a photographic lineup, they more accurately recognize the White faces than the Black faces.

I am White. When I first read this research I thought, of course: White people *are* more physically diverse than Blacks. But my reaction was apparently just an illustration of the phenomenon. For if my reaction were correct, Black people, too, would better recognize a White face among a lineup of Whites than a Black face in a lineup of Blacks. But in fact, Blacks more easily recognize another Black than they do a White (Bothwell & others, 1989). And Hispanics more readily recognize another Hispanic whom they saw a couple of hours earlier than they do an Anglo (Platz & Hosch, 1988).

Distinctive Stimuli

Other ways we perceive our worlds also breed stereotypes. Distinctive people and vivid or extreme occurrences often capture attention and distort judgments.

Distinctive People Draw Attention

Have you ever found yourself in a situation where you were the only person present of your sex, race, or nationality? If so, your difference from the others probably made you more noticeable and the object of more attention. A Black in an otherwise White group, a man in an otherwise female group, or a woman in an otherwise male group seems more prominent and influential and to have exaggerated good and bad qualities (Crocker & McGraw, 1984; S. E. Taylor & others, 1979). This occurs because when someone in a group is made salient (conspicuous), we tend to see that person as causing whatever happens (Taylor & Fiske, 1978). If we are positioned to look at Joe, an average group member, Joe will seem to have a greater than average influence upon the group. People who capture our attention seem more responsible for what happens.

Have you noticed that people also define you by your most distinctive traits and behaviors? Tell people about someone who is a sky diver and a tennis player, report Lori Nelson and Dale Miller (1997), and they will think of the person as a sky diver. Asked to choose a gift book for the person, they will pick a skydiving book over a tennis book. A person who has both a pet snake and a pet dog is seen more as a snake owner than a dog owner. People also take note of those who violate expectations (Bettencourt & others, 1997). "Like a flower blooming in winter, intellect is more readily noticed where it is not expected," reflected Stephen Carter (1993, p. 54) on his experience as an African American intellectual. Such perceived distinctiveness makes it easier for highly capable job applicants from low-status groups to get noticed, though they also must work harder to prove their abilities are genuine (Biernat & Kobrynowicz, 1997).

Ellen Langer and Lois Imber (1980) cleverly demonstrated the attention paid to distinctive people. They asked Harvard students to watch a video of a man reading. The students paid closer attention when they were led to think he was out of the ordinary—a cancer patient, a homosexual, or a millionaire. They detected characteristics that other viewers ignored, and their evaluation of him was more extreme. Those who thought the man was a cancer patient noticed distinctive facial characteristics and bodily movements and thus perceived him as much more "different from most people" than did the other viewers. The extra attention we pay to distinctive people creates an illusion that they differ more from others than they really do. If people thought you had the IQ of a genius, they would probably notice things about you that otherwise would pass them by unnoticed.

When surrounded by European Americans, African Americans sometimes detect people reacting to their distinctiveness. Many report being stared or glared at, being subject to insensitive comments, and receiving bad service (Swim & others, 1998). However, sometimes we perceive others as reacting to our distinctiveness when actually they aren't. At Dartmouth College, researchers Robert Kleck and Angelo Strenta (1980) discovered this when they led college women to feel disfigured. The women thought the purpose of the experiment was to assess how someone would react to a facial scar created with theatrical makeup; the scar was on the right cheek, running from the ear to the mouth. Actually, the purpose was to see how the women themselves, when made to feel deviant, would perceive others' behavior toward them. After applying the makeup, the experimenter gave each subject a small hand mirror so she could see the authentic-looking scar. When she put the mirror down, he then applied some "moisturizer" to "keep the makeup from cracking." What the "moisturizer" really did was remove the scar.

The scene that followed was poignant. A young woman, feeling terribly self-conscious about her supposedly disfigured face, talked with another woman who saw no such disfigurement and knew nothing of what has gone before. If you have ever felt similarly self-conscious—perhaps about a physical disability, acne, even just a bad hair day—then perhaps you can sympathize with the self-conscious woman. Compared to women who have been led to believe their conversational partner merely thought they had an allergy, the "disfigured" women became acutely sensitive to how their conversation partners were looking at them. They rated their partners as more tense, distant, and patronizing. But in fact, observers who later analyzed videotapes of how the partners treated "disfigured" persons could find no such differences in treatment. Self-conscious about being different, the "disfigured" women misinterpreted mannerisms and comments they would otherwise not notice.

Vivid, Distinctive Cases

Our minds also use distinctive cases as a shortcut to judging groups. Are Blacks good athletes? "Well, there's Barry Sanders and Sheryl Swoopes and Michael Jordan. Yeah, I'd say so." Note the thought processes at work here: Given limited experience with a particular social group, we recall examples of it and generalize from those (Sherman, 1996). Moreover, encountering examplars of negative stereotypes (a hostile Black person, in one recent experiment) can prime such stereotypes, leading people to minimize contact with the group (Hendersen-King & Nisbett, 1996). Such generalizing from single cases can cause problems. Vivid instances, though more available in memory, are seldom representative of the larger group. Exceptional athletes, though distinctive and memorable, are not the best basis for judging the distribution of athletic talent among an entire group.

Myron Rothbart and his colleagues (1978) showed how distinctive cases also fuel stereotypes. They had University of Oregon students view 50 slides, each of which stated the man's height. For one group of students, 10 of the men were slightly over 6 feet (up to 6 feet, 4 inches). For other students, these 10 men were well over 6 feet (up to 6 feet, 11 inches). When asked later how many of the men were over 6 feet, those given the moderately tall examples recalled 5 percent too many. In a follow-up experiment, students read descriptions of the actions of 50 men, 10 of whom had committed either nonviolent crimes, such as forgery, or violent crimes, such as rape. Of those shown the list with the violent crimes, most overestimated the number of criminal acts.

Because they are distinctive, we most easily remember extreme cases; and because they alone are newsworthy, they dominate our images of various groups. The attention-getting power of distinctive, extreme cases helps explain why middle-class people so greatly exaggerate the dissimilarities between themselves and the underclass. Contrary to stereotypes of "welfare queens" driving Cadillacs, people living in poverty generally share the aspirations of the middle class and would rather provide for themselves than accept public assistance (Cook & Curtin, 1987). Moreover, the less we know about a group, the more we are influenced by a few vivid cases (Quattrone & Jones, 1980). To see is to believe.

Attribution: Is It a Just World?

In explaining others' actions, we frequently commit the fundamental attribution error. We attribute their behavior so much to their inner dispositions that we discount important situational forces. The error occurs partly because our attention focuses on the persons, not on the situation. A person's race or sex is vivid and attention-getting; the situational forces working upon that person are usually less visible. Slavery was often overlooked as an explanation for slave behavior; the behavior was instead attributed to the slaves' own nature. Until recently, the same was true of how we explained the perceived differences between women and men. Because gender-role constraints were hard to see, we attributed men's and women's behavior solely to their innate dispositions.

In a series of experiments conducted at the Universities of Waterloo and Kentucky, Melvin Lerner and his colleagues (Lerner & Miller, 1978; Lerner, 1980) discovered that merely *observing* another person being innocently victimized is enough to make the victim seem less worthy. Imagine that you, along with some others, are participating in one of Lerner's studies— supposedly on the perception of emotional cues (Lerner & Simmons, 1966). One of the participants, a confederate, is selected by lottery to perform a memory task. This person apparently receives painful shocks whenever she gives a wrong answer. You and the others note her emotional responses.

After watching the victim seemingly receive painful shocks, the experimenter asks you to evaluate her. How would you respond? With compassionate sympathy? We might expect so. As Ralph Waldo Emerson wrote, "The martyr cannot be dishonored." On the contrary, the experiments revealed that martyrs *can* be dishonored. When observers were powerless to alter the victim's fate, they often rejected and devalued the victim. Juvenal, the Roman satirist, anticipated these results: "The Roman mob follows after Fortune . . . and hates those who have been condemned."

Linda Carli and her colleagues (1989, 1990) report that this **just-world phenomenon** colors our impressions of rape victims. Carli had people read detailed descriptions of interactions between a man and a woman. For example, a woman and her boss meet for dinner, go to his home and each have a glass of wine. Some read a scenario that has a happy ending: "Then he led me to the couch. He held my hand and asked me to marry him." In hindsight, people find the ending unsurprising and admire the man's and woman's character traits. Others read the same scenario with a different ending: "But then he became very rough and pushed me onto the couch. He held me down on the couch and raped me." Given this ending, people see it as more inevitable and blame the woman for behavior that seems faultless when it has a happier outcome.

Lerner (1980) believes such disparaging of hapless victims results from our need to believe that "I am a just person living in a just world, a world where people get what they deserve." From early childhood, he argues, we are taught that good is rewarded and evil punished: Hard work and virtue pay dividends; laziness and immorality do not. From this it is but a short leap to assuming that those who flourish must be good and those who suffer must deserve their fate. The classic illustration is the Old Testament story of Job, a good person who suffers terrible misfortune. Job's friends surmise that, this being a just world, Job must have done something wicked to elicit such terrible suffering.

This suggests that people are indifferent to social injustice not because they have no concern for justice but because they *see* no injustice. Those who assume this is a just world believe that rape victims must have behaved seductively (Borgida & Brekke, 1985), that battered spouses must have provoked their beatings (Summers & Feldman, 1984), that poor people don't deserve better (Furnham & Gunter, 1984), and that sick people are responsible for their illness (Gruman & Sloan, 1983). Such beliefs enable successful people to reassure themselves that they, too, deserve what they have. The wealthy and healthy can see their own good fortune, and others' misfortune, as justly deserved. Linking good fortune with virtue and misfortune with moral failure enables the fortunate to feel pride and to avoid responsibility for the unfortunate.

Social psychologists have been more successful in explaining prejudice than in alleviating it. Because prejudice results from many interrelated factors, there is no simple remedy. Nevertheless, we can now anticipate techniques for reducing prejudice (discussed further in modules to come): If unequal status breeds prejudice, then we can seek to create cooperative, equal-status relationships. If prejudice often rationalizes discriminatory behavior, then we can mandate nondiscrimination. If outgroups seem more unlike one's own group than they really are, then we can make efforts to personalize their members. These are some of the antidotes for the poison of prejudice.

Since the end of World War II in 1945, a number of these antidotes have been applied, and racial and gender prejudices have indeed diminished. It now remains to be seen whether, during the next century, progress will continue—or whether, as could easily happen in a time of increasing population and diminishing resources, antagonisms will again erupt into open hostility.

CONCEPTS TO REMEMBER

Stereotype threat A disruptive concern, when facing a negative stereotype, that one will verify the stereotype.

Social identity The "we" aspect of our self-concept. The part of our answer to "Who am I?" that comes from our group memberships. Examples: "I am Australian." "I am Catholic."

Ingroup "Us." A group of people who share a sense of belonging, a feeling of common identity.

Outgroup "Them." A group that people perceive as distinctively different from or apart from their in group.

In group bias The tendency to favor one's own group.

Realistic group conflict theory The theory that prejudice arises from competition between groups for scarce resources.

Ethnocentrism A belief in the superiority of one's own ethnic and cultural group, and a corresponding disdain for all other groups.

Outgroup homogeneity effect A perception of outgroup members as being more similar to one another than in group members are. "They are alike; we are diverse."

Just-world phenomenon The tendency of people to believe the world is just and that people therefore get what they deserve and deserve what they get.

❖

The Nature and Nurture of Aggression

O ur behavior toward one another seems increasingly destructive. Woody Allen's prediction that "by 1990 kidnapping will be the dominant mode of social interaction" has not been fulfilled, but images of 1990s violence have horrified people across the world. In the United States, where increases in policing and imprisonment as well as an economic boom led to a decline in crime in the mid 1990s, reported assaults still exceed 1 million annually. Worldwide, we humans spend on arms and armies $1.4 million per minute—$1.4 million per minute that could daily feed, educate, and protect the environment of the world's impoverished millions.

To a social psychologist, **aggression** is *any physical or verbal behavior intended to hurt someone.* This excludes things like auto accidents, dental treatments, and unintentional sidewalk collisions. It includes slaps, direct insults, even gossipy "digs," whether done coolly (as a calculated means to some end) or in an emotional outburst. When Iraqis killed Kuwaitis while invading their country, and when Allied forces killed 100,000 Iraqis while rousting them from Kuwait, their motives were instrumental: killing people was simply a way to seize territory. But their behavior was nevertheless aggressive.

Aggression, like other human behaviors, emerges from the mix of nature and nurture. For a gun to fire, or for a person to explode in a rage, a trigger must be pulled. With some people, as with hair-trigger guns, the trigger pulls easily. Let's consider biological factors that influence how easily our trigger pulls, and psychological factors that pull it.

BIOLOGICAL INFLUENCES ON AGGRESSION

Is Aggression an Instinct?

Philosophers have long debated whether our human nature is fundamentally that of a benign, contented "noble savage" or that of a potentially explosive brute. The first view, argued by eighteenth-century French philosopher Jean-Jacques Rousseau, blames society, not human nature, for social evils. The second, associated with English philosopher Thomas Hobbes (1588–1679), sees society's laws as necessary to restrain and control the human brute. In this century, the "brutish" view—that aggressive drive is inborn and thus inevitable—was argued by Sigmund Freud in Vienna and Konrad Lorenz in Germany.

Freud speculated that human aggression springs from our redirecting toward others the energy of a primitive death urge (which, loosely speaking, he called the "death instinct"). Lorenz, who studied animal behavior, saw aggression as adaptive rather than self-destructive. But both agreed that aggressive energy is instinctual. If not discharged, it supposedly builds up until it explodes or until an appropriate stimulus "releases" it, like a mouse setting off a mousetrap. Although Lorenz (1976) also argued that we have innate mechanisms for inhibiting aggression (such as making ourselves defenseless), he feared the implications of arming our "fighting instinct" without arming our inhibitions.

The idea that aggression is an instinct collapsed as the list of supposed human instincts grew to include nearly every conceivable human behavior and as scientists became aware how much behavior varies from person to person and culture to culture. Yet biology clearly does influence behavior, just as nurture works upon nature. Our experiences interact with the nervous system engineered by our genes.

Neural Influences

Aggression is a complex behavior, and no one spot in the brain controls it. But in both animals and humans, researchers have found neural systems that facilitate aggression. When they activate these areas in the brain, hostility increases; when they deactivate them, hostility decreases. Docile animals can thus be provoked into rage, and raging animals into submission.

In one experiment, researchers placed an electrode in an aggression-inhibiting area of a domineering monkey's brain. Given a button that activated the electrode, one small monkey learned to push it every time the tyrant monkey became intimidating. Brain activation works with humans, too. After receiving painless electrical stimulation in her amygdala (a part of the brain core), one woman became enraged and smashed her guitar against the wall, barely missing her psychiatrist's head (Moyer, 1976, 1983).

Genetic Influences

Heredity influences the neural system's sensitivity to aggressive cues. It has long been known that animals of many species can be bred for aggressiveness. Sometimes this is done for practical purposes (the breeding of fighting cocks). Sometimes, breeding is done for research. Finnish psychologist Kirsti Lagerspetz (1979) took normal albino mice and bred the most aggressive ones together and bred the least aggressive ones together. After repeating the procedure for 26 generations, she had one set of fierce mice and one set of placid mice.

Aggressiveness similarly varies among primates and humans (Asher, 1987; Olweus, 1979). Our temperament—how intense and reactive we are—is partly something we bring with us into the world, influenced by our sympathetic nervous system's reactivity (Kagan, 1989). Identical twins, when asked separately, are more likely than fraternal twins to agree on whether they have "a violent temper" (Rushton & others, 1986).

Blood Chemistry

Blood chemistry also influences neural sensitivity to aggressive stimulation. Both laboratory experiments and police data indicate that when people are provoked, alcohol unleashes aggression (Bushman & Cooper, 1990; Bushman, 1993; Taylor & Chermack, 1993). Violent people are more likely (1) to drink, and (2) to become aggressive when intoxicated (White & others, 1993).

In experiments, intoxicated people administer stronger supposed shocks or higher levels of pain. In the real world, people who have been drinking commit about half of all rapes and other violent crimes (Abbey & others, 1993, 1996; Seto & Barbaree, 1995). In 65 percent of homicides, the murderer and/or the victim had been drinking (American Psychological Association, 1993). If spouse-battering alcoholics cease their problem drinking after treatment, their violent behavior typically ceases as well (Murphy & O'Farrell, 1996). Alcohol enhances aggressiveness by reducing people's self-awareness, and by reducing their ability to consider consequences (Hull & Bond, 1986; Ito & others, 1996; Steele & Southwick, 1985). Alcohol deindividuates, and it disinhibits.

There are other biochemical influences. Low blood sugar can boost aggressiveness. Aggressiveness also correlates with the male sex hormone testosterone. Although hormonal influences appear much stronger in lower animals than in humans, drugs that diminish testosterone levels in violent human males will subdue their aggressive tendencies. After people reach age 25, their testosterone and rates of violent crime decrease together. Among prisoners convicted of unprovoked violent crimes, testosterone levels tend to be higher than among those imprisoned for nonviolent crimes (Dabbs, 1992; Dabbs & others, 1995, 1997). And among the normal range of teen boys and adult men, those with high testosterone levels are more prone to delinquency, hard drug use, and aggressive responses to provocation (Archer, 1991; Dabbs & Morris, 1990; Olweus & others, 1988). Injecting a man with testosterone won't make him aggressive, yet men with low testosterone are somewhat less likely to react aggressively when provoked (Geen, 1998). Testosterone is roughly like battery power. Supercharging a portable tape player's batteries won't make it play faster, yet low batteries will make for slow play.

So, there exist important neural, genetic, and biochemical influences on aggression. Biological influences predispose some people more than others to react aggressively to conflict and provocation. But is aggression so much a part of human nature that it makes peace unattainable? The American Psychological Association and the International Council of Psychologists have joined other organizations in unanimously endorsing a statement on violence developed by scientists from a dozen nations (Adams, 1991): "It is scientifically incorrect [to say that] war or any other violent behavior is genetically programmed into our human nature [or that] war is caused by 'instinct' or any single motivation." Thus there are, as we will see, ways to reduce human aggression.

PSYCHOLOGICAL INFLUENCES ON AGGRESSION

Frustration and Aggression

It is a warm evening. Tired and thirsty after two hours of studying, you borrow some change from a friend and head for the nearest soft-drink machine. As the machine devours the change, you can almost taste the cold, refreshing cola. But when you push the button, nothing happens. You push it again. Then you flip the coin return button. Still nothing. Again, you hit the buttons. You slam them. And finally you shake and whack the machine. You stomp back to your studies, empty-handed and short-changed. Should your roommate beware? Are you now more likely to say or do something hurtful?

One of the first psychological theories of aggression, the popular frustration-aggression theory, answers yes. "Frustration always leads to some form of aggression," said John Dollard and his colleagues (1939, p. 1). **Frustration** is anything (such as the malfunctioning vending machine) that blocks our attaining a goal. Frustration grows when our motivation to achieve a goal is very strong, when we expected gratification, and when the blocking is complete.

As Figure 21-1 suggests, the aggressive energy need not explode directly against its source. We learn to inhibit direct retaliation, especially when others might disapprove or punish; instead we *displace* our hostilities onto safer targets. **Displacement** occurs in the old anecdote about a man who, humiliated by his boss, berates his wife, who yells at their son, who kicks the dog, which bites the mail carrier.

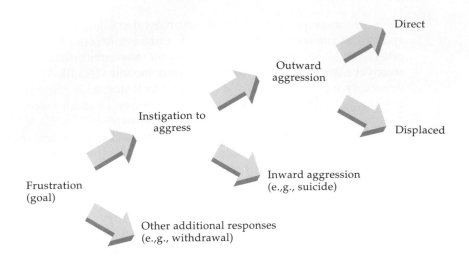

FIGURE 21-1
The classic frustration-aggression theory. Frustration creates a motive to aggress. Fear of punishment or disapproval for aggressing against the source of frustration can cause the aggressive drive to be displaced against some other target or even redirected against oneself. (Based on Dollard & others, 1939, and Miller, 1941.)

Laboratory tests of the frustration-aggression theory produced mixed results: Sometimes frustration increased aggressiveness, sometimes not. For example, if the frustration was understandable—if, as in one experiment by Eugene Burnstein and Philip Worchel (1962), a confederate disrupted a group's problem solving because his hearing aid malfunctioned (rather than just because he paid no attention)—then frustration led to irritation, not aggression.

Leonard Berkowitz (1978, 1989) realized that the original theory overstated the frustration-aggression connection, so he revised it. Berkowitz theorized that frustration produces *anger,* an emotional readiness to aggress. Anger arises when someone who frustrates us could have chosen to act otherwise (Averill, 1983; Weiner, 1981). A frustrated person is especially likely to lash out when aggressive cues pull the cork, releasing bottled-up anger. Sometimes the cork will blow without such cues. But cues associated with aggression amplify aggression (Carlson & others, 1990).

Berkowitz (1968, 1981, 1995) and others have found that the sight of a weapon is such a cue, especially when perceived as an instrument of violence rather than recreation. In one experiment, children who had just played with toy guns became more willing to knock down another child's blocks. In another, angered University of Wisconsin men gave more supposed electric shocks to their tormenter when a rifle and a revolver (supposedly left over from a previous experiment) were nearby than when badminton racquets had been left behind (Berkowitz & LePage, 1967).

Guns prime hostile thoughts (Anderson & others, 1996). Thus, Berkowitz is also not surprised that half of all U.S. murders are committed with handguns, and that handguns in homes are far more likely to kill household members than intruders. "Guns not only permit violence," he reported, "they can stimulate it as well. The finger pulls the trigger, but the trigger may also be pulling the finger."

Berkowitz is also not surprised that countries that ban handguns have lower murder rates. Compared to the United States, Britain has one-fourth as many people and one-sixteenth as many murders. The United States has 10,000 handgun homicides a year; Britain has about 10. Vancouver, British Columbia, and Seattle, Washington, have similar populations, climates, economies, and rates of criminal activity and assault—except that Vancouver, which carefully restricts handgun ownership, has had one-fifth as many handgun murders as Seattle and thus a 40 percent lower overall murder rate (Sloan & others, 1988). When Washington, D.C., adopted a law restricting handgun possession, the numbers of gun-related murders and suicides each abruptly dropped about 25 percent. There were no declines in the numbers of other methods of murder and suicide, nor did adjacent areas outside the reach of this law experience any such declines (Loftin & others, 1991).

Guns not only serve as aggression cues, they also put psychological distance between aggressor and victim. As Milgram's obedience studies taught us, remoteness from the victim facilitates cruelty. A knife can kill someone, but a knife attack is more difficult to carry out than pulling a trigger from a distance.

The Learning of Aggression

Theories of aggression based on instinct and frustration assume that hostile urges erupt from inner emotions, which naturally "push" aggression from within. Social psychologists contend that learning also "pulls" aggression out of us.

The Rewards of Aggression

By experience and by observing others, we learn that aggression often pays. Experiments have transformed animals from docile creatures into ferocious fighters. Severe defeats, on the other hand, create submissiveness (Ginsburg & Allee, 1942; Kahn, 1951; Scott & Marston, 1953).

People, too, can learn the rewards of aggression. A child whose aggressive acts successfully intimidate other children will likely become increasingly aggressive (Patterson & others, 1967). Aggressive hockey players—the ones sent most often to the penalty box for rough play—score more goals than nonaggressive players (McCarthy & Kelly, 1978a, 1978b). Canadian teenage hockey players whose fathers applaud physically aggressive play show the most aggressive attitudes and style of play (Ennis & Zanna, 1991). In these cases, aggression is instrumental in achieving certain rewards.

Collective violence can also pay. After the 1980 riot in Miami's Liberty City neighborhood, President Carter came to the neighborhood to assure residents personally of his concern and of forthcoming federal aid. After the 1967 Detroit riot, the Ford Motor Company accelerated its efforts to hire minority workers, prompting comedian Dick Gregory to joke, "Last summer the fire got too close to the Ford plant. Don't scorch the Mustangs, baby." After the 1985 riots in South Africa became severe, the government repealed laws forbidding mixed marriages, offered to restore Black "citizenship rights" (not including the right to vote), and eliminated the hated pass laws controlling the movement of Blacks. The point is not that people consciously plan riots for their instrumental value but that aggression sometimes has payoffs. If nothing more, it gets attention.

The same is true of terrorist acts, which enable powerless people to garner widespread attention. "Kill one, frighten ten thousand," asserts an ancient Chinese proverb. In this age of global communications, killing only a few can frighten tens of millions—as happened when the terrorist-caused deaths of 25 Americans in several incidents during 1985 struck more fear into the hearts of travelers than the car-accident deaths of 46,000, or when the 1995 Oklahoma City bombing of a federal building captured a nation's attention. Deprived of what Margaret Thatcher called "the oxygen of publicity," terrorism would surely diminish, concluded Jeffrey Rubin (1986). It's like the 1970s incidents of naked spectators "streaking" onto football fields for a few seconds of television exposure. Once the networks decided to ignore the incidents, the phenomenon ended.

Observational Learning

Albert Bandura (1997) proposed a **social learning theory** of aggression. He believes that we learn aggression not only by experiencing its payoffs but also by observing others. As with most social behaviors, we learn to aggress by watching others act and noting the consequences.

Bandura (1979) believes that everyday life exposes us to aggressive models in (1) the family, (2) the subculture, and (3) the mass media. Children of physically punitive parents tend to use aggression when relating to others. Many of these parents themselves had parents who were physically punitive (Bandura & Walters, 1959; Straus & Gelles, 1980). Although most abused children do not become criminals or abusive parents, 30 percent do later abuse their own children; this is four times the national rate (Kaufman & Zigler, 1987; Widom, 1989). Within families, violence often leads to violence.

The social environment outside the home also provides models. In communities where "macho" images are admired, aggression is readily transmitted to new generations (Cartwright, 1975; Short, 1969). The violent subculture of teenage gangs, for instance, provides its junior members with aggressive models. At sporting events such as soccer games, player violence precedes most incidents of fan violence (Goldstein, 1982).

Richard Nisbett (1990, 1993) and Dov Cohen (1996) have explored the subculture effect. Within the United States, they report, the sober, cooperative White folk who settled New England and the Middle Atlantic region produced a different culture than the swashbuckling, honor-preserving White folk (many of them my Scots-Irish ancestral cousins) who settled much of the South. The former were genteel farmer-artisans, the latter aggressive hunters and herders. To the present, American cities and areas that were populated by Southerners have much higher White homicide rates than those populated by Northerners.

So, people learn aggressive responses both by experience and by observing aggressive models. But when will aggressive responses actually occur? Bandura (1979) contends that aggressive acts are motivated by a variety of aversive experiences, including frustration, pain, and insults. Such experiences arouse us emotionally. But whether we act aggressively depends upon the consequences we anticipate. Aggression is most likely when we are aroused *and* it seems safe and rewarding to aggress.

Environmental Influences

Social learning theory offers a perspective from which we can examine specific influences on aggression. Under what conditions do we aggress? What environmental influences pull our trigger?

Painful incidents

Researcher Nathan Azrin wanted to know if switching off foot shocks would reinforce two rats' positive interactions with each other. Azrin planned to turn on the shock and then, once the rats approached each other, cut off the pain. To his great surprise, the experiment proved impossible. As soon as the rats felt pain, they attacked each other, before the experimenter could switch off the shock.

Is this true of rats alone? The researchers found that with a wide variety of species, the cruelty the animals imposed upon each other matched zap for zap the cruelty imposed upon them. As Azrin (1967) explained, the pain-attack response occurred

> in many different strains of rats. Then we found that shock produced attack when pairs of the following species were caged together: some kinds of mice, hamsters, opossums, raccoons, marmosets, foxes, nutria, cats, snapping turtles, squirrel monkeys, ferrets, red squirrels, bantam roosters, alligators, crayfish, amphiuma (an amphibian), and several species of snakes including the boa constrictor, rattlesnake, brown rat-snake, cottonmouth, copperhead, and black snake. The shock-attack reaction was clearly present in many very different kinds of creatures. In all the species in which shock produced attack it was fast and consistent, in the same "push-button" manner as with the rats.

The animals were not choosy about their targets. They would attack animals of their own species and also those of a different species, or stuffed dolls, or even tennis balls.

The researchers also varied the source of pain. They found that not just shocks induce attack; intense heat and "psychological pain"—for example, suddenly not rewarding hungry pigeons that have been trained to expect a grain reward after pecking at a disk—brought the same reaction as shocks. "Psychological pain" is, of course, what we call frustration.

Pain heightens aggressiveness in humans, also. Many of us can recall such a reaction after stubbing a toe or suffering a headache. Leonard Berkowitz and his associates demonstrated this by having University of Wisconsin students hold one hand in lukewarm water or painfully cold water. Those whose hands were submerged in the cold water reported feeling more irritable and more annoyed, and they were more willing to blast another person with unpleasant noise. In view of such results, Berkowitz (1983, 1989) now believes that aversive stimulation rather than frustration is the basic trigger of hostile aggression. Frustration is certainly one important type of unpleasantness. But any aversive event, whether a dashed expectation, a personal insult, or physical pain, can incite an emotional outburst. Even the torment of a depressed state increases the likelihood of hostile aggressive behavior.

Heat
An uncomfortable environment also heightens aggressive tendencies. Offensive odors, cigarette smoke, and air pollution have all been linked with aggressive behavior (Rotton & Frey, 1985). But the most-studied environmental irritant is heat. William Griffitt (1970; Griffitt & Veitch, 1971) found that, compared to students who answered questionnaires in a room with a normal temperature, those who did so in an uncomfortably hot room (over 90°F.) reported feeling more tired and aggressive and expressed more hostility toward a stranger. Follow-up experiments revealed that heat also triggers retaliatory actions (Bell, 1980; Rule & others, 1987).

Does uncomfortable heat increase aggression in the real world as well as in the laboratory? Consider:

- The riots in 79 U.S. cities between 1967 and 1971, were more likely on hot than on cool days.
- When the weather is hot, more violent crimes occur. This has been found true in
  - Des Moines (Cotton, 1981),
  - Dayton (Rotton & Frey, 1985),
  - Houston (Anderson & Anderson, 1984),
  - Indianapolis (Cotton, 1986),
  - Dallas (Harries & Stadler, 1988); and
  - Minneapolis (Cohn, 1993).
- Not only do hotter days have more violent crimes, so do hotter seasons of the year, hotter summers, hotter years, hotter cities, and hot-

ter regions of western Europe (Anderson & Anderson, 1996; Anderson & Anderson, 1998). Assuming that predicted global warming occurs, Craig Anderson, Brad Bushman, and Ralph Groom (1997) project that by the middle of the twenty-first century, there will annually be at least 115,000 more serious assaults in the United States alone.

- In heat-stricken Phoenix, Arizona, drivers without air conditioning are more likely to honk at a stalled car (Kenrick & MacFarlane, 1986).

- During the 1986 to 1988 major league baseball seasons, two-thirds more batters were hit by a pitch in games played when temperatures were in the 90s than in games played below 80° (Reifman & others, 1991). Pitchers weren't wilder on hot days—they had no more walks and wild pitches—they just clobbered more batters.

Attacks

Being attacked or insulted is especially conducive to aggression. Experiments at Kent State University by Stuart Taylor (Taylor & Pisano, 1971), at Washington State University by Harold Dengerink (Dengerink & Myers, 1977), and at Osaka University by Kennichi Ohbuchi and Toshihiro Kambara (1985) confirm that intentional attacks breed retaliatory attacks. In most of these experiments, one person competes with another in a reaction-time contest. After each test trial, the winner chooses how much shock to give the loser. Actually, each subject is playing a programmed opponent, who steadily escalates the amount of shock. Do the real subjects respond charitably? Hardly. Extracting "an eye for an eye" is the more likely response.

Crowding

Crowding, the subjective feeling of not having enough space, is stressful. Crammed in the back of a bus, trapped in slow-moving freeway traffic, or living three to a small room in a college dorm diminishes one's sense of control (Baron & others, 1976; McNeel, 1980). Might such experiences also heighten aggression?

The stress experienced by animals allowed to overpopulate a confined environment does heighten aggressiveness (Calhoun, 1962; Christian & others, 1960). But it is a rather large leap from rats in an enclosure or deer on an island to humans in a city. Nevertheless, it's true that dense urban areas do have higher rates of crime and emotional distress (Fleming & others, 1987; Kirmeyer, 1978). Even when they don't suffer higher crime rates, residents of crowded cities can *feel* more fearful. Toronto's crime rate has been four times higher than Hong Kong's. Yet compared to Toronto people, people from Hong Kong—which is four times more densely populated—have reported feeling more fearful on their city's streets (Gifford & Peacock, 1979).

REDUCING AGGRESSION

We have examined instinct, frustration-aggression, and social learning theories of aggression, and we have scrutinized influences on aggression. How, then, can we reduce aggression? Do theory and research suggest ways to control aggression?

Catharsis?

"Youngsters should be taught to vent their anger." So advised Ann Landers (1969). If a person "bottles up his rage, we have to find an outlet. We have to give him an opportunity of letting off steam." So asserted the prominent psychiatrist Fritz Perls (1973). Both statements assume the "hydraulic model"—accumulated aggressive energy that, like dammed-up water, needs a release.

The concept of catharsis is usually credited to Aristotle. Although Aristotle actually said nothing about aggression, he did argue that we can purge emotions by experiencing them and that viewing the classic tragedies therefore enabled a catharsis ("purgation") of pity and fear. To have an emotion excited, he believed, is to have that emotion released (Butcher, 1951). The catharsis hypothesis has been extended to include the emotional release supposedly obtained not only by observing drama but also through recalling and reliving past events, through expressing emotions, and through various actions.

Catharsis sometimes occurs. Confiding is good for both soul and body. Even expressing anger can temporarily calm us, *if* it doesn't leave us feeling guilty or anxious about retaliation (Geen & Quanty, 1977; Hokanson & Edelman, 1966). But in the long run expressing anger is more likely to breed anger. For example, Robert Arms and his associates report that Canadian and American spectators of football, wrestling, and hockey games exhibit *more* hostility after viewing the event than before (Arms & others, 1979; Goldstein & Arms, 1971; Russell, 1983). Not even war seems to purge aggressive feelings. After a war, a nation's murder rate tends to jump (Archer & Gartner, 1976).

In experiments, too, aggressing has led to heightened aggression. Ebbe Ebbesen and his co-researchers (1975) interviewed 100 engineers and technicians shortly after they were angered by layoff notices. Some were asked questions that gave them an opportunity to express hostility against their employer or supervisor, such as "What instances can you think of where the company has not been fair with you?" Afterward, they answered a questionnaire assessing attitudes toward the company and the supervisor. Did the previous opportunity to "vent" or "drain off" their hostility reduce it? To the contrary, their hostility increased. Expressing hostility bred more hostility.

Sound familiar? Recall from Module 9 on behavior and belief that cruel acts beget cruel attitudes. Furthermore, as we noted in analyzing

Stanley Milgram's obedience experiments, little aggressive acts can breed their own justification. People derogate their victims, rationalizing further aggression. Even if retaliation sometimes (in the short run) reduces tension, in the long run it reduces inhibitions.

Should we therefore bottle up anger and aggressive urges? Silent sulking is hardly more effective, because it allows us to continue reciting our grievances as we conduct conversations in our head. Fortunately, there are nonaggressive ways to express our feelings and to inform others how their behavior affects us. Across cultures, those who reframe accusatory "you" messages as "I" messages—"I'm angry," or "When you talk like that I feel irritated"—communicate their feelings in a way that better enables the other person to make a positive response (Kubany & others, 1995). We can be assertive without being aggressive.

A Social Learning Approach

If aggressive behavior is learned, then there is hope for its control. Let us briefly review factors that influence aggression and speculate how to counteract them.

Aversive experiences such as frustrated expectations and personal attacks predispose hostile aggression. So it is wise to refrain from planting false, unreachable expectations in people's minds. Anticipated rewards and costs influence instrumental aggression. This suggests that we should reward cooperative, nonaggressive behavior. In experiments, children become less aggressive when caregivers ignore their aggressive behavior and reinforce their nonaggressive behavior (Hamblin & others, 1969).

But there are limits to punishment's effectiveness. Most murderous aggression is impulsive, hot aggression—the result of an argument, an insult, or an attack. Thus, we must *prevent* aggression before it happens. We must teach nonaggressive conflict-resolution strategies. If only mortal aggression were cool and instrumental, we could hope that waiting until it happens and severely punishing the criminal afterward would deter such acts. In that world, states that impose the death penalty might have a lower murder rate than states without the death penalty. But in our world of hot homicide, that is not so (Costanzo, 1998).

To foster a gentler world, we could model and reward sensitivity and cooperation from an early age, perhaps by teaching parents how to discipline without violence. Training programs encourage parents to reinforce desirable behaviors and to frame statements positively ("When you finish cleaning your room, you can go play" rather than "If you don't clean your room, you're grounded.") One "aggression-replacement program" has reduced re-arrest rates of juvenile offenders and gang members by teaching the youths and their parents communication skills, training them to control anger, and raising their level of moral reasoning (Goldstein & Glick, 1994).

If observing aggressive models lowers inhibitions and elicits imitation, then we might also reduce brutal, dehumanizing portrayals in films and on television, just as we have already taken steps to reduce racist and sexist portrayals. We can also inoculate children against the effects of media violence. Despairing that the TV networks would ever "face the facts and change their programming," Eron and Huesmann (1984) taught 170 Oak Park, Illinois, children that television portrays the world unrealistically, that aggression is less common and effective than TV suggests, and that aggressive behavior is undesirable. (Drawing upon attitude research, Eron and Huesmann encouraged children to draw these inferences themselves and to attribute their expressed criticisms of television to their own convictions.) When restudied two years later, these children were less influenced by TV violence than were untrained children.

Aggressive stimuli also trigger aggression. This suggests reducing the availability of weapons such as handguns. Jamaica in 1974 implemented a sweeping anticrime program that included strict gun control and censorship of gun scenes from television and movies (Diener & Crandall, 1979). In the following year, robberies dropped 25 percent, nonfatal shootings 37 percent. In Sweden, the toy industry has discontinued the sale of war toys. The Swedish Information Service (1980) stated the national attitude: "Playing at war means learning to settle disputes by violent means."

Suggestions such as these can help us minimize aggression. But given the complexity of aggression's causes and the difficulty of controlling them, who can feel the optimism expressed by Andrew Carnegie's forecast that in the twentieth century, "To kill a man will be considered as disgusting as we in this day consider it disgusting to eat one." Since Carnegie uttered those words in 1900, some 200 million human beings have been killed. It is a sad irony that although today we understand human aggression better than ever before, humanity's inhumanity is hardly diminished.

CONCEPTS TO REMEMBER

Aggression   Physical or verbal behavior intended to hurt someone.

Frustration   The blocking of goal-directed behavior.

Displacement   The redirection of aggression to a target other than the source of the frustration. Generally, the new target is a safer or more socially acceptable target.

Social learning theory   The theory that we learn social behavior by observing and imitating and by being rewarded and punished.

Crowding   A subjective feeling that there is not enough space per person.

MODULE

22

❖

Do the Media Influence Social Behavior?

I n several countries there was an increase in reported violent crime from 1960 to the early 1990s. Why the change? What social forces have caused the mushrooming violence?

Alcohol contributes to aggression, but alcohol use has not appreciably changed since 1960 (McAneny, 1994). Might the surging violence instead be fueled by the growth in individualism and materialism? by the growing gap between the powerful rich and the powerless poor? by the decline in two-parent families and the increase in father absence? by the media's increasing modeling of violence and unrestrained sexuality? The latter question arises because increased rates of violence and sexual coercion have coincided with increases in media mayhem and sexual suggestion. Is the historical correlation a coincidence? What are the social consequences of pornography (which *Webster's* defines as "erotic depictions intended to excite sexual arousal")? And what are the effects of the modeling of violence in movies and on television?

PORNOGRAPHY AND SEXUAL VIOLENCE

Repeated exposure to fictional eroticism has several effects. It can decrease one's attraction to one's less exciting real-life partner (Kenrick & others, 1989). It can also increase one's acceptance of extramarital sex and of women's sexual submission to men (Zillmann, 1989). Rock video images of macho men and sexually acquiescent women similarly color viewers' perceptions of men and women (Hansen, 1989; Hansen & Hansen 1988,

1990; St. Lawrence & Joyner, 1991). But social-psychological research has focused mostly on depictions of sexual violence.

A typical sexually violent episode shows a man forcing himself upon a woman. She at first resists and tries to fight off her attacker. Gradually she becomes sexually aroused, and her resistance melts. By the end she is in ecstasy, pleading for more. We have all viewed or read nonpornographic versions of this sequence: She resists, he persists. Dashing man grabs and forcibly kisses protesting woman. Within moments, the arms that were pushing him away are clutching him tight, her resistance overwhelmed by her unleashed passion. In *Gone with the Wind*, Scarlett O'Hara is carried to bed protesting and kicking, and wakes up singing.

Social psychologists report that viewing such fictional scenes of a man overpowering and arousing a woman can (1) distort one's perceptions of how women actually respond to sexual coercion and (2) increase men's aggression against women, at least in laboratory settings.

Distorted Perceptions of Sexual Reality

Does viewing sexual violence reinforce the myth that some women would welcome sexual assault—that " 'no' doesn't really mean no"? To find out, Neil Malamuth and James Check (1981) showed University of Manitoba men either two nonsexual movies or two movies depicting a man sexually overcoming a woman. A week later, when surveyed by a different experimenter, those who saw the films with mild sexual violence were more accepting of violence against women.

Viewing slasher movies has much the same effect. Men shown films such as *Texas Chainsaw Massacre* become desensitized to brutality and more likely to view rape victims unsympathetically (Linz & others, 1988, 1989). While spending three evenings watching sexually violent movies, male viewers in an experiment by Charles Mullin and Daniel Linz (1995) became progressively less bothered by the raping and slashing. Compared to others who were not exposed to the films, they also, three days later, expressed less sympathy for domestic violence victims and they rated the victims' injuries as less severe. In fact, said researchers Edward Donnerstein, Daniel Linz, and Steven Penrod (1987), what better way for an evil character to get people to react calmly to the torture and mutilation of women than to show a gradually escalating series of such films?

Aggression Against Women

Evidence also is accumulating that pornography can contribute to men's actual aggression toward women. Correlational studies raise that possibility. John Court (1984) noted that across the world, as pornography became more widely available during the 1960s and 1970s, the rate of reported rapes sharply increased—except in countries and areas where pornography was controlled. (The examples that counter this trend—such as Japan, where violent pornography is available but the rape rate is low—remind us that other factors are also important.) In Hawaii, the number of reported rapes rose ninefold between 1960 and 1974, dropped when restraints on pornography were temporarily imposed, and rose again when the restraints were lifted.

In another correlational study, Larry Baron and Murray Straus (1984) discovered that the sales of sexually explicit magazines (such as *Hustler* and *Playboy*) in the 50 states correlated with state rape rates. After controlling for other factors, such as the percentage of young males in each state, a positive relationship remained. Alaska ranked first in sex magazine sales and first in rape. Nevada was second on both measures.

When interviewed, Canadian and American sexual offenders commonly acknowledge pornography use. For example, William Marshall (1989) reported that Ontario rapists and child molesters used pornography much more than men who were not sexual offenders. An FBI study also reports considerable exposure to pornography among serial killers, as does the Los Angeles Police Department among most child sex abusers (Bennett, 1991; Ressler & others, 1988). Of course, this *correlation* cannot prove that pornography is a contributing *cause* of rape. Maybe the offenders' use of pornography is merely a symptom, and not a cause, of their basic deviance. Moreover, the evidence is mixed: Some studies find prior pornography use (including childhood exposure to pornography) uncorrelated with sexual aggression (Bauserman, 1996).

Although limited to the sorts of short-term behaviors that can be studied in the laboratory, controlled experiments reveal cause and effect. A consensus statement by 21 leading social scientists sums up the results: "Exposure to violent pornography increases punitive behavior toward women" (Koop, 1987). One of these social scientists, Edward Donnerstein (1980), had shown 120 University of Wisconsin men a neutral, an erotic, or an aggressive-erotic (rape) film. Then the men, supposedly as part of another experiment, "taught" a male or female confederate some nonsense syllables by choosing how much shock to administer for incorrect answers. Especially when angered, the men who had watched the rape film administered markedly stronger shocks—but only to female victims (Figure 22-1).

If the ethics of conducting such experiments trouble you, rest assured that these researchers appreciate the controversial and powerful experience they are giving participants. Only after giving their knowing consent do people participate. Moreover, after the experiment, researchers debunk any myths the film communicated. One hopes that such debriefing sufficiently offsets the vivid image of a supposedly euphoric rape victim. Judging from studies with University of Manitoba and Winnipeg students by James Check and Neil Malamuth (1984; Malamuth & Check, 1984), it does. Those who read erotic rape stories and were then fully debriefed became *less* accepting of the "women-enjoy-rape" myth. Other studies confirm the effectiveness of debriefing (Allen & others, 1996). For example, Donnerstein and

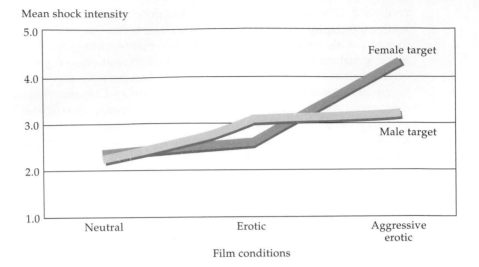

FIGURE 22-1
After viewing an aggressive-erotic film, college men delivered stronger shocks than before, especially to a woman. (Data from Donnerstein, 1980.)

Berkowitz (1981) found that Wisconsin students who viewed pornography *and* were then thoroughly debriefed were later *less* likely than other students to agree that "being roughed up is sexually stimulating to many women."

Justification for this experimentation is not only scientific but also humanitarian. In a careful national survey, 22 percent of women reported having been forced by a man to do something sexual (Laumann & others, 1994). In surveys of 6,200 college students nationwide and 2,200 Ohio working women, Mary Koss and her colleagues (1988, 1990, 1993) found that 28 percent of the women reported an experience that met the legal definition of rape or attempted rape. Surveys in other industrialized countries produce similar results. Three in four stranger rapes and nearly all acquaintance rapes went unreported to police. Thus the known rape rate *greatly* underestimates the actual rape rate. Moreover, many more women—half in one survey of college women (Sandberg & others, 1985)—report having suffered some form of sexual assault while on a date, and even more have experienced verbal sexual coercion or harassment (Craig, 1990; Pryor, 1987). Men who behave in sexually coercive, aggressive ways typically desire dominance, exhibit hostility toward women, and are sexually promiscuous (Anderson & others, 1997; Malamuth & others, 1995).

Malamuth, Donnerstein, and Zillmann are among those alarmed by women's increasing risk of being sexually harassed or raped. They caution against oversimplifying the complex causes of rape, which is no more attributable to any one cause than is cancer. Yet they conclude that viewing violence, especially sexual violence, can have antisocial effects. Just as most Germans quietly tolerated the degrading anti-Semitic images that fed the Holocaust, so most people today tolerate media images of women that feed what some call the growing "female holocaust" of sexual harassment, abuse, and rape.

Is the answer censorship? Most people support censorship in instances where one person's rights are trampled by another's free expression (as in cases involving child pornography, slander, and false advertising). In 1992 the Supreme Court of Canada extended such protection to women when it unanimously upheld an antipornography law that suppresses materials deemed harmful to the equal rights of women. "If true equality between male and female persons is to be achieved, we cannot ignore the threat to equality resulting from exposure to audiences of certain types of violent and degrading materials," the court declared.

In the contest of individual versus collective rights, people in most Western nations side with individual rights. So, as an alternative to censorship, many psychologists favor "media awareness training." Recall that pornography researchers have successfully resensitized and educated participants to women's actual responses to sexual violence. Could educators similarly promote critical viewing skills? By sensitizing people to the view of women that predominates in pornography and to issues of sexual harassment and violence, it should be possible to counter the myth that women enjoy being coerced. "Our utopian and perhaps naive hope," say Edward Donnerstein, Daniel Linz, and Steven Penrod (1987, p. 196), "is that in the end the truth revealed through good science will prevail and the public will be convinced that these images not only demean those portrayed but also those who view them."

Is such a hope naive? Consider: With no ban on cigarettes, the number of U.S. smokers dropped from 43 percent in 1972 to 27 percent in 1994 (Gallup, 1994). Without censorship of racism, once-common media images of African Americans as childlike, superstitious buffoons have nearly disappeared. As public consciousness changed, scriptwriters, producers, and media executives decided that exploitative images of minorities were not good. More recently they have decided that drugs are not glamorous, as many films and songs from the 1960s and 1970s implied, but dangerous— and high school seniors' marijuana use during the previous month dropped from 37 percent in 1979 to 11 percent in 1992, before rebounding to 22 percent in 1996 as the cultural antidrug voice softened and drug use became reglamorized in some music and films (Johnston, 1996). Will we one day look back with embarrassment on the time when movies entertained people with scenes of exploitation, mutilation, and sexual coercion?

Picture this scene from one of Bandura's experiments (Bandura & others, 1961). A Stanford nursery school child is put to work on an interesting art activity. An adult is in another part of the room, where there are Tinker Toys, a mallet, and a big inflated doll. After a minute of working with the Tinker Toys, the adult gets up and for almost 10 minutes attacks the inflated doll. She pounds it with the mallet, kicks it, and throws it, all the while yelling, "Sock him in the nose. . . . Knock him down. . . . Kick him."

After observing this outburst, the child goes to a different room with many very attractive toys. But after two minutes the experimenter interrupts, saying these are her best toys and she must "save them for the other children." The frustrated child now goes into another room with various toys for aggressive and nonaggressive play, two of which are a Bobo doll and a mallet.

Seldom did children not exposed to the aggressive adult model display any aggressive play or talk. Although frustrated, they nevertheless played calmly. Those who had observed the aggressive adult were many times more likely to pick up the mallet and lash out at the doll. Watching the adult's aggressive behavior lowered their inhibitions. Moreover, the children often reproduced the model's acts and said her words. Observing aggressive behavior had both lowered their inhibitions and taught them ways to aggress.

TELEVISION

If watching an aggressive model can unleash children's aggressive urges and teach them new ways to aggress, would watching aggressive models on television similarly affect children?

Consider these few facts about watching television. In 1945, a Gallup poll asked Americans, "Do you know what television is?" (Gallup, 1972, p. 551). Today, in America, as in much of the industrialized world, 98 percent of households have a TV set, more than have bathtubs or telephones. In the average home, the set is on seven hours a day, and individual household members watch for an average four hours per day each.

During all those hours, what social behaviors are modeled? Since 1967, George Gerbner and other TV watchers (1993, 1994) at the University of Pennsylvania have been sampling U.S. network prime-time and Saturday morning entertainment programs. Their findings? Two out of three programs contain violence ("physically compelling action that threatens to hurt or kill, or actual hurting or killing"). What does it add up to? By the end of elementary school, the average child has viewed some 8,000 TV murders and 100,000 other violent acts (Huston & others, 1992). Reflecting on his 22 years of cruelty counting, Gerbner (1994) lamented: "Humankind has had more bloodthirsty eras but none as filled with *images* of violence as the present. We are awash in a tide of violent representations the world has never seen . . . drenching every home with graphic scenes of expertly choreographed brutality."

Does it matter? Does prime-time crime stimulate the behavior it depicts? Or, do the shows drain off aggressive energy as viewers vicariously participate in aggressive acts?

The latter idea, a variation on the **catharsis** hypothesis, maintains that watching violent drama enables people to release their pent-up hostilities. Defenders of the media cite this theory frequently and remind us that violence predates television. In an imaginary debate with one of television's critics, the medium's defender might argue, "Television played no role in the genocides of Jews and Native Americans. Television just reflects and caters to our tastes." "Agreed," responds the critic, "but it's also true that during America's TV age, reported violent crime has increased several times faster than the population rate. Surely you don't mean the popular arts are mere passive reflections, without any power to influence public consciousness." The defender replies: "The violence epidemic results from many factors. TV might even reduce aggression by keeping people off the streets and by offering them a harmless opportunity to vent their aggression."

Television's Effects on Behavior

Do viewers imitate violent models? Examples abound of people reenacting television crimes. In one survey of 208 prison convicts, 9 of 10 admitted that they learned new criminal tricks by watching crime programs. And 4 out of 10 said they had attempted specific crimes seen on television (*TV Guide*, 1977).

Correlating TV Viewing and Behavior

Crime stories are not scientific evidence. Researchers therefore use correlational and experimental studies to examine the effects of viewing violence. One technique, commonly used with schoolchildren, asks whether their TV watching predicts their aggressiveness. To some extent it does. The more violent the content of the child's TV viewing, the more aggressive the child (Eron, 1987; Turner & others, 1986). The relationship is modest but consistently found in the United States, Europe, and Australia.

So can we conclude that a diet of violent TV fuels aggression? Perhaps you are already thinking that because this is a correlational study, the cause-effect relation could also work in the opposite direction. Maybe aggressive children prefer aggressive programs. Or maybe some underlying third factor, such as lower intelligence, predisposes some children both to prefer aggressive programs and to act aggressively.

Researchers have developed two ways to test these alternative explanations. They test the "hidden third factor" explanation by statistically pulling out the influence of some of these possible factors. For example, British researcher William Belson (1978; Muson, 1978) studied 1,565 London boys. Compared to those who watched little violence, those who watched a great deal (especially realistic rather than cartoon violence) admitted to 50 percent more violent acts during the preceding six months (for example, "I busted the telephone in a telephone box"). Belson also examined 22 likely third factors, such as family size. The heavy and light viewers still differed after equating

Seriousness of criminal acts by age 30

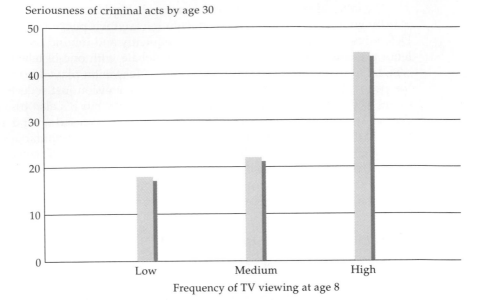

Frequency of TV viewing at age 8

FIGURE 22-2
Children's television viewing and later criminal activity. Violence viewing at age 8 was a predictor of a serious criminal offense by age 30. (Data from Eron & Huesmann, 1984.)

them with respect to potential third factors. So Belson surmised that the heavy viewers were indeed more violent *because* of their TV exposure.

Similarly, Leonard Eron and Rowell Huesmann (1980, 1985) found that violence viewing among 875 eight-year-olds correlated with aggressiveness even after statistically pulling out several obvious possible third factors. Moreover, when they restudied these individuals as 19-year-olds, they discovered that viewing violence at age 8 modestly predicted aggressiveness at age 19, but that aggressiveness at age 8 did *not* predict viewing violence at age 19. Aggression followed viewing, not the reverse. They confirmed these findings in follow-up studies of 758 Chicago-area and 220 Finnish youngsters (Huesmann & others, 1984). What is more, when Eron and Huesmann (1984) examined the later criminal conviction records of their initial sample of 8-year-olds, they found that at age 30, those men who as children had watched a great deal of violent television were more likely to have been convicted of a serious crime (Figure 22-2).

Even murder rates increase when and where television comes. In Canada and the United States, the homicide rate doubled between 1957 and 1974 as violent television spread. In census regions where television came later, the homicide rate jumped later, too. In White areas of South Africa, where television was not introduced until 1975, a similar near doubling of the homicide rate did not begin until after 1975 (Centerwall, 1989).

And in a closely studied rural Canadian town where television came late, playground aggression doubled soon after (Williams, 1986).

Notice that these studies illustrate how researchers are now using correlational findings to *suggest* cause and effect. An infinite number of possible third factors could be creating a merely coincidental relation between viewing violence and aggression; fortunately, however, the experimental method can control these extraneous factors. If we randomly assign some children to watch a violent film and others a nonviolent film, any later aggression difference between the two groups will be due to the only factor that distinguishes them: what they watched.

TV Viewing Experiments

The pioneering experiments by Albert Bandura and Richard Walters (1963) sometimes had young children view the adult pounding the inflated doll on film instead of observing it live, with much the same effect. Then Leonard Berkowitz and Russell Geen (1966) found that angered college students who viewed a violent film acted more aggressively than did similarly angered students who viewed nonaggressive films. These laboratory experiments, coupled with growing public concern, were sufficient to prompt the U.S. Surgeon General to commission 50 new research studies during the early 1970s. By and large, these studies confirmed that viewing violence amplifies aggression.

In a later series of experiments, research teams led by Ross Parke (1977) in the United States and Jacques Leyens (1975) in Belgium showed institutionalized American and Belgian delinquent boys a series of either aggressive or nonaggressive commercial films. Their consistent finding: "Exposure to movie violence . . . led to an increase in viewer aggression". Compared to the week preceding the film series, physical attacks increased sharply in cottages where boys were viewing violent films.

Chris Boyatzis and his colleagues (1995) observed a similar effect when they showed some elementary school children, but not others, an episode of television's most popular, and most violent, children's program, "Power Rangers." Immediately after viewing the episode, the viewers committed seven times as many aggressive acts per two-minute interval as the nonviewers. As in Bandura's pioneering Bobo doll studies, the boy viewers often precisely imitated the characters' acts, such as their flying karate kicks. In Norway in 1994, a five-year-old girl was stoned, kicked, and left to freeze in the snow by playmates reportedly imitating acts seen on the show—triggering the show's banning by three Scandinavian countries (Blucher, 1994).

The Convergence of Evidence

Television research has involved a variety of methods and participants. Researchers Susan Hearold (1986) and Wendy Wood and colleagues (1991) assembled the results of correlational and experimental studies.

Their conclusion: Viewing antisocial portrayals is indeed associated with antisocial behavior. The effect is not overwhelming; in fact, at times it is so modest that some critics doubt it exists (Freedman, 1988; McGuire, 1986). Moreover, the aggression provoked in these experiments is not assault and battery; it's more on the scale of a shove in the lunch line, a cruel comment, a threatening gesture.

Nevertheless, the convergence of evidence is striking. "The irrefutable conclusion," said a 1993 American Psychological Association youth violence commission, is "that viewing violence increases violence." This is especially so among people with aggressive tendencies (Bushman, 1995). The violence viewing effect also is strongest when an attractive person commits justified, realistic violence that goes unpunished and that shows no pain or harm (Donnerstein, 1998). Violent entertainment often creates these conditions for antisocial effects, but not always. By depicting unjustified violence by unattractive perpetrators on suffering Holocaust victims, *Schindler's List* is unlikely to have encouraged violent acts.

Why Does TV Viewing Affect Behavior?

We know from experiments that prolonged violence viewing has two effects on thinking. It desensitizes people to cruelty. (Emotionally numbed, they say, "It doesn't bother me at all.") And it distorts their perceptions of reality. (They exaggerate the frequency of violence and become more fearful.) But why does violence viewing also affect *behavior?* The conclusion drawn by the surgeon general and by the researchers we have cited is *not* that television is the primary cause of social violence, any more than cyclamates are a primary cause of cancer. Rather, they say, television is *a* cause. Even if it is just one ingredient in a complex recipe for violence, it is one that, like cyclamates, is potentially controllable. Given the convergence of correlational and experimental evidence, researchers have explored *why* viewing violence has this effect.

Consider three possibilities (Geen & Thomas, 1986). One is that it's not the violent content itself that causes social violence but the *arousal* it produces (Mueller & others, 1983; Zillmann, 1989). As we noted earlier, arousal tends to spill over: One type of arousal energizes other behaviors.

Other research shows that viewing violence *disinhibits*. In Bandura's experiment, the adult's punching the Bobo doll seemed to legitimate such outbursts and to lower the children's own inhibitions. Viewing violence primes the viewer for aggressive behavior by activating violence-related thoughts (Berkowitz, 1984; Bushman & Geen, 1990; Josephson, 1987). Listening to music with sexually violent lyrics seems to have a similar effect, predisposing younger males to behave more aggressively (Barongan & Hall, 1995; Johnson, 1995).

Media portrayals also evoke *imitation*. The children in Bandura's experiments reenacted the specific behaviors they had witnessed. The commercial television industry is hard-pressed to dispute that television leads viewers to imitate what they have seen: Its advertisers model consumption. Television's critics agree—and are troubled that on TV programs acts of assault outnumber affectionate acts 4 to 1 and that, in other ways as well, television models an unreal world. They love to recount seeming examples of imitation, as when two Utah men three times viewed the movie *Magnum Force,* in which the caustic cleaner liquid Drano is used to kill a woman. Later that month, the men reenacted the scene, murdering three people by forcing them to drink Drano (Bushman, 1996).

If the ways of relating and problem solving modeled on television do trigger imitation, especially among young viewers, then modeling **prosocial behavior** on TV should be socially beneficial. Happily, it is: Television's subtle influence can indeed teach children positive lessons in behavior. Susan Hearold (1986) statistically combined 108 comparisons of prosocial programs with neutral programs or no program. She found that, on average, "if the viewer watched prosocial programs instead of neutral programs, he would [at least temporarily] be elevated from the 50th to the 74th percentile in prosocial behavior—typically altruism."

In one such study, researchers Lynette Friedrich and Aletha Stein (1973; Stein & Friedrich, 1972) showed preschool children episodes of *Mister Rogers' Neighborhood* each day for four weeks as part of their nursery school program. (*Mister Rogers' Neighborhood* is an educational program designed to enhance young children's social and emotional development.) During this viewing period, children from less educated homes became more cooperative, helpful, and likely to state their feelings. In a follow-up study, kindergartners who viewed four *Mister Rogers* programs were able to state its prosocial content, both on a test and in puppet play (Friedrich & Stein, 1975; also Coates & others, 1976).

CONCEPTS TO REMEMBER

Catharsis Emotional release. The catharsis view of aggression is that aggressive drive is reduced when one "releases" aggressive energy, either by acting aggressively or by fantasizing aggression.

Prosocial behavior Positive, constructive, helpful social behavior; the opposite of antisocial behavior.

23

❖

Causes of Conflict

There is a speech that has been given in many languages by the leaders of many countries. It goes like this: "The intentions of our country are entirely peaceful. Yet, we are also aware that other nations, with their new weapons, threaten us. Thus we must defend ourselves against attack. By so doing, we shall protect our way of life and preserve the peace" (Richardson, 1969). Almost every nation claims concern only for peace but, mistrusting other nations, arms itself in self-defense. The result: a world that has seen 110 million war-related deaths this century, a world still with a nuclear weapons stockpile equal to 700 times the explosive power used in World War II and the Korean and Vietnam Wars combined, a world that spends $1.4 million per minute on arms and armies (Sivard, 1996).

The elements of such **conflict** (a perceived incompatibility of actions or goals) are similar at all levels, from nations in an arms race, to Bosnian Serbs warring against Muslims, to corporate executives and workers disputing salaries, to a feuding married couple. Let's consider these conflict elements.

SOCIAL DILEMMAS

Several of the problems that most threaten our human future—nuclear arms, global warming, overpopulation, natural resource depletion—arise as various parties pursue their self-interest, ironically, to their collective detriment. Anyone can think: "It would cost me lots to buy expensive pollution controls. Besides, by itself my pollution is trivial." Many others reason similarly, and the result is unclean air and water.

Thus, choices that are individually rewarding become collectively punishing when others choose the same. We therefore have an urgent dilemma: How can we reconcile individuals' well-being, including their right to pursue their personal interests, with communal well-being?

To isolate and illustrate this dilemma, social psychologists have used laboratory games that expose the heart of many real social conflicts. By showing us how well-meaning people become trapped in mutually destructive behavior, they illuminate some fascinating, yet troubling, paradoxes of human existence. Consider two examples: the Prisoner's Dilemma and the Tragedy of the Commons.

The Prisoner's Dilemma

One dilemma derives from an anecdote concerning two suspects questioned separately by the district attorney (Rapoport, 1960). They are jointly guilty; however, the DA has only enough evidence to convict them of a lesser offense. So the DA creates an incentive for each to confess privately: If one confesses and the other doesn't, the DA will grant the confessor immunity (and will use the confession to convict the other of a maximum offense). If both confess, each will receive a moderate sentence. If neither confesses, each will receive a very light sentence. The matrix of Figure 23-1 summarizes the choices. Faced with such a dilemma, would you confess?

To minimize their own sentence, many would, despite the fact that mutual confession elicits more severe sentences than mutual nonconfession. Note from the matrix that no matter what the other prisoner decides, each is better off confessing. If the other confesses, one then gets a moderate sentence instead of a severe one. If the other does not confess, one goes free. Of course, each prisoner reasons the same way. Hence, the social trap.

In some 2,000 studies (Dawes, 1991), university students have faced variations of the Prisoner's Dilemma with the outcomes being not prison terms but chips, money, or course points. As Figure 23-2 illustrates, on any given decision, a person is better off defecting (because such behavior exploits the other's cooperation or protects against the other's exploitation). However—and here's the rub—by not cooperating, both parties end up far worse off than if they trusted each other and gained a joint profit. This dilemma often traps each one in a maddening predicament in which both realize they *could* mutually profit but, mistrusting one another, become "locked in" to not cooperating.

The Tragedy of the Commons

Many social dilemmas involve more than two parties. The greenhouse effect stems from widespread deforestation and from the carbon dioxide emitted by the world's cars, oil burners, and coal-fired power plants. Each

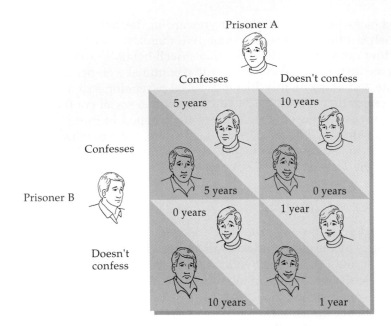

FIGURE 23-1
The Prisoner's Dilemma. In each box, the number above the diagonal is
prisoner A's outcome. Thus, if both prisoners confess, both get five years.
If neither confesses, each gets a year. If one confesses, that prisoner is set
free in exchange for evidence used to convict the other of a crime bringing
a 10-year sentence. If you were one of the prisoners, would you confess?

gas-guzzling car contributes infinitesimally to the problem, and the harm
each does is diffused over many people. To model such social predicaments, researchers have developed laboratory dilemmas that involve multiple people.

A metaphor for the insidious nature of social dilemmas is what ecolo-
gist Garrett Hardin (1968) called the "tragedy of the commons." He derived the name from the centrally located pasture area in old English
towns, but the "commons" can be air, water, whales, cookies, or any shared
and limited resource. If all use the resource in moderation, it can replenish
itself as rapidly as it's harvested. The grass will grow, the whales will reproduce, and the cookie jar gets restocked.

Imagine 100 farmers surrounding a commons capable of sustaining
100 cows. When each farmer grazes one cow, the common feeding ground
is optimally used. But then someone reasons: "If I put a second cow in the
pasture, I'll double my output, minus the mere 1 percent overgrazing." So
this farmer adds a second cow. So do each of the other farmers. The inevitable result? The Tragedy of the Commons—a grassless mud field.

Many real predicaments parallel this story. Internet congestion occurs
as unregulated individuals, seeking to maximize their own gain, surf the

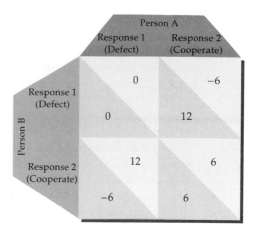

FIGURE 23-2
Laboratory version of the Prisoner's Dilemma. The numbers represent some reward, such as money. In each box, the number above the diagonal lines is the outcome for person A.

Web, filling its pipelines with graphical information (Huberman & Lukose, 1997). Likewise, environmental pollution is the sum of many minor pollutions, each of which benefits the individual polluters much more than they could benefit themselves (and the environment) if they stopped polluting. We litter public places—dorm lounges, parks, zoos—while keeping our personal spaces clean. And we deplete our natural resources because the immediate personal benefits of, say, taking a long, hot shower outweigh the seemingly inconsequential costs. Whalers knew others would exploit the whales if they didn't and figured that taking a few whales would hardly diminish the species. Therein lay the tragedy. Everybody's business (conservation) became nobody's business.

The elements of the commons dilemma have been isolated in laboratory games. Put yourself in the place of Arizona State University students playing Julian Edney's Nuts Game (1979). You and several others sit around a shallow bowl that initially has 10 metal nuts. The experimenter explains that your goal is to accumulate as many nuts as possible. Each of you at any time may take as many as you want, and every 10 seconds the number of nuts remaining in the bowl will be doubled. Would you leave the nuts in the bowl to regenerate, thus producing a greater harvest for all?

Likely not. Unless they were given time to devise and agree upon a conservation strategy, 65 percent of Edney's groups never reached the first 10-second replenishment. Often the people knocked the bowl on the floor grabbing for their share.

Edney's nut bowl reminds me of the cookie jar in our home. What we *should* have done is conserve cookies during the interval between weekly restockings, so that each day we could each munch two or three. Lacking regulation and fearing that other family members would soon deplete the resource, what we actually did was maximize our individual cookie consumption by downing one after the other. The result: Within 24 hours the cookie glut would end, the jar sitting empty.

The Prisoner's Dilemma and the Tragedy of the Commons have several similar features. First, both tempt people to explain their own behavior situationally ("I had to protect myself against exploitation by my opponent") and to explain their partners' behavior dispositionally ("She was greedy," "He was untrustworthy"). Most never realize that their counterparts are viewing them with the same fundamental attribution error (Hine & Gifford, 1996).

Second, motives often change. At first, people are eager to make some easy money, then to minimize their losses, and finally to save face and avoid defeat (Brockner & others, 1982; Teger, 1980). These shifting motives are strikingly similar to President Johnson's apparently shifting motives during the buildup of the Vietnam War in the 1960s. At first, his speeches described America's concern for democracy, freedom, and justice. As the conflict escalated, his expressed concern became protecting America's honor and avoiding the national humiliation of losing a war.

Third, most real-life conflicts, like the Prisoner's Dilemma and the Tragedy of the Commons, are **non-zero-sum games.** The two sides' profits and losses need not add up to zero. Both can win; both can lose. Each game pits the immediate interests of individuals against the well-being of the group. Each is a diabolical social trap that shows how, even when individuals behave "rationally," harm can result. No malicious person planned for Los Angeles to be smothered in smog, or for the earth's atmosphere to be warmed by a blanket of carbon dioxide.

Not all self-serving behavior leads to collective doom. In a plentiful commons, as in the world of eighteenth-century capitalist economist Adam Smith (1776), individuals who seek to maximize their own profit can also give the community what it needs: "It is not from the benevolence of the butcher, the brewer, or the baker, that we expect our dinner," Smith observed, "but from their regard to their own interest" (p. 18).

Resolving Social Dilemmas

In those situations that are indeed social traps, how can we induce people to cooperate for their mutual betterment? Research with the laboratory dilemmas reveals several ways (Gifford & Hine, 1997).

Regulation
If taxes were entirely voluntary, how many would pay their full share? Surely, many would not, which is why modern societies do not depend on charity to pay for social and military security.

We also develop laws and regulations for our common good. An International Whaling Commission sets an agreed-upon "harvest" that enables whales to regenerate.

Small Is Beautiful

There is another way to resolve social dilemmas: Make the group small. In small commons, each person feels more responsible and effective (Kerr, 1989). In small groups, people also feel more identified with a group's success. Anything else that enhances group identity will also increase cooperation. Even just a few minutes of discussion or just believing that one shares similarities with others in the group can increase "we feeling," and cooperation (Brewer, 1987; Orbell & others, 1988).

On the Puget Sound island where I grew up, our small neighborhood shared a communal water supply. On hot summer days when the reservoir ran low, a light came on, signaling our 15 families to conserve. Recognizing our responsibility to one another, and feeling like our conservation really mattered, each of us conserved. Never did the reservoir run dry. In a much larger commons—say, a city—voluntary conservation is less successful.

Communication

To escape a social trap, people must communicate. In the laboratory, group communication sometimes degenerates into threats and name calling (Deutsch & Krauss, 1960).

Without communication, those who expect others not to cooperate will usually refuse to cooperate themselves (Messé & Sivacek, 1979; Pruitt & Kimmel, 1977). One who mistrusts almost has to be uncooperative (to protect against exploitation). Noncooperation, in turn, feeds further mistrust ("What else could I do? It's a dog-eat-dog world"). In experiments, communication reduces mistrust, enabling people to reach agreements that lead to their common betterment.

Changing the Payoffs

Cooperation rises when experimenters change the payoff matrix to make cooperation more rewarding, exploitation less rewarding (Komorita & Barth, 1985; Pruitt & Rubin, 1986). Changing payoffs also helps resolve actual dilemmas. In some cities, freeways get clogged and skies get smogged because people prefer the convenience of driving themselves directly to work. Each knows that one more car does not add noticeably to the congestion and pollution. To alter the personal cost-benefit calculations, many cities now give carpoolers incentives, such as designated freeway lanes or reduced tolls.

Appeals to Altruistic Norms

When cooperation obviously serves the public good, one can usefully appeal to the social-responsibility norm (Lynn & Oldenquist, 1986). When, for example, people believe public transportation can save time, they will be more likely to use it if they also believe it reduces pollution (Van Vugt & others, 1996). In the struggle for civil rights, many marchers willingly agreed, for the sake of the larger group, to suffer harassment, beatings, and jail. In wartime, people make great personal sacrifices for the good of their group. As Winston Churchill said of the Battle of Britain, the actions of the Royal Air Force pilots were genuinely altruistic: A great many people owed a great deal to those who flew into battle knowing there was a high probability they would not return.

To summarize, we can minimize destructive entrapment in social dilemmas by establishing rules that regulate self-serving behavior, by keeping groups small, by enabling people to communicate, by changing payoffs to make cooperation more rewarding, and by invoking altruistic norms.

COMPETITION

In the module on prejudice we noted that racial hostilities often arise when groups compete for jobs and housing. When interests clash, conflict erupts.

But does competition by itself provoke hostile conflict? Real-life situations are so complex that it is hard to be sure. If competition is indeed responsible, then it should be possible to provoke in an experiment. We could randomly divide people into two groups, have the groups compete for a scarce resource, and note what happens. This is precisely what Muzafer Sherif (1966) and his colleagues did in a dramatic series of experiments with typical 11- and 12-year-old boys. The inspiration for these experiments dated back to Sherif's witnessing, as a teenager, Greek troops invading his Turkish province in 1919.

> They started killing people right and left. [That] made a great impression on me. There and then I became interested in understanding why these things were happening among human beings. . . . I wanted to learn whatever science or specialization was needed to understand this intergroup savagery. (Quoted by Aron & Aron, 1989, p. 131)

After studying the social roots of savagery, Sherif introduced the seeming essentials into several three-week summer camping experiences. In one such study, he divided 22 unacquainted Oklahoma City boys into two groups, took them to a Boy Scout camp in separate buses, and settled them in bunkhouses about a half-mile apart. For most of the first week, each group was unaware of the other group's existence. By cooperating in various activities—preparing meals, camping out, fixing up a swimming hole, building a rope bridge—each group soon became close-knit. They gave themselves names: "Rattlers" and "Eagles." Typifying the good feeling, a sign appeared in one cabin: "Home Sweet Home."

Group identity thus established, the stage was set for the conflict. Toward the end of the first week, the Rattlers "discovered the Eagles on 'our' baseball field." When the camp staff then proposed a tournament of competitive activities between the two groups (baseball games, tugs-of-war, cabin inspections, treasure hunts, and so forth), both groups responded enthusiastically. This was a win-lose competition. The spoils (medals, knives) would all go to the tournament victor.

The result? The camp gradually degenerated into open warfare. It was like a scene from William Golding's novel *Lord of the Flies,* which depicts the social disintegration of boys marooned on an island. In Sherif's study, the conflict began with each side calling the other names during the competitive activities. Soon it escalated to dining hall "garbage wars," flag burnings, cabin ransackings, even fistfights. Asked to describe the other group, the boys said "they" were "sneaky," "smart alecks," "stinkers"; they referred to their own group as "brave," "tough," "friendly."

The win-lose competition had produced intense conflict, negative images of the outgroup, and strong ingroup cohesiveness and pride. All this occurred without any cultural, physical, or economic differences between the two groups and with boys who were their communities' "cream of the crop." Sherif (1966) noted that had we visited the camp at this point, we would have concluded these "were wicked, disturbed, and vicious bunches of youngsters" (p. 85). Actually, their evil behavior was triggered by an evil situation. Fortunately, as we will see, Sherif not only made strangers into enemies; he then made the enemies into friends.

PERCEIVED INJUSTICE

"That's unfair!" "What a ripoff!" "We deserve better!" Such comments typify conflicts bred by perceived injustice. But what is "justice"? According to some social-psychological theorists, people perceive justice as *equity*—the distribution of rewards in proportion to individuals' contributions (Walster & others, 1978). If you and I have a relationship (employer-employee, teacher-student, husband-wife, colleague-colleague), it is equitable if:

$$\frac{\text{My outcomes}}{\text{My inputs}} = \frac{\text{Your outcomes}}{\text{Your inputs}}$$

If you contribute more and benefit less than I do, you will feel exploited and irritated; I might feel exploitative and guilty. Chances are, though, that you, more than I, will be sensitive to the inequity (Greenberg, 1986; Messick & Sentis, 1979).

We might agree with the equity principle's definition of justice yet disagree on whether our relationship is equitable. If two people are colleagues, what will each consider a relevant input? The one who is older might favor basing pay on seniority, the other on current productivity. Given such a disagreement, whose definition is likely to prevail? More

TABLE 23-1 GALLUP POLLS REVEAL INCREASED PERCEPTIONS OF GENDER INEQUALITY

All things considered, who has a better life in this country—men or women?

	1972	1993
Men	29%	60%
Women	35	21
Same	30	15
No opinion	6	5

SOURCE: From Roper Center for Public Opinion Research, 1997.

often than not, those with social power convince themselves and others that they deserve what they're getting (Mikula, 1984). This has been called a "golden" rule: Whoever has the gold makes the rules.

As this suggests, exploiters can relieve their guilt by valuing or devaluing inputs to justify the existing outcomes. Men might perceive the lower pay of women as equitable, given women's "less important" inputs. Those who inflict harm might blame the victim and thus maintain their belief in a just world.

And how do those who are exploited react? Elaine Hatfield, William Walster, and Ellen Berscheid (1978) detected three possibilities. They can accept and justify their inferior position ("We're poor; it's what we deserve, but we're happy"). They can demand compensation, perhaps by harassing, embarrassing, even cheating their exploiter. If all else fails, they could try to restore equity by retaliating.

An interesting implication of equity theory—an implication that has been confirmed experimentally—is that the more competent and worthy people feel (the more they value their inputs), the more they will feel underbenefited and thus eager to retaliate (Ross & others, 1971). Intense social protests generally come from those who believe themselves worthy of more than they are receiving.

Since 1970, professional opportunities for women have significantly increased. Ironically, though understandably to an equity theorist, so have people's feelings that women's status is *in*equitable (Table 23-1). So long as women compared their opportunities and earnings with other women, they felt generally satisfied, as they still do with their disproportionate share of family labor (Jackson, 1989; Major, 1989, 1993). Now that women are more likely to see themselves as men's equals, their sense of relative deprivation has grown. If secretarial work and truck driving have "comparable worth" (for the skills required), then they deserve comparable pay; that's equity, say advocates of gender equality (Lowe & Wittig, 1989).

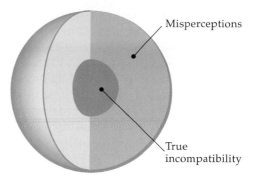

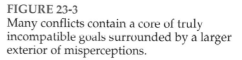

FIGURE 23-3
Many conflicts contain a core of truly
incompatible goals surrounded by a larger
exterior of misperceptions.

MISPERCEPTION

Recall that conflict is a *perceived* incompatibility of actions or goals. Many
conflicts contain but a small core of truly incompatible goals; the bigger
problem is the misperceptions of the other's motives and goals. The Eagles
and the Rattlers did indeed have some genuinely incompatible aims, but
their perceptions subjectively magnified their differences (Figure 23-3).

In earlier modules we considered the seeds of such misperception. *Self-
serving bias* leads individuals and groups to accept credit for their good deeds
and shuck responsibility for bad deeds, without according others the same
benefit of the doubt. A tendency to *self-justify* further inclines people to deny
the wrong of their evil acts that cannot be shucked off. Thanks to the *fundamental attribution error,* each side sees the other's hostility as reflecting an evil
disposition. One then filters the information and interprets it to fit one's *preconceptions.* Groups frequently *polarize* these self-serving, self-justifying, bias-
ing tendencies. One symptom of *groupthink* is the tendency to perceive one's
own group as moral and strong, the opposition as evil and weak. Terrorist
acts that are despicable brutality to most people are "holy war" to others. Indeed, the mere fact of being in a group triggers an *ingroup bias.* And negative
stereotypes, once formed, are often resistant to contradictory evidence.

So it should not surprise us, though it should sober us, to discover that
people in conflict form distorted images of one another. Even the types of
misperception are intriguingly predictable.

Mirror-Image Perceptions

To a striking degree, the misperceptions of those in conflict are mutual. People in conflict attribute similar virtues to themselves and vices to the other.
When American psychologist Urie Bronfenbrenner (1961) visited the former

Soviet Union in 1960 and conversed with many ordinary citizens in Russian, he was astonished to hear them saying the same things about America that Americans were saying about the Soviets. The Soviets said that the U.S. government was militarily aggressive; that it exploited and deluded the American people; that in diplomacy it was not to be trusted. "Slowly and painfully, it forced itself upon one that the Russians' distorted picture of us was curiously similar to our view of them—a mirror image."

When two sides have clashing perceptions, at least one of the two is misperceiving the other. And when such misperceptions exist, noted Bronfenbrenner, "It is a psychological phenomenon without parallel in the gravity of its consequences . . . for *it is characteristic of such images that they are self-confirming.*" If A expects B to be hostile, A might treat B in such a way that B fulfills A's expectations, thus beginning a vicious circle. Morton Deutsch (1986) explains:

> You hear the false rumor that a friend is saying nasty things about you; you snub him; he then badmouths you, confirming your expectation. Similarly, if the policymakers of East and West believe that war is likely and either attempts to increase its military security vis-à-vis the other, the other's response will justify the initial move.

Negative **mirror-image perceptions** have been an obstacle to peace in many places:

- Both sides of the Arab-Israeli conflict insisted that "we" are motivated by our need to protect our security and our territory, while "they" want to obliterate us and gobble up our land (Heradstveit, 1979; R. K. White, 1977). Given such intense mistrust, negotiation is difficult.
- At Northern Ireland's University of Ulster, J. A. Hunter and his colleagues (1991) showed Catholic and Protestant students videos of a Protestant attack at a Catholic funeral and a Catholic attack at a Protestant funeral. Most students attributed the other side's attack to "bloodthirsty" motives but its own side's attack to retaliation or self-defense.
- Muslims and Hindus in Bangladesh exhibit the same ingroup-favoring perceptions (Islam & Hewstone, 1993).

Destructive mirror-image perceptions also operate in conflicts between small groups and between individuals. As we saw in the dilemma games, both parties might say, "We want to cooperate. But their refusal to cooperate forces us to react defensively." In a study of executives, Kenneth Thomas and Louis Pondy (1977) uncovered such attributions. Asked to describe a significant recent conflict, only 12 percent felt the other party was cooperative; 74 percent perceived themselves as cooperative. The executives explained that they had "suggested," "informed," and "recommended" but that their antagonist had "demanded," "disagreed with everything I said," and "refused."

International conflicts are often fueled by an illusion that the enemy's top leaders are evil but their people, though controlled and manipulated, are pro-us. This *evil leader–good people* perception characterized Americans' and Soviets' views of each other during the cold war. "The American people are good, but the leaders are bad," explained one Baghdad grocer after the late 1998 bombing of his country (Kinzer, 1998).

Another type of mirror-image perception is each side's exaggeration of the other's position. People with opposing views on issues such as abortion, capital punishment, and government budget cuts often differ less than they suppose. Each side overestimates the extremity of the other's views, especially those of the group seeking change. And each presumes that "our" beliefs *follow* from the facts while "their" ideology *dictates* their interpretation of facts (Keltner & Robinson, 1996; Robinson & others, 1995). From such exaggerated perceptions arise culture wars. Ralph White (1996) reports that the Serbs started the war in Bosnia partly out of an exaggerated fear of the relatively secularized Bosnian Muslims, whose beliefs they wrongly associated with Middle Eastern Islamic fundamentalism and fanatical terrorism.

Shifting Perceptions

If misperceptions accompany conflict, then they should appear and disappear as conflicts wax and wane. And they do, with startling ease. The same processes that create the enemy's image can reverse that image when the enemy becomes an ally. Thus the "bloodthirsty, cruel, treacherous, bucktoothed little Japs" of World War II soon became—in American minds (Gallup, 1972) and in the American media—our "intelligent, hardworking, self-disciplined, resourceful allies." Our World War II allies, the Soviets, then became the "warlike, treacherous" ones.

The Germans, whom Americans after two world wars hated, then admired, and then again hated, were once again admired—apparently no longer plagued by what earlier was presumed to be cruelty in their national character. So long as Iraq was attacking Iran, even while using chemical weapons and massacring its own Kurds, many nations supported it. Our enemy's enemy is our friend. When Iraq ended its war with Iran and invaded oil-rich Kuwait, Iraq's behavior suddenly became "barbaric." Clearly, images of our enemies not only justify our actions but also change with amazing ease.

The extent of misperceptions during conflict provides a chilling reminder that people need not be insane or abnormally evil to form these distorted images of their antagonists. When in conflict with another nation, another group, or simply a roommate or parent, we readily develop misperceptions that allow us to perceive our own motives and actions as wholly good and the other's as totally evil. Our antagonists usually form a mirror-image perception of us. So, trapped in a social dilemma, competing for scarce resources, or perceiving injustice, the conflict continues until something enables both parties to peel away their misperceptions and work at reconciling their actual differences. Good advice, then, is this: When in conflict, do not assume that the other fails to share your values and morality; rather, compare perceptions, assuming that the other is likely perceiving the situation differently.

CONCEPTS TO REMEMBER

Conflict   A perceived incompatibility of actions or goals.

Non-zero-sum games   Games in which outcomes need not sum to zero. With cooperation, both can win; with competition, both can lose. (Also called *mixed-motive situations*.)

Mirror-image perceptions   Reciprocal views of one another often held by parties in conflict; for example, each might view itself as moral and peace-loving and the other as evil and aggressive.

24

❖

Blessed Are the Peacemakers

We have seen how conflicts are ignited: by social traps, competition, perceived injustices, and misperceptions. Although grim, the picture is not hopeless. Sometimes closed fists become open arms as hostilities evolve into friendship. Social psychologists have focused on four strategies for helping enemies become comrades. We can remember these as the four C's of peacemaking: contact, cooperation, communication, conciliation.

CONTACT

Might putting two conflicting individuals or groups into close contact enable them to know and like each other? We have seen why it might. We have seen that proximity—and the accompanying interaction, anticipation of interaction, and mere exposure—boosts liking. We have noted that the recent downturn in blatant racial prejudice in the United States followed closely on the heels of desegregation, showing that "attitudes follow behavior."

During the last 30 years in the United States, segregation and prejudice have diminished together. But was interracial contact the *cause* of these improved attitudes? Were those who actually experienced desegregation affected by it?

Does Desegregation Improve Racial Attitudes?

School desegregation has produced measurable benefits, such as leading more Blacks to attend and succeed in college (Stephan, 1988). Does desegregation of schools, neighborhoods, and workplaces also produce favorable *social* results? The evidence is mixed.

On the one hand, many studies conducted during and shortly after the desegregation following World War II found Whites' attitudes toward Blacks improving markedly. Whether the people were department store clerks and customers, merchant marines, government workers, police officers, neighbors, or students, racial contact led to diminished prejudice (Amir, 1969; Pettigrew, 1969). For example, near the end of World War II, the Army partially desegregated some of its rifle companies (Stouffer & others, 1949). When asked their opinions of such desegregation, 11 percent of the White soldiers in segregated companies approved. Of those in desegregated companies, 60 percent approved.

Surveys of nearly 4,000 Europeans reveal that friendship is a key to successful contact: If you have a minority-group friend, you become much more likely to express sympathy and support for the friend's group, and even somewhat more support for immigration by that group. It's true of West Germans' attitudes toward Turks, French people's attitudes toward Asians and North Africans, Netherlanders' attitudes toward Surinamers and Turks, and Britishers' attitudes toward West Indians and Asians (Hamberger & Hewstone, 1997; Pettigrew, 1997). Likewise, antigay feeling is lower among people who know gays personally (Herek, 1993). Additional studies of attitudes toward the elderly, the mentally ill, AIDs patients, and those with disabilities confirm that contact often predicts positive attitudes (Pettigrew, 1998).

Findings such as these influenced the Supreme Court's 1954 decision to desegregate U.S. schools and helped fuel the civil rights movement of the 1960s (Pettigrew, 1986). Yet studies of the effects of school desegregation have been less encouraging. Social psychologist Walter Stephan (1986) reviewed all such studies and concluded that racial attitudes have been little affected by desegregation. For Blacks the more noticeable consequence of desegregated schooling is their increased likelihood of attending integrated (or predominantly White) colleges, living in integrated neighborhoods, and working in integrated settings.

So, sometimes desegregation improves racial attitudes, sometimes it doesn't. Such disagreements excite the scientist's detective spirit. What explains the difference? So far, we've been lumping all kinds of desegregation together. Actual desegregation occurs in many ways and under vastly different conditions.

When Does Desegregation Improve Racial Attitudes?

Might the amount of interracial *contact* be a factor? Indeed it seems to be. Researchers have gone into dozens of desegregated schools and observed with whom children of a given race eat, loiter, and talk. Race influences contact. Whites disproportionately associate with Whites, Blacks with Blacks (Schofield, 1982, 1986). Academic tracking programs often amplify resegregation by separating academically advantaged White students into predominantly White classes.

In contrast, the more encouraging older studies of store clerks, soldiers, and housing project neighbors involved considerable interracial contact, more than enough to reduce the anxiety that marks initial intergroup contact. Other studies involving prolonged, personal contact— between Black and White prison inmates and between Black and White girls in an interracial summer camp—show similar benefits (Clore & others, 1978; Foley, 1976). Among American students who have studied in Germany or Britain, the more contact they had with host-country people, the more positive their attitudes (Stangor & others, 1996).

The social psychologists who advocated desegregation never claimed that contact of *any* sort would improve attitudes. They expected poor results when contacts were competitive, unsupported by authorities, and unequal (Pettigrew, 1988; Stephan, 1987). Before 1954, many prejudiced Whites had frequent contacts with Blacks—as shoeshine men and domestic workers. Contacts on such an unequal basis breed attitudes that merely justify the continuation of inequality. So it's important that the contact be **equal-status contact,** like that between the store clerks, the soldiers, the neighbors, the prisoners, and the summer campers.

COOPERATION

Although equal-status contact can help, it is sometimes not enough. It didn't help when Muzafer Sherif stopped the Eagles-versus-Rattlers competition and brought the groups together for noncompetitive activities, such as watching movies, shooting off fireworks, and eating. By this time, their hostility was so strong that what contact provided was the opportunity for taunts and attacks. When an Eagle was bumped by a Rattler, his fellow Eagles urged him to "brush off the dirt." Obviously, desegregating the two groups had hardly promoted their social integration.

Given entrenched hostility, what can a peacemaker do? Think back to the successful and unsuccessful desegregation efforts. The Army's racial mixing of rifle companies not only brought Blacks and Whites into equal-status contact but also made them interdependent. Together, they were fighting a common enemy, striving toward a shared goal.

Contrast this interdependence with the competitive situation in the typical classroom, desegregated or not. Is the following scene familiar (Aronson, 1980)? Students compete for good grades, teacher approval, and various honors and privileges. The teacher asks a question. Several students' hands shoot up; other students sit, eyes downcast, trying to look invisible. When the teacher calls on one of the eager faces, the others hope for a wrong answer, giving them a chance to display their knowledge. The losers in this academic sport often resent the "nerds" or "geeks" who succeed. The situation abounds with both competition and painfully obvious status inequalities; we could hardly design it better to create divisions among the children.

Does this suggest a second factor that predicts whether the effect of desegregation will be favorable? Does competitive contact divide and *cooperative* contact unite? Consider what happens to people who together face a common predicament.

Common External Threats

Together with others, have you ever been victimized by the weather, harassed as part of your initiation into a group, punished by a teacher, or persecuted and ridiculed because of your social, racial, or religious identity? If so, you might recall feeling close to those with whom you shared the predicament. Perhaps previous social barriers were dropped as you helped one another dig out of the snow or struggled to cope with a common enemy.

Such friendliness is common among those who experience a shared threat. John Lanzetta (1955) observed this when he put four-man groups of Naval ROTC cadets to work on problem-solving tasks and then began informing them over a loudspeaker that their answers were wrong, their productivity inexcusably low, their thinking stupid. Other groups did not receive this harassment. Lanzetta observed that the group members under duress became friendlier to one another, more cooperative, less argumentative, less competitive. They were in it together. And the result was a cohesive spirit.

Having a common enemy unified the groups of competing boys in Sherif's camping experiments and in many subsequent experiments (Dion, 1979). Americans' feelings of patriotism and unity were aroused by conflicts with Germany and Japan during World War II, with the Soviet Union during the cold war, with Iran during 1980, and with Iraq during 1991. Soldiers who together face combat often maintain lifelong ties with their comrades (Elder & Clipp, 1988). Few things so unite a people as having a common hatred.

Times of interracial strife can therefore be times of heightened group pride. For Chinese university students in Toronto, facing discrimination heightens a sense of kinship with other Chinese (Pak & others, 1991). Just being reminded of an outgroup (say, a rival school) heightens people's responsiveness to their own group (Wilder & Shapiro, 1984). When keenly conscious of who "they" are, we also know who "we" are.

Superordinate Goals

Closely related to the unifying power of an external threat is the unifying power of **superordinate goals,** goals compelling for all in a group and requiring cooperative effort. To promote harmony among his warring campers, Sherif introduced such goals. He created a problem with the camp water supply, necessitating their cooperation to restore the water. Given an opportunity to rent a movie, one expensive enough to require the joint resources of both groups, they again cooperated. When a truck "broke down" on a camping trip, a staff member casually left the tug-of-war rope nearby, prompting one boy to suggest that they all pull the truck to get it started. When it started, a backslapping celebration ensued over their victorious "tug-of-war against the truck."

After working together to achieve such superordinate goals, the boys ate together and enjoyed themselves around a campfire. Friendships sprouted across group lines. Hostilities plummeted. On the last day, the boys decided to travel home together on one bus. During the trip they no longer sat by groups. As the bus approached Oklahoma City and home, they, as one, spontaneously sang "Oklahoma" and then bade their friends farewell. With isolation and competition, Sherif made strangers into bitter enemies. With superordinate goals, he made enemies into friends.

Are Sherif's experiments mere child's play? Or can pulling together to achieve superordinate goals be similarly beneficial with adults in conflict? Robert Blake and Jane Mouton (1979) wondered. So in a series of two-week experiments involving more than 1,000 executives in 150 different groups, they re-created the essential features of the situation experienced by the Rattlers and Eagles. Each group first engaged in activities by itself, then competed with another group, and then cooperated with the other group in working toward jointly chosen superordinate goals. Their results provided "unequivocal evidence that adult reactions parallel those of Sherif's younger subjects."

Extending these findings, Samuel Gaertner, John Dovidio, and their collaborators (1993, 1998) report that working cooperatively has especially favorable effects under conditions that lead people to define a new, inclusive group that dissolves their former subgroups. Old feelings of bias against another group diminish when members of the two groups sit alternately around a table (rather than on opposite sides), give their new group a single name, and then work together under conditions that foster a good mood. "Us" and "them" become "we."

Cooperative Learning

So far we have noted the apparently meager social benefits of typical school desegregation and the apparently dramatic social benefits of successful, cooperative contacts between members of rival groups. Could putting these two findings together suggest a constructive alternative to traditional desegregation practices? Several independent research teams speculated yes. Each wondered whether, without affecting academic achievement, we could promote interracial friendships by replacing competitive learning situations with cooperative ones. Given the diversity of their methods—all involving students on integrated study teams, sometimes in competition with other teams—the results are striking and very heartening.

One research team, led by Elliot Aronson (1978, 1979; Aronson & Gonzalez, 1988), elicited similar group cooperation with a "jigsaw" technique. In experiments in Texas and California elementary schools, they assigned children to racially and academically diverse six-member groups. The subject they were studying was then divided into six parts, with each student becoming the expert on his or her part. In a unit on Chile, one student might be the expert on Chile's history, another on its geography, another on its culture. First, the various "historians," "geographers," and so forth got together to master their material. Then each returned to the home group to teach it to their classmates. Each group member held, so to speak, a piece of the jigsaw. The self-confident students therefore had to listen to and learn from the reticent students, who in turn soon realized they had something important to offer their peers.

With cooperative learning, students learn not only the material but other lessons as well. Cross-racial friendships also begin to blossom. The exam scores of minority students improve (perhaps because academic achievement is now peer-supported). After the experiments are over, many teachers continue using cooperative learning (D. W. Johnson & others, 1981; Slavin, 1990). "It is clear," wrote race-relations expert John McConahay (1981), that cooperative learning "is the most effective practice for improving race relations in desegregated schools that we know of to date."

So, cooperative, equal-status contacts exert a positive influence on boy campers, industrial executives, college students, and schoolchildren. Does the principle extend to all levels of human relations? Are families unified by pulling together to farm the land, restore an old house, or sail a sloop? Are communal identities forged by barn raisings, group singing, or cheering on the football team? Is international understanding bred by international collaboration in science and space, by joint efforts to feed the world and conserve resources, by friendly personal contacts between people of different nations? Indications are that the answer to all these questions is yes (Brewer & Miller, 1988; Desforges & others, 1991, 1997; Deutsch, 1985, 1994). Thus an important challenge facing our divided world is to identify and agree on our superordinate goals and to structure cooperative efforts to achieve them.

COMMUNICATION

Conflicting parties have other ways to resolve their differences. When husband and wife, or labor and management, or nation X and nation Y disagree, they can **bargain** with one another directly. They can ask a third party to **mediate** by making suggestions and facilitating their negotiations. Or they can **arbitrate** by submitting their disagreement to someone who will study the issues and impose a settlement.

Bargaining

If you or I want to buy or sell a new car, are we better off adopting a tough bargaining stance—opening with an extreme offer so that splitting the difference will yield a favorable result? Or are we better off beginning with a sincere "good-faith" offer?

Experiments suggest no simple answer. On the one hand, those who demand more will often get more. Tough bargaining can lower the other party's expectations, making the other side willing to settle for less (Yukl, 1974).

But toughness can sometimes backfire. Many a conflict is not over a pie of fixed size but over a pie that shrinks if the conflict continues. When a strike is prolonged, both labor and management lose. Being tough can also diminish the chances of actually reaching an agreement. If the other party responds with an equally extreme stance, both can be locked into positions from which neither can back down without losing face. In the weeks before the 1991 Persian Gulf war, President Bush threatened, in the full glare of publicity, to "kick Saddam's ass." Saddam Hussein, no less macho, threatened to make "infidel" Americans "swim in their own blood." After such belligerent statements, it was difficult for either side to evade war and save face.

Mediation

A third-party mediator can offer suggestions that enable conflicting parties to make concessions and still save face (Pruitt, 1998). If my concession can be attributed to a mediator, who is gaining an equal concession from my antagonist, then neither of us will be viewed as caving in to the other's demands.

Turning Win-Lose into Win-Win

Mediators also help resolve conflicts by facilitating constructive communication. Their first task is to help the parties rethink the conflict and gain information about the other interests (Thompson, 1998). Typically, people on both sides have a competitive "win-lose" orientation: They think they are successful if their opponent is unhappy with the result, and unsuccessful if their opponent is pleased (Thompson & others, 1995). The mediator aims to replace this win-lose orientation with a cooperative "win-win" orientation, by prodding them to set aside their conflicting demands and instead to think about each other's underlying needs, interests, and goals. In experiments, Leigh Thompson (1990) found that, with experience, negotiators become better able to make mutually beneficial tradeoffs and thus to achieve win-win resolutions.

A classic story of such a resolution concerns two sisters who quarreled over an orange (Follett, 1940). Finally they compromised and split the orange in half, whereupon one sister squeezed her half for juice while the other used the peel to make a cake. In experiments at the State University of New York at Buffalo, Dean Pruitt and his associates induced bargainers to search for **integrative agreements.** If the sisters had agreed to split the orange so that one sister got all the juice and the other got all the peel, they would have hit on such an agreement, one that integrates both parties' interests (Kimmel & others, 1980; Pruitt & Lewis, 1975, 1977). Compared to compromises, in which each party sacrifices something important, integrative agreements are more enduring. Because they are mutually rewarding, they also lead to better ongoing relationships (Pruitt, 1986).

Unraveling Misperceptions with Controlled Communications

Communication often helps reduce self-fulfilling misperceptions. Perhaps you can recall experiences similar to that of this college student:

> Often, after a prolonged period of little communication, I perceive Martha's silence as a sign of her dislike for me. She, in turn, thinks that my quietness is a result of my being mad at her. My silence induces her silence, which makes me even more silent . . . until this snowballing effect is broken by some occurrence that makes it necessary for us to interact. And the communication then unravels all the misinterpretations we had made about one another.

The outcome of such conflicts often depends on *how* people communicate their feelings to one another. Roger Knudson and his colleagues (1980) invited married couples to come to the University of Illinois psychology laboratory and relive, through role playing, one of their past conflicts. Before, during, and after their conversation (which often generated as much emotion as the actual previous conflict), the couples were closely observed and questioned. Couples who evaded the issue, by failing to make their positions clear or failing to acknowledge their spouse's position, left with the illusion that they were more in harmony and agreement than they really were. Often, they came to believe they now agreed more when actually they agreed less. In contrast, those who engaged the issue—by making their positions clear and by taking one another's views into account—achieved more actual agreement and gained more accurate information about one another's perceptions. That helps explain why couples who communicate their concerns directly and openly are usually happily married (Grush & Glidden, 1987).

Conflict researchers report that a key factor is *trust* (Ross & Ward, 1995). If you believe the other person is well-intentioned, you are more likely to divulge your needs and concerns. Lacking such trust, you might fear that being open will give the other party information that might be used against you.

When the two parties mistrust each other and communicate unproductively, a third-party mediator—a marriage counselor, a labor mediator, a diplomat—sometimes helps. After coaxing the conflicting parties to rethink their perceived win-lose conflict, the mediator often has each party identify and rank its goals. When goals are compatible, the ranking procedure makes it easier for each to concede on less important goals so that both achieve their chief goals (Erickson & others, 1974; Schulz & Pruitt, 1978).

Once labor and management both believe that management's goal of higher productivity and profit is compatible with labor's goal of better wages and working conditions, they can begin to work for an integrative win-win solution.

When the parties then convene to communicate directly, they are usually *not* set loose in the hope that, eyeball to eyeball, the conflict will resolve itself. In the midst of a threatening, stressful conflict, emotions often disrupt the ability to understand the other party's point of view. Communication can become most difficult just when it is most needed (Tetlock, 1985). Often the mediator will therefore structure the encounter to help each party understand and feel understood by the other. The mediator might ask the conflicting parties to restrict their arguments to statements of fact, including statements of how they feel and how they respond when the other acts in a given way: "I enjoy having music on. When you play it loud, I find it hard to concentrate. That makes me crabby." Also, the mediator might ask people to reverse roles and argue the other's position, or to restate one another's positions before replying with their own: "My turning up the stereo bugs you."

Neutral third parties can also suggest mutually agreeable proposals that would be dismissed—"reactively devalued"—if offered by either side. Constance Stillinger and her colleagues (1991) found that a nuclear disarmament proposal that Americans dismissed when it was attributed to the Soviet Union seemed more acceptable when it was attributed to a neutral third party. Likewise, people will often reactively devalue a concession offered by an adversary ("They must not value it"); the same concession can seem less like a token gesture when suggested by a third party.

These peacemaking principles, based partly on laboratory experiments, partly on practical experience, have helped mediate both international and industrial conflicts (Blake & Mouton, 1962, 1979; Fisher, 1994; Wehr, 1979). One small team of Arab and Jewish Americans, led by social psychologist Herbert Kelman (1997), has conducted workshops bringing together influential Arabs and Israelis, and Pakistanis and Indians. Using methods such as those we've considered, Kelman and colleagues counter misperceptions and have participants creatively seek solutions for their common good. Isolated, the participants are free to speak directly to their adversaries without fear of their constituents' second-guessing what they are saying. The result? Those from both sides typically come to understand the other's perspective and how the other side responds to their own group's actions.

In 1976, Kelman drove an Egyptian social scientist, Boutros Boutros-Ghali (who in 1991 became the UN secretary general), to the Boston airport. En route, they formulated plans for an Egyptian conference on misperceptions in Arab-Israeli relations. The conference later took place, and Kelman conveyed its promising results to influential Israelis. A year later, Boutros-Ghali became Egypt's acting foreign minister, and Egyptian President Anwar Sadat made his historic trip to Israel, opening a road to peace. Afterward, Boutros-Ghali said happily to Kelman, "You see the process that we started at the Boston airport last year" (Armstrong, 1981).

A year later, mediator Jimmy Carter secluded Sadat and Israeli Prime Minister Menachem Begin at Camp David. Rather than begin by having each side state its demands, Carter had them identify their underlying interests and goals—security for Israel, authority over its historic territory for Egypt. Thirteen days later, the trio emerged with "A Framework for Peace in the Middle East," granting each what they desired—security in exchange for territory (Rubin, 1989). Six months later, after further mediation by President Carter during visits to both countries, Begin and Sadat signed a treaty ending a state of war that had existed since 1948.

Arbitration

Some conflicts are so intractable, the underlying interests so divergent, that a mutually satisfactory resolution is unattainable. Bosnian Serbs and Muslims could not both have jurisdiction over the same homelands. In a divorce dispute over custody of a child, both parents cannot enjoy full custody. In these and many other cases (disputes over tenants' repair bills, athletes' wages, and national territories), a third-party mediator might—or might not—help resolve the conflict.

If not, the parties might turn to *arbitration* by having the mediator or another third party *impose* a settlement. Disputants usually prefer to settle their differences without arbitration so they retain control over the outcome. Neil McGillicuddy and others (1987) observed this preference in an experiment involving disputants coming to the Dispute Settlement Center in Buffalo, New York. When people knew they would face an arbitrated settlement if mediation failed, they tried harder to resolve the problem, exhibited less hostility, and thus were more likely to reach agreement.

In cases where differences seem large and irreconcilable, the prospect of arbitration can have an opposite effect (Pruitt, 1986). The disputants might freeze their positions, hoping to gain an advantage when the arbitrator chooses a compromise. To combat this tendency, some disputes, such as those involving salaries of individual baseball players, are settled with "final-offer arbitration" in which the third party chooses one of the two final offers. Final-offer arbitration motivates each party to make a reasonable proposal.

Typically, however, the final offer is not so reasonable as it would be if each party, free of self-serving bias, saw its own proposal through others' eyes. Negotiation researchers report that most disputants are made stubborn by "optimistic overconfidence" (Kahneman & Tversky, 1995). Successful mediation is hindered when, as often happens, both parties believe they have a two-thirds chance of winning a final-offer arbitration (Bazerman, 1986, 1990).

CONCILIATION

Sometimes tension and suspicion run so high that communication, much less resolution, becomes all but impossible. Each party might threaten, coerce, or retaliate against the other. Unfortunately, such acts tend to be reciprocated, thus escalating the conflict. So, would a strategy of appeasing the other party by being unconditionally cooperative produce a satisfying result? Often not. In laboratory games, those who are 100 percent cooperative often get exploited. Politically, a one-sided pacifism is out of the question anyway.

Grit

Social psychologist Charles Osgood (1962, 1980) advocated a third alternative—one that is conciliatory, rather than retaliatory, yet strong enough to discourage exploitation. Osgood called it "graduated and reciprocated initiatives in tension reduction," nicknamed **GRIT,** a label that suggests the determination it requires. GRIT aims to reverse the "conflict spiral" by triggering reciprocal deescalation.

GRIT requires one side to initiate a few small deescalatory actions, after *announcing a conciliatory intent.* The initiator states its desire to reduce tension, declares each conciliatory act prior to making it, and invites the adversary to reciprocate. Such announcements create a framework that helps the adversary correctly interpret what otherwise might be seen as weak or tricky actions. They also bring public pressure on the adversary to follow the reciprocity norm.

Next, the initiator establishes credibility and genuineness by carrying out, exactly as announced, several verifiable *conciliatory acts.* This intensifies the pressure to reciprocate. Making conciliatory acts diverse—perhaps offering medical information, closing a military base, and lifting a trade ban—keeps the initiator from making a significant sacrifice in any one area and leaves the adversary freer to choose its own means of reciprocation. If the adversary reciprocates voluntarily, its own conciliatory behavior can soften its attitudes.

GRIT *is* conciliatory. But it is not "surrender on the installment plan." The remaining aspects of the plan protect each side's self-interest by *maintaining retaliatory capability.* The initial conciliatory steps entail some small risk but do not jeopardize either side's security; rather, they are calculated to begin edging both sides down the tension ladder. If one side takes an aggressive action, the other side reciprocates in kind, making it clear it will not tolerate exploitation. Yet the reciprocal act is not an overresponse that would reescalate the conflict. If the adversary offers its own conciliatory acts, these, too, are matched or even slightly exceeded. Conflict expert Morton Deutsch (1993) captures the spirit of GRIT in advising negotiators to be "'firm, fair, and friendly': *firm* in resisting intimidation, exploitation, and dirty tricks; *fair* in holding to one's moral principles and not reciprocating the other's immoral behavior despite his or her provocations; and *friendly* in the sense that one is willing to initiate and reciprocate cooperation."

Does GRIT really work? In laboratory dilemma games, a successful strategy has proved to be simple "tit-for-tat," which begins with a cooperative opening play and thereafter matches the other party's last response (Axelrod & Dion, 1988; Komorita & others, 1992; Smith, 1987). Cooperate-unless-you've-just-been-exploited is another successful strategy that tries to cooperate and is forgiving, yet does not tolerate exploitation (Nowak & Sigmund, 1993). In a lengthy series of experiments at Ohio University, Svenn Lindskold and his associates (1976 to 1988) have tested other aspects of the GRIT strategy. Lindskold (1978) reports that his own and others' studies provide "strong support for the various steps in the GRIT proposal." In laboratory games, announcing cooperative intent *does* boost cooperation. Repeated conciliatory acts *do* breed greater trust (although self-serving biases often make one's own acts seem more conciliatory and less hostile than those of the adversary). Maintaining an equality of power *does* protect against exploitation.

GRIT-like strategies have occasionally been tried outside the laboratory, with promising results. To many, the most significant attempt at GRIT was the so-called Kennedy experiment (Etzioni, 1967). On June 10, 1963, President Kennedy gave a major speech, "A Strategy for Peace." In it he noted, "Our problems are man-made . . . and can be solved by man," and then announced his first conciliatory act: The United States was stopping all atmospheric nuclear tests and would not resume them unless another country did. In the Soviet Union, Kennedy's speech was published in full. Five days later Premier Khrushchev reciprocated, announcing he had halted production of strategic bombers. There soon followed further reciprocal gestures: The United States agreed to sell wheat to Russia, the Soviets agreed to a "hot line" between the two countries, and the two countries soon achieved a test-ban treaty. For a time, these conciliatory initiatives warmed relations between the two countries.

As they warmed again, within all our memories, President Bush in 1991 ordered the elimination of all land-based U.S. tactical nuclear warheads and took strategic bombers off high alert, putting their bombs in storage. Although leaving intact his least vulnerable and most extensive nuclear arsenal—submarine-based missiles—he invited Mikhail Gorbachev to reciprocate. Eight days later Gorbachev did, taking his bombers off alert, storing their bombs, and announcing the removal of nuclear weapons from short-range rockets, ships, and submarines.

Might conciliatory efforts also help reduce tension between individuals? There is every reason to expect so. When a relationship is strained and communication nonexistent, it sometimes takes only a conciliatory gesture—a soft answer, a warm smile, a gentle touch—for both parties to begin easing down the tension ladder, to a rung where contact, cooperation, and communication again become possible.

CONCEPTS TO REMEMBER

Equal-status contact   Contact made on an equal basis. Just as a relationship between people of unequal status breeds attitudes consistent with their relationship, so do relationships between those of equal status. Thus, to reduce prejudice, interracial contact should be between persons equal in status.

Superordinate goal   A shared goal that necessitates cooperative effort; a goal that overrides people's differences from one another.

Bargaining   Seeking an agreement through direct negotiation between parties to a conflict.

Mediation   An attempt by a neutral third party to resolve a conflict by facilitating communication and offering suggestions.

Arbitration   Resolution of a conflict by a neutral third party who studies both sides and imposes a settlement.

Integrative agreements   Win-win agreements that reconcile both parties' interests to their mutual benefit.

GRIT   Acronym for "graduated and reciprocated initiatives in tension reduction"—a strategy designed to deescalate international tensions.

MODULE

25

❖

Who Likes Whom?

At our beginning there was attraction—the attraction between a particular man and a particular woman to which we each owe our existence. Our lifelong dependence on one another puts relationships at the core of our existence. Asked "What is it that makes your life meaningful?" or "What is necessary for your happiness?" most people mention, before anything else, satisfying close relationships with friends, family, or romantic partners (Berscheid, 1985; Berscheid & Peplau, 1983).

What predisposes one person to like, or to love, another? So much has been written about liking and loving that almost every conceivable explanation, and its opposite, has been already proposed. Does absence make the heart grow fonder? Or is someone who is out of sight also out of mind? Is it likes that attract? Or opposites?

Consider a simple but powerful *reward theory of attraction:* We like those whose behavior is rewarding to us, or whom we associate with rewarding events. Friends reward each other. Without keeping score, they do favors for one another. Likewise, we develop a liking for those whom we associate with pleasant happenings and surroundings. Thus, surmised researchers Elaine Hatfield and William Walster (1978), "romantic dinners, trips to the theatre, evenings at home together, and vacations never stop being important. . . . If your relationship is to survive, it's important that you *both* continue to associate your relationship with good things."

But as with most sweeping generalizations, the reward theory of attraction leaves many questions unanswered. What, precisely, *is* rewarding? Is it usually more rewarding to be with someone who differs from us or someone who is similar to us? to be lavishly flattered or constructively criticized? What factors have fostered *your* close relationships?

PROXIMITY

One of the most powerful predictors of whether any two people are friends is sheer **proximity.** Proximity can also breed hostility; most assaults and murders involve people living close together. But far more often, proximity kindles liking. Though it might seem trivial to those pondering the mysterious origins of romantic love, sociologists have found that most people marry someone who lives in the same neighborhood, or works at the same company or job, or sits in the same class (Bossard, 1932; Burr, 1973; Clarke, 1952; Katz & Hill, 1958). Look around. If you marry, it will likely be to someone who has lived or worked or studied within walking distance.

Interaction

Actually, it is not geographical distance that is critical but "functional distance"—how often people's paths cross. We frequently become friends with those who use the same entrances, parking lots, and recreation areas. Randomly assigned college roommate, who of course can hardly avoid frequent interaction, are far more likely to become good friends than enemies (Newcomb, 1961). Such interaction enables people to explore their similarities, to sense one another's liking, and to perceive themselves as a social unit (Arkin & Burger, 1980).

At the college where I teach, the male and female students once lived on opposite sides of the campus. They understandably bemoaned the lack of cross-sex friendships. Now that they occupy different areas of the same dormitories and share common sidewalks, lounges, and laundry facilities, cross-sex friendships are far more frequent. So, if you're new in town and want to make friends, try to get an apartment near the mailboxes, an office desk near the coffee pot, a parking spot near the main buildings. Such is the architecture of friendship.

But why does proximity breed liking? One factor is availability; obviously there are fewer opportunities to get to know someone who attends a different school or lives in another town. But there is more to it than that. Most people like their roommates, or those one door away, better than those two doors away. Those just a few doors away, or even a floor below, hardly live at an inconvenient distance. Moreover, those close by are potential enemies as well as friends. So why does proximity encourage affection more than animosity?

Anticipation of Interaction

Already we have noted one answer: Proximity enables people to discover commonalities and exchange rewards. What is more, merely *anticipating* interaction boosts liking. John Darley and Ellen Berscheid (1967) discovered this when they gave University of Minnesota women ambiguous information about two other women, one of whom they expected to talk with intimately. Asked how much they liked each one, the women preferred the person they expected to meet. Expecting to date someone similarly boosts liking (Berscheid & others, 1976). Anticipatory liking—expecting that someone will be pleasant and compatible—increases the chance of a rewarding relationship (Knight & Vallacher, 1981; Klein & Kunda, 1992; Miller & Marks, 1982).

The phenomenon is adaptive. Our lives are filled with relationships with people whom we might not have chosen but with whom we need to have continuing interactions—roommates, grandparents, teachers, classmates, coworkers. Liking such people is surely conducive to better relationships with them, which in turn makes for happier, more productive living.

Mere Exposure

Proximity leads to liking for yet another reason: More than 200 experiments reveal that, contrary to the old proverb, familiarity does not breed contempt. Rather it breeds fondness (Bornstein, 1989). **Mere exposure** to all sorts of novel stimuli—nonsense syllables, Chinese characters, musical selections, faces—boosts people's ratings of them. Do the supposed Turkish words *nansoma, saricik,* and *afworbu* mean something better or something worse than the words *iktitaf, biwojni,* and *kadirga*? University of Michigan students tested by Robert Zajonc (1968, 1970) preferred whichever of these words they had seen most frequently. The more times they had seen a meaningless word or a Chinese ideograph, the more likely they were to say it meant something good (Figure 25-1). Or consider this: What are your favorite letters of the alphabet? People of differing nationalities, languages, and ages prefer the letter appearing in their own name and those that frequently appear in their own language (Hoorens & others, 1990, 1993; Kitayama & Karasawa, 1997; Nuttin, 1987). French students rate capital *W,* the least frequent letter in French, as their least favorite letter. Japanese students not only prefer letters from their name, but numbers corresponding to their birthdate.

The mere-exposure effect violates the commonsense prediction of *decreased* interest in repeatedly heard music or tasted foods (Kahneman & Snell, 1992). But unless the repetitions are incessant ("Even the best song becomes tiresome if heard too often," says a Korean proverb), liking usually increases. When completed in 1889, the Eiffel Tower in Paris was mocked as grotesque (Harrison, 1977). Today it is the beloved symbol of Paris. Such changes make one wonder about initial reactions to new things. Do visitors to the Louvre in Paris really adore the *Mona Lisa,* or are they simply delighted to find a familiar face? It might be both: To know her is to like her.

The mere exposure effect has "enormous adaptive significance," notes Zajonc (1998). It is a "hardwired" phenomenon that predisposes our at-

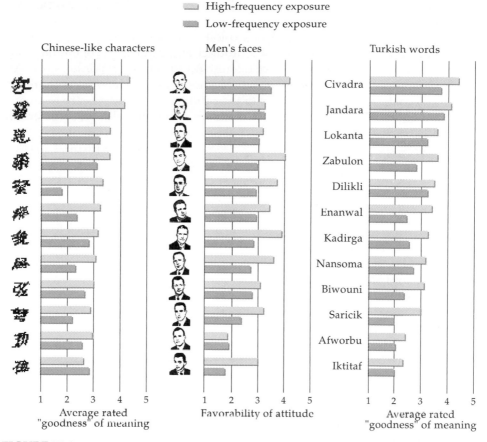

FIGURE 25-1

The mere-exposure effect. Students rates stimuli more positively after being shown them repeatedly. (From Zajonc, 1968.)

tractions and our attachments, and that helped our ancestors categorize things and people as either familiar and safe, or unfamiliar and possibly dangerous. Of course, the phenomenon's darker side is our wariness of the unfamiliar, which could explain the primitive, automatic prejudice people often feel when confronting those who are different.

The mere-exposure effect colors our evaluations of others: We like familiar people more (Swap, 1977). We even like ourselves better when we are the way we're used to seeing ourselves. In a delightful experiment, Theodore Mita, Marshall Dermer, and Jeffrey Knight (1977) photographed women students at the University of Wisconsin–Milwaukee and later showed each one her actual picture along with a mirror image of it. Asked which picture they liked better, most preferred the mirror image—the image they were used to seeing. (No wonder our photographs never look quite right.) When close friends of the subjects were shown the same two pictures, they preferred the true picture—the image *they* were used to seeing.

Advertisers and politicians exploit this phenomenon. When people have no strong feelings about a product or a candidate, repetition alone can increase sales or votes (McCullough & Ostrom, 1974; Winter, 1973). After endless repetition of a commercial, shoppers often have an unthinking, automatic, favorable response to the product. If candidates are relatively unknown, those with the most media exposure usually win (Patterson, 1980; Schaffner & others, 1981). Political strategists who understand the mere-exposure effect have replaced reasoned argument with brief ads that hammer home a candidate's name and sound-bite message.

The respected Washington state Supreme Court Chief Justice Keith Callow learned this lesson when in 1990 he lost to a nominal opponent, Charles Johnson. Johnson, an unknown attorney who handled minor criminal cases and divorces, filed for the seat on the principle that judges "need to be challenged." Neither man campaigned, and the media ignored the race. On election day the two candidates' names appeared without any identification— just one name next to the other. The result: a 53 percent to 47 percent Johnson victory. "There are a lot more Johnsons out there than Callows," offered the ousted judge afterward to a stunned legal community. Indeed, a Seattle newspaper counted 27 Charles Johnsons in Seattle alone. There was Charles Johnson, the King County judge. And down in Tacoma there was television anchorman Charles Johnson, whose broadcasts were seen on statewide cable TV. Forced to choose between two unknown names, many voters preferred the comfortable, familiar name of Charles Johnson.

*P*HYSICAL ATTRACTIVENESS

What do (or did) you look for in a potential date? Sincerity? Good looks? Character? Conversational ability? Sophisticated, intelligent people are unconcerned with such superficial qualities as good looks; they know "Beauty is only skin deep" and "You can't judge a book by its cover." At least they know that's how they *ought* to feel. As Cicero counseled, "resist appearance."

The belief that looks matter little might be another instance of our denying real influences upon us, for there is now a file cabinet full of research studies showing that appearance *does* matter. The consistence and pervasiveness of this effect is disconcerting. Good looks are a great asset.

Attractiveness and Dating

Like it or not, a young woman's physical attractiveness is a moderately good predictor of how frequently she dates. A young man's attractiveness is slightly less a predictor of how frequently he dates (Berscheid & others,

1971; Krebs & Adinolfi, 1975; Reis & others, 1980, 1982; Walster & others, 1966). Does this imply, as many have surmised, that women are better at following Cicero's advice? Or does it merely reflect the fact that men more often do the inviting? If women were to indicate their preferences among various men, would looks be as important to them as they are to men? Philosopher Bertrand Russell (1930, p. 139) thought not: "On the whole women tend to love men for their character while men tend to love women for their appearance."

To see whether, indeed, men are more influenced by looks, researchers have provided female and male students with various pieces of information about someone of the other sex, including a picture of the person. Or they have briefly introduced a man and a woman and later asked each about their interest in dating the other. In such experiments, men do put somewhat more value on opposite-sex physical attractiveness (Feingold, 1990, 1991; Sprecher & others, 1994). Perhaps sensing this, women worry more about their appearance and constitute nearly 90 percent of cosmetic surgery patients (Crowley, 1996; Dion & others, 1990). But women, too, respond to a man's looks.

In one ambitious study, Elaine Hatfield and her co-workers (1966) matched 752 University of Minnesota first-year students for a "Welcome Week" computer dance. The researchers gave each student personality and aptitude tests but then matched the couples randomly. On the night of the dance, the couples danced and talked for two and a half hours and then took a brief intermission to evaluate their dates. How well did the personality and aptitude tests predict attraction? Did people like someone better who was high in self-esteem, or low in anxiety, or different from themselves in outgoingness? The researchers examined a long list of possibilities. But so far as they could determine, only one thing mattered: how physically attractive the person was. The more attractive the woman was, the more he liked her and wanted to date her again. And the more attractive the man was, the more she liked him and wanted to date him again. Pretty pleases.

To say that attractiveness is important, other things being equal, is not to say that physical appearance always outranks other qualities. Attractiveness probably most affects first impressions. But first impressions are important, and are becoming more so as societies become increasingly mobile and urbanized and as contacts with people become more fleeting (Berscheid, 1981).

Though interviewers might deny it, attractiveness and grooming affects first impressions in job interviews (Cash & Janda, 1984; Mack & Rainey, 1990; Marvelle & Green, 1980). This helps explain why attractive people have more prestigious jobs and make more money (Umberson & Hughes, 1987). Patricia Roszell and her colleagues (1990) looked at the attractiveness of a national sample of Canadians whom interviewers had rated on a 1 (homely) to 5 (strikingly attractive) scale. They found that for each additional scale unit of rated attractiveness, people earned, on average, an additional $1,988 annually. Irene Hanson Frieze and her associates (1991) did the same analysis with 737 MBA graduates after rating them on a similar 1-to-5 scale using student picture book photos. For each additional scale unit of rated attractiveness, men earned an added $2,600 and women earned an added $2,150.

The Matching Phenomenon

Not everyone can end up paired with someone stunningly attractive. So how do people pair off? Judging from research by Bernard Murstein (1986) and others, they pair off with people who are about as attractive as they are. Several studies have found a strong correspondence between the attractiveness of husbands and wives, of dating partners, and even of those within particular fraternities (Feingold, 1988). People tend to select as friends, and especially to marry, those who are a "good match" not only to their level of intelligence but also to their level of attractiveness.

Experiments confirm this **matching phenomenon.** When choosing whom to approach, knowing the other is free to say yes or no, people usually approach someone whose attractiveness roughly matches their own (Berscheid & others, 1971; Huston, 1973; Stroebe & others, 1971). Good physical matches can also be conducive to good relationships, as Gregory White (1980) found in a study of UCLA dating couples. Those who were most similar in physical attractiveness were most likely, nine months later, to have fallen more deeply in love.

So, who might we expect to be most closely matched for attractiveness—married couples or couples casually dating? White found, as have other researchers, that married couples are better matched.

Perhaps this research prompts you to think of happy couples who are not equally attractive. In such cases, the less attractive person often has compensating qualities. Each partner brings assets to the social marketplace, and the value of the respective assets creates an equitable match. Personal advertisements exhibit this exchange of assets (Cicerello & Sheehan, 1995; Koestner & Wheeler, 1988; Rajecki & others, 1991). Men typically offer wealth or status and seek youth and attractiveness; women more often do the reverse: "Attractive, bright woman, 26, slender, seeks warm, professional male." Moreover, men who advertise their income and education, and women who advertise their youth and looks, receive more responses to their ads (Baize & Schroeder, 1995). The asset-matching process helps explain why beautiful young women often marry older men of higher social status (Elder, 1969).

The Physical-Attractiveness Stereotype

Does the attractiveness effect spring entirely from sexual attractiveness? Clearly not, as Vicky Houston and Ray Bull (1994) discovered when they used a makeup artist to give an accomplice an apparently scarred, bruised, or birthmarked face. When riding on a Glasgow commuter rail line, people of *both* sexes avoided sitting next to the accomplice when she appeared facially disfigured. Moreover, just as adults are biased toward attractive adults, young children are biased toward attractive children (Dion, 1973; Dion & Berscheid, 1974; Langlois & Stephan, 1981). To judge from how long they gaze at different people, even babies prefer attractive faces (Langlois & others, 1987).

Adults show a similar bias when judging children. Margaret Clifford and Elaine Hatfield (Clifford & Walster, 1973) gave Missouri fifth-grade teachers identical information about a girl or boy but with the photograph of an attractive or unattractive child attached. The teachers perceived the attractive child as more intelligent and successful in school. Think of yourself as a playground supervisor having to discipline an unruly child. Might you, like the women studied by Karen Dion (1972), show less warmth and tact to an unattractive child? The sad truth is that most of us assume what we might call a "Bart Simpson effect"—that homely children are less able and socially competent than their beautiful peers.

What is more, we assume that beautiful people possess certain desirable traits. Other things being equal, we guess beautiful people are happier, sexually warmer, and more outgoing, intelligent, and successful, though not more honest or concerned for others (Eagly & others, 1991; Feingold, 1992b; Jackson & others, 1995). In collectivist Korea, where concern for others and integrity are valued above assertiveness, those are traits people associate with attractiveness (Wheeler & Kim, 1997). Added together, the findings define a **physical-attractiveness stereotype:** What is beautiful is good. Children learn the stereotype quite early. Snow White and Cinderella are beautiful—and kind. The witch and the stepsisters are ugly—and wicked. As one kindergarten girl put it when asked what it means to be pretty, "It's like to be a princess. Everybody loves you" (Dion, 1979). Think Princess Diana.

If physical attractiveness is this important, then permanently changing people's attractiveness should change the way others react to them. But is it ethical to alter someone's looks? Such manipulations are performed millions of times a year by plastic surgeons and orthodontists. With teeth and nose straightened, hair replaced and dyed, face lifted, fat liposuctioned, and (for more than 1 million American women) breasts enlarged, can a self-dissatisfied person now find happiness?

To examine the effect of such alterations, Michael Kalick (1977) had Harvard students rate their impressions of eight women based on profile photographs taken before or after cosmetic surgery. Not only did they judge the women as more physically attractive after the surgery but also as kinder, more sensitive, more sexually warm and responsive, more likable, and so on. Ellen Berscheid (1981) noted that although such cosmetic improvements can boost self-image, they can also be temporarily disturbing:

> Most of us—at least those of us who have *not* experienced swift alterations of our physical appearance—can continue to believe that our physical attractiveness level plays a minor role in how we are treated by others. It is harder,

however, for those who have actually experienced swift changes in appearance to continue to deny and to minimize the influence of physical attractiveness in their own lives—and the fact of it may be disturbing, even when the changes are for the better.

Do beautiful people indeed have desirable traits? Or was Leo Tolstoy correct when he wrote that it's "a strange illusion . . . to suppose that beauty is goodness"? There is some truth to the stereotype. Attractive children and young adults are somewhat more relaxed and socially polished (Feingold, 1992b). William Goldman and Philip Lewis (1977) demonstrated this by having 60 University of Georgia men call and talk for five minutes with each of three women students. Afterward the men and women rated their unseen telephone partners who happened to be most attractive as somewhat more socially skilled and likeable. Physically attractive individuals tend also to be more popular, more outgoing, and more gender-typed (more traditionally masculine if male, more feminine if female) (Langlois & others, 1996).

These small average differences between attractive and unattractive people probably result from self-fulfilling prophecies. Attractive people are valued and favored, and therefore many develop more social self-confidence. By this analysis, what's crucial to your social skill is not how you look but how people treat you and how you feel about yourself—whether you accept yourself, like yourself, feel comfortable with yourself.

Despite all the advantages of being beautiful, attraction researchers Elaine Hatfield and Susan Sprecher (1986) report there is also an ugly truth about beauty. Exceptionally attractive people can suffer unwelcome sexual advances, and resentment from others of their own sex. They can be unsure whether others are responding to their performance, their inner qualities, or just their looks, which in time will fade (Satterfield & Muehlenhard, 1997). Moreover, if they can coast on their looks, they can be less motivated to develop themselves in other ways. Ellen Berscheid wonders whether we might still be lighting our houses with candles if Charles Steinmetz, the homely and exceptionally short genius of electricity, had instead been subjected to the social enticements experienced by a Tom Cruise.

Who Is Attractive?

I have described attractiveness as if it were an objective quality like height, which some people have more of, some less. Strictly speaking, attractiveness is whatever the people of any given place and time find attractive. This, of course, varies. The beauty standards by which Miss Universe is judged hardly apply to the whole planet. Even in a given place and time, people (fortunately) disagree about who's attractive (Morse & Gruzen, 1976).

But there is also some agreement. Generally, "attractive" facial and bodily features do not deviate too drastically from average (Beck & others,

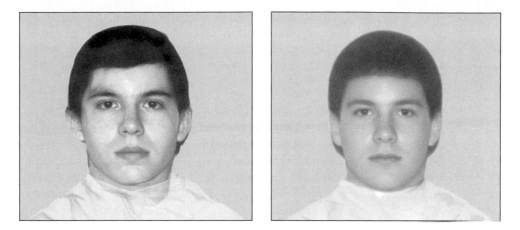

FIGURE 25-2
Is beauty merely in the eye of the beholder? Which of these faces is most attractive? People everywhere agree that the symmetrical face on the right (a composite of 32 male faces) is better looking, note Judith Langlois and her collaborators (1996). To evolutionary psychologists, such agreement suggests some universal standards of beauty rooted in our ancestral history.

1976; Graziano & others, 1978; Symons, 1981). People perceive noses, legs, or statures that are not unusually large or small as relatively attractive. Judith Langlois and Lori Roggman (1990, 1994) showed this by digitizing the faces of up to 32 college students and using a computer to average them. Students judged the composite faces as more appealing than 96 percent of the individual faces (Figure 25-2). Computer-averaged faces tend also to be perfectly symmetrical—another characteristic of strikingly attractive people (Gangestad & Thornhill, 1997; Grammer & Thornhill, 1994; Shackelford & Larsen, 1997). So in some respects, perfectly average is quite attractive.

Evolution and Attraction
Psychologists working from the evolutionary perspective explain these gender differences in terms of reproductive strategy. They assume that beauty signals biologically important information: health, youth, and fertility. Over time, men who preferred fertile-looking women out-reproduced those who were as happy to mate with prepubescent or post-menopausal females. And they assume evolution predisposes women to favor male traits that signify an ability to provide and protect resources. That, David Buss (1989) believes, explains why the males he studied in 37 cultures—from Australia to Zambia—did indeed prefer female character-istics that signify reproductive capacity. And it explains why physically at-tractive females tend to marry high-status males and why men compete with such determination to achieve fame and fortune.

In every culture the beauty business is big business that shows no signs of abating. We are, evolutionary psychologists suggest, driven by primal attractions. Like eating and breathing, attraction and mating are too important to leave to the whims of culture.

The Contrast Effect

Although our mating psychology has biological wisdom, attraction is not all hardwired. What's attractive to you also depends on your comparison standards. Douglas Kenrick and Sara Gutierres (1980) had male confederates interrupt Montana State University men in their dormitory rooms and explain, "We have a friend coming to town this week and we want to fix him up with a date, but we can't decide whether to fix him up with her or not, so we decided to conduct a survey. . . . We want you to give us your vote on how attractive you think she is . . . on a scale of 1 to 7." Shown a picture of an average young woman, those who had just been watching three beautiful women on televisions's *Charlie's Angels* rated her less attractive than those who hadn't.

Laboratory experiments confirm this "contrast effect." To men who have recently been gazing at centerfolds, average women—or even their own wives—seem less attractive (Kenrick & others, 1989). Viewing pornographic films simulating passionate sex similarly decreases satisfaction with one's own partner (Zillmann, 1989). Being sexually aroused can *temporarily* make a person of the other sex seem more attractive, but the lingering effect of exposure to perfect "10s," or of unrealistic sexual depictions, is to make one's own partner seem less appealing—more like a "6" than an "8." It works the same way with our self-perceptions. After viewing a superattractive person of the same sex, people *feel* less attractive than after viewing a homely person (Brown & others, 1992; Thornton & Moore, 1993).

The Attractiveness of Those We Love

Let's conclude our discussion of attractiveness on an upbeat note. Not only do we perceive attractive people as likeable, we also perceive likeable people as attractive. Perhaps you can recall individuals who, as you grew to like them, became more attractive. Their physical imperfections were no longer so noticeable. Alan Gross and Christine Crofton (1977) had University of Missouri–St. Louis students view someone's photograph after reading a favorable or unfavorable description of the person's personality. When portrayed as warm, helpful, and considerate, people *looked* more attractive. Discovering someone's similarities to us also makes the person seem more attractive (Beaman & Klentz, 1983; Klentz & others, 1987).

Moreover, love sees loveliness: The more in love a woman is with a man, the more physically attractive she finds him (Price & others, 1974). And the more in love people are, the *less* attractive they find all others of the opposite sex (Johnson & Rusbult, 1989; Simpson & others, 1990). "The grass may be greener on the other side," note Rowland Miller and Jeffry Simpson (1990), "but happy gardeners are less likely to notice." To paraphrase Benjamin Franklin, when Jill's in love, she finds Jack more handsome than his friends.

SIMILARITY VERSUS COMPLEMENTARITY

From our discussion so far, one might surmise that Leo Tolstoy was entirely correct: "Love depends . . . on frequent meetings, and on the style in which the hair is done up, and on the color and cut of the dress." However, as people get to know one another, other factors influence whether acquaintance develops into friendship. Thus, men's initial liking for one another after the first week of living in the same boardinghouse does *not* predict very well their ultimate liking four months later (Nisbett & Smith, 1989). Their similarity, however, does.

Do Birds of a Feather Flock Together?

Of this much we can be sure: Birds that flock together are of a feather. Friends, engaged couples, and spouses are far more likely than people randomly paired to share common attitudes, beliefs, and values. Furthermore, the greater the similarity between husband and wife, the happier they are and the less likely they are to divorce (Byrne, 1971; Caspi & Herbener, 1990). Such correlational findings are intriguing, but cause and effect remain an enigma. Does similarity lead to liking? Or does liking lead to similarity?

Likeness Begets Liking
To discern cause and effect, we experiment. Imagine that at a campus party Laura gets involved in a long discussion of politics, religion, and personal likes and dislikes with Les and Larry. She discovers that she and Les agree on almost everything, she and Larry on few things. Afterward, she reflects: "Les is really intelligent . . . and so likeable . . . hope we meet again." In experiments, Donn Byrne (1971) and his colleagues captured the essence of Laura's experience. Over and over again they found that the more similar someone's attitudes are to your own, the more likeable you will find the person. Likeness produces liking not only for college students but also for children and the elderly, for people of various occupations, and for those of various cultures.

The likeness-leads-to-liking effect has been tested in real-life situations by noting who comes to like whom. At the University of Michigan, Theodore Newcomb (1961) studied two groups of 17 unacquainted male transfer students. After 13 weeks of living together in a boardinghouse, those whose agreement was initially highest were most likely to have formed close friendships. One group of friends was composed of five liberal arts students, each a political liberal with strong intellectual interests. Another was made up of three conservative veterans who were all enrolled in the engineering college.

William Griffitt and Russell Veitch (1974) compressed the getting-to-know-you process by confining 13 unacquainted men in a fallout shelter. (The men were paid volunteers.) Knowing the men's opinions on various issues, the researchers could predict with better-than-chance accuracy those each man would most like and most dislike. As in the boarding-house, the men liked best those most like themselves. Similarity breeds content. Surely you have noticed this upon discovering a special someone who shares your ideas, values, and desires, a soul mate who likes the same music, the same activities, even the same foods you do.

Do Opposites Attract?

But are we not also attracted to people who are in some ways *different* from ourselves, in ways that complement our own characteristics? Researchers have explored this question by comparing not only friends' and spouses' attitudes and beliefs but also their age, religion, race, smoking behavior, economic level, education, height, intelligence, and appearance. In all these ways and more, similarity still prevails (Buss, 1985; Kandel, 1978). Smart birds flock together. So do rich birds, Protestant birds, tall birds, pretty birds.

Still we resist: Are we not attracted to people whose needs and personalities complement our own? Would a sadist and a masochist find true love? Even *Reader's Digest* has told us that "opposites attract . . . Socializers pair with loners, novelty-lovers with those who dislike change, free spenders with scrimpers, risk-takers with the very cautious" (Jacoby, 1986). Sociologist Robert Winch (1958) reasoned that the needs of someone who is outgoing and domineering would naturally complement those of someone who is shy and submissive. The logic seems compelling, and most of us can think of couples who view their differences as complementary: "My husband and I are perfect for each other. I'm Aquarius—a decisive person. He's Libra—can't make decisions. But he's always happy to go along with arrangements I make."

Some **complementarity** can evolve as a relationship progresses (even a relationship between two identical twins). Yet people seem slightly more prone to like and to marry those whose needs and personalities are *similar* (Botwin & others, 1997; Buss, 1984; Fishbein & Thelen, 1981a, 1981b; Nias, 1979). Perhaps we shall yet discover some ways (other than heterosexuality) in which differences commonly breed liking. Dominance/submissiveness might be one such way (Dryer & Horowitz, 1997). But researcher David Buss (1985) doubts it: "The tendency of opposites to marry, or mate . . . has never been reliably demonstrated, with the single exception of sex." So it seems that the "opposites-attract" rule, if it's ever true, is of hardly any importance compared to the powerful tendency of likes to attract.

*L*IKING THOSE WHO LIKE US

With hindsight, the reward principle explains our conclusions so far:

- *Proximity* is rewarding. It costs less time and effort to receive friendship's benefits with someone who lives or works close by.
- We like *attractive* people because we perceive that they offer other desirable traits and because we benefit by associating with them.
- If others have *similar* opinions, we feel rewarded because we presume that they like us in return. Moreover, those who share our views help validate them.

If we like those whose behavior is rewarding, then we ought to adore those who like and admire us. The best friendships should be mutual admiration societies. Do we in fact like those who like us? Indeed, one person's liking for another predicts the other's liking in return (Kenny & Nasby, 1980). Liking is mutual.

But does one person's liking another *cause* the other to return the appreciation? People's reports of how they fell in love suggest yes (Aron & others, 1989). Discovering that an appealing someone really likes you seems to awaken romantic feelings. Experiments confirm it: Those told that certain others like or admire them usually feel a reciprocal affection (Berscheid & Walster, 1978).

And consider this finding by Ellen Berscheid and her colleagues (1969): People like even better another student who says eight positive things about them than one who says seven positive things and one negative thing. We are sensitive to the slightest hint of criticism. Writer Larry L. King speaks for many in noting, "I have discovered over the years that good reviews strangely fail to make the author feel as good as bad reviews make him feel bad." Whether we are judging ourselves or others, negative information carries more weight because, being less usual, it grabs more attention (Yzerbyt & Leyens, 1991). People's votes are more influenced by their impressions of presidential candidates' weaknesses than by their impressions of strengths (Klein, 1991), a phenomenon that has not been lost on those who design negative campaigns.

That we like those we perceive as liking us was recognized long ago. Observers from the ancient philosopher Hecato ("If you wish to be loved, love") to Ralph Waldo Emerson ("The only way to have a friend is to be one") to Dale Carnegie ("Dole out praise lavishly") anticipated the findings. What they did not anticipate was the precise conditions under which the principle works.

Self-Esteem and Attraction

Elaine Hatfield (Walster, 1965) wondered if another's approval is especially rewarding after we have been deprived of approval, much as eating is most powerfully rewarding after fasting. To test this idea, she gave some Stanford University women either very favorable or very unfavorable analyses of their personalities, affirming some and wounding others. Then she asked them to evaluate several people, including an attractive male confederate who just before the experiment had struck up a warm conversation with each woman and had asked each for a date. (Not one turned him down.) Which women most liked the man? Those whose self-esteem had been temporarily shattered and who were presumably hungry for social approval. This helps explain why people sometimes fall passionately in love on the rebound, after an ego-bruising rejection. (After this experiment Dr. Hatfield spent almost an hour explaining the experiment and talking with each woman. She reports that, in the end, none remained disturbed by the temporary ego blow or the broken date.)

Proximity, attractiveness, similarity, being liked—these are factors known to influence our friendship formation. Sometimes friendship deepens into the passion and intimacy of love. What is love? And why does it sometimes flourish and sometimes fade? To those questions we turn next.

CONCEPTS TO REMEMBER

Reward theory of attraction   The theory that we like those whose behavior we find rewarding or whom we associate with rewarding events.

Proximity   Geographical nearness. Proximity (more precisely, "functional distance") powerfully predicts liking.

Mere-exposure effect   The tendency for novel stimuli to be liked more or rated more positively after the rate has been repeatedly exposed to them.

Matching phenomenon   The tendency for men and women to choose as partners those who are a "good match" in attractiveness and other traits.

Physical-attractiveness stereotype   The presumption that physically attractive people possess other socially desirable traits as well: What is beautiful is good.

Complementarity   The popularly supposed tendency, in a relationship between two people, for each to complete what is missing in the other. The questionable complementarity hypothesis proposes that people attract those whose needs are different, in ways that complement their own.

MODULE
26

❖

The Ups and Downs of Love

W hat is this thing called "love"? Loving is more complex than liking and thus more difficult to measure, more perplexing to study. People yearn for it, live for it, die for it. Yet only in the last few years has loving become a serious topic in social psychology.

Most attraction researchers have studied what is most easily studied—responses during brief encounters between strangers. The influences on our initial liking of another—proximity, attractiveness, similarity, being liked—also influence our long-term, close relationships. The impressions that dating couples quickly form of each other therefore provide a clue to their long-term future (Berg, 1984; Berg & McQuinn, 1986). Indeed, if North American romances flourished *randomly*, without regard to proximity and similarity, then most Catholics (being a minority) would marry Protestants, most Blacks would marry Whites, and college graduates would be as apt to marry high school dropouts as fellow graduates.

So first impressions are important. Nevertheless, long-term loving is not merely an intensification of initial liking. Social psychologists have therefore shifted their attention from the mild attraction experienced during first encounters to the study of enduring, close relationships.

One line of investigation compares the nature of love in various close relationships—same-sex friendships, parent-child relationships, and spouses or lovers (Davis, 1985; Maxwell, 1985; Sternberg & Grajek, 1984). These investigations reveal elements that are common to all loving relationships: mutual understanding, giving and receiving support, valuing and enjoying being with the loved one. Although such ingredients of love apply equally to love between best friends or between husband and wife, they are spiced differently depending on the relationship. Passionate love, especially in its initial phase, is distinguished by physical affection, an expectation of exclusiveness, and an intense fascination with the loved one.

*P*ASSIONATE LOVE

The first step in scientifically studying romantic love, as in studying any variable, is to decide how to define and measure it. We have ways to measure aggression, altruism, prejudice, and liking, but how do we measure love?

Elizabeth Barrett Browning asked a similar question: "How do I love thee? Let me count the ways." Social scientists have counted various ways. In psychologist Robert Sternberg's (1988) "triangular" theory of love, love has three sides: passion, intimacy, and commitment (Figure 26-1). Drawing from ancient philosophy and literature, sociologist John Alan Lee (1988) and psychologists Clyde Hendrick and Susan Hendrick (1993) identify three primary love styles—*eros* (self-disclosing passion), *ludus* (uncommitted game playing), and *storge* (friendship)—which, like the primary colors, combine to form secondary love styles. Some love styles, notably eros, predict high relationship satisfaction; others, such as ludus, predict low satisfaction (Hendrick & Hendrick, 1997).

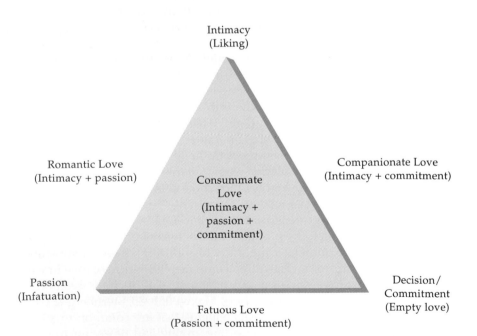

FIGURE 26-1
In Robert Sternberg's (1988) conception, the kinds of loving are combinations of three basic components of love.

Pioneering love researcher Zick Rubin (1970, 1973) discerned some-what different factors and wrote questionnaire items to tap these factors:

1. *Attachment* (for example, "If I were lonely, my first thought would be to seek _____ out.")
2. *Caring* (for example, "If _____ were feeling bad, my first duty would be to cheer him [her] up.")
3. *Intimacy* (for example, "I feel that I can confide in _____ about virtually everything.")

Rubin gave his Love Scale to hundreds of University of Michigan dat-ing couples. Later, from behind a one-way mirror in a laboratory waiting room, he clocked eye-contact among "weak-love" and "strong-love" cou-ples. His result will not surprise you: The strong-love couples gave them-selves away by gazing long into one another's eyes.

Passionate love is emotional, exciting, intense. Hatfield (1988) defines it as *"a state of intense longing for union with another"* (p. 193). If reciprocated, one feels fulfilled and joyous; if not, one feels empty or despairing. Like other forms of emotional excitement, passionate love involves a mix of ela-tion and gloom, tingling exhilaration and dejected misery.

A Theory of Passionate Love

To explain passionate love, Hatfield notes that a given state of arousal can be steered into any of several emotions, depending on how we attribute the arousal. An emotion involves both body and mind, both arousal and how we interpret and label the arousal. Imagine yourself with pounding heart and trembling hands: Are you experiencing fear, anxiety, joy? Phys-iologically, one emotion is quite similar to another. You might therefore ex-perience the arousal as joy if you are in a euphoric situation, anger if your environment is hostile, and passionate love if the situation is romantic. In this view, passionate love is the psychological experience of being biolog-ically aroused by someone we find attractive.

If indeed passion is a revved-up state that's labeled "love," then what-ever revs one up should intensify feelings of love. In several experiments, college men aroused sexually by reading or viewing erotic materials had a heightened response to a woman (for example, by scoring much higher on Rubin's Love Scale when describing their girlfriend) (Carducci & others, 1978; Dermer & Pyszczynski, 1978; Stephan & others, 1971). Proponents of the **two-factor theory of emotion** argue that when the revved-up men re-sponded to a woman, they easily misattributed some of their arousal to her.

According to this theory, being aroused by *any* source should intensify passionate feelings, provided the mind is free to attribute some of the arousal to a romantic stimulus. Donald Dutton and Arthur Aron (1974,

1989) invited University of British Columbia men to participate in a learning experiment. After meeting their attractive female partner, some were frightened with the news that they would be suffering some "quite painful" electric shocks. Before the experiment was to begin, the researcher gave a brief questionnaire "to get some information on your present feelings and reactions, since these often influence performance on the learning task." Asked how much they would like to date and kiss their female partner, the aroused (frightened) men expressed more intense attraction toward the woman.

Does this phenomenon occur outside the laboratory? Dutton and Aron (1974) had an attractive young woman approach individual young men as they crossed a narrow, wobbly 450-foot-long suspension walkway hanging 230 feet above British Columbia's rocky Capilano River. The woman asked each man to help her fill out a class questionnaire. When he had finished, she scribbled her name and phone number and invited him to call if he wanted to hear more about the project. Most accepted the phone number, and half who did so called. By contrast, men approached by the woman on a low, solid bridge, and men approached on the high bridge by a *male* interviewer, rarely called. Once again, physical arousal accentuated romantic responses. Adrenaline makes the heart grow fonder.

Variations in Love

Time and Culture
There is always a temptation to assume that most others share our feelings and ideas. We assume, for example, that love is a precondition for marriage. But this assumption is not shared in cultures that practice arranged marriages. Moreover, until recently in North America, marital choices, especially those by women, were strongly influenced by considerations of economic security, family background, and professional status. This is still true to varying degrees in collectivist countries such as Pakistan, India, and Thailand (Levine & others, 1995). But by the mid 1980s, almost 9 in 10 North American young adults surveyed indicated that love was essential for marriage (Simpson & others, 1986).

Cultures vary in the importance they place upon romantic love. Most cultures—89 percent in one analysis of 166 cultures—have a concept of romantic love, as reflected in flirtation or couples running off together (Jankowiak & Fischer, 1992). But not all cultures build marriage on romance. In Western, individualistic cultures today, love generally precedes marriage; in others, it more often follows.

Self-Monitoring
Within any given place and time, individuals also vary in their approach to heterosexual relationships. Some seek a succession of short involvements; others value the intimacy of an exclusive and enduring relationship. In a

series of studies, Mark Snyder and his colleagues (1985, 1988; Snyder & Simpson, 1985) identified a personality difference linked with these two approaches to romance. Some people, those high in **self-monitoring,** skillfully monitor their own behavior to create the desired effect in any given situation. Others, those low in self-monitoring, are more internally guided, more likely to report that they act the same way regardless of the situation.

Which type of person—someone high or low in self-monitoring— would you guess to be more affected by a prospect's physical appearance? to be more willing to end a relationship in favor of a new partner and therefore to date more people for shorter periods of time? to be more sexually promiscuous?

Snyder and Simpson report that in each case the answer is the person high in self-monitoring. Such people are skilled in managing first impressions but tend to be less committed to deep and enduring relationships. Low self-monitors, being less externally focused, are more committed and display more concern for people's inner qualities. When reading folders with information on potential dates or employees, they place a higher premium on personal attributes than on appearance. Given a choice between someone who shares their attitudes or their preferred activities, low self-monitors (unlike high self-monitors) feel drawn to those with kindred attitudes (Jamieson & others, 1987).

Gender

Do males and females differ in how they experience passionate love? Studies of men and women falling in and out of love reveal some surprises. Most people, including the writer of the following letter to a newspaper advice columnist, suppose that women fall in love more readily:

> Dear Dr. Brothers:
>
> Do you think it's effeminate for a 19-year-old guy to fall in love so hard it's like the whole world's turned around? I think I'm really crazy because this has happened several times now and love just seems to hit me on the head from nowhere. . . . My father says this is the way girls fall in love and that it doesn't happen this way with guys—at least it's not supposed to. I can't change how I am in this way but it kind of worries me.—P.T. (quoted by Dion & Dion, 1985)

P.T. would be reassured by the repeated finding that it is actually *men* who tend to fall more readily in love (Dion & Dion, 1985; Peplau & Gordon, 1985). Men also seem to fall out of love more slowly and are less likely than women to break up a premarital romance. However, women in love are typically as emotionally involved as their partners, or more so. They are more likely to report feeling euphoric and "giddy and carefree," as if they were "floating on a cloud." Women are also somewhat more likely than men to focus on the intimacy of the friendship and on their concern for their partner. Men are more likely than women to think about the playful and physical aspects of the relationship (Hendrick & Hendrick, 1995).

COMPANIONATE LOVE

Although passionate love burns hot, it inevitably simmers down. The longer a relationship endures, the fewer its emotional ups and downs (Berscheid & others, 1989). The high of romance might be sustained for a few months, even a couple of years. But as we noted in the discussion of adaptation, no high lasts forever. The intense absorption in the other, the thrill of the romance, the giddy "floating on a cloud" feeling, fades. After two years of marriage, spouses express affection about half as often as when they were newlyweds (Huston & Chorost, 1994). About four years after marriage the divorce rate peaks in cultures worldwide (Fisher, 1994). If a close relationship is to endure, it will settle to a steadier but still warm afterglow that Hatfield calls **companionate love.**

Unlike the wild emotions of passionate love, companionate love is lower key; it's a deep, affectionate attachment. And it is just as real. Even if one develops a tolerance for a drug, withdrawal can be painful. So it is with close relationships. Mutually dependent couples who no longer feel the flame of passionate love will often, upon divorce or death, discover that they have lost more than they expected. Having focused on what was not working, they stopped noticing what was (Carlson & Hatfield, 1992).

The cooling of passionate love over time and the growing importance of other factors, such as shared values, can be seen in the feelings of those who enter arranged versus love-based marriages in India. Usha Gupta and Pushpa Singh (1982) asked 50 couples in Jaipur, India, to complete Zick Rubin's Love Scale. They found that those who married for love reported diminishing feelings of love if they had been married more than five years. By contrast, those in arranged marriages reported *more* love if they were not newlyweds (Figure 26-2).

The cooling of intense romantic love often triggers a period of disillusionment, especially among those who regard such love as essential both for a marriage and for its continuation. Jeffry Simpson, Bruce Campbell, and Ellen Berscheid (1986) suspect "the sharp rise in the divorce rate in the past two decades is linked, at least in part, to the growing importance of intense positive emotional experiences (e.g., romantic love) in people's lives, experiences that may be particularly difficult to sustain over time." Compared to North Americans, Asians tend to focus less on personal feelings and more on the practical aspects of social attachments (Dion & Dion, 1988; Sprecher & others, 1994). Thus, they are less vulnerable to disillusion. Asians are also less prone to the self-focused individualism that in the long run can undermine a relationship and lead to divorce (Dion & Dion, 1991, 1996; Triandis & others, 1988).

The decline in intense mutual fascination might be natural and adaptive for species survival. The result of passionate love frequently is children, whose survival is aided by the parents' waning obsession with one another (Kenrick & Trost, 1987). Nevertheless, for those married more than

Scores on Rubin's Love Scale
(9-item version; possible range 9 to 91)

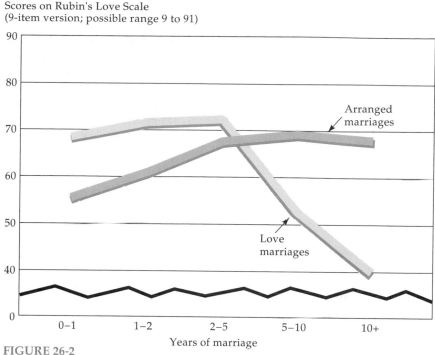

FIGURE 26-2
Romantic love between partners in arranged or love marriages in Jaipur, India.
(Data from Gupta & Singh, 1982.)

20 years, some of the lost romantic feeling is often renewed as the family nest empties and the parents are once again free to focus their attention on each other (Hatfield & Sprecher, 1986). "No man or woman really knows what love is until they have been married a quarter of a century," said Mark Twain. If the relationship has been intimate and mutually rewarding, companionate love rooted in a rich history of shared experiences deepens. But what is "intimacy"? And what is "mutually rewarding"?

MAINTAINING CLOSE RELATIONSHIPS

What factors influence the ups and downs of our close relationships? Let's consider two: equity and intimacy.

Equity

If both partners in a relationship pursue their personal desires willy-nilly, the friendship will die. Therefore, our society teaches us to exchange rewards by what Elaine Hatfield, William Walster, and Ellen Berscheid (1978) have called an **equity** principle of attraction: What you and your partner get out of a relationship should be proportional to what you each put into it. If two people receive equal outcomes, they should contribute equally; otherwise one or the other will feel it is unfair. If both feel their outcomes correspond to the assets and efforts each contributes, then both perceive equity.

Strangers and casual acquaintances maintain equity by exchanging benefits: You lend me your class notes; later, I'll lend you mine. I invite you to my party; you invite me to yours. Those in an enduring relationship, including roommates and those in love, do not feel bound to trade similar benefits—notes for notes, parties for parties (Berg, 1984). They feel freer to maintain equity by exchanging a variety of benefits ("When you drop by to lend me your notes, why don't you stay for dinner?") and eventually to stop keeping track of who owes whom.

Long-Term Equity

Is it crass to suppose that friendship and love are rooted in an equitable exchange of rewards? Don't we sometimes give in response to a loved one's need, without expecting any sort of return? Indeed, those involved in an equitable long-term relationship are unconcerned with short-term equity. Margaret Clark and Judson Mills (1979, 1993; Clark, 1984, 1986) argue that people even take pains to *avoid* calculating any exchange benefits. When we help a good friend, we do not want instant repayment. If someone has us for dinner, we wait before reciprocating, lest the person attribute the motive for our return invitation to be merely paying off a social debt. True friends tune into one another's needs even when reciprocation is impossible (Clark & others, 1986, 1989). One clue that an acquaintance is becoming such a friend is the person's sharing when sharing is unexpected (Miller & others, 1989). Happily married people tend *not* to keep score of how much they are giving and getting (Buunk & Van Yperen, 1991).

Previously we noted an equity rule at work in the matching phenomenon: People usually bring equal assets to romantic relationships. Recall that often they are matched for attractiveness, status, and so forth. If they are mismatched in one area, such as attractiveness, they tend to be mismatched in some other area, such as status. But in total assets, they are an equitable match. No one says, and few even think, "I'll trade you my good looks for your big income." But especially in relationships that last, equity is the rule.

Perceived Equity and Satisfaction

Those in an equitable relationship are more content (Fletcher & others, 1987; Hatfield & others, 1985; Van Yperen & Buunk, 1990). Those who perceive their relationship as *in*equitable feel discomfort: The one who has the better deal might feel guilty and the one who senses a raw deal might feel strong irritation. (Given self-serving bias, the person who is "overbenefited" is less sensitive to the inequity.)

Robert Schafer and Patricia Keith (1980) surveyed several hundred married couples of all ages, noting those who felt their marriage was somewhat unfair because one spouse contributed too little to the cooking, housekeeping, parenting, or providing. Inequity took its toll: Those who perceived inequity also felt more distressed and depressed. During the child-rearing years, when wives often feel underbenefited and husbands overbenefited, marital satisfaction tends to dip. During the honeymoon and empty-nest stages, spouses are more likely to perceive equity and to feel satisfaction with their marriage (Feeney & others, 1994). When both partners freely give and receive, and make decisions together, the odds of sustained, satisfying love are good.

Self-Disclosure

Deep, companionate relationships are intimate. They enable us to be known as we truly are and feel accepted. We discover this delicious experience in a good marriage or a close friendship—a relationship where trust displaces anxiety and where we are therefore free to open ourselves without fear of losing the other's affection (Holmes & Rempel, 1989). Such relationships are characterized by what the late Sidney Jourard called **self-disclosure** (Derlega & others, 1993). As a relationship grows, self-disclosing partners reveal more and more of themselves to one another; their knowledge of one another penetrates to deeper and deeper levels until it reaches an appropriate depth. Lacking opportunities for intimacy, we experience the pain of loneliness (Berg & Peplau, 1982; Solano & others, 1982).

Experiments have probed both the *causes* and the *effects* of self-disclosure. When are people most willing to disclose intimate information concerning "what you like and don't like about yourself" or "what you're most ashamed and most proud of"? And what effects do such revelations have upon those who reveal and receive them?

The most reliable finding is the **disclosure reciprocity** effect: Disclosure begets disclosure (Berg, 1987; Miller, 1990; Reis & Shaver, 1988). We reveal more to those who have been open with us. But intimacy is seldom instant. (If it is, the person might seem indiscreet and unstable.) Appropriate intimacy progresses like a dance: I reveal a little, you reveal a little—but not too much. You then reveal more, and I reciprocate.

Some people, most of them women, are especially skilled "openers"—they easily elicit intimate disclosures from others, even from those who normally don't reveal very much of themselves (Miller & others, 1983; Pegalis & others, 1994; Shaffer & others, 1996). Such people tend to be good listeners. During conversation they maintain attentive facial expressions and appear to be comfortably enjoying themselves (Purvis & others, 1984). They might also express interest by uttering supportive phrases while their conversational partner is speaking. They are what psychologist Carl Rogers (1980) called "growth-promoting" listeners—people who are *genuine* in revealing their own feelings, who are *accepting* of others' feelings, and who are *empathic,* sensitive, reflective listeners.

What are the effects of such self-disclosure? Jourard (1964) argued that dropping our masks, letting ourselves be known as we are, nurtures love. He presumed that it is gratifying to open up to another and then to receive the trust another implies by being open with us. For example, having an intimate friend with whom we can discuss threats to our self-image seems to help us survive such stresses (Swann & Predmore, 1985). A true friendship is a special relationship that helps us cope with our other relationships. "When I am with my friend," reflected the Roman playwright Seneca, "methinks I am alone, and as much at liberty to speak anything as to think it." At its best, marriage is such a friendship, sealed by commitment.

Although intimacy is rewarding, the results of many experiments caution us not to presume that self-disclosure will automatically kindle love. It is just not that simple. It is true that we like best those to whom we've disclosed ourselves (R. L. Archer & others, 1980). But we are not always fond of those who most intimately reveal themselves to us (Archer & Burleson, 1980; Archer & others, 1980). Someone who early in an acquaintanceship rushes to tell us intimate details can seem indiscreet, immature, even unstable (Dion & Dion, 1978; Miell & others, 1979). Usually, though, people prefer an open, self-disclosing person to one who holds back. This is especially so when the disclosure is appropriate to the conversation. We feel pleased when a normally reserved person says that something about us "made me feel like opening up" and shares confidential information (Archer & Cook, 1986; D. Taylor & others, 1981). It is gratifying to be singled out for another's disclosure.

Intimate self-disclosure is one of companionate love's delights. Dating and married couples who most reveal themselves to one another express most satisfaction with their relationship and are more likely to endure in it (Berg & McQuinn, 1986; Hendrick & others, 1988; Sprecher, 1987). In a Gallup national marriage survey, 75 percent of those who prayed with their spouse (and 57 percent of those who didn't) reported their marriage as very happy (Greeley, 1991). Among believers, shared prayer from the heart is a humbling, intimate, soulful exposure. Those who pray together also more often say they discuss their marriage together, respect their spouse, and rate their spouse as a skilled lover.

Researchers have also found that women are often more willing to disclose their fears and weaknesses than men are (Cunningham, 1981). As Kate Millett (1975) put it, "Women express, men repress." Nevertheless, men today, particularly men with egalitarian gender-role attitudes, seem increasingly willing to reveal intimate feelings and to enjoy the satisfactions that accompany a relationship of mutual trust and self-disclosure. And that, say Arthur Aron and Elaine Aron (1994), is the essence of love— two selves connecting, disclosing, and identifying with one another; two selves, each retaining their individuality, yet sharing activities, delighting in similarities, and mutually supporting.

ENDING RELATIONSHIPS

Often love dies. What factors predict marital dissolution? How do couples typically detach or renew their relationships?

In 1971, a man wrote a love poem to his bride, slipped it into a bottle, and dropped it into the Pacific Ocean between Seattle and Hawaii. A decade later, a jogger found it on a Guam beach:

> If, by the time this letter reaches you, I am old and gray, I know that our love will be as fresh as it is today.
>
> It may take a week or it may take years for this note to find you. . . . If this should never reach you, it will still be written in my heart that I will go to extreme means to prove my love for you. Your husband, Bob.

The woman to whom the love note was addressed was reached by phone. The note was read to her. She burst out laughing. And the more she heard, the harder she laughed. "We're divorced," she finally said, and slammed down the phone.

So it often goes. Comparing their unsatisfying relationship with the support and affection they imagine is available elsewhere, people are now divorcing more often—at double the 1960 rate. Slightly more than half of American marriages and roughly 40 percent of Canadian marriages now end in divorce. Enduring relationships are rooted in enduring love and satisfaction, but also in inattention to possible alternative partners, fear of the costs of termination, and a sense of moral obligation (Adams & Jones, 1997; Miller, 1997). As economic and social barriers to divorce weakened during the 1960s and 1970s, thanks partly to women's increasing employment, divorce rates rose. "We are living longer, but loving more briefly," quips Os Guiness (1993, p. 309).

Sociologist Norval Glenn (1991) analyzed national opinion data gathered on thousands of Americans from 1972 to 1988. He followed the course of marriages that began in the early 1970s. By the late 1980s, only a third of the starry-eyed newlyweds were both still married *and* proclaiming their marriages "very happy." Allowing for some overreporting of marital happiness (it's easier to tell an interviewer you've succeeded than failed in your marriage), Glenn concludes that "the real proportion of those marriages that were successful . . . may well have been under a fourth." From a 1988 national survey, the Gallup Organization offers a similarly dismal conclusion: Two out of three 35- to 54-year-olds had divorced, separated, or been close to separation (Colasanto & Shriver, 1989). If this pattern continues, said the Gallup researchers, "our nation will soon reach the point where the dominant experience of adults will have been marital instability."

Britain's royal House of Windsor knows well the hazards of modern marriage. The fairy-tale marriages of Princess Margaret, Princess Anne, Prince Charles, and Prince Andrew all crumbled, smiles replaced with stony stares. Shortly after her 1986 marriage to Prince Andrew, Sarah

Ferguson gushed, "I love his wit, his charm, his looks. I worship him." Andrew reciprocated her euphoria: "She is the best thing in my life." Six years later, Andrew, having decided her friends were "philistines," and Sarah, having derided Andrew's boorish behavior as "terribly gauche," called it quits (*Time*, 1992).

Who Divorces?

Divorce rates vary widely by country, ranging from 0.01 percent of the population annually in Bolivia, the Philippines, and Spain to 4.7 percent in the world's most divorce-prone country, the United States. To predict a culture's divorce rates, it helps to know its values (Triandis, 1994). Individualistic cultures (where love is a feeling and people ask, "What does my heart say?") have more divorce than do communal cultures (where love entails obligation and people ask, "What will other people say?"). Individualists marry "for as long as we both shall love," collectivists more often for life. Individualists expect more passion and personal fulfillment in a marriage, which puts the relationship under greater pressure (Dion & Dion, 1993). "Keeping romance alive" was rated as important to a good marriage by 78 percent of American women surveyed and 29 percent of Japanese women (*American Enterprise*, 1992).

Risk of divorce also depends on who marries whom (Fergusson & others, 1984; Myers, 2000; Tzeng, 1992). People usually stay married if they

- married after age 20,
- both grew up in stable, two-parent homes,
- dated for a long while before marriage,
- are well and similarly educated,
- enjoy a stable income from a good job,
- live in a small town or on a farm,
- did not cohabit or become pregnant before marriage,
- are religiously committed, and
- are of similar age, faith, and education.

None of these predictors, by itself, is essential to a stable marriage. But if none of these things is true for someone, marital breakdown is an almost sure bet. If all are true, they are *very* likely to stay together until death. The English perhaps had it right, several centuries ago, when presuming that the temporary intoxication of passionate love was a foolish basis for permanent marital decisions. Better, they felt, to choose a mate based on stable friendship and compatible backgrounds, interests, habits, and values (Stone, 1977).

The Detachment Process

Severing bonds produces a predictable sequence of agitated preoccupation with the lost partner, followed by deep sadness and, eventually, the
beginnings of emotional detachment and a return to normal living (Hazan
& Shaver, 1994). Even newly separated couples who have long ago ceased
feeling affection are often surprised at their desire to be near the former
partner. Deep and longstanding attachments seldom break quickly; de-
taching is a process, not an event.

Among dating couples, the closer and longer the relationship and the
fewer the available alternatives, the more painful the breakup (Simpson,
1987). Surprisingly, Roy Baumeister and Sara Wotman (1992) report that
months or years later people recall more pain over spurning someone's
love than over having been spurned. Their distress arises from guilt over
hurting someone, from upset over the heartbroken lover's persistence, or
from uncertainty over how to respond. Among married couples, breakup
has additional costs: shocked parents and friends, guilt over broken vows,
possibly restricted parental rights. Still, each year millions of couples are
willing to pay such costs to extricate themselves from what they perceive
as the greater costs of continuing a painful, unrewarding relationship.
Such costs include, in one study of 328 married couples, a tenfold increase
in depression symptoms when a marriage is marked by discord rather
than satisfaction (O'Leary & others, 1994).

When relationships suffer, there are alternatives to divorce. Caryl Rusbult and her colleagues (1986, 1987) have explored three other ways of coping with a failing relationship. Some people exhibit *loyalty*, by waiting for
conditions to improve. The problems are too painful to speak of and the risks
of separation are too great, so the loyal partner perseveres, hoping the good
old days will return. Others (especially men) exhibit *neglect;* they ignore the
partner and allow the relationship to deteriorate. When painful dissatisfac-
tions are ignored, an insidious emotional uncoupling ensues as the partners
talk less and begin redefining their lives without each other. Still others will
voice their concerns and take active steps to improve the relationship by discussing problems, seeking advice, and attempting to change.

Study after study—in fact, 115 studies of 45,000 couples—reveal that
unhappy couples disagree, command, criticize, and put down. Happy
couples more often agree, approve, assent, and laugh (Karney & Bradbury, 1995; Noller & Fitzpatrick, 1990). After observing 2,000 couples,
John Gottman (1994) noted that healthy marriages were not necessarily
devoid of conflict. Rather, they were marked by an ability to reconcile differences and to overbalance criticism with affection. In successful marriages, positive interactions (smiling, touching, complimenting, laughing) outnumbered negative interactions (sarcasm, disapproval, insults)
by at least a 5-to-1 ratio.

Successful couples have learned, sometimes aided by communication training, to restrain the cancerous putdowns and gut-level fire-with-fire reactions, to fight fair (by stating feelings without insulting), and to depersonalize conflict with comments like "I know it's not your fault" (Markman & others, 1988; Notarius & Markman, 1993; Yovetich & Rusbult, 1994). Would unhappy relationships get better if the partners agreed to *act* more as happy couples do, by complaining and criticizing less? by affirming and agreeing more? by setting times aside to voice their concerns? by praying or playing together daily? As attitudes trail behaviors, do affections trail actions?

Joan Kellerman, James Lewis, and James Laird (1989) wondered. They knew that among couples passionately in love, eye gazing is typically prolonged and mutual (Rubin, 1973). Would intimate eye gazing similarly stir feelings between those not in love (much as 45 minutes of escalating self-disclosure evoked feelings of closeness among those unacquainted students)? To find out, they asked unacquainted male-female pairs to gaze intently for two minutes either at one another's hands or in one another's eyes. When they separated, the eye gazers reported a tingle of attraction and affection toward each other. Simulating love had begun to stir it.

By enacting and expressing love, researcher Robert Sternberg (1988) believes the passion of initial romance can evolve into enduring love:

> "Living happily ever after" need not be a myth, but if it is to be a reality, the happiness must be based upon different configurations of mutual feelings at various times in a relationship. Couples who expect their passion to last forever, or their intimacy to remain unchallenged, are in for disappointment. . . . We must constantly work at understanding, building, and rebuilding our loving relationships. Relationships are constructions, and they decay over time if they are not maintained and improved. We cannot expect a relationship simply to take care of itself, any more than we can expect that of a building. Rather, we must take responsibility for making our relationships the best they can be.
>
> Given the psychological ingredients of marital happiness—kindred minds, social and sexual intimacy, equitable giving and receiving of emotional and material resources—it does, however, become possible to contest the French saying, "Love makes the time pass and time makes love pass." But it takes effort to stem love's decay. It takes effort to carve out time each day to talk over the day's happenings. It takes effort to forgo nagging and bickering and instead to disclose and hear one another's hurts, concerns, and dreams. It takes time to make a relationship into "a classless utopia of social equality" (Sarnoff & Sarnoff, 1989), in which both partners freely give and receive, share decision making, and enjoy life together.

CONCEPTS TO REMEMBER

Passionate love A state of intense longing for union with another. Passionate lovers are absorbed in one another, feel ecstatic at attaining their partner's love, and are disconsolate on losing it.

Two-factor theory of emotion   Arousal × label = emotion. (Emotional experience is a product of physiological arousal and how we cognitively label the arousal.)

Self-monitoring   Being attuned to the way one presents oneself in social situations and adjusting one's performance to create the desired impression.

Companionate love   The affection we feel for those with whom our lives are deeply intertwined.

Equity   A condition in which the outcomes people receive from a relationship are proportional to what they contribute to it. (Note: Equitable outcomes needn't always be equal outcomes.)

Self-disclosure   Revealing intimate aspects of oneself to others.

Disclosure reciprocity   The tendency for one person's intimacy of self-disclosure to match that of a conversational partner.

MODULE

27

❖

When Do People Help?

On March 13, 1964, bar manager Kitty Genovese was set upon by a knife-wielding rapist as she returned to her Queens, New York, apartment house at 3:00 A.M. Her screams of terror and pleas for help—"Oh my God, he stabbed me! Please help me! Please help me!"—aroused 38 of her neighbors. Many went to their windows and watched while, for 35 minutes, she struggled to escape her attacker. Not until her attacker departed did anyone so much as call the police. Soon after, she died.

Eleanor Bradley tripped and broke her leg while shopping. Dazed and in pain, she pleaded for help. For 40 minutes the stream of shoppers simply parted and flowed around her. Finally, a cab driver helped her to a doctor (Darley & Latané, 1968).

What is shocking is not that in these cases some people failed to help but that almost 100 percent of those involved failed to respond. Why? In the same or similar situations, would you or I react as they did? Or would we be heroes, like Everett Sanderson? Hearing the rumble of an approaching New York subway train, Everett Sanderson leapt down onto the tracks and raced toward the approaching headlights to rescue Michelle De Jesus, a 4-year-old who had fallen from the platform. Three seconds before the train would have run her over, Sanderson flung Michelle into the crowd above. As the train roared in, he himself failed in his first effort to jump back to the platform. At the last instant, bystanders pulled him to safety (Young, 1977).

Or consider the hillside in Jerusalem where 800 trees form a simple line, the Avenue of the Righteous. Beneath each tree is a plaque with the name of a European Christian who gave refuge to one or more Jews during the Nazi Holocaust. These "righteous Gentiles" knew that if the refugees were discovered, Nazi policy dictated that both host and refugee would suffer a common fate. Many did (Hellman, 1980; Wiesel, 1985).

Less dramatic acts of comforting, caring, and helping abound: Without asking anything in return, people offer directions, donate money, give blood, volunteer time. Why, and when, will people perform altruistic acts? And what can be done to lessen indifference and increase altruism?

Altruism is selfishness in reverse. An altruistic person is concerned and helpful even when no benefits are offered or expected in return. Jesus' parable of the Good Samaritan provides the classic illustration:

> A man was going down from Jerusalem to Jericho, and fell into the hands of robbers, who stripped him, beat him, and went away, leaving him half dead. Now by chance a priest was going down that road; and when he saw him, he passed by on the other side. So likewise a Levite, when he came to the place and saw him, passed by on the other side. But a Samaritan while traveling came near him; and when he saw him, he was moved with pity. He went to him and bandaged his wounds, having poured oil and wine on them. Then he put him on his own animal, brought him to an inn, and took care of him. The next day he took out two denarii, gave them to the innkeeper, and said, "Take care of him; and when I come back, I will repay you whatever more you spend." (Luke 10:30–35)

The Samaritan illustrates pure altruism. Filled with compassion, he gives a total stranger time, energy, and money while expecting neither repayment nor appreciation.

WHY DO PEOPLE HELP?

What motivates altruism? One idea, called **social-exchange theory,** is that we help after doing a cost-benefit analysis. As part of an exchange of benefits, helpers aim to maximize their rewards and minimize their costs. When donating blood, we weigh the costs (the inconvenience and discomfort) against the benefits (the social approval and noble feeling). If the anticipated rewards exceed the costs, we help.

You might object: Social-exchange theory takes the selflessness out of altruism. It seems to imply that a helpful act is never genuinely altruistic; we merely call it "altruistic" when the rewards are inconspicuous. If we know people are tutoring only to alleviate guilt or gain social approval, we hardly credit them for a good deed. We laud people for their altruism only when we can't otherwise explain it.

From babyhood onward, however, people sometimes exhibit a natural **empathy,** by feeling distress when seeing someone in distress and relief when their suffering ends. Loving parents (unlike child abusers and other perpetrators of cruelty) suffer when their children suffer and rejoice over their children's joys (Miller & Eisenberg, 1988). Although some helpful acts are indeed done to gain rewards or relieve guilt, experiments suggest that other helpful acts aim simply to increase another's welfare, producing satisfaction for oneself merely as a by-product (Batson, 1991). In these experiments, empathy often produces helping only when helpgivers believe the other will actually receive the needed help and regardless of whether the recipient knows who helped.

Social norms also motivate helping. They prescribe how we *ought* to behave. We learn the **reciprocity norm**—that we should return help to those who have helped us. Thus we expect that those who receive favors (gifts, invitations, help) should later return them. The reciprocity norm is qualified by our awareness that some people are incapable of reciprocal giving and receiving. Thus we also feel a **social-responsibility norm**—that we should help those who really need it, without regard to future exchanges. When we pick up the dropped books for the person on crutches, we expect nothing in return.

These suggested reasons for helping make biological sense. The empathy that parents feel for their children and other relatives promotes the survival of their shared genes. Likewise, say evolutionary psychologists, reciprocal altruism in small groups boosts everyone's survival.

WHEN DO PEOPLE HELP?

Social psychologists were curious and concerned about bystanders' lack of involvement during such events as the Kitty Genovese rape-murder. So they undertook experiments to identify when people will help in an emergency. Then they broadened the question to ask: Who is likely to help in nonemergencies—by such deeds as giving money, donating blood, or contributing time (Myers, 1993)? Among their answers: Helping often increases among people who are

- feeling guilty, thus providing a way to relieve the guilt or restore self-image;
- in a good mood; or
- deeply religious (evidenced by higher rates of charitable giving and volunteerism).

Social psychologists also study the *circumstances* that enhance helpfulness. The odds of our helping someone increase in these circumstances:

- We have just observed a helpful model.
- We are not hurried.
- The victim appears to need and deserve help.

- The victim is similar to ourselves.
- We are in a small town or rural area.
- There are few other bystanders.

NUMBER OF BYSTANDERS

Bystander passivity during emergencies has prompted social commentators to lament people's "alienation," "apathy," "indifference," and "unconscious sadistic impulses." By attributing the nonintervention to the bystanders' dispositions, we can reassure ourselves that as caring people, we *would* have helped. But were the bystanders such inhuman characters?

Social psychologists Bibb Latané and John Darley (1970) were unconvinced. So they staged ingenious emergencies and found that a single situational factor—the presence of other bystanders—greatly decreased intervention. By 1980 some four dozen experiments had compared help given by bystanders who perceived themselves to be either alone or with others. In about 90 percent of these comparisons, involving nearly 6,000 people, lone bystanders were more likely to help (Latané & Nida, 1981).

Sometimes the victim was less likely to get help when many people were around. When Latané and James Dabbs (1975) and 145 collaborators "accidentally" dropped coins or pencils during 1,497 elevator rides, they were helped 40 percent of the time when one other person was on the elevator and less than 20 percent of the time when there were six passengers. Why? Latané and Darley surmised that as the number of bystanders increases, any given bystander is less likely to *notice* the incident, less likely to *interpret* the incident as a problem or emergency, and less likely to *assume responsibility* for taking action (Figure 27-1).

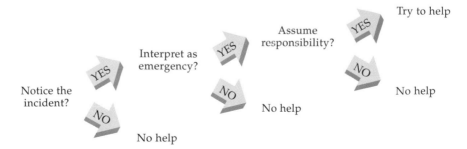

FIGURE 27-1
Latané and Darley's decision tree. Only one path up the tree leads to helping. At each fork of the path, the presence of other bystanders may divert a person down a branch toward not helping. (Adapted from Darley & Latané, 1968.)

Noticing

Twenty minutes after Eleanor Bradley has fallen and broken her leg on a crowded city sidewalk, you come along. Your eyes are on the backs of the pedestrians in front of you (it is bad manners to stare at those you pass) and your private thoughts are on the day's events. Would you therefore be less likely to notice the injured woman than if the sidewalk were virtually deserted?

To find out, Latané and Darley (1968) had Columbia University men fill out a questionnaire in a room, either by themselves or with two strangers. While they were working (and being observed through a one-way mirror), there was a staged emergency: Smoke poured into the room through a wall vent. Solitary students, who often glanced idly about the room while working, noticed the smoke almost immediately—usually in less than five seconds. Those in groups kept their eyes on their work. It typically took them about 20 seconds to *notice* the smoke.

Interpreting

Once we notice an ambiguous event, we must interpret it. Put yourself in the room filling with smoke. Though worried, you don't want to embarrass yourself by getting flustered. You glance at the others. They look calm, indifferent. Assuming everything must be okay, you shrug it off and go back to work. Then one of the others notices the smoke and, noting your apparent unconcern, reacts similarly. This is yet another example of informational influence. Each person uses others' behavior as clues to reality.

So it happened in the actual experiment (Latané & Darley, 1968). When those working alone noticed the smoke, they usually hesitated a moment, then got up, walked over to the vent, felt, sniffed, and waved at the smoke, hesitated again, and then went to report it. In dramatic contrast, those in groups of three did not move. Among the 24 men in 8 groups, only one person reported the smoke within the first four minutes (Figure 27-2). By the end of the six-minute experiment, the smoke was so thick it was obscuring the men's vision and they were rubbing their eyes and coughing. Still, in only three of the eight groups did even a single person leave to report the problem.

Equally interesting, the group's passivity affected its members' interpretations. What caused the smoke? "A leak in the air conditioning." "Chemistry labs in the building." "Steam pipes." "Truth gas." They offered many explanations. Not one said "Fire." The group members, in serving as nonresponsive models, influenced each other's interpretation.

This experimental dilemma parallels dilemmas each of us face. Are the shrieks outside merely playful antics or the desperate screams of someone being assaulted? Is the boys' scuffling a friendly tussle or a vicious fight? Is the person slumped in the doorway sleeping, high on drugs, or seriously ill, perhaps in a diabetic coma? That surely was the question confronting those who passed by Sidney Brookins (Goleman, 1993). Brookins, who had

Proportion having reported smoke, percent

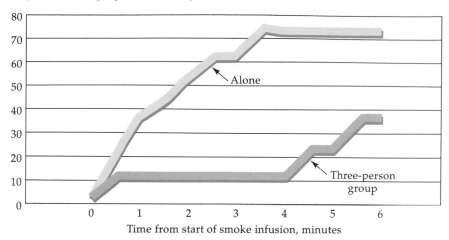

FIGURE 27-2
The smoke-filled room experiment. Smoke pouring into the testing room was
much more likely to be reported by individuals working alone than by three-
person groups. (Data from Latané & Darley, 1968.)

been beaten and suffered a concussion, died after lying near the door to a
Minneapolis apartment house for two days.

Assuming Responsibility

Misinterpretation is not the only cause of the **bystander effect**—the inaction of strangers faced with ambiguous emergencies. And what about
those times when an emergency is obvious? Those who saw and heard
Kitty Genovese's pleas for help correctly interpreted what was happening.
But the lights and silhouetted figures in neighboring windows told them
that others were also watching. This diffused the responsibility for action.

Few of us have observed a murder. But all of us have at times been
slower to react to a need when others were present. Passing a stranded motorist on a highway, we are less likely to offer help than on a country road.
To explore bystander inaction in clear emergencies, Darley and Latané
(1968) simulated the Genovese drama. They placed people in separate
rooms from which the participants would hear a victim crying for help. To
create this situation, Darley and Latané asked some New York University
students to discuss their problems with university life over a laboratory in-
tercom. They told the students that to guarantee their anonymity, no one
would be visible, nor would the experimenter eavesdrop. During the
ensuing discussion, the participants heard one person, when the experimenter turned his microphone on, lapse into an epileptic seizure. With increasing intensity and speech difficulty, he pleaded for someone to help.

Of those led to believe they were the only listener, 85 percent left their room to seek help. Of those who believed four others also overheard the victim, only 31 percent went for help. Were those who didn't respond apathetic and indifferent? When the experimenter came in to end the experiment, she did not find this response. Most immediately expressed concern. Many had trembling hands and sweating palms. They believed an emergency had occurred but were undecided whether to act.

After the smoke-filled room, the woman-in-distress, and the seizure experiments, Latané and Darley asked the participants whether the presence of others had influenced them. We know the others had a dramatic effect. Yet the participants almost invariably denied the influence. The typical reply? "I was aware of the others, but I would have reacted just the same if they weren't there." This response reinforces a familiar point: We often do not know why we do what we do. That is why experiments such as these are revealing. A survey of uninvolved bystanders following a real emergency would have left the bystander effect hidden.

These experiments raise again the issue of research ethics. Is it right to force hundreds of subway riders to witness someone's apparent collapse? Were the researchers in the seizure experiment ethical when they forced people to decide whether to abort the discussion to report the problem? Would you object to being in such a study? Note that it would have been impossible to get your "informed consent"; doing so would have destroyed the cover for the experiment.

In defense of the researchers, they were always careful to debrief the laboratory participants. After explaining the seizure experiment, probably the most stressful, the experimenter gave the participants a questionnaire. Every single one of them said the deception was justified and that they would be willing to take part in similar experiments in the future. None of the participants reported feeling angry at the experimenter. Other researchers similarly report that the overwhelming majority of participants in such experiments say afterward that their participation was both instructive and ethically justified (Schwartz & Gottlieb, 1981). In field experiments, an accomplice assisted the victim if no one else did, thus reassuring bystanders that the problem was being dealt with.

Remember that the social psychologist has a twofold ethical obligation: to protect the participants and to enhance human welfare by discovering influences upon human behavior. Such discoveries can alert us to unwanted influences and show us how we might exert positive influences. The ethical principle thus seems to be this: After protecting participants' welfare, social psychologists fulfill their responsibility to society by doing such research.

Will learning about the factors that inhibit altruism reduce their influence? Experiments with University of Montana students by Arthur Beaman and his colleagues (1978) revealed that once people understand why the presence of bystanders inhibits helping, they become more likely to help in group situations. The researchers used a lecture to explain to some students how bystander inaction can affect our interpretation of an emergency and our feelings of responsibility. Other students heard either an irrelevant lecture or no lecture at all. Two weeks later, as part of a different experiment in a different location, the participants found themselves walking (with an unresponsive confederate) past someone slumped over or past a person sprawled beneath a bicycle. Of those who had not heard the helping lecture, one-fourth paused to offer help; twice as many of those who had been "enlightened" did so.

Having read this module, you, too, have perhaps changed. As you come to understand what influences people's responses, will your attitudes and your behavior be the same? Coincidentally, shortly before I wrote the last paragraph, a former student, now living in Washington, D.C., stopped by. She mentioned that she recently found herself part of a stream of pedestrians striding past a man lying unconscious on the sidewalk. "It took my mind back to our social psych class and the accounts of why people fail to help in such situations. Then I thought, well, if I just walk by, too, who's going to help him?" So she made a call to an emergency help number and waited with the victim—and other bystanders who now joined her—until help arrived.

Another student, happening upon a drunk man beating up a street person near midnight in a Vienna subway station, flowed by with the crowd.

> Finally, I was convinced enough of the truth we learned in social psychology to go back and pull the drunk off the street person. Suddenly he was very mad at me and chased me through the subway until police came, arrested him, and got an ambulance for the victim. It was pretty exciting and made me feel good. But the coolest part was how a little insight into social-psychological aspects of our own behavior can help us overcome the power of the situation and change our predicted actions.

So, how will learning about social influences upon good and evil affect you? Will the knowledge you've gained affect your actions? I hope so.

CONCEPTS TO REMEMBER

Altruism   A motive to increase another's welfare without conscious regard for one's self-interests.

Social-exchange theory   The theory that human interactions are transactions that aim to maximize one's rewards and minimize one's costs.

Empathy   Vicariously experiencing another's feelings; putting oneself in another's shoes.

Reciprocity norm   An expectation that people will help, not hurt, those who have helped them.

Social-responsibility norm   An expectation that people will help those dependent upon them.

Bystander effect   The finding that a person is less likely to provide help when there are other bystanders.

❖

PART FIVE

Social Psychology Applied

Throughout this book, I have aimed to link laboratory and life by relating social psychology's principles and findings to everyday happenings. We now conclude by recollecting a number of these big ideas and applying and relating them to other realms. Modules 28 and 29 apply social psychology to the clinic, by asking how a social psychologist might help explain and treat depression, loneliness, and anxiety, and what social and psychological factors predict human happiness. Module 30 concludes the book with a recap of social psychology's biggest themes, and by suggesting how these relate to religious ideas about human nature.

28

❖

Who Is Miserable – and Why?

I f you are a typical college student, you might occasionally feel mildly depressed—dissatisfied with your life, discouraged about the future, sad, lacking appetite and energy, unable to concentrate, perhaps even wondering if life is worth it. Maybe you think disappointing grades have jeopardized your career goals. Perhaps the breakup of a relationship has left you in despair. At such times your self-focused brooding only worsens your feelings. For some 10 percent of men and nearly twice that many women, life's down times are not just temporary blue moods but one or more major depressive episodes that last for weeks without any obvious cause.

One of psychology's most intriguing research frontiers concerns the cognitive processes that accompany psychological disorders. What are the memories, attributions, and expectations of depressed, lonely, shy, or illness-prone people? In the case of depression, the most heavily researched disorder, dozens of new studies are providing some answers.

SOCIAL COGNITION AND DEPRESSION

As we all know from experience, depressed people are negative thinkers. They view life through dark-colored glasses. With seriously depressed people—those who are feeling worthless, lethargic, uninterested in friends and family, and unable to sleep or eat normally—the negative thinking becomes self-defeating. Their intensely pessimistic outlook leads them to magnify bad experiences and minimize good ones. These words of a depressed young woman illustrate: "The real me is worthless and inadequate. I can't move forward with my work because I become frozen with doubt" (Burns, 1980, p. 29).

Distortion or Realism?

Are all depressed people unrealistically negative? To find out, Lauren Al-loy and Lyn Abramson (1979) studied college students who were either mildly depressed or not depressed. They had the students observe whether their pressing a button was linked with a light coming on. Sur-prisingly, the depressed students were quite accurate in estimating their degree of control. It was the *non*depressives whose judgments were dis-torted, who exaggerated the extent of their control.

This surprising phenomenon of **depressive realism,** nicknamed the "sadder-but-wiser effect," shows up in various judgments of one's control or skill (Ackermann & DeRubeis, 1991; Alloy & others, 1990). Shelley Tay-lor (1989, p. 214) explains:

> Normal people exaggerate how competent and well liked they are. Depressed people do not. Normal people remember their past behavior with a rosy glow. Depressed people [unless severely depressed] are more evenhanded in recall-ing their successes and failures. Normal people describe themselves primarily positively. Depressed people describe both their positive and negative quali-ties. Normal people take credit for successful outcomes and tend to deny re-sponsibility for failure. Depressed people accept responsibility for both suc-cess and failure. Normal people exaggerate the control they have over what goes on around them. Depressed people are less vulnerable to the illusion of control. Normal people believe to an unrealistic degree that the future holds a bounty of good things and few bad things. Depressed people are more realis-tic in their perceptions of the future. In fact, on virtually every point on which normal people show enhanced self-regard, illusions of control, and unrealis-tic visions of the future, depressed people fail to show the same biases. "Sad-der but wiser" does indeed appear to apply to depression.

Underlying the thinking of depressed people are their attributions of responsibility. Consider: If you fail an exam and blame yourself, you might conclude that you are stupid or lazy, and feel depressed. If you attribute the failure to an unfair exam or to other circumstances beyond your con-trol, you are more likely to feel angry. In over 100 studies involving 15,000 subjects (Sweeney & others, 1986), depressed people have been more likely than nondepressed people to exhibit a negative **explanatory style** (Figure 28-1). They are more likely to attribute failure and setbacks to causes that are *stable* ("It's going to last forever"), *global* ("It's going to affect every-thing I do"), and *internal* ("It's all my fault"). The result of this pessimistic, overgeneralized, self-blaming thinking, say Abramson and her colleagues (1989), is a depressing sense of hopelessness.

Is Negative Thinking a Cause
or a Result of Depression?

The cognitive accompaniments of depression raise a chicken-and-egg question: Do depressed moods cause negative thinking, or does negative thinking cause depression?

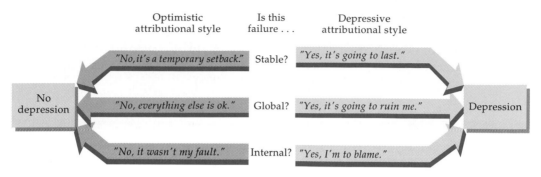

FIGURE 28-1
Depressive explanatory style. Depression is linked with a negative, pessimistic way of explaining and interpreting failures.

Depressed Moods Cause Negative Thinking

Without doubt, our moods definitely color our thinking. When we *feel* happy, we *think* happy. We see and recall a good world. But let our mood turn gloomy, and our thoughts switch to a different track. Off come the rose-colored glasses; on come the dark glasses. Now the bad mood primes our recollections of negative events (Bower, 1987; Johnson & Magaro, 1987). Our relationships seem to sour, our self-image takes a dive, our hopes for the future dim, other people's behavior seems more sinister (Brown & Taylor, 1986; Mayer & Salovey, 1987). As depression increases, memories and expectations plummet; when depression lifts, thinking brightens (Barnett & Gotlib, 1988; Kuiper & Higgins, 1985). Thus, *currently* depressed people recall their parents as having been rejecting and punitive. But *formerly* depressed people recall their parents in the same positive terms as do never-depressed people (Lewinsohn & Rosenbaum, 1987).

As Edward Hirt and his colleagues (1992) demonstrated in a study of some rabid Indiana University basketball fans, a bad mood induced by rejection or defeat can darken our thinking. After the fans were either depressed by watching their team lose or elated by a victory, the researchers asked them to predict the team's future performance, and their own. After a loss, people offered bleaker assessments not only of the team's future but also of their own likely performance at throwing darts, solving anagrams, and getting a date. When things aren't going our way, it can seem as though they never will.

A depressed mood also affects behavior. The person who is withdrawn, glum, and complaining does not elicit joy and warmth in others. Stephen Strack and James Coyne (1983) found that depressed people were realistic in thinking that others didn't appreciate their behavior. Their pessimism and bad moods trigger social rejection (Carver & others, 1994). Depressed behavior can also trigger reciprocal depression in others. College students who have depressed roommates tend to become a little depressed themselves (Burchill & Stiles, 1988; Joiner, 1994; Sanislow & others, 1989).

Depressed people are therefore at risk for being divorced, fired, or shunned, thus magnifying their depression (Coyne & others, 1991; Gotlib & Lee, 1989; Sacco & Dunn, 1990). They might also seek out those whose unfavorable views of them verify, and further magnify, their low self-image (Lineham, 1997; Swann & others, 1991).

Negative Thinking Causes Depressed Moods

Many people feel depressed when experiencing severe stress—losing a job, getting divorced or rejected, suffering physical trauma—anything that disrupts their sense of who they are and why they are a worthy human being (Hamilton & others, 1993; Kendler & others, 1993). Such brooding can be adaptive; insights gained during times of depressed inactivity can later result in better strategies for interacting with the world. But depression-prone people respond to bad events in an especially self-focused, self-blaming way (Pyszczynski & others, 1991; Wood & others, 1990a,b). Their self-esteem fluctuates more rapidly up with boosts and down with threats (Butler & others, 1994).

Why are some people so affected by *minor* stresses? Evidence suggests that a negative explanatory style contributes to depressive reactions. Colin Sacks and Daphne Bugental (1987) asked some young women to get acquainted with a stranger who sometimes acted cold and unfriendly, creating an awkward social situation. Unlike optimistic women, those with a pessimistic explanatory style—who characteristically offered stable, global, and internal attributions for bad events—reacted to the social failure by feeling depressed. Moreover, they then behaved more antagonistically toward the next person they met. Their negative thinking led to a negative mood response, which then led to negative behavior.

Outside the laboratory, studies of children, teenagers, and adults confirm that those with a pessimistic explanatory style are more likely to become depressed when bad things happen (Alloy & Clements, 1992; Brown & Siegel, 1988; Nolen-Hoeksema & others, 1986). "A recipe for severe depression is preexisting pessimism encountering failure," notes Martin Seligman (1991, p. 78). Moreover, patients who end therapy no longer feeling depressed but still with a negative explanatory style tend to relapse as bad events occur (Seligman, 1992). If those with a more optimistic explanatory style relapse, they often recover quickly (Metalsky & others, 1993; Needles & Abramson, 1990).

Researcher Peter Lewinsohn and his colleagues (1985) have assembled these findings into a coherent psychological understanding of depression. In their view, the negative self-image, attributions, and expectations of a depressed person are an essential link in a vicious cycle that is triggered by negative experience—perhaps academic or vocational failure, or family conflict, or social rejection (Figure 28-2). In those vulnerable to depression, such stresses trigger brooding, self-focused, self-blaming thoughts (Pyszczynski &

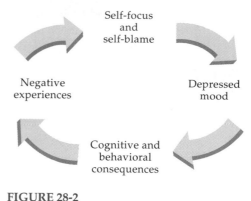

FIGURE 28-2
The vicious cycle of depression.

others, 1991; Wood & others, 1990a,b). Such ruminations create a depressed mood that drastically alters the way the person thinks and acts,
which then fuels further negative experiences, self-blame, and depressed
mood. In experiments, mildly depressed people's moods brighten when a
task diverts their attention to something external (Nix & others, 1995).
(Happiness seems best pursued by focusing not on oneself but beyond
oneself.) Depression is therefore *both* a cause and a consequence of negative cognitions.

Martin Seligman (1991) believes that self-focus and self-blame help
explain the near-epidemic levels of depression in the Western world today. In North America, for example, young adults today are three times
as likely as their grandparents to have suffered depression, despite having lived far fewer years than their grandparents (Cross-National Collaborative Group, 1992). Seligman believes that the decline of religion
and family, plus the growth of individualism, breeds hopelessness and
self-blame when things don't go well. Failed courses, careers, and marriages produce despair when we stand alone, with nothing and no one to
fall back on. If, as a macho *Fortune* ad declared, you can "make it on your
own," on "your own drive, your own guts, your own energy, your own
ambition," then whose fault is it if you *don't* make it? In nonwestern cultures, where close-knit relationships and cooperation are the norm, major depression is less common and less tied to guilt and self-blame over
perceived failure. In Japan, for example, depressed people instead tend
to report feeling shame over letting down their family or co-workers
(Draguns, 1990).

These insights into the thinking style linked with depression have
prompted social psychologists to study thinking patterns associated with
other problems. How do those who are plagued with excessive loneliness,
shyness, or substance abuse view themselves? How well do they recall

their successes and their failures? To what do they attribute their ups and downs? Where is their attention focused—on themselves or on others?

SOCIAL COGNITION AND LONELINESS

If depression is the "common cold of psychological disorders," then loneliness is the headache. Loneliness, whether chronic or temporary, is a painful awareness that our social relationships are less numerous or meaningful than we desire. Jenny de Jong-Gierveld (1987) observed in her study of Dutch adults that unmarried and unattached people are more likely to feel lonely. This prompted her to speculate that the modern emphasis on individual fulfillment and the depreciation of marriage and family life can be "loneliness-provoking" (as well as depression-provoking). Job-related mobility also makes for fewer long-term family and social ties and increased loneliness (Dill & Anderson, 1998).

But loneliness need not coincide with aloneness. One can feel lonely in the middle of a party. And one can be utterly alone—as I am while writing these words in the solitude of an isolated turret office at a British university 5,000 miles from home—without feeling lonely. To feel lonely is to feel excluded from a group, unloved by those around you, unable to share your private concerns, or different and alienated from those in your surroundings (Beck & Young, 1978; Davis & Franzoi, 1986).

Like depressed people, chronically lonely people seem caught in a vicious cycle of self-defeating social cognitions and social behaviors. They have some of the negative explanatory style of the depressed; they blame themselves for their poor social relationships and see most things as beyond their control (Anderson & others, 1994; Snodgrass, 1987). Moreover, they perceive others in negative ways. When paired with a stranger of the same sex or with a first-year college roommate, lonely students are more likely to perceive the other person negatively (Jones & others, 1981; Wittenberg & Reis, 1986). As Figure 28-3 illustrates, loneliness, depression, and shyness sometimes feed one another.

These negative views can both reflect and color the lonely person's experience. Believing in their social unworthiness and feeling pessimistic about others inhibits lonely people from acting to reduce their loneliness. Lonely people often do find it hard to introduce themselves, make phone calls, and participate in groups (Rook, 1984; Spitzberg & Hurt, 1987; Nurmi & others, 1996, 1997). They tend to be self-conscious and to have low self-esteem (Check & Melchior, 1990; Vaux, 1988). When talking with a stranger, they spend more time talking about themselves and take less interest in their conversational partners than do nonlonely people (Jones & others, 1982). After such conversations, the new acquaintances often come away with more negative impressions of the lonely people (Jones & others, 1983).

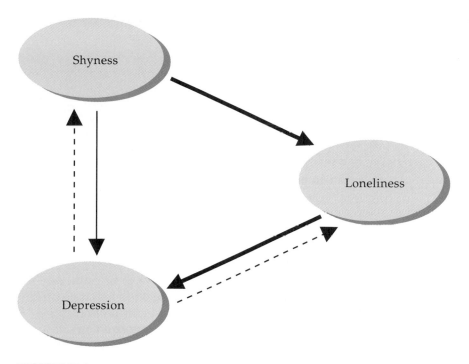

FIGURE 28-3
The interplay of chronic shyness, loneliness, and depression. Solid arrows indicate primary cause-effect direction, as summarized by Jody Dill and Craig Anderson (1998).

SOCIAL COGNITION AND ANXIETY

Being interviewed for a much-wanted job, dating someone for the first time, stepping into a roomful of strangers, performing before an important audience, or (the most common phobia) giving a speech can make almost anyone feel anxious. Some people, especially those who are shy or easily embarrassed, feel anxious in almost any situation in which they might be evaluated. For these people, anxiety is more a trait than a temporary state.

What causes us to feel anxious in social situations? Why are some people shackled in the prison of their own shyness? Barry Schlenker and Mark Leary (1982b, 1985; Leary & Kowalski, 1995) answer these questions by applying self-presentation theory. Self-presentation theory assumes that we are eager to present ourselves in ways that make a good impression. The implications for social anxiety are straightforward: *We feel anxious when we are motivated to impress others but doubt our ability to do so.* This simple principle helps explain a variety of research findings, each of which might ring true in your own experience. We feel most anxious in these circumstances:

- When dealing with powerful, high-status people—people whose impressions of us matter
- In evaluative contexts, as when making a first impression on the parents of our fiancé
- When feeling self-conscious (as shy people often do) and our attention is focused on ourselves and how we are coming across
- In an interaction that focuses on something central to our self-image, as when a college professor presents ideas before peers at a professional convention
- In novel or unstructured situations, such as a first school dance or first formal dinner, where we are unsure of the social rules

The natural tendency in all such situations is to be cautiously self-protective: to talk less; to avoid topics that reveal one's ignorance; to be guarded about oneself; to be unassertive, agreeable, and smiling.

Shyness is a form of social anxiety characterized by self-consciousness and worry about what others think (Anderson & Harvey, 1988; Asendorpf, 1987; Carver & Scheier, 1986). Compared to people who are not shy, shy self-conscious people (whose numbers include many adolescents) see incidental events as somehow relevant to themselves (Fenigstein, 1984; Fenigstein & Vanable, 1992). They overpersonalize situations, a tendency that breeds anxious concern and, in extreme cases, paranoia. Shown someone they think is interviewing them live (actually a videotaped interviewer), they perceive the interviewer as less accepting and interested in them (Pozo & others, 1991). They also overestimate the extent to which other people are watching and evaluating them. If their hair won't comb right or they have a facial blemish, they assume everyone else notices and judges them accordingly.

To reduce social anxiety, some people turn to alcohol. Alcohol lowers anxiety as it reduces self-consciousness (Hull & Young, 1983). Thus, chronically self-conscious people are especially likely to drink following a failure. If they become alcoholics, they are more likely than those low in self-consciousness to relapse from treatment when they again experience stress or failure.

Symptoms as diverse as anxiety and alcohol abuse can also serve a self-handicapping function. Labeling oneself as anxious, shy, depressed, or under the influence of alcohol can provide an excuse for failure (Snyder & Smith, 1986). Behind a barricade of symptoms, the person's ego stands secure. "Why don't I date? Because I'm shy, so people don't easily get to know the real me." The symptom is an unconscious strategic ploy to explain away negative outcomes.

What if we were to remove the need for such a ploy by providing people with a handy alternative explanation for their anxiety and therefore for possible failure? Would a shy person no longer need to be shy? That is precisely what Susan Brodt and Philip Zimbardo (1981) found when they brought shy and not-shy college women to the laboratory and had them converse with a handsome male who posed as another subject. Before the conversation, the women were cooped up in a small chamber and blasted with loud noise. Some of the shy women (but not others) were told that the noise would leave them with a pounding heart, a common symptom of social anxiety. Thus when these women later talked with the man, they could attribute their pounding heart and any conversational difficulties to the noise, not to their shyness or social inadequacy. Compared to the shy women who were not given this handy explanation for their pounding hearts, these women were no longer so shy. They talked fluently once the conversation got going and asked questions of the man. In fact, unlike the other shy women (whom the man could easily spot as shy), these women were to him indistinguishable from the not-shy women.

SOCIAL-PSYCHOLOGICAL APPROACHES TO TREATMENT

So far, we have considered patterns of social thinking that are linked with problems in living, ranging from serious depression to everyday shyness. Do these maladaptive thought patterns suggest any treatments? There is no social-psychological therapy. But therapy is a social encounter, and social psychologists are now suggesting how their principles might be integrated into existing treatment techniques (Forsyth & Leary, 1997; Strong & others, 1992).

Inducing Internal Change Through External Behavior

In Module 9, we reviewed a broad range of evidence for a simple but powerful principle: Our actions affect our attitudes. The roles we play, the things we say and do, and the decisions we make influence who we are.

Consistent with this attitudes-follow-behavior principle, several psychotherapy techniques prescribe action. Behavior therapists try to shape behavior and assume that inner dispositions will tag along after the behavior changes. Assertiveness training employs the foot-in-the-door procedure. The individual first role-plays assertiveness in a supportive context, then gradually becomes assertive in everyday life. Rational-emotive therapy assumes that we generate our own emotions, and clients receive "homework" assignments to talk and act in new ways that will generate new emotions: Challenge that overbearing relative. Stop telling yourself you're an unattractive person and ask someone out. Self-help groups subtly induce participants to behave in new ways in front of the group—to express anger, cry, act with high self-esteem, express positive feelings.

Experiments confirm that what we say about ourselves can affect how we feel. In one experiment, students were induced to write self-laudatory essays (Mirels & McPeek, 1977). These students, more than others who wrote essays about a current social issue, later expressed higher self-esteem when privately rating themselves for a different experimenter. In several more experiments, Edward Jones and his associates (1981; Rhode-walt & Agustsdottir, 1986) influenced students to present themselves to an interviewer in either self-enhancing or self-deprecating ways. Again, the public displays, whether upbeat or downbeat, carried over to later private responses on a test of actual self-esteem. Saying is believing, even when we talk about ourselves. This was especially true when the students were made to feel responsible for how they presented themselves. So, the most therapeutic commitments are both uncoerced and effortful.

Breaking Vicious Cycles

If depression, loneliness, and social anxiety maintain themselves through a vicious cycle of negative experiences, negative thinking, and self-defeating behavior, it should be possible to break the cycle at any of several points—by changing the environment, by training the person to behave more constructively, by reversing negative thinking. And it is. Several therapy methods help free people from depression's vicious cycle.

Social Skills Training

Depression, loneliness, and shyness are not just problems in someone's mind. To be around a depressed person for any length of time can be irritating and depressing. As lonely and shy people suspect, they can indeed come across poorly in social situations. In these cases, social skills training can help. By observing and then practicing new behaviors in safe situations, the person can develop the confidence to behave more effectively in other situations.

The person who begins to enjoy the rewards of behaving more skillfully develops a more positive self-perception. Frances Haemmerlie and Robert Montgomery (1982, 1984, 1986) demonstrated this in several heartwarming studies with shy, anxious heterosexual college students. Those who are inexperienced and nervous around those of the other sex might say to themselves: "I don't date much, so I must be socially inadequate, so I shouldn't try reaching out to anyone." To reverse this negative sequence, Haemmerlie and Montgomery enticed such students into pleasant interactions with people of the other sex.

In one experiment, college men completed social anxiety questionnaires and then came to the laboratory on two different days. Each day they enjoyed 12-minute conversations with each of six young women. The men thought the women were also subjects. Actually, the women had been asked to carry on a natural, positive, friendly conversation with each of the men.

The effect of these two and a half hours of conversation was remarkable. As one subject wrote afterward, "I had never met so many girls that I could have a good conversation with. After a few girls, my confidence grew to the point where I didn't notice being nervous like I once did." Such comments were supported by a variety of measures. Unlike men in a control condition, those who experienced the conversations reported considerably less female-related anxiety when retested one week and six months later. Placed alone in a room with an attractive female stranger, they also became much more likely to start a conversation. Outside the laboratory they actually began occasional dating.

Haemmerlie and Montgomery note that not only did all this occur without any counseling, but it might very well have occurred *because* there was no counseling. Having behaved successfully on their own, the men could now perceive themselves as socially competent. Although seven months later the researchers did debrief the participants, by that time the men had presumably enjoyed enough social success to maintain their internal attributions for success. "Nothing succeeds like success," concluded Haemmerlie (1987), "as long as there are no external factors present that the client can use as an excuse for that success!"

Explanatory Style Therapy

The vicious cycles that maintain depression, loneliness, and shyness can be broken by social skills training, by positive experiences that alter self-perceptions, *and* by changing negative thought patterns. Some people have social skills, but their experiences with hypercritical friends and family have convinced them they do not. For such people it can be enough to help them reverse their negative beliefs about themselves and their futures. One of the cognitive therapies with this aim is an *explanatory style therapy* proposed by social psychologists (Abramson, 1988; Försterling, 1986; Greenberg & others, 1992).

One such program taught depressed college students to change their typical attributions. Mary Anne Layden (1982) first explained the advantages of making attributions more like those of the typical nondepressed person (by accepting credit for successes and seeing how circumstances can make things go wrong). After assigning a variety of tasks, she helped the students see how they typically interpreted success and failure. Then came the treatment phase: Layden instructed each person to keep a diary of daily successes and failures, noting how they contributed to their own successes and noting external reasons for their failures. When retested after a month of this attributional retraining and compared with an untreated control group, their self-esteem had risen and their attributional style had become more positive. And the more their explanatory style improved, the more their depression lifted. By changing their attributions, they had changed their emotions.

Having emphasized what changed behavior and thought patterns can accomplish, we do well to remind ourselves of their limits. Social skills training and positive thinking cannot transform us into consistent winners who are loved and admired by everyone. Furthermore, temporary depression, loneliness, and shyness are perfectly appropriate responses to profoundly sad events. It is when such feelings exist chronically and without any discernible cause that there is reason for concern and a need to change the self-defeating thoughts and behaviors.

CONCEPTS TO REMEMBER

Depressive realism   The tendency of mildly depressed people to make accurate rather than self-serving judgments, attributions, and predictions.

Explanatory style   One's habitual way of explaining life events. A negative, pessimistic, depressive explanatory style attributes failures to stable, global, and internal causes.

MODULE

29

❖

Who Is Happy –
and Why?

Who is happy? Is happiness showered on those of a particular age, gender, or income level? Does it come with certain genetically predisposed traits? with supportive close relationships? with a spiritual perspective?

Such questions not only went unanswered during most of psychology's first century, they went largely unasked as psychology focused on illness more than health, on fear more than courage, on aggression more than love. An electronic search of *Psychological Abstracts* since 1967 turned up 5,548 articles on anger, 41,416 on anxiety, and 54,040 on depression—whereas only 415 abstracts mentioned joy, 1,710 mentioned happiness, and 2,582 mentioned life satisfaction. In this sampling, negative emotions trounced positive emotions by a 21-to-1 ratio (even greater than the 8-to-1 margin by which "treatment" exceeded "prevention").

Although human suffering understandably focuses much of our attention on the understanding and alleviation of misery, one sees harbingers of a more positive dimension to psychology. For example, a new scientific pursuit of happiness and life satisfaction (together called "subjective well-being") has begun by asking two simple questions: How happy are people? And who are the happy people—what characteristics, traits, and circumstances mark happy lives?

---

[1] I adapted this module from my article, "The Funds, Friends, and Faith of Happy People," in the *American Psychologist* millennium issue (January, 2000) and from "The Science of Happiness" (co-authored by Ed Diener) in *The Futurist*, September–October, 1997.

*H*OW HAPPY ARE PEOPLE?

A long tradition views life as tragedy, extending from Sophocles' observing (in *Oedipus at Colonus*) that "Not to be born is, past all prizing, best" to Woody Allen's discerning (in *Annie Hall*) two kinds of lives: the horrible and the merely miserable. Albert Camus, Allen Drury, Tennessee Williams, and other novelists and playwrights similarly give us images of unhappy people.

Many social observers concur. "Our pains greatly exceed our pleasures," it seemed to Rousseau, "so that, all things considered, human life is not at all a valuable gift." "We are not born for happiness," agreed Samuel Johnson. In *The Conquest of Happiness* (1930), philosopher Bertrand Russell echoed that most people are *un*happy. Recent warmhearted books for the would-be-happy (often written by people who generalize from their counseling of those unhappy) concur. In *Are You Happy?* (1986), Dennis Wholey reports that experts he interviewed believe that perhaps 20 percent of Americans are happy. "I'm surprised!" responded psychologist Archibald Hart in his *15 Principles for Achieving Happiness* (1988). "I would have thought the proportion was much lower!" In *Happiness Is an Inside Job* (1989), Father John Powell agrees: "One-third of all Americans wake up depressed every day. Professionals estimate that only 10 to 15 percent of Americans think of themselves as truly happy." Thomas Szasz (quoted by Winokur, 1987) speaks for many in surmising, "Happiness is an imaginary condition, formerly attributed by the living to the dead, now usually attributed by adults to children, and by children to adults."

But when asked about their happiness, people across the world paint a much rosier picture. For example, in periodic National Opinion Research Center surveys, 3 in 10 Americans say they are *very* happy. Only 1 in 10 say "not too happy." The remaining 6 in 10 describe themselves as "pretty happy." Yet the idea that others are not so happy persists: More than two-thirds of a representative sample of Minnesotans rate their "capacity for happiness" in the upper 35 percent "of other people of your age and sex" (Lykken, 1999).

Most people are similarly upbeat about their satisfaction with life (Inglehart, 1990; Myers, 1993). In western Europe and North America, 8 in 10 rate themselves as more satisfied than dissatisfied. Fewer than 1 in 10 rate themselves as more dissatisfied than satisfied. Likewise, some three-fourths of people say, yes, they've felt excited, proud, or pleased at some point during the past few weeks; no more than a third say they've felt lonely, bored, or depressed.

Ed Diener (Myers & Diener, 1996) has aggregated data from 916 surveys of 1.1 million people in 45 nations representing most of humanity. He recalibrated subjective well-being onto a 0-to-10 scale (where 0 is the low extreme, such as "very unhappy" or "completely dissatisfied with life," 5 is neutral, and 10 is the high extreme). The average response on this 10-point scale: 6.7.

A 1998 survey of 1,003 American adults by Opinion Research Corporation painted a similarly upbeat picture (Black & McCafferty, 1998). Asked, "Who of the following people do you think is the happiest?" people responded: "Oprah Winfrey" (23 percent), "Bill Gates" (7 percent), "the Pope" (12 percent), "Chelsea Clinton" (3 percent), and "Yourself" (49 percent, with the remaining 6 percent "Don't know").

These above-neutral reports characterize all ages, both sexes, all races studied, and all strategies for assessing subjective well-being, including those that sample people's experience using pagers. (The few exceptions, note Diener and Diener, 1996, include hospitalized alcoholics, newly incarcerated inmates, new therapy clients, South African Blacks living under apartheid, and students living under conditions of political suppression.) This positivity contradicts the intuitions of psychology students, half of whom wrongly think the elderly are "mostly unhappy." Another third wrongly guess the same of African Americans, as do 9 in 10 students of "unemployed men."

Are these happy-seeming people merely "in denial" of their actual misery? By definition, the final judge of someone's *subjective* well-being is whoever lives inside that person's skin. "If you feel happy," noted Jonathan Freedman (1978), "you are happy—that's all we mean by the term." Yet those who report themselves happy do *seem* so to their family members and close friends (Pavot & others, 1991; Sandvik, Diener, & Seidlitz, 1993). Their daily mood ratings reveal mostly positive emotions, and their self-reported happiness predicts other indicators of well-being. Compared to people who are depressed, happy people are less self-focused, less hostile and abusive, and less vulnerable to disease. They also are more loving, forgiving, trusting, energetic, decisive, creative, sociable, and helpful (Myers, 1993; Veenhoven, 1988).

But aren't depression rates on the rise? They are. Nevertheless, in one multination census of psychiatric disorders, the *lifetime* rate of depression was only 9 percent in the most vulnerable young adult age group (Cross-National Collaborative Group, 1992). At any time, only about 2 percent of people suffer major depression or bipolar disorder (Goodwin & others, 1993).

Ergo, the set-point for mood seems slightly positive. And for good reason: Positive emotions are conducive to healthy immune systems, sociability, and optimistic goal-striving. And they define an emotional background against which negative emotions, in response to threats, gain signal value. When something goes awry, the stone in the emotional shoe alerts the organism to act to alleviate the negative mood.

WHO IS HAPPY?

Although many people believe there are unhappy times of life—times of adolescent stress, midlife crisis, or old age decline—repeated surveys across the industrialized world reveal that no time of life is notably happiest and most satisfying (Myers & Diener, 1995). Emotionality changes with maturity, and the predictors of happiness change somewhat (in later life, satisfaction with social relations and health become more important). Yet in every age group there are many happy and some unhappy people.

Like age, gender gives little clue to happiness. Despite the well-known gender gaps in misery—men more often act antisocial or become alcoholic, women more often ruminate and get depressed or anxious—women and men are equally likely to declare themselves "very happy" and "satisfied" with their lives. This conclusion is grounded in surveys of 170,000 adults in 16 countries (Inglehart, 1990), in surveys of 18,000 university students in 39 countries (Michalos, 1991), and in a meta-analysis of 146 other studies (Haring, Stock, & Okun, 1984).

So who are the relatively happy people? As Diener (2000) indicates, some cultures (especially affluent cultures marked by political freedom) are conducive to increased satisfaction with life, if not more positive emotions. And certain traits and temperaments appear to predispose to happiness. Those who have followed lives through time find that some people, through varying circumstances, are persistently happier than others. Especially in Westernized cultures, such people tend to express high *self-esteem* (which, as we might expect from the better-than-neutral levels of self-reported well-being, most people do). They typically exhibit an *internal locus of control*; they feel empowered rather than helpless and victimized. They typically are *optimistic*. Those who agree, for example, to the proposition "When I undertake something new, I expect to succeed" tend to indeed to be more successful, and to be healthier and happier. And they tend to be *extraverted*. Although we might have expected that introverts would live happily in the serenity of their less-stressed contemplative lives, extraverts report somewhat more happiness—whether living alone or with others, whether working in solitary or social occupations.

Some of these traits, notably extraversion, are known to be genetically influenced, which helps explain Lykken and Tellegen's (1996) finding that about 50 percent of the variation in current happiness is heritable. Like cholesterol levels, happiness is genetically influenced but not genetically fixed.

So what else might influence personal happiness? Mihaly Csikszentmihalyi (1990) has observed increased quality of life when work and leisure engage one's skills. Between the anxiety of being overwhelmed and stressed, and the apathy of being underwhelmed and bored, lies a zone in which people experience "flow." When their experience is sampled using electronic pagers, people report greatest enjoyment not when mindlessly passive, but when unselfconsciously absorbed in a mindful challenge.

Additional research has focused on three other possible correlates of happiness. Even if money can't buy happiness, is there nevertheless an association between wealth and well-being? How important are supportive, close relationships for a sense of well-being? And what connections, if any, exist between religiosity and happiness? Simply said, do funds, friends, or faith predict happiness?

WEALTH AND WELL-BEING

"Could money buy you happiness?" Most deny it. But ask a different question—"Would a *little* more money make you a *little* happier?"—and many will smirk and nod yes. There is, we believe, some connection between wealth and well-being. Asked in a Roper survey (1984) how satisfied they were with 13 aspects of their lives, including friends, house, and schooling, Americans expressed least satisfaction with "the amount of money you have to live on." What would improve your quality of life? "More money" was the most frequent response to a University of Michigan national survey (Campbell, 1981, p. 41). The more the better. In one Gallup Poll (Gallup & Newport, 1990), 1 in 2 women, 2 in 3 men, and 4 in 5 people earning more than $75,000 would like to be rich. Asked by the Roper Organization what annual income they needed to fulfill their dreams, the average American suggested $102,000. Thus the modern American dream: life, liberty, and the purchase of happiness. Although most realize that the happy-seeming lifestyle of the rich and famous is beyond their reach, they do imagine "the good life" that might become possible when they achieve greater wealth.

The clearest evidence of this "greening of America" comes from the annual UCLA/American Council on Education survey of nearly a quarter million entering collegians. Those agreeing that a "very important" reason for their going to college was "to make more money" rose from 1 in 2 in 1971 to 3 in 4 in 1997 (Astin & others, 1987; Sax & others, 1998). And the proportion who consider it "very important or essential" that they become "very well off financially" rose from 39 percent in 1970 to 75 percent in 1997. Of 19 listed objectives, this was number one, outranking "developing a meaningful philosophy of life," "becoming an authority in my field," "helping others in difficulty," and "raising a family." For today's young Americans, money matters.

Does being well off indeed produce, or at least correlate with, psychological well-being? Would people be happier if they could exchange a middle-class lifestyle for one with palatial surroundings, Aspen ski vacations, and executive-class travel? Would they be happier if they won a publishers' sweepstake and could choose among its suggested indulgences: a 40-foot yacht, deluxe motorhome, designer wardrobe, luxury car, and private housekeeper? "Whoever said money can't buy happiness isn't spending it right," proclaimed a Lexus ad.

As Diener (1999) reports, there is some tendency for wealthy nations to have more satisfied people. The Swiss and Scandinavians, for instance, are generally prosperous and satisfied. When people in poorer nations compare themselves with the abundance of the rich nations, they might become more aware of their relative poverty. But among nations with more than $8,000 GNP per person, the correlation between national wealth and well-being evaporates. Better (so far as happiness and life satisfaction go) to be Irish than Bulgarian. But whether one is Irish, Belgian,

Norwegian, or American hardly matters. Indeed, the Irish during the 1980s reported consistently greater life satisfaction than the doubly wealthy but less satisfied West Germans (Inglehart, 1990). Moreover, note Diener, Diener, & Diener (1995), national wealth is entangled with civil rights, literacy, and the number of continuous years of democracy. For a clearer look at money and happiness, researchers have therefore asked whether, across individuals and over time, people's well-being rises with their wealth.

Are Rich People Happier?

In poor countries such as India, where low income more often threatens basic human needs, being relatively well off does predict greater well-being (Argyle, 1999). Psychologically as well as materially, it is better to be high caste than low. But in affluent countries, where most can afford life's necessities, affluence matters surprisingly little. In the United States, Canada, and Europe, the correlation between income and personal happiness, notes Ronald Inglehart (1990, p. 242), "is surprisingly weak (indeed, virtually negligible)." Happiness tends to be lower among the very poor. But once comfortable, more money provides diminishing returns. Summarizing his own studies of happiness, David Lykken (1999, p. 17) observes that "People who go to work in their overalls and on the bus are just as happy, on the average, as those in suits who drive to work in their own Mercedes."

Even very rich people—the *Forbes* 100 wealthiest Americans surveyed by Diener, Horwitz, and Emmons (1985)—are only slightly happier than average. Although having more than enough money to buy many things they don't need and hardly care about, 4 in 5 of the 49 super rich responding to the survey agreed that "Money can increase OR decrease happiness, depending on how it is used." And some were indeed unhappy. One fabulously wealthy man could not remember ever having been happy. One woman reported that money could not undo the misery caused by her children's problems. When sailing on the Titanic, even first class cannot get you where you want to go.

Our human capacity for adaptation (Diener, 1999) helps explain a major conclusion of subjective well-being research, as expressed by the late Richard Kammann (1983): "Objective life circumstances have a negligible role to play in a theory of happiness." Good and bad events (a pay hike, being rejected for tenure) do temporarily influence our moods, and people often seize upon such short-run influences to explain their happiness. Yet in less time than most people suppose, the emotional impact of significant events and circumstances dissipates (Gilbert & others, 1998). In a society where everyone lived in 4,000-square-foot houses, people would likely be no happier than in a society in which everyone lived in 2,000-square-foot houses. Thanks to our capacity to adapt to ever greater fame and fortune, yesterday's luxuries can soon become today's necessities and tomorrow's relics.

Does Economic Growth Improve Human Morale?

Over time, does happiness rise with affluence? Will Frank and Shirley Mae Capaci be enduringly happier for having in 1998 won the $195 million Powerball lottery? Likely not as much as they initially supposed. Lottery winners typically gain only a temporary jolt of joy from their winnings (Brickman, Coates, & Janoff-Bulman, 1978; Argyle, 1986). Although they are delighted to have won, their euphoria eventually fades. Likewise, those whose incomes have increased over the previous decade are not happier than those whose income has not increased (Diener & others, 1993).

If one is not surrounded by wealth, the pain of simplification can also be short-lived. Economist Robert Frank (1996) experienced this:

> As a young man fresh out of college, I served as a Peace Corps Volunteer in rural Nepal. My one-room house had no electricity, no heat, no indoor toilet, no running water. The local diet offered little variety and virtually no meat. . . . Yet, although my living conditions in Nepal were a bit startling at first, the most salient feature of my experience was how quickly they came to seem normal. Within a matter of weeks, I lost all sense of impoverishment. Indeed, my $40 monthly stipend was more than most others had in my village, and with it I experienced a feeling of prosperity that I have recaptured only in recent years.

If enduring personal happiness generally does not rise with personal affluence, does collective happiness float upward with a rising economic tide? Are Americans happier today than in 1940, when two out of five homes lacked a shower or bathtub, heat often meant feeding a furnace wood or coal, and 35 percent of homes had no toilet (U.S. Bureau of the Census, 1994)? Or consider 1957, when economist John Galbraith was about to describe the United States as *The Affluent Society*. Americans' per-person income, expressed in today's dollars, was about $9,000. Today, it is $20,000, thanks to increased real wages into the 1970s, increased nonwage income, and the doubling of married women's employment. Compared to 1957, Americans are therefore "the doubly affluent society," with double what money buys. Although income disparity has increased between rich and poor, the rising tide has lifted most boats. Americans today own twice as many cars per person and eat out more than twice as often, and many enjoy microwave ovens, big-screen color TVs, and home computers. From 1960 to 1997, the percentage of homes with

- dishwashers increased from 7 to 50 percent,
- clothes dryers increased from 20 to 71 percent, and
- air conditioning increased from 15 to 73 percent (U.S. Bureau of the Census, 1979, 1998).

So, believing that it is "very important" to be very well-off financially, and having seen their affluence ratchet upward little by little over four decades, are Americans now happier?

They are not. In National Opinion Research Center surveys, those reporting themselves "very happy" declined slightly between 1957 and 1998, from 35 to 32 percent. Twice as rich and no happier. Meanwhile, the divorce rate doubled. Teen suicide tripled. Arrests for juvenile crime quadrupled. And depression rates have soared, especially among youth and young adults (Seligman, 1989; Klerman & Wiessman, 1989; Cross-National Collaborative Group, 1992). Compared to their grandparents, today's young adults have grown up with much more affluence, slightly less happiness, and much greater risk of depression and assorted social pathologies.

It is hard to avoid a startling conclusion: Our becoming much better off over the last four decades has not been accompanied by one iota of increased subjective well-being. The same is true of the European countries and Japan, reports Richard Easterlin (1995). In Britain, for example, sharp increases in the percentage of households with cars, central heating, and telephones have not been accompanied by increased happiness. The conclusion is startling because it challenges modern materialism. So far as happiness goes, it is not, as the motto of one recent presidential campaign implied, "the economy, stupid." *Economic growth in affluent countries has provided no apparent boost to human morale.*

CLOSE RELATIONSHIPS AND WELL-BEING

One can easily imagine why the stress of close relationships might exacerbate illness and misery. "Hell is other people," mused Jean-Paul Sartre. Thus, people might fret over dysfunctional relationships. Pop psychology books warn us against the yoke of co-dependent connections, marked by too much support and loyalty to a troubled partner at the cost of one's self-fulfillment. Recognizing how the "chains" of marriage and the "shackles" of commitment can put people in "bondage," modern individualism advises us to give priority to enhancing our own identity and self-expression. "The only question which matters," declared Carl Rogers (quoted by Wallach & Wallach, 1985), "is, 'Am I living in a way which is deeply satisfying to me, and which truly expresses me?' "

Without disputing the human quest for personal identity, social and evolutionary psychologists remind us that we are also, as Aristotle recognized, social animals. We have a deep "need to belong."

Friendships and Well-Being

Do the correlates of social support include psychological as well as physical well-being? Being attached to friends and partners with whom we can share intimate thoughts has two effects, believed Francis Bacon (1625): "It redoubleth joys, and cutteth griefs in half." Three hundred and fifty years later, John Lennon and Paul McCartney (1967) sang the same idea: "I get by with a little help from my friends."

Indeed, people report happier feelings when with others (Pavot, Diener, & Fujita, 1990). When asked by the National Opinion Research Center,[1] "How many close friends would you say you have?" (excluding family members), 26 percent of those reporting fewer than five friends and 38 percent of those reporting five or more said they were "very happy."

Other findings confirm the correlation between social support and well-being. For example, those who enjoy close relationships cope better with various stresses, including bereavement, rape, job loss, and illness (Abbey & Andrews, 1985; Perlman & Rook, 1987). And among 800 college alumni surveyed, those with "Yuppie values"—who preferred a high income and occupational success and prestige to having very close friends and a close marriage—were twice as likely as their former classmates to describe themselves as "fairly" or "very" *un*happy.

Marriage and Well-Being

For more than 9 in 10 people worldwide, reports the United Nations' *Demographic Yearbook* one eventual example of a close relationship is marriage. Given our seeming need to belong, and the resulting links between friendship and well-being, does marriage predict greater well-being? Or is happiness more often associated with independence?

A mountain of data reveal that most people are happier attached than unattached. Repeated surveys in Europe and North America have produced a consistent result: Compared to the never married, and especially compared to those separated or divorced, married people report being happier and more satisfied with life. For example, among the 32,139 Americans surveyed by the National Opinion Research Center between 1972 and 1994, 40 percent of married adults declared themselves very happy—nearly double the 24 percent of never-married adults who said the same. Pooling data from national surveys of 20,800 people in 19 countries, Arne Mastekaasa (1994) confirmed the correlation between marriage and happiness. Married people are also at decreased risk of depression.

Even less happy than those unmarried or divorced are those in not-very-happy marriages. But those reporting their marriage as "very happy" are among the happiest of people—57 percent of them declaring life as a whole to be very happy. Henry Ward Beecher would not have been surprised: "Well-married a person is winged; ill-matched, shackled." As it happens, 3 in 4 married Americans say their spouse is their best friend, and 4 in 5 say they would marry the same person again (Greeley, 1991; Glenn, 1996).

---

[1] I analyzed National Opinion Research Center General Social Survey data for this paper via http://www.icpsr.umich.edu/gss/ and http://csa.berkeley.edu:7502/.

So, why are married people happier? Is marriage conducive to happiness? Or is happiness conducive to marriage? The traffic between marriage and happiness appears to be two-way.

First, happy people might be more appealing as marriage partners. Because they are more good-natured, more outgoing, and more focused on others (Veenhoven, 1988), they generally are socially attractive. Unhappy people are more often socially rejected. Misery might love company, but research on the social consequences of depression reveals that company does not love misery. An unhappy (and therefore self-focused, irritable, and withdrawn) spouse or roommate is often not perceived as fun to be around (Gotlib, 1992; Segrin & Dillard, 1992). For such reasons, positive, happy people more readily form happy relationships.

Yet "the prevailing opinion of researchers," reports Mastekaasa (1995), is that the marriage–happiness correlation is "mainly due" to the beneficial effects of marriage. Consider: If the happiest people marry sooner and more often, then as people age (and progressively less happy people move into marriage), the average happiness of both married and never-married people should decline. (The older, less happy newlyweds would pull down the average happiness of married people, leaving the unhappiest people in the unmarried group.) But the data do not support this prediction, which suggests that marital intimacy, commitment, and support do, for most people, pay emotional dividends. Marriage offers new roles, providing new stresses but also additional rewards and sources of identity and self-esteem (Crosby, 1987). And when marked by intimacy, marriage—friendship sealed by commitment—reduces loneliness and offers a dependable lover and companion (Hendrick & Hendrick, 1997).

FAITH AND WELL-BEING

Freud (1928/1964, p. 71) surmised that religion is corrosive to happiness—creating an "obsessional neurosis" that entails guilt, repressed sexuality, and suppressed emotions. Was he right? Or is religion more often associated with joy?

Accumulating evidence reveals that some forms of religious experience correlate with prejudice and guilt, but that, in general, an active religiosity is associated with several mental health criteria. First, actively religious North Americans are much less likely than irreligious people to become delinquent, to abuse drugs and alcohol, to divorce, and to commit suicide (Batson, Schoenrade, & Ventis, 1993; Colasanto & Shriver, 1989). Thanks in part to their lower rates of smoking and drinking, religiously active people even tend to be physically healthier and to live longer (Koenig, 1997; Matthews & Larson, 1997).

Other studies have probed the correlation between faith and coping with crises. Compared to religiously inactive widows, recently widowed women who worship regularly report more joy in their lives (Harvey, Barnes, & Greenwood, 1987; McGloshen & O'Bryant, 1988; Siegel & Kuykendall, 1990). Among mothers of children with developmental disabilities, those with a deep religious faith are less vulnerable to depression (Friedrich, Cohen, & Wilturner, 1988). People of faith also tend to retain or recover greater happiness after suffering divorce, unemployment, serious illness, or bereavement (Ellison, 1991; McIntosh, Silver, & Wortman, 1993). In later life, according to one meta-analysis, the two best predictors of life satisfaction have been health and religiousness (Okun & Stock, 1987).

In surveys in various nations, religiously active people also report somewhat higher levels of happiness (Inglehart, 1990). Consider a Gallup Organization (1984) U.S. survey. Those responding with highest scores on a spiritual commitment scale (by agreeing, for example, that "My religious faith is the most important influence in my life") were twice as likely as those lowest in spiritual commitment to declare themselves very happy. National Opinion Research Center surveys reveal higher levels of "very happy" people among those who feel "close to God." Self-rated spirituality and happiness might both be socially desirable responses, however. So, would the happiness correlation extend to a behavioral measure of religiosity? Among some 32,000 Americans randomly sampled from 1972 to 1994, the percentage who reported themselves to be "very happy" ranged from 27 percent among those who reported attending religious services "less than monthly" up to 47 percent among those attending "several times weekly."

What explains this positive correlation between faith and well-being? Possible explanations include the supportive close relationships often enjoyed by those active in faith communities, the motivation to focus beyond self, the sense of meaning that many people derive from their faith, and the hope it provides when facing the "terror" of one's mortality.

The correlational evidence that marks the new scientific pursuit of happiness leaves many fields for future researchers to plow as they explore the roots and fruits of happiness. But this much we now know: Age, gender, and income (assuming people have enough to afford life's necessities) give little clue to someone's happiness. William Cowper's 1782 hunch appears correct: "Happiness depends, as Nature shows, Less on exterior things than most suppose." Better clues come from knowing people's traits and the quality of their work and leisure experiences (Diener, 1999; Csikszentmihalyi, 2000), from knowing whether they enjoy a supportive network of close relationships, and from knowing whether the person has a faith that encompasses social support, purpose, and hope. Research on subjective well-being complements society's emphases on physical and material well-being and psychology's historic preoccupation with negative emotions. By asking who is happy, and why, the scientific pursuit of happiness can help our culture rethink its priorities and envision a world that enhances human well-being.

30

❖

Big Ideas in Social Psychology and Religion

In any academic field, the results of tens of thousands of studies, the conclusions of thousands of investigators, the insights of hundreds of theorists, can usually be boiled down to a few overriding ideas. Biology offers us principles such as natural selection and adaptation. Sociology builds upon concepts such as social structure, cultural relativity, and societal organization. Music exploits our ideas of rhythm, melody, and harmony.

Which concepts might we include on our short list of social psychology's big ideas? What basic principles are worth remembering long after you have forgotten most of what you learned in this book? And how well do these big ideas about human nature connect with those found in other fields, such as religious studies? Every religious tradition offers answers to some big questions: Who are we? Why are we here? What ought we to do? So let's ask, how do some of social psychology's big ideas connect with those of the Jewish-Christian religious tradition that prevails in Europe and the Americas?[1]

My list of "great ideas we ought never forget" includes four truths, each two-sided. As Pascal reminded us 300 years ago, no single truth is ever sufficient, because the world is not simple. Any truth separated from its complementary truth is a half-truth. It is in the union of partial truths— of what the Chinese call yin and yang (complementary opposites)—that we glimpse the larger reality.

---

[1]One could similarly relate social psychology's view of human nature to ideas derived from other religious traditions. I chose the Judeo-Christian tradition because of its familiarity to me and to most of my readers.

RATIONALITY AND IRRATIONALITY

How "noble in reason!" and "infinite in faculties!" is the human intellect, rhapsodized Shakespeare's Hamlet. In some ways, indeed, *our cognitive capacities are awesome.* The three-pound tissue in our skulls contains circuitry more complex than all the phone networks on the planet, enabling us to process information either effortfully or automatically, to remember vast quantities of information, and to make snap judgments using rule-of-thumb heuristics. One of the most human of tendencies is our urge to explain behavior, to attribute it to some cause, and therefore to make it seem orderly, predictable, and controllable. As intuitive scientists, we make our attributions efficiently and with enough accuracy for our daily needs.

Yes, echo Jewish and Christian theologians. We are *made in the divine image* and given stewardship for the earth and its creatures. We are the summit of the Creator's work, God's own children.

Yet our explanations are vulnerable to error, insist social psychologists. In ways we are often unaware of, *our explanations and social judgments are vulnerable to error.* When observing others, we are sometimes too prone to be biased by our preconceptions, to "see" illusory relationships and causes, to treat people in ways that trigger their fulfilling our expectations, to be swayed more by vivid anecdotes than by statistical reality, and to attribute their behavior to their dispositions (for example, to think that someone who acts strangely must *be* strange). Failing to recognize such sources of error in our social thinking, we are prone to overconfidence in our social judgments.

Such conclusions have a familiar ring to theologians, who remind us that *we are finite creatures* of the one who declares "I am God, and there is none like me" and that "as the heavens are higher than the earth, so are my ways higher than your ways and my thoughts than your thoughts" (Isaiah 46:9 and 55:9). As God's children we have dignity, but not deity. Thus we must be skeptical of those who claim for themselves godlike powers of omniscience (reading others' minds, foretelling the future), omnipresence (viewing happenings in remote locations), and omnipotence (creating or altering physical reality with mental power). We should be wary even of those who idolize their religion, presuming their doctrinal fine points to be absolute truth. Always, we see reality through a dim mirror.

SELF-SERVING BIAS AND SELF-ESTEEM

Our views of ourselves are fragile containers of truth. Heeding the ancient admonition to "know thyself," we analyze our behavior, but hardly impartially. Our human tendency to *self-serving bias* appears in our differing explanations for our successes and failures, for our good deeds and bad. On any socially desirable dimension, we commonly view ourselves as relatively superior—as, say, more ethical, socially skilled, and tolerant than our average peer. Moreover, we justify our past behaviors; we have an inflated confidence in the accuracy of our beliefs; we misremember our own past in self-enhancing ways; and we overestimate how virtuously we would behave in situations that draw less-than-virtuous behavior out of most people. Researcher Anthony Greenwald (1984) speaks for dozens of researchers: "People experience life through a self-centered filter."

That conclusion echoes a very old religious idea—that *self-righteous pride is the fundamental sin,* the original sin, the deadliest of the seven deadly sins. Thus the Psalmist could declare that "no one can see his own errors" and the Pharisee could thank God "that I am not like other men" (and you and I can thank God that we are not like the Pharisee). Pride goes before a fall. It corrodes our relations with one another, as in conflicts between partners in marriage, management and labor, nations at war. Each side views its motives alone as pure, its actions beyond reproach. But so does its opposition, continuing the conflict.

Yet *self-esteem pays dividends.* Self-affirmation is often adaptive. It helps maintain our confidence and minimize our depression. To doubt our efficacy and to blame ourselves for our failures is a recipe for failure, loneliness, or dejection. People made to feel secure and valued exhibit less prejudice and contempt for others.

Again, there is a religious parallel, in the idea that to sense an *ultimate acceptance* (divine "grace"—the religious parallel to psychology's "unconditional positive regard") is to be liberated from both self-protective pride and self-condemnation. To feel profoundly affirmed, just as I am, lessens my need to define my self-worth in terms of achievements, prestige, or material and physical well-being. It's rather like insecure Pinocchio saying to his maker, Geppetto, "Papa, I am not sure who I am. But if I'm all right with you, then I guess I'm all right with me."

ATTITUDES AND BEHAVIOR

Studies during the 1960s shocked social psychologists with revelations that our attitudes sometimes lie dormant, overwhelmed by other influences. But follow-up research was reassuring. *Our attitudes influence our behavior,*—when they are relevant and brought to mind. Thus our political attitudes influence our behavior in the voting booth. Our smoking attitudes influence our susceptibility to peer pressures to smoke. Our attitudes toward famine victims influence our contributions. Change the way people think and—whether we call such persuasion "education" or "propaganda"—the impact can be considerable.

If social psychology has taught us anything, it is that the reverse is also true: We are as likely to act ourselves into a way of thinking as to think ourselves into action. We are as likely to believe in what we have stood up for as to stand up for what we believe. Especially when we feel responsible for how we have acted, *our attitudes follow our behavior.* This self-persuasion enables all sorts of people—political campaigners, lovers, even terrorists—to believe more strongly in that for which they have witnessed or suffered.

The realization that inner attitude and outer behavior, like chicken and egg, generate one another parallels the Jewish-Christian idea that inner faith and outer action likewise feed one another. Thus, *faith is a source of action.* Elijah is overwhelmed by the Holy as he huddles in a cave. Paul is converted on the Damascus Road. Ezekiel, Isaiah, and Jeremiah undergo an inner transformation. In each case, a new spiritual consciousness produces a new pattern of behavior.

But *faith is also a consequence of action.* Throughout the Old and New Testaments, faith is seen as nurtured by obedient action. For example, in the Old Testament the Hebrew word for "know" is usually a verb, designating something one does. To *know* love, one must not only know about love, one must *act* lovingly. Philosophers and theologians note how faith grows as people act on what little faith they have. Rather than insist that people believe before they pray, Talmudic scholars would tell rabbis, get them to pray and their belief will grow. "The proof of Christianity really consists in 'following,' " declared Søren Kierkegaard (1851). To attain faith, said Pascal (1670), "follow the way by which [the committed] began; by acting as if they believed, taking the holy water, having masses said, etc. Even this will naturally make you believe. . . ." C. S. Lewis (1960) concurred:

> Believe in God and you will have to face hours when it seems *obvious* that this material world is the only reality; disbelieve in Him and you must face hours when this material world seems to shout at you that it is not all. No conviction, religious or irreligious, will, of itself, end once and for all [these doubts] in the soul. Only the practice of Faith resulting in the habit of Faith will gradually do that.

PERSONS AND SITUATIONS

On this incomplete list of big ideas, my final two-sided truth is that people and situations interact. We see this, first, in the evidence that social influences powerfully affect our behavior. *We are the creatures of our social worlds.*

Recall the studies of conformity, role playing, persuasion, and group influence. The most dramatic findings come from experiments that put well-intentioned people in evil situations to see whether good or evil prevailed. To a dismaying extent, evil pressures overwhelm good intentions, inducing people to conform to falsehoods or capitulate to cruelty. Faced with a powerful situation, nice people often don't behave so nicely. Depending on the social context, most of us are capable of acting kindly or brutally, independently or submissively, wisely or foolishly. In one irony-laden experiment, even most seminary students en route to recording an extemporaneous talk on the Good Samaritan parable failed to stop and give aid to a slumped, groaning person—*if* they had been pressed to hurry (Darley & Batson, 1973). External social forces shape our social behavior.

The social-psychological idea that there are powers greater than the individual is paralleled by the religious idea of *transcendent good and evil powers,* symbolized in the creation story as a seductive demonic force. Evil involves not only individual rotten apples here and there. It also is a product of "principalities and powers"—corrosive forces—that can make a whole barrel of apples go bad. And because evil is collective as well as personal, responding to it takes a communal religious life.

Although powerful situations can override people's individual dispositions, social psychologists do not view humans as mere passive tumbleweeds, blown this way and that by the social winds. Facing the same situation, different people might react differently, depending on their personality and culture. Feeling coerced by blatant pressure, they will sometimes react in ways that restore their sense of freedom. In a numerical minority, they will sometimes oppose and sway the majority. When they believe in themselves, maintaining an "internal locus of control," they sometimes work wonders. Moreover, people choose their situations—their college environments, their jobs, their locales. And their social expectations are sometimes self-fulfilling, as when we expect someone to be warm or hostile and they become so. In such ways, *we are the creators of our social worlds.*

To most religious traditions, that rings true. *We are morally responsible—* accountable for how we use whatever freedom we have. What we decide matters. The stream of causation from past to future runs through our choices.

Faced with these pairs of complementary ideas, framed either psychologically or religiously, we are like someone stranded in a deep well with two ropes dangling down. If we grab either one alone, we sink deeper into the well. Only when we hold both ropes can we climb out, because at the top, beyond where we can see, they come together around a pulley. Grabbing only the rope of rationality or irrationality, of self-serving pride or self-esteem, of attitudes-first or behavior-first, of personal or situational causation, plunges us to the bottom of a well. So instead we grab both ropes, perhaps without yet fully grasping how they come together. In doing so, we might be comforted by knowing that in both science and religion a confused acceptance of complementary principles is sometimes more honest than an oversimplified theory that ignores half the evidence. In the scissors of truth, the cutting edge lies between the blades of yin and yang.

References

ABBEY, A., & ANDREWS, F. M. (1985). Modeling the psychological determinants of life quality. *Social Indicators Research, 16,* 1–34.

ABBEY, A., ROSS, L. T., & McDUFFIE, D. (1993). Alcohol's role in sexual assault. In R. R. Watson (Ed.), *Drug and alcohol abuse reviews: Vol 5. Addictive behaviors in women.* Totowa, NJ: Humana Press.

ABBEY, A., ROSS, L. T., McDUFFIE, D., & McAUSLAN, P. (1996). Alcohol and dating risk factors for sexual assault among college women. *Psychology of Women Quarterly, 20,* 147–169.

ABELSON, R. P., KINDER, D. R., PETERS, M. D., & FISKE, S. T. (1982). Affective and semantic components in political person perception. *Journal of Personality and Social Psychology, 42,* 619–630.

ABRAMS, D. (1991). *AIDS: What young people believe and what they do.* Paper presented at the British Association for the Advancement of Science conference.

ABRAMS, D., WETHERELL, M., COCHRANE, S., HOGG, M. A., & TURNER, J. C. (1990). Knowing what to think by knowing who you are: Self-categorization and the nature of norm formation, conformity and group polarization. *British Journal of Social Psychology, 29,* 97–119.

ABRAMSON, L. Y. (Ed.). (1988). *Social cognition and clinical psychology: A synthesis.* New York: Guilford.

ABRAMSON, L. Y., METALSKY, G. I., & ALLOY, L. B. (1989). Hopelessness depression: A theory-based subtype. *Psychological Review, 96,* 358–372.

ACKERMANN, R., & DeRUBEIS, R. J. (1991). Is depressive realism real? *Clinical Psychology Review, 11,* 565–584.

ADAIR, J. G., DUSHENKO, T. W., & LINDSAY, R. C. L. (1985). Ethical regulations and their impact on research practice. *American Psychologist, 40,* 59–72.

ADAMS, D. (Ed.) (1991). *The Seville statement on violence: Preparing the ground for the constructing of peace.* Geneva: UNESCO.

ADAMS, J. M., & JONES, W. H. (1997). The conceptualization of marital commitment: An integrative analysis. *Journal of Personality and Social Psychology, 72,* 1177–1196.

ADLER, N. E., BOYCE, T., CHESNEY, M. A., COHEN, S., FOLKMAN, S., KAHN, R. L., & SYME, S. L. (1993). Socioeconomic inequalities in health: No easy solution. *Journal of the American Medical Association, 269,* 3140–3145.

ADLER, N. E., BOYCE, T., CHESNEY, M. A., COHEN, S., FOLKMAN, S., KAHN, R. L., & SYME, S. L. (1994). Socioeconomic status and health: The challenge of the gradient. *American Psychologist, 49,* 15–24.

ADLER, R. P., LESSER, G. S., MERINGOFF, L. K., ROBERTSON, T. S., & WARD, S. (1980). *The effects of television advertising on children.* Lexington, MA: Lexington Books.

ADORNO, T., FRENKEL-BRUNSWIK, E., LEVINSON, D., & SANFORD, R. N. (1950). *The authoritarian personality.* New York: Harper.

AIELLO, J. R., THOMPSON, D. E., & BRODZINSKY, D. M. (1983). How funny is crowding anyway? Effects of room size, group size, and the introduction of humor. *Basic and Applied Social Psychology, 4,* 193–207.

ALICKE, M. D., KLOTZ, M. L., BREITENBECHER, D. L., YURAK, T. J., & VREDENBURG, D. S. (1995). Personal contact, individuation and the better than average effect. *Journal of Personality and Social Psychology, 68,* 804–825.

ALLEE, W. C., & MASURE, R. M. (1936). A comparison of maze behavior in paired and isolated shell-parakeets (*Melopsittacus undulatus Shaw*) in a two-alley problem box. *Journal of Comparative Psychology, 22,* 131–155.

ALLEN, M., D'ALESSIO, D., EMMERS, T. M., & GEBHARDT, L. (1996). The role of educational briefings in mitigating effects of experimental exposure to violent sexually explicit material: A meta-analysis. *Journal of Sex Research, 33,* 133–141.

ALLISON, S. T., MACKIE, D. M., MULLER, M. M., & WORTH, L. T. (1993). Sequential correspondence biases and perceptions of change: The Castro studies revisited. *Personality and Social Psychology Bulletin, 19,* 151–157.

ALLISON, S. T., MESSICK, D. M., & GOETHALS, G. R. (1989). On being better but not smarter than others: The Muhammad Ali effect. *Social Cognition, 7,* 275–296.

ALLOY, L. B., & ABRAMSON, L. Y. (1979). Judgment of contingency in depressed and nondepressed students: Sadder but wiser? *Journal of Experimental Psychology: General, 108,* 441–485.

ALLOY, L. B., ALBRIGHT, J. S., ABRAMSON, L. Y., & DYKMAN, B. M. (1990). Depressive realism and nondepressive optimistic illusions: The role of the self. In R. E. Ingram (Ed.), *Contemporary psychological approaches to depression: Theory, research and treatment.* New York: Plenum Press.

ALLOY, L. B., & CLEMENTS, C. M. (1992). Illusion of control: Invulnerability to negative affect and depressive symptoms after laboratory and natural stressors. *Journal of Abnormal Psychology, 101,* 234–245.

ALLPORT, G. W. (1958). *The nature of prejudice* (abridged). Garden City, NY: Anchor Books.

ALTEMEYER, B. (1988). *Enemies of freedom: Understanding right-wing authoritarianism.* San Francisco: Jossey-Bass.

ALTEMEYER, B. (1992). *Six studies of right-wing authoritarianism among American state legislators.* Unpublished manuscript, University of Manitoba.

AMABILE, T. M., & GLAZEBROOK, A. H. (1982). A negativity bias in interpersonal evaluation. *Journal of Experimental Social Psychology, 18,* 1–22.

AMERICAN PSYCHOLOGICAL ASSOCIATION. (1981). Ethical principles of psychologists. *American Psychologist, 36,* 633–638.

AMERICAN PSYCHOLOGICAL ASSOCIATION. (1992). Ethical principles of psychologists and code of conduct. Washington, D.C.: *American Psychologist, 47,* 1597–1611.

AMERICAN PSYCHOLOGICAL ASSOCIATION. (1993). *Violence and youth: Psychology's response. Vol. 1: Summary report of the American Psychological Assocation Commission on Violence and Youth.* Washington D.C.: American Psychological Association, Public Interest Directorate.

AMIR, Y. (1969). Contact hypothesis in ethnic relations. *Psychological Bulletin, 71,* 319–342.

ANDERSON, C. A., & ANDERSON, D. C. (1984). Ambient temperature and violent crime: Tests of the linear and curvilinear hypotheses. *Journal of Personality and Social Psychology, 46,* 91–97.

ANDERSON, C. A., & ANDERSON, K. B. (1996). Violent crime rate studies in philosophical context: A destructive testing approach to heat and southern culture of violence effects. *Journal of Personality and Social Psychology, 70,* 740–756.

ANDERSON, C. A., & ANDERSON, K. B. (1998). Temperature and aggression: Paradox, controversy, and a (fairly) clear picture. In R. Geen & E. Donnerstein (Eds.), *Human aggression: Theories, research, and implications for social policy.* San Diego: Academic Press.

ANDERSON, C. A., ANDERSON, K. B., & DEUSER, W. E. (1996). Examining an affective aggression framework: Weapon and temperature effects on aggressive thoughts, affect, and attitudes. *Personality and Social Psychology Bulletin, 22,* 366–376.

ANDERSON, C. A., BUSHMAN, B. J., & GROOM, R. W. (1997). Hot years and serious and deadly assault: Empirical tests of the heat hypothesis. *Journal of Personality and Social Psychology, 73,* 1213–1223.

ANDERSON, C. A., & HARVEY, R. J. (1988). Discriminating between problems in living: An examination of measures of depression, loneliness, shyness, and social anxiety. *Journal of Social and Clinical Psychology, 6,* 482–491.

ANDERSON, C. A., HOROWITZ, L. M., & FRENCH, R. D. (1983). Attributional style of lonely and depressed people. *Journal of Personality and Social Psychology, 45,* 127–136.

ANDERSON, C. A., MILLER, R. S., RIGER, A. L., DILL, J. C., & SEDIKIDES, C. (1994). Behavioral and characterological attributional styles as predictors of depression and loneliness: Review, refinement, and test. *Journal of Personality and Social Psychology, 66,* 549–558.

ANDERSON, K. B., COOPER, H., & OKAMURA, L. (1997). Individual differences and attitudes toward rape: A meta-analytic review. *Personality and Social Psychology Review, 23,* 295–315.

ARCHER, D., & GARTNER, R. (1976). Violent acts and violent times: A comparative approach to postwar homicide rates. *American Sociological Review, 41,* 937–963.

ARCHER, D., IRITANI, B., KIMES, D. B., & BARRIOS, M. (1983). Face-ism: Five studies of sex differences in facial prominence. *Journal of Personality and Social Psychology, 45,* 725–735.

ARCHER, J. (1991). The influence of testosterone on human aggression. *British Journal of Psychology, 82,* 1–28.

ARCHER, R. L., BERG, J. M., & BURLESON, J. A. (1980). *Self-disclosure and attraction: A self-perception analysis.* Unpublished manuscript, Univ. of Texas at Austin.

ARCHER, R. L., & COOK, C. E. (1986). Personalistic self-disclosure and attraction: Basis for relationship or scarce resource. *Social Psychology Quarterly, 49,* 268–272.

ARENDT, H. (1963). *Eichmann in Jerusalem: A report on the banality of evil.* New York: Viking Press.

ARGYLE, M. (1986), *The psychology of happiness.* London: Methuen.

ARGYLE, M. (1999). Causes and correlates of happiness. In D. Kahneman, E. Diener, & N. Schwartz (Eds.), *Foundations of hedonic psychology: Scientific perspectives on enjoyment and suffering.* New York: Russell Sage Foundation.

ARGYLE, M., SHIMODA, K., & LITTLE, B. (1978). Variance due to persons and situations in England and Japan. *British Journal of Social and Clinical Psychology, 17,* 335–337.

ARKIN, R. M., APPLEMAN, A., & BURGER, J. M. (1980). Social anxiety, self-presentation, and the self-serving bias in causal attribution. *Journal of Personality and Social Psychology, 38,* 23–35.

ARKIN, R. M., & BAUMGARDNER, A. H. (1985). Self-handicapping. In J. H. Harvey & C. Weary (Eds.), *Attribution: Basic issues and applications.* New York: Academic Press.

ARKIN, R. M., & BURGER, J. M. (1980). Effects of unit relation tendencies on interpersonal attraction. *Social Psychology Quarterly, 43,* 380–391.

ARKIN, R. M., COOPER, H., & KOLDITZ, T. (1980). A statistical review of the literature concerning the self-serving attribution bias in interpersonal influence situations. *Journal of Personality, 48,* 435–448.

ARKIN, R. M., LAKE, E. A., & BAUMGARDNER, A. H. (1986). Shyness and self-presentation. In W. H. Jones, J. M. Cheek, & S. R. Briggs (Eds.), *Shyness: Perspectives on research and treatment.* New York: Plenum Press.

ARKIN, R. M., & MARUYAMA, G. M. (1979). Attribution, affect, and college exam performance. *Journal of Educational Psychology, 71,* 85–93.

ARMOR, D. A., & TAYLOR, S. E. (1998). Situated optimism: Specific outcome expectancies and self-regulation. In M. P. Zanna (Ed.), *Advances in experimental social psychology* (Vol. 30). San Diego: Academic Press.

ARMS, R. L., RUSSELL, G. W., & SANDILANDS, M. L. (1979). Effects on the hostility of spectators of viewing aggressive sports. *Social Psychology Quarterly, 42,* 275–279.

ARMSTRONG, B. (1981, January). An interview with Herbert Kelman. *APA Monitor,* pp. 4–5, 55.

ARON, A., & ARON, E. (1989). *The heart of social psychology* (2nd ed.). Lexington, MA: Lexington Books.

ARON, A., & ARON, E. N. (1994). Love. In A. L. Weber & J. H. Harvey (Eds.), *Perspective on close relationships.* Boston: Allyn & Bacon.

ARON, A., DUTTON, D. G., ARON, E. N., & IVERSON, A. (1989). Experiences of falling in love. *Journal of Social and Personal Relationships, 6,* 243–257.

ARONSON, E. (1980). *The social animal.* New York: Freeman.

ARONSON, E., BLANEY, N., STEPHAN, C., SIKES, J., & SNAPP, M. (1978). *The jigsaw classroom.* Beverly Hills, CA: Sage.

ARONSON, E., BREWER, M., & CARLSMITH, J. M. (1985). Experimentation in social psychology. In G. Lindzey & E. Aronson (Eds.), *Handbook of social psychology* (Vol. 1). Hillsdale, NJ: Erlbaum.

ARONSON, E., & BRIDGEMAN, D. (1979). Jigsaw groups and the desegregated classroom: In pursuit of common goals. *Personality and Social Psychology Bulletin, 5,* 438–446.

ARONSON, E., & GONZALEZ, A. (1988). Desegregation, jigsaw, and the Mexican-American experience. In P. A. Katz & D. Taylor (Eds.), *Towards the elimination of racism: Profiles in controversy.* New York: Plenum Press.

ARONSON, E., & MILLS, J. (1959). The effect of severity of initiation on liking for a group. *Journal of Abnormal and Social Psychology, 59,* 177–181.

ASCH, S. E. (1955, November). Opinions and social pressure. *Scientific American,* pp. 31–35.

ASENDORPF, J. B. (1987). Videotape reconstruction of emotions and cognitions related to shyness. *Journal of Personality and Social Psychology, 53,* 541–549.

ASHER, J. (1987, April). Born to be shy? *Psychology Today,* pp. 56–64.

ASTIN, A. W., GREEN, K. C., & KORN, W. S. (1987). *The American freshman: Twenty year trends.* Los Angeles: UCLA, Graduate School of Education, Higher Education Research Institute.

ASTIN, A. W., GREEN, K. C., KORN, W. S., & SCHALIT, M. (1987). *The American freshman: National norms for fall 1987.* Los Angeles: UCLA, Higher Education Research Institute.

ATWELL, R. H. (1986, July 28). Drugs on campus: A perspective. *Higher Education and National Affairs,* p. 5.

AVERILL, J. R. (1983). Studies on anger and aggression: Implications for theories of emotion. *American Psychologist, 38,* 1145–1160.

AXELROD, R., & DION, D. (1988). The further evolution of cooperation. *Science, 242,* 1385–1390.

AXSOM, D., YATES, S., & CHAIKEN, S. (1987). Audience response as a heuristic cue in persuasion. *Journal of Personality and Social Psychology, 53,* 30–40.

AYRES, I. (1991). Fair driving: Gender and race discrimination in retail car negotiations. *Harvard Law Review, 104,* 817–872.

AZRIN, N. H. (1967, May). Pain and aggression. *Psychology Today,* pp. 27–33.

BABAD, E., HILLS, M., & O'DRISCOLL, M. (1992). Factors influencing wishful thinking and predictions of election outcomes. *Basic and Applied Social Psychology, 13,* 461–476.

BACHMAN, J. G., & O'MALLEY, P. M. (1977). Self-esteem in young men: A longitudinal analysis of the impact of educational and occupational attainment. *Journal of Personality and Social Psychology, 35,* 365–380.

BACON, F. (1625). Of friendship. *Essays.* New York: Oxford University Press.

BAER, R., HINKLE, S., SMITH, K., & FENTON, M. (1980). Reactance as a function of actual versus projected autonomy. *Journal of Personality and Social Psychology, 38,* 416–422.

BAILEY, J. M., GAULIN, S., AGYEI, Y., & GLADUE, B. A. (1994). Effects of gender and sexual orientation on evolutionary relevant aspects of human mating psychology. *Journal of Personality and Social Psychology, 66,* 1081–1093.

BAIZE, H. R., JR., & SCHROEDER, J. E. (1995). Personality and mate selection in personal ads: Evolutionary preferences in a public mate selection process. *Journal of Social Behavior and Personality, 10,* 517–536.

BAKER, L. A., & EMERY, R. E. (1993). When every relationship is above average: Perceptions and expectations of divorce at the time of marriage. *Law and Human Behavior, 17,* 439–450.

BANDURA, A. (1979). The social learning perspective: Mechanisms of aggression. In H. Toch (Ed.), *Psychology of crime and criminal justice.* New York: Holt, Rinehart & Winston.

BANDURA, A. (1986). *Social foundations of thought and action: A social cognitive theory.* Englewood Cliffs, NJ: Prentice Hall.

BANDURA, A. (1997). *Self-efficacy: The exercise of control.* New York: Freeman.

BANDURA, A., ROSS, D., & ROSS, S. A. (1961). Transmission of aggression through imitation of aggressive models. *Journal of Abnormal and Social Psychology, 63,* 575–582.

BANDURA, A., & WALTERS, R. H. (1959). *Adolescent aggression.* New York: Ronald Press.

BANDURA, A., & WALTERS, R. H. (1963). *Social learning and personality development.* New York: Holt, Rinehart & Winston.

BARGH, J. A. (1994). The four horsemen of automaticity: Awareness, intention, efficiency, and control in social cognition, In R. S. Wyer & T. K. Srull (Eds.), *Handbook of social cognition* (2nd ed., Vol. 1). Hillsdale, NJ: Erlbaum.

BARGH, J. A., CHEN, M., & BURROWS, L. (1996). Automaticity of social behavior: Direct effects of trait construct and stereotype activation on action. *Journal of Personality and Social Psychology, 71,* 230–244.

BARNETT, P. A., & GOTLIB, I. H. (1988). Psychosocial functioning and depression: Distinguishing among antecedents, concomitants, and consequences. *Psychological Bulletin, 104,* 97–126.

BARON, L., & STRAUS, M. A. (1984). Sexual stratification, pornography, and rape in the United States. In N. M. Malamuth & E. Donnerstein (Eds.), *Pornography and sexual aggression.* New York: Academic Press.

BARON, R. M., MANDEL, D. R., ADAMS, C. A., & GRIFFEN, L. M. (1976). Effects of social density in university residential environments. *Journal of Personality and Social Psychology, 34,* 434–446.

BARON, R. S. (1986). Distraction-conflict theory: Progress and problems. In L. Berkowitz (Ed.), *Advances in experimental social psychology,* Orlando, FL: Academic Press.

BARON, R. S., DAVID, J. P., INMAN, M., & BRUNSMAN, B. M. (1997). Why listeners hear less than they are told: Attentional load and the teller-listener extremity effect. *Journal of Personality and Social Psychology, 72,* 826–838.

BARONGAN, C., & HALL, G. C. N. (1995). The influence of misogynous rap music on sexual aggression against women. *Psychology of Women Quarterly, 19,* 195–207.

BARRY, D. (1995, January). Bored stiff. *Funny Times,* p. 5.

BATSON, C. D. (1991). *The altruism question: Toward a social-psychological answer.* Hillsdale, NJ: Erlbaum.

BATSON, C. D., SCHOENRADE, P. A., & VENTIS, W. L. (1993). *Religion and the individual: A social-psychological perspective.* New York: Oxford University Press.

BAUMEISTER, R. (1996). Should schools try to boost self-esteem? Beware the dark side. *American Educator, 20,* 14–19, 43.

BAUMEISTER, R. F., CHESNER, S. P., SENDERS, P. S., & TICE, D. M. (1988). Who's in charge here? Group leaders do lend help in emergencies. *Personality and Social Psychology Bulletin, 14,* 17–22.

BAUMEISTER, R. F., & SCHER, S. J. (1988). Self-defeating behavior patterns among normal individuals: Review and analysis of common self-destructive tendencies. *Psychological Bulletin, 104,* 3–22.

BAUMEISTER, R. F., SMART, L., & BODEN, J. (1996). Relation of threatened egotism to violence and aggression: The dark side of high self-esteem. *Psychological Review, 103*, 5–33.

BAUMEISTER, R. F., & WOTMAN, S. R. (1992). *Breaking hearts: The two sides of unrequited love.* New York: Guilford Press.

BAUMGARDNER, A. H. (1991). Claiming depressive symptoms as a self-handicap: A protective self-presentation strategy. *Basic and Applied Social Psychology, 12,* 97–113.

BAUMGARDNER, A. H., & BROWNLEE, E. A. (1987). Strategic failure in social interaction: Evidence for expectancy disconfirmation process. *Journal of Personality and Social Psychology, 52,* 525–535.

BAUMGARDNER, A. H., KAUFMAN, C. M., & LEVY, P. E. (1989). Regulating affect interpersonally: When low esteem leads to greater enhancement. *Journal of Personality and Social Psychology, 56,* 907–921.

BAUMHART, R. (1968). *An honest profit.* New York: Holt, Rinehart & Winston.

BAUSERMAN, R. (1996). Sexual aggression and pornography: A review of correlational research. *Basic and Applied Social Psychology, 18,* 405–427.

BAXTER, T. L., & GOLDBERG, L. R. (1987). Perceived behavioral consistency underlying trait attributions to oneself and another: An extension of the actor-observer effect. *Personality and Social Psychology Bulletin, 13,* 437–447.

BAYER, E. (1929). Beiträge zur zeitkomponenten theorie des hungers [Time components in hunger theory]. *Zeitschrift fur Psychologie, 112,* 1–54.

BAZERMAN, M. H. (1986, June). Why negotiations go wrong. *Psychology Today,* pp. 54–58.

BAZERMAN, M. H. (1990). *Judgment in managerial decision making* (2nd ed.). New York: Wiley.

BEAMAN, A. L., BARNES, P. J., KLENTZ, B., & MCQUIRK, B. (1978). Increasing helping rates through information dissemination: Teaching pays. *Personality and Social Psychology Bulletin, 4,* 406–411.

BEAMAN, A. L., & KLENTZ, B. (1983). The supposed physical attractiveness bias against supporters of the women's movement: A meta-analysis. *Personality and Social Psychology Bulletin, 9,* 544–550.

BEAMAN, A. L., KLENTZ, B., DIENER, E., & SVANUM, S. (1979). Self-awareness and transgression in children: Two field studies. *Journal of Personality and Social Psychology, 37,* 1835–1846.

BEAUREGARD, K. S., & DUNNING, D. (1998). Turning up the contrast: Self-enhancement motives prompt egocentric contrast effects in social judgments. *Journal of Personality and Social Psychology, 74* (3), 606–621.

BEAUVOIS, J. L., & DUBOIS, N. (1988). The norm of internality in the explanation of psychological events. *European Journal of Social Psychology, 18,* 299–316.

BECK, A. T., & YOUNG, J. E. (1978, September). College blues. *Psychology Today,* pp. 80–92.

BECK, S. B., WARD-HULL, C. I., & MCLEAR, P. M. (1976). Variables related to women's somatic preferences of the male and female body. *Journal of Personality and Social Psychology, 34,* 1200–1210.

BELL, P. A. (1980). Effects of heat, noise, and provocation on retaliatory evaluative behavior. *Journal of Social Psychology, 110,* 97–100.

BELSON, W. A. (1978). *Television violence and the adolescent boy.* Westmead, England: Saxon House, Teakfield Ltd.

BEM, D. J. (1972). Self-perception theory. In L. Berkowitz (Ed.), *Advances in experimental social psychology* (Vol. 6). New York: Academic Press.

BEM, D. J., & McCONNELL, H. K. (1970). Testing the self-perception explanation of dissonance phenomena: On the salience of premanipulation attitudes. *Journal of Personality and Social Psychology, 14,* 23–31.

BENNETT, R. (1991, February). *Pornography and extrafamilial child sexual abuse: Examining the relationship.* Unpublished manuscript, Los Angeles Police Department Sexually Exploited Child Unit.

BENNIS, W. (1984). Transformative power and leadership. In T. J. Sergiovani & J. E. Corbally (Eds.), *Leadership and organizational culture.* Urbana: University of Illinois Press.

BERG, J. H. (1984). Development of friendship between roommates. *Journal of Personality and Social Psychology, 46,* 346–356.

BERG, J. H. (1987). Responsiveness and self-disclosure. In V. J. Derlega & J. H. Berg (Eds.), *Self-disclosure: Theory, research, and therapy.* New York: Plenum Press.

BERG, J. H., & McQUINN, R. D. (1986). Attraction and exchange in continuing and noncontinuing dating relationships. *Journal of Personality and Social Psychology, 50,* 942–952.

BERG, J. H., & PEPLAU, L. A. (1982). Loneliness: The relationship of self-disclosure and androgyny. *Personality and Social Psychology Bulletin, 8,* 624–630.

BERGER, P. (1963). *Invitation to sociology: A humanistic perspective.* Garden City, NY: Doubleday Anchor Books.

BERGLAS, S., & JONES, E. E. (1978). Drug choice as a self-handicapping strategy in response to noncontingent success. *Journal of Personality and Social Psychology, 36,* 405–417.

BERKOWITZ, L. (1968, September). Impulse, aggression and the gun. *Psychology Today,* pp. 18–22.

BERKOWITZ, L. (1978). Whatever happened to the frustration-aggression hypothesis? *American Behavioral Scientists, 21,* 691–708.

BERKOWITZ, L. (1981, June). How guns control us. *Psychology Today,* pp. 11–12.

BERKOWITZ, L. (1983). Aversively stimulated aggression: Some parallels and differences in research with animals and humans. *American Psychologist, 38,* 1135–1144.

BERKOWITZ, L. (1984). Some effects of thoughts on anti- and prosocial influences of media events: A cognitive-neoassociation analysis, *Psychological Bulletin, 95,* 410–427.

BERKOWITZ, L. (1989). Frustration-aggression hypothesis: Examination and reformulation. *Psychological Bulletin, 106,* 59–73.

BERKOWITZ, L. (1995). A career on aggression. In G. G. Brannigan & M. R. Merrens (Eds.), *The social psychologists: Research adventures.* New York: McGraw-Hill.

BERKOWITZ, L., & GEEN, R. G. (1966). Film violence and the cue properties of available targets. *Journal of Personality and Social Psychology, 3,* 525–530.

BERKOWITZ, L., & LePAGE, A. (1967). Weapons as aggression-eliciting stimuli. *Journal of Personality and Social Psychology, 7,* 202–207.

BERRY, J. W., & KALIN, R. (1995). Multicultural and ethnic attitudes in Canada: An overview of the 1991 national survey. *Canadian Journal of Behavioural Science, 27,* 301–320.

BERSCHEID, E. (1981). An overview of the psychological effects of physical attractiveness and some comments upon the psychological effects of knowledge of the effects of physical attractiveness. In W. Lucker, K. Ribbens, & J. A.

McNamera (Eds.), *Logical aspects of facial form (craniofacial growth series)*. Ann Arbor: University of Michigan Press.

BERSCHEID, E. (1985). Interpersonal attraction. In G. Lindzey & E. Aronson (Eds.), *The handbook of social psychology*. New York: Random House.

BERSCHEID, E., BOYE, D., & WALSTER, E. (1968). Retaliation as a means of restoring equity. *Journal of Personality and Social Psychology, 10,* 370–376.

BERSCHEID, E., DION, K., WALSTER, E., & WALSTER, G. W. (1971). Physical attractiveness and dating choice: A test of the matching hypothesis. *Journal of Experimental Social Psychology, 7,* 173–189.

BERSCHEID, E., GRAZIANO, W., MONSON, T., & DERMER, M. (1976). Outcome dependency: Attention, attribution, and attraction. *Journal of Personality and Social Psychology, 34,* 978–989.

BERSCHEID, E., & PEPLAU, L. A. (1983). The emerging science of relationships. In H. H. Kelley et al. (Eds.), *Close relationships*. New York: Freeman.

BERSCHEID, E., SNYDER, M., & OMOTO, A. M. (1989). Issues in studying close relationships: Conceptualizing and measuring closeness. In C. Hendrick (Ed.), *Review of personality and social psychology* (Vol. 10). Newbury Park, CA: Sage.

BERSCHEID, E., & WALSTER, E. (1978). *Interpersonal attraction*. Reading, MA: Addison-Wesley.

BERSCHEID, E., WALSTER, G. W., & HATFIELD, E. (1969). *Effects of accuracy and positivity of evaluation on liking for the evaluator*. Unpublished manuscript. Summarized by E. Berscheid and E. Walster (1978), *Interpersonal attraction*. Reading, MA: Addison-Wesley.

BETTENCOURT, B. A., DILL, K. E., GREATHOUSE, S. A., CHARLTON, K., & MULHOLLAND, A. (1997). Evaluations of ingroup and outgroup members: The role of category-based expectancy violation. *Journal of Experimental Social Psychology, 33,* 244–275.

BIERBRAUER, G. (1979). Why did he do it? Attribution of obedience and the phenomenon of dispositional bias. *European Journal of Social Psychology 9,* 67–84.

BIERLY, M. M. (1985). Prejudice toward contemporary outgroups as a generalized attitude. *Journal of Applied Social Psychology, 15,* 189–199.

BIERNAT, M. (1991). Gender stereotypes and the relationship between masculinity and femininity: A developmental analysis. *Journal of Personality and Social Psychology, 61,* 351–365.

BIERNAT, M., & KOBRYNOWICZ, D. (1997). Gender- and race-based standards of competence: Lower minimum standards but higher ability standards for devalued groups. *Journal of Personality and Social Psychology, 72,* 544–557.

BIERNAT, M., VESCIO, T. K., & GREEN, M. L. (1996). Selective self-stereotyping. *Journal of Personality and Social Psychology, 71,* 1194–1209.

BIERNAT, M., & WORTMAN, C. B. (1991). Sharing of home responsibilities between professionally employed women and their husbands. *Journal of Personality and Social Psychology, 60,* 844–860.

BILLIG, M., & TAJFEL, H. (1973). Social categorization and similarity in intergroup behaviour. *European Journal of Social Psychology, 3,* 27–52.

BINER, P. M., ANGLE, S. T., PARK, J. H., MELLINGER, A. E., & BARBER, B. C. (1995). Need state and the illusion of control. *Personality and Social Psychology Bulletin, 21,* 899–907.

BLACK, A. L., & MCCAFFERTY, D. (1998, July 3–5). The age of contentment. *USA Weekend,* pp. 4–6.

BLACKBURN, R. T., PELLINO, G. R., BOBERG, A., & O'CONNELL, C. (1980). Are instructional improvement programs off target? *Current Issues in Higher Education, 1,* 31–48.

BLAIR, I. V., & BANAJI, M. R. (1996). Automatic and controlled processes in stereotype priming. *Journal of Personality and Social Psychology, 70,* 1142–1163.

BLAKE, R. R., & MOUTON, J. S. (1962). The intergroup dynamics of win-lose conflict and problem-solving collaboration in union-management relations. In M. Sherif (Ed.), *Intergroup relations and leadership.* New York: Wiley.

BLAKE, R. R., & MOUTON, J. S. (1979). Intergroup problem solving in organizations: From theory to practice. In W. G. Austin & S. Worchel (Eds.), *The social psychology of intergroup relations.* Monterey, CA: Brooks/Cole.

BLANCHARD, F. A., & COOK, S. W. (1976). Effects of helping a less competent member of a cooperating interracial group on the development of interpersonal attraction. *Journal of Personality and Social Psychology, 34,* 1245–1255.

BLASS, T. (1996). Stanley Milgram: A life of inventiveness and controversy. In G. A. Kimble, C. A. Boneau, & M. Wertheimer (Eds.), *Portraits of pioneers in psychology* (Vol. 2). Washington, DC: American Psychological Association.

BLOCK, J., & FUNDER, D. C. (1986). Social roles and social perception: Individual differences in attribution and error. *Journal of Personality and Social Psychology, 51,* 1200–1207.

BLUCHER, J. (1994, October 27). Tuning in to violence: Are "Power Rangers" and other TV shows making children more aggressive? *Anchorage Daily News,* pp. E1–E2.

BODENHAUSEN, G. V. (1990). Stereotypes as judgmental heuristics: Evidence of circadian variations in discrimination. *Psychological Science, 1,* 319–322.

BODENHAUSEN, G. V. (1993). Emotions, arousal, and stereotypic judgments: A heuristic model of affect and stereotyping. In D. M. Mackie & D. L. Hamilton (Eds.), *Affect, cognition, and stereotyping: Interactive processes in group perception.* San Diego: Academic Press.

BOLT, M., & BRINK, J. (1991, November 1). Personal correspondence.

BOND, C. F., JR., & TITUS, L. J. (1983). Social facilitation: A meta-analysis of 241 studies. *Psychological Bulletin, 94,* 265–292.

BORGIDA, E., & BREKKE, N. (1985). Psycholegal research on rape trials. In A. W. Burgess (Ed.), *Rape and sexual assault: A research handbook.* New York: Garland.

BORNSTEIN, G., RAPOPORT, A., KERPEL, L., & KATZ, T. (1989). Within- and between-group communication in intergroup competition for public goods. *Journal of Experimental Social Psychology, 25,* 422–436.

BOSSARD, J. H. S. (1932). Residential propinquity as a factor in marriage selection. *American Journal of Sociology, 38,* 219–224.

BOTHWELL, R. K., BRIGHAM, J. C., & MALPASS, R. S. (1989). Cross-racial identification. *Personality and Social Psychology Bulletin, 15,* 19–25.

BOTVIN, G. J., SCHINKE, S., & ORLANDI, M. A. (1995). School-based health promotion: Substance abuse and sexual behavior. *Applied and Preventive Psychology, 4,* 167–184.

BOTWIN, M. D., BUSS, D. M., & SHACKELFORD, T. K. (1997). Personality and mate preferences: Five factors in mate selection and marital satisfaction. *Journal of Personality, 65,* 107–136.

BOWER, G. H. (1987). Commentary on mood and memory. *Behavioral Research and Therapy, 25,* 443–455.

BOYATZIS, C. J., MATILLO, G. M., & NESBITT, K. M. (1995). Effects of the "Mighty Morphin Power Rangers" on children's aggression with peers. *Child Study Journal, 25,* 45–55.

BREHM, S., & BREHM, J. W. (1981). *Psychological reactance: A theory of freedom and control.* New York: Academic Press.

BRENNER, S. N., & MOLANDER, E. A. (1977, January–February). Is the ethics of business changing? *Harvard Business Review,* pp. 57–71.

BREWER, M. B. (1987). Collective decisions. *Social Science, 72,* 140–143.

BREWER, M. B., & MILLER, N. (1988). Contact and cooperation: When do they work? In P. A. Katz & D. Taylor (Eds.), *Towards the elimination of racism: Profiles in controversy.* New York: Plenum Press.

BREWER, M. B., & SILVER, M. (1978). In-group bias as a function of task characteristics. *European Journal of Social Psychology, 8,* 393–400.

BRICKMAN, P., COATES, D., & JANOFF-BULMAN, R. J. (1978). Lottery winners and accident victims: Is happiness relative? *Journal of Personality and Social Psychology, 36,* 917–927.

BRIGHAM, J. C., & WILLIAMSON, N. L. (1979). Cross-racial recognition and age: When you're over 60, do they still all look alike? *Personality and Social Psychology Bulletin, 5,* 218–222.

BRISCOE, D. (1997, February 16). Women lawmakers still not in charge. *Grand Rapids Press,* p. A23.

BRITISH PSYCHOLOGICAL SOCIETY. (1991). *Code of conduct ethical principles and guidelines.* Leicester.

BROCKNER, J., & HULTON, A. J. B. (1978). How to reverse the vicious cycle of low self-esteem: The importance of attentional focus. *Journal of Experimental Social Psychology, 14,* 564–578.

BROCKNER, J., RUBIN, J. Z., FINE, J., HAMILTON, T. P., THOMAS, B., & TURETSKY, B. (1982). Factors affecting entrapment in escalating conflicts: The importance of timing. *Journal of Research in Personality, 16,* 247–266.

BRODT, S. E., & ZIMBARDO, P. G. (1981). Modifying shyness-related social behavior through symptom misattribution. *Journal of Personality and Social Psychology, 41,* 437–449.

BRONFENBRENNER, U. (1961). The mirror image in Soviet-American relations. *Journal of Social Issues, 17* (3), 45–56.

BROWN, J. D. (1986). Evaluations of self and others: Self-enhancement biases in social judgments. *Social Cognition, 4,* 353–376.

BROWN, J. D. (1991). Accuracy and bias in self-knowledge: Can knowing the truth be hazardous to your health? In C. R. Snyder & D. F. Forsyth (Eds.), *Handbook of social and clinical psychology: The health perspective.* New York: Pergamon Press.

BROWN, J. D., & SIEGEL, J. M. (1988). Attributions for negative life events and depression: The role of perceived control. *Journal of Personality and Social Psychology, 54,* 316–322.

BROWN, J. D., COLLINS, R. L., & SCHMIDT, G. W. (1988). Self-esteem and direct versus indirect forms of self-enhancement. *Journal of Personality and Social Psychology, 55,* 445–453.

BROWN, J. D., NOVICK, N. J., LORD, K. A., & RICHARDS, J. M. (1992). When Gulliver travels: Social context, psychological closeness, and self-appraisals. *Journal of Personality and Social Psychology, 62,* 717–727.

BROWN, J. D., & TAYLOR, S. E. (1986). Affect and the processing of personal information: Evidence for mood-activated self-schemata. *Journal of Experimental Social Psychology, 22,* 436–452.

BROWN, L. R., HANE, H., & AYRES, E. (Eds.). (1993). *Vital signs 1993: The trends that are shaping our future.* New York: W. W. Norton.

BROWN, R., & WOOTTON-MILLWARD, L. (1993). Perceptions of group homogeneity during group formation and change. *Social Cognition, 11,* 126–149.

BROWNING, C. (1992). *Ordinary men: Reserve police battalion 101 and the final solution in Poland.* New York: HarperCollins.

BUEHLER, R., GRIFFIN, D., & ROSS, M. (1994). Exploring the "planning fallacy": When people underestimate their task completion times. *Journal of Personality and Social Psychology, 67,* 366–381.

BURCHILL, S. A. L., & STILES, W. B. (1988). Interactions of depressed college students with their roommates: Not necessarily negative. *Journal of Personality and Social Psychology, 55,* 410–419.

BUREAU OF THE CENSUS. (1979). *Statistical abstract of the United States 1978* (Table 1383). Washington, DC: Superintendent of Documents.

BUREAU OF THE CENSUS. (1996). *Statistical abstract of the United States 1996.* Washington, DC: U.S. Government Printing Office.

BUREAU OF THE CENSUS. (1998). *Statistical abstract of the United States 1996* (Table 1223). Washington, DC: Superintendent of Documents.

BURGER, J. M. (1987). Increased performance with increased personal control: A self-presentation interpretation. *Journal of Experimental Social Psychology, 23,* 350–360.

BURGER, J. M. (1991). Changes in attributions over time: The ephemeral fundamental attribution error. *Social Cognition, 9,* 182–193.

BURGER, J. M., & BURNS, L. (1988). The illusion of unique invulnerability and the use of effective contraception. *Personality and Social Psychology Bulletin, 14,* 264–270.

BURGER, J. M., & PALMER, M. L. (1991). Changes in and generalization of unrealistic optimism following experiences with stressful events: Reactions to the 1989 California earthquake. *Personality and Social Psychology Bulletin, 18,* 39–43.

BURGER, J. M., & PAVELICH, J. L. (1994). Attributions for presidential elections: The situational shift over time. *Basic and Applied Social Psychology, 15,* 359–371.

BURN, S. M. (1992). Locus of control, attributions, and helplessness in the homeless. *Journal of Applied Social Psychology, 22,* 1161–1174.

BURNS, D. D. (1980). *Feeling good: The new mood therapy.* New York: Signet.

BURNSTEIN, E., & KITAYAMA, S. (1989). Persuasion in groups. In T. C. Brock & S. Shavitt (Eds.), *The psychology of persuasion.* San Francisco: Freeman.

BURNSTEIN, E., & VINOKUR, A. (1977). Persuasive argumentation and social comparison as determinants of attitude polarization. *Journal of Experimental Social Psychology, 13,* 315–332.

BURNSTEIN, E., & WORCHEL, P. (1962). Arbitrariness of frustration and its consequences for aggression in a social situation. *Journal of Personality, 30,* 528–540.

BURR, W. R. (1973). *Theory construction and the sociology of the family.* New York: Wiley.

BURROS, M. (1988, February 24). Women: Out of the house but not out of the kitchen. *New York Times.*

BUSHMAN, B. J. (1993). Human aggression while under the influence of alcohol and other drugs: An integrative research review. *Current Directions in Psychological Science, 2,* 148–152.

BUSHMAN, B. J. (1995). Moderating role of trait aggressiveness in the effects of violent media on aggression. *Journal of Personality and Social Psychology, 69,* 950–960.

BUSHMAN, B. J. (1996). Individual differences in the extent and development of aggressive cognitive-associative networks. *Personality and Social Psychology Bulletin, 22,* 811–819.

BUSHMAN, B. J., & BAUMEISTER, R. (1998). Threatened egotism, narcissism, self-esteem, and direct and displaced aggression: Does self-love or self-hate lead to violence? *Journal of Personality and Social Psychology, 75,* 219–229.

BUSHMAN, B. J., & COOPER, H. M. (1990). Effects of alcohol on human aggression: An integrative research review. *Psychological Bulletin, 107,* 341–354.

BUSHMAN, B. J., & GEEN, R. G. (1990). Role of cognitive-emotional mediators and individual differences in the effects of media violence on aggression. *Journal of Personality and Social Psychology, 58,* 156–163.

BUSS, D. M. (1984). Toward a psychology of person-environment (PE) correlation: The role of spouse selection. *Journal of Personality and Social Psychology, 47,* 361–377.

BUSS, D. M. (1985). Human mate selection. *American Scientist, 73,* 47–51.

BUSS, D. M. (1989). Sex differences in human mate preferences: Evolutionary hypotheses tested in 37 cultures. *Behavioral and Brain Sciences, 12,* 1–49.

BUSS, D. M. (1994). *The evolution of desire: Strategies of human mating.* New York: Basic Books.

BUTCHER, S. H. (1951). *Aristotle's theory of poetry and fine art.* New York: Dover.

BUTLER, A. C., HOKANSON, J. E., & FLYNN, H. A. (1994). A comparison of self-esteem lability and low trait self-esteem as vulnerability factors for depression. *Journal of Personality and Social Psychology, 66,* 166–177.

BUUNK, B. P., & VAN DER EIJNDEN, R. J. J. M. (1997). Perceived prevalence, perceived superiority, and relationship satisfaction: Most relationships are good, but ours is the best. *Personality and Social Psychology Bulletin, 23,* 219–228.

BUUNK, B. P., & VAN YPEREN, N. W. (1991). Referential comparisons, relational comparisons, and exchange orientation: Their relation to marital satisfaction. *Personality and Social Psychology Bulletin, 17,* 709–717.

BYRNE, D. (1971). *The attraction paradigm.* New York: Academic Press.

BYRNE, D., & WONG, T. J. (1962). Racial prejudice, interpersonal attraction, and assumed dissimilarity of attitudes. *Journal of Abnormal and Social Psychology, 65,* 246–253.

BYTWERK, R. L. (1976). Julius Streicher and the impact of *Der Stürmer. Wiener Library Bulletin, 29,* 41–46.

CACIOPPO, J. T., CLAIBORN, C. D., PETTY, R. E., & HEESACKER, M. (1991). General framework for the study of attitude change in psychotherapy. In C. R. Snyder & D. R. Forsyth (Eds.), *Handbook of social and clinical psychology.* New York: Pergamon Press.

CACIOPPO, J. T., PETTY, R. E., FEINSTEIN, J. A., & JARVIS, W. B. G. (1996). Dispositional differences in cognitive motivation: The life and times of individuals varying in need for cognition. *Psychological Bulletin, 119,* 197–253.

CACIOPPO, J. T., PETTY, R. E., & MORRIS, K. J. (1983). Effects of need for cognition on message evaluation, recall, and persuasion. *Journal of Personality and Social Psychology, 45,* 805–818.

CALHOUN, J. B. (1962, February). Population density and social pathology. *Scientific American,* pp. 139–148.

CAMPBELL, A. (1981). *The sense of well-being in America.* New York: McGraw-Hill.

CAMPBELL, E. Q., & PETTIGREW, T. F. (1959). Racial and moral crisis: The role of Little Rock ministers. *American Journal of Sociology, 64,* 509–516.

CANTRIL, H., & BUMSTEAD, C. H. (1960). *Reflections on the human venture.* New York: New York University Press.

CARDUCCI, B. J., COSBY, P. C., & WARD, D. D. (1978). Sexual arousal and interpersonal evaluations. *Journal of Experimental Social Psychology, 14,* 449–457.

CARLI, L. L. (1991). Gender, status, and influence. In E. J. Lawler & B. Markovsky (Ed.), *Advances in group processes: Theory and research* (Vol. 8). Greenwich, CT: JAI Press.

CARLI, L. L., COLUMBO, J., DOWLING, S., KULIS, M., & MINALGA, C. (1990). *Victim derogation as a function of hindsight and cognitive bolstering.* Paper presented at the meeting of the American Psychological Association.

CARLI, L. L., & LEONARD, J. B. (1989). The effect of hindsight on victim derogation. *Journal of Social and Clinical Psychology, 8,* 331–343.

CARLSON, J., & HATFIELD, E. (1992). *The psychology of emotion.* Fort Worth: Holt, Rinehart & Winston.

CARLSON, M., MARCUS-NEWHALL, A., & MILLER, N. (1990). Effects of situational aggression cues: A quantitative review. *Journal of Personality and Social Psychology, 58,* 622–633.

CARLSTON, D. E., & SHOVAR, N. (1983). Effects of performance attributions on others' perceptions of the attributor. *Journal of Personality and Social Psychology, 44,* 515–525.

CARROLL, D., DAVEY SMITH, G., & BENNETT, P. (1994, March). Health and socioeconomic status. *Psychologist,* pp. 122–125.

CARTER, S. L. (1993). *Reflections of an affirmative action baby.* New York: Basic Books.

CARTWRIGHT, D. S. (1975). The nature of gangs. In D. S. Cartwright, B. Tomson, & H. Schwartz (Eds.), *Gang delinquency.* Monterey, CA: Brooks/Cole.

CARVER, C. S., KUS, L. A., & SCHEIER, M. F. (1994). Effect of good versus bad mood and optimistic versus pessimistic outlook on social acceptance versus rejection. *Journal of Social and Clinical Psychology, 13,* 138–151.

CARVER, C. S., & SCHEIER, M. F. (1986). Analyzing shyness: A specific application of broader self-regulatory principles. In W. H. Jones, J. M. Cheek, & S. R. Briggs (Eds.), *Shyness: Perspectives on research and treatment.* New York: Plenum Press.

CASH, T. F., & JANDA, L. H. (1984, December). The eye of the beholder. *Psychology Today,* pp. 46–52.

CASPI, A., & HERBENER, E. S. (1990). Continuity and change: Assortative marriage and the consistency of personality in adulthood. *Journal of Personality and Social Psychology, 58,* 250–258.

CENTERWALL, B. S. (1989). Exposure to television as a risk factor for violence. *American Journal of Epidemiology, 129,* 643–652.

CHAIKEN, S. (1979). Communicator physical attractiveness and persuasion. *Journal of Personality and Social Psychology, 37,* 1387–1397.

CHAIKEN, S. (1980). Heuristic versus systematic information processing and the use of source versus message cues in persuasion. *Journal of Personality and Social Psychology, 39,* 752–766.

CHAIKEN, S., & MAHESWARAN, D. (1994). Neuristic processing can bias systematic processing: Effects of source credibility, argument ambiguity, and task importance on attitude judgment. *Journal of Personality and Social Psychology, 66,* 460–473.

CHANCE, J. E., & GOLDSTEIN, A. G. (1981). Depth of processing in response to own- and other-race faces. *Personality and Social Psychology Bulletin, 7,* 475–480.

CHAPMAN, L. J., & CHAPMAN, J. P. (1969). Genesis of popular but erroneous psychodiagnostic observations. *Journal of Abnormal Psychology, 74,* 272–280.

CHAPMAN, L. J., & CHAPMAN, J. P. (1971, November). Test results are what you think they are. *Psychology Today,* pp. 18–22, 106–107.

CHECK, J., & MALAMUTH, N. (1984). Can there be positive effects of participation in pornography experiments? *Journal of Sex Research, 20,* 14–31.

CHECK, J. M., & MELCHIOR, L. A. (1990). Shyness, self-esteem, and self-consciousness. In H. Leitenberg (Ed.), *Handbook of social and evaluation anxiety.* New York: Plenum Press.

CHEN, H. C., REARDON, R., & REA, C. (1992). Forewarning of content and involvement: Consequences for persuasion and resistance to persuasion. *Journal of Experimental Social Psychology, 28,* 523–541.

CHEN, S. C. (1937). Social modification of the activity of ants in nest-building. *Physiological Zoology, 10,* 420–436.

CHICKERING, A. W., & McCORMICK, J. (1973). Personality development and the college experience. *Research in Higher Education,* No. 1, 62–64.

CHODOROW, N. J. (1978). *The reproduction of mother: Psychoanalysis and the sociology of gender.* Berkeley: University of California Press.

CHODOROW, N. J. (1989). *Feminism and psychoanalytic theory.* New Haven, CT: Yale University Press.

CHRISTENSEN, L. (1988). Deception in psychological research: When is its use justified? *Personality and Social Psychology Bulletin, 14,* 664–675.

CHRISTIAN, J. J., FLYGER, V., & DAVIS, D. E. (1960). Factors in the mass mortality of a herd of sika deer, *Cervus Nippon. Chesapeake Science, 1,* 79–95.

CHUA-EOAN, H. (1997, April 7). Imprisoned by his own passions. *Time,* pp. 40–42.

CHURCH, G. J. (1986, January 6). China. *Time,* pp. 6–19.

CIALDINI, R. B. (1988). *Influence: Science and practice.* Glenview, IL: Scott, Foresman/ Little, Brown.

CIALDINI, R. B., CACIOPPO, J. T., BASSETT, R., & MILLER, J. A. (1978). Lowball procedure for producing compliance: Commitment then cost. *Journal of Personality and Social Psychology, 36,* 463–476.

CIALDINI, R. B., & RICHARDSON, K. D. (1980). Two indirect tactics of image management: Basking and blasting. *Journal of Personality and Social Psychology, 39,* 406–415.

CICERELLO, A., & SHEEHAN, E. P. (1995). Personal advertisements: A content analysis. *Journal of Social Behavior and Personality, 10,* 751–756.

CLANCY, S. M., & DOLLINGER, S. J. (1993). Photographic depictions of the self: Gender and age differences in social connectedness. *Sex Roles, 29,* 477–495.

CLARK, K., & CLARK, M. (1947). Racial identification and preference in Negro children. In T. M. Newcomb & E. L. Hartley (Eds.), *Readings in social psychology.* New York: Holt.

CLARK, M. S. (1984). Record keeping in two types of relationships. *Journal of Personality and Social Psychology, 47,* 549–557.

CLARK, M. S. (1986). Evidence for the effectiveness of manipulations of desire for communal versus exchange relationships. *Personality and Social Psychology Bulletin, 12,* 414–425.

CLARK, M. S., & BENNETT, M. E. (1992). Research on relationships: Implications for mental health. In D. Ruble & P. Costanzo (Eds.), *The social psychology of mental health.* New York: Guilford.

CLARK, M. S., & MILLS, J. (1979). Interpersonal attraction in exchange and communal relationships. *Journal of Personality and Social Psychology, 37,* 12–24.

CLARK, M. S., & MILLS, J. (1993). The difference between communal and exchange relationships: What it is and is not. *Personality and Social Psychology Bulletin, 19,* 684–691.

CLARK, M. S., MILLS, J., & CORCORAN, D. (1989). Keeping track of needs and inputs of friends and strangers. *Personality and Social Psychology Bulletin, 15,* 533–542.

CLARK, M. S., MILLS, J., & POWELL, M. C. (1986). Keeping track of needs in communal and exchange relationships. *Journal of Personality and Social Psychology, 51,* 333–338.

CLARK, R. D., III (1995). A few parallels between group polarization and minority influence. In S. Moscovici, H. Mucchi-Faina, & A. Maass (Eds.), *Minority influence.* Chicago: Nelson-Hall.

CLARK, R. D., III, & MAASS, A. (1990). The effects of majority size on minority influence. *European Journal of Social Psychology, 20,* 99–117.

CLARKE, A. C. (1952). An examination of the operation of residual propinquity as a factor in mate selection. *American Sociological Review, 27,* 17–22.

CLIFFORD, M. M., & WALSTER, E. H. (1973). The effect of physical attractiveness on teacher expectation. *Sociology of Education, 46,* 248–258.

CLORE, G. L., BRAY, R. M., ITKIN, S. M., & MURPHY, P. (1978). Interracial attitudes and behavior at a summer camp. *Journal of Personality and Social Psychology, 36,* 107–116.

COATES, B., PUSSER, H. E., & GOODMAN, I. (1976). The influence of "Sesame Street" and "Mister Rogers' Neighborhood" on children's social behavior in the preschool. *Child Development, 47,* 138–144.

COATS, E. J., & FELDMAN, R. S. (1996). Gender differences in nonverbal correlates of social status. *Personality and Social Psychology Bulletin, 22,* 1014–1022.

CODOL, J.-P. (1976). On the so-called superior conformity of the self behavior: Twenty experimental investigations. *European Journal of Social Psychology, 5,* 457–501.

COHEN, D. (1996). Law, social policy, and violence: The impact of regional cultures. *Journal of Personality and Social Psychology, 70,* 961–978.

COHEN, M., & DAVIS, N. (1981). *Medication errors: Causes and prevention.* Philadelphia: G. F. Stickley Co. Cited by R. B. Cialdini (1989). *Agents of influence: Bunglers, smugglers, and sleuths.* Paper presented at the American Psychological Association convention.

COHEN, S. (1980). *Training to understand TV advertising: Effects and some policy implications.* Paper presented at the American Psychological Association convention.

COHN, E. G. (1993). The prediction of police calls for service: The influence of weather and temporal variables on rape and domestic violence. *Environmental Psychology, 13,* 71–83.

COLASANTO, D., & SHRIVER, J. (1989, May). Mirror of America: Middle-aged face marital crisis. *Gallup Report* (No. 284), pp. 34–38.

COLOMBO, J. R. (Ed.). (1994). *The 1994 Canadian global almanac.* Toronto: Macmillan Canada.

COLVIN, C. R., BLOCK, J., & FUNDER, D. C. (1995). Overly-positive self evaluations and personality: Negative implications for mental health. *Journal of Personality and Social Psychology, 68,* 1152–1162.

COMER, D. R. (1995). A model of social loafing in real work group. *Human Relations, 48, 647–667.*

CONWAY, F., & SIEGELMAN, J. (1979). *Snapping: America's epidemic of sudden personality change.* New York: Delta Books.

CONWAY, M., & ROSS, M. (1986). Remembering one's own past: The construction of personal histories. In R. Sorrentino & E. T. Higgins (Eds.), *Handbook of motivation and cognition.* New York: Guilford Press.

COOK, T. D., & CURTIN, T. R. (1987). The mainstream and the underclass: Why are the differences so salient and the similarities so unobtrusive? In J. C. Masters & W. P. Smith (Eds.), *Social comparison, social justice, and relative deprivation: Theoretical, empirical, and policy perspectives.* Hillsdale, NJ: Erlbaum.

COOK, T. D., & FLAY, B. R. (1978). The persistence of experimentally induced attitude change. In L. Berkowitz (Ed.), *Advances in experimental social psychology* (Vol. 11). New York: Academic Press.

COOPER, H. (1983). Teacher expectation effects. In L. Bickman (Ed.), *Applied social psychology annual* (Vol. 4). Beverly Hills, CA: Sage.

COSTANZO, M. (1998). *Just revenge.* New York: St. Martins Press.

COTA, A. A., & DION, K. L. (1986). Salience of gender and sex composition of ad hoc groups: An experimental test of distinctiveness theory. *Journal of Personality and Social Psychology, 50, 770–776.*

COTTON, J. L. (1981). *Ambient temperature and violent crime.* Paper presented at the Midwestern Psychological Association convention.

COTTON, J. L. (1986). Ambient temperature and violent crime. *Journal of Applied Social Psychology, 16, 786–801.*

COTTRELL, N. B., WACK, D. L., SEKERAK, G. J., & RITTLE, R. M. (1968). Social facilitation of dominant responses by the presence of an audience and the mere presence of others. *Journal of Personality and Social Psychology, 9, 245–250.*

COURT, J. H. (1984). Sex and violence: A ripple effect. In N. M. Malamuth & E. Donnerstein (Eds.), *Pornography and sexual aggression.* New York: Academic Press.

COYNE, J. C., BURCHILL, S. A. L., & STILES, W. B. (1991). In C. R. Snyder & D. O. Forsyth (Eds.), *Handbook of social and clinical psychology: The health perspective.* New York: Pergamon Press.

CRAIG, M. E. (1990). Coercive sexuality in dating relationships: A situational model. *Clinical Psychology Review, 10, 395–423.*

CRANDALL, C. S. (1994). Prejudice against fat people: Ideology and self-interest. *Journal of Personality and Social Psychology, 66, 882–894.*

CROCKER, J. (1981). Judgment of covariation by social perceivers. *Psychological Bulletin, 90, 272–292.*

CROCKER, J., & McGRAW, K. M. (1984). What's good for the goose is not good for the gander: Solo status as an obstacle to occupational achievement for males and females. *American Behavioral Scientist, 27, 357–370.*

CROCKER, J., THOMPSON, L. L., McGRAW, K. M., & INGERMAN, C. (1987). Downward comparison, prejudice, and evaluations of others: Effects of self-esteem and threat. *Journal of Personality and Social Psychology, 52, 907–916.*

CROSBY, F. J. (Ed.). (1987). *Spouse, parent, worker: On gender and multiple roles.* New Haven, CT: Yale University Press.

CROSBY, F. J., BROMLEY, S., & SAXE, L. (1980). Recent unobtrusive studies of black and white discrimination and prejudice: A literature review. *Psychological Bulletin, 87, 546–563.*

CROSBY, F. J., PUFALL, A., SNYDER, R. C., O'CONNELL, M., & WHALEN, P. (1989). The denial of personal disadvantage among you, me, and all the other ostriches. In M. Crawford & M. Gentry (Eds.), *Gender and thought.* New York: Springer-Verlag.

CROSS, P. (1977, Spring). Not *can* but *will* college teaching be improved? *New Directions for Higher Education,* No. 17, pp. 1–15.

CROSS-NATIONAL COLLABORATIVE GROUP. (1992). The changing rate of major depression. *Journal of the American Medical Association, 268,* 3098–3105.

CROSS-NATIONAL COLLABORATIVE GROUP. (1992). The changing rate of major depression. *Journal of the American Medical Association, 268,* 3098–3105.

CROWLEY, G. (1996, June 3). The biology of beauty. *Newsweek,* pp. 61–69.

CROXTON, J. S., & MILLER, A. G. (1987). Behavioral disconfirmation and the observer bias. *Journal of Social Behavior and Personality, 2,* 145–152.

CROXTON, J. S., & MORROW, N. (1984). What does it take to reduce observer bias? *Psychological Reports, 55,* 135–138.

CSIKSZENTMIHALYI, M. (1990). *Flow: The psychology of optimal experience.* New York: Harper & Row.

CUNNINGHAM, J. D. (1981). Self-disclosure intimacy: Sex, sex-of-target, cross-national, and generational differences. *Personality and Social Psychology Bulletin, 7,* 314–319.

DABBS, J. M., & JANIS, I. L. (1965). Why does eating while reading facilitate opinion change? An experimental inquiry. *Journal of Experimental Social Psychology, 1,* 133–144.

DABBS, J. M., JR. (1992). Testosterone measurements in social and clinical psychology. *Journal of Social and Clinical Psychology, 11,* 302–321.

DABBS, J. M., JR., CARR, T. S., FRADY, R. L., & RIAD, J. K. (1995). Testosterone, crime, and misbehavior among 692 male prison inmates. *Personality and Individual Differences, 18,* 627–633.

DABBS, J. M., JR., DE LA RUE, D., & WILLIAMS, P. M. (1990). Testosterone and occupational choice: Actors, ministers, and other men. *Journal of Personality and Social Psychology, 59,* 1261–1265.

DABBS, J. M., JR., & HARGROVE, M. F. (1997). Age, testosterone, and behavior among female prison inmates. *Psychosomatic Medicine, 59,* 477–480.

DABBS, J. M., JR., HARGROVE, M. F., & HEUSEL, C. (1993). *Testosterone differences among college fraternities: Well-behaved vs. rambunctious.* Unpublished manuscript, Georgia State University.

DABBS, J. M., JR., & MORRIS, R. (1990). Testosterone, social class, and antisocial behavior in a sample of 4,462 men. *Psychological Science, 1,* 209–211.

DALY, M., & WILSON, M. (1989). Killing the competition: Female/female and male/male homicide. *Human Nature, 1,* 81–107.

DAMON, D. (1995). *Greater expectations: Overcoming the culture of indulgence in America's homes and schools.* New York: Free Press.

DARLEY, J. M., & BATSON, C. D. (1973). From Jerusalem to Jericho: A study of situational and dispositional variables in helping behavior. *Journal of Personality and Social Psychology, 27,* 100–108.

DARLEY, J. M., & BERSCHEID, E. (1967). Increased liking as a result of the anticipation of personal contact. *Human Relations, 20,* 29–40.

DARLEY, J. M., & LATANÉ, B. (1968). Bystander intervention in emergencies: Diffusion of responsibility. *Journal of Personality and Social Psychology, 8,* 377–383.

DARLEY, S., & COOPER, J. (1972). Cognitive consequences of forced noncompliance. *Journal of Personality and Social Psychology, 24,* 321–326.

DASHIELL, J. F. (1930). An experimental analysis of some group effects. *Journal of Abnormal and Social Psychology, 25,* 190–199.

DAVIS, B. M., & GILBERT, L. A. (1989). Effect of dispositional and situational influences on women's dominance expression in mixed-sex dyads. *Journal of Personality and Social Psychology, 57,* 294–300.

DAVIS, K. E. (1985, February). Near and dear: Friendship and love compared. *Psychology Today,* pp. 22–30.

DAVIS, K. E., & JONES, E. E. (1960). Changes in interpersonal perception as a means of reducing cognitive dissonance. *Journal of Abnormal and Social Psychology, 61,* 402–410.

DAVIS, L., & GREENLEES, C. (1992). *Social loafing revisited: Factors that mitigate—and reverse—performance loss.* Paper presented at the Southwestern Psychological Association convention.

DAVIS, M. H. (1979). *The case for attributional egotism.* Paper presented at the American Psychological Association convention.

DAVIS, M. H., & FRANZOI, S. L. (1986). Adolescent loneliness, self-disclosure, and private self-consciousness: A longitudinal investigation. *Journal of Personality and Social Psychology, 51,* 595–608.

DAVIS, M. H., & STEPHAN, W. G. (1980). Attributions for exam performance. *Journal of Applied Social Psychology, 10,* 235–248.

DAWES, R. M. (1976). Shallow psychology. In J. S. Carroll & J. W. Payne (Eds.), *Cognition and social behavior.* Hillsdale, NJ: Erlbaum.

DAWES, R. M. (1990). The potential nonfalsity of the false consensus effect. In R. M. Hogarth (Ed.), *Insights in decision making: A tribute to Hillel J. Einhorn.* Chicago: University of Chicago Press.

DAWES, R. M. (1991). Social dilemmas, economic self-interest, and evolutionary theory. In D. R. Brown & J. E. Keith Smith (Eds.), *Frontiers of mathematical psychology: Essays in honor of Clyde Coombs.* New York: Springer-Verlag.

DAWES, R. M. (1994). *House of cards: Psychology and psychotherapy built on myth.* New York: Free Press.

DAWES, R. M. (1988, October). The social usefulness of self-esteem: A skeptical view. *Harvard Mental Health Letter,* pp. 4–5.

DAWES, R. M., FAUST, D., & MEEHL, P. E. (1989). Clinical versus actuarial judgment. *Science, 243,* 1668–1674.

DAWSON, N. V., ARKES, H. R., SICILIANO, C., BLINKHORN, R., LAKSHMANAN, M., & PETRELLI, M. (1988). Hindsight bias: An impediment to accurate probability estimation in clinicopathologic conferences. *Medical Decision Making, 8,* 259–264.

DEAUX, K., & LAFRANCE, M. (1998). Gender. In D. Gilbert, S. Fiske, & G. Lindzey (Eds.), *The handbook of social psychology* (4th ed.). Hillsdale, NJ: Erlbaum.

DECI, E. L., & RYAN, R. M. (1987). The support of autonomy and the control of behavior. *Journal of Personality and Social Psychology, 53,* 1024–1037.

DE JONG-GIERVELD, J. (1987). Developing and testing a model of loneliness. *Journal of Personality and Social Psychology, 53,* 119–128.

DEMBROSKI, T. M., LASATER, T. M., & RAMIREZ, A. (1978). Communicator similarity, fear arousing communications, and compliance with health care recommendations. *Journal of Applied Social Psychology, 8,* 254–269.

DENGERINK, H. A., & MYERS, J. D. (1977). Three effects of failure and depression on subsequent aggression. *Journal of Personality and Social Psychology, 35,* 88–96.

DePAULO, B. M., KENNY, D. A., HOOVER, C. W., WEBB, W., & OLIVER, P. V. (1987). Accuracy of person perception: Do people know what kinds of impressions they convey? *Journal of Personality and Social Psychology, 52,* 303–315.

DERLEGA, V., METTS, S., PETRONIO, S., & MARGULIS, S. T. (1993). *Self-disclosure.* Newbury Park, CA: Sage.

DERMER, M., & PYSZCZYNSKI, T. A. (1978). Effects of erotica upon men's loving and liking responses for women they love. *Journal of Personality and Social Psychology, 36,* 1302–1309.

DESFORGES, D. M., LORD, C. G., PUGH, M. A., SIA, T. L., SCARBERRY, N. C., & RATCLIFF, C. D. (1997). Role of group representativeness in the generalization part of the contact hypothesis. *Basic and Applied Social Psychology, 19,* 183–204.

DESFORGES, D. M., LORD, C. G., RAMSEY, S. L., MASON, J. A., VAN LEEUWEN, M. D., WEST, S. C., & LEPPER, M. R. (1991). Effects of structured cooperative contact on changing negative attitudes toward stigmatized social groups. *Journal of Personality and Social Psychology, 60,* 531–544.

DeSTEFANO, L., & COLASANTO, D. (1990, February). Unlike 1975, today most Americans think men have it better. *Gallup Poll Monthly,* No. 293, 25–36.

DeSTENO, D. A., & SALOVEY, P. (1996). Jealousy and the characteristics of one's rival: A self-evaluation maintenance perspective. *Personality and Social Psychology Bulletin, 22,* 920–932.

DEUTSCH, M. (1985). *Distributive justice: A social psychological perspective.* New Haven: Yale University Press.

DEUTSCH, M. (1986). Folie à deux: A psychological perspective on Soviet-American relations. In M. P. Kearns (Ed.), *Persistent patterns and emergent structures in a waving century.* New York: Praeger.

DEUTSCH, M. (1993). Educating for a peaceful world. *American Psychologist, 48,* 510–517.

DEUTSCH, M. (1994). Constructive conflict resolution: Principles, training, and research. *Journal of Social Issues, 50,* 13–32.

DEUTSCH, M., & KRAUSS, R. M. (1960). The effect of threat upon interpersonal bargaining. *Journal of Abnormal and Social Psychology, 61,* 181–189.

DEVINE, P. G. (1989). Stereotypes and prejudice: Their automatic and controlled components. *Journal of Personality and Social Psychology, 56,* 5–18.

DEVINE, P. G. (1995). Prejudice and outgroup perception. In A. Tesser (Ed.), *Advanced social psychology.* New York: McGraw-Hill.

DE VRIES, N. K., & VAN KNIPPENBERG, A. (1987). Biased and unbiased self-evaluations of ability: The effects of further testing. *British Journal of Social Psychology, 26,* 9–15.

DIEKMANN, K. A., SAMUELS, S. M., ROSS, L., & BAZERMAN, M. H. (1997). Self-interest and fairness in problems of resource allocation: Allocators versus recipients. *Journal of Personality and Social Psychology, 72,* 1061–1074.

DIENER, E. (1976). Effects of prior destructive behavior, anonymity, and group presence on deindividuation and aggression. *Journal of Personality and Social Psychology, 33,* 497–507.

DIENER, E. (1979). Deindividuation, self-awareness, and disinhibition. *Journal of Personality and Social Psychology, 37,* 1160–1171.

DIENER, E. (1980). Deindividuation: The absence of self-awareness and self-regulation in group members. In P. Paulus (Ed.), *The psychology of group influence*. Hillsdale, NJ: Erlbaum.

DIENER, E. (2000). Subjective well-being: The science of happiness, and some policy implications. *American Psychologist, 55*.

DIENER, E., & CRANDALL, R. (1979). An evaluation of the Jamaican anticrime program. *Journal of Applied Social Psychology, 9*, 135–146.

DIENER, E., & DIENER, C. (1996). Most people are happy. *Psychological Science, 7*, 181–185.

DIENER, E., DIENER, M., & DIENER, C. (1995). Factors predicting the subjective well-being of nations. *Journal of Personality and Social Psychology, 69*, 653–663.

DIENER, E., FRASER, S. C., BEAMAN, A. L., & KELEM, R. T. (1976). Effects of deindividuation variables on stealing among Halloween trick-or-treaters. *Journal of Personality and Social Psychology, 33*, 178–183.

DIENER, E., HORWITZ, J., & EMMONS, R. A. (1985). Happiness of the very wealthy. *Social Indicators, 16*, 263–274.

DIENER, E., SANDVIK, E., SEIDLITZ, L., & DIENER, M. (1993). The relationship between income and subjective well-being: Relative or absolute? *Social Indicators Research, 28*, 195–223.

DIENER, E., & WALLBOM, M. (1976). Effects of self-awareness on antinormative behavior. *Journal of Research in Personality, 10*, 107–111.

DILL, J. C., & ANDERSON, C. A. (1998). Loneliness, shyness, and depression: The etiology and interrelationships of everyday problems in living. In T. Joiner & J. C. Coyne (Eds.), *Recent advances in interpersonal approaches to depression*. Washington, DC: American Psychological Association.

DINDIA, K., & ALLEN, M. (1992). Sex differences in self-disclosure: A meta-analysis. *Psychological Bulletin, 112*, 106–124.

DION, K. K. (1972). Physical attractiveness and evaluations of children's transgressions. *Journal of Personality and Social Psychology, 24*, 207–213.

DION, K. K. (1973). Young children's stereotyping of facial attractiveness. *Developmental Psychology, 9*, 183–188.

DION, K. K. (1979). Physical attractiveness and interpersonal attraction. In M. Cook & G. Wilson (Eds.), *Love and attraction*. New York: Pergamon Press.

DION, K. K., & BERSCHEID, E. (1974). Physical attractiveness and peer perception among children. *Sociometry, 37*, 1–12.

DION, K. K., & DION, K. L. (1985). Personality, gender, and the phenomenology of romantic love. In P. R. Shaver (Ed.), *Review of personality and social psychology* (Vol. 6). Beverly Hills, CA: Sage.

DION, K. K., & DION, K. L. (1991). Psychological individualism and romantic love. *Journal of Social Behavior and Personality, 6*, 17–33.

DION, K. K., & DION, K. L. (1993). Individualistic and collectivistic perspectives on gender and the cultural context of love and intimacy. *Journal of Social Issues, 49*, 53–69.

DION, K. K., & DION, K. L. (1996). Cultural perspectives on romantic love. *Personal Relationships, 3*, 5–17.

DION, K. K., & STEIN, S. (1978). Physical attractiveness and interpersonal influence. *Journal of Experimental Social Psychology, 14*, 97–109.

DION, K. L. (1979). Intergroup conflict and intragroup cohesiveness. In W. G. Austin & S. Worchel (Eds.), *The social psychology of intergroup relations*. Monterey, CA: Brooks/Cole.

DION, K. L. (1987). What's in a title? The Ms. stereotype and images of women's titles of address. *Psychology of Women Quarterly, 11,* 21–36.

DION, K. L., & COTA, A. A. (1991). The Ms. stereotype: Its domain and the role of explicitness in title preference. *Psychology of Women Quarterly, 15,* 403–410.

DION, K. L., & DION, K. K. (1988). Romantic love: Individual and cultural perspectives. In R. J. Sternberg & M. L. Barnes (Eds.), *The psychology of love.* New Haven, CT: Yale University Press.

DION, K. L., DION, K. K., & KEELAN, J. P. (1990). Appearance anxiety as a dimension of social-evaluative anxiety: Exploring the ugly duckling syndrome. *Contemporary Social Psychology, 14* (4), 220–224.

DION, K. L., & KAWAKAMI, K. (1996). Ethnicity and perceived discrimination in Toronto: Another look at the personal/group discrimination controversy. *Canadian Journal of Behavioural Science, 28,* 203–213.

DION, K. L., & SCHULLER, R. A. (1991). The Ms. stereotype: Its generality and its relation to managerial and marital status stereotypes. *Canadian Journal of Behavioural Science, 23,* 25–40.

DITTO, P. H. (1994). *Walking the line between passion and reason: Motivated judgment in an adaptive context.* Paper presented to the American Psychological Society convention.

DITTO, P. H., SCEPANSKY, J. A., MUNRO, G. D., APANOVITCH, A. M., & LOCKHART, L. K. (1997). *Motivated sensitivity to preference-inconsistent information.* Unpublished manuscript, Kent State University.

DOLLARD, J., DOOB, L., MILLER, N., MOWRER, O. H., & SEARS, R. R. (1939). *Frustration and aggression.* New Haven, CT: Yale University Press.

DONNERSTEIN, E. (1980). Aggressive erotica and violence against women. *Journal of Personality and Social Psychology, 39,* 269–277.

DONNERSTEIN, E. (1998). *Why do we have those new ratings on television?* Invited address to the National Institute on the Teaching of Psychology.

DONNERSTEIN, E., & BERKOWITZ, L. (1981). Victim reactions in aggressive erotic films as a factor in violence against women. *Journal of Personality and Social Psychology, 41,* 710–724.

DONNERSTEIN, E., LINZ, D., & PENROD, S. (1987). *The question of pornography.* London: Free Press.

DOOB, A. N., & ROBERTS, J. (1988). Public attitudes toward sentencing in Canada. In N. Walker & M. Hough (Eds.), *Sentencing and the public.* London: Gower.

DOTY, R. M., PETERSON, B. E., & WINTER, D. G. (1991). Threat and authoritarianism in the United States, 1978–1987. *Journal of Personality and Social Psychology, 61,* 629–640.

DOVIDIO, J. R., BRIGHAM, J. C., JOHNSON, B. T., & GAERTNER, S. L. (1996). Stereotyping, prejudice, and discrimination: Another look. In N. Macrae, M. Hewstone, & C. Stangor (Eds.), *Stereotypes and stereotyping.* New York: Guilford.

DRAGUNS, J. G. (1990). Normal and abnormal behavior in cross-cultural perspective: Specifying the nature of their relationship. *Nebraska Symposium on Motivation 1989, 37,* 235–277.

DRAKULIC, S. (1992, December 13). Rape after rape after rape. *New York Times,* Section 4, p. 17.

DRYER, D. C., & HOROWITZ, L. M. (1997). When do opposites attract? Interpersonal complementarity versus similarity. *Journal of Personality and Social Psychology, 72,* 592–603.

DUNCAN, B. L. (1976). Differential social perception and attribution of intergroup violence: Testing the lower limits of stereotyping of blacks. *Journal of Personality and Social Psychology, 34,* 590–598.

DUNNING, D. (1995). Trait importance and modifiability as factors influencing self-assessment and self-enhancement motives. *Personality and Social Psychology Bulletin, 21,* 1297–1306.

DUNNING, D., GRIFFIN, D. W., MILOJKOVIC, J. D., & ROSS, L. (1990). The overconfidence effect in social prediction. *Journal of Personality and Social Psychology, 58,* 568–581.

DUNNING, D., MEYEROWITZ, J. A., & HOLZBERG, A. D. (1989). Ambiguity and self-evaluation. *Journal of Personality and Social Psychology, 57,* 1082–1090.

DUNNING, D., PERIE, M., & STORY, A. L. (1991). Self-serving prototypes of social categories. *Journal of Personality and Social Psychology, 61,* 957–968.

DUTTON, D. G., & ARON, A. P. (1974). Some evidence for heightened sexual attraction under conditions of high anxiety. *Journal of Personality and Social Psychology, 30,* 510–517.

DUTTON, D. G., & ARON, A. (1989). Romantic attraction and generalized liking for others who are sources of conflict-based arousal. *Canadian Journal of Behavioural Science, 21,* 246–257.

EAGLY, A. H. (1987). *Sex differences in social behavior: A social-role interpretation.* Hillsdale, NJ: Erlbaum.

EAGLY, A. H. (1994). *Are people prejudiced against women?* Donald Campbell Award invited address, American Psychological Association convention.

EAGLY, A. H. (1997). *Sex differences in social behavior: Social psychology meets evolutionary psychology.* Midwestern Psychological Association invited address.

EAGLY, A. H., ASHMORE, R. D., MAKHIJANI, M. G., & LONGO, L. C. (1991). What is beautiful is good, but . . . : A meta-analytic review of research on the physical attractiveness stereotype. *Psychological Bulletin, 110,* 109–128.

EAGLY, A. H., & CHAIKEN, S. (1993). *The psychology of attitudes.* San Diego: Harcourt Brace Jovanovich.

EAGLY, A. H., & CROWLEY, M. (1986). Gender and helping behavior: A meta-analytic review of the social psychological literature. *Psychological Bulletin, 100,* 283–308.

EAGLY, A. H., & JOHNSON, B. T. (1990). Gender and leadership style: A meta-analysis. *Psychological Bulletin, 108,* 233–256.

EAGLY, A. H., & KARAU, S. J. (1991). Gender and the emergence of leaders: A meta-analysis. *Journal of Personality and Social Psychology, 60,* 685–710.

EAGLY, A. H., KARAU, S. J., & MAKHIJANI, M. G. (1995). Gender and the effectiveness of leaders: A meta-analysis. *Psychological Bulletin, 117,* 125–145.

EAGLY, A. H., MLADINIC, A., & OTTO, S. (1991). Are women evaluated more favorably than men? *Psychology of Women Quarterly, 15,* 203–216.

EAGLY, A. H., & WOOD, W. (1991). Explaining sex differences in social behavior: A meta-analytic perspective. *Personality and Social Psychology Bulletin, 17,* 306–315.

EASTERLIN, R. (1995). Will raising the incomes of all increase the happiness of all? *Journal of Economic Behavior and Organization, 27,* 35–47.

EBBESEN, E. B., DUNCAN, B., & KONECNI, V. J. (1975). Effects of content of verbal aggression on future verbal aggression: A field experiment. *Journal of Experimental Social Psychology, 11,* 192–204.

EDNEY, J. J. (1979). The nuts game: A concise commons dilemma analog. *Environmental Psychology and Nonverbal Behavior, 3,* 252–254.

EISENBERG, N., & LENNON, R. (1983). Sex differences in empathy and related capacities. *Psychological Bulletin, 94,* 100–131.

EISER, J. R., SUTTON, S. R., & WOBER, M. (1979). Smoking, seat-belts, and beliefs about health. *Addictive Behaviors, 4,* 331–338.

ELDER, G. H., JR. (1969). Appearance and education in marriage mobility. *American Sociological Review, 34,* 519–533.

ELDER, G. H., JR., & CLIPP, E. C. (1988). Wartime losses and social bonding: Influences across 40 years in men's lives. *Psychiatry, 51,* 177–197.

ELLICKSON, P. L., & BELL, R. M. (1990). Drug prevention in junior high: A multisite longitudinal test. *Science, 247,* 1299–1305.

ELLIS, B. J., & SYMONS, D. (1990). Sex difference in sexual fantasy: An evolutionary psychological approach. *Journal of Sex Research, 27,* 490–521.

ELLIS, H. D. (1981). Theoretical aspects of face recognition. In G. H. Davies, H. D. Ellis, & J. Shepherd (Eds.), *Perceiving and remembering faces.* London: Academic Press.

ELLISON, C. G. (1991). Religious involvement and subjective well-being. *Journal of Health and Social Behavior, 32,* 80–99.

ELLYSON, S. L., DOVIDIO, J. F., & BROWN, C. E. (1991). The look of power: Gender differences and similarities in visual dominance behavior. In C. Ridgeway (Ed.), *Gender and interaction: The role of microstructures in inequality.* New York: Springer-Verlag.

ELMS, A. C. (1995). Obedience in retrospect. *Journal of Social Issues, 51,* 21–31.

ENGS, R., & HANSON, D. J. (1989). Reactance theory: A test with collegiate drinking. *Psychological Reports, 64,* 1083–1086.

ENNIS, B. J., & VERRILLI, D. B., JR. (1989). *Motion for leave to file brief amicus curiae and brief of Society for the Scientific Study of Religion, American Sociological Association, and others. U.S. Supreme Court Case No. 88-1600, Holy Spirit Association for the Unification of World Christianity, et al., v. David Molko and Tracy Leal. On petition for write of certiorari to the Supreme Court of California.* Washington, DC: Jenner & Block, 21 Dupont Circle NW.

ENNIS, R., & ZANNA, M. P. (1991). *Hockey assault: Constitutive versus normative violations.* Paper presented at the Canadian Psychological Association convention.

EPSTEIN, S., & FEIST, G. J. (1988). Relation between self- and other-acceptance and its moderation by identification. *Journal of Personality and Social Psychology, 54,* 309–315.

ERICKSON, B., HOLMES, J. G., FREY, R., WALKER, L., & THIBAUT, J. (1974). Functions of a third party in the resolution of conflict: The role of a judge in pretrial conferences. *Journal of Personality and Social Psychology, 30,* 296–306.

ERNST, J. M., & HEESACKER, M. (1993). Application of the elaboration likelihood model of attitude change to assertion training. *Journal of Counseling Psychology, 40,* 37–45.

ERON, L. D. (1987). The development of aggressive behavior from the perspective of a developing behaviorism. *American Psychologist, 42,* 425–442.

ERON, L. D., & HUESMANN, L. R. (1980). Adolescent aggression and television. *Annals of the New York Academy of Sciences, 347,* 319–331.

ERON, L. D., & HUESMANN, L. R. (1984). The control of aggressive behavior by changes in attitudes, values, and the conditions of learning. In R. J. Blanchard & C. Blanchard (Eds.), *Advances in the study of aggression* (Vol. 1). Orlando, FL: Academic Press.

ERON, L. D., & HUESMANN, L. R. (1985). The role of television in the development of prosocial and antisocial behavior. In D. Olweus, M. Radke-Yarrow, J. Block (Eds.), *Development of antisocial and prosocial behavior*. Orlando, FL: Academic Press.

ERON, L., HUESMANN, L. R., & GUERRA, N. (1997). Poverty and violence. In S. Feshbach & J. Zagrodzka (Eds.), *Human aggression: Biological and social roots*. New York: Plenum Press.

ESSER, J. K., & LINDOERFER, J. S. (1989). Groupthink and the space shuttle *Challenger* accident: Toward a quantitative case analysis. *Journal of Behavioral Decision Making, 2,* 167–177.

ESSES, V. M., HADDOCK, G., & ZANNA, M. P. (1993b). The role of mood in the expression of intergroup stereotypes. In M. P. Zanna & J. M. Olson (Eds.), *The psychology of prejudice: The Ontario symposium* (Vol. 7). Hillsdale, NJ: Erlbaum.

ESSES, V. M., & ZANNA, M. P. (1995). Mood and the expression of ethnic stereotypes. *Journal of Personality and Social Psychology, 69,* 1052–1068.

ETZIONI, A. (1967). The Kennedy experiment. *Western Political Quarterly, 20,* 361–380.

EVANS, G. W. (1979). Behavioral and physiological consequences of crowding in humans. *Journal of Applied Social Psychology, 9,* 27–46.

EVANS, R. I., SMITH, C. K., & RAINES, B. E. (1984). Deterring cigarette smoking in adolescents: A psycho-social-behavioral analysis of an intervention strategy. In A. Baum, J. Singer, & S. Taylor (Eds.), *Handbook of psychology and health: Social psychological aspects of health* (Vol. 4). Hillsdale, NJ: Erlbaum.

EXLINE, J. J., & LOBEL, M. (in press). The perils of outperformance: Sensitivity about being the target of a threatening upward comparison. *Psychological Bulletin.*

FALBO, T., POSTON, D. L., JR., TRISCARI, R. S., & ZHANG, X. (1997). Self-enhancing illusions among Chinese schoolchildren. *Journal of Cross-Cultural Psychology, 28,* 172–191.

FAULKNER, S. L., & WILLIAMS, K. D. (1996). *A study of social loafing in industry.* Paper presented to the Midwestern Psychological Association convention.

FAUST, D., & ZISKIN, J. (1988). The expert witness in psychology and psychiatry. *Science, 241,* 31–35.

FAZIO, R. H. (1990). Multiple processes by which attitudes guide behavior: The mode model as an integrative framework. *Advances in Experimental Social Psychology, 23,* 75–109.

FAZIO, R. H., EFFREIN, E. A., & FALENDER, V. J. (1981). Self-perceptions following social interaction. *Journal of Personality and Social Psychology, 41,* 232–242.

FAZIO, R. H., JACKSON, J. R., DUNTON, B. C., & WILLIAMS, C. J. (1995). Variability in automatic activation as an unobtrusive measure of racial attitudes: A bona fide pipeline? *Journal of Personality and Social Psychology, 69,* 1013–1027.

FEATHER, N. T. (1983). Causal attributions for good and bad outcomes in achievement and affiliation situations. *Australian Journal of Psychology, 35,* 37–48.

FEENEY, J., PETERSON, C., & NOLLER, P. (1994). Equity and marital satisfaction over the family life cycle. *Personality Relationships, 1,* 83–99.

FEIN, S., HILTON, J. L., & MILLER, D. T. (1990). Suspicion of ulterior motivation and the correspondence bias. *Journal of Personality and Social Psychology, 58,* 753–764.

FEINGOLD, A. (1988). Matching for attractiveness in romantic partners and same-sex friends: A meta-analysis and theoretical critique. *Psychological Bulletin, 104,* 226–235.

FEINGOLD, A. (1990). Gender differences in effects of physical attractiveness on romantic attraction: A comparison across five research paradigms. *Journal of Personality and Social Psychology, 59,* 981–993.

FEINGOLD, A. (1991). Sex differences in the effects of similarity and physical attractiveness on opposite-sex attraction. *Basic and Applied Social Psychology, 12,* 357–367.

FEINGOLD, A. (1992a). Gender differences in mate selection preferences: A test of the parental investment model. *Psychological Bulletin, 112,* 125–139.

FEINGOLD, A. (1992b). Good-looking people are not what we think. *Psychological Bulletin, 111,* 304–341.

FELDMAN, K. A., & NEWCOMB, T. M. (1969). *The impact of college on students.* San Francisco: Jossey-Bass.

FELSON, R. B. (1984). The effect of self-appraisals of ability on academic performance. *Journal of Personality and Social Psychology, 47,* 944–952.

FENIGSTEIN, A. (1984). Self-consciousness and the overperception of self as a target. *Journal of Personality and Social Psychology, 47,* 860–870.

FENIGSTEIN, A., & VANABLE, P. A. (1992). Paranoia and self-consciousness. *Journal of Personality and Social Psychology, 62,* 129–138.

FERGUSSON, D. M., HORWOOD, L. J., & SHANNON, F. T. (1984). A proportional hazards model of family breakdown. *Journal of Marriage and the Family, 46,* 539–549.

FESHBACH, N. D. (1980). *The child as "psychologist" and "economist": Two curricula.* Paper presented at the American Psychological Association convention.

FESHBACH, S. (1980). *Television advertising and children: Policy issues and alternatives.* Paper presented at the American Psychological Association convention.

FESTINGER, L. (1954). A theory of social comparison processes. *Human Relations, 7,* 117–140.

FESTINGER, L. (1957). *A theory of cognitive dissonance.* Stanford: Stanford University Press.

FESTINGER, L., & MACCOBY, N. (1964). On resistance to persuasive communications. *Journal of Abnormal and Social Psychology, 68,* 359–366.

FESTINGER, L., PEPITONE, A., & NEWCOMB, T. (1952). Some consequences of deindividuation in a group. *Journal of Abnormal and Social Psychology, 47,* 382–389.

FIEBERT, M. S. (1990). Men, women and housework: The Roshomon effect. *Men's Studies Review, 8,* 6.

FIEDLER, F. E. (1987, September). When to lead, when to stand back. *Psychology Today,* pp. 26–27.

FIEDLER, K., SEMIN, G. R., & KOPPETSCH, C. (1991). Language use and attributional biases in close personal relationships. *Personality and Social Psychology Bulletin, 17,* 147–155.

FIELDS, J. M., & SCHUMAN, H. (1976). Public beliefs about the beliefs of the public. *Public Opinion Quarterly, 40,* 427–448.

FINCH, J. F., & CIALDINI, R. B. (1989). Another indirect tactic of (self-) image management: Boosting. *Personality and Social Psychology Bulletin, 15,* 222–232.

FINCHAM, F. D., & JASPARS, J. M. (1980). Attribution of responsibility: From man the scientist to man as lawyer. In L. Berkowitz (Ed.), *Advances in experimental social psychology* (Vol. 13). New York: Academic Press.

FINDLEY, M. J., & COOPER, H. M. (1983). Locus of control and academic achievement: A literature review. *Journal of Personality and Social Psychology, 44,* 419–427.

FINEBERG, H. V. (1988). Education to prevent AIDS: Prospects and obstacles. *Science, 239,* 592–596.

FISCHHOFF, B. (1982). Debiasing. In D. Kahneman, P. Slovic, & A. Tversky (Eds.), *Judgment under uncertainty: Heuristics and biases.* New York: Cambridge University Press.

FISHBEIN, D., & THELEN, M. H. (1981a). *Husband-wife similarity and marital satisfaction: A different approach.* Paper presented at the Midwestern Psychological Association convention.

FISHBEIN, D., & THELEN, M. H. (1981b). Psychological factors in mate selection and marital satisfaction: A review (Ms. 2374). *Catalog of Selected Documents in Psychology, 11,* 84.

FISHER, H. (1994, April). The nature of romantic love. *Journal of NIH Research,* pp. 59–64.

FISHER, R. J. (1994). Generic principles for resolving intergroup conflict. *Journal of Social Issues, 50,* 47–66.

FLAY, B. R., RYAN, K. B., BEST, J. A., BROWN, K. S., KERSELL, M. W., d'AVERNAS, J. R., & ZANNA, M. P. (1985). Are social-psychological smoking prevention programs effective? The Waterloo study. *Journal of Behavioral Medicine, 8,* 37–59.

FLEMING, I., BAUM, A., & WEISS, L. (1987). Social density and perceived control as mediators of crowding stress in high-density residential neighborhoods. *Journal of Personality and Social Psychology, 52,* 899–906.

FLETCHER, G. J. O., FINCHAM, F. D., CRAMER, L., & HERON, N. (1987). The role of attributions in the development of dating relationships. *Journal of Personality and Social Psychology, 53,* 481–489.

FOLEY, L. A. (1976). Personality and situational influences on changes in prejudice: A replication of Cook's railroad game in a prison setting. *Journal of Personality and Social Psychology, 34,* 846–856.

FOLLETT, M. P. (1940). Constructive conflict. In H. C. Metcalf & L. Urwick (Eds.), *Dynamic administration: The collected papers of Mary Parker Follett.* New York: Harper.

FORGAS, J. P., & FIEDLER, K. (1996a). Mood effects on intergroup discrimination: The role of affect in reward allocation decisions. *Journal of Personality and Social Psychology, 70,* 28–40.

FORGAS, J. P., & FIEDLER, K. (1996b). Us and them: Mood effects on intergroup discrimination. *Journal of Personality and Social Psychology, 70,* 28–40.

FÖRSTERLING, F. (1986). Attributional conceptions in clinical psychology. *American Psychologist, 41,* 275–285.

FORSYTH, D. R., BERGER, R. E., & MITCHELL, T. (1981). The effects of self-serving vs. other-serving claims of responsibility on attraction and attribution in groups. *Social Psychology Quarterly, 44,* 59–64.

FORSYTH, D. R., & LEARY, M. R. (1997). Achieving the goals of the scientist-practitioner model: The seven interfaces of social and counseling psychology. *Counseling Psychologist, 25,* 180–200.

FRANK, M. G., & GILOVICH, T. (1988). The dark side of self and social perception: Black uniforms and aggression in professional sports. *Journal of Personality and Social Psychology, 54,* 74–85.

FRANK, M. G., & GILOVICH, T. (1989). Effect of memory perspective on retrospective causal attributions. *Journal of Personality and Social Psychology, 57,* 399–403.

FRANK, R. H. (1996). *The empty wealth of nations.* Unpublished manuscript, Johnson Graduate School of Management, Cornell University.

FRANKEL, A., & SNYDER, M. L. (1987). *Egotism among the depressed: When self-protection becomes self-handicapping.* Paper presented at the American Psychological Association convention.

FREEDMAN, J. (1978). *Happy people.* New York: Harcourt Brace Jovanovich.

FREEDMAN, J. L. (1988). Television violence and aggression: What the evidence shows. In S. Oskamp (Ed.), *Television as a social issue. Applied social psychology annual* (Vol. 8). Newbury Park, CA: Sage.

FREEDMAN, J. L., BIRSKY, J., & CAVOUKIAN, A. (1980). Environmental determinants of behavioral contagion: Density and number. *Basic and Applied Social Psychology, 1,* 155–161.

FREEDMAN, J. L., & FRASER, S. C. (1966). Compliance without pressure: The foot-in-the-door technique. *Journal of Personality and Social Psychology, 4,* 195–202.

FREEDMAN, J. L., & PERLICK, D. (1979). Crowding, contagion, and laughter. *Journal of Experimental Social Psychology, 15,* 295–303.

FREEDMAN, J. L., & SEARS, D. O. (1965). Warning, distraction, and resistance to influence. *Journal of Personality and Social Psychology, 1,* 262–266.

FREEDMAN, J. S. (1965). Long-term behavioral effects of cognitive dissonance. *Journal of Experimental Social Psychology, 1,* 145–155.

FRENCH, J. R. P. (1968). The conceptualization and the measurement of mental health in terms of self-identity theory. In S. B. Sells (Ed.), *The definition and measurement of mental health.* Washington, D.C.: Department of Health, Education, and Welfare. (Cited by M. Rosenberg, 1979, *Conceiving the self.* New York: Basic Books.)

FREUD, S. (1964). *The future of an illusion.* Garden City, NY: Doubleday.

FRIEDRICH, J. (1996). On seeing oneself as less self-serving than others: The ultimate self-serving bias? *Teaching of Psychology, 23,* 107–109.

FRIEDRICH, L. K., & STEIN, A. H. (1973). Aggressive and prosocial television programs and the natural behavior of preschool children. *Monographs of the Society of Research in Child Development, 38* (4, Serial No. 151).

FRIEDRICH, L. K., & STEIN, A. H. (1975). Prosocial television and young children: The effects of verbal labeling and role playing on learning and behavior. *Child Development, 46,* 27–38.

FRIEDRICH, W. N., COHEN, D. S., & WILTURNER, L. T. (1988). Specific beliefs as moderator variables in maternal coping with mental retardation. *Children's Health Care, 17,* 40–44.

FRIEZE, I. H., OLSON, J. E., & RUSSELL, J. (1991). Attractiveness and income for men and women in management. *Journal of Applied Social Psychology, 21,* 1039–1057.

FURNHAM, A. (1982). Explanations for unemployment in Britain. *European Journal of Social Psychology, 12,* 335–352.

FURNHAM, A., & GUNTER, B. (1984). Just world beliefs and attitudes towards the poor. *British Journal of Social Psychology, 23,* 265–269.

GABRENYA, W. K., JR., WANG, Y.-E., & LATANÉ, B. (1985). Social loafing on an optimizing task: Cross-cultural differences among Chinese and Americans. *Journal of Cross-Cultural Psychology, 16,* 223–242.

GAERTNER, S. L., DOVIDIO, J. F., ANASTASIO, P. A., BACHMAN, B. A., & RUST, M. C. (1993). The Common Ingroup Identity Model: Recategorization and the reduction of intergroup bias. In W. Stroebe & M. Hewstone (Eds.), *European Review of Social Psychology* (Vol. 4). London: Wiley.

GAERTNER, S. L., DOVIDIO, J. F., NIER, J. A., WARD, C. M., & BANKER, B. S. (1998). Across cultural divides: The value of superordinate identity. In D. Prentice & D. Miller (Eds.), *Cultural divides: The social psychology of intergroup contact.* New York: Russell Sage Foundation.

GALANTER, M. (1989). *Cults: Faith, healing, and coercion.* New York: Oxford University Press.

GALANTER, M. (1990). Cults and zealous self-help movements: A psychiatric perspective. *American Journal of Psychiatry, 147,* 543–551.

GALIZIO, M., & HENDRICK, C. (1972). Effect of musical accompaniment on attitude: The guitar as a prop for persuasion. *Journal of Applied Social Psychology, 2,* 350–359.

GALLUP, G., JR. (1984, March). Commentary on the state of religion in the U.S. today. *Religion in America: The Gallup Report* (No. 222).

GALLUP, G. G., JR., & NEWPORT, F. (1990, July). Americans widely disagree on what constitutes rich. *Gallup Poll Monthly,* pp. 28–36.

GALLUP, G. H. (1972). *The Gallup poll: Public opinion 1935–1971* (Vol. 3). New York: Random House, pp. 551, 1716.

GALLUP ORGANIZATION. (1990). April 19–22 survey reported in *American Enterprise,* September/October, 1990, p. 92.

GAMSON, W. A., FIREMAN, B., & RYTINA, S. (1982). *Encounters with unjust authority.* Homewood, IL: Dorsey Press.

GANGESTAD, S. W., & THORNHILL, R. (1997). Human sexual selection and developmental stability. In J. A. Simpson & D. T. Kenrick (Eds.), *Evolutionary social psychology.* Mahway, NJ: Erlbaum.

GARB, H. N. (1994). Judgment research: Implications for clinical practice and testimony in court. *Applied and Preventive Psychology, 3,* 173–183.

GARDNER, M. (1997, July/August). Heaven's Gate: The UFO cult of Bo and Peep. *Skeptical Inquirer,* pp. 15–17.

GASTORF, J. W., SULS, J., & SANDERS, G. S. (1980). Type A coronary-prone behavior pattern and social facilitation. *Journal of Personality and Social Psychology, 8,* 773–780.

GATES, M. F., & ALLEE, W. C. (1933). Conditioned behavior of isolated and grouped cockroaches on a simple maze. *Journal of Comparative Psychology, 15,* 331–358.

GAZZANIGA, M. S. (1992). *Nature's mind: The biological roots of thinking, emotions, sexuality, language, and intelligence.* New York: Basic Books.

GECAS, V. (1989). The social psychology of self-efficacy. *Annual Review of Sociology, 15,* 291–316.

GEEN, R. G. (1998). Aggression and antisocial behavior. In D. Gilbert, S. Fiske, & G. Lindzey (Eds.), *Handbook of social psychology* (4th ed.). New York: McGraw-Hill.

GEEN, R. G., & GANGE, J. J. (1983). Social facilitation: Drive theory and beyond. In H. H. Blumberg, A. P. Hare, V. Kent, & M. Davies (Eds.), *Small groups and social interaction* (Vol. 1). London: Wiley.

GEEN, R. G., & QUANTY, M. B. (1977). The catharsis of aggression: An evaluation of a hypothesis. In L. Berkowitz (Ed.), *Advances in experimental social psychology* (Vol. 10). New York: Academic Press.

GEEN, R. G., & THOMAS, S. L. (1986). The immediate effects of media violence on behavior. *Journal of Social Issues, 42* (3), 7–28.

GERARD, H. B., & MATHEWSON, G. C. (1966). The effects of severity of initiation on liking for a group: A replication. *Journal of Experimental Social Psychology, 2,* 278–287.

GERBNER, G. (1993, June). *Women and minorities on television: A study in casting and fate.* A report to the Screen Actors Guild and the American Federation of Radio and Television Artists.

GERBNER, G. (1994). The politics of media violence: Some reflections. In C. Hamelink & O. Linne (Eds.), *Mass communication research: On problems and policies.* Norwood, NJ: Ablex.

GIBBONS, F. X., EGGLESTON, T. J., & BENTHIN, A. C. (1997). Cognitive reactions to smoking relapse: The reciprocal relation between dissonance and self-esteem. *Journal of Personality and Social Psychology, 72,* 184–195.

GIFFORD, R., & HINE, D. W. (1997). Toward cooperation in commons dilemmas. *Canadian Journal of Behavioural Science, 29,* 167–179.

GIFFORD, R., & PEACOCK, J. (1979). Crowding: More fearsome than crime-provoking? Comparison of an Asian city and a North American city. *Psychologia, 22,* 79–83.

GIGONE, D., & HASTIE, R. (1993). The common knowledge effect: Information sharing and group judgment. *Journal of Personality and Social Psychology, 65,* 959–974.

GILBERT, D. T., & HIXON, J. G. (1991). The trouble of thinking: Activation and application of stereotypic beliefs. *Journal of Personality and Social Psychology, 60,* 509–517.

GILBERT, D. T., & JONES, E. E. (1986). Perceiver-induced constraint: Interpretations of self-generated reality. *Journal of Personality and Social Psychology, 50,* 269–280.

GILBERT, D. T., McNULTY, S. E., GIULIANO, T. A., & BENSON, J. E. (1992). Blurry words and fuzzy deeds: The attribution of obscure behavior. *Journal of Personality and Social Psychology, 62,* 18–25.

GILBERT, D. T., PELHAM, B. W., & KRULL, D. S. (1988). On cognitive busyness: When person perceivers meet persons perceived. *Journal of Personality and Social Psychology, 54,* 733–740.

GILBERT, D. T., PINEL, E. C., WILSON, T. D., BLUMBERG, S. J., & WHEATLEY, T. P. (1998). Immune neglect: A source of durability bias in affective forecasting. *Journal of Personality and Social Psychology, 75,* 617–638.

GILLIGAN, C. (1982). *In a different voice: Psychological theory and women's development.* Cambridge, MA: Harvard University Press.

GILLIGAN, C., LYONS, N. P., & HANMER, T. J. (Eds.). (1990). *Making connections: The relational worlds of adolescent girls at Emma Willard School.* Cambridge, MA: Harvard University Press.

GILLIS, J. S., & AVIS, W. E. (1980). The male-taller norm in mate selection. *Personality and Social Psychology Bulletin, 6,* 396–401.

GILMOR, T. M., & REID, D. W. (1979). Locus of control and causal attribution for positive and negative outcomes on university examinations. *Journal of Research in Personality, 13*, 154–160.

GILOVICH, T. (1987). Secondhand information and social judgment. *Journal of Experimental Social Psychology, 23*, 59–74.

GILOVICH, T., & DOUGLAS, C. (1986). Biased evaluations of randomly determined gambling outcomes. *Journal of Experimental Social Psychology, 22*, 228–241.

GILOVICH, T., KERR, M., & MEDVEC, V. H. (1993). Effect of temporal perspective on subjective confidence. *Journal of Personality and Social Psychology, 64*, 552–560.

GINSBURG, B., & ALLEE, W. C. (1942). Some effects of conditioning on social dominance and subordination in inbred strains of mice. *Physiological Zoology, 15*, 485–506.

GLASS, D. C. (1964). Changes in liking as a means of reducing cognitive discrepancies between self-esteem and aggression. *Journal of Personality, 32*, 531–549.

GLENN, N. D. (1980). Aging and attitudinal stability. In O. G. Brim, Jr., & J. Kagan (Eds.), *Constancy and change in human development.* Cambridge, MA: Harvard University Press.

GLENN, N. D. (1981). Personal communication.

GLENN, N. D. (1991). The recent trend in marital success in the United States. *Journal of Marriage and the Family, 53*, 261–270.

GLENN, N. D. (1996). Values, attitudes, and the state of American marriage. In D. Popenoe, J. B. Elshtain, & D. Blankenhorn (Eds.), *Promises to keep: Decline and renewal of marriage in America.* Lanham, MD: Rowman & Littlefield.

GLICK, D., GOTTESMAN, D., & JOLTON, J. (1989). The fault is not in the stars: Susceptibility of skeptics and believers in astrology to the Barnum effect. *Personality and Social Psychology Bulletin, 15*, 572–583.

GOETHALS, G. R., MESSICK, D. M., & ALLISON, S. T. (1991). The uniqueness bias: Studies of constructive social comparison. In J. Suls & T. A. Wills (Eds.), *Social comparison: Contemporary theory and research.* Hillsdale, NJ: Erlbaum.

GOETHALS, G. R., & ZANNA, M. P. (1979). The role of social comparison in choice shifts. *Journal of Personality and Social Psychology, 37*, 1469–1476.

GOGGIN, W. C., & RANGE, L. M. (1985). The disadvantages of hindsight in the perception of suicide. *Journal of Social and Clinical Psychology, 3*, 232–237.

GOLDHAGEN, D. J. (1996). *Hitler's willing executioners.* New York: Knopf.

GOLDMAN, W., & LEWIS, P. (1977). Beautiful is good: Evidence that the physically attractive are more socially skillful. *Journal of Experimental Social Psychology, 13*, 125–130.

GOLDSTEIN, A. P., & GLICK, B. (1994). Aggression replacement training: Curriculum and evaluation. *Simulation and Gaming, 25*, 9–26.

GOLDSTEIN, J. H. (1982). Sports violence. *National Forum, 62* (1), 9–11.

GOLDSTEIN, J. H., & ARMS, R. L. (1971). Effects of observing athletic contests on hostility. *Sociometry, 34*, 83–90.

GOODHART, D. E. (1986). The effects of positive and negative thinking on performance in an achievement situation. *Journal of Personality and Social Psychology, 51*, 117–124.

GOODWIN, F. K., ET AL. (1993). Health care reform for Americans with severe mental illness: Report of the National Advisory Mental Health Council. *American Journal of Psychiatry, 150*, 1447–1465.

GOTLIB, I. H. (1992). Interpersonal and cognitive aspects of depression. *Current Directions in Psychological Science, 1*, 149–154.

GOTLIB, I. H., & LEE, C. M. (1989). The social functioning of depressed patients: A longitudinal assessment. *Journal of Social and Clinical Psychology, 8,* 223–237.

GOTTMAN, J., & SILVER, N. (1994). *Why marriages succeed or fail.* New York: Simon & Schuster.

GOULD, R., BROUNSTEIN, P. J., & SIGALL, H. (1977). Attributing ability to an opponent: Public aggrandizement and private denigration. *Sociometry, 40,* 254–261.

GRAHAM, S., WEINER, B., & ZUCKER, G. S. (1997). An attributional analysis of punishment goals and public reactions to O. J. Simpson. *Personality and Social Psychology Bulletin, 23,* 331–346.

GRAMMER, K., & THORNHILL, R. (1994). Human facial attractiveness and sexual selection: The role of symmetry and averageness. *Journal of Comparative Psychology, 108,* 233–242.

GRAY, J. D., & SILVER, R. C. (1990). Opposite sides of the same coin: Former spouses' divergent perspectives in coping with their divorce. *Journal of Personality and Social Psychology, 59,* 1180–1191.

GRAZIANO, W., BROTHEN, T., & BERSCHEID, E. (1978). Height and attraction: Do men and women see eye-to-eye? *Journal of Personality, 46,* 128–145.

GREELEY, A. M. (1991). *Faithful attraction.* New York: Tor Books.

GREELEY, A. M., & SHEATSLEY, P. B. (1971). Attitudes toward racial integration. *Scientific American, 225* (6), 13–19.

GREENBERG, J. (1986). Differential intolerance for inequity from organizational and individual agents. *Journal of Applied Social Psychology, 16,* 191–196.

GREENBERG, J., PYSZCZYNSKI, T., BURLING, J., & TIBBS, K. (1992). Depression, self-focused attention, and the self-serving attributional bias. *Personality and Individual Differences, 13,* 959–965.

GREENBERG, J., PYSZCZYNSKI, T., SOLOMON, S., ROSENBLATT, A., VEEDER, M., KIRKLAND, S., & LYON, D. (1990). Evidence for terror management theory: II. The effects of mortality salience on reactions to those who threaten or bolster the cultural worldview. *Journal of Personality and Social Psychology, 58,* 308–318.

GREENWALD, A. G. (1980). The totalitarian ego: Fabrication and revision of personal history. *American Psychologist, 35,* 603–618.

GREENWALD, A. G. (1984, June 12). Quoted by D. Goleman, A bias puts self at center of everything. *New York Times,* pp. C1, C4.

GREENWALD, A. G., & BANAJI, M. R. (1995). Implicit social cognition: Attitudes, self-esteem, and stereotypes. *Psychological Review, 102,* 4–27.

GREENWALD, A. G., CARNOT, C. G., BEACH, R., & YOUNG, B. (1987). Increasing voting behavior by asking people if they expect to vote. *Journal of Applied Psychology, 72,* 315–318.

GREENWALD, A. G., SPANGENBERG, E. R., PRATKANIS, A. R., & ESKENAZI, J. (1991). Double-blind tests of subliminal self-help audiotapes. *Psychological Science, 2,* 119–122.

GRIFFIN, B. Q., COMBS, A. L., LAND, M. L., & COMBS, N. N. (1983). Attribution of success and failure in college performance. *Journal of Psychology, 114,* 259–266.

GRIFFITT, W. (1970). Environmental effects on interpersonal affective behavior. Ambient effective temperature and attraction. *Journal of Personality and Social Psychology, 15,* 240–244.

GRIFFITT, W. (1987). Females, males, and sexual responses. In K. Kelley (Ed.), *Females, males, and sexuality: Theories and research.* Albany: State University of New York Press.

GRIFFITT, W., & VEITCH, R. (1971). Hot and crowded: Influences of population density and temperature on interpersonal affective behavior. *Journal of Personality and Social Psychology, 17,* 92–98.

GRIFFITT, W., & VEITCH, R. (1974). Preacquaintance attitude similarity and attraction revisited: Ten days in a fallout shelter. *Sociometry, 37,* 163–173.

GROSS, A. E., & CROFTON, C. (1977). What is good is beautiful. *Sociometry, 40,* 85–90.

GROVE, J. R., HANRAHAN, S. J., & MCINMAN, A. (1991). Success/failure bias in attributions across involvement categories in sport. *Personality and Social Psychology Bulletin, 17,* 93–97.

GRUDER, C. L., COOK, T. D., HENNIGAN, K. M., FLAY, B., ALESSIS, C., & KALAMAJ, J. (1978). Empirical tests of the absolute sleeper effect predicted from the discounting cue hypothesis. *Journal of Personality and Social Psychology, 36,* 1061–1074.

GRUMAN, J. C., & SLOAN, R. P. (1983). Disease as justice: Perceptions of the victims of physical illness. *Basic and Applied Social Psychology, 4,* 39–46.

GRUNBERGER, R. (1971). *The 12-year-Reich: A social history of Nazi Germany 1933–1945.* New York: Holt, Rinehart & Winston.

GRUSH, J. E., & GLIDDEN, M. V. (1987). *Power and satisfaction among distressed and nondistressed couples.* Paper presented at the Midwestern Psychological Association convention.

GUDYKUNST, W. B. (1989). Culture and intergroup processes. In M. H. Bond (Ed.), *The cross-cultural challenge to social psychology.* Newbury Park, CA: Sage.

GUERIN, B. (1993). *Social facilitation.* Paris: Cambridge University Press.

GUERIN, B. (1994). What do people think about the risks of driving? Implications for traffic safety interventions. *Journal of Applied Social Psychology, 24,* 994–1021.

GUERIN, B., & INNES, J. M. (1982). Social facilitation and social monitoring: A new look at Zajonc's mere presence hypothesis. *British Journal of Social Psychology, 21,* 7–18.

GUINESS, O. (1993). *The American hour: A time of reckoning and the once and future role of faith.* New York: Free Press.

GUPTA, U., & SINGH, P. (1982). Exploratory study of love and liking and type of marriages. *Indian Journal of Applied Psychology, 19,* 92–97.

HACKMAN, J. R. (1986). The design of work teams. In J. Lorsch (Ed.), *Handbook of organizational behavior.* Englewood Cliffs, NJ: Prentice Hall.

HADDOCK, G., & ZANNA, M. P. (1994). Preferring "housewives" to "feminists." *Psychology of Women Quarterly, 18,* 25–52.

HAEMMERLIE, F. M. (1987). *Creating adaptive illusions in counseling and therapy using a self-perception theory perspective.* Paper presented at the Midwestern Psychological Association, Chicago.

HAEMMERLIE, F. M., & MONTGOMERY, R. L. (1982). Self-perception theory and unobtrusively biased interactions: A treatment for heterosocial anxiety. *Journal of Counseling Psychology, 29,* 362–370.

HAEMMERLIE, F. M., & MONTGOMERY, R. L. (1984). Purposefully biased interventions: Reducing heterosocial anxiety through self-perception theory. *Journal of Personality and Social Psychology, 47,* 900–908.

HAEMMERLIE, F. M., & MONTGOMERY, R. L. (1986). Self-perception theory and the treatment of shyness. In W. H. Jones, J. M. Cheek, & S. R. Briggs (Eds.), *A sourcebook on shyness: Research and treatment.* New York: Plenum Press.

HAGIWARA, S. (1983). Role of self-based and sample-based consensus estimates as mediators of responsibility judgments for automobile accidents. *Japanese Psychological Research, 25,* 16–28.

HALL, J. A. (1984). *Nonverbal sex differences: Communication accuracy and expressive style.* Baltimore: Johns Hopkins University Press.

HALL, T. (1985, June 25). The unconverted: Smoking of cigarettes seems to be becoming a lower-class habit. *Wall Street Journal,* pp. 1, 25.

HALLAHAN, M., LEE, F., & HERZOG, T. (1997). It's not just whether you win or lose, it's also where you play the game: A naturalistic, cross-cultural examination of the positivity bias. *Journal of Cross-Cultural Psychology, 28,* 768–778.

HALLMARK CARDS. (1990). Cited in Odds and trends. *Time,* Fall special issue on women, p. 26.

HAMBERGER, J., & HEWSTONE, M. (1997). Inter-ethnic contact as a predictor of blatant and subtle prejudice: Tests of a model in four West European nations. *British Journal of Social Psychology, 36,* 173–190.

HAMBLIN, R. L., BUCKHOLDT, D., BUSHELL, D., ELLIS, D., & FERITOR, D. (1969, January). Changing the game from get the teacher to learn. *Transaction,* pp. 20–25, 28–31.

HAMILTON, V. L., HOFFMAN, W. S., BROMAN, C. L., & RAUMA, D. (1993). Unemployment, distress, and coping: A panel study of autoworkers. *Journal of Personality and Social Psychology, 65,* 234–247.

HANSEN, C. H. (1989). Priming sex-role stereotypic event schemas with rock music videos: Effects on impression favorability, trait inferences, and recall of a subsequent male/female interaction. *Basic and Applied Social Psychology, 10* (4), 371–391.

HANSEN, C. H., & HANSEN, R. D. (1988). Priming stereotypic appraisal of social interactions: How rock music videos can change what's seen when boy meets girl. *Sex Roles, 19,* 287–316.

HANSEN, C. H., & HANSEN, R. D. (1990). Rock music videos and antisocial behavior. *Basic and Applied Social Psychology, 11,* 357–369.

HARDIN, G. (1968). The tragedy of the commons. *Science, 162,* 1243–1248.

HARDY, C., & LATANÉ, B. (1986). Social loafing on a cheering task. *Social Science, 71,* 165–172.

HARING, M. J., STOCK, W. A., & OKUN, M. A. (1984). A research synthesis of gender and social class as correlates of subjective well-being. *Human Relations, 37,* 645–657.

HARITOS-FATOUROS, M. (1988). The official torturer: A learning model for obedience to the authority of violence. *Journal of Applied Social Psychology, 18,* 1107–1120.

HARKINS, S. G. (1981). *Effects of task difficulty and task responsibility on social loafing.* Presentation to the First International Conference on Social Processes in Small Groups, Kill Devil Hills, North Carolina.

HARKINS, S. G., & JACKSON, J. M. (1985). The role of evaluation in eliminating social loafing. *Personality and Social Psychology Bulletin, 11,* 457–465.

HARKINS, S. G., LATANÉ, B., & WILLIAMS, K. (1980). Social loafing: Allocating effort or taking it easy? *Journal of Experimental Social Psychology, 16,* 457–465.

HARKINS, S. G., & PETTY, R. E. (1981). Effects of source magnification of cognitive effort on attitudes: An information-processing view. *Journal of Personality and Social Psychology, 40,* 401–413.

HARKINS, S. G., & PETTY, R. E. (1982). Effects of task difficulty and task uniqueness on social loafing. *Journal of Personality and Social Psychology, 43,* 1214–1229.

HARKINS, S. G., & PETTY, R. E. (1987). Information utility and the multiple source effect. *Journal of Personality and Social Psychology, 52,* 260–268.

HARKINS, S. G., & SZYMANSKI, K. (1989). Social loafing and group evaluation. *Journal of Personality and Social Psychology, 56,* 934–941.

HARMON-JONES, E., BREHM, J. W., GREENBERG, J., SIMON, L., & NELSON, D. E. (1996). Evidence that the production of aversive consequences is not necessary to create cognitive dissonance. *Journal of Personality and Social Psychology, 70,* 5–16.

HARRIES, K. D., & STADLER, S. J. (1988). Heat and violence: New findings from Dallas field data, 1980–1981. *Journal of Applied Social Psychology, 18,* 129–138.

HARRIS, J. R. (1998). *The nurture assumption.* New York: Free Press.

HARRIS, M. J., & ROSENTHAL, R. (1985). Mediation of interpersonal expectancy effects: 31 meta-analyses. *Psychological Bulletin, 97,* 363–386.

HARRIS, M. J., & ROSENTHAL, R. (1986). Four factors in the mediation of teacher expectancy effects. In R. S. Feldman (Ed.), *The social psychology of education.* New York: Cambridge University Press.

HARRISON, A. A. (1977). Mere exposure. In L. Berkowitz (Ed.), *Advances in experimental social psychology* (Vol. 10). New York: Academic Press.

HART, A. (1988). *Fifteen principles for achieving happiness.* Dallas: Word.

HARVEY, C. D., BARNES, G. E., & GREENWOOD, L. (1987). Correlates of morale among Canadian widowed persons. *Social Psychiatry, 22,* 65–72.

HARVEY, J. H., TOWN, J. P., & YARKIN, K. L. (1981). How fundamental is the fundamental attribution error? *Journal of Personality and Social Psychology, 40,* 346–349.

HASLAM, S. A., & OAKES, P. J. (1995). How context-independent is the group homogeneity effect? A response to Bartsch and Judd. *European Journal of Social Psychology, 25,* 469–475.

HATFIELD, E. (1988). Passionate and compassionate love. In R. J. Sternberg & M. L. Barnes (Eds.), *The psychology of love.* New Haven, CT: Yale University Press.

HATFIELD, E., & SPRECHER, S. (1986). *Mirror, mirror: The importance of looks in everyday life.* Albany: State University of New York Press.

HATFIELD, E., TRAUPMANN, J., SPRECHER, S., UTNE, M., & HAY, J. (1985). Equity and intimate relations: Recent research. In W. Ickes (Ed.), *Compatible and incompatible relationships.* New York: Springer-Verlag.

HATFIELD, E., WALSTER, G. W., & BERSCHEID, E. (1978). *Equity: Theory and research.* Boston: Allyn & Bacon.

HAZAN, C., & SHAVER, P. R. (1994). Attachment as an organizational framework for research on close relationships. *Psychological Inquiry, 5,* 1–22.

HEADEY, B., & WEARING, A. (1987). The sense of relative superiority—Central to well-being. *Social Indicators Research, 20,* 497–516.

HEAROLD, S. (1986). A synthesis of 1043 effects of television on social behavior. In G. Comstock (Ed.), *Public communication and behavior* (Vol. 1). Orlando, FL: Academic Press.

HEESACKER, M. (1989). Counseling and the elaboration likelihood model of attitude change. In J. F. Cruz, R. A. Goncalves, & P. P. Machado (Eds.), *Psychology and education: Investigations and interventions.* (Proceedings of the International Conference on Interventions in Psychology and Education, Porto, Portugal, July 1987.) Porto, Portugal: Portuguese Psychological Association.

HEILMAN, M. E. (1976). Oppositional behavior as a function of influence attempt intensity and retaliation threat. *Journal of Personality and Social Psychology, 33,* 574–578.

HEINE, S. J., & LEHMAN, D. R. (1995). Cultural variation in unrealistic optimism: Does the West feel more invulnerable than the East? *Journal of Personality and Social Psychology, 68,* 595–607.

HEINE, S. J., & LEHMAN, D. R. (1997). The cultural construction of self-enhancement: An examination of group-serving biases. *Journal of Personality and Social Psychology, 72,* 1268–1283.

HELLMAN, P. (1980). *Avenue of the righteous of nations.* New York: Atheneum.

HENDERSON-KING, E. I., & NISBETT, R. E. (1996). Anti-black prejudice as a function of exposure to the negative behavior of a single black person. *Journal of Personality and Social Psychology, 71,* 654–664.

HENDRICK, C. (1988). Roles and gender in relationships. In S. Duck (Ed.), *Handbook of personal relationships.* Chichester, England: Wiley.

HENDRICK, C., & HENDRICK, S. (1993). *Romantic love.* Newbury Park, CA: Sage.

HENDRICK, S. S., & HENDRICK, C. (1995). Gender differences and similarities in sex and love. *Personal Relationships, 2,* 55–65.

HENDRICK, S. S., & HENDRICK, C. (1997). Love and satisfaction. In R. J. Sternberg & M. Hojjat (Eds.), *Satisfaction in close relationships.* New York: Guilford.

HENDRICK, S. S., HENDRICK, C., & ADLER, N. L. (1988). Romantic relationships: Love, satisfaction, and staying together. *Journal of Personality and Social Psychology, 54,* 980–988.

HENDRICK, S. S., HENDRICK, C., SLAPION-FOOTE, J., & FOOTE, F. H. (1985). Gender differences in sexual attitudes. *Journal of Personality and Social Psychology, 48,* 1630–1642.

HENRY, W. A. III (1994, June 27). Pride and prejudice. *Time,* pp. 54–59.

HENSLIN, M. (1967). Craps and magic. *American Journal of Sociology, 73,* 316–330.

HEPWORTH, J. T., & WEST, S. G. (1988). Lynchings and the economy: A time-series reanalysis of Hovland and Sears (1940). *Journal of Personality and Social Psychology, 55,* 239–247.

HERADSTVEIT, D. (1979). *The Arab-Israeli conflict: Psychological obstacles to peace* (Vol. 28). Oslo, Norway: Universitetsforlaget. Reviewed by R. K. White, *Contemporary Psychology,* 1980, 25, 11–12.

HEWSTONE, M., HANTZI, A., & JOHNSTON, L. (1991). Social categorisation and person memory: The pervasiveness of race as an organizing principle. *European Journal of Social Psychology, 21,* 517–528.

HIGBEE, K. L., MILLARD, R. J., & FOLKMAN, J. R. (1982). Social psychology research during the 1970s: Predominance of experimentation and college students. *Personality and Social Psychology Bulletin, 8,* 180–183.

HIGGINS, E. T., & MCCANN, C. D. (1984). Social encoding and subsequent attitudes, impressions and memory: "Context-driven" and motivational aspects of processing. *Journal of Personality and Social Psychology, 47,* 26–39.

HIGGINS, E. T., & RHOLES, W. S. (1978). Saying is believing: Effects of message modification on memory and liking for the person described. *Journal of Experimental Social Psychology, 14,* 363–378.

HILL, T., SMITH, N. D., & LEWICKI, P. (1989). The development of self-image bias: A real-world demonstration. *Personality and Social Psychology Bulletin, 15,* 205–211.

HINE, D. W., & GIFFORD, R. (1996). Attributions about self and others in commons dilemmas. *European Journal of Social Psychology, 26,* 429–445.

HINSZ, V. B., TINDALE, R. S., & VOLLRATH, D. A. (1997). The emerging conceptualization of groups as information processors. *Psychological Bulletin, 121,* 43–64.

HIRSCHMAN, R. S., & LEVENTHAL, H. (1989). Preventing smoking behavior in school children: An initial test of a cognitive-development program. *Journal of Applied Social Psychology, 19,* 559–583.

HIRT, E. R. (1990). Do I see only what I expect? Evidence for an expectancy-guided retrieval model. *Journal of Personality and Social Psychology, 58,* 937–951.

HIRT, E. R., ZILLMANN, D., ERICKSON, G. A., & KENNEDY, C. (1992). Costs and benefits of allegiance: Changes in fans' self-ascribed competencies after team victory versus defeat. *Journal of Personality and Social Psychology, 63,* 724–738.

HOFFMAN, C., & HURST, N. (1990). Gender stereotypes: Perception or rationalization? *Journal of Personality and Social Psychology, 58,* 197–208.

HOFFMAN, L. W. (1977). Changes in family roles, socialization, and sex differences. *American Psychologist, 32,* 644–657.

HOFLING, C. K., BROTZMAN, E., DAIRYMPLE, S., GRAVES, N., & PIERCE, C. M. (1966). An experimental study in nurse-physician relationships. *Journal of Nervous and Mental Disease, 143,* 171–180.

HOGAN, R., CURPHY, G. J., & HOGAN, J. (1994). What we know about leadership: Effectiveness and personality. *American Psychologist, 49,* 493–504.

HOGG, M. A. (1992). *The social psychology of group cohesiveness: From attraction to social identity.* London: Harvester Wheatsheaf.

HOGG, M. A. (1996). Intragroup processes, group structure and social identity. In W. P. Robinson (Ed.), *Social groups and identities: Developing the legacy of Henri Tajfel.* Oxford: Butterworth Heinemann.

HOGG, M. A., TURNER, J. C., & DAVIDSON, B. (1990). Polarized norms and social frames of reference: A test of the self-categorization theory of group polarization. *Basic and Applied Social Psychology, 11,* 77–100.

HOKANSON, J. E., & EDELMAN, R. (1966). Effects of three social responses on vascular processes. *Journal of Personality and Social Psychology, 3,* 442–447.

HOLMBERG, D., & HOLMES, J. G. (1994). Reconstruction of relationship memories: A mental models approach. In N. Schwarz & S. Sudman (Eds.), *Autobiographical memory and the validity of retrospective reports.* New York: Springer-Verlag.

HOLMES, J. G., & REMPEL, J. K. (1989). Trust in close relationships. In C. Hendrick (Ed.), *Review of personality and social psychology* (Vol. 10). Newbury Park, CA: Sage.

HOLTGRAVES, T., & SRULL, T. K. (1989). The effects of positive self-descriptions on impressions: General principles and individual differences. *Personality and Social Psychology Bulletin, 15,* 452–462.

HOORENS, V. (1993). Self-enhancement and superiority biases in social comparison. In W. Stroebe & M. Hewstone (Eds.), *European review of social psychology* (Vol. 4). Chichester: Wiley.

HOORENS, V. (1995). Self-favoring biases, self-presentation and the self-other asymmetry in social comparison. *Journal of Personality, 63,* 793–817.

HOORENS, V., & NUTTIN, J. M. (1993). Overvaluation of own attributes: Mere ownership or subjective frequency? *Social Cognition, 11,* 177–200.

HOORENS, V., NUTTIN, J. M., HERMAN, I. E., & PAVAKANUN, U. (1990). Mastery pleasure versus mere ownership: A quasi-experimental cross-cultural and cross-alphabetical test of the name letter effect. *European Journal of Social Psychology, 20,* 181–205.

HORMUTH, S. E. (1986). Lack of effort as a result of self-focused attention: An attributional ambiguity analysis. *European Journal of Social Psychology, 16,* 181–192.

HOUSE, R. J., & SINGH, J. V. (1987). Organizational behavior: Some new directions for I/O psychology. *Annual Review of Psychology, 38,* 669–718.

HOUSTON, V., & BULL, R. (1994). Do people avoid sitting next to someone who is facially disfigured? *European Journal of Social Psychology, 24,* 279–284.

HOVLAND, C. I., LUMSDAINE, A. A., & SHEFFIELD, F. D. (1949). *Experiments on mass communication. Studies in social psychology in World War II* (Vol. 3). Princeton, NJ: Princeton University Press.

HOVLAND, C. I., & SEARS, R. (1940). Minor studies of aggression: Correlation of lynchings with economic indices. *Journal of Psychology, 9,* 301–310.

HUBERMAN, B., & LUKOSE, R. (1997). Social dilemmas and internet congestion. *Science, 277,* 535–537.

HUDDY, L., & VIRTANEN, S. (1995). Subgroup differentiation and subgroup bias among Latinos as a function of familiarity and positive distinctiveness. *Journal of Personality and Social Psychology, 68,* 97–108.

HUESMANN, L. R., LAGERSPETZ, K., & ERON, L. D. (1984). Intervening variables in the TV violence-aggression relation: Evidence from two countries. *Developmental Psychology, 20,* 746–775.

HULL, J. G., & BOND, C. F., JR. (1986). Social and behavioral consequences of alcohol consumption and expectancy: A meta-analysis. *Psychological Bulletin, 99,* 347–360.

HULL, J. G., LEVENSON, R. W., YOUNG, R. D., & SHER, K. J. (1983). Self-awareness-reducing effects of alcohol consumption. *Journal of Personality and Social Psychology, 44,* 461–473.

HULL, J. G., & YOUNG, R. D. (1983). The self-awareness-reducing effects of alcohol consumption: Evidence and implications. In J. Suls & A. G. Greenwald (Eds.), *Psychological perspectives on the self* (Vol. 2). Hillsdale, NJ: Erlbaum.

HUNT, M. (1993). *The story of psychology.* New York: Doubleday.

HUNT, P. J., & HILLERY, J. M. (1973). Social facilitation in a location setting: An examination of the effects over learning trials. *Journal of Experimental Social Psychology, 9,* 563–571.

HUNTER, J. A., STRINGER, M., & WATSON, R. P. (1991). Intergroup violence and intergroup attributions. *British Journal of Social Psychology, 30,* 261–266.

HURTADO, S., DEY, E. L., & TREVINO, J. G. (1994). *Exclusion or self-segregation? Interaction across racial/ethnic groups on college campuses.* Paper presented at the American Educational Research Association annual meeting.

HUSTON, A. C., DONNERSTEIN, E., FAIRCHILD, H., FESHBACH, N. D., KATZ, P. A., & MURRAY, J. P. (1992). *Big world, small screen: The role of television in American society.* Lincoln: University of Nebraska Press.

HUSTON, T. L. (1973). Ambiguity of acceptance, social desirability, and dating choice. *Journal of Experimental Social Psychology, 9,* 32–42.

HUSTON, T. L., & CHOROST, A. F. (1994). Behavioral buffers on the effect of negativity on marital satisfaction: A longitudinal study. *Personal Relationships, 1,* 223–239.

HYMAN, H. H., & SHEATSLEY, P. B. (1956 & 1964). Attitudes toward desegregation. *Scientific American, 195* (6), 35–39; *211* (1), 16–23.

ICKES, B. (1980). *On disconfirming our perceptions of others.* Paper presented at the American Psychological Association convention.

ICKES, W., & LAYDEN, M. A. (1978). Attributional styles. In J. H. Harvey, W. Ickes, & R. F. Kidd (Eds.), *New directions in attribution research* (Vol. 2). Hillsdale, NJ: Erlbaum.

ICKES, W., LAYDEN, M. A., & BARNES, R. D. (1978). Objective self-awareness and individuation: An empirical link. *Journal of Personality, 46,* 146–161.

ICKES, W., SNYDER, M., & CARCIA, S. (1990). Personality influences on the choice of situations. In S. Briggs, R. Hogan, & W. Jones (Eds.), *Handbook of personality psychology.* New York: Academic Press.

IMAI, Y. (1994). Effects of influencing attempts on the perceptions of powerholders and the powerless. *Journal of Social Behavior and Personality, 9,* 455–468.

INGHAM, A. G., LEVINGER, G., GRAVES, J., & PECKHAM, V. (1974). The Ringelmann effect: Studies of group size and group performance. *Journal of Experimental Social Psychology, 10,* 371–384.

INGLEHART, R. (1990). *Culture shift in advanced industrial society.* Princeton, NJ: Princeton University Press.

INGLEHART, R. (1997). *Modernization and postmodernization: Cultural, economic, and political change in societies.* Princeton, NJ: Princeton University Press.

ISLAM, M. R., & HEWSTONE, M. (1993). Dimensions of contact as predictors of intergroup anxiety, perceived out-group variability, and out-group attitude: An integrative model. *Personality and Social Psychology Bulletin, 19,* 700–710.

ISOZAKI, M. (1984). The effect of discussion on polarization of judgments. *Japanese Psychological Research, 26,* 187–193.

ISR Newsletter (1975). [Institute for Social Research, University of Michigan], *3* (4), 4–7.

ITO, T. A., MILLER, N., & POLLOCK, V. E. (1996). Alcohol and aggression: A meta-analysis on the moderating effects of inhibitory cues, triggering events, and self-focused attention. *Psychological Bulletin, 120,* 60–82.

JACKMAN, M. R., & SENTER, M. S. (1981). Beliefs about race, gender, and social class different, therefore unequal: Beliefs about trait differences between groups of unequal status. In D. J. Treiman & R. V. Robinson (Eds.), *Research in stratification and mobility* (Vol. 2). Greenwich, CT: JAI Press.

JACKSON, J. M., & LATANÉ, B. (1981). All alone in front of all those people: Stage fright as a function of number and type of co-performers and audience. *Journal of Personality and Social Psychology, 40,* 73–85.

JACKSON, L. A. (1989). Relative deprivation and the gender wage gap. *Journal of Social Issues, 45* (4), 117–133.

JACKSON, L. A., HUNTER, J. E., & HODGE, C. N. (1995). Physical attractiveness and intellectual competence: A meta-analytic review. *Social Psychology Quarterly, 58,* 108–122.

JACOBY, S. (1986, December). When opposites attract. *Reader's Digest,* pp. 95–98.

JAIN, U. (1990). Social perspectives on causal attribution. In G. Misra (Ed.), *Applied social psychology in India.* New Delhi: Sage.

JAMIESON, D. W., LYDON, J. E., STEWART, G., & ZANNA, M. P. (1987). Pygmalion revisited: New evidence for student expectancy effects in the classroom. *Journal of Educational Psychology, 79,* 461–466.

JAMIESON, D. W., LYDON, J. E., & ZANNA, M. P. (1987). Attitude and activity preference similarity: Differential bases of interpersonal attraction for low and high self-monitors. *Journal of Personality and Social Psychology, 53,* 1052–1060.

JANIS, I. L. (1971, November). Groupthink. *Psychology Today,* pp. 43–46.

JANIS, I. L. (1982). Counteracting the adverse effects of concurrence-seeking in policy-planning groups: Theory and research perspectives. In H. Brandstatter, J. H. Davis, & G. Stocker-Kreichgauer (Eds.), *Group decision making*. New York: Academic Press.

JANIS, I. L., KAYE, D., & KIRSCHNER, P. (1965). Facilitating effects of eating while reading on responsiveness to persuasive communications. *Journal of Personality and Social Psychology, 1*, 181–186.

JANKOWIAK, W. R., & FISCHER, E. F. (1992). A cross-cultural perspective on romantic love. *Ethnology, 31*, 149–155.

JEFFERY, R. (1964). The psychologist as an expert witness on the issue of insanity. *American Psychologist, 19*, 838–843.

JELLISON, J. M., & GREEN, J. (1981). A self-presentation approach to the fundamental attribution error: The norm of internality. *Journal of Personality and Social Psychology, 40*, 643–649.

JENNINGS, D. L., AMABILE, T. M., & ROSS, L. (1982). Informal covariation assessment: Data-based vs theory-based judgments. In D. Kahneman, P. Slovic, & A. Tversky (Eds.), *Judgment under uncertainty: Heuristics and biases*. New York: Cambridge University Press.

JOHNSON, B. T., & EAGLY, A. H. (1990). Involvement and persuasion: Types, traditions, and the evidence. *Psychological Bulletin, 107*, 375–384.

JOHNSON, D. J., & RUSBULT, C. E. (1989). Resisting temptation: Devaluation of alternative partners as a means of maintaining commitment in close relationships. *Journal of Personality and Social Psychology, 57*, 967–980.

JOHNSON, D. W., MARUYAMA, G., JOHNSON, R., NELSON, D., & SKON, L. (1981). Effects of cooperative, competitive, and individualistic goal structures on achievement: A meta-analysis. *Psychological Bulletin, 89*, 47–62.

JOHNSON, J. D., ADAMS, M. S., ASHBURN, L., & REED, W. (1995). Differential gender effects of exposure to rap music on African American adolescents' acceptance of teen dating violence. *Sex Roles, 33*, 597–605.

JOHNSON, J. T., JEMMOTT, J. B., III, & PETTIGREW, T. F. (1984). Causal attribution and dispositional inference: Evidence of inconsistent judgments. *Journal of Experimental Social Psychology, 20*, 567–585.

JOHNSON, M. H., & MAGARO, P. A. (1987). Effects of mood and severity on memory processes in depression and mania. *Psychological Bulletin, 101*, 28–40.

JOHNSON, R. D., & DOWNING, L. L. (1979). Deindividuation and valence of cues: Effects of prosocial and antisocial behavior. *Journal of Personality and Social Psychology, 37*, 1532–1538.

JOHNSTON, L. D. (1996, December 19). Monitoring the future study of drug use. News and Information Services, University of Michigan.

JOINER, T. E., JR. (1994). Contagious depression: Existence, specificity to depressed symptoms, and the role of reassurance seeking. *Journal of Personality and Social Psychology, 67*, 287–296.

JONES, E. E. (1976). How do people perceive the causes of behavior? *American Scientist, 64*, 300–305.

JONES, E. E., & HARRIS, V. A. (1967). The attribution of attitudes. *Journal of Experimental Social Psychology, 3*, 2–24.

JONES, E. E., & NISBETT, R. E. (1971). *The actor and the observer: Divergent perceptions of the cases of behavior.* Morristown, NJ: General Learning Press.

JONES, E. E., RHODEWALT, F., BERGLAS, S., & SKELTON, J. A. (1981). Effects of strategic self-presentation on subsequent self-esteem. *Journal of Personality and Social Psychology, 41*, 407–421.

JONES, J. M. (1983). The concept of race in social psychology: From color to culture. In L. Wheeler & P. Shaver (Eds.), *Review of personality and social psychology* (Vol. 4). Beverly Hills, CA: Sage.

JONES, W. H., CARPENTER, B. N., & QUINTANA, D. (1985). Personality and interpersonal predictors of loneliness in two cultures. *Journal of Personality and Social Psychology, 48*, 1503–1511.

JONES, W. H., FREEMON, J. E., & GOSWICK, R. A. (1981). The persistence of loneliness: Self and other determinants. *Journal of Personality, 49*, 27–48.

JONES, W. H., HOBBS, S. A., & HOCKENBURY, D. (1982). Loneliness and social skill deficits. *Journal of Personality and Social Psychology, 42*, 682–689.

JONES, W. H., SANSONE, C., & HELM, B. (1983). Loneliness and interpersonal judgments. *Personality and Social Psychology Bulletin, 9*, 437–441.

JOSEPHSON, W. L. (1987). Television violence and children's aggression: Testing the priming, social script, and disinhibition predictions. *Journal of Personality and Social Psychology, 53*, 882–890.

JOURARD, S. M. (1964), *The transparent self.* Princeton, NJ: Van Nostrand.

JOURDEN, F. J., & HEATH, C. (1996). The evaluation gap in performance perceptions: Illusory perceptions of groups and individuals. *Journal of Applied Psychology, 81*, 369–379.

JUDD, C. M., PARK, B., RYAN, C. S., BRAUER, M., & KRAUS, S. (1995). Stereotypes and ethnocentrism: Diverging interethnic perceptions of African American and White American youth. *Journal of Personality and Social Psychology, 69*, 460–481.

JUDD, C. M., RYAN, C. S., & PARK, B. (1991). Accuracy in the judgment of in-group and out-group variability. *Journal of Personality and Social Psychology, 61*, 366–379.

JUSSIM, L. (1986). Self-fulfilling prophecies: A theoretical and integrative review. *Psychological Review, 93*, 429–445.

JUSSIM, L. (1989). Teacher expectations: Self-fulfilling prophecies, perceptual biases, and accuracy. *Journal of Personality and Social Psychology, 57*, 469–480.

JUSSIM, L. (1991). Social perception and social reality: A reflection-construction model. *Psychological Review, 98*, 54–73.

JUSSIM, L., ECCLES, J., & MADON, S. (1996). Social perception, social stereotypes, and teacher expectations: Accuracy and the quest for the powerful self-fulfilling prophecy. *Advances in Experimental Social Psychology, 29*, 281–388.

KAGAN, J. (1989). Temperamental contributions to social behavior. *American Psychologist, 44*, 668–674.

KAHN, M. W. (1951). The effect of severe defeat at various age levels on the aggressive behavior of mice. *Journal of Genetic Psychology, 79*, 117–130.

KAHNEMAN, D., & SNELL, J. (1992). Predicting a changing taste: Do people know what they will like? *Journal of Behavioral Decision Making, 5*, 187–200.

KAHNEMAN, D., & TVERSKY, A. (1979). Intuitive prediction: Biases and corrective procedures. *Management Science, 12*, 313–327.

KAHNEMAN, D., & TVERSKY, A. (1995). Conflict resolution: A cognitive perspective. In K. Arrow, R. Mnookin, L. Ross, A. Tversky, & R. Wilson (Eds.), *Barriers to the negotiated resolution of conflict.* New York: W. W. Norton.

KALICK, S. M. (1977). *Plastic surgery, physical appearance, and person perception.* Unpublished doctoral dissertation, Harvard University. Cited by E. Berscheid in An overview of the psychological effects of physical attractiveness and some comments upon the psychological effects of knowledge of the effects of physical attractiveness. In W. Lucker, K. Ribbens, & J. A. McNamera (Eds.), *Logical aspects of facial form* (craniofacial growth series). Ann Arbor: University of Michigan Press, 1981.

KAMEDA, T., & SUGIMORI, S. (1993). Psychological entrapment in group decision making: An assigned decision rule and a groupthink phenomenon. *Journal of Personality and Social Psychology, 65,* 282–292.

KAMMANN, R. (1983). Objective circumstances, life satisfactions, and sense of well-being: Consistencies across time and place. *New Zealand Journal of Psychology, 12,* 14–22.

KAMMER, D. (1982). Differences in trait ascriptions to self and friend: Unconfounding intensity from variability. *Psychological Reports, 51,* 99–102.

KANDEL, D. B. (1978). Similarity in real-life adolescent friendship pairs. *Journal of Personality and Social Psychology, 36,* 306–312.

KAPLAN, M. F. (1989). Task, situational, and personal determinants of influence processes in group decision making. In E. J. Lawler (Ed.), *Advances in group processes* (Vol. 6). Greenwich, CT: JAI Press.

KAPLAN, M. F., WANSHULA, L. T., & ZANNA, M. P. (1993). Time pressure and information integration in social judgment: The effect of need for structure. In O. Svenson & J. Maule (Eds.), *Time pressure and stress in human judgment and decision making.* Cambridge, England: Cambridge University Press.

KARAU, S. J., & WILLIAMS, K. D. (1993). Social loafing: A meta-analytic review and theoretical integration. *Journal of Personality and Social Psychology, 65,* 681–706.

KARNEY, B. R., & BRADBURY, T. N. (1995). The longitudinal course of marital quality and stability: A review of theory, method, and research. *Psychological Bulletin, 118,* 3–34.

KATZ, A. M., & HILL, R. (1958). Residential propinquity and marital selection: A review of theory, method, and fact. *Marriage and Family Living, 20,* 237–335.

KAUFMAN, J., & ZIGLER, E. (1987). Do abused children become abusive parents? *American Journal of Orthopsychiatry, 57,* 186–192.

KEATING, J. P., & BROCK, T. C. (1974). Acceptance of persuasion and the inhibition of counterargumentation under various distraction tasks. *Journal of Experimental Social Psychology, 10,* 301–309.

KELLERMAN, J., LEWIS, J., & LAIRD, J. D. (1989). Looking and loving: The effects of mutual gaze on feelings of romantic love. *Journal of Research in Personality, 23,* 145–161.

KELLEY, H. H., & STAHELSKI, A. J. (1970). The social interaction basis of cooperators' and competitors' beliefs about others. *Journal of Personality and Social Psychology, 16,* 66–91.

KELMAN, H. C. (1997). Group processes in the resolution of international conflicts: Experiences from the Israeli-Palestinian case. *American Psychologist, 52,* 212–220.

KELTNER, D., & ROBINSON, R. J. (1996). Extremism, power, and the imagined basis of social conflict. *Current Directions in Psychological Science, 5,* 101–105.

KENDLER, K. S., NEALE, M., KESSLER, R., HEATH, A., & EAVES, L. (1993). A twin study of recent life events and difficulties. *Archives of General Psychiatry, 50,* 789–796.

KENNY, D. A., & ALBRIGHT, L. (1987). Accuracy in interpersonal perception: A social relations analysis. *Psychology Bulletin, 102,* 390–402.

KENNY, D. A., & DEPAULO, B. M. (1993). Do people know how others view them? An empirical and theoretical account. *Psychological Bulletin, 114,* 145–161.

KENNY, D. A., & NASBY, W. (1980). Splitting the reciprocity correlation. *Journal of Personality and Social Psychology, 38,* 249–256.

KENRICK, D. T. (1987). Gender, genes, and the social environment: A biosocial interactionist perspective. In P. Shaver & C. Hendrick (Eds.), *Sex and gender: Review of personality and social psychology* (Vol. 7). Beverly Hills, CA: Sage.

KENRICK, D. T., & GUTIERRES, S. E. (1980). Contrast effects and judgments of physical attractiveness: When beauty becomes a social problem. *Journal of Personality and Social Psychology, 38,* 131–140.

KENRICK, D. T., GUTIERRES, S. E., & GOLDBERG, L. L. (1989). Influence of popular erotica on judgments of strangers and mates. *Journal of Experimental Social Psychology, 25,* 159–167.

KENRICK, D. T., & MACFARLANE, S. W. (1986). Ambient temperature and horn-honking: A field study of the heat/aggression relationship. *Environment and Behavior, 18,* 179–191.

KENRICK, D. T., & TROST, M. R. (1987). A biosocial theory of heterosexual relationships. In K. Kelly (Ed.), *Females, males, and sexuality.* Albany: State University of New York Press.

KERR, N. L. (1983). Motivation losses in small groups: A social dilemma analysis. *Journal of Personality and Social Psychology, 45,* 819–828.

KERR, N. L. (1989). Illusions of efficacy: The effects of group size on perceived efficacy in social dilemmas. *Journal of Experimental Social Psychology, 25,* 287–313.

KERR, N. L., & BRUUN, S. E. (1981). Ringelmann revisited: Alternative explanations for the social loafing effect. *Personality and Social Psychology Bulletin, 7,* 224–231.

KERR, N. L., & BRUUN, S. E. (1983). Dispensibility of member effort and group motivation losses: Free-rider effects. *Journal of Personality and Social Psychology, 44,* 78–94.

KERR, N. L., HARMON, D. L., & GRAVES, J. K. (1982). Independence of multiple verdicts by jurors and juries. *Journal of Applied Social Psychology, 12,* 12–29.

KIDD, J. B., & MORGAN, J. R. (1969). A predictive information system for management. *Operational Research Quarterly, 20,* 149–170.

KIERKEGAARD, S. (1851/1944). *For self-examination* and *Judge for yourself.* Trans. W. Lowrie. Princeton, NJ: Princeton University Press.

KIESLER, C. A. (1971). *The psychology of commitment: Experiments linking behavior to belief.* New York: Academic Press.

KIMMEL, M. J., PRUITT, D. G., MAGENAU, J. M., KONAR-GOLDBAND, E., & CARNEVALE, P. J. D. (1980). Effects of trust, aspiration, and gender on negotiation tactics. *Journal of Personality and Social Psychology, 38,* 9–22.

KINDER, D. R., & SEARS, D. O. (1985). Public opinion and political action. In G. Lindzey & E. Aronson (Eds.), *The handbook of social psychology* (3rd ed.). New York: Random House.

KINZER, S. (1998, December 21). This time, little damage is to be seen in Baghdad. *New York Times.* (Retrieved from the World Wide Web: www.nytimes.com.)

KIRMEYER, S. L. (1978). Urban density and pathology: A review of research. *Environment and Behavior, 10,* 257–269.

KITAYAMA, S., & KARASAWA, M. (1997). Implicit self-esteem in Japan: Name letters and birthday numbers. *Personality and Social Psychology Bulletin, 23,* 736–742.

KLAAS, E. T. (1978). Psychological effects of immoral actions: The experimental evidence. *Psychological Bulletin, 85,* 756–771.

KLASEN, S. (1994). "Missing women" reconsidered. *World Development, 22,* 1061–1071.

KLECK, R. E., & STRENTA, A. (1980). Perceptions of the impact of negatively valued physical characteristics on social interaction. *Journal of Personality and Social Psychology, 39,* 861–873.

KLEIN, J. G. (1991). Negative effects in impression formation: A test in the political arena. *Personality and Social Psychology Bulletin, 17,* 412–418.

KLEIN, W. M., & KUNDA, Z. (1992). Motivated person perception: Constructing justifications for desired beliefs. *Journal of Experimental Social Psychology, 28,* 145–168.

KLEINKE, C. L. (1977). Compliance to requests made by gazing and touching experimenters in field settings. *Journal of Experimental Social Psychology, 13,* 218–223.

KLENTZ, B., BEAMAN, A. L., MAPELLI, S. D., & ULLRICH, J. R. (1987). Perceived physical attractiveness of supporters and nonsupporters of the women's movement: An attitude-similarity-mediated error (AS-ME). *Personality and Social Psychology Bulletin, 13,* 513–523.

KLERMAN, G. L., & WEISSMAN, M. M. (1989). Increasing rates of depression. *Journal of the American Medical Association, 261,* 229–235.

KNIGHT, G. P., FABES, R. A., & HIGGINS, D. A. (1996). Concerns about drawing causal inferences from meta-analyses: An example in the study of gender differences in aggression. *Psychological Bulletin, 119,* 410–421.

KNIGHT, J. A., & VALLACHER, R. R. (1981). Interpersonal engagement in social perception: The consequences of getting into the action. *Journal of Personality and Social Psychology, 40,* 990–999.

KNOWLES, E. S. (1983). Social physics and the effects of others: Tests of the effects of audience size and distance on social judgment and behavior. *Journal of Personality and Social Psychology, 45,* 1263–1279.

KNUDSON, R. M., SOMMERS, A. A., & GOLDING, S. L. (1980). Interpersonal perception and mode of resolution in marital conflict. *Journal of Personality and Social Psychology, 38,* 751–763.

KOEHLER, D. J. (1991). Explanation, imagination, and confidence in judgment. *Psychological Bulletin, 110,* 499–519.

KOENIG, H. G. (1997). *Is religion good for your health? The effects of religion on physical and mental health.* Binghamton, NY: Haworth Press.

KOESTNER, R., & WHEELER, L. (1988). Self-presentation in personal advertisements: The influence of implicit notions of attraction and role expectations. *Journal of Social and Personal Relationships, 5,* 149–160.

KOESTNER, R. F. (1993). *False consensus effects for the 1992 Canadian referendum.* Paper presented at the American Psychological Association.

KOMORITA, S. S., & BARTH, J. M. (1985). Components of reward in social dilemmas. *Journal of Personality and Social Psychology, 48,* 364–373.

KOMORITA, S. S., PARKS, C. D., & HULBERT, L. G. (1992). Reciprocity and the induction of cooperation in social dilemmas. *Journal of Personality and Social Psychology, 62,* 607–617.

KOOP, C. E. (1987). Report of the Surgeon General's workshop on pornography and public health. *American Psychologist, 42,* 944–945.

KORIAT, A., LICHTENSTEIN, S., & FISCHHOFF, B. (1980). Reasons for confidence. *Journal of Experimental Social Psychology: Human Learning and Memory, 6,* 107–118.

KORN, J. H., & NICKS, S. D. (1993). *The rise and decline of deception in social psychology.* Poster presented at the American Psychological Society convention.

KOSS, M. P. (1990, August 29). *Rape incidence: A review and assessment of the data.* Testimony on behalf of the American Psychological Association before the U.S. Senate Judiciary Committee.

KOSS, M. P. (1993). Rape: Scope, impact, interventions, and public policy responses. *American Psychologist, 48,* 1062–1069.

KOSS, M. P., DINERO, T. E., SEIBEL, C. A., & COX, S. L. (1988). Stranger and acquaintance rape. *Psychology of Women, 12,* 1–24.

KRACKOW, A., & BLASS, T. (1995). When nurses obey or defy inappropriate physician orders: Attributional differences. *Journal of Social Behavior and Personality, 10,* 585–594.

KRAUT, R. E., & POE, D. (1980). Behavioral roots of person perception: The deception judgments of customs inspectors and laymen. *Journal of Personality and Social Psychology, 39,* 784–798.

KRAVITZ, D. A., & MARTIN, B. (1986). Ringelmann rediscovered: The original article. *Journal of Personality and Social Psychology, 50,* 936–941.

KREBS, D., & ADINOLFI, A. A. (1975). Physical attractiveness, social relations, and personality style. *Journal of Personality and Social Psychology, 31,* 245–253.

KRISTOF, N. (1993, July 22). China faces huge surplus of males as scans hold key to missing girls. *Guardian* (England), p. 22.

KROSNICK, J. A., & ALWIN, D. F. (1989). Aging and susceptibility to attitude change. *Journal of Personality and Social Psychology, 57,* 416–425.

KRUEGER, J. (1996). Personal beliefs and cultural stereotypes about racial characteristics. *Journal of Personality and Social Psychology, 71,* 536–548.

KRUEGER, J., & CLEMENT, R. W. (1994). Memory-based judgments about multiple categories: A revision and extension of Tajfel's accentuation theory. *Journal of Personality and Social Psychology, 67,* 35–47.

KRUGLANSKI, A. W., & WEBSTER, D. M. (1991). Group members' reactions to opinion deviates and conformists at varying degrees of proximity to decision deadline and of environmental noise. *Journal of Personality and Social Psychology, 61,* 212–225.

KRUGLANSKI, A. W., WEBSTER, D. M., & KLEM, A. (1993). Motivated resistance and openness to persuasion in the presence or absence of prior information. *Journal of Personality and Social Psychology, 65,* 861–876.

KUBANY, E. S., BAUER, G. B., PANGILINAN, M. E., MUROKA, M. Y., & ENRIQUEZ, V. G. (1995). Impact of labeled anger and blame in intimate relationships. *Journal of Cross-Cultural Psychology, 26,* 65–83.

KUIPER, N. A., & HIGGINS, E. T. (1985). Social cognition and depression: A general integrative perspective. *Social Cognition, 3,* 1–15.

KUNDA, Z. (1990). The case for motivated reasoning. *Psychological Bulletin, 108,* 480–498.

LAGERSPETZ, K. (1979). Modification of aggressiveness in mice. In S. Feshbach & A. Fraczek (Eds.), *Aggression and behavior change.* New York: Praeger.

LALONDE, R. N. (1992). The dynamics of group differentiation in the face of defeat. *Personality and Social Psychology Bulletin, 18,* 336–342.

LAMAL, P. A. (1979). College student common beliefs about psychology. *Teaching of Psychology, 6,* 155–158.

LANDERS, A. (1969, April 8). Syndicated newspaper column. April 8, 1969. Cited by L. Berkowitz in, The case for bottling up rage. *Psychology Today,* September, 1973, pp. 24–31.

LANGER, E. J. (1977). The psychology of chance. *Journal for the Theory of Social Behavior, 7,* 185–208.

LANGER, E. J., & IMBER, L. (1980). The role of mindlessness in the perception of deviance. *Journal of Personality and Social Psychology, 39,* 360–367.

LANGER, E. J., JANIS, I. L., & WOFER, J. A. (1975). Reduction of psychological stress in surgical patients. *Journal of Experimental Social Psychology, 11,* 155–165.

LANGER, E. J., & RODIN, J. (1976). The effects of choice and enhanced personal responsibility for the aged: A field experiment in an institutional setting. *Journal of Personality and Social Psychology, 334,* 191–198.

LANGLOIS, J. H., KALAKANIS, L., RUBENSTEIN, A., LARSON, A., HALLAM, M., & SMOOT, M. (1996). *Maxims and myths of beauty: A meta-analytic and theoretical review.* Paper presented to the American Psychological Society convention.

LANGLOIS, J. H., & ROGGMAN, L. A. (1990). Attractive faces are only average. *Psychological Science, 1,* 115–121.

LANGLOIS, J. H., ROGGMAN, L. A., & MUSSELMAN, L. (1994). What is average and what is not average about attractive faces? *Psychological Science, 5,* 214–220.

LANGLOIS, J. H., ROGGMAN, L. A., CASEY, R. J., RITTER, J. M., RIESER-DANNER, L. A., & JENKINS, V. Y. (1987). Infant preferences for attractive faces: Rudiments of a stereotype? *Developmental Psychology, 23,* 363–369.

LANGLOIS, J. H., & STEPHAN, C. W. (1981). Beauty and the beast: The role of physical attractiveness in the development of peer relations and social behavior. In S. S. Brehm, S. M. Kassin, & F. X. Gibbons (Eds.), *Developmental social psychology.* New York: Oxford University Press.

LANZETTA, J. T. (1955). Group behavior under stress. *Human Relations, 8,* 29–53.

LARSON, J. R., JR., FOSTER-FISHMAN, P. G., & KEYS, C. B. (1994). Discussion of shared and unshared information in decision-making groups. *Journal of Personality and Social Psychology, 67,* 446–461.

LARSSON, K. (1956). *Conditioning and sexual behavior in the male albino rat.* Stockholm: Almqvist & Wiksell.

LARWOOD, L. (1978). Swine flu: A field study of self-serving biases. *Journal of Applied Social Psychology, 18,* 283–289.

LARWOOD, L., & WHITTAKER, W. (1977). Managerial myopia: Self-serving biases in organizational planning. *Journal of Applied Psychology, 62,* 194–198.

LASSITER, G. D., & DUDLEY, K. A. (1991). The *a priori* value of basic research: The case of videotaped confessions. *Journal of Social Behavior and Personality, 6,* 7–16.

LASSITER, G. D., & IRVINE, A. A. (1986). Videotaped confessions: The impact of camera point of view on judgments of coercion. *Journal of Applied Social Psychology, 16,* 268–276.

LATANÉ, B., & DABBS, J. M., JR. (1975). Sex, group size and helping in three cities. *Sociometry, 38,* 180–194.

LATANÉ, B., & DARLEY, J. M. (1968). Group inhibition of bystander intervention in emergencies. *Journal of Personality and Social Psychology, 10,* 215–221.

LATANÉ, B., & DARLEY, J. M. (1970). *The unresponsive bystander: Why doesn't he help?* New York: Appleton-Century-Crofts.

LATANÉ, B., & NIDA, S. (1981). Ten years of research on group size and helping. *Psychological Bulletin, 89,* 308–324.

LATANÉ, B., WILLIAMS, K., & HARKINS, S. (1979). Many hands make light the work: The causes and consequences of social loafing. *Journal of Personality and Social Psychology, 37,* 822–832.

LAUMANN, E. O., GAGNON, J. H., MICHAEL, R. T., & MICHAELS, S. (1994). *The social organization of sexuality: Sexual practices in the United States.* Chicago: University of Chicago Press.

LAYDEN, M. A. (1982). Attributional therapy. In C. Antaki & C. Brewin (Eds.), *Attributions and psychological change: Applications of attributional theories to clinical and educational practice.* London: Academic Press.

LAZARSFELD, P. F. (1949). *The American soldier—An expository review.* Public Opinion Quarterly, 13, 377–404.

LEARY, M. R. (1998). The social and psychological importance of self-esteem. In R. M. Kowalski and M. R. Leary (Eds.), *The social psychology of emotional and behavioral problems.* Washington, DC: APA Books.

LEARY, M. R., & KOWALSKI, R. M. (1995). *Social anxiety.* New York: Guilford.

LEARY, M. R., TCHVIDJIAN, L. R., & KRAXBERGER, B. E. (1994). Self-presentation can be hazardous to your health: Impression management and health risk. *Health Psychology, 13,* 461–470.

LEDOUX, J. (1994, June). Emotion, memory and the brain. *Scientific American,* pp. 50–57.

LEDOUX, J. (1996). *The emotional brain: The mysterious underpinnings of emotional life.* New York: Simon & Schuster.

LEE, F., HALLAHAN, M., & HERZOG, T. (1996). Explaining real-life events: How culture and domain shape attributions. *Personality and Social Psychology Bulletin, 22,* 732–741.

LEE, J. A. (1988). Love-styles. In R. J. Sternberg & M. L. Barnes (Eds.), *The psychology of love.* New Haven: Yale University Press.

LEE, Y-T., & SELIGMAN, M. E. P. (1997). Are Americans more optimistic than the Chinese? *Personality and Social Psychology Bulletin, 23,* 32–40.

LEFCOURT, H. M. (1982). *Locus of control: Current trends in theory and research.* Hillsdale, NJ: Erlbaum.

LEFEBVRE, L. M. (1979). Causal attributions for basketball outcomes by players and coaches. *Psychological Belgica, 19,* 109–115.

LEIPPE, M. R., & ELKIN, R. A. (1987). *Dissonance reduction strategies and accountability to self and others: Ruminations and some initial research.* Presentation to the Fifth International Conference on Affect, Motivation, and Cognition, Nags Head Conference Center.

LEMYRE, L., & SMITH, P. M. (1985). Intergroup discrimination and self-esteem in the minimal group paradigm. *Journal of Personality and Social Psychology, 49,* 660–670.

LENIHAN, K. J. (1965). *Perceived climates as a barrier to housing desegregation.* Unpublished manuscript, Bureau of Applied Social Research, Columbia University.

LENNON, J., & McCARTNEY, P. (1967). *Sgt. Pepper's lonely hearts club band* [Record album].

LERNER, M. J. (1980). *The belief in a just world: A fundamental delusion.* New York: Plenum Press.

LERNER, M. J., & MILLER, D. T. (1978). Just world research and the attribution process: Looking back and ahead. *Psychological Bulletin, 85,* 1030–1051.

LERNER, M. J., & SIMMONS, C. H. (1966). Observer's reaction to the "innocent victim": Compassion or rejection? *Journal of Personality and Social Psychology, 4,* 203–210.

LERNER, M. J., SOMERS, D. G., REID, D., CHIRIBOGA, D., & TIERNEY, M. (1991). Adult children as caregivers: Egocentric biases in judgments of sibling contributions. *Gerontologist, 31,* 746–755.

LEVENTHAL, H. (1970). Findings and theory in the study of fear communications. In L. Berkowitz (Ed.), *Advances in experimental social psychology* (Vol. 5). New York: Academic Press.

LEVER, J. (1978). Sex differences in the complexity of children's play and games. *American Sociological Review, 43,* 471–483.

LEVINE, J. M. (1989). Reaction to opinion deviance in small groups. In P. Paulus (Ed.), *Psychology of group influence: New perspectives.* Hillsdale, NJ: Erlbaum.

LEVINE, J. M., & MORELAND, R. L. (1985). Innovation and socialization in small groups. In S. Moscovici, G. Mugny, & E. Van Avermaet (Eds.), *Perspectives on minority influence.* Cambridge, England: Cambridge University Press.

LEVINE, J. M., & RUSSO, E. M. (1987). Majority and minority influence. In C. Hendrick (Ed.) *Group processes: Review of personality and social psychology* (Vol. 8). Newbury Park, CA: Sage.

LEVINE, R., SATO, S., HASHIMOTO, T., & VERMA, J. (1995). Love and marriage in eleven cultures. *Journal of Cross-Cultural Psychology, 26,* 554–571.

LEVINE, R., & ULEMAN, J. S. (1979). Perceived locus of control, chronic self-esteem, and attributions to success and failure. *Journal of Personality and Social Psychology, 5,* 69–72.

LEVY-LEBOYER, C. (1988). Success and failure in applying psychology. *American Psychologist, 43,* 779–785.

LEWICKI, P. (1983). Self-image bias in person perception. *Journal of Personality and Social Psychology, 45,* 384–393.

LEWINSOHN, P. M., HOBERMAN, H., TERI, L., & HAUTZINER, M. (1985). An integrative theory of depression. In S. Reiss & R. Bootzin (Eds.), *Theoretical issues in behavior therapy.* New York: Academic Press.

LEWINSOHN, P. M., MISCHEL, W., CHAPLINE, W., & BARTON, R. (1980). Social competence and depression: The role of illusionary self-perceptions. *Journal of Abnormal Psychology, 89,* 203–212.

LEWINSOHN, P. M., & ROSENBAUM, M. (1987). Recall of parental behavior by acute depressives, remitted depressives, and nondepressives. *Journal of Personality and Social Psychology, 52,* 611–619.

LEWIS, C. S. (1960). *Mere Christianity.* New York: Macmillan.

LEYENS, J. P., CAMINO, L., PARKE, R. D., & BERKOWITZ, L. (1975). Effects of movie violence on aggression in a field setting as a function of group dominance and cohesion. *Journal of Personality and Social Psychology, 32,* 346–360.

LICHTENSTEIN, S., & FISCHHOFF, B. (1980). Training for calibration. *Organizational Behavior and Human Performance, 26,* 149–171.

LIEBERT, R. M., & BARON, R. A. (1972). Some immediate effects of televised violence on children's behavior. *Developmental Psychology, 6,* 469–475.

LIEBRAND, W. B. G., MESSICK, D. M., & WOLTERS, F. J. M. (1986). Why we are fairer than others: A cross-cultural replication and extension. *Journal of Experimental Social Psychology, 22,* 590–604.

LINDSKOLD, S. (1978). Trust development, the GRIT proposal, and the effects of conciliatory acts on conflict and cooperation. *Psychological Bulletin, 85,* 772–793.

LINDSKOLD, S. (1979a). Conciliation with simultaneous or sequential interaction: Variations in trustworthiness and vulnerability in the prisoner's dilemma. *Journal of Conflict Resolution, 27,* 704–714.

LINDSKOLD, S. (1979b). Managing conflict through announced conciliatory initiatives backed with retaliatory capability. In W. G. Austin & S. Worchel (Eds.), *The social psychology of intergroup relations.* Monterey, CA: Brooks/Cole.

LINDSKOLD, S. (1981). *The laboratory evaluation of GRIT: Trust, cooperation, aversion to using conciliation.* Paper presented at the American Association for the Advancement of Science convention.

LINDSKOLD, S. (1983). Cooperators, competitors, and response to GRIT. *Journal of Conflict Resolution, 27,* 521–532.

LINDSKOLD, S., & ARONOFF, J. R. (1980). Conciliatory strategies and relative power. *Journal of Experimental Social Psychology, 16,* 187–198.

LINDSKOLD, S., BENNETT, R., & WAYNER, M. (1976). Retaliation level as a foundation for subsequent conciliation. *Behavioral Science, 21,* 13–18.

LINDSKOLD, S., BETZ, B., & WALTERS, P. S. (1986). Transforming competitive or cooperative climate. *Journal of Conflict Resolution, 30,* 99–114.

LINDSKOLD, S., & COLLINS, M. G. (1978). Inducing cooperation by groups and individuals. *Journal of Conflict Resolution, 22,* 679–690.

LINDSKOLD, S., & FINCH, M. L. (1981). Styles of announcing conciliation. *Journal of Conflict Resolution, 25,* 145–155.

LINDSKOLD, S., & HAN, G. (1988). GRIT as a foundation for integrative bargaining. *Personality and Social Psychology Bulletin, 14,* 335–345.

LINDSKOLD, S., HAN, G., & BETZ, B. (1986a). The essential elements of communication in the GRIT strategy. *Personality and Social Psychology Bulletin, 12,* 179–186.

LINDSKOLD, S., HAN, G., & BETZ, B. (1986b). Repeated persuasion in interpersonal conflict. *Journal of Personality and Social Psychology, 51,* 1183–1188.

LINDSKOLD, S., WALTERS, P. S., KOUTSOURAIS, H., & SHAYO, R. (1981). *Cooperators, competitors, and response to GRIT.* Unpublished manuscript, Ohio University.

LINEHAM, M. M. (1997). Self-verification and drug abusers: Implications for treatment. *Psychological Science, 8,* 181–184.

LINVILLE, P. W., GISCHER, G. W., & SALOVEY, P. (1989). Perceived distributions of the characteristics of in-group and out-group members: Empirical evidence and a computer simulation. *Journal of Personality and Social Psychology, 57,* 165–188.

LINZ, D. G., DONNERSTEIN, E., & ADAMS, S. M. (1989). Physiological desensitization and judgments about female victims of violence. *Human Communication Research, 15,* 509–522.

LINZ, D. G., DONNERSTEIN, E., & PENROD, S. (1988). Effects of long term exposure to violent and sexually degrading depictions of women. *Journal of Personality and Social Psychology, 55,* 758–768.

LIPSITZ, A., KALLMEYER, K., FERGUSON, M., & ABAS, A. (1989). Counting on blood donors: Increasing the impact of reminder calls. *Journal of Applied Social Psychology, 19,* 1057–1067.

LOCKE, E. A., & LATHAM, G. P. (1990). Work motivation and satisfaction: Light at the end of the tunnel. *Psychological Science, 1,* 240–246.

LOCKSLEY, A., ORTIZ, V., & HEPBURN, C. (1980). Social categorization and discriminatory behavior: Extinguishing the minimal intergroup discrimination effect. *Journal of Personality and Social Psychology, 39,* 773–783.

LOEWENSTEIN, G., & SCHKADE, D. (1999). Wouldn't it be nice? Predicting future feelings. In D. Kahneman, E. Diener, & N. Schwarz (Eds.), *Understanding well-being: Scientific perspectives on enjoyment and suffering.* New York: Russell Sage Foundation.

LOFLAND, J., & STARK, R. (1965). Becoming a worldsaver: A theory of conversion to a deviant perspective. *American Sociological Review, 30,* 862–864.

LOFTIN, C., McDOWALL, D., WIERSEMA, B., & COTTEY, T. J. (1991). Effects of restrictive licensing of handguns on homicide and suicide in the District of Columbia. *New England Journal of Medicine, 325,* 1615–1620.

LOFTUS, E. F., & KLINGER, M. R. (1992). Is the unconscious smart or dumb? *American Psychologist, 47,* 761–765.

LORD, C. G., ROSS, L., & LEPPER, M. (1979). Biased assimilation and attitude polarization: The effects of prior theories on subsequently considered evidence. *Journal of Personality and Social Psychology, 37,* 2098–2109.

LORENZ, K. (1976). *On aggression.* New York: Bantam Books.

LOVETT, F. (1997). Thinking about values (report of December 13, 1996 *Wall Street Journal* national survey). *The Responsive Community, 7* (2), 87.

LOWE, R. H., & WITTIG, M. A. (1989). Comparable worth: Individual, interpersonal, and structural considerations. *Journal of Social Issues, 45,* 223–246.

LUEPTOW, L. B., GAROVICH, L., & LUEPTOW, M. B. (1995). The persistence of gender stereotypes in the face of changing sex roles: Evidence contrary to the sociocultural model. *Ethology and Sociobiology, 16,* 509–530.

LYDON, J., & DUNKEL-SCHETTER, C. (1994). Seeing is committing: A longitudinal study of bolstering commitment in amniocentesis patients. *Personality and Social Psychology Bulletin, 20,* 218–227.

LYKKEN, D. (1999). *Happiness.* New York: Golden Books.

LYKKEN, D., & TELLEGAN, A. (1996). Happiness is a stochastic phenomenon. *Psychological Science, 7,* 186–189.

LYNN, M., & OLDENQUIST, A. (1986). Egoistic and nonegoistic motives in social dilemmas. *American Psychologist, 41,* 529–534.

MAASS, A., & CLARK, R. D., III (1984). Hidden impact of minorities: Fifteen years of minority influence research. *Psychological Bulletin, 95,* 428–450.

MAASS, A., & CLARK, R. D., III (1986). Conversion theory and simultaneous majority/minority influence: Can reactance offer an alternative explanation? *European Journal of Social Psychology, 16,* 305–309.

MAASS, A., VOLPARO, C., & MUCCHI-FAINA, A. (1996). Social influence and the verifiability of the issue under discussion: Attitudinal versus objective items. *British Journal of Social Psychology, 35,* 15–26.

MACK, D., & RAINEY, D. (1990). Female applicants' grooming and personnel selection. *Journal of Social Behavior and Personality, 5,* 399–407.

MACKAY, J. L. (1980). Selfhood: Comment on Brewster Smith. *American Psychologist, 35,* 106–107.

MACKIE, D. M. (1987). Systematic and nonsystematic processing of majority and minority persuasive communications. *Journal of Personality and Social Psychology, 53,* 41–52.

MACRAE, C. N., BODENHAUSEN, G. V., MILNE, A. B., & JETTEN, J. (1994). Out of mind but back in sight: Stereotypes on the rebound. *Journal of Personality and Social Psychology, 67,* 808–817.

MACRAE, C. N., STANGOR, C., & MILNE, A. B. (1994). Activating social stereotypes: A functional analysis. *Journal of Experimental Social Psychology, 30,* 370–389.

MADDUX, J. E. (1991). Personal efficacy. In V. Derlega, B. Winstead, & W. Jones (Eds.), *Personality: Contemporary theory and research* (2nd ed.). New York: Nelson-Hall.

MADDUX, J. E. (1993). The mythology of psychopathology: A social cognitive view of deviance, difference, and disorder. *General Psychologist, 29* (2), 34–45.

MADDUX, J. E., & ROGERS, R. W. (1983). Protection motivation and self-efficacy: A revised theory of fear appeals and attitude change. *Journal of Experimental Social Psychology, 19,* 469–479.

MAGNUSON, E. (1986, March 10). "A serious deficiency": The Rogers Commission faults NASA's "flawed" decision-making process. *Time* [international ed.], pp. 40–42.

MAJOR, B. (1989). Gender differences in comparisons and entitlement: Implications for comparable worth. *Journal of Social Issues, 45,* 99–116.

MAJOR, B. (1993). Gender, entitlement, and the distribution of family labor. *Journal of Social Issues, 49,* 141–159.

MAJOR, B., SCHMIDLIN, A. M., & WILLIAMS, L. (1990). Gender patterns in social touch: The impact of setting and age. *Journal of Personality and Social Psychology, 58,* 634–643.

MALAMUTH, N. M., & CHECK, J. V. P. (1981). The effects of media exposure on acceptance of violence against women: A field experiment. *Journal of Research in Personality, 15,* 436–446.

MALAMUTH, N. M., & CHECK, J. V. P. (1984). Debriefing effectiveness following exposure to pornographic rape depictions. *Journal of Sex Research, 20,* 1–13.

MALAMUTH, N. M., LINZ, D., HEAVEY, C. L., BARNES, G., & ACKER, M. (1995). Using the confluence model of sexual aggression to predict men's conflict with women: A 10-year follow-up study. *Journal of Personality and Social Psychology, 69,* 353–369.

MALKIEL, B. G. (1985). *A random walk down Wall Street* (4th ed.). New York: W. W. Norton.

MALKIEL, B. G. (1995, June). Returns from investing in equity mutual funds 1971 to 1991. *Journal of Finance,* pp. 549–572.

MANN, L. (1981). The baiting crowd in episodes of threatened suicide. *Journal of Personality and Social Psychology, 41,* 703–709.

MARCUS, S. (1974, January 13). Review of *Obedience to authority. New York Times Book Review,* pp. 1–2.

MARKMAN, H. J., FLOYD, F. J., STANLEY, S. M., & STORAASLI, R. D. (1988). Prevention of marital distress: A longitudinal investigation. *Journal of Consulting and Clinical Psychology, 56,* 210–217.

MARKS, G., & MILLER, N. (1987). Ten years of research on the false-consensus effect: An empirical and theoretical review. *Psychological Bulletin, 102,* 72–90.

MARKS, G., MILLER, N., & MARUYAMA, G. (1981). Effect of targets' physical attractiveness on assumptions of similarity. *Journal of Personality and Social Psychology, 41,* 198–206.

MARKUS, G. B. (1986). Stability and change in political attitudes: Observe, recall, and "explain." *Political Behavior, 8,* 21–44.

MARKUS, H., & KITAYAMA, S. (1991). Culture and the self: Implications for cognition, emotion, and motivation. *Psychological Review, 98,* 224–253.

MARSH, H. W., & YOUNG, A. S. (1997). Causal effects of academic self-concept on academic achievement: Structural equation models of longitudinal data. *Journal of Educational Psychology, 89,* 41–54.

MARSHALL, W. L. (1989). Pornography and sex offenders. In D. Zillmann & J. Bryant (Eds.), *Pornography: Research advances and policy considerations.* Hillsdale, NJ: Erlbaum.

MARTIN, C. L. (1987). A ratio measure of sex stereotyping. *Journal of Personality and Social Psychology, 52,* 489–499.

MARTIN, R. (1996). Minority influence and argument generation. *British Journal of Social Psychology, 35,* 91–103.

MARUYAMA, G., RUBIN, R. A., & KINGBURY, G. (1981). Self-esteem and educational achievement: Independent constructs with a common cause? *Journal of Personality and Social Psychology, 40,* 962–975.

MARVELLE, K., & GREEN, S. (1980). Physical attractiveness and sex bias in hiring decisions for two types of jobs. *Journal of the National Association of Women Deans, Administrators, and Counselors, 44* (1), 3–6.

MARX, G. (1960). *Groucho and me.* New York: Dell.

MASTEKAASA, A. (1994). Marital status, distress, and well-being: An international comparison. *Journal of Comparative Family Studies, 25,* 183–206.

MASTEKAASA, A. (1995). Age variations in the suicide rates and self-reported subjective well-being of married and never married persons. *Journal of Community and Applied Social Psychology, 5,* 21–39.

MATTHEWS, D. A., & LARSON, D. B. (1997). *The faith factor: An annotated bibliography of clinical research on spiritual subjects* (Vols. 1–4). Rockville, MD: National Institute for Healthcare Research and Georgetown University Press.

MAXWELL, G. M. (1985). Behaviour of lovers: Measuring the closeness of relationships. *Journal of Personality and Social Psychology, 2,* 215–238.

MAYER, J. D., & SALOVEY, P. (1987). Personality moderates the interaction of mood and cognition. In K. Fiedler & J. Forgas (Eds.), *Affect, cognition, and social behavior.* Toronto: Hogrefe.

MCALISTER, A., PERRY, C., KILLEN, J., SLINKARD, L. A., & MACCOBY, N. (1980). Pilot study of smoking, alcohol and drug abuse prevention. *American Journal of Public Health, 70,* 719–721.

MCANENY, L. (1994, June). Alcohol in America: Number of drinkers holding steady, but drinking less. *Gallup Poll Monthly,* pp. 14–19.

MCCARREY, M., EDWARDS, H. P., & ROZARIO, W. (1982). Ego-relevant feedback, affect, and self-serving attributional bias. *Personality and Social Psychology Bulletin, 8,* 189–194.

MCCARTHY, J. D., & HOGE, D. R. (1984). The dynamics of self-esteem and delinquency. *American Journal of Sociology, 90,* 396–410.

MCCARTHY, J. F., & KELLY, B. R. (1978a). Aggression, performance variables, and anger self-report in ice hockey players. *Journal of Psychology, 99,* 97–101.

MCCARTHY, J. F., & KELLY, B. R. (1978b). Aggressive behavior and its effect on performance over time in ice hockey athletes: An archival study. *International Journal of Sport Psychology, 9,* 90–96.

McCAULEY, C. (1989). The nature of social influence in groupthink: Compliance and internalization. *Journal of Personality and Social Psychology, 57,* 250–260.

McCAULEY, C. R., & SEGAL, M. E. (1987). Social psychology of terrorist groups. In C. Hendrick (Ed.), *Group processes and intergroup relations: Review of personality and social psychology* (Vol. 9). Newbury Park, CA: Sage.

McCONAHAY, J. B. (1981). Reducing racial prejudice in desegregated schools. In W. D. Hawley (Ed.), *Effective school desegregation.* Beverly Hills, CA: Sage.

McCULLOUGH, J. L., & OSTROM, T. M. (1974). Repetition of highly similar messages and attitude change. *Journal of Applied Psychology, 59,* 395–397.

McFARLAND, C., & ROSS, M. (1985). *The relation between current impressions and memories of self and dating partners.* Unpublished manuscript, University of Waterloo.

McFARLAND, S. G., AGEYEV, V. S., & ABALAKINA-PAAP, M. A. (1992). Authoritarianism in the former Soviet Union. *Journal of Personality and Social Psychology, 63,* 1004–1010.

McFARLAND, S. G., AGEYEV, V. S., & DJINTCHARADZE, N. (1996). Russian authoritarianism two years after communism. *Personality and Social Psychology Bulletin, 22,* 210–217.

McGILLICUDDY, N. B., WELTON, G. L., & PRUITT, D. G. (1987). Third-party intervention: A field experiment comparing three different models. *Journal of Personality and Social Psychology, 53,* 104–112.

McGLOSHEN, T. H., & O'BRYANT, S. L. (1988). The psychological well-being of older, recent widows. *Psychology of Women Quarterly, 12,* 99–116.

McGUIRE, W. J. (1964). Inducing resistance to persuasion: Some contemporary approaches. In L. Berkowitz (Ed.), *Advances in experimental social psychology* (Vol. 1). New York: Academic Press.

McGUIRE, W. J. (1986). The myth of massive media impact: Savagings and salvagings. In G. Comstock (Ed.), *Public communication and behavior* (Vol. 1). Orlando, FL: Academic Press.

McGUIRE, W. J., & McGUIRE, C. V. (1986). Differences in conceptualizing self versus conceptualizing other people as manifested in contrasting verb types used in natural speech. *Journal of Personality and Social Psychology, 51,* 1135–1143.

McGUIRE, W. J., McGUIRE, C. V., CHILD, P., & FUJIOKA, T. (1978). Salience of ethnicity in the spontaneous self-concept as a function of one's ethnic distinctiveness in the social environment. *Journal of Personality and Social Psychology, 36,* 511–520.

McGUIRE, W. J., McGUIRE, C. V., & WINTON, W. (1979). Effects of household sex composition on the salience of one's gender in the spontaneous self-concept. *Journal of Experimental Social Psychology, 15,* 77–90.

McGUIRE, W. J., & PADAWER-SINGER, A. (1978). Trait salience in the spontaneous self-concept. *Journal of Personality and Social Psychology, 33,* 743–754.

McINTOSH, D. N., SILVER, R. C., & WORTMAN, C. B. (1993). Religion's role in adjustment to a negative life event: Coping with the loss of a child. *Journal of Personality and Social Psychology, 65,* 812–821.

McKENNA, F. P., & MYERS, L. B. (1997). Illusory self-assessments—Can they be reduced? *British Journal of Psychology, 88,* 39–51.

McNEEL, S. P. (1980). *Tripling up: Perceptions and effects of dormitory crowding.* Paper presented at the American Psychological Association convention.

McNEILL, B. W., & STOLTENBERG, C. D. (1988). A test of the elaboration likelihood model for therapy. *Cognitive Therapy and Research, 12,* 69–79.

MEEHL, P. E. (1954). *Clinical vs. statistical prediction: A theoretical analysis and a review of evidence.* Minneapolis: University of Minnesota Press.

MEEHL, P. E. (1986). Causes and effects of my disturbing little book. *Journal of Personality Assessment, 50,* 370–375.

MEINDL, J. R., & LERNER, M. J. (1984). Exacerbation of extreme responses to an outgroup. *Journal of Personality and Social Psychology, 47,* 71–84.

MENAND, L. (1991, May 20). Illiberalisms. *New Yorker,* pp. 101–107.

MESSÉ, L. A., & SIVACEK, J. M. (1979). Predictions of others' responses in a mixed-motive game: Self-justification or false consensus? *Journal of Personality and Social Psychology, 37,* 602–607.

MESSICK, D. M., BLOOM, S., BOLDIZAR, J. P., & SAMUELSON, C. D. (1985). Why we are fairer than others. *Journal of Experimental Social Psychology, 21,* 480–500.

MESSICK, D. M., & SENTIS, K. P. (1979). Fairness and preference. *Journal of Experimental Social Psychology, 15,* 418–434.

METALSKY, G. I., JOINER, T. E., JR., HARDIN, T. S., & ABRAMSON, L. Y. (1993). Depressive reactions to failure in a naturalistic setting: A test of the hopelessness and self-esteem theories of depression. *Journal of Abnormal Psychology, 102,* 101–109.

MICHAELS, J. W., BLOMMEL, J. M., BROCATO, R. M., LINKOUS, R. A., & ROWE, J. S. (1982). Social facilitation and inhibition in a natural setting. *Replications in Social Psychology, 2,* 21–24.

MICHALOS, A. (1991). *Life satisfaction and happiness. Vol. 1 of global report on student well-being.* New York: Springer-Verlag.

MIELL, E., DUCK, S., & LA GAIPA, J. (1979). Interactive effects of sex and timing in self disclosure. *British Journal of Social and Clinical Psychology, 18,* 355–362.

MIKULA, G. (1984). Justice and fairness in interpersonal relations: Thoughts and suggestions. In H. Taijfel (Ed.), *The social dimension: European developments in social psychology* (Vol. 1). Cambridge, England: Cambridge University Press.

MILGRAM, S. (1965). Some conditions of obedience and disobedience to authority. *Human Relations, 18,* 57–76.

MILGRAM, S. (1974). *Obedience to authority.* New York: Harper & Row.

MILGRAM, S., & SABINI, J. (1983). On maintaining social norms: A field experiment in the subway. In H. H. Blumberg, A. P. Hare, V. Kent, & M. Davies (Eds.), *Small groups and social interaction* (Vol. 1). London: Wiley.

MILLER, A. G. (1986). *The obedience experiments: A case study of controversy in social science.* New York: Praeger.

MILLER, A. G., ASHTON, W., & MISHAL, M. (1990). Beliefs concerning the features of constrained behavior: A basis for the fundamental attribution error. *Journal of Personality and Social Psychology, 59,* 635–650.

MILLER, J. B. (1986). *Toward a new psychology of women* (2nd ed.). Boston, MA: Beacon Press.

MILLER, J. G. (1984). Culture and the development of everyday social explanation. *Journal of Personality and Social Psychology, 46,* 961–978.

MILLER, K. I., & MONGE, P. R. (1986). Participation, satisfaction, and productivity: A meta-analytic review. *Academy of Management Journal, 29,* 727–753.

MILLER, L. C. (1990). Intimacy and liking: Mutual influence and the role of unique relationships. *Journal of Personality and Social Psychology, 59,* 50–60.

MILLER, L. C., BERG, J. H., & ARCHER, R. L. (1983). Openers: Individuals who elicit intimate self-disclosure. *Journal of Personality and Social Psychology, 44,* 1234–1244.

MILLER, L. C., BERG, J. H., & RUGS, D. (1989). *Selectivity and sharing: Needs and norms in developing friendships.* Unpublished manuscript, Scripps College.

MILLER, N., & MARKS, G. (1982). Assumed similarity between self and other: Effect of expectation of future interaction with that other. *Social Psychology Quarterly, 45,* 100–105.

MILLER, N. E. (1941). The frustration-aggression hypothesis. *Psychological Review, 48,* 337–342.

MILLER, N. E., & BUGELSKI, R. (1948). Minor studies of aggression: II. The influence of frustrations imposed by the in-group on attitudes expressed toward out-groups. *Journal of Psychology, 25,* 437–442.

MILLER, P. A., & EISENBERG, N. (1988). The relation of empathy to aggressive and externalizing/antisocial behavior. *Psychological Bulletin, 103,* 324–344.

MILLER, P. C., LEFCOURT, H. M., HOLMES, J. G., WARE, E. E., & SALEY, W. E. (1986). Marital locus of control and marital problem solving. *Journal of Personality and Social Psychology, 51,* 161–169.

MILLER, R. L., BRICKMAN, P., & BOLEN, D. (1975). Attribution versus persuasion as a means for modifying behavior. *Journal of Personality and Social Psychology, 31,* 430–441.

MILLER, R. S. (1997). Inattentive and contented: Relationship commitment and attention to alternatives. *Journal of Personality and Social Psychology, 73,* 758–766.

MILLER, R. S., & SCHLENKER, B. R. (1985). Egotism in group members: Public and private attributions of responsibility for group performance. *Social Psychology Quarterly, 48,* 85–89.

MILLER, R. S., & SIMPSON, J. A. (1990). *Relationship satisfaction and attentiveness to alternatives.* Paper presented at the American Psychological Association convention.

MILLETT, K. (1975, January). The shame is over. *Ms.,* pp. 26–29.

MINARD, R. D. (1952). Race relationships in the Pocohontas coal field. *Journal of Social Issues, 8* (1), 29–44.

MIRELS, H. L., & MCPEEK, R. W. (1977). Self-advocacy and self-esteem. *Journal of Consulting and Clinical Psychology, 45,* 1132–1138.

MITA, T. H., DERMER, M., & KNIGHT, J. (1977). Reversed facial images and the mere-exposure hypothesis. *Journal of Personality and Social Psychology, 35,* 597–601.

MITCHELL, T. R., & THOMPSON, L. (1994). A theory of temporal adjustments of the evaluation of events: Rosy prospection and rosy retrospection. In C. Stubbart, J. Porac, & J. Meindl (Eds.), *Advances in managerial cognition and organizational information processing.* Greenwich, CT: JAI Press.

MITCHELL, T. R., THOMPSON, L., PETERSON, E., & CRONK, R. (1997). Temporal adjustments in the evaluation of events: The "rosy view." *Journal of Experimental Social Psychology, 33,* 421–448.

MONSON, T. C., & SNYDER, M. (1977). Actors, observers, and the attribution process: Toward a reconceptualization. *Journal of Experimental Social Psychology, 13,* 89–111.

MOODY, K. (1980). *Growing up on television: The TV effect.* New York: Times Books.

MOORE, D. L., & BARON, R. S. (1983). Social facilitation: A physiological analysis. In J. T. Cacioppo & R. Petty (Eds.), *Social psychophysiology.* New York: Guilford Press.

MORIER, D., & SEROY, C. (1994). The effect of interpersonal expectancies on men's self-presentation of gender role attitudes to women. *Sex Roles, 31,* 493–504.

MORRISON, D. M. (1989). Predicting contraceptive efficacy: A discriminant analysis of three groups of adolescent women. *Journal of Applied Social Psychology, 19,* 1431–1452.

MORSE, S. J., & GRUZEN, J. (1976). The eye of the beholder: A neglected variable in the study of physical attractiveness. *Journal of Psychology, 44,* 209–225.

MOSCOVICI, S. (1985). Social influence and conformity. In G. Lindzey & E. Aronson (Eds.), *The handbook of social psychology* (3rd ed.). Hillsdale, NJ: Erlbaum.

MOSCOVICI, S., LAGE, S., & NAFFRECHOUX, M. (1969). Influence of a consistent minority on the responses of a majority in a color perception task. *Sociometry, 32,* 365–380.

MOSCOVICI, S., & ZAVALLONI, M. (1969). The group as a polarizer of attitudes. *Journal of Personality and Social Psychology, 12,* 124–135.

MOYER, K. E. (1976). *The psychobiology of aggression.* New York: Harper & Row.

MOYER, K. E. (1983). The physiology of motivation: Aggression as a model. In C. J. Scheier & A. M. Rogers (Eds.), *G. Stanley Hall Lecture Series* (Vol. 3). Washington, DC: American Psychological Association.

MUCCHI-FAINA, A., MAASS, A., & VOLPATO, C. (1991). Social influence: The role of originality. *European Journal of Social Psychology, 21,* 183–197.

MUELLER, C. W., DONNERSTEIN, E., & HALLAM, J. (1983). Violent films and prosocial behavior. *Personality and Social Psychology Bulletin, 9,* 83–89.

MULLEN, B. (1986a). Atrocity as a function of lynch mob composition: A self-attention perspective. *Personality and Social Psychology Bulletin, 12,* 187–197.

MULLEN, B. (1986b). Stuttering, audience size, and the other-total ratio: A self-attention perspective. *Journal of Applied Social Psychology, 16,* 139–149.

MULLEN, B., & BAUMEISTER, R. F. (1987). Group effects on self-attention and performance: Social loafing, social facilitation, and social impairment. In C. Hendrick (Ed.), *Group processes and intergroup relations: Review of personality and social psychology* (Vol. 9). Newbury Park, CA: Sage.

MULLEN, B., BROWN, R., & SMITH, C. (1992). Ingroup bias as a function of salience, relevance, and status: An integration. *European Journal of Social Psychology, 22,* 103–122.

MULLEN, B., BRYANT, B., & DRISKELL, J. E. (1997). Presence of others and arousal: An integration. *Group Dynamics: Theory, Research, and Practice, 1,* 52–64.

MULLEN, B., & COPPER, C. (1994). The relation between group cohesiveness and performance: An integration. *Psychological Bulletin, 115,* 210–227.

MULLEN, B., & GOETHALS, G. R. (1990). Social projection, actual consensus and valence. *British Journal of Social Psychology, 29,* 279–282.

MULLEN, B., & RIORDAN, C. A. (1988). Self-serving attributions for performance in naturalistic settings: A meta-analytic review. *Journal of Applied Social Psychology, 18,* 3–22.

MULLEN, B., SALAS, E., & DRISKELL, J. E. (1989). Salience, motivation, and artifact as contributions to the relation between participation rate and leadership. *Journal of Experimental Social Psychology, 25,* 545–559.

MULLER, S., & JOHNSON, B. T. (1990). *Fear and persuasion: A linear relationship?* Paper presented to the Eastern Psychological Association convention.

MULLIN, C. R., & LINZ, D. (1995). Desensitization and resensitization to violence against women: Effects of exposure to sexually violent films on judgments of domestic violence victims. *Journal of Personality and Social Psychology, 69,* 449–459.

MURPHY, C. (1990, June). New findings: Hold on to your hat. *Atlantic,* pp. 22–23.

MURPHY, C. M., & O'FARRELL, T. J. (1996). Marital violence among alcoholics. *Current Directions in Psychological Science, 5,* 183–187.

MURPHY-BERMAN, V., & SHARMA, R. (1986). Testing the assumptions of attribution theory in India. *Journal of Social Psychology, 126,* 607–616.

MURRAY, S. L., HOLMES, J. G., & GRIFFIN, D. W. (1996). The self-fulfilling nature of positive illusions in romantic relationships: Love is not blind, but prescient. *Journal of Personality and Social Psychology, 71,* 1155–1180.

MURSTEIN, B. L. (1986). *Paths to marriage.* Newbury Park, CA: Sage.

MUSON, G. (1978, March). Teenage violence and the telly. *Psychology Today,* pp. 50–54.

MYERS, D. G. (1993). *The pursuit of happiness.* New York: Avon.

MYERS, D. G. (1995). Who is happy? *Psychology Science, 6,* 10–19.

MYERS, D. G. (1998). *Psychology* (5th ed.). New York: Worth.

MYERS, D. G. (2000). *The American paradox.* New Haven, CT: Yale University Press.

MYERS, D. G., & BISHOP, G. D. (1970). Discussion effects on racial attitudes. *Science, 169,* 778–789.

MYERS, D. G., & DIENER E. (1996, May). The pursuit of happiness. *Scientific American,* pp. 54–56.

NADLER, A., GOLDBERG, M., & JAFFE, Y. (1982). Effect of self-differentiation and anonymity in group on deindividuation. *Journal of Personality and Social Psychology, 42,* 1127–1136.

NAGAR, D., & PANDEY, J. (1987). Affect and performance on cognitive task as a function of crowding and noise. *Journal of Applied Social Psychology, 17,* 147–157.

NAIL, P. R., & VAN LEEUWEN, M. D. (1993). An analysis and restructuring of the diamond model of social response. *Personality and Social Psychology Bulletin, 19,* 106–116.

NAPOLITAN, D. A., & GOETHALS, G. R. (1979). The attribution of friendliness. *Journal of Experimental Social Psychology, 15,* 105–113.

NATIONAL COUNCIL FOR RESEARCH ON WOMEN. (1994). Women and philanthropy fact sheet. *Issues Quarterly, 1* (2), 9.

NATIONAL OPINION RESEARCH CENTER. (1996). *General social survey.* Chicago: University of Chicago, NORC.

NATIONAL SAFETY COUNCIL. (1991). *Accident facts.* Chicago: Author.

NAYLOR, T. H. (1990). Redefining corporate motivation, Swedish style. *Christian Century, 107,* 566–570.

NEEDLES, D. J., & ABRAMSON, L. Y. (1990). Positive life events, attributional style, and hopefulness: Testing a model of recovery from depression. *Journal of Abnormal Psychology, 99,* 156–165.

NEIMEYER, G. J., MACNAIR, R., METZLER, A. E., & COURCHAINE, K. (1991). Changing personal beliefs: Effects of forewarning, argument quality, prior bias, and personal exploration. *Journal of Social and Clinical Psychology, 10,* 1–20.

NELSON, L. J., & MILLER, D. T. (1997). The distinctiveness effect in social categorization: You are what makes you unusual. *Psychological Science, 6,* 246–249.

NEMETH, C. (1979). The role of an active minority in intergroup relations. In W. G. Austin & S. Worchel (Eds.), *The social psychology of intergroup relations.* Monterey, CA: Brooks/Cole.

NEMETH, C., & WACHTLER, J. (1974). Creating the perceptions of consistency and confidence: A necessary condition for minority influence. *Sociometry, 37,* 529–540.

NEWCOMB, T. M. (1961). *The acquaintance process.* New York: Holt, Rinehart Winston.

NEWMAN, H. M., & LANGER, E. J. (1981). Post-divorce adaptation and the attribution of responsibility. *Sex Roles, 7,* 223–231.

NEWMAN, L. S. (1993). How individualists interpret behavior: Idiocentrism and spontaneous trait inference. *Social Cognition, 11,* 243–269.

NIAS, D. K. B. (1979). Marital choice: Matching or complementation? In M. Cook & G. Wilson (Eds.), *Love and attraction.* Oxford: Pergamon Press.

NIEMI, R. G., MUELLER, J., & SMITH, T. W. (1989). *Trends in public opinion: A compendium of survey data.* New York: Greenwood Press.

NISBETT, R. (1988, Fall). The Vincennes incident: Congress hears psychologists. *Science Agenda* (American Psychological Association), p. 4.

NISBETT, R. E. (1990). Evolutionary psychology, biology, and cultural evolution. *Motivation and emotion, 14,* 255–263.

NISBETT, R. E. (1993). Violence and U.S. regional culture. *American Psychologist, 48,* 441–449.

NISBETT, R. E., BORGIDA, E., CRANDALL, R., & REED, H. (1976). Popular induction: Information is not necessarily informative. In J. S. Carroll & J. W. Payne (Eds.), *Cognition and social behavior.* Hillsdale, NJ: Erlbaum.

NISBETT, R. E., & ROSS, L. (1991). *The person and the situation.* New York: McGraw-Hill.

NISBETT, R. E., & SCHACHTER, S. (1966). Cognitive manipulation of pain. *Journal of Experimental Social Psychology, 2,* 227–236.

NISBETT, R. E., & SMITH, M. (1989). Predicting interpersonal attraction from small samples: A reanalysis of Newcomb's acquaintance study. *Social Cognition, 7,* 67–73.

NISBETT, R. E., & WILSON, T. D. (1977). Telling more than we can know: Verbal reports on mental processes. *Psychological Review, 84,* 231–259.

NIX, G., WATSON, C., PYSZCZYNSKI, T., & GREENBERG, J. (1995). Reducing depressive affect through external focus of attention. *Journal of Social and Clinical Psychology, 14,* 36–52.

NOLEN-HOEKSEMA, S., GIRGUS, J. S., & SELIGMAN, M. E. P. (1986). Learned helplessness in children: A longitudinal study of depression, achievement, and explanatory style. *Journal of Personality and Social Psychology, 51,* 435–442.

NOLLER, P., & FITZPATRICK, M. A. (1990). Marital communication in the eighties. *Journal of Marriage and the Family, 52,* 832–843.

NOREM, J. K., & CANTOR, N. (1986). Defensive pessimism: Harnessing anxiety as motivation. *Journal of Personality and Social Psychology, 51,* 1208–1217.

NOTARIUS, C., & MARKMAN, H. J. (1993). *We can work it out.* New York: Putnam.

NOWAK, M., & SIGMUND, K. (1993). A strategy of win-stay, lose-shift that outperforms tit-for-tat in the Prisoner's Dilemma game. *Nature, 364,* 56–58.

NURMI, J-E., & SALMELA-ARO, K. (1997). Social strategies and loneliness: A prospective study. *Personality and Individual Differences, 23,* 205–215.

NURMI, J-E., TOIVONEN, S., SALMELA-ARO, K., & ERONEN, S. (1996). Optimistic, approach-oriented, and avoidance strategies in social situations: Three studies on loneliness and peer relationships. *European Journal of Personality, 10,* 201–219.

NUTTIN, J. M., JR. (1987). Affective consequences of mere ownership: The name letter effect in twelve European languages. *European Journal of Social Psychology, 17,* 318–402.

O'DEA, T. F. (1968). Sects and cults. In D. L. Sills (Ed.), *International encyclopedia of the social sciences* (Vol. 14). New York: Macmillan.

O'GORMAN, H. J., & GARRY, S. L. (1976). Pluralistic ignorance—A replication and extension. *Public Opinion Quarterly, 40,* 449–458.

OHBUCHI, K., & KAMBARA, T. (1985). Attacker's intent and awareness of outcome, impression management, and retaliation. *Journal of Experimental Social Psychology, 21,* 321–330.

OKUN, M. A., & STOCK, W. A. (1987). Correlates and components of subjective well-being among the elderly. *Journal of Applied Gerontology, 6,* 95–112.

O'LEARY, K. D., CHRISTIAN, J. L., & MENDELL, N. R. (1994). A closer look at the link between marital discord and depressive symptomatology. *Journal of Social and Clinical Psychology, 13,* 33–41.

OLSON, J. M., ROESE, N. J., & ZANNA, M. P. (1996). Expectancies. In E. T. Higgins & A. W. Kruglanski (Eds.), *Social psychology: Handbook of basic principles.* New York: Guilford Press.

OLSON, J. M., & ZANNA, M. P. (1981, November). *Promoting physical activity: A social psychological perspective.* Report prepared for the Ministry of Culture and Recreation, Sports and Fitness Branch, 77 Bloor St. West, 8th Floor, Toronto, Ontario M7A 2R9.

OLWEUS, D. (1979). Stability of aggressive reaction patterns in males: A review. *Psychological Bulletin, 86,* 852–875.

OLWEUS, D., MATTSSON, A., SCHALLING, D., & LOW, H. (1988). Circulating testosterone levels and aggression in adolescent males: A causal analysis. *Psychosomatic Medicine, 50,* 261–272.

ORBELL, J. M., VAN DE KRAGT, A. J. C., & DAWES, R. M. (1988). Explaining discussion-induced cooperation. *Journal of Personality and Social Psychology, 54,* 811–819.

ORIVE, R. (1984). Group similarity, public self-awareness, and opinion extremity: A social projection explanation of deindividuation effects. *Journal of Personality and Social Psychology, 47,* 727–737.

ORNSTEIN, R. (1991). *The evolution of consciousness: Of Darwin, Freud, and cranial fire: The origins of the way we think.* New York: Prentice Hall.

OSBERG, T. M., & SHRAUGER, J. S. (1986). Self-prediction: Exploring the parameters of accuracy. *Journal of Personality and Social Psychology, 51,* 1044–1057.

OSBERG, T. M., & SHRAUGER, J. S. (1990). The role of self-prediction in psychological assessment. In J. N. Butcher & C. D. Spielberger (Eds.), *Advances in Personality Assessment* (Vol. 8). Hillsdale, NJ: Erlbaum.

OSGOOD, C. E. (1962). *An alternative to war or surrender.* Urbana: University of Illinois Press.

OSGOOD, C. E. (1980). GRIT: *A strategy for survival in mankind's nuclear age?* Paper presented at the Pugwash Conference on New Directions in Disarmament, Racine, WI.

OSKAMP, S. (1991). *Curbside recycling: Knowledge, attitudes, and behavior.* Paper presented at the Society for Experimental Social Psychology meeting, Columbus, Ohio.

OSTERHOUSE, R. A., & BROCK, T. C. (1970). Distraction increases yielding to propaganda by inhibiting counterarguing. *Journal of Personality and Social Psychology, 15,* 344–358.

OSTROM, T. M., & SEDIKIDES, C. (1992). Out-group homogeneity effects in natural and minimal groups. *Psychological Bulletin, 112,* 536–552.

OZER, E. M., & BANDURA, A. (1990). Mechanisms governing empowerment effects: A self-efficacy analysis. *Journal of Personality and Social Psychology, 58,* 472–486.

PADGETT, V. R. (1989). *Predicting organizational violence: An application of 11 powerful principles of obedience.* Paper presented at the American Psychological Association Convention.

PAK, A. W., DION, K. L., & DION, K. K. (1991). Social-psychological correlates of experienced discrimination: Test of the double jeopardy hypothesis. *International Journal of Intercultural Relations, 15,* 243–254.

PALLAK, S. R., MURRONI, E., & KOCH, J. (1983). Communicator attractiveness and expertise, emotional versus rational appeals, and persuasion: A heuristic versus systematic processing interpretation. *Social Cognition, 2,* 122–141.

PALMER, D. L. (1996). Determinants of Canadian attitudes toward immigration: More than just racism? *Canadian Journal of Behavioural Science, 28,* 180–192.

PALMER, E. L., & DORR, A. (Eds.) (1980). *Children and the faces of television: Teaching, violence, selling.* New York: Academic Press.

PANDEY, J., SINHA, Y., PRAKASH, A., & TRIPATHI, R. C. (1982). Right-left political ideologies and attribution of the causes of poverty. *European Journal of Social Psychology, 12,* 327–331.

PAPASTAMOU, S., & MUGNY, G. (1990). Synchronic consistency and psychologization in minority influence. *European Journal of Social Psychology, 20,* 85–98.

PARK, B., & ROTHBART, M. (1982). Perception of out-group homogeneity and levels of social categorization: Memory for the subordinate attributes of in-group and out-group members. *Journal of Personality and Social Psychology, 42,* 1051–1068.

PARKE, R. D., BERKOWITZ, L., LEYENS, J. P., WEST, S. G., & SEBASTIAN, J. (1977). Some effects of violent and nonviolent movies on the behavior of juvenile delinquents. In L. Berkowitz (Ed.), *Advances in experimental social psychology* (Vol. 10). New York: Academic Press.

PASCAL, B. (1670/1965). *Thoughts* (trans. W. F. Trotter). In M. Mack (Ed.), *World masterpieces.* New York: W. W. Norton.

PASCARELLA, E. T., & TERENZINI, P. T. (1991). *How collects affects students: Findings and insights from twenty years of research.* San Francisco: Jossey-Bass.

PATTERSON, G. R., LITTMAN, R. A., & BRICKER, W. (1967). Assertive behavior in children: A step toward a theory of aggression. *Monographs of the Society of Research in Child Development* (Serial No. 113), 32, 5.

PATTERSON, T. E. (1980). The role of the mass media in presidential campaigns: The lessons of the 1976 election. *Items, 34,* 25–30. Social Science Research Council, 605 Third Avenue, New York, N.Y. 10016.

PAVOT, W., DIENER, E., COLVIN, C. R., & SANDVIK, E. (1991). Further validation of the satisfaction with life scale: Evidence for the cross-method convergence of well-being measures. *Journal of Personality Assessment, 57,* 149–161.

PAVOT, W., DIENER, E., & FUJITA, F. (1990). Extraversion and happiness. *Personality and Individual Differences, 11,* 1299–1306.

PEGALIS, L. J., SHAFFER, D. R., BAZZINI, D. G., & GREENIER, K. (1994). On the ability to elicit self-disclosure: Are there gender-based and contextual limitations on the opener effect? *Personality and Social Psychology Bulletin, 20,* 412–420.

PEPLAU, L. A., & GORDON, S. L. (1985). Women and men in love: Gender differences in close heterosexual relationships. In V. E. O'Leary, R. K. Unger, & B. S. Wallston (Eds.), *Women, gender, and social psychology.* Hillsdale, NJ: Erlbaum.

PERLMAN, D., & ROOK, K. S. (1987). Social support, social deficits, and the family: Toward the enhancement of well-being. In S. Oskamp (Ed.), *Family processes and problems: Social psychological aspects.* Newbury Park, CA: Sage.

PERLOFF, L. S. (1987). Social comparison and illusions of invulnerability. In C. R. Snyder & C. R. Ford (Eds.), *Coping with negative life events: Clinical and social psychological perspectives.* New York: Plenum Press.

PERLS, F. S. (1973). *Ego, hunger and aggression: The beginning of Gestalt therapy.* Random House, 1969. Cited by Berkowitz in The case for bottling up rage. *Psychology Today,* July, pp. 24–30.

PESSIN, J. (1933). The comparative effects of social and mechanical stimulation on memorizing. *American Journal of Psychology, 45,* 263–270.

PESSIN, J., & HUSBAND, R. W. (1933). Effects of social stimulation on human maze learning. *Journal of Abnormal and Social Psychology, 28,* 148–154.

PETERSON, B. E., DOTY, R. M., & WINTER, D. G. (1993). Authoritarianism and attitudes toward contemporary social issues. *Personality and Social Psychology Bulletin, 19,* 174–184.

PETERSON, C., SCHWARTZ, S. M., & SELIGMAN, M. E. P. (1981). Self-blame and depression symptoms. *Journal of Personality and Social Psychology, 41,* 253–259.

PETERSON, R. S., & NEMETH, C. J. (1996). Focus versus flexibility: Majority and minority influence can both improve performance. *Personality and Social Psychology Bulletin, 22,* 14–23.

PETTIGREW, T. F. (1958). Personality and socio-cultural factors in intergroup attitudes: A cross-national comparison. *Journal of Conflict Resolution, 2,* 29–42.

PETTIGREW, T. F. (1969). Racially separate or together? *Journal of Social Issues, 2,* 43–69.

PETTIGREW, T. F. (1978). Three issues in ethnicity: Boundaries, deprivations, and perceptions. In J. M. Yinger & S. J. Cutler (Eds.), *Major social issues: A multidisciplinary view.* New York: Free Press.

PETTIGREW, T. F. (1986). The intergroup contact hypothesis reconsidered. In M. Hewstone & R. Brown (Eds.), *Contact and conflict in intergroup encounters.* Oxford: Basil Blackwell.

PETTIGREW, T. F. (1988). *Advancing racial justice: Past lessons for future use.* Paper for the "Opening Doors: An Appraisal of Race Relations in America" conference, University of Alabama.

PETTIGREW, T. F. (1997). Generalized intergroup contact effects on prejudice. *Personality and Social Psychology Bulletin, 23,* 173–185.

PETTIGREW, T. F., JACKSON, J. S., BRIKA, J. B., LEMAINE, G., MEERTENS, R. W., WAGNER, U., & ZICK, A. (1998). Outgroup prejudice in Western Europe. *European Review of Social Psychology, 8,* 241–273.

PETTIGREW, T. F., & MEERTENS, R. W. (1995). Subtle and blatant prejudice in Western Europe. *European Journal of Social Psychology, 25,* 57–76.

PETTY, R. E., & CACIOPPO, J. T. (1977). Forewarning cognitive responding, and resistance to persuasion. *Journal of Personality and Social Psychology, 35,* 645–655.

PETTY, R. E., & CACIOPPO, J. T. (1979). Effects of forewarning of persuasive intent and involvement on cognitive response and persuasion. *Personality and Social Psychology Bulletin, 5,* 173–176.

PETTY, R. E., & CACIOPPO, J. T. (1986). *Communication and persuasion: Central and peripheral routes to attitude change.* New York: Springer-Verlag.

PETTY, R. E., CACIOPPO, J. T., & GOLDMAN, R. (1981). Personal involvement as a determinant of argument-based persuasion. *Journal of Personality and Social Psychology, 41,* 847–855.

PETTY, R. E., HAUGTVEDT, C. P., & SMITH, S. M. (1995). Elaboration as a determinant of attitude strength: Creating attitudes that are persistent, resistant, and predictive of behavior. In R. E. Petty & J. A. Krosnick (Eds.), *Attitude strength: Antecedents and consequences.* Hillsdale, NJ: Erlbaum.

PETTY, R. E., SCHUMANN, D. W., RICHMAN, S. A., & STRATHMAN, A. J. (1993). Positive mood and persuasion: Different roles for affect under high and low elaboration conditions. *Journal of Personality and Social Psychology, 64,* 5–20.

PETTY, R. E., & WEGENER, D. T. (1998). Attitude change: Multiple roles for persuasion variables. In D. Gilbert, S. Fiske, & G. Lindzey (Eds.), *Handbook of social psychology* (4th ed.). New York: McGraw-Hill.

PHILLIPS, S. T., & ZILLER, R. C. (1997). Toward a theory and measure of the nature of nonprejudice. *Journal of Personality and Social Psychology, 72,* 420–434.

PLATZ, S. J., & HOSCH, H. M. (1988). Cross-racial/ethnic eyewitness identification: A field study. *Journal of Applied Social Psychology, 18,* 972–984.

PLECK, J. H., SONENSTEIN, F. L., & KU, L. C. (1993). Masculinity ideology: Its impact on adolescent males' heterosexual relationships. *Journal of Social Issues, 49,* 11–29.

PLINER, P., HART, H., KOHL, J., & SAARI, D. (1974). Compliance without pressure: Some further data on the foot-in-the-door technique. *Journal of Experimental Social Psychology, 10,* 17–22.

POMERLEAU, O. F., & RODIN, J. (1986). Behavioral medicine and health psychology. In S. L. Garfield & A. E. Bergin (Eds.), *Handbook of psychotherapy and behavior change* (3rd ed.). New York: Wiley.

PORTER, N., GEIS, F. L., & JENNINGS, J. (1983). Are women invisible as leaders? *Sex Roles, 9,* 1035–1049.

POWELL, J. (1989). *Happiness is an inside job.* Valencia, CA: Tabor.

ROPER ORGANIZATION. (1984, August/September). Survey reported in *Public Opinion,* p. 25.

POZO, C., CARVER, C. S., WELLENS, A. R., & SCHEIER, M. F. (1991). Social anxiety and social perception: Construing others' reactions to the self. *Personality and Social Psychology Bulletin, 17,* 355–362.

PRAGER, I. G., & CUTLER, B. L. (1990). Attributing traits to oneself and to others: The role of acquaintance level. *Personality and Social Psychology Bulletin, 16,* 309–319.

PRATKANIS, A. R., GREENWALD, A. G., LEIPPE, M. R., & BAUMGARDNER, M. H. (1988). In search of reliable persuasion effects: III. The sleeper effect is dead. Long live the sleeper effect. *Journal of Personality and Social Psychology, 54,* 203–218.

PRATTO, F. (1996). Sexual politics: The gender gap in the bedroom, the cupboard, and the cabinet. In D. M. Buss & N. M. Malamuth (Eds.), *Sex, power, conflict: Evolutionary and feminist perspectives.* New York: Oxford University Press.

PRATTO, F., SIDANIUS, J., STALLWORTH, L. M., & MALLE, B. F. (1994). Social dominance orientation: A personality variable predicting social and political attitudes. *Journal of Personality and Social Psychology, 67,* 741–763.

PRATTO, F., STALLWORTH, L. M., & SIDANIUS, J. (1997a). The gender gap: Differences in political attitudes and social dominance orientation. *British Journal of Social Psychology, 36,* 49–68.

PRATTO, F., STALLWORTH, L. M., SIDANIUS, J., & SIERS, B. (1997b). The gender gap in occupational role attainment: A social dominance approach. *Journal of Personality and Social Psychology, 72,* 37–53.

PRENTICE-DUNN, S., & ROGERS, R. W. (1980). Effects of deindividuating situational cues and aggressive models on subjective deindividuation and aggression. *Journal of Personality and Social Psychology, 39,* 104–113.

PRENTICE-DUNN, S., & ROGERS, R. W. (1989). Deindividuation and the self-regulation of behavior. In P. B. Paulus (Ed.), *Psychology of group influence* (2nd ed.). Hillsdale, NJ: Erlbaum.

PRESSON, P. K., & BENASSI, V. A. (1996). Illusion of control: A meta-analytic review. *Journal of Social Behavior and Personality, 11,* 493–510.

PRICE, G. H., DABBS, J. M., JR., CLOWER, B. J., & RESIN, R. P. (1974). *At first glance—Or, is physical attractiveness more than skin deep?* Paper presented at the Eastern Psychological Association convention. Cited by K. L. Dion & K. K. Dion (1979). Personality and behavioral correlates of romantic love. In M. Cook & G. Wilson (Eds.), *Love and attraction.* Oxford: Pergamon.

PROHASKA, V. (1994). "I know I'll get an A": Confident overestimation of final course grades. *Teaching of Psychology, 21,* 141–143.

PRUITT, D. G. (1986b, July). Trends in the scientific study of negotiation. *Negotiation Journal,* pp. 237–244.

PRUITT, D. G. (1986a). Achieving integrative agreements in negotiation. In R. K. White (Ed.), *Psychology and the prevention of nuclear war.* New York: New York University Press.

PRUITT, D. G. (1998). Social conflict. In D. Gilbert, S. T. Fiske, & G. Lindzey (Eds.), *Handbook of social psychology* (4th ed.). New York: McGraw-Hill.

PRUITT, D. G., & KIMMEL, M. J. (1977). Twenty years of experimental gaming: Critique, synthesis, and suggestions for the future. *Annual Review of Psychology, 28,* 363–392.

PRUITT, D. G., & LEWIS, S. A. (1975). Development of integrative solutions in bilateral negotiation. *Journal of Personality and Social Psychology, 31,* 621–633.

PRUITT, D. G., & LEWIS, S. A. (1977). The psychology of integrative bargaining. In D. Druckman (Ed.), *Negotiations: A social-psychological analysis.* New York: Halsted.

PRUITT, D. G., & RUBIN, J. Z. (1986). *Social conflict.* San Francisco: Random House.

PRYOR, J. B. (1987). Sexual harassment proclivities in men. *Sex Roles, 17,* 269–290.

PURVIS, J. A., DABBS, J. M., JR., & HOPPER, C. H. (1984). The "opener": Skilled user of facial expression and speech pattern. *Personality and Social Psychology Bulletin, 10,* 61–66.

PYSZCZYNSKI, T., & GREENBERG, J. (1983). Determinants of reduction in intended effort as a strategy for coping with anticipated failure. *Journal of Research in Personality, 17,* 412–422.

PYSZCZYNSKI, T., GREENBERG, J., & HOLT, K. (1985). Maintaining consistency between self-serving beliefs and available data: A bias in information evaluation. *Personality and Social Psychology Bulletin, 11,* 179–190.

PYSZCZYNSKI, T., HAMILTON, J. C., GREENBERG, J., & BECKER, S. E. (1991). Self-awareness and psychological dysfunction. In C. R. Snyder & D. O. Forsyth (Eds.), *Handbook of social and clinical psychology: The health perspective.* New York: Pergamon Press.

QUATTRONE, G. A. (1982). Behavioral consequences of attributional bias. *Social Cognition, 1,* 358–378.

QUATTRONE, G. A., & JONES, E. E. (1980). The perception of variability within in-groups and out-groups: Implications for the law of small numbers. *Journal of Personality and Social Psychology, 38,* 141–152.

RAJECKI, D. W., BLEDSOE, S. B., & RASMUSSEN, J. L. (1991). Successful personal ads: Gender differences and similarities in offers, stipulations, and outcomes. *Basic and Applied Social Psychology, 12,* 457–469.

RANK, S. G., & JACOBSON, C. K. (1977). Hospital nurses' compliance with medication overdose orders: A failure to replicate. *Journal of Health and Social Behavior, 18,* 188–193.

RAPOPORT, A. (1960). *Fights, games, and debates.* Ann Arbor: University of Michigan Press.

RCAGENDA (1979, November–December). p. 11. 475 Riverside Drive, New York, NY 10027.

REEDER, G. D., FLETCHER, G. J., & FURMAN, K. 1989. The role of observers' expectations in attitude attribution. *Journal of Experimental Social Psychology, 25,* 168–188.

REGAN, D. T., & CHENG, J. B. (1973). Distraction and attitude change: A resolution. *Journal of Experimental Social Psychology, 9,* 138–147.

REIFMAN, A. S., LARRICK, R. P., & FEIN, S. (1991). Temper and temperature on the diamond: The heat-aggression relationship in major league baseball. *Personality and Social Psychology Bulletin, 17,* 580–585.

REIS, H. T., NEZLEK, J., & WHEELER, L. (1980). Physical attractiveness in social interaction. *Journal of Personality and Social Psychology, 38,* 604–617.

REIS, H. T., & SHAVER, P. (1988). Intimacy as an interpersonal process. In S. Duck (Ed.), *Handbook of personal relationships: Theory, relationships and interventions.* Chichester, England: Wiley.

REIS, H. T., WHEELER, L., SPIEGEL, N., KERNIS, M. H., NEZLEK, J., & PERRI, M. (1982). Physical attractiveness in social interaction: II. Why does appearance affect social experience? *Journal of Personality and Social Psychology, 43,* 979–996.

REITZES, D. C. (1953). The role of organizational structures: Union versus neighborhood in a tension situation. *Journal of Social Issues, 9* (1), 37–44.

RENAUD, H., & ESTESS, F. (1961). Life history interviews with one hundred normal American males: "Pathogenecity" of childhood. *American Journal of Orthopsychiatry, 31,* 786–802.

RESSLER, R. K., BURGESS, A. W., & DOUGLAS, J. E. (1988). *Sexual homicide patterns.* Boston: Lexington Books.

RHODEWALT, F. (1987). *Is self-handicapping an effective self-protective attributional strategy?* Paper presented at the American Psychological Association convention.

RHODEWALT, F., & AGUSTSDOTTIR, S. (1986). Effects of self-presentation on the phenomenal self. *Journal of Personality and Social Psychology, 50,* 47–55.

RHODEWALT, F., SALTZMAN, A. T., & WITTMER J. (1984). Self-handicapping among competitive athletes: The role of practice in self-esteem protection. *Basic and Applied Social Psychology, 5,* 197–209.

RHOLES, W. S., NEWMAN, L. S., & RUBLE, D. N. (1990). Understanding self and others: Developmental and motivational aspects of perceiving persons in terms of invariant dispositions. In E. T. Higgins & R. M. Sorrentino (Eds.), *Handbook of motivation and cognition: Foundations of social behavior* (Vol. 2). New York: Guilford.

RICE, B. (1985, September). Performance review: The job nobody likes. *Psychology Today*, pp. 30–36.

RICHARDSON, L. F. (1960). Generalized foreign policy. *British Journal of Psychology Monographs Supplements, 23*. Cited by A. Rapoport in *Fights, games, and debates.* Ann Arbor: Univ. of Michigan Press, 1960, p. 15.

RIESS, M., ROSENFELD, P., MELBURG, V., & TEDESCHI, J. T. (1981). Self-serving attributions: Biased private perceptions and distorted public descriptions. *Journal of Personality and Social Psychology, 41*, 224–231.

RIGGS, J. M. (1992). Self-handicapping and achievement. In A. K. Boggiano & T. S. Pittman (Eds.), *Achievement and motivation: A social-developmental perspective.* New York: Cambridge University Press.

ROBBERSON, M. R., & ROGERS, R. W. (1988). Beyond fear appeals: Negative and positive persuasive appeals to health and self-esteem. *Journal of Applied Social Psychology, 18*, 277–287.

ROBINS, R. W., SPRANCA, M. D., & MENDELSOHN, G. A. (1996). The actor-observer effect revisited: Effects of individual differences and repeated social interactions on actor and observer attributions. *Journal of Personality and Social Psychology, 71*, 375–389.

ROBINSON, R. J., KELTNER, D., WARD, A., & ROSS, L. (1995). Actual versus assumed differences in construal: "Naive realism" in intergroup perception and conflict. *Journal of Personality and Social Psychology, 68*, 404–417.

ROCHAT, F. (1993). *How did they resist authority? Protecting refugees in Le Chambon during World War II.* Paper presented at the American Psychological Association convention.

ROCHAT, F., & MODIGLIANI, A. (1995). The ordinary quality of resistance: From Milgram's laboratory to the village of Le Chambon. *Journal of Social Issues, 51*, 195–210.

ROGERS, C. R. (1958). Reinhold Niebuhr's *The self and the dramas of history:* A criticism. *Pastoral Psychology, 9*, 15–17.

ROGERS, C. R. (1980). *A way of being.* Boston: Houghton Mifflin.

ROGERS, R. W., & MEWBORN, C. R. (1976). Fear appeals and attitude change: Effects of a threat's noxiousness, probability of occurrence, and the efficacy of coping responses. *Journal of Personality and Social Psychology, 34*, 54–61.

ROGERS, R. W., & PRENTICE-DUNN, S. (1981). Deindividuation and anger-mediated interracial aggression: Unmasking regressive racism. *Journal of Personality and Social Psychology, 41*, 63–73.

ROKEACH, M., & MEZEI, L. (1966). Race and shared beliefs as factors in social choice. *Science, 151*, 167–172.

ROOK, K. S. (1984). Promoting social bonding: Strategies for helping the lonely and socially isolated. *American Psychologist, 39*, 1389–1407.

ROSENFELD, D. (1979). *The relationship between self-esteem and egotism in males and females.* Unpublished manuscript, Southern Methodist University.

ROSENHAN, D. L. (1973). On being sane in insane places. *Science, 179*, 250–258.

ROSENTHAL, R. (1985). From unconscious experimenter bias to teacher expectancy effects. In J. B. Dusek, V. C. Hall, & W. J. Meyer (Eds.), *Teacher expectancies.* Hillsdale, NJ: Erlbaum.

ROSENTHAL, R. (1991). Teacher expectancy effects: A brief update 25 years after the Pygmalion experiment. *Journal of Research in Education, 1,* 3–12.

ROSENZWEIG, M. R. (1972). Cognitive dissonance. *American Psychologist, 27,* 769.

ROSS, L. (1977). The intuitive psychologist and his shortcomings: Distortions in the attribution process. In L. Berkowitz (Ed.), *Advances in experimental social psychology* (Vol. 10). New York: Academic Press.

ROSS, L. (1981). The "intuitive scientist" formulation and its developmental implications. In J. H. Havell & L. Ross (Eds.), *Social cognitive development: Frontiers and possible futures.* Cambridge, England: Cambridge University Press.

ROSS, L. (1988). Situationist perspectives on the obedience experiments: Review of A. G. Miller's *The obedience experiments. Contemporary Psychology, 33,* 101–104.

ROSS, L., AMABILE, T. M., & STEINMETZ, J. L. (1977). Social roles, social control, and biases in social-perception processes. *Journal of Personality and Social Psychology, 35,* 485–494.

ROSS, L., & WARD, A. (1995). Psychological barriers to dispute resolution. In M. P. Zanna (ed.), *Advances in experimental social psychology* (Vol. 27). San Diego: Academic Press.

ROSS, M., & BUEHLER, R. (1994). Creative remembering. In U. Neisser & R. Fivush (Eds.), *The remembering self.* New York: Cambridge University Press.

ROSS, M., McFARLAND, C., & FLETCHER, G. J. O. (1981). The effect of attitude on the recall of personal histories. *Journal of Personality and Social Psychology, 40,* 627–634.

ROSS, M., & SICOLY, F. (1979). Egocentric biases in availability and attribution. *Journal of Personality and Social Psychology, 37,* 322–336.

ROSS, M., THIBAUT, J., & EVENBECK, S. (1971). Some determinants of the intensity of social protest. *Journal of Experimental Social Psychology, 7,* 401–418.

ROSSI, A. S., & ROSSI, P. H. (1990). *Of human bonding: Parent-child relations across the life course.* Hawthorne, NY: Aldine de Gruyter.

ROTHBART, M., & BIRRELL, P. (1977). Attitude and perception of faces. *Journal of Research Personality, 11,* 209–215.

ROTHBART, M., FULERO, S., JENSEN, C., HOWARD, J., & BIRRELL, P. (1978). From individual to group impressions: Availability heuristics in stereotype formation. *Journal of Experimental Social Psychology, 14,* 237–255.

ROTHBART, M., & TAYLOR, M. (1992). Social categories and social reality. In G. R. Semin & K. Fielder (eds.), *Language, interaction and social cognition.* London: Sage.

ROTTER, J. (1973). Internal-external locus of control scale. In J. P. Robinson & R. P. Shaver (Eds.), *Measures of social psychological attitudes.* Ann Arbor: University of Michigan, Institute for Social Research.

ROTTON, J., & FREY, J. (1985). Air pollution, weather, and violent crimes: Concomitant time-series analysis of archival data. *Journal of Personality and Social Psychology, 49,* 1207–1220.

RUBACK, R. B., CARR, T. S., & HOPER, C. H. (1986). Perceived control in prison: Its relation to reported crowding, stress, and symptoms. *Journal of Applied Social Psychology, 16,* 375–386.

RUBIN, J. Z. (1986). *Can we negotiate with terrorists? Some answers from psychology.* Paper presented at the American Psychological Association convention.

RUBIN, J. Z. (1989). Some wise and mistaken assumptions about conflict and negotiation. *Journal of Social Issues, 45,* 195–209.

RUBIN, L. B. (1985). *Just friends: The role of friendship in our lives.* New York: Harper & Row.

RUBIN, Z. (1970). Measurement of romantic love. *Journal of Personality and Social Psychology, 16,* 265–273.

RUBIN, Z. (1973). *Liking and loving: An invitation to social psychology.* New York: Holt, Rinehart & Winston.

RULE, B. G., TAYLOR, B. R., & DOBBS, A. R. (1987). Priming effects of heat on aggressive thoughts. *Social Cognition, 5,* 131–143.

RUSBULT, C. E., JOHNSON, D. J., & MORROW, G. D. (1986). Impact of couple patterns of problem solving on distress and nondistress in dating relationships. *Journal of Personality and Social Psychology, 50,* 744–753.

RUSBULT, C. E., MORROW, G. D., & JOHNSON, D. J. (1987). Self-esteem and problem-solving behaviour in close relationships. *British Journal of Social Psychology, 26,* 293–303.

RUSHTON, J. P., FULKER, D. W., NEALE, M. C., NIAS, D. K. B., & EYSENCK, H. J. (1986). Altruism and aggression: The heritability of individual differences. *Journal of Personality and Social Psychology, 50,* 1192–1198.

RUSSELL, B. (1930/1980). *The conquest of happiness.* London: Unwin Paperbacks.

RUSSELL, G. W. (1983). Psychological issues in sports aggression. In J. H. Goldstein (Ed.), *Sports violence.* New York: Springer-Verlag.

RUZZENE, M., & NOLLER, P. (1986). Feedback motivation and reactions to personality interpretations that differ in favorability and accuracy. *Journal of Personality and Social Psychology, 51,* 1293–1299.

RYAN, C. S. (1996). Accuracy of black and white college students' in-group and out-group stereotypes. *Personality and Social Psychology Bulletin, 22,* 1114–1127.

SABINI, J., & SILVER, M. (1982). *Moralities of everyday life.* New York: Oxford University Press.

SACCO, W. P., & DUNN, V. K. (1990). Effect of actor depression on observer attributions: Existence and impact of negative attributions toward the depressed. *Journal of Personality and Social Psychology, 59,* 517–524.

SACKS, C. H., & BUGENTAL, D. P. (1987). Attributions as moderators of affective and behavioral responses to social failure. *Journal of Personality and Social Psychology, 53,* 939–947.

SALES, S. M. (1972). Economic threat as a determinant of conversion rates in authoritarian and nonauthoritarian churches. *Journal of Personality and Social Psychology, 23,* 420–428.

SALES, S. M. (1973). Threat as a factor in authoritarianism: An analysis of archival data. *Journal of Personality and Social Psychology, 28,* 44–57.

SANDBERG, G. G., JACKSON, T. L., & PETRETIC-JACKSON, P. (1985). *Sexual aggression and courtship violence in dating relationships.* Paper presented at the Midwestern Psychological Association convention.

SANDE, G. N., GOETHALS, G. R., & RADLOFF, C. E. (1988). Perceiving one's own traits and others': The multifaceted self. *Journal of Personality and Social Psychology, 54,* 13–20.

SANDERS, G. S. (1981a). Driven by distraction: An integrative review of social facilitation and theory and research. *Journal of Experimental Social Psychology, 17,* 227–251.

SANDERS, G. S. (1981b). Toward a comprehensive account of social facilitation: Distraction/conflict does not mean theoretical conflict. *Journal of Experimental Social Psychology, 17,* 262–265.

SANDERS, G. S., & BARON, R. S. (1977). Is social comparison irrelevant for producing choice shifts? *Journal of Experimental Social Psychology, 13,* 303–314.

SANDERS, G. S., BARON, R. S., & MOORE, D. L. (1978). Distraction and social comparison as mediators of social facilitation effects. *Journal of Experimental Social Psychology, 14,* 291–303.

SANDVIK, E., DIENER, E., & SEIDLITZ, L. (1993). Subjective well-being: The convergence and stability of self-report and non-self-report measures. *Journal of Personality, 61,* 317–342.

SANISLOW, C. A., III, PERKINS, D. V., & BALOGH, D. W. (1989). Mood induction, interpersonal perceptions, and rejection in the roommates of depressed, nondepressed-disturbed, and normal college students. *Journal of Social and Clinical Psychology, 8,* 345–358.

SANITIOSO, R., KUNDA, Z., & FONG, G. T. (1990). Motivated recruitment of autobiographical memories. *Journal of Personality and Social Psychology, 59,* 229–241.

SARNOFF, I., & SARNOFF, S. (1989). *Love-centered marriage in a self-centered world.* New York: Hemisphere.

SARTRE, J-P. (1946/1948). *Anti-Semite and Jew.* New York: Shocken Books.

SATTERFIELD, A. T., & MUEHLENHARD, C. L. (1997). Shaken confidence: The effects of an authority figure's flirtatiousness on women's and men's self-rated creativity. *Psychology of Women Quarterly, 21,* 395–416.

SAX, L. J., ASTIN, A. W., KORN, W. S., & MAHONEY, K. M. (1997). *The American freshman: National norms for fall 1997.* Los Angeles: UCLA, Higher Education Research Institute.

SAX, L. J., ASTIN, A. W., KORN, W. S., & MAHONEY, K. M. (1998). *The American freshman: National norms for fall 1998.* Los Angeles: UCLA, Higher Education Research Institute.

SCHACHTER, S. (1951). Deviation, rejection and communication. *Journal of Abnormal and Social Psychology, 46,* 190–207.

SCHAFER, R. B., & KEITH, P. M. (1980). Equity and depression among married couples. *Social Psychology Quarterly, 43,* 430–435.

SCHAFFNER, P. E., WANDERSMAN, A., & STANG, D. (1981). Candidate name exposure and voting: Two field studies. *Basic and Applied Social Psychology, 2,* 195–203.

SCHEIER, M. F., & CARVER, C. S. (1992). Effects of optimism on psychological and physical well-being: Theoretical overview and empirical update. *Cognitive Therapy and Research, 16,* 201–228.

SCHEIN, E. H. (1956). The Chinese indoctrination program for prisoners of war: A study of attempted brainwashing. *Psychiatry, 19,* 149–172.

SCHIFFENBAUER, A., & SCHIAVO, R. S. (1976). Physical distance and attraction: An intensification effect. *Journal of Experimental Social Psychology, 12,* 274–282.

SCHLENKER, B. R., & LEARY, M. R. (1982a). Audiences' reactions to self-enhancing, self-denigrating, and accurate self-presentations. *Journal of Experimental Social Psychology, 18,* 89–104.

SCHLENKER, B. R., & LEARY, M. R. (1982b). Social anxiety and self-presentation: A conceptualization and model. *Psychological Bulletin, 92,* 641–669.

SCHLENKER, B. R., & LEARY, M. R. (1985). Social anxiety and communication about the self. *Journal of Language and Social Psychology, 4,* 171–192.

SCHLENKER, B. R., & WEIGOLD, M. F. (1992). Interpersonal processes involving impression regulation and management. *Annual Review of Psychology, 43,* 133–168.

SCHLENKER, B. R., WEIGOLD, M. F., & HALLAM, J. R. (1990). Self-serving attribu-
tions in social context: Effects of self-esteem and social pressure. *Journal of Per-
sonality and Social Psychology, 58,* 855–863.
SCHLESINGER, A., JR. (1949). The statistical soldier. *Partisan Review, 16,* 852–856.
SCHLESINGER, A. M., JR. (1965). *A thousand days.* Boston: Houghton Mifflin. Cited
by I. L. Janis (1972) in *Victims of groupthink.* Boston: Houghton Mifflin.
SCHOENFELD, B. (1995, May 14). The loneliness of being white. *New York Times
Magazine,* 34–37.
SCHOFIELD, J. W. (1982). *Black and white in school: Trust, tension, or tolerance?* New
York: Praeger.
SCHOFIELD, J. W. (1986). Causes and consequences of the colorblind perspective.
In J. F. Dovidio & S. L. Gaertner (Eds.), *Prejudice, discrimination, and racism.* Or-
lando, FL: Academic Press.
SCHULZ, J. W., & PRUITT, D. G. (1978). The effects of mutual concern on joint wel-
fare. *Journal of Experimental Social Psychology, 14,* 480–492.
SCHUMAN, H., & SCOTT, J. (1989). Generations and collective memories. *American
Sociological Review, 54,* 359–381.
SCHUMAN, H., STEEH, C., BOBO, L., & KRYSAN, M. (1998). *Racial attitudes in Amer-
ica: Trends and interpretations.* Cambridge, MA: Harvard University Press.
SCHWARTZ, S. H., & GOTTLIEB, A. (1981). Participants' post-experimental reac-
tions and the ethics of bystander research. *Journal of Experimental Social Psy-
chology, 17,* 396–407.
SCHWARZ, N., BLESS, H., & BOHNER, G. (1991). Mood and persuasion: Affective
states influence the processing of persuasive communications. In M. Zanna (Ed.),
Advances in experimental social psychology (Vol. 24). New York: Academic Press.
SCHWARZ, N., & KURZ, E. (1989). What's in a picture? The impact of face-ism on
trait attribution. *European Journal of Social Psychology, 19,* 311–316.
SCHWARZWALD, J., BIZMAN, A., & RAZ, M. (1983). The foot-in-the-door paradigm:
Effects of second request size on donation probability and donor generosity.
Personality and Social Psychology Bulletin, 9, 443–450.
SCOTT, J. P., & MARSTON, M. V. (1953). Nonadaptive behavior resulting from a series
of defeats in fighting mice. *Journal of Abnormal and Social Psychology, 48,* 417–428.
SEARS, D. O. (1979). *Life stage effects upon attitude change, especially among the elderly.*
Manuscript prepared for Workshop on the Elderly of the Future, Committee
on Aging, National Research Council, Annapolis, MD, May 3–5.
SEARS, D. O. (1986). College sophomores in the laboratory: Influences of a narrow
data base on social psychology's view of human nature. *Journal of Personality
and Social Psychology, 51,* 515–530.
SEDIKIDES, C. (1993). Assessment, enhancement, and verification determinants of
the self-evaluation process. *Journal of Personality and Social Psychology, 65,*
317–338.
SEGAL, H. A. (1954). Initial psychiatric findings of recently repatriated prisoners of
war. *American Journal of Psychiatry, 61,* 358–363.
SEGALL, M. H., DASEN, P. R., BERRY, J. W., & POORTINGA, Y. H. (1990). *Human behavior in global perspective: An introduction to cross-cultural psychology.* New
York: Pergamon Press.
SEGRIN, C., & DILLARD, J. P. (1992). The interactional theory of depression: A meta-
analysis of the research literature. *Journal of Social and Clinical Psychology, 11,*
43–70.

SELIGMAN, M. E. P. (1975). *Helplessness: On depression, development and death.* San Francisco: W. H. Freeman.

SELIGMAN, M. E. P. (1989). Explanatory style: Predicting depression, achievement, and health. In M. D. Yapko (Ed.), *Brief therapy approaches to treating anxiety and depression.* New York: Brunner/Mazel.

SELIGMAN, M. E. P. (1991). *Learned optimism.* New York: Knopf.

SELIGMAN, M. E. P. (1992). Power and powerlessness: Comments on "Cognates of personal control." *Applied and Preventive Psychology, 1,* 119–120.

SELIGMAN, M. E. P. (1994). *What you can change and what you can't.* New York: Knopf.

SEMIN, G. R., & DE POOT, C. J. (1997). Bringing partiality to light: Question wording and choice as indicators of bias. *Social Cognition, 15,* 91–106.

SENTYRZ, S. M., & BUSHMAN, B. J. (1997). *Mirror, mirror on the wall, who's the thinnest one of all? Effects of self-awareness on consumption of fatty, reduced-fat, and fat-free products.* Unpublished manuscript, Iowa State University.

SETA, C. E., & SETA, J. J. (1992). Increments and decrements in mean arterial pressure levels as a function of audience composition: An averaging and summation analysis. *Personality and Social Psychology Bulletin, 18,* 173–181.

SETA, J. J. (1982). The impact of comparison processes on coactors' task performance. *Journal of Personality and Social Psychology, 42,* 281–291.

SETO, M. C., & BARBAREE, H. E. (1995). The role of alcohol in sexual aggression. *Clinical Psychology Review, 15,* 545–566.

SHACKELFORD, T. K., & LARSEN, R. J. (1997). Facial asymmetry as an indicator of psychological, emotional, and physiological distress. *Journal of Personality and Social Psychology, 72,* 456–466.

SHAFFER, D. R., PEGALIS, L. J., & BAZZINI, D. G. (1996). When boy meets girls (revisited): Gender, gender-role orientation, and prospect of future interaction as determinants of self-disclosure among same- and opposite-sex acquaintances. *Personality and Social Psychology Bulletin, 22,* 495–506.

SHARMA, N. (1981). Some aspect of attitude and behaviour of mothers. *Indian Psychological Review, 20,* 35–42.

SHARPE, D., ADAIR, J. G., & ROESE, N. J. (1992). Twenty years of deception research: A decline in subjects' trust? *Personality and Social Psychology Bulletin, 18,* 585–590.

SHEPPERD, J. A. (1993). Student derogation of the Scholastic Aptitude Test: Biases in perceptions and presentations of College Board Scores. *Basic and Applied Social Psychology, 14,* 455–473.

SHEPPERD, J. A., & ARKIN, R. M. (1991). Behavioral other-enhancement: Strategically obscuring the link between performance and evaluation. *Journal of Personality and Social Psychology, 60,* 79–88.

SHEPPERD, J. A., OULLETTE, J. A., & FERNANDEZ, J. K. (1996). Abandoning unrealistic optimism: Performance estimates and the temporal proximity of self-relevant feedback. *Journal of Personality and Social Psychology, 70,* 844–855.

SHEPPERD, J. A., & WRIGHT, R. A. (1989). Individual contributions to a collective effort: An incentive analysis. *Personality and Social Psychology Bulletin, 15,* 141–149.

SHERIF, M. (1966). *In common predicament: Social psychology of intergroup conflict and cooperation.* Boston: Houghton Mifflin.

SHERMAN, J. W. (1996). Development and mental representation of stereotypes. *Journal of Personality and Social Psychology, 70,* 1126–1141.

SHORT, J. F., JR. (ED.) (1969). *Gang delinquency and delinquent subcultures*. New York: Harper & Row.

SHOWERS, C., & RUBEN, C. (1987). *Distinguishing pessimism from depression: Negative expectations and positive coping mechanisms*. Paper presented at the American Psychological Association convention.

SHRAUGER, J. S. (1983). *The accuracy of self-prediction: How good are we and why?* Paper presented at the Midwestern Psychological Association convention.

SIDANIUS, J., PRATTO, F., & BOBO, L. (1996). Racism, conservatism, affirmative action, and intellectual sophistication: A matter of principled conservatism or group dominance? *Journal of Personality and Social Psychology, 70*, 476–490.

SIEGEL, J. M., & KUYKENDALL, D. H. (1990). Loss, widowhood, and psychological distress among the elderly. *Journal of Consulting and Clinical Psychology, 58*, 519–524.

SILVER, M., & GELLER, D. (1978). On the irrelevance of evil: The organization and individual action. *Journal of Social Issues, 34*, 125–136.

SIMONTON, D. K. (1994). *Greatness: Who makes history and why*. New York: Guilford.

SIMPSON, J. A. (1987). The dissolution of romantic relationships: Factors involved in relationship stability and emotional distress. *Journal of Personality and Social Psychology, 53*, 683–692.

SIMPSON, J. A., CAMPBELL, B., & BERSCHEID, E. (1986). The association between romantic love and marriage: Kephart (1967) twice revisited. *Personality and Social Psychology Bulletin, 12*, 363–372.

SIMPSON, J. A., GANGESTAD, S. W., & LERMA, M. (1990). Perception of physical attractiveness: Mechanisms involved in the maintenance of romantic relationships. *Journal of Personality and Social Psychology, 59*, 1192–1201.

SINGER, M. (1979, July-August). Interviewed by M. Freeman. Of cults and communication: A conversation with Margaret Singer. *APA Monitor*, pp. 6–7. *(b)*

SINGER, M. (1979). *Cults and cult members*. Address to the American Psychological Association convention. *(a)*

SIVARD, R. L. (1995). *Women—A world survey* (2nd ed.). Washington, DC: World Priorities.

SIVARD, R. L. (1996). *World military and social expenditures 1996* (16th ed.). Washington, DC: World Priorities.

SKAALVIK, E. M., & HAGTVET, K. A. (1990). Academic achievement and self-concept: An analysis of causal predominance in a developmental perpsective. *Journal of Personality and Social Psychology, 58*, 292–307.

SLAVIN, R. E. (1990, December/January). Research on cooperative learning: Consensus and controversy. *Educational Leadership*, pp. 52–54.

SLOAN, J. H., KELLERMAN, A. L., REAY, D. T., FERRIS, J. A., KOEPSELL, T., RIVARA, F. P., RICE, C., GRAY, L., & LOGERFO, J. (1988). Handgun regulations, crime, assaults, and homicide: A tale of two cities. *New England Journal of Medicine, 319*, 1256–1261.

SLOVIC, P. (1972). From Shakespeare to Simon: Speculations—and some evidence—about man's ability to process information. *Oregon Research Institute Research Bulletin, 12* (2).

SLOVIC, P., & FISCHHOFF, B. (1977). On the psychology of experimental surprises. *Journal of Experimental Psychology: Human Perception and Performance, 3*, 544–551.

SMEDLEY, J. W., & BAYTON, J. A. (1978). Evaluative race-class stereotypes by race and perceived class of subjects. *Journal of Personality and Social Psychology, 3*, 530–535.

SMITH, A. (1976). *The wealth of nations* (Book 1). Chicago: University of Chicago Press. (Originally published, 1776)

SMITH, D. E., GIER, J. A., & WILLIS, F. N. (1982). Interpersonal touch and compliance with a marketing request. *Basic and Applied Social Psychology, 3,* 35–38.

SMITH, H. (1976). *The Russians.* New York: Balantine Books. Cited by B. Latané, K. Williams, and S. Harkins in, Many hands make light the work. *Journal of Personality and Social Psychology, 1979, 37,* 822–832.

SMITH, H. J., & TYLER, T. R. (1997). Choosing the right pond: The impact of group membership on self-esteem and group-oriented behavior. *Journal of Experimental Social Psychology, 33,* 146–170.

SMITH, P. B., & TAYEB, M. (1989). Organizational structure and processes. In M. Bond (Ed.), *The cross-cultural challenge to social psychology.* Newbury Park, CA: Sage.

SMITH, T. W. (1997). Personal correspondence. Data from the General Social Survey, National Opinion Research Center, University of Chicago.

SMITH, W. P. (1987). Conflict and negotiation: Trends and emerging issues. *Journal of Applied Social Psychology, 17,* 641–677.

SMOKE CIGARETTES—TREND. (1994, July). Gallup Poll Monthly, p. 53.

SNODGRASS, M. A. (1987). The relationships of differential loneliness, intimacy, and characterological attributional style to duration of loneliness. *Journal of Social Behavior and Personality, 2,* 173–186.

SNYDER, C. R. (1978). The "illusion" of uniqueness. *Journal of Humanistic Psychology, 18,* 33–41.

SNYDER, C. R. (1980, March). The uniqueness mystique. *Psychology Today,* pp. 86–90.

SNYDER, C. R., & FROMKIN, H. L. (1980). *Uniqueness; The human pursuit of difference.* New York: Plenum Press.

SNYDER, C. R., & HIGGINS, R. L. (1988). Excuses: Their effective role in the negotiation of reality. *Psychological Bulletin, 104,* 23–35.

SNYDER, C. R., & SMITH, T. W. (1986). On being "shy like a fox": A self-handicapping analysis. In W. H. Jones et al. (Eds.), *Shyness: Perspectives on research and treatment.* New York: Plenum Press.

SNYDER, M. (1981). Seek, and ye shall find: Testing hypotheses about other people. In E. T. Higgins, C. P. Herman, & M. P. Zanna (Eds.), *Social cognition: The Ontario symposium on personality and social psychology.* Hillsdale, NJ: Erlbaum.

SNYDER, M. (1983). The influence of individuals on situations: Implications for understanding the links between personality and social behavior. *Journal of Personality, 51,* 497–516.

SNYDER, M. (1984). When belief creates reality. In L. Berkowitz (Ed.), *Advances in experimental social psychology* (Vol. 18). New York: Academic Press.

SNYDER, M. (1989). Selling images versus selling products: Motivational foundations of behavioral confirmation. *Advances in Experimental Social Psychology, 26,* 206–311.

SNYDER, M., & DEBONO, K. G. (1987). A functional approach to attitudes and persuasion. In M. P. Zanna, J. M. Olson, & C. P. Herman (Eds.), *Social influence: The Ontario symposium* (Vol. 5). Hillsdale, NJ: Erlbaum.

SNYDER, M., & ICKES, W. (1985). Personality and social behavior. In G. Lindzey & E. Aronson (Eds.), *Handbook of social psychology* (3rd ed.). New York: Random House.

SNYDER, M., BERSCHEID, E., & GLICK, P. (1985). Focusing on the exterior and the interior: Two investigations of the initiation of personal relationships. *Journal of Personality and Social Psychology, 48,* 1427–1439.

SNYDER, M., BERSCHEID, E., & MATWYCHUK, A. (1988). Orientations toward personnel selection: Differential reliance on appearance and personality. *Journal of Personality and Social Psychology, 54,* 972–979.

SNYDER, M., CAMPBELL, B., & PRESTON, E. (1982). Testing hypotheses about human nature: Assessing the accuracy of social stereotypes. *Social Cognition, 1,* 256–272.

SNYDER, M., & SIMPSON, J. (1985). Orientations toward romantic relationships. In S. Duckk & D. Perlman (Eds.), *Understanding personal relationships.* Beverly Hills, CA: Sage.

SNYDER, M., TANKE, E. D., & BERSCHEID, E. (1977). Social perception and interpersonal behavior: On the self-fulfilling nature of social stereotypes. *Journal of Personality and Social Psychology, 35,* 656–666.

SOKOLL, G. R., & MYNATT, C. R. (1984). *Arousal and free throw shooting.* Paper presented at the Midwestern Psychological Association convention, Chicago.

SOLANO, C. H., BATTEN, P. G., & PARISH, E. A. (1982). Loneliness and patterns of self-disclosure. *Journal of Personality and Social Psychology, 43,* 524–531.

SORRENTINO, R. M., BOBOCEL, D. R., GITTA, M. Z., OLSEN, J. M., & HEWITT, E. C. (1988). Uncertainty orientation and persuasion: Individual differences in the effects of personal relevance on social judgments. *Journal of Personality and Social Psychology, 55,* 357–371.

SPARRELL, J. A., & SHRAUGER, J. S. (1984). *Self-confidence and optimism in self-prediction.* Paper presented at the American Psychological Association convention.

SPECTOR, P. E. (1986). Perceived control by employees: A meta-analysis of studies concerning autonomy and participation at work. *Human Relations, 39,* 1005–1016.

SPEER, A. (1971). *Inside the Third Reich: Memoirs* (P. Winston & C. Winston, Trans.). New York: Avon Books.

SPENCER, S. J., & STEELE, C. M. (1997). *Under suspicion of inability: Stereotype vulnerability and women's math performance.* Unpublished manuscript, University of Waterloo.

SPIEGEL, H. W. (1971). *The growth of economic thought.* Durham, NC: Duke University Press.

SPITZBERG, B. H., & HURT, H. T. (1987). The relationship of interpersonal competence and skills to reported loneliness across time. *Journal of Social Behavior and Personality, 2,* 157–172.

SPIVAK, J. (1979, June 6). *Wall Street Journal.*

SPIVEY, C. B., & PRENTICE-DUNN, S. (1990). Assessing the directionality of deindividuated behavior: Effects of deindividuation, modeling, and private self-consciousness on aggressive and prosocial responses. *Basic and Applied Social Psychology, 11,* 387–403.

SPRECHER, S. (1987). The effects of self-disclosure given and received on affection for an intimate partner and stability of the relationship. *Journal of Personality and Social Psychology, 4,* 115–127.

SPRECHER, S., ARON, A., HATFIELD, E., CORTESE, A., POTAPOVA, E., & LEVITSKAYA, A. (1994). Love: American style, Russian style, and Japanese style. *Personal Relationships, 1,* 349–369.

SPRECHER, S., SULLIVAN, Q., & HATFIELD, E. (1994). Mate selection preferences: Gender differences examined in a national sample. *Journal of Personality and Social Psychology, 66,* 1074–1080.

ST. LAWRENCE, J. S., & JOYNER, D. J. (1991). The effects of sexually violent rock music on males' acceptance of violence against women. *Psychology of Women Quarterly, 15* (1), 49–63.

STANGOR, C., JONAS, K., STROEBE, W., & HEWSTONE, M. (1996). Influence of student exchange on national stereotypes, attitudes and perceived group variability. *European Journal of Social Psychology, 26,* 663–675.

STANGOR, C., LYNCH, L., DUAN, C., & GLASS, B. (1992). Categorization of individuals on the basis of multiple social features. *Journal of Personality and Social Psychology, 62,* 207–218.

STARK, R., & BAINBRIDGE, W. S. (1980). Networks of faith: Interpersonal bonds and recruitment of cults and sects. *American Journal of Sociology, 85,* 1376–1395.

STASSER, G. (1991). Pooling of unshared information during group discussion. In S. Worchel, W. Wood, & J. Simpson (Eds.), *Group process and productivity.* Beverly Hills, CA: Sage.

STAUB, E. (1989). *The roots of evil: The origins of genocide and other group violence.* Cambridge, England: Cambridge University Press.

STAUB, E. (1997). Blind versus constructive patriotism: Moving from embeddedness in the group to critical loyalty and action. In D. Bar-Tal & E. Staub (eds.), *Patriotism in the lives of individuals and nations.* Chicago: Nelson-Hall.

STEELE, C. M., & SOUTHWICK, L. (1985). Alcohol and social behavior: I. The psychology of drunken excess. *Journal of Personality and Social Psychology, 48,* 18–34.

STEIN, A. H., & FRIEDRICH, L. K. (1972). Television content and young children's behavior. In J. P. Murray, E. A. Rubinstein, & G. A. Comstock (Eds.), *Television and social learning.* Washington, DC: Government Printing Office.

STEIN, D. D., HARDYCK, J. A., & SMITH, M. B. (1965). Race and belief: An open and shut case. *Journal of Personality and Social Psychology, 1,* 281–289.

STEPHAN, W. G. (1986). The effects of school desegregation: An evaluation 30 years after *Brown.* In R. Kidd, L. Saxe, & M. Saks (Eds.), *Advances in applied social psychology.* New York: Erlbaum.

STEPHAN, W. G. (1987). The contact hypothesis in intergroup relations. In C. Hendrick (Ed.), *Group processes and intergroup relations.* Newbury Park, CA: Sage.

STEPHAN, W. G. (1988). *School desegregation: Short-term and long-term effects.* Paper presented at the national conference "Opening Doors: An Appraisal of Race Relations in America," University of Alabama.

STEPHAN, W. G., BERSCHEID, E., & WALSTER, E. (1971). Sexual arousal and heterosexual perception. *Journal of Personality and Social Psychology, 20,* 93–101.

STERNBERG, R. J. (1988). Triangulating love. In R. J. Sternberg & M. L. Barnes (Eds.), *The psychology of love.* New Haven, CT: Yale University Press.

STERNBERG, R. J., & GRAJEK, S. (1984). The nature of love. *Journal of Personality and Social Psychology, 47,* 312–329.

STILLINGER, C., EPELBAUM, M., KELTNER, D., & ROSS, L. (1991). *The "reactive devaluation" barrier to conflict resolution.* Unpublished manuscript, Stanford University.

STONE, A. A., HEDGES, S. M., NEALE, J. M., & SATIN, M. S. (1985). Prospective and cross-sectional mood reports offer no evidence of a "blue Monday" phenomenon. *Journal of Personality and Social Psychology, 49,* 129–134.

STONE, L. (1977). *The family, sex and marriage in England, 1500–1800*. New York: Harper & Row.

STONER, J. A. F. (1961). *A comparison of individual and group decisions involving risk.* Unpublished master's thesis, Massachusetts Institute of Technology. Cited by D. G. Marquis in, Individual responsibility and group decisions involving risk. *Industrial Management Review, 1962, 3,* 8–23.

STORMS, M. D. (1973). Videotape and the attribution process: Reversing actors' and observers' points of view. *Journal of Personality and Social Psychology, 27,* 165–175.

STORMS, M. D., & THOMAS, G. C. (1977). Reactions to physical closeness. *Journal of Personality and Social Psychology, 35,* 412–418.

STOUFFER, S. A., SUCHMAN, E. A., DEVINNEY, L. C., STAR, S. A., & WILLIAMS, R. M., JR. (1949). *The American soldier: Adjustment during army life* (Vol. 1.). Princeton, NJ: Princeton University Press.

STRACK, S., & COYNE, J. C. (1983). Social confirmation of dysphoria: Shared and private reactions to depression. *Journal of Personality and Social Psychology, 44,* 798–806.

STRAUS, M. A., & GELLES, R. J. (1980). *Behind closed doors: Violence in the American family.* New York: Anchor/Doubleday.

STROEBE, W., INSKO, C. A., THOMPSON, V. D., & LAYTON, B. D. (1971). Effects of physical attractiveness, attitude similarity, and sex on various aspects of interpersonal attraction. *Journal of Personality and Social Psychology, 18,* 79–91.

STROESSNER, S. J., HAMILTON, D. L., & LEPORE, L. (1990). *Intergroup categorization and intragroup differentiation: Ingroup-outgroup differences.* Paper presented at the American Psychological Association convention.

STROESSNER, S. J., & MACKIE, D. M. (1993). Affect and perceived group variability: Implications for stereotyping and prejudice. In D. M. Mackie & D. L. Hamilton (Eds.), *Affect, cognition, and stereotyping: Interactive processes in group perception.* San Diego: Academic Press.

STRONG, S. R. (1968). Counseling: An interpersonal influence process. *Journal of Counseling Psychology, 17,* 81–87.

STRONG, S. R. (1978). Social psychological approach to psychotherapy research. In S. L. Garfield & A. E. Bergin (Eds.), *Handbook of psychotherapy and behavior change* (2nd ed.). New York: Wiley.

STRONG, S. R., WELSH, J. A., CORCORAN, J. L., & HOYT, W. T. (1992). Social psychology and counseling psychology: The history, products, and promise of an interface. *Journal of Personality and Social Psychology, 39,* 139–157.

SULS, J., WAN, C. K., & SANDERS, G. S. (1988). False consensus and false uniqueness in estimating the prevalence of health-protective behaviors. *Journal of Applied Social Psychology, 18,* 66–79.

SUMMERS, G., & FELDMAN, N. S. (1984). Blaming the victim versus blaming the perpetrator: An attributional analysis of spouse abuse. *Journal of Social and Clinical Psychology, 2,* 339–347.

SUNDSTROM, E., DE MEUSE, K. P., & FUTRELL, D. (1990). Work teams: Applications and effectiveness. *American Psychologist, 45,* 120–133.

SVENSON, O. (1981). Are we all less risky and more skillful than our fellow drivers? *Acta Psychologica, 47,* 143–148.

SWANN, W. B., JR. (1996). *Self-traps: The elusive quest for higher self-esteem.* New York: Freeman.

SWANN, W. B., JR. (1997). The trouble with change: Self-verification and allegiance to the self. *Psychological Science, 8,* 177–180.

SWANN, W. B., JR., & GILL, M. J. (1997). Confidence and accuracy in person perception: Do we know what we think we know about our relationship partners? *Journal of Personality and Social Psychology, 73,* 747–757.

SWANN, W. B., JR., GIULIANO, T., & WEGNER, D. M. (1982). Where leading questions can lead: The power of conjecture in social interaction. *Journal of Personality and Social Psychology, 42,* 1025–1035.

SWANN, W. B., JR., & PREDMORE, S. C. (1985). Intimates as agents of social support: Sources of consolation or despair? *Journal of Personality and Social Psychology, 49,* 1609–1617.

SWANN, W. B., JR., WENZLAFF, R. M., KRULL, D. S., & PELHAM, B. W. (1991). Seeking truth, reaping despair: Depression, self-verification and selection of relationship partners. *Journal of Abnormal Psychology, 101,* 293–306.

SWAP, W. C. (1977). Interpersonal attraction and repeated exposure to rewarders and punishers. *Personality and Social Psychology Bulletin, 3,* 248–251.

SWEDISH INFORMATION SERVICE (1980, September). *Social change in Sweden,* No. 19, p. 5. (Published by the Swedish Consulate General, 825 Third Avenue, New York, N.Y. 10022.)

SWEENEY, J. (1973). An experimental investigation of the free rider problem. *Social Science Research, 2,* 277–292.

SWEENEY, P. D., ANDERSON, K., & BAILEY, S. (1986). Attributional style in depression: A meta-analytic review. *Journal of Personality and Social Psychology, 50,* 947–991.

SWIM, J. K. (1994). Perceived versus meta-analytic effect sizes: An assessment of the accuracy of gender stereotypes. *Journal of Personality and Social Psychology, 66,* 21–36.

SWIM, J. K., AIKIN, K. J., HALL, W. S., & HUNTER, B. A. (1995). Sexism and racism: Old-fashioned and modern prejudices. *Journal of Personality and Social Psychology, 68,* 199–214.

SWIM, J. K., & COHEN, L. L. (1997). Overt, covert, and subtle sexism. *Psychology of Women Quarterly, 21,* 103–118.

SWIM, J. K., COHEN, L. L., & HYERS, L. L. (1998). Experiencing everyday prejudice and discrimination. In J. K. Swim & C. Stangor (Eds.), *Prejudice: The target's perspective.* San Diego: Academic Press.

SWIM, J. K., & HYERS, L. L. (1998). Excuse me—What did you just say?!: Women's public and private reactions to sexist remarks. *Journal of Experimental Social Psychology, 31,* 68–88.

SWIM, J. K., & STANGOR, C. (Eds.) (1998). *Prejudice: The target's perspective.* San Diego: Academic Press.

SYMONS, D. (INTERVIEWED BY S. KEEN). (1981, February). Eros and alley cop. *Psychology Today,* p. 54.

TAJFEL, H. (1970, November). Experiments in intergroup discrimination. *Scientific American,* pp. 96–102.

TAJFEL, H. (1981). *Human groups and social categories: Studies in social psychology.* London: Cambridge University Press.

TAJFEL, H. (1982). Social psychology of intergroup relations. *Annual Review of Psychology, 33,* 1–39.

TAJFEL, H., & BILLIG, M. (1974). Familiarity and categorization in intergroup behavior. *Journal of Experimental Social Psychology, 10,* 159–170.

TANNEN, D. (1990). *You just don't understand: Women and men in conversation.* New York: Morrow.

TAYLOR, D. A., GOULD, R. J., & BROUNSTEIN, P. J. (1981). Effects of personalistic self-disclosure. *Personality and Social Psychology Bulletin, 7,* 487–492.

TAYLOR, D. G., SHEATSLEY, P. B., & GREELEY, A. M. (1978). Attitudes toward racial integration. *Scientific American, 238* (6), 42–49.

TAYLOR, D. M., & DORIA, J. R. (1981). Self-serving and group-serving bias in attribution. *Journal of Social Psychology, 113,* 201–211.

TAYLOR, D. M., WRIGHT, S. C., MOGHADDAM, F. M., & LALONDE, R. N. (1990). The personal/group discrimination discrepancy: Perceiving my group, but not myself, to be a target for discrimination. *Personality and Social Psychology Bulletin, 16,* 254–262.

TAYLOR, S. E. (1979). Remarks at symposium on social psychology and medicine, American Psychological Association convention.

TAYLOR, S. E. (1981). A categorization approach to stereotyping. In D. L. Hamilton (Ed.), *Cognitive processes in stereotyping and intergroup behavior.* Hillsdale, NJ: Erlbaum.

TAYLOR, S. E. (1989). *Positive illusions: Creative self-deception and the healthy mind.* New York: Basic Books.

TAYLOR, S. P., & CHERMACK, S. T. (1993). Alcohol, drugs and human physical aggression. *Journal of Studies on Alcohol,* Supplement No. 11, 78–88.

TAYLOR, S. E., CROCKER, J., FISKE, S. T., SPRINZEN, M., & WINKLER, J. D. (1979). The generalizability of salience effects. *Journal of Personality and Social Psychology, 37,* 357–368.

TAYLOR, S. E., & FISKE, S. T. (1978). Salience, attention, and attribution: Top of the head phenomena. In L. Berkowitz (Ed.), *Advances in experimental social psychology* (Vol. 11). New York: Academic Press.

TAYLOR, S. E., FISKE, S. T., ETCOFF, N. L., & RUDERMAN, A. J. (1978). Categorical and contextual bases of person memory and stereotyping. *Journal of Personality and Social Psychology, 36,* 778–793.

TAYLOR, S. P., & PISANO, R. (1971). Physical aggression as a function of frustration and physical attack. *Journal of Social Psychology, 84,* 261–267.

TEGER, A. I. (1980). *Too much invested to quit.* New York: Pergamon Press.

TEIGEN, K. H. (1986). Old truths or fresh insights? A study of students' evaluations of proverbs. *British Journal of Social Psychology, 25,* 43–50.

TELCH, M. J., KILLEN, J. D., MCALISTER, A. L., PERRY, C. L., & MACCOBY, N. (1981). *Long-term follow-up of a pilot project on smoking prevention with adolescents.* Paper presented at the American Psychological Association convention.

TESSER, A. (1988). Toward a self-evaluation maintenance model of social behavior. In L. Berkowitz (Ed.), *Advances in experimental social psychology* (Vol. 21). San Diego: Academic Press.

TETLOCK, P. E. (1985). Integrative complexity of American and Soviet foreign policy rhetoric: A time-series analysis. *Journal of Personality and Social Psychology, 49,* 1565–1585.

THOMAS, K. W., & PONDY, L. R. (1977). Toward an "intent" model of conflict management among principal parties. *Human Relations, 30,* 1089–1102.

THOMAS, L. (1978). Hubris in science? *Science, 200,* 1459–1462.

THOMPSON, L. (1990a). An examination of naive and experienced negotiators. *Journal of Personality and Social Psychology, 59,* 82–90.

THOMPSON, L. (1990b). The influence of experience on negotiation performance. *Journal of Experimental Social Psychology, 26,* 528–544.

THOMPSON, L. (1998). *The mind and heart of the negotiator.* Upper Saddle River, NJ: Prentice Hall.

THOMPSON, L. L., & CROCKER, J. (1985). *Prejudice following threat to the self-concept: Effects of performance expectations and attributions.* Unpublished manuscript, Northwestern University.

THORNTON, B., & MOORE, S. (1993). Physical attractiveness contrast effect: Implications for self-esteem and evaluations of the social self. *Personality and Social Psychology Bulletin, 19,* 474–480.

Time (1992, March 30). The not so merry wife of Windsor. pp. 38–39.

TIMKO, C., & MOOS, R. H. (1989). Choice, control, and adaptation among elderly residents of sheltered care settings. *Journal of Applied Social Psychology, 19,* 636–655.

Toronto News (1977, July 26).

TRAVIS, L. E. (1925). The effect of a small audience upon eye-hand coordination. *Journal of Abnormal and Social Psychology, 20,* 142–146.

TRIANDIS, H. C. (1994). *Culture and social behavior.* New York: McGraw-Hill.

TRIANDIS, H. C., BONTEMPO, R., VILLAREAL, M. J., ASAI, M., & LUCCA, N. (1988). Individualism and collectivism: Cross-cultural perspectives on self-ingroup relationships. *Journal of Personality and Social Psychology, 54,* 323–338.

TRIPLETT, N. (1898). The dynamogenic factors in pacemaking and competition. *American Journal of Psychology, 9,* 507–533.

TROLIER, T. K., & HAMILTON, D. L. (1986). Variables influencing judgments of correlational relations. *Journal of Personality and Social Psychology, 50,* 879–888.

TROST, M. R., MAASS, A., & KENRICK, D. T. (1992). Minority influence: Personal relevance biases cognitive processes and reverses private acceptance. *Journal of Experimental Social Psychology, 28,* 234–254.

TUMIN, M. M. (1958). Readiness and resistance to desegregation: A social portrait of the hard core. *Social Forces, 36,* 256–273.

TURNER, C. W., HESSE, B. W., & PETERSON-LEWIS, S. (1986). Naturalistic studies of the long-term effects of television violence. *Journal of Social Issues, 42* (3), 51–74.

TURNER, J. C. (1981). The experimental social psychology of intergroup behaviour. In J. Turner & H. Giles (Eds.), *Intergroup behavior.* Oxford, England: Blackwell.

TURNER, J. C. (1987). *Rediscovering the social group: A self-categorization theory.* New York: Basil Blackwell.

TURNER, J. C. (1991). *Social influence.* Milton Keynes, England: Open University Press.

TURNER, M. E., & PRATKANIS, A. R. (1993). Effects of preferential and meritorious selection on performance: An examination of intuitive and self-handicapping perspectives. *Personality and Social Psychology Bulletin, 19,* 47–58.

TURNER, M. E., & PRATKANIS, A. R. (1994). Affirmative action as help: A review of recipient reactions to preferential selection and affirmative action. *Basic and Applied Social Psychology, 15,* 43–69.

TURNER, M. E., PRATKANIS, A. R., PROBASCO, P., & LEVE, C. (1992). Threat cohesion, and group effectiveness: Testing a social identity maintenance perspective on groupthink. *Journal of Personality and Social Psychology, 63,* 781–796.

TV Guide. (1977, January 26). pp. 5–10.

TVERKSY, A., & KAHNEMAN, D. (1974). Judgment under uncertainty: Heuristics and biases. *Science, 185,* 1123–1131.

TZENG, M. (1992). The effects of socioeconomic heterogamy and changes on marital dissolution for first marriages. *Journal of Marriage and the Family, 54,* 609–619.

UMBERSON, D., & HUGHES, M. (1987). The impact of physical attractiveness on achievement and psychological well-being. *Social Psychology Quarterly, 50,* 227–236.

UNITED NATIONS. (1991). *The world's women 1970–1990: Trends and statistics.* New York: Author.

UPI. (1970/1967). September 23, 1967. Cited by P. G. Zimbardo, in The human choice: Individuation, reason, and order versus deindividuation, impulse, and chaos. In W. J. Arnold & D. Levine (Eds.), *Nebraska symposium on motivation, 1969.* Lincoln: University of Nebraska Press.

VAILLANT, G. E. (1977). *Adaptation to life.* Boston: Little, Brown.

VALLONE, R. P., GRIFFIN, D. W., LIN, S., & ROSS, L. (1990). Overconfident prediction of future actions and outcomes by self and others. *Journal of Personality and Social Psychology, 58,* 582–592.

VALLONE, R. P., ROSS, L., & LEPPER, M. R. (1985). The hostile media phenomenon: Biased perception and perceptions of media bias in coverage of the "Beirut Massacre." *Journal of Personality and Social Psychology, 49,* 577–585.

VANCOUVER, J. B., RUBIN, B., & KERR, N. L. (1991). Sex composition of groups and member motivation: III. Motivational losses at a feminine task. *Basic and Applied Social Psychology, 12,* 133–144.

VANDERSLICE, V. J., RICE, R. W., & JULIAN, J. W. (1987). The effects of participation in decision-making on worker satisfaction and productivity: An organizational simulation. *Journal of Applied Social Psychology, 17,* 158–170.

VANITY FARE. (1984, August/September). *Public Opinion,* p. 22.

VAN KNIPPENBERG, D., & WILKE, H. (1992). Prototypicality of arguments and conformity to ingroup norms. *European Journal of Social Psychology, 22,* 141–155.

VAN LANGE, P. A. M. (1991). Being better but not smarter than others: The Muhammad Ali effect at work in interpersonal situations. *Personality and Social Psychology Bulletin, 17,* 689–693.

VAN LANGE, P. A. M., TARIS, T. W., & VONK, R. (1997). Dilemmas of academic practice: perceptions of superiority among social psychologists. *European Journal of Social Psychology, 27,* 675–685.

VAN VUGT, M., VAN LANGE, P. A. M., & MEERTENS, R. M. (1996). Commuting by car or public transportation? A social dilemma analysis of travel mode judgements. *European Journal of Social Psychology, 26,* 373–395.

VAN YPEREN, N. W., & BUUNK, B. P. (1990). A longitudinal study of equity and satisfaction in intimate relationships. *European Journal of Social Psychology, 20,* 287–309.

VAUX, A. (1988). Social and personal factors in loneliness. *Journal of Social and Clinical Psychology, 6,* 462–471.

VEENHOVEN, R. (1988). The utility of happiness. *Social Indicators Research, 20,* 333–354.

VERPLANKEN, B. (1991). Persuasive communication of risk information: A test of cue versus message processing effects in a field experiment. *Personality and Social Psychology Bulletin, 17,* 188–193.

VITELLI, R. (1988). The crisis issue assessed: An empirical analysis. *Basic and Applied Social Psychology, 9*, 301–309.

WAGSTAFF, G. F. (1983). Attitudes to poverty, the Protestant ethic, and political affiliation: A preliminary investigation. *Social Behavior and Personality, 11*, 45–47.

WALLACH, M. A., & WALLACH, L. (1985, February). How psychology sanctions the cult of the self. *Washington Monthly*, pp. 46–56.

WALSTER, E. (1965). The effect of self-esteem on romantic liking. *Journal of Experimental Social Psychology, 1*, 184–197.

WALSTER, E., & WALSTER, G. W. (1978). *A new look at love.* Reading, MA: Addison-Wesley.

WALSTER, E., ARONSON, V., ABRAHAMS, D., & ROTTMAN, L. (1966). Importance of physical attractiveness in dating behavior. *Journal of Personality and Social Psychology, 4*, 508–516.

WALSTER, E., WALSTER, G. W., & BERSCHEID, E. (1978). *Equity: Theory and research.* Boston: Allyn & Bacon.

WARD, W. C., & JENKINS, H. M. (1965). The display of information and the judgment of contingency. *Canadian Journal of Psychology, 19*, 231–241.

WASON, P. C. (1960). On the failure to eliminate hypotheses in a conceptual task. *Quarterly Journal of Experimental Psychology, 12*, 129–140.

WATSON, D. (1982). The actor and the observer: How are their perceptions of causality divergent? *Psychological Bulletin, 92*, 682–700.

WATSON, R. I., JR. (1973). Investigation into deindividuation using a cross-cultural survey technique. *Journal of Personality and Social Psychology, 25*, 342–345.

WEARY, G., HARVEY, J. H., SCHWIEGER, P., OLSON, C. T., PERLOFF, R., & PRITCHARD, S. (1982). Self-presentation and the moderation of self-serving biases. *Social Cognition, 1*, 140–159.

WEBSTER, D. M. (1993). Motivated augmentation and reduction of the overattribution bias. *Journal of Personality and Social Psychology, 65*, 261–271.

WEGNER, D. M., & ERBER, R. (1992). The hyperaccessibility of suppressed thoughts. *Journal of Personality and Social Psychology, 63*, 903–912.

WEHR, P. (1979). *Conflict regulation.* Boulder, CO: Westview Press.

WEINER, B. (1981). *The emotional consequences of causal ascriptions.* Unpublished manuscript, UCLA.

WEINSTEIN, N. D. (1980). Unrealistic optimism about future life events. *Journal of Personality and Social Psychology, 39*, 806–820.

WEINSTEIN, N. D. (1982). Unrealistic optimism about susceptibility to health problems. *Journal of Behavioral Medicine, 5*, 441–460.

WEISS, J., & BROWN, P. (1976). *Self-insight error in the explanation of mood.* Unpublished manuscript, Harvard University.

WENER, R., FRAZIER, W., & FARBSTEIN, J. (1987, June). Building better jails. *Psychology Today*, pp. 40–49.

WHEELER, L., & KIM, Y. (1997). What is beautiful is culturally good: The physical attractiveness stereotype has different content in collectivistic cultures. *Personality and Social Psychology Bulletin, 23*, 795–800.

WHITE, G. L. (1980). Physical attractiveness and courtship progress. *Journal of Personality and Social Psychology, 39*, 660–668.

WHITE, H. R., BRICK, J., & HANSELL, S. (1993). A longitudinal investigation of alcohol use and aggression in adolescence. *Journal of Studies on Alcohol*, Supplement No. 11, 62–77.

WHITE, J. A., & PLOUS, S. (1995). Self-enhancement and social responsibility: On caring more, but doing less, than others. *Journal of Applied Social Psychology, 25,* 1297–1318.

WHITE, P. A., & YOUNGER, D. P. (1988). Differences in the ascription of transient internal states to self and other. *Journal of Experimental Social Psychology, 24,* 292–309.

WHITE, R. K. (1977). Misperception in the Arab-Israeli conflict. *Journal of Social Issues, 33* (1), 190–221.

WHITE, R. K. (1996). Why the Serbs fought: Motives and misperceptions. *Peace and Conflict: Journal of Peace Psychology, 2,* 109–128.

WHITLEY, B. E., JR., & FRIEZE, I. H. (1985). Children's causal attributions for success and failure in achievement settings: A meta-analysis. *Journal of Educational Psychology, 77,* 608–616.

WHITLEY, B. E., JR., & LEE, S. E. (1997). *The relationship of authoritarianism and related constructs to attitudes toward homosexuality.* Unpublished manuscript, Ball State University.

WHITMAN, D. (1996, December 16). I'm OK, you're not. *U.S. News and World Report,* p. 24.

WHITMAN, R. M., KRAMER, M., & BALDRIDGE, B. (1963). Which dream does the patient tell? *Archives of General Psychology, 8,* 277–282.

WHOLEY, D. (1986). *Are you happy?* Boston: Houghton Mifflin.

WHYTE, G. (1993). Escalating commitment in individual and group decision making: A prospect theory approach. *Organizational Behavior and Human Decision Processes, 54,* 430–455.

WICKER, A. W. (1971). An examination of the "other variables" explanation of attitude-behavior inconsistency. *Journal of Personality and Social Psychology, 19,* 18–30.

WIDOM, C. S. (1989). Does violence beget violence? A critical examination of the literature. *Psychological Bulletin, 106,* 3–28.

WIEGMAN, O. (1985). Two politicians in a realistic experiment: Attraction, discrepancy, intensity of delivery, and attitude change. *Journal of Applied Social Psychology, 15,* 673–686.

WIESEL, E. (1985, April 6). The brave Christians who saved Jews from the Nazis. *TV Guide,* pp. 4–6.

WILDER, D. A. (1978). Perceiving persons as a group: Effect on attributions of causality and beliefs. *Social Psychology, 41,* 13–23.

WILDER, D. A. (1981). Perceiving persons as a group: Categorization and intergroup relations. In. D. L. Hamilton (Ed.). *Cognitive processes in stereotyping and intergroup behavior.* Hillsdale, NJ: Erlbaum.

WILDER, D. A. (1990). Some determinants of the persuasive power of in-groups and out-groups: Organization of information and attribution of independence. *Journal of Personality and Social Psychology, 59,* 1202–1213.

WILDER, D. A., & SHAPIRO, P. N. (1984). Role of out-group cues in determining social identity. *Journal of Personality and Social Psychology, 47,* 342–348.

WILLIAMS, J. E., & BEST, D. L. (1990a). *Measuring sex stereotypes: A multination study.* Newbury Park, CA: Sage.

WILLIAMS, J. E., & BEST, D. L. (1990b). *Sex and psyche: Gender and self viewed cross-culturally.* Newbury Park, CA: Sage.

WILLIAMS, K. D., HARKINS, S., & LATANÉ, B. (1981). Identifiability as a deterrent to social loafing: Two cheering experiments. *Journal of Personality and Social Psychology, 40,* 303–311.

WILLIAMS, K. D., & KARAU, S. J. (1991). Social loafing and social compensation: The effects of expectations of coworker performance. *Journal of Personality and Social Psychology, 61,* 570–581.

WILLIAMS, K. D., NIDA, S. A., BACA, L. D., & LATANÉ, B. (1989). Social loafing and swimming: Effects of identifiability on individual and relay performance of intercollegiate swimmers. *Basic and Applied Social Psychology, 10,* 73–81.

WILLIAMS, T. M. (Ed.) (1986). *The impact of television: A natural experiment in three communities.* Orlando, FL: Academic Press.

WILLIS, F. N., & HAMM, H. K. (1980). The use of interpersonal touch in securing compliance. *Journal of Nonverbal Behavior, 5,* 49–55.

WILLS, T. A. (1981). Downward comparison principles in social psychology. *Psychological Bulletin, 90,* 245–271.

WILSON, D. K., KAPLAN, R. M., & SCHNEIDERMAN, L. J. (1987). Framing of decisions and selections of alternatives in health care. *Social Behaviour, 2,* 51–59.

WILSON, D. K., PURDON, S. E., & WALLSTON, K. A. (1988). Compliance to health recommendations: A theoretical overview of message framing. *Health Education Research, 3,* 161–171.

WILSON, R. C., GAFT, J. G., DIENST, E. R., WOOD, L., & BAVRY, J. L. (1975). *College professors and their impact on students.* New York: Wiley.

WILSON, T. D., LASER, P. S., & STONE, J. I. (1982). Judging the predictors of one's mood: Accuracy and the use of shared theories. *Journal of Experimental Social Psychology, 18,* 537–556.

WINCH, R. F. (1958). *Mate selection: A study of complementary needs.* New York: Harper & Row.

WINTER, F. W. (1973). A laboratory experiment of individual attitude response to advertising exposure. *Journal of Marketing Research, 10,* 130–140.

WITTENBERG, M. T., & REIS, H. T. (1986). Loneliness, social skills, and social perception. *Personality and Social Psychology Bulletin, 12,* 121–130.

WITTENBRINK, B., JUDD, C. M., & PARK, B. (1997). Evidence for racial prejudice at the implicit level and its relationship with questionnaire measures. *Journal of Personality and Social Psychology, 72,* 262–274.

WIXON, D. R., & LAIRD, J. D. (1976). Awareness and attitude change in the forced-compliance paradigm: The importance of when. *Journal of Personality and Social Psychology, 34,* 376–384.

WOLF, S. (1987). Majority and minority influence: A social impact analysis. In M. P. Zanna, J. M. Olson, & C. P. Herman (Eds.), *Social influence: The Ontario symposium on personality and social psychology* (Vol. 5). Hillsdale, NJ: Erlbaum.

WOLF, S., & LATANÉ, B. (1985). Conformity, innovation and the psycho-social law. In S. Moscovici, G. Mugny, & E. Van Avermaet (Eds.), *Perspectives on minority influence.* Cambridge, England: Cambridge University Press.

WOMEN, MEN, MARRIAGES AND MINISTERS. (1992, January/February). *American Enterprise,* p. 106.

WOMEN OF OUR WORLD. (1998). New York: Population Reference Bureau.

WOOD, J. V., SALTZBERG, J. A., & GOLDSAMT, L. A. (1990). Does affect induce self-focused attention? *Journal of Personality and Social Psychology, 58,* 899–908.

WOOD, J. V., SALTZBERG, J. A., NEALE, J. M., STONE, A. A., & RACHMIEL, T. B. (1990). Self-focused attention, coping responses, and distressed mood in everyday life. *Journal of Personality and Social Psychology, 58,* 1027–1036.

WOOD, W., & RHODES, N. (1991). Sex differences in interaction style in task groups. In C. Ridgeway (Ed.), *Gender and interaction: The role of microstructures in inequality.* New York: Springer-Verlag.

WOOD, W., LUNDGREN, S., OUELLETE, J. A., BUSCEME, S., & BLACKSTONE, T. (1994). Minority influence: A meta-analytic review of social influence processes. *Psychological Bulletin, 115,* 323–345.

WOOD, W., POOL, G. J., LECK, K., & PURVIS, D. (1996). Self-definition, defensive processing, and influence: The normative impact of majority and minority groups. *Journal of Personality and Social Psychology, 71,* 1181–1193.

WOOD, W., WONG, F. Y., & CHACHERE, J. G. (1991). Effects of media violence on viewers' aggression in unconstrained social interaction. *Psychological Bulletin, 109,* 371–383.

WORCHEL, S., & BROWN, E. H. (1984). The role of plausibility in influencing environmental attributions. *Journal of Experimental Social Psychology, 20,* 86–96.

WORD, C. O., ZANNA, M. P., & COOPER, J. (1974). The nonverbal mediation of self-fulfilling prophecies in interracial interaction. *Journal of Experimental Social Psychology, 10,* 109–120.

WORRINGHAM, C. J., & MESSICK, D. M. (1983). Social facilitation of running: An unobtrusive study. *Journal of Social Psychology, 121,* 23–29.

WU, D. Y. H., & TSENG, W. S. (1985). Introduction: The characteristics of Chinese culture. In D. Y. H. Wu & W. S. Tseng (Eds.), *Chinese culture and mental health.* San Diego: Academic Press.

WYLIE, R. C. (1979). *The self-concept. Vol. 2. Theory and research on selected topics.* Lincoln: University of Nebraska Press.

YOUNG, W. R. (1977, February). There's a girl on the tracks! *Reader's Digest,* pp. 91–95.

YOVETICH, N. A., & RUSBULT, C. E. (1994). Accommodative behavior in close relationships: Exploring transformation of motivation. *Journal of Experimental Social Psychology, 30,* 138–164.

YUKL, G. (1974). Effects of the opponent's initial offer, concession magnitude, and concession frequency on bargaining behavior. *Journal of Personality and Social Psychology, 30,* 323–335.

YZERBYT, V. Y., & LEYENS, J-P. (1991). Requesting information to form an impression: The influence of valence and confirmatory status. *Journal of Experimental Social Psychology, 27,* 337–356.

YZERBYT, V. Y., ROCHER, S., & SCHADRON, G. (1997). Stereotypes as explanations: A subjective essentialistic view of group perception. In R. Spears, P. J. Oakes, N. Ellemers, & S. A. Haslam (Eds.), *The social psychology of stereotyping and group life.* Oxford, England: Blackwell.

ZAJONC, R. B. (1965). Social facilitation. *Science, 149,* 269–274.

ZAJONC, R. B. (1968). Attitudinal effects of mere exposure. *Journal of Personality and Social Psychology, 9* (Monograph Suppl. No. 2, part 2).

ZAJONC, R. B. (1970, February). Brainwash: Familiarity breeds comfort. *Psychology Today,* pp. 32–35, 60–62.

ZAJONC, R. B. (1998). Emotions. In D. Gilbert, S. T. Fiske, & G. Lindzey (Eds.), *Handbook of social psychology* (4th ed.). New York: McGraw-Hill.

ZAJONC, R. B., & SALES, S. M. (1966). Social facilitation of dominant and subordinate responses. *Journal of Experimental Social Psychology, 2,* 160–168.

ZANNA, M. P., & PACK, S. J. (1975). On the self-fulfilling nature of apparent sex differences in behavior. *Journal of Experimental Social Psychology, 11,* 583–591.

ZEBROWITZ-MCARTHUR, L. (1988). Person perception in cross-cultural perspective. In M. H. Bond (Ed.), *The cross-cultural challenge to social psychology.* Newbury Park, CA: Sage.

ZILLMANN, D. (1989a). Aggression and sex: Independent and joint operations. In H. L. Wagner & A. S. R. Manstead (Eds.), *Handbook of psychophysiology: Emotion and social behavior.* Chichester: Wiley.

ZILLMANN, D. (1989b). Effects of prolonged consumption of pornography. In D. Zillmann & J. Bryant (Eds.), *Pornography: Research advances and policy considerations.* Hillsdale, NJ: Erlbaum.

ZILLMANN, D., & PAULUS, P. B. (1993). Spectators: Reactions to sports events and effects on athletic performance. In R. N. Singer, N. Murphey, & L. K. Tennant (Eds.), *Handbook of research on sport psychology.* New York: Macmillan.

ZIMBARDO, P. G. (1970). The human choice: Individuation, reason, and order versus deindividuation, impulse, and chaos. In W. J. Arnold & D. Levine (Eds.), *Nebraska symposium on motivation, 1969.* Lincoln: University of Nebraska Press.

ZIMBARDO, P. G. (1971). *The psychological power and pathology of imprisonment.* A statement prepared for the U.S. House of Representatives Committee on the Judiciary, Subcommittee No. 3: Hearings on Prison Reform, San Francisco, October 25.

ZIMBARDO, P. G. (1972). The Stanford prison experiment. A slide/tape presentation produced by Philip G. Zimbardo, Inc., P. O. Box 4395, Stanford, Calif. 94305.

ZIMBARDO, P. G., EBBESEN, E. B., & MASLACH, C. (1977). *Influencing attitudes and changing behavior.* Reading, MA: Addison-Wesley.

ZUCKER, G. S., & WEINER, B. (1993). Conservatism and perceptions of poverty: An attributional analysis. *Journal of Applied Social Psychology, 23,* 925–943.

ZUWERINK, J. R., & DEVINE, P. G. (1996). Attitude importance and resistance to persuasion: It's not just the thought that counts. *Journal of Personality and Social Psychology, 70,* 931–940.

Credits

— ❖ —

Name Index

❖

Note: page numbers followed by *n* indicate notes.

Subject Index

———— ❖ ————